Object-Oriented Programming Using C++
Third Edition

Joyce Farrell

THOMSON

COURSE TECHNOLOGY

Australia • Canada • Mexico • Singapore • Spain • United Kingdom • United States

D1307642

Object-Oriented Programming Using C++, Third Edition is published by Thomson Course Technology.

Executive Editor
Bob Woodbury

Managing Editor
William Pitkin III

Senior Product Manager
Tricia Coia

Production Editor
Danielle Chouhan

Developmental Editor
Lisa Ruffolo

Associate Product Manager
Sarah Santoro

Product Marketing Manager
Brian Berkeley

Editorial Assistant
Allison Murphy

Senior Manufacturing Coordinator
Justin Palmeiro

Cover Designer
Steve Deschene

Compositor
GEX Publishing Services

Copyeditor
Gary Michael Stahl

Proofreader
John Bosco

Indexer
Sharon Hilgenberg

BRIEF
Contents

TABLE OF

Contents

CHAPTER THREE
Making Decisions   **81**

CHAPTER EIGHT
Class Features and Design Issues   313

CHAPTER NINE
Understanding Friends and Overloading Operators   363

CHAPTER TWELVE
Handling Exceptions   519

CHAPTER THIRTEEN
Advanced Input and Output   565

Preface

Oobject-Oriented Programming Using C++, Third Edition is designed for many levels of programming students and a variety of programming teaching styles. Readers who are new to programming will find the basics of programming logic and the C++ programming language covered thoroughly and clearly. Clear, thorough explanations, multiple programming examples, and step-by-step programming lessons provide beginning readers with a solid C++ background. Users who know some C++ syntax, but are new to object-oriented programming, will find objects explored thoroughly from the first chapters. Objects are introduced early, so those who want to learn objects at the start of their programming experience can do so. Users who want to postpone objects can simply omit the later sections of each chapter and cover the basic programming structures with simple data types before returning to the more complex objects later on.

Organization and Coverage

Object-Oriented Programming Using C++ contains 14 chapters and five appendices that present clear text explanation, directed hands-on instruction, and a wealth of exercises. In these chapters, readers learn about programming logic in general, C++ syntax in particular, and gain an appreciation for and understanding of the object-oriented approach. When readers complete the book, they will have an understanding of object-oriented concepts as they apply to programming, and the ability to use these concepts to develop C++ programs.

Chapter 1 provides an overview of programming in general and C++ in particular. You work with variables, comments, input and output, and data structures. This book distinguishes itself from other C++ books by introducing structure objects in Chapter 1 so that students start thinking in an object-oriented manner from the beginning of the course.

Chapter 2 focuses on evaluating C++ expressions. Chapters 3, 4, and 5 discuss decisions, loops, and arrays, strings, and pointers—all fundamental building blocks of C++ programs. Chapter 6 provides a solid foundation in writing and using functions including passing parameters by value and by reference and returning values from functions.

Once students understand C++ basics they are ready for Chapters 7 and 8, which delve more completely into the object-oriented aspects of C++, featuring classes, objects, and design issues. Friend functions and operator overloading are covered in Chapter 9, and inheritance, another important OO feature, is explained in Chapter 10.

Advanced C++ features such as templates, exception handling, and advanced input and output techniques, including writing objects to files, are covered in Chapters 11, 12, and 13. Chapter 14 presents some interesting adjuncts to C++ that make it such a powerful language, including creating enumerations, working with bits, and understanding recursion.

Five appendices offer further explanation to topics mentioned in the chapters. Appendices A and B describe how to get started with various C++ compilers. Appendix C contains a handy table of precedence and associativity. Appendix D contains information on formatting output, and Appendix E is a lesson in generating random numbers—an important skill in creating scientific simulations as well as in creating games.

Approach

Object-Oriented Programming Using C++ teaches object-oriented concepts using C++ as a tool to demonstrate these concepts. This book teaches programming concepts using a task-driven rather than a command-driven approach. Structures are introduced in Chapter 1 so that students start thinking about objects right from the start. However, discussion of objects is reserved for the last sections of the first six chapters, so that instructors who prefer to start with a procedural approach can omit these sections at first, then go back to cover them after the first six chapters have been completed.

Features

Object-Oriented Programming Using C++ is an exceptional textbook because it also includes the following features:

- **Objectives.** A brief list of objectives appears at the beginning of each chapter so the student has an overview of the main topics to be covered.

- **Tips.** These provide additional information about a procedure or topic, such as an alternative method of performing a procedure.

- **Figures.** Each chapter averages over 30 figures that contain code, working programs, or screen shots of the programs' execution.

- **You Do It.** After students study each chapter's concepts, they are invited to create small applications that illustrate the concepts. Each application is explained step-by-step as the students add appropriate code to interesting applications.

- **Summaries.** A summary that recaps the programming concepts and commands covered follows each chapter.

- **Key Terms.** Each chapter contains a list of all the key terms defined in the chapter, along with explanation and presented in the order covered in the chapter. The list of Key Terms serves as an additional chapter summary.

- **Review Questions.** Each chapter includes 20 multiple choice review questions that test students' understanding of what they learned in the chapter.

- **Exercises.** Each chapter contains interesting exercises that provide students with the opportunity to apply the concepts they have mastered by writing C++ programs.

- **Debugging Exercises.** Each chapter ends with debugging exercises—programs with a few syntax or logical errors. The student can find the errors and fix them, developing crucial skills of reading others' programs, analyzing error messages and probable cause of errors, and solving problems.

- **Running Cases.** The book contains two running cases in which the student develops large classes, adding appropriate features as each new concept is introduced. By the end of the book the student has created two substantial working classes.

Teaching Tools

The following teaching tools are available when this book is used in a classroom setting. All of the teaching tools available with this book are provided to the instructor on a single CD-ROM.

- **Instructor's Manual.** Additional instructional material to assist in class preparation, including suggestions for lecture topics, including a 14 and 16 week syllabus outline.

- **Solution Files.** Solutions to all end-of-chapter materials. (Due to the nature of programming, students' solutions may differ from these solutions and still be correct.)

- **Data Files.** Data files, containing all of the data that students will use for the exercises in this book, are provided on the Thomson Course Technology Web site and on the Instructor's Resource CD-ROM. Additionally, all complete programs that are presented as figures in the book are included so that students can execute the files and experiment with them without a lot of tedious typing. See the "Read This Before You Begin" section for more information on Data Files.

- **ExamView Test Bank.** This textbook is accompanied by ExamView, a powerful testing software package that allows instructors to create and administer printed, computer (LAN-based), and Internet exams. ExamView includes hundreds of questions that correspond to the topics covered in this text, enabling students to generate detailed study guides that include page references for further review. The computer-based and Internet testing components allow students to take exams at their computers, and also save time for the instructor by grading each exam automatically.

- **PowerPoint Presentations.** This book comes with Microsoft PowerPoint slides for each chapter. These are included as a teaching aid for classroom presentation, to make available to students on the network for chapter review, or to be printed for classroom distribution. Instructors can add their own slides for additional topics they introduce to the class.

ACKNOWLEDGMENTS

I would like to thank all of the people who have this book a reality, especially Lisa Ruffolo, my Developmental Editor who has kept up her good humor through the last two editions of this book as well as several others. She makes me look good. Thanks also to Tricia Coia, Senior Product Manager, whose help and friendship have been immeasurable not just on this book, but for the decade I have been associated with Thomson Course Technology. Thanks to Danielle Chouhan, Production Editor, Mary Franz, Managing Editor, and Will Pitkin, Managing Editor, as well as the testers in Quality Assurance who play a big part in making sure we produce a high-quality programming text.

Thank you to the reviewers who provided helpful and insightful comments during the development of this book, including Steve Chadwick, Embry-Riddle Aeronautical University; Robert Dollinger, University of Wisconsin Stevens Point; Stephen P. Leach, Florida State University; Paul Turnage, Schoolcraft College; Catherine Wyman, DeVry University.

Thank you to my husband Geoff who runs all the errands so I can compile just one more program.

Finally, this book is dedicated to Jann Patton, my cousin and friend.

Read This Before You Begin

TO THE USER

Data Files

To complete some of the steps and exercises in this book, you will need data files that have been created for this book. Your instructor will provide the data files to you. You also can obtain the files electronically from the Thomson Course Technology Web site by connecting to www.course.com and then searching for this book by title, author, or ISBN.

Each chapter in this book has its own set of data files, which is stored in a separate folder. For example, the files for Chapter 3 are stored in the Chapter 3 folder. You can use a computer in your school lab or your own computer to complete the labs and exercises in this book.

Using Your Own Computer

To use your own computer to complete the steps and exercises in this book, you will need the following:

- A personal computer. This book was written and quality assurance tested using Microsoft Windows 2000 and XP and Linux.

- A C++ compiler. Almost all examples in this book will work with any C++ compiler. This book was written using Microsoft Visual Studio 2005 Express Edition (beta) and quality assurance tested using Linux and Microsoft Visual C++ .NET 2003 Standard Edition, as well as Microsoft Visual C++ 2005 Express Edition (final). If your book came with a copy of Microsoft Visual Basic 2005 Express Edition, then you may install that on your computer and use it to complete the material. If you purchased a copy of the text, then you also received Microsoft Visual C++ 2005 Standard Edition on CD-ROM. Appendix A contains instructions on getting started with Microsoft Visual Studio. Appendix B contains instructions on getting started with some other compilers and suggests minor modifications you might have to make to your programs to get them to work correctly using different compilers.

- Data files. You will not be able to complete the steps and exercises in this book using your own computer unless you have the data files. You can get the data files from your instructor, or you can obtain the data files electronically from the Thomson Course Technology Web site by connecting to www.course.com and then searching for this book title.

Visit Our World Wide Web Site

Additional materials might be available for your course on the Web. Visit the Thomson Course Technology Web site—www.course.com—and periodically search this site for more details.

TO THE INSTRUCTOR

To complete the labs and exercises in this book, your students must use a set of data files. These files are included on the Teaching Tools CD-ROM. They may also be obtained electronically through the Thomson Course Technology Web site at www.course.com. Follow the instructions in the Help file to copy the data files to your server or standalone computer. You can view the Help file using a text editor such as WordPad or Notepad. Once the files are copied, you should instruct your users how to copy the files to their own computers or workstations.

Thomson Course Technology Data Files

You are granted a license to copy the data files to any computer or computer network used by individuals who have purchased this book.

1

AN OVERVIEW OF OBJECT-ORIENTED PROGRAMMING AND C++

In this chapter, you will:

♦ Learn about the task of programming

♦ Examine programming universals

♦ Explore procedural programming

♦ Be introduced to object-oriented programming

♦ Get started in the C++ programming environment

♦ Work with variables and the `const` qualifier

♦ Create comments

♦ Examine the differences between ANSI/ISO C++ and Standard C++

♦ Produce C++ output with `cout` and provide input with `cin`

♦ Begin to work with data structures and classes

Whether you are new to programming or have already had a class in logic or a programming language other than C++, this chapter introduces you to the fundamental concepts of programming, including procedural and object-oriented programming. After learning or reviewing what it means to program, you will examine the characteristics of procedural programs and consider a few examples. Then you will compare procedural and object-oriented programs and learn the additional features object-orientation provides.

In the rest of the chapter, you will consider the basic principles behind object-oriented programming techniques, including objects, classes, inheritance, and polymorphism. Then you will get started in the C++ programming environment by applying what you have learned. For example, you will learn how to create a `main()` function, work with variables and constants, and create comments. Finally, you will learn how to produce output and process input with C++, and learn how to create your first objects.

THE TASK OF PROGRAMMING

Programming a computer involves writing instructions that enable a computer to carry out a single task or a group of tasks. Writing these sets of instructions, which are known as **programs** or **software**, requires using a computer programming language and resolving errors in the instructions so that the programs work correctly. Programs are also frequently called **application programs**, or simply **applications**, because you apply them to a task such as preparing payroll checks, creating inventory reports, or—as in the case of game programs—even entertaining someone.

As with any language, learning a computer **programming language** requires learning both vocabulary and syntax. People speak a variety of languages, such as English and Japanese; similarly, programmers use many different programming languages, including Java, Visual Basic, C#, and C++.

The rules of any language make up its **syntax**. Writing in a programming language requires correct use of that language's syntax. In English, using incorrect syntax—that is, committing a **syntax error**—might make communication more difficult but usually does not prevent it altogether. If you ask, "Name yours what is?" most people can still figure out what you mean. If you are vague or spell a word wrong when writing, most people will nevertheless understand your message. Computers are not nearly as flexible as most people. As a result, using correct syntax in a computer program is not just important—it's essential.

Most of today's programming languages follow syntax rules that are close enough to human language to make them accessible to anyone willing to learn and practice them. The statements you write in an English-like programming language must be subsequently translated into machine language. **Machine language** is the language that computers can understand; it consists of 1s and 0s. A translator program (called either a compiler or an interpreter) checks your program for syntax errors. If there are no errors, the translator changes your written program statements into machine language. Therefore, syntax errors are not a big problem; you always have an opportunity to fix them before you actually attempt to run the program. For example, if you write a computer program in C++ but spell a word incorrectly or reverse the required order of two words, the compiler informs you of such errors and will not let you run the program until you have corrected them.

 An **interpreter** is a program that translates programming language instructions one line at a time; a **compiler** works by translating the entire program at one time. Usually, you do not choose whether to use a compiler or an interpreter; instead, the software you use to develop programs in a particular language contains one or the other. C++ is usually thought of as a compiled language, although interpreter programs are available for it.

Finding logical errors is much more time consuming for a programmer than finding syntax errors. A **logical error** occurs when you use a statement that, although syntactically correct, doesn't do what you intended. For a program that is supposed to add two numbers and show the sum, logical errors arise when multiplication is used instead of addition, or when the sum is given before the arithmetic occurs. The language compiler will not tell you when you have committed a logical error; only running and testing your program will enable you to find inappropriate statements. You **run** a program by issuing a command to **execute**—that is, to carry out—the program statements. You **test** a program by using sample data to determine whether the program results are correct.

Programmers call some logical errors **semantic errors**. For example, if you misspell a programming language word, you commit a syntax error, but if you use a correct word in the wrong context, you commit a semantic error.

Selecting data for testing is an art in itself. For example, imagine that you write a program to add two numbers, and test the program with the values 2 and 2. You cannot be sure that the program is free of logical errors just because the answer is 4. Perhaps you used the multiplication symbol rather than the addition symbol. You can confirm your program's accuracy by testing the program several times using a variety of data.

PROGRAMMING UNIVERSALS

All modern programming languages share common characteristics. For example, all programming languages provide methods for directing **output**—the information produced by a program—to a desired object, such as a monitor screen, printer, or file. Similarly, all programming languages provide methods for sending **input**—the data provided by an outside source, such as a keyboard, scanner, or file—into the computer program so that it can be manipulated.

In addition, all programming languages provide a way to name locations in computer memory. These locations are commonly called **variables**. For example, if a person asks, "What is yourAge?" yourAge is considered a variable for two reasons: yourAge has different (varied) values for different people, and any person can have a change in the value of yourAge. When writing a computer program, yourAge becomes the name of a position or location in computer memory; the *value at* that location or the *state of* that location might be 18 or 80, or it might be unknown.

A variable or attribute is also an object, although it is a much simpler object than a monitor or file.

When discussing the variable yourAge, the separate words "your" and "Age" are run together on purpose. All modern programming languages require that variable names be one word; that is, although they do not have to match any word found in a conventional dictionary, they cannot include any embedded spaces. Each programming language has other specific rules as to which characters are not allowed, how many characters may be used in the variable name, and whether capitalization makes a difference.

 Ideally, variables have meaningful names, although no programming language actually requires that they meet this standard. A payroll program, for example, is easier to read if a variable that is meant to hold your salary is called `yourSalary`, but it is legal—that is, acceptable to the language-translating software—to call the variable `ImHungry` or `jqxBr`.

A variable may have only one value at a time, but it is the ability of memory variables to *change* in value that makes computers and programming worthwhile. Because one memory location, or variable, can be used repeatedly with different values, program instructions can be written once and then used for thousands of problems. Thus, one set of payroll instructions at your company might produce thousands of individual paychecks each week, and a variable for hourly wage, perhaps called `hourlyWage`, can be reused for each employee, holding a different value as each individual employee's paycheck is calculated.

In many computer programming languages, including C++, variables must be explicitly **declared**, that is, given a data type as well as a name, before they can be used. The **data type** of a variable defines what kind of values may be stored in a variable and what kind of operations can be performed on it. Most computer languages allow at least two types: one for numbers and one for characters. **Numeric variables** hold values like 13 or –6. **Character variables** hold values like 'A' or '&'. Many languages include even more specialized types, such as **integer** (for storing whole numbers) or **floating point** (for storing numbers with decimal places). Some languages, including C++, also let you create your own types. The distinction between variable types is important because computers handle the various types of data differently; each type of variable requires a different amount of storage and answers to different rules for manipulation. When you declare a variable with a type, you aren't merely naming it; you are giving it a set of characteristics and allowable values.

 Numeric values like 13 and –6 are called numeric constants; they always appear without quotes. Character values like 'A' and '&' are character constants and, in C++, always appear within single quotes.

PROCEDURAL PROGRAMMING

For most of the history of computer programming, which now covers roughly 60 years, most programs were written procedurally. **Procedural programs** consist of a series of steps or procedures that take place one after the other. The programmer determines the exact conditions under which a procedure takes place, how often it takes place, and when the program stops.

Programmers write procedural programs in many programming languages, such as COBOL, BASIC, FORTRAN, and RPG. You can also write procedural programs in C++. Although each language has a different syntax, they all share many elements.

Over the years, as programmers have sought better ways to accommodate the way people work best on computers, procedural programming techniques have evolved into object-oriented techniques. Some older languages do not support object-oriented techniques, but several newer languages do, including Visual Basic, Java, C#, and C++.

Early Procedural Programs

When programming languages were first used, the programmer's job was to break a task into small, specific steps. Each step was then coded in an appropriate language.

Consider a program that creates customer bills for a small business. Assume that the business sells only one product that costs exactly $7.99. Each customer order must contain the desired quantity of the item and the customer's name and address. If you could write the program in English rather than in a programming language, a simple version of the program might look something like Figure 1-1.

```
Declare variables quantityOrdered, customerName, customerAddress,
   and balanceDue
Read in quantityOrdered, customerName, and customerAddress
   from disk
Print "From:"
Print "ABC Company"
Print "Stevens Point, WI"
Print "Send To:"
Print customerName
Print customerAddress
Multiply quantityOrdered by 7.99 giving balanceDue
Print balanceDue
```

Figure 1-1   English language version of a simple procedural billing program

The programmer creates every step needed to produce a bill. He or she also chooses unique, descriptive variable names, such as `customerName` and `balanceDue`.

TIP

In a real-life program used by a business, often called a **production program**, the data stored in variables such as `customerName` and `customerAddress` would most likely be divided into appropriate subfields. Most companies would store `firstName` and `lastName` in separate fields, but use both on a customer bill. Similarly, `streetAddress`, `city`, `state`, and `zipCode` are likely to be separate variables. The example in Figure 1-1 uses `customerName` and `customerAddress` to limit the number of statements.

Basic logic components used in programs are called **control structures**. Three basic control structures are used in procedural programming. In the **sequence structure**, program steps execute one after another, without interruption. The order of some of the statements is important; for example, when producing a bill, you must determine the `balanceDue` before you can print it out. For some other statements, however, order is unimportant. In the process shown in Figure 1-1, you can print the "From:" and "Send To:" information, compute the `balanceDue`, and then print the `balanceDue`, but you can instead compute the `balanceDue` first, print the "From:" and "Send To:" information, and then print the `balanceDue` with no difference in the resulting bill.

Procedural programs can also include a second control structure called a **selection structure**, which you use to perform different tasks based on a condition. Perhaps you give a $5 discount to any customer who orders more than a dozen of an item. Figure 1-2 shows how this is accomplished. The selection occurs in the second statement from the bottom of the program.

 Programmers also call a selection a decision or an if-then.

TIP

```
Declare variables quantityOrdered, customerName, customerAddress,
  and balanceDue
Read in quantityOrdered, customerName, and customerAddress
  from disk
Print "From:"
Print "ABC Company"
Print "Stevens Point, WI"
Print "Send To:"
Print customerName
Print customerAddress
Multiply quantityOrdered by 7.99 giving balanceDue
If quantityOrdered is greater than 12 then
  subtract 5 from balanceDue
Print balanceDue
```

Figure 1-2   Adding a selection structure to the simple procedural billing program

In the example shown in Figure 1-2, $5 is deducted from the `balanceDue` if—and only if—the customer orders more than 12 items. The actual program that produces bills for a company might have many more selection statements than this example and is usually far more detailed. What if you're out of stock? What about taxes? What if the customer has a credit balance that should be applied to this order? What if one of the data items like `quantityOrdered` or `customerAddress` has been left blank? Some programs contain dozens or even hundreds of selection statements.

The third control structure used in computer programs is the **loop structure**, which repeats actions while some condition remains unchanged. When companies bill customers, they usually bill many customers at one time. The relevant program accesses a customer record from an input file, produces a bill, and continues to repeat the same steps until no more customers remain in the file. The example in Figure 1-3 shows a program that loops.

```
Declare variables quantityOrdered, customerName, customerAddress,
  and balanceDue
Repeat until there are no more input records on the disk
   Read in quantityOrdered, customerName, and customerAddress from disk
   Print "From:"
   Print "ABC Company"
   Print "Stevens Point, WI"
   Print "Send To:"
   Print customerName
   Print customerAddress
   Multiply quantityOrdered by 7.99 giving balanceDue
   If quantityOrdered is greater than 12 then
    subtract 5 from balanceDue
   Print balanceDue
```

Figure 1-3   Adding a loop to a simple procedural billing program

Some programmers call the loop structure a repetition or iteration structure.

The indentation shown in the code in Figure 1-3 indicates that all ten statements, from "Read" until "`Print balanceDue`", occur repeatedly "`until there are no more input records on the disk`".

In reality, production programmers structure their loops a little differently to avoid printing one useless customer bill after the last data record is read from the disk. You will become comfortable with this concept after you learn about writing C++ loops.

The billing program shown in Figure 1-3 does not contain nearly as many sequential steps, selections, or loops as a full-blown production program would, but even as it stands, the billing program contains quite a few statements. As programs grow more complicated, they can contain many hundreds or even thousands of separate statements, and are difficult to follow. Luckily, all modern programming languages allow programmers to break their programs into smaller, easier-to-follow modules.

Modularity and Abstraction

Programming in the oldest procedural languages had two major disadvantages:

- The programming process involved so much detail that the programmer (and any person reading the program) lost sight of the big picture.

- Similar statements required in various parts of the program had to be rewritten in more than one place.

Writing programs became easier when programming languages began to allow the programmer to write **methods**—groups of statements that can be executed as a unit. Using methods allows programmers to group statements together into modules, which are known in various programming languages as functions, procedures, methods, subprograms, subroutines, or simply routines. For example, you can create a module named `printReturnAddress`, as shown in the sample code in Figure 1-4.

```
module printReturnAddress
        Print "From:"
        Print "ABC Company"
        Print "Stevens Point, WI"
endModule
```

Figure 1-4   The `printReturnAddress` module

 In general, C++ programmers use the term "functions" when referring to methods. "Methods" is the more generic term. You will learn more about functions later in this chapter.

TIP

You can then change the customer billing program so it looks like the sample code in Figure 1-5. The highlighted statement executes the entire `printReturnAddress` module that performs the three actions listed in Figure 1-4.

```
Declare variables quantityOrdered, customerName, customerAddress,
   and balanceDue
Repeat until there are no more input records on the disk
   Read in quantityOrdered, customerName, and customerAddress from disk
   printReturnAddress
   Print "Send To:"
   Print customerName
   Print customerAddress
   Multiply quantityOrdered by 7.99 giving balanceDue
   If quantityOrdered is greater than 12 then
      subtract 5 from balanceDue
   Print balanceDue
```

Figure 1-5   Billing program that uses the `printReturnAddress` module

The program that includes the `printReturnAddress` module is slightly shorter than the original program because three separate statements are summarized by a single module name. The use of the method name in the program represents a **call to the method**—using the method's name to cause execution of the statements within the method.

Modular programs are easier to read than nonmodular ones, because one descriptive group name represents an entire series of detailed steps. If more modules are created, the main program can change as shown in Figure 1-6. The `printSendToAddress` module contains the statements that print "Send To:" as well as print the `customerName` and the `customerAddress` values. The `computeBalance` module contains both the multiplication statement and the discount-determining decision.

```
Declare variables quantityOrdered, customerName, customerAddress,
   and balanceDue
Repeat until there are no more input records on the disk
   Read in quantityOrdered, customerName,
   and customerAddress from disk
   printReturnAddress
   printSendToAddress
   computeBalance
   Print balanceDue
```

Figure 1-6   The procedural billing program containing several module calls

The new program in Figure 1-6 is more concise and more understandable at first glance; it is also more abstract. **Abstraction** is the process of paying attention to important properties while ignoring details. You employ abstraction in your daily life when you make a to-do list containing tasks like "grocery shop" and "wash car." Each of those tasks requires multiple steps and decisions, but you don't write down every detail involved in those tasks in your list. Of course, you must attend to the details at some point, and in modularized programs, the individual modules must eventually be written in a step-by-step process. However, the main program can be written by using abstract concepts to represent sets of finer details.

TIP   Programming in the oldest programming languages—machine language and assembly language—is called low-level programming because you must deal with the details of how the machine physically works. In contrast, programming languages such as COBOL and BASIC are called high-level because the programmer need not worry about hardware details. Although C++ is a high-level language, it is sometimes referred to as mid-level because it contains features that allow you to use it on either a high or a low level.

When you work with real-world objects, you take abstraction for granted. For example, you talk on the telephone without considering how the signals are transmitted. If you had to worry about every low-level detail—from how the words are formed in your mouth, to how the signals are transmitted across the phone lines, to how the phone charges are billed to your account—you would never complete a call.

Programming in a high-level programming language allows you to take advantage of abstraction. When you write a command to send output to a printer, you don't instruct the printer how to actually function—how to form-feed the paper, dispense ink, and print each character. Instead, you simply write an instruction such as `Print balanceDue`, and the hardware operations are carried out automatically. Every programming language contains a print (or similar) command that takes care of the low-level printing details. You simply carry abstraction one step further when you create a command such as `printReturnAddress`, which takes care of the lower-level return-address details.

Besides the advantage of abstraction, modular programs can be written more quickly because different programmers can be assigned to write different modules. If the program contains four modules, four programmers can work simultaneously, with each handling one-fourth of the job.

An additional advantage to modularization is that a well-written module may be called from multiple places within the same program or from another program. Many applications can use the module that prints a company's return address, for example. Whether you are preparing job estimates, year-end tax returns, or stockholder reports, you need to print the company name and address; when a well-written module is stored, any application can use it.

Encapsulation

Modules or procedures act somewhat like relatively autonomous mini-programs. Not only can modular routines contain their own sets of instructions, but most programming languages allow them to contain their own variables as well. The variables and instructions within a module are hidden and contained—that is, **encapsulated**—which helps to make the module independent of all other modules and therefore reusable.

You can find many real-world examples of encapsulation. When you build a house, you don't invent plumbing fixtures and heating systems. Rather, you reuse previously designed and tested systems. You don't need to know the fine details of how the systems work; they are self-contained units you incorporate in your house by plugging them in through some standard **interface**, or means of entry, such as an electrical outlet. This type of encapsulation certainly reduces the time and effort necessary to build a house. Assuming the plumbing fixtures and heating systems you choose are already in use in other houses, using existing systems also improves your house's **reliability**—that is, dependability and trustworthiness. Besides not needing to know how your furnace works, if you replace one model with another, you don't care if its internal operations differ. The result—a warm house—is what's important.

Similarly, reusable software saves time and money and enhances reliability. If the `printReturnAddress` routine in Figure 1-6 has been tested before, you can be confident that it will produce correctly spaced and aligned output. If another programmer creates a new and improved `printReturnAddress` routine, you don't care how it works as long as it prints the data correctly.

When you use modules within procedural programs, you are still limited in your programming. You must know the names of the modules to call, and you can't reuse those names for other modules within the same program. If you need a similar but slightly different procedure, you must create a new module with a different name, and use the new name when you call the similar module. The group of techniques called object-oriented programming greatly reduces these limitations.

OBJECT-ORIENTED PROGRAMMING

Object-oriented programs use all the features of procedural programs you just read about: they contain variables that are operated on by instructions written in sequence, selection, and loop statements. However, **object-oriented programming** requires a different way of thinking and adds several new concepts to programming:

- You analyze the objects with which you are working—both the attributes of those objects and the tasks that need to be performed with and on those objects.

- You pass messages to objects, requesting the objects to take action.

- The same message works differently (and appropriately) when applied to the various objects.

- A method can work appropriately with different types of data it receives, without the need for separate method names.

- Objects can assume or **inherit** traits of previously created objects, thereby reducing the time it takes to create new objects.

- Information hiding is more complete than in procedural programs.

The basic principles behind using object-oriented programming techniques involve:

- Objects
- Classes
- Inheritance
- Polymorphism

Each of these principles is complex. As you work through the lessons and exercises in this text, you will gain mastery of these concepts as they apply to C++. For now, the following sections provide a brief overview of each concept.

Objects and Classes

It is difficult to discuss objects without mentioning classes; it is equally difficult to discuss classes without bringing up objects. An **object** is any *thing*. A **class** consists of a *category* of things. An object is a specific item that belongs to a class; it is called an **instance** of a class. A class defines the characteristics of its objects and the methods that can be applied to its objects.

For example, `Dish` is a class. You know that you can hold a `Dish` object in your hand, that you can eat from a `Dish`, and that you can wash it. `Dish` objects have attributes like size and color. They also have methods like `fill` and `wash`. `myBlueCerealBowl` is an object and a member of—or a specific instance of—the `Dish` class. This situation is considered an **is-a relationship** because you can say, "`myBlueCerealBowl` is a `Dish`." For example, `yourBlueCerealBowl` is another instance of the `Dish` class, as is `myPewterSaladPlate`. Because `myBlueCerealBowl`, `yourBlueCerealBowl`, and `myPewterSaladPlate` are examples of a `Dish`, they share characteristics. Each has a size and color; each can be filled and washed.

If I tell you I am buying my grandmother a `scarletWindsor`, you probably have no way of organizing its characteristics in your brain. Is it something you eat? Is it a piece of clothing? If I tell you a `scarletWindsor` "is a" `Dish`, you have a beginning frame of reference because of your knowledge of the `Dish` class in general. If it "is a" `Dish`, you assume it has a size and color and that it can be filled and washed.

Similarly, each button on the toolbar of a word-processing program is an instance of a `Button` class, and each button shares some general characteristics that all buttons possess. Even if you have never used a particular piece of software before, if you are presented with a screen containing a button, you know how to use it.

In a program used to manage a hotel, `thePenthouse` and `theBridalSuite` are specific instances of `HotelRoom`. Organizing program components into classes and objects reflects a natural way of thinking.

It is conventional, but not required, to begin object names with a lowercase letter and to begin class names with an uppercase letter.

Inheritance

The concept of using classes provides a useful way to organize objects; it is especially useful because classes are reusable. That is, you can extend them—they are **extensible**. You can create new classes that extend or are **descendents** of existing classes. The descendent classes can **inherit** all the attributes of the original (or **parent**) class, or they can override inappropriate attributes.

In geometry, a `Cube` is a descendent of a `Square`. A `Cube` has all of a `Square`'s attributes, plus one additional characteristic: depth. A `Cube`, however, has a different method of calculating `totalArea` (or volume) than does a `Square`. A `DisposableDish` class has all the characteristics of a `Dish`, plus some special ones. In business, a `PartTimeEmployee` contains all the attributes of an `Employee`, plus more specialized attributes.

Because object-oriented programming languages allow inheritance, you can build classes that are extensions of existing classes; you don't have to start fresh each time you want to create a class.

Polymorphism

Programming modules might occasionally need to change the way they operate depending on the context. Object-oriented programs use **polymorphism** to carry out the same operation in a manner customized to the object. Such differentiation is never allowed in languages that aren't object oriented.

Without polymorphism, you would have to use a separate module or method name for a method that multiplies two numbers and one that multiplies three numbers. Without polymorphism, you would have to create separate module names for a method that cleans a `Dish` object, one that cleans a `Car` object, and one that cleans a `Baby` object. Just as your blender can produce juice regardless of whether you insert two fruits or three vegetables, using a polymorphic, object-oriented multiplication function call will produce a correct product whether you send it two integers or three floating-point numbers. Furthermore, using a polymorphic, object-oriented clean method will operate correctly and appropriately on a `Dish`, a `Car`, or a `Baby`. This is how the English language works; you understand words based on their context. When you master polymorphism in an object-oriented programming language, you take a big step toward producing objects that function like their real-world counterparts.

GETTING STARTED IN THE C++ PROGRAMMING ENVIRONMENT

The main work area in any C++ programming environment is the editor. An **editor** is a simplified version of a word processor in which you type your program statements, or **source code**. When you save what you have written on a disk, you typically save C++ source code files with a filename that has a .cpp extension.

TIP
After you enter the source code for a program, you must compile the program. When you **compile** a program, the code you have written is transformed into machine language—the language that the computer can understand. The output from the compilation is **object code**—statements that have been translated into something the computer can use.

A runnable, or **executable**, program needs the object code as well as code from any out-side sources (other files) to which it refers. The process of integrating these outside refer-ences is called **linking**. An executable file contains the same filename as the source code and the object code, but carries the extension .exe to distinguish it as a program.

When you compile a C++ program, **error messages** and/or **warnings** might appear. A C++ program with errors will not execute; you must eliminate all error messages before you can run the program. Error messages notify you of **fatal errors**—errors that are so severe that they prevent a program from executing. Although a warning will not prevent a program from executing (a warning is a **non-fatal error**), it's important that you exam-ine every warning closely, as each probably indicates a problem. For example, if you try to display a variable that does not exist, C++ will issue an error message such as "Undefined symbol", and you cannot run the program. If you attempt to display a variable that exists but has not been assigned a valid value, C++ will not issue an error message but will issue a warning, such as "Possible use of variable before definition." You can run the program, but the variable value that is given will be meaningless.

If you have purposely included statements within a program that produce warning mes-sages, for example, to experiment with what will happen, then it's okay to ignore warn-ings and run your program. However, in professional production programs, you should eliminate all warnings.

Creating a `main()` Function

C++ programs consist of modules called **functions**. Every statement within every C++ program is contained in a function.

Every function consists of two parts: a function header and a function body. The initial line of code in a C++ function makes up the **function header**, which always has three parts:

- Return type of the function

- Name of the function

- Types and names of any variables enclosed in parentheses, and which the func-tion receives

A C++ program may contain many functions, but every C++ program contains at least one function, and that function is called **main()**. If the `main()` function does not pass values to other programs or receives values from outside the program, then `main()` receives and returns a **void** type. (In this context, **void** simply means nothing; more lit-erally, it means "empty.") Many C++ programs begin with the header `void main(void)` or, for simplicity, `void main()`. Many C++ programmers prefer to use the header `int main()`. Using this header implies that the `main()` function will return an integer value to the operating system in which you are running the program. If you do not explicitly state the value to be returned, the value is 0, which means "everything went smoothly." This book follows the popular convention of using `int main()` as the `main()` func-tion header.

You do not need to understand the terms int, void, or return type to successfully run C++ programs. The purpose of these components will become apparent when you learn to write your own functions. For now, you can begin each program with the header int main().

The body of every function in a C++ program is contained in curly braces. Therefore, the simplest program you can write has the form shown in Figure 1-7. It contains the header int main() and an empty body.

```
int main()
{
}
```

Figure 1-7   The simplest C++ program

In Chapter 6, you will learn that, usually, functions that begin with int must include a return statement. The main() function is an exception; it does not require a return statement. You might have a teacher or boss who requests that you include a return statement in your main() functions, but for simplicity, and following a common convention, this book will omit it.

Placing the **main()** header and the pair of braces on three separate lines is a matter of style. This style, in which the braces in a function each occupy a line of their own and align to the left, is called the **exdented style**.

The following program, written on a single line, works as well as one written on three lines:

```
int main() { }
```

Another style places the opening curly brace on the same line as the function header:

```
int main() {
}
```

Other programmers prefer that the curly braces align but be indented a few spaces, as in the following:

```
int main()
    {
    }
```

The most important style issues are that you observe the style guidelines in the place you work (or those of your instructor in the classroom), and that you apply the style consistently. As a matter of style, this book will give int main() a line of its own, and then give each brace a line of its own, aligned to the left.

The function shown in Figure 1-7 doesn't actually do anything because it contains no C++ statements. A **statement** is a segment of C++ code that performs a task; it is similar to an

English sentence. To create a program that does something, you must place one or more C++ statements between the opening and closing braces.

Every complete C++ statement ends with a semicolon. Frequently, a statement occupies a single line in the editor, but a statement can run across multiple lines in the editor, and you also can place multiple statements on a line if they are short enough. Often several statements must be grouped together, as when several statements must occur in a loop. In such a case, the statements have their own set of opening and closing braces within the main braces, forming a **block**. One universal C++ truth is that every C++ program must contain exactly the same number of opening braces as closing braces.

It is easy to forget to type the closing curly brace to a function, especially if you have typed many statements since typing the opening brace. Therefore, many programmers recommend typing the closing curly brace immediately after you type the opening one. Then you can go back and insert needed statements between them.

Don't block statements unless you have a reason to do so. Place statements in a block within a function only if they form a unit whose execution depends on a selection or a loop.

WORKING WITH VARIABLES AND THE const QUALIFIER

In C++, you must provide a name, also called an **identifier**, to each variable before you can use it. The ability to use identifiers is a key feature of all modern programming languages; without them, you would need to memorize a value's computer memory address. Just as it is easier for you to remember that your friend's house is the `whiteAluminumSidedRanchWithTheGreenTrim` than it is to remember her street address, it is also easier to remember a descriptive identifier than it is to remember a memory address.

Besides variables, you also provide identifiers for C++ functions, structures, and classes.

Identifiers for C++ variables can include letters, numbers, and underscores, but must begin with a letter or underscore. No spaces or other special characters are allowed within a C++ variable name. `Age`, `lastName`, `tax_2006`, `ready2go`, `salary`, `Salary`, and `SALARY` are all valid identifiers. Note that `salary`, `Salary`, and `SALARY` could all be used within the same C++ function without conflict because C++ is case-sensitive. (However, using multiple identifiers whose only difference is the case of some of the letters would be confusing and is not recommended.) C++ programmers typically use all lowercase letters for variable names, or else capitalize only the first letter of each new word (after the first word) in a variable name, as in lastYearGross.

TIP There is an art to selecting appropriate and useful identifiers. In Chapter 8, you will learn more about style issues in C++ programs.

TIP Beginning an identifier with a lowercase letter and capitalizing subsequent words within the identifier is a style known as **camel casing**. An identifier such as lastName resembles a camel because of the "hump" in the middle.

Every programming language contains a few vocabulary words, or **keywords**, that you need in order to use the language. A C++ keyword cannot be used as a variable name. Common C++ keywords are listed in Table 1-1. Keywords vary for each C++ compiler, so some of the terms listed in Table 1-1 might not be keywords in your system. However, it is best not to use any of these terms as variables. That way, your code will be portable to other compilers.

Table 1-1   Common C++ keywords

and	continue	If	public	try
and_eq	default	inline	register	typedef
asm	delete	Int	reinterpret_cast	typeid
auto	do	Long	return	typename
bitand	double	mutable	short	uchar_t
bitor	dynamiccast	namespace	signed	union
bool	else	New	sizeof	unsigned
break	enum	Not	state_cast	using
case	explicit	not_eq	static	virtual
catch	extern	operator	struct	void
char	false	Or	switch	volatile
class	float	or_eq	template	wchar_t
compl	for	overload	this	while
const	friend	private	throw	xor
constcast	goto	protected	true	xor_eq

TIP On some older computer systems, only the first 31 characters of a variable name are actually used. Thus, to ensure portability, you might choose to limit variable names to 31 characters, or at least make them unique within the first 31 characters.

Besides an identifier, each named variable must have a data type. C++ supports three simple data types: integral, floating point, and enumeration.

The integral and floating-point data types are discussed in this chapter. You will learn about the enumeration type in Chapter 14. In addition to the simple data types, C++ supports structured data types and pointers. You will learn about structured data types later in this chapter, and about pointers in future chapters.

TIP

An **integral data type** is a type that holds an **integer**—a number (either positive or negative) without a decimal point. Integral data types include nine categories: `char`, `short`, `int`, `long`, `bool`, `unsigned char`, `unsigned short`, `unsigned int`, and `unsigned long`. Each of these categories has a different set of values associated with it as well as a specific number of bytes of memory it occupies, and you might choose one over the other if limiting memory usage is important in an application. For example, the amount of memory required by `short` and `long` might be shorter or longer than that required by an `int`—it depends on the computer system. However, the integer types are meant to be relative. Therefore, a `short` might take less memory than an `int`, and a `long` might take more than an `int`. (But maybe not! The amount of memory used depends on your system.)

This book will use only three integral types: `int`, `char`, and `bool`.

You can declare a variable that is meant to hold a whole number as `int`, `short`, `long`, `unsigned int`, `unsigned short`, or `unsigned long`. If you use a constant whole-number value, such as 12, in a C++ program, it is an `int` by default.

TIP

The int Data Type

An integer value may be stored in an **integer data type variable**, declared with the keyword **int**. Examples are 4, 15, +5000, and −10. Integers do not include decimal points, and they cannot be written with commas, dollar signs, or any symbols other than a leading + or −. (Of course, if a + symbol is not used, the integer is assumed to be positive.) You can also declare an integer variable using `short int` and `long int`.

You can determine the size of variables in your system with the `sizeof()` operator. For example, to find out how much memory an integer uses, you can place the following statement in a program:

TIP

`cout<<"Integer size is " <<sizeof(int)<<" on this computer";`

Output might then be: `Integer size is 4 on this computer`.

When an integer is stored in four bytes, the 32 bits used can form only 4,294,967,296 combinations (2 to the 32nd power); thus, only 4,294,967,296 different integer values can be stored. One bit indicates whether the value is positive or negative; the other 31 bits can represent values from –2,147,483,648 through +2,147,483,647. Problems arise when a programmer forgets those limits. If you store a value of 5000000000 (5 billion) in an integer named `salary` and then print it out, C++ will not produce an error message but will show 705032704 rather than 5000000000. Because 5,000,000,000 is larger than 4,294,967,296, C++ misinterprets `salary` as a negative number.

The char Data Type

Characters may be stored in **character data type variables**, declared with the keyword **char**. (Most programmers pronounce this keyword "care" because it comes from "character"; others pronounce it "char" [as in "to scorch"] because of the way it is spelled. Others say "car," like an automobile.) A **char** may hold any single symbol in the ASCII character set. Often it contains a letter of the alphabet, but it could include a space, a digit, a punctuation mark, an arithmetic symbol, or any other special symbol. In C++, a character value is always expressed in single quotes, such as 'A' or '&'.

A single character, such as 'D', is contained in single quotes. A string value, such as "Donna", uses double quotes.

The bool Data Type

A **Boolean data type variable** can be declared using the **bool** data type, which has only two possible values—**true** or **false**. When you assign a value to a Boolean variable, you can use **true** or **false**, as in the following examples:

```
bool isDriverInsured = true;
bool isPremiumPaid = false;
```

However, when you display the value stored in a Boolean variable, a 0 or 1 displays, for **false** and **true** respectively. You will learn much more about how to use this data type in Chapter 3.

George Boole was a mathematician who lived from 1815 to 1864. He approached logic more simply than his predecessors did, by expressing logical selections with common algebraic symbols. He is considered the founder of "Boolean algebra," or what some call "mathematical logic," and Boolean (true/false) expressions are named for him.

Some older compilers do not support the `bool` data type.

Floating-Point Data Types

Real numbers, or **floating-point numbers**, are numbers that include decimal positions, such as 98.6, 1000.0002, and −3.85. They may be stored in variables with types **float**, **double**, and **long double**. The amount of storage required for each of these types varies from computer to computer. Usually a `double` occupies more memory space than a `float` (allowing a `double` to provide more decimal places, which is called providing greater **precision**, or accuracy). The maximum number of decimal places allowed in a `float` is usually 6 or 7, and the maximum in a `double` is usually 15. This book uses the `double` data type to manipulate floating-point numbers.

`Float` values are called single-precision numbers, and `double` values are called double-precision numbers.

You can declare a variable that is meant to hold a floating-point number as `float` or `double`. If you use a floating-point number constant value, such as 12.25, in a C++ program, it is a `double` by default.

When you use different compilers, the amount of storage allocated for different data types can differ. For example, on many newer compilers, `long double` and `double` are the same. A `double` never takes less storage space than a `float`, and a `double` never takes more space than a `long double`.

Declaring Variables

Before you can use a variable within any C++ method, you must declare it—that is, provide it with both a data type and an identifier. A variable declaration is a C++ statement, so it must end with a semicolon. For example, `int myTestScore;` is a complete C++ statement that declares an integer variable named `myTestScore`. Remember, C++ allows any one-word identifier to be used as a variable name, but your programs will be clearer and your work will be considered more professional if you use descriptive names like `myTestScore` instead of cryptic variable names such as `x`.

If you write a function that contains variables of diverse types, each variable must be declared in a statement of its own. If you want to declare two or more variables of the same type, you may declare them in the same statement, separated by commas. A declaration statement may include only one data type; you must declare variables of different types in separate statements.

Variables may be declared anywhere in a C++ program, but cannot be used until after they are declared. Commonly, variables are declared at the beginning of a function, just after the opening curly braces. This traditional format makes the variables easier to locate when reading the function later. The code following this paragraph shows the beginning of a typical C++ program that will use variables of several types.

```
int main()
{
    int myAge;
    int yourAge;
    char myMiddleInitial;
    double myMoney, yourMoney;
}
```

TIP In the C programming language, which was a predecessor to C++, all variables had to be declared within a function before any executable statements could be included. Although C++ does not require this rigid format, many programmers still think it is good form to declare all variables at the beginning of every function.

Notice that the integer variables **myAge** and **yourAge** are each declared in a separate statement. On the other hand, the two **double** variables, **myMoney** and **yourMoney**, are declared in the same statement. When you declare two variables within the same statement, you separate the variable names with a comma and place the semicolon at the end of the list of all the variables of that type. Either style of variable declaration (separate statements or a shared statement) is acceptable when you declare multiple variables of the same type.

As a matter of style, some programmers prefer always to declare each variable in its own statement. This makes it easier to remove a single variable if it is no longer needed. Others prefer a style in which variables of the same type are declared in the same statement but each is listed in a separate line, as in the following example:

```
int myAge,
    yourAge,
    hisAge;
```

These three variables are declared in a single statement—notice no semicolon appears until the end of the last line. By using separate lines, it is easier to see each variable, and by indenting the second and third lines, it is easier to see they are continuations of the statement started in the first line.

Explicitly stating the value of a variable is called **assignment** and is achieved with the **assignment operator** =. You can assign a value to a variable in the same statement that declares the variable, or assign the value later in another statement. For instance, in Figure 1-8, the variable **midtermScore** is declared in one statement and assigned a value in a separate statement. The variable **finalScore** is declared and assigned a value at the same time. Assigning a value to a variable upon creation is often referred to as **initializing** the variable.

```
int midtermScore;
int finalScore = 100;
midtermScore = 76;
int quiz1Score = 10,
    quiz2Score = 5;
```

Figure 1-8   Declaring, initializing, and assigning values to variables

 TIP Unlike most other programming languages, C++ allows you to assign values to several variables in one statement. For example, `tot = sum = amount = 0;` assigns a value of 0 to all three variables listed in the statement.

Assignment always takes place from right to left; that is, a value on the right side of the assignment operator is stored in the memory location (variable) on the left side of the assignment operator. Although midtermScore = 76 and 76 = midtermScore are equivalent statements in algebra, C++ does not allow the second statement. C++ refers to locations where values may be stored as **Lvalues** because these values are located on the left side of assignment statements.

Figure 1-8 also shows two integer variables, `quiz1Score` and `quiz2Score`, being declared and initialized in the same statement. After C++ programmers become accustomed to placing a semicolon at the end of each statement, they sometimes get carried away and put a semicolon at the end of every line. However, sometimes a statement extends across several lines. A declaration is complete only when you have listed as many variables as you want for that type; use a semicolon only when the entire statement is complete.

 TIP You also might have noticed that semicolons never follow function headers such as `int main()`. Function headers are not C++ statements. You can think of C++ statements as full actions, so you do not place a semicolon at the end of a function header, nor at the end of any line with a statement that continues on the next line.

 TIP Because numeric constants that contain decimal places are `doubles` by default, some compilers will issue a warning message if you assign a constant double to a `float`, as in `float value = 12.34;`. You can suppress the warning message by using an `f` following the constant, as in `float value = 12.34f;`.

 TIP When you declare a variable between any set of curly braces, the variable is usable only from the point of declaration to the closing curly brace. This area is referred to as the **scope of the variable**, or the region of the program in which the variable exists.

The const Qualifier

A variable that does not change in a program should not be declared as a variable. (After all, it won't vary.) Instead, it should be a **named constant**—a named memory location whose contents cannot change during execution of the program. The statement `const double MINIMUM_WAGE = 5.75;` declares a constant named `MINIMUM_WAGE` that can be used like a variable but cannot be changed during a program. For example, if you declare `const double MINIMUM_WAGE = 5.75;` within a function, then it is illegal to write the statement `MINIMUM_WAGE = 6.00;` later in the same function. The keyword `const` is an example of a **qualifier**—a word that qualifies, or restricts, the ordinary capabilities of the named type (such as `double`).

TIP

In some languages, such as Java, programmers usually use all uppercase letters for a constant name; that way, constants are easily identified in a program and not mistaken for variables. However, such capitalization is not required. In C++, constants have traditionally been lowercase, although many programmers recommend using uppercase identifiers, as in Java. What's most important is that you develop a consistent style within your programs.

CREATING COMMENTS

Comments are statements that do not affect the compiling or running of a program—that is, they do not show up when the program runs. Comments are simply explanatory remarks that the programmer includes in a program to make notes, explain programming choices, or clarify what is taking place. These remarks are useful to other programmers who read your programs because that might help explain the intent of a particular statement or the purpose of the entire program. In addition, comments could indicate who wrote the program and when. They often help the programmer remember why something was done a certain way when the program was written weeks or months earlier.

C++ supports both line comments and block comments. A **line comment** begins with two slashes (//) and continues to the end of the line on which it is placed. It might take up an entire line, or it might begin after some executable C++ code and take up the rest of the line. A **block comment** begins with a single slash and an asterisk (/*) and ends with an asterisk and a slash (*/); it might be contained on a single line or continued across many lines. Like a line comment, a block comment might take up an entire line, or it might occur on a line along with executable code, either before or after the code. Figure 1-9 shows a program that contains only one executable statement: the highlighted statement that declares the variable `myAge`.

```
// this is a comment on one line
/* this comment is on a different line */
/* this is in front */   int myAge;    //this is in back
/* this comment runs across
     three lines of code just to show
     that it can be done !        */
```

Figure 1-9   Demonstrating comments

When using block comments, don't start a comment that never ends. Using /* without a corresponding end */ makes everything following the /* in the program a nonexecuting comment.

TIP

Throughout this text, comments are used to point out features in code examples. Sometimes a comment even indicates that a statement is invalid. This type of comment is for instruction only; you wouldn't use such comments in professional programs.

TIP

The end of a function is sometimes hard to notice because the single closing curly brace on a line by itself does not stand out. Some programmers help mark the end of a function by placing a comment to the right of the closing curly brace, such as the following:

TIP

```
// end of main function
```

ANSI/ISO Standard C++

The C++ programming language evolved from a language named C. C++ was designed by Bjarne Stoustrup at Bell Laboratories in the 1980s. During its early years, several compilers were developed for C++, and the language evolved in slightly different ways in different compilers. Because of this, C++ programs written in one compiler were not always portable to another compiler.

In the early 1990s, a joint committee of the American National Standards Institute (ANSI) and the International Standard Organization (ISO) standardized the syntax used in C++. The standardized rules are known as the **ANSI/ISO Standard**. Most newer compilers use the new standard, most older compilers use the older standard, and some compilers allow you to use whichever you prefer. The features of the language are almost entirely the same using any C++ compiler, but to access certain features, notably input and output operations, you must begin your C++ programs with slightly different statements.

Using Libraries, Preprocessor Directives, and namespace

C++ programs often refer to variables and code that lie outside the source code the programmer actually writes. C++ is powerful in part because many of its functions have already been written for you. For example, finding the square root of a number can be a fairly complicated mathematical task, but the creators of C++ have written a function that calculates square roots. You can include this function, **sqrt()**, in your own C++ programs—but only if your programs can find it when you link to outside files to create executable files.

Header files are files that contain predefined values and routines, such as **sqrt()**. Their filenames usually have no extension or end in .h. In order for your C++ program to use these predefined routines, you must include a **preprocessor directive**—a statement that tells a program, called the **preprocessor**, what to do before compiling the program. In C++, all preprocessor directives begin with a pound sign (#), which is also called an **octothorp**.

The **#include** preprocessor directive tells the compiler to include a file as part of the finished product. In any program, you might include a special-purpose file you wrote, or you might include a file that is packaged with your C++ compiler. For example, to use the **sqrt()** function, you might use **#include <math.h>** or **#include <cmath>** depending on whether your compiler is old or new. You will need another include directive, **#include <iostream.h>** or **#include <iostream>**, to use C++ input and output statements.

The angle brackets in **#include <math.h>** indicate that the math.h file is found in the standard folder that holds include files. You could use quotation marks in place of the angle brackets, but the compiler would take a little longer to find your file, and you would be using an unconventional format for the include statement.

TIP

Do not include a semicolon at the end of any preprocessor directive. A preprocessor directive is not a C++ statement.

TIP

Be careful that you do not include spaces around the filename within the angle brackets in an include statement. The compiler will search for a filename that begins and ends with spaces, and will not be able to find the file you intend to include.

TIP

To use specific C++ features in ANSI/ISO C++, you must also learn to access a namespace. A **namespace** is a mechanism for grouping features you want to include in a program. For example, to use the standard C++ input and output statements (which you will learn about in the next section), you can type the following near the top of your program file:

```
using namespace std;
```

This book uses the ANSI/ISO Standard, but you might see C++ programs that follow the older conventions. You will certainly be able to understand older C++ programs if you encounter them; the differences are minor and are summarized in Table 1-2.

Table 1-2   Differences between ANSI/ISO C++ programs and Standard C++ programs

ANSI/ISO C++	Standard C++
The `include` preprocessor directives do not typically use file extensions, for example `#include<iostream>`	The `include` preprocessor directives typically use file extensions, for example `#include<iostream.h>`
Uses the statement `using namespace std;`	Does not use the `using namespace std;` statement

The `main()` function header is `int main()`	The `main()` function header might be any of the following:
	`int main()`
	`int main(void)`
	`void main()`
	`void main(void)`

The `main()` function does not require a `return` statement	The `main()` function does not have a `return` statement if the function type (first word in the header) is void. The `main()` function ends with a statement such as `return 0;` if the `main()` function type is `int`.

PRODUCING C++ OUTPUT

C++ provides several objects for producing output. The simplest object is called **cout**, pronounced "see out." The name comes from Console OUTput and `cout` shows whatever is passed to it. When contained in a complete C++ program, the statement `cout<<"Hi there";` places the phrase "Hi there" on the monitor. The **insertion operator** (<<) says "insert whatever is to my right into the object `cout`."

TIP   If you think like a computer (rather than a person), the direction of the brackets used with `cout` makes sense. In the statement `cout<<"Hi there";` the phrase is being sent to the output device, so the insertion symbol points to and inserts characters into the `cout` object.

TIP   A phrase such as "Hi there" that is included within double quotes is a string. You will learn more about strings in Chapter 5.

The object **cout** is contained in the header file iostream (in ANSI/ISO C++) or iostream.h (in Standard C++). The term iostream is short for Input Output STREAM. The preprocessor directive to `#include one of the iostream files` must appear at the top of any program that uses `cout`. Two complete programs that print "Hi there" are shown in Figure 1-10. If you type one of these programs into a C++ editor, compile it, and run it, the words "Hi there" will appear on the monitor.

```
// Program that displays "Hi there" using an ANSI/ISO C++ compiler
#include<iostream>
using namespace std;
int main()
{
    cout<<"Hi there";
}
// Program that displays "Hi there" using a Standard C++ compiler
#include<iostream.h>
void main()
{
    cout<<"Hi there";
}
```

Figure 1-10   Programs that use `cout`

TIP

With some compilers, the screen output appears but is gone so quickly that you don't get a chance to read the output message. If this happens to you, include the line `#include<conio>` or `#include<conio.h>` as the first line in your file, and include the line `getch();` immediately after the statement `cout<<"Hi there";`. This pauses the execution of your program and waits for one character to be input from the keyboard before the output screen closes down.

You can see in Figure 1-10 that the programs are very similar. The only differences are in the extension in the included filename and the addition of the `using namespace std;` statement in the ANSI/ISO version. To avoid much duplication, the examples in the rest of this text will use the ANSI/ISO versions.

You could replace the `cout` statement in Figure 1-10 with two `cout` statements:

```
cout<<"Hi ";
cout<<"there";
```

Even though this replacement version of the program uses two `cout` statements, nothing indicates that any output should be placed on a new line. The character string "Hi " (notice the space included before the last quotation mark) would print on the monitor, followed immediately by the character string "there". To indicate a **newline** character—that is, the invisible character that forces the next output to appear on a new line—you can use the escape sequence \n. The backslash removes the usual meaning of the letter *n* (which is simply to produce the letter *n*, as in the statement `cout<<'n';`) and causes the output to move to a new line. The statement `cout<<"Hi\nthere";` shows "Hi" and "there" on two separate lines.

TIP

An **escape sequence** is a sequence of characters in which the first character serves only to "escape" from the usual meaning of the second character. Other commonly used escape sequences are \t for Tab, \" for a double quote, and \' for a single quote. To actually show a backslash, use \\.

Another way to advance output to a new line is to use the end line manipulator **endl**. Inserting `endl` into the output stream causes a new line plus all waiting output to become visible, a process called **flushing the buffer**. The following code produces "Hi" and "there" on two separate lines:

```
cout<<"Hi";
cout<<endl;
cout<<"there";
```

TIP   It's a good idea to add an `endl` manipulator to the end of the last `cout` statement in every C++ program. When you do so, you make sure that all waiting output is displayed before the program ends.

A single `cout` object might show more than one item, as long as each item is preceded by its own insertion symbol. For example, `cout<<"Hi"<<endl<<"there";` displays "Hi", goes to a new line, and displays "there" on the next line.

In addition to strings, you can output numbers and variables. Thus, the following three statements of code together produce 1, 2, 3, and 4, each displayed on its own line.

```
int number = 3;
cout<<1<<endl;
cout<<2<<endl<<number<<endl<<4<<endl;
```

PROVIDING C++ INPUT

A program in which the programmer predetermines all variable values is not very useful. Many programs rely on input from a **user**—a person who runs, and probably benefits from, the output provided by a program. These are called **interactive programs** because the user interacts with the program statements. The program must provide a way for the user to enter responses to program **prompts**—statements that request input from the user, often explaining what is expected. You create prompts by using the `cout` object; you retrieve user responses by using the `cin` object. The **cin** (pronounced "see in") object fetches values from the keyboard; it is used with the **extraction operator** (>>). Like `cout`, `cin` is contained in the iostream header file.

TIP   According to computer logic, the direction of the brackets in `cin` makes sense. For example, the statement `cin>>quantity;` places a value into the variable `quantity`.

Figure 1-11 shows a program that declares a variable that stores an age; prompts the user for a value; and then **echoes**, or repeats, the user's input as output.

```
#include<iostream>

using namespace std;

int main()
{
    int age;
    cout<<"How old are you? ";
    cin>>age;
    cout<<"Your age is "<<age<<endl;
}
```

Figure 1-11   A program with a prompt, input, and output

TIP   A space often appears within the quotes at the end of a prompt. The purpose of the space is cosmetic. As the program user enters a data value, that value appears on the monitor immediately to the right of the prompt. A space after the prompt, yet before the data, makes the screen easier to read.

In the program shown in Figure 1-11, after the prompt is given, the program pauses until a user types a number and presses Enter. Then the age is echoed. Figure 1-12 shows a typical execution of the program.

Figure 1-12   Typical execution of the program in Figure 1-11

TIP   Your compiler might automatically pause and produce a phrase similar to "Press any key to continue." This phrase appears on all the output shown in this book.

Similarly to `cout`, one `cin` object may be used to enter more than one value, as in the following example:

```
int score1, score2, score3;
cout<<"Please enter three scores. Use a space between them. ";
cin>>score1>>score2>>score3;
```

At the prompt "Please enter three scores. Use a space between them. ", the user may enter three integers with any whitespace between them. **Whitespace** consists of any number of spaces, tabs, and Enter characters. Although this code segment allows the user to enter three scores, it is almost always a better practice to ask a user for one value at a time. That is, first provide a prompt, then add a `cin` statement to read the first value. Then provide the second prompt and its `cin`, followed by the third prompt and its `cin`.

A FIRST LOOK AT DATA STRUCTURES AND CLASSES

When you use data types like `int`, `char`, and `double` within a program, you are using the C++ built-in **primitive** or **scalar** data types. A major feature of object-oriented languages is the ability to create your own complex data types. C++ supports two ways to create your own complex data types: **data structures**—or, more simply, **structures**—and **classes**.

Although both contain the term "structure," control structures and data structures are very different. The control structures sequence, selection, and loop describe the logical flow of a program's instructions. Data structures are used to encapsulate separate related data fields.

Data structures and classes can become quite complex. Both can contain many simpler data types within them, as well as any number of functions. For example, you might create an `Employee` structure or class with components such as `firstName`, `lastName`, `hourlySalary`, `numberOfDependents`, and `hireDate`. The relationship between these components, or **fields**, of the `Employee` class is often called a **has-a relationship** because every `Employee` "has a" `firstName`, `lastName`, and so on.

Consider a very simple `Employee` structure or class that contains only two components: `idNumber` and `hourlySalary`. You could define such a structure or class with two types, as shown in Figure 1-13. You use the C++ keyword `struct` or `class` and follow it with an identifier you choose. Between curly braces, you name the individual fields that will be part of the `struct` or `class`. Each field type and identifier ends with a semicolon, and the `struct` or `class` definition itself ends with a semicolon after the closing curly brace. Notice, in Figure 1-13, that in this case, the only difference in the definition of the data structure and class is in the first highlighted word.

You would not create both a struct and a class with the same name in the same program. Both are shown in Figure 1-13 for comparison purposes.

```
struct Employee                class Employee
{                              {
   int idNumber;                  int idNumber;
   double hourlySalary;           double hourlySalary;
};                             };
```

Figure 1-13   A simple `Employee` struct and class

The semicolon after the closing curly brace in the struct and class definitions is important; your program will not compile without it. Unfortunately, this semicolon is easy to forget, because when closing curly braces appear in other places in C++ programs—for example, at the end of functions—they are seldom followed by a semicolon.

TIP

When you declare a structure type, you are not required to give it a name, but if you use this technique, you must declare all the structure objects immediately after the closing curly brace and before the semicolon. This book will always provide a name for structure data types.

The `Employee` class definition shown in Figure 1-13 indicates that an `Employee` has two components: an integer `idNumber` and a double `hourlySalary`. If you declare an `int` within a C++ program, it can hold only a whole number value, such as 2345. If you declare a `double` within a C++ program, it can contain only a floating-point number value, such as 12.95. However, if you create an `Employee` object, it can hold two values: an `int` and a `double`. Figure 1-14 shows a `main()` function that declares two objects: an integer and an `Employee`. Note that whether you declare a primitive type variable, a structure, or a class object, the syntax is the same: type, identifier, semicolon.

```
int main()
{
   int companyStaffSize;
   Employee oneStaffMember;
}
```

Figure 1-14   A `main()` function that declares an integer and an `Employee`

Whether you use a structure or a class, after you declare an `Employee` named `oneStaffMember`, you refer to the individual fields of `oneStaffMember` by using the object name, a **dot operator** (or period), and the field name. For example, the `idNumber` of the `oneStaffMember` object is referenced with the identifier `oneStaffMember.idNumber`.

There is an important difference in the way `struct`s and `class`es treat their data members. If you write the program in Figure 1-14 to include the `Employee` structure, and include a new statement such as `oneStaffMember.idNumber = 2345;`, then 2345 will be assigned to the `idNumber` of `oneStaffMember`. However, if you use the `Employee` class instead of the data structure and include the same assignment statement, then you will receive an error message that indicates the `idNumber` is not accessible from within your program. The reason is that, by default, all structure fields are **public,** or available to functions (like the `main()` function) that are outside the structure. Conversely, all class fields are **private**. That means they are not available for use outside the class. When you create a class, you can declare some fields to be private and some to be public. For example, in the real world, you might want your name to be public knowledge but your Social Security number, salary, or age to be private.

Object-oriented C++ programmers use classes more frequently than structures, and as you continue your study of C++, you will learn that most class fields are made private the majority of the time. You will also learn how to access these private fields. For now, you can use structures to group individual fields into specialized complex data types. Figure 1-15 shows a complete program that declares a data structure with public fields, and uses that structure within a **main()** function. Figure 1-16 shows the output.

```
// The Employee struct and
// a main() function that declares and uses an Employee
#include<iostream>
using namespace std;
struct Employee
{
    int idNumber;
    double hourlySalary;
};
int main()
{
    Employee oneStaffMember;
    oneStaffMember.idNumber = 2345;
    oneStaffMember.hourlySalary = 12.95;
    cout<<"ID number is "<<oneStaffMember.idNumber<<endl;
    cout<<"Hourly rate is "<<oneStaffMember.hourlySalary<<endl;
}
```

Figure 1-15   A structure and a **main()** method that uses the structure

Figure 1-16   Output of program in Figure 1-15

Creating structures and classes provides a means to group data fields in a logical way. When you think of an **Employee**, you think of an actual human employee as encapsulating, or encompassing, an ID number and a salary (and usually even more fields). Similarly, a **Student** encapsulates a credit hour field as well as a grade point average field. Creating entities that mimic their real-world counterparts is a hallmark of object-oriented programming. As you continue your studies of C++ (or other object-oriented languages), you will learn how to encapsulate more fields and even actions, or functions, into a class.

When you first learn about structures or classes, they seem to provide few advantages—and the drawback of additional typing. For now, you just have to trust that as you continue to study C++, you will find many advantages to encapsulating your data and functions into reusable objects.

YOU DO IT

In the steps that follow, you will create your first executable C++ program. For help in getting started with your compiler, see Appendix A (for an ANSI/ISO C++ compiler) or Appendix B (for a Standard C++ complier).

TIP

If you are using Microsoft Visual Studio 2005, be sure to also include the following line as the first line in your program file:

```
#include "stdafx.h"
```

If you are using Microsoft Visual Studio 6.0, do not include this line.

Creating a Program That Displays Variable Values

To create a program that declares two variables, assigns values to them, and creates output:

1. Create a project named **Output1**. In your C++ editor, type the following comment to explain the purpose of the program:

    ```
    // A first C++ program demonstrating variable use
    ```

    Add any comments your instructor requests or that you think enhance the program documentation. For example, you might want to include your name and the date you are writing the program.

2. On the next lines, type the preprocessor directive and the `using namespace` statement that you need to use `cout`.

    ```
    #include<iostream>
    using namespace std;
    ```

3. As shown below, type the `main()` function header. Press **Enter** to move to a new line, and type the opening curly brace of the `main()` function. Then press the **Enter** key again.

    ```
    int main()
    {
    ```

4. Indent three spaces to the right of the opening curly brace on the previous line. Declare two variables. One variable is an integer named `creditHours`, and the other is a `double` variable named `gradePointAverage`.

    ```
    int creditHours;
    double gradePointAverage;
    ```

5. Press **Enter** to start a new line. Then assign values to the two declared variables.

    ```
    creditHours = 15;
    gradePointAverage = 3.25;
    ```

6. Add statements that show the assigned values with an explanation on two separate lines.

```
cout<<"The number of credit hours is "<<creditHours<<endl;
cout<<"The grade point average is "<<gradePointAverage<<endl;
```

7. Add a closing curly brace as the last line in the program. Align it vertically with the opening curly brace seven lines above it. The complete program is shown in Figure 1-17.

```
// A first C++ program demonstrating variable use
#include<iostream>
using namespace std;
int main()
{
   int creditHours;
   double gradePointAverage;
   creditHours = 15;
   gradePointAverage = 3.25;
   cout<<"The number of credit hours is "<<creditHours<<endl;
   cout<<"The grade point average is "<<gradePointAverage<<endl;
}
```

Figure 1-17   A program that displays some variable values

8. Save the file.

9. Compile the program. If you receive any error messages, correct the errors.

10. Run the program and observe the output. It should look like Figure 1-18.

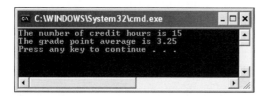

Figure 1-18   Output of the Output1.cpp program

TIP   If your output screen flashes quickly and disappears, then add `#include<conio.h>` at the top of your file and `getch();` as the last statement in your program, before the closing curly brace. This statement pauses the program until you type a keyboard character, providing time for you to view the output.

11. Change the values assigned to the variables `creditHours` and `gradePointAverage`. Compile and run the program again. Confirm that the new output shows the new values you assigned to the variables.

Introducing Errors into a Program

Next, you will purposely introduce errors into your C++ program so that you can become familiar with the types of warnings and error messages you will see when you accidentally make similar errors.

1. Open the **Output1.cpp** file if it is not already open on your system.

2. Remove the parentheses after `main` in the `main()` function header, and then compile the program. Make a note of the error message generated. For example, in Microsoft Visual Studio 2005, the message is "`'main' : looks like a function definition, but there is no formal parameter list; skipping apparent body`". This means that, although `main` looks like a function, it is incomplete.

3. Replace the parentheses and compile the program again. All error messages are gone.

4. Continue to introduce each of the following errors. Compile the program, note the error, fix the error, and compile the program again. Save the document with your list of error messages and their causes as **CommonCompilerErrorMessages.doc**.

5. Change the spelling of `main()` to `man()`.

6. Remove the opening parenthesis of the `main()` function.

7. Remove the statement that declares the `creditHours` variable.

8. Remove the statement that assigns 15 to `creditHours`.

9. Remove the preprocessor directive `#include<iostream>`.

10. Misspell cout in one of the `cout` statements.

11. Remove the last semicolon in the program.

12. Experiment with any more errors you like—for example, removing a quotation mark, assignment operator, or insertion operator. Make sure that all errors are corrected and the program executes before proceeding to the next set of steps.

Modifying a Program to Accept Input Values

In the next steps, you will add prompts and interactive input to the Output1.cpp program.

1. Open the **Output1.cpp** file if it is not already open on your system.

2. Delete the following two lines. Your program will no longer assign values to these variables; instead, it will prompt the user to enter values.

```
creditHours = 15;
gradePointAverage = 3.25;
```

3. In place of the two deleted statements, insert a prompt for the credit hours value.

```
cout<<"Please enter your credit hours ";
```

4. On the next line, type the following statement that reads the `creditHours` in from the keyboard.

```
cin>>creditHours;
```

5. On the next line, add the statements below that prompt for and read the `gradePointAverage`.

```
cout<<"Please enter your grade point average ";
cin>>gradePointAverage;
```

6. Save the file as **Output2.cpp**.

7. Compile the program and correct any errors. Remember that C++ is case-sensitive; some of your errors might be due to incorrect capitalization. When you have corrected any errors, save the file and compile it again.

8. Run the program. Enter data at the prompts—for example, **26** for the `creditHours` variable and **3.78** for the `gradePointAverage` variable. The output should look like Figure 1-19.

Figure 1-19   Execution of the Output2.cpp program

Creating a Simple Structure

In the next steps, you will create a `Student` structure—a new data type that holds two pieces of data about a student—and then you will create a program that uses a `Student`.

1. Open a new project named **Student**. Type the comment below:

```
// Demonstrating a Student struct
```

2. Type the preprocessor directives to include the iostream file so that `cout` and `cin` will work correctly. Also include the `using namespace` statement you need.

```
#include<iostream>
using namespace std;
```

3. Define a `Student` structure that will contain two fields: one that holds credit hours for a student, and another that holds the grade point average.

```
struct Student
{
        int creditHours;
        double gradePointAverage;
};
```

4. Next begin the `main()` function, and declare a `Student` identified as `oneSophomore`.

```
int main()
{
    Student oneSophomore;
```

5. Write the statements that prompt for and allow entry of the `Student`'s data.

```
cout<<"Please enter a student's credit hours ";
cin>>oneSophomore.creditHours;
cout<<"Please enter the student's grade point average ";
cin>>oneSophomore.gradePointAverage;
```

6. Add the statements that echo the data just entered.

```
cout<<"The number of credit hours is "<<
    oneSophomore.creditHours<<endl;
cout<<"The grade point average is "<<
    oneSophomore.gradePointAverage<<endl;
```

TIP

Add `#include<conio.h>` at the top of the file and the `getch();` statement at the end of the program if you need to hold the output screen. You might also choose to include a `cout` statement such as `cout<<"Press any key to continue";` so the user knows what to do.

7. Add the closing curly brace for the program, and then save the file.

8. Compile the program. When it is error-free, run the program. Depending on the data you use for input, the output should look similar to Figure 1-20.

```
C:\WINDOWS\system32\cmd.exe                        _ □ ×
Please enter a student's credit hours 15
Please enter the student's grade point average 3.2
The number of credit hours is 15
The grade point average is 3.2
Press any key to continue . . .
```

Figure 1-20   Output of the Student.cpp program

CHAPTER SUMMARY

❑ Programming a computer involves learning the syntax of a computer programming language and resolving logical errors. To create a working program, you first write the program, and then compile it and test it.

❑ All programming languages provide methods for input and output of variable values. You declare a variable by providing it with a name and a type.

❑ Procedural programs consist of a series of steps or procedures that take place one after the other. Procedural programs use control structures named sequence, selection, and loop. Within programs, you can call modules or subroutines.

❑ Object-oriented programming adds several new programming concepts including objects, classes, inheritance, and polymorphism. An object is an instance of a class. Inheritance provides a means of extending a class to make more specific classes. Polymorphism is the feature that allows program modules to operate appropriately based on the context.

❑ You write a C++ program by typing source code into an editor and compiling the program. When you compile a program, the compiler might issue warnings or errors, which you must rectify before you can run the program.

❑ C++ modules are called functions, and each function contains a header and a body. Every C++ program contains a `main()` function.

❑ C++ variables must be given a type and a name. Simple types include integer for whole numbers, `double` and `float` for floating-point values, and character for any character. Variables must be given a one-word name that is not a C++ keyword. You can assign a value to a variable using the assignment operator, the equal sign. Values that do not vary are called constants.

❑ Comments are nonexecuting program statements. C++ supports line comments and block comments.

❑ A preprocessor directive tells the compiler to do something, such as to include a header file, before compiling the program.

❑ The `cout` statement (along with an insertion operator) is used to display values. The `cin` statement (along with an extraction operator) is used to read values into variables.

❑ When you create a data structure or class, you create your own C++ data type, which is a complex type composed of simpler types. When you create a structure, its fields are public by default, and you access the fields with a dot operator.

KEY TERMS

Programming a computer involves writing instructions that enable a computer to carry out a single task or a group of tasks.

Programs or **software** are the instructions written to perform computerized tasks.

Programs that you apply to a task are called **application programs**, or simply **applications**.

A computer **programming language** defines both vocabulary and syntax.

The rules of any language make up its **syntax**.

A **syntax error** is the incorrect application of a language's rules.

Machine language is the language that computers can understand; it consists of 1s and 0s.

An **interpreter** is a program that translates programming language instructions one line at a time.

A **compiler** is a program that translates an entire program at one time.

A **logical error** occurs when you use a statement that, although syntactically correct, doesn't do what you intended.

You **run** a program by issuing a command to execute, or carry out, the program statements.

To **execute** program statements is to carry them out.

You **test** a program by using sample data to determine whether the program results are correct.

Semantic errors occur when you use a correct word in the wrong context.

Output is the information produced by a program.

Input is the data provided by an outside source into the computer program so that it can be manipulated.

Variables are named memory locations whose contents can change.

When a variable is explicitly **declared**, it is given a data type as well as a name; a variable must be declared before it can be used.

The **data type** of a variable defines what kind of values may be stored in a variable and what kind of operations can be performed on it.

Numeric variables hold values like 13 or −6.

Character variables hold values like 'A' or '&'.

Integer variables store whole numbers.

Floating-point variables store numbers with decimal places.

Procedural programs consist of a series of steps or procedures that take place one after the other.

A **production program** is a real-life program in use by a business.

Control structures are the basic logic components used in programs.

Using the **sequence structure**, you program steps to execute one after another, without interruption.

Using the **selection structure**, you perform different tasks based on a condition.

Using the **loop structure**, you repeat actions while some condition remains unchanged.

Methods are groups of statements that can be executed as a unit.

You make a **call to the method** by using the method's name to execute the statements coded within the method.

Abstraction is the process of paying attention to important properties while ignoring details.

The variables and instructions within a module are hidden and contained—that is, **encapsulated**—which helps to make the module independent of all other modules, and therefore reusable.

An **interface** is a means of entry into a method.

The **reliability** of a module is its dependability and trustworthiness.

The group of techniques known as **object-oriented programming** requires you to analyze the objects with which you are working, organize them into classes, and learn about inheritance and polymorphism.

Objects can assume or **inherit** traits of previously created objects, thereby reducing the time it takes to create new objects.

An **object** is any thing.

A **class** consists of a category of things.

An object is a specific item that belongs to a class; it is called an **instance** of a class.

An **is-a relationship** is one in which one item is an object that is an instance of a class.

When a class is **extensible**, it is extendable; that is, you can create a new class that inherits from it.

You can create new classes that extend or are **descendents** of existing classes.

A descendent class can **inherit** all the attributes of the original (or parent) class, or they can override inappropriate attributes.

A **parent** class is an original class that has been extended, or inherited from.

Object-oriented programs use **polymorphism** to carry out the same operation in a manner customized to the object.

An **editor** is a simplified version of a word processor in which you type your program statements.

Program statements are called **source code**.

When you **compile**, the code you have written is transformed into machine language.

The output from compilation is **object code**—statements that have been translated into something the computer can use.

An **executable** program is runnable.

The process of integrating outside references to a program is called **linking**.

Error messages are notifications of fatal errors from the compiler.

Warnings are notifications of non-fatal errors from the compiler.

Fatal errors prevent a program from executing.

A **non-fatal error** is a warning; a program containing only warnings and no errors can execute.

C++ programs consist of modules called **functions**.

The initial line of code in a C++ function makes up the **function header**, which always has three parts.

A C++ program may contain many functions, but every C++ program contains at least one function, and that function is called **main()**.

As a keyword, **void** means "nothing" or "empty."

The program coding style in which the braces in a function each occupy a line of their own and align to the left is called the **exdented style**.

A **statement** is a segment of C++ code that performs a task; it is similar to an English sentence.

A **block** is a group of statements between a set of opening and closing braces.

An **identifier** is a name provided to a variable or other C++ element.

Camel casing is the style of naming identifiers in which the name begins with a lowercase letter and subsequent words within the identifier are capitalized.

Keywords are the words that are part of a programming language.

An **integral data type** is a type that holds an integer—a number (either positive or negative) without a decimal point.

An **integer** is a number (either positive or negative) without a decimal point.

An integer value may be stored in an **integer data type variable**, declared with the keyword `int`.

The keyword **int** is used to declare an integer variable.

Characters may be stored in **character data type variables**, declared with the keyword `char`.

The keyword **char** is used to declare a character variable.

A **Boolean data type variable** can be declared using the `bool` data type, which has only two possible values—true or false.

The keyword **bool** is used to declare Boolean variables, which have only two possible values—true or false.

Real numbers, or **floating-point numbers**, are numbers that include decimal positions, such as 98.6, 1000.0002, and −3.85.

The keyword **float** is used to declare floating-point values.

The keyword **double** is used to declare floating-point values.

The keyword **long double** is used to declare floating-point values.

Precision is a measure of accuracy, referring to the number of significant digits of floating-point numbers.

Assignment is the act of explicitly stating the value of a variable.

The **assignment operator** is the equals sign (=).

Assigning a value to a variable upon creation is often referred to as **initializing** the variable.

Lvalues are variables that are located on the left side of assignment statements to which values can legally be assigned.

The **scope of the variable** is the region of the program in which the variable exists.

A **named constant** is a named memory location whose contents cannot change during execution of the program.

A **qualifier** is a word that qualifies, or restricts, the ordinary capabilities of the named type.

Comments are statements that do not affect the compiling or running of a program; they are explanatory remarks that the programmer includes in a program to make notes, explain programming choices, or clarify what is taking place.

A **line comment** begins with two slashes (//) and continues to the end of the line on which it is placed.

A **block comment** begins with a single slash and an asterisk (/*) and ends with an asterisk and a slash (*/); it might be contained on a single line or continued across many lines.

The **ANSI/ISO Standard** is a set of C++ syntax rules developed by a joint committee of the American National Standards Institute (ANSI) and the International Standard Organization (ISO).

Header files are files that contain predefined values and routines.

A **preprocessor directive** is a statement that tells a program, called the preprocessor, what to do before compiling the program.

A program called the **preprocessor** runs before a C++ program is compiled.

The **octothorp** is the pound sign (#).

The **#include** preprocessor directive tells the compiler to include a file as part of the finished product.

A **namespace** is a mechanism for grouping features you want to include in a program.

The simplest object used for C++ output is **cout**.

The **insertion operator** (<<) is used to insert whatever is to the right into a cout object.

A **newline** character is the invisible character that forces the next output to appear on a new line.

The escape sequence **\n** indicates a new line in C++.

An **escape sequence** is a sequence of characters in which the first character serves only to "escape" from the usual meaning of the second character.

The end line manipulator is **endl**; inserting endl into the output stream causes a new line plus all waiting output to become visible.

Flushing the buffer is the process of forcing all waiting output to become visible.

A **user** is a person who runs, and probably benefits from, the output provided by a program.

Interactive programs are programs in which the user interacts with the program statements.

Prompts are statements that request input from the user, often explaining what is expected.

The **cin** object fetches values from the keyboard.

The **extraction operator** (>>) is used with **cin** to obtain input.

To **echo** input is to repeat it as output.

Whitespace consists of any number of spaces, tabs, and Enter characters.

Primitive or **scalar** data types are built-in, simple types, such as **int, char**, and **double**.

Data structures, or **structures**, are user-defined, complex data types. By default, their data fields are public.

Classes are user-defined, complex data types. By default, their data fields are private.

Fields are the simple components that are attributes of a class.

A **has-a relationship** describes the relationship of a class to its fields.

A **dot operator** is a period (.), and is used to separate an object and a field name.

Public fields are available to functions outside the class.

Private fields are not available for use outside the class.

REVIEW QUESTIONS

1. Writing instructions that enable a computer to carry out a task or group of tasks is known as _____.

    a. processing

    b. programming

    c. editing

    d. compiling

2. The physical components of a computer system are called _____.

    a. hardware

    b. software

    c. firmware

    d. programs

3. Another term for programs is _____.

    a. input

    b. floppy disks

    c. hardware

    d. software

4. C++, Visual Basic, Java, and C# are all _____.

    a. operating systems

    b. codes

    c. programming languages

    d. hardware

5. The rules of any programming language are its _____.

    a. syntax

    b. interpretation

    c. logic

    d. customs

6. A translator that notes whether you have used a language correctly might be called a _____.

    a. thesaurus

    b. compiler

    c. coder

    d. decoder

7. Using a correctly written statement at the wrong time creates a(n) _____ error.

    a. logical

    b. syntax

    c. object-oriented

    d. language

8. When a programmer determines the exact sequence in which events will take place, the program is said to be _____.

    a. compiled

    b. interpreted

    c. procedural

    d. object oriented

9. Which type of statement does not occur in computer programs?

    a. sequence

    b. loop

    c. denial

    d. selection

10. Paying attention to the important properties while ignoring unessential details is known as _____.

    a. selectiveness

    b. polymorphism

    c. abstraction

    d. summarizing

1

11. Object-oriented programmers primarily focus on _____.

a. procedures to be performed

b. the step-by-step statements needed to solve a problem

c. objects and the tasks that must be performed with those objects

d. the physical orientation of objects within a program

12. An object is _____.

a. a category of classes

b. a name given to a class

c. an instance of a class

d. the same as a class

13. Object is to class as _____.

a. library is to book

b. mother is to daughter

c. Plato is to philosopher

d. president is to Lincoln

14. The feature that allows the same operations to be carried out differently depending on the context is _____.

a. polymorphism

b. polygamy

c. inheritance

d. multitasking

15. Which English-language example best represents polymorphism?

a. taking a nap as opposed to taking a bribe

b. killing time as opposed to killing a bug

c. ordering a pizza as opposed to ordering a soldier

d. all of the above

16. All of the following are C++ data types except _____.

a. letter

b. double

c. char

d. int

17. All of the following are program control structures except _____.

    a. sequence

    b. loop

    c. perpetuation

    d. selection

18. The symbol used with the **cout** object << is called the _____ operator.

    a. insertion

    b. extraction

    c. modification

    d. dot

19. When you create a data structure or class object, you access the object's fields using the _____ operator.

    a. insertion

    b. extraction

    c. modification

    d. dot

20. If you create a structure named **Luggage** and an object named **myBlueOvernightBag**, which of the following could output your overnight bag's price?

    a. cout>>Luggage.price;

    b. cout>>price.myBlueOvernightBag;

    c. cout<<Luggage.myBlueOvernightBag;

    d. cout<<myBlueOvernightBag.price;

EXERCISES

1. List the steps to perform each of the following tasks. Include at least one example of a loop and one example of a selection in this process.

    a. shopping for new shoes

    b. filling a customer's catalog order

    c. computing the amount of federal income tax you owe

2. Many systems are modular. Name some modules within each of the following systems:

   a. a stereo

   b. a college

   c. a payroll system

3. Name a class that contains each of these objects:

   a. William Shakespeare

   b. a customer letter indicating that an item has been back-ordered

   c. a refund check to a customer who has overpaid

4. Name three objects in each of these classes:

   a. musical group

   b. business transaction

   c. year-end report

5. Write a C++ program that displays your name on the output screen. Save the file as **Name.cpp**.

6. Write a C++ program that displays your name, street address, and city and state on three separate lines on the screen. Save the file as **NameAndAddress.cpp**.

7. Write a C++ program that displays the following pattern on the screen:

   ```
       *
     *   *
   *   *   *
     *   *
       *
   ```

   Save the file as **Diamond.cpp**.

8. Write a C++ program that displays the following pattern on the screen:

   ```
      X
      XXX
     XXXXX
   XXXXXXX
        X
   ```

   Save the file as **Tree.cpp**.

9. Write a C++ program that displays your initials on the screen. Compose each initial with five lines of initials, as in the following example:

```
    J       FFFFFF

    J       F

    J       FFFF

J   J       F

JJJJJJ      F
```

Save the file as **Initials.cpp**.

10. Write a C++ program that displays all the objectives listed at the beginning of this chapter. Save the file as **Objectives.cpp**.

11. From 1925 through 1963, Burma Shave advertising signs appeared next to highways all across the United States. There were always four or five signs in a row containing pieces of a rhyme, followed by a final sign that read "Burma Shave". For example, one set of signs that has been preserved by the Smithsonian Institution reads as follows:

Shaving brushes
You'll soon see 'em
On a shelf
In some museum

Burma Shave

Find a classic Burma Shave rhyme on the Web. Write a C++ program that displays the slogan on five lines. Save the file as **BurmaShave.cpp**.

12. Write a C++ program that declares a variable that can hold the amount of money in your pocket right now. Assign a value to the variable. Display the value, with explanation, on the screen. For example, the output might be "In my pocket, I have $4.36." Save the file as **SpareChange.cpp**.

13. Write a C++ program that declares a value that can hold the price of a lunch. Prompt a user to enter the amount he or she spent on lunch. Read in the value, and display it with explanation. Save the file as **Lunch.cpp**.

14. Write a program that declares a variable that can hold the letter grade a student will receive in this class. Prompt the user to enter the letter. Then read it in, and echo it with explanation. Save the file as **LetterGrade.cpp**.

15. Write a program that declares two integer variables that can hold the ages of two people. Prompt a user to enter the ages of his or her two best friends, and echo the numbers with explanation. Save the file as **TwoAges.cpp**.

16. Create a data structure named `Car` that contains two public fields: an `int` field for model year and a `double` field for miles per gallon. Write a program that declares a `Car`. Assign values to the car's two data fields, and display the values with explanation. Save the file as **Car.cpp**.

17. Create a data structure named `College` that contains three public fields: the year the college was founded, the current student population, and the annual tuition. Write a program that declares a `College`. Prompt the user for values for the fields, and echo them. Save the file as **College.cpp**.

18. Create a data structure named `Computer`. Decide on at least three fields that you want to include within your `Computer` structure. Each of the fields must be an `int` or a `double`. Write a program that declares two `Computers`. Prompt the user for values for the fields for each `Computer`, and echo them. Save the file as **Computer.cpp**.

19. Each of the following files in the Chapter01 folder of your Data Disk contains syntax and/or logical errors. Determine the problem in each case, and fix the program. Save your solutions by adding "Fixed" to the file name, as in **DEBUG1-1Fixed.cpp**.

   a. DEBUG1-1.cpp

   b. DEBUG1-2.cpp

   c. DEBUG1-3.cpp

   d. DEBUG1-4.cpp

CASE PROJECT 1

CASE PROJECTS

Teacher's Pet is a software firm that specializes in children's educational programs. The firm has decided to develop a series of products that will help children discover the properties of fractions. As you plan the program series, you realize that a fraction contains at least two data properties: a numerator and a denominator. Therefore, you begin to think of specific fractions as objects that belong to the class called `Fraction`. For now, though, you decide to work with `structs`. Develop the `Fraction struct` so that it contains public data fields that hold the integers `numerator` and `denominator`. (In later chapters, you will change your data structure to a class and learn to make these data fields private.) Write a `main()` function that declares a `Fraction` and allows you to enter data values for the two `Fraction` fields. Echo the input. Save the file as **Fraction.cpp**.

CASE PROJECT 2

CASE PROJECTS

Parkville Bank is a full-service bank that has decided to computerize its banking processes. One object needed is a `BankAccount`. Develop a `struct` so that it contains public data fields that hold the `int` account number and `double` account balance. (In later chapters, you will convert `BankAccount` to a class and learn to make these data fields private.) Write a `main()` function that declares a `BankAccount` and allows you to enter data values for the `BankAccount` fields. Echo the input. Save the file as **BankAccount.cpp**.

2

EVALUATING C++ EXPRESSIONS

> **In this chapter, you will:**
> ♦ Use C++ binary arithmetic operators
> ♦ Learn about the precedence and associativity of arithmetic operations
> ♦ Examine shortcut arithmetic operators
> ♦ Use other unary operators
> ♦ Evaluate Boolean expressions
> ♦ Perform operations on struct fields

When you write a program, you use variable names to create locations where you can store data. You can use assignment and input statements to provide values for the variables, and you can use output statements to display those values on the screen. In most programs that you write, you will want to do more than input and output variable values, you also might want to evaluate those values and create expressions that use the values. For example, you might want to perform arithmetic with values, or base decisions on values that users input.

In this chapter, you will learn to use the C++ operators to create arithmetic expressions and study the results they produce. You will also learn about the valuable shortcut arithmetic operators in C++. Then you will concentrate on the Boolean expressions you can use to control C++ decisions and loops—the topics of the next two chapters.

USING C++ BINARY ARITHMETIC OPERATORS

Often after data values are input, you perform calculations with them. C++ provides five simple arithmetic operators for creating arithmetic expressions:

- the **addition operator** (+)
- the **subtraction operator** (–)
- the **multiplication operator** (*)
- the **division operator** (/)
- the **modulus operator** (%)

Each of these symbols is an **arithmetic operator**—a symbol that performs arithmetic. Each is also a **binary operator**—an operator that takes two operands, one on each side of the operator, as in 12 + 9 or 16.2 * 1.5.

 Some arithmetic operators are not binary and some binary operators are not arithmetic. You will learn about some of these operators later in this chapter.

 Do not confuse binary operators with the binary numbering system. Binary operators take two operands; the binary numbering system is a system that uses only two values, 0 and 1.

The results of an arithmetic operation can be used immediately or stored in a variable in computer memory. For example, each **cout** statement in the program shown in Figure 2-1 produces the value 21 as output, as you can see in Figure 2-2. In the first statement within the **main()** function, the result, 21, is calculated within the **cout** statement and output immediately, without being stored. In the second **cout** statement, the value of a variable is shown. The advantage to this approach is that the result of the addition calculation is stored in the variable named **sum** and can be accessed again later within the same program, if necessary. For example, you might need **sum** again if its value is required as part of a subsequent calculation.

```
#include<iostream>
using namespace std;
int main()
{
   cout<<12+9<<endl; // displays the value 21
   int sum=12+9;     // calculates sum whose value becomes 21
   cout<<sum<<endl;  // displays the value of sum
}
```

Figure 2-1   Program that uses two ways to produce 21

Figure 2-2   Output of program in Figure 2-1

TIP

If you will use a calculated value later in a program, it is inefficient not to store it. For example, in the following code, the net-pay calculation is performed twice because the value is used in the last two output statements. It would be more efficient to declare a variable to hold the difference between salary and deductions, perform the arithmetic once, and then use the calculated variable value in both output statements.

```
double salary = 1000.00;
double deductions = 385.00;
cout<<"Salary is "<<salary;
cout<<"Deductions are "<<deductions<<endl;
cout<<"The difference is "<<(salary - deductions)<<endl;
cout<<"So, your net pay is "<<(salary - deductions)<<endl;
```

Addition, subtraction, multiplication, division, or modulus of any two integers results in an integer. For example, the expression $7 + 3$ results in 10, $7 - 3$ results in 4, and $7 * 3$ results in 21. These results are the ones you might expect, but the result of integer division is less obvious. For example, the expression $7 / 3$ results in 2, not 2.333333. When two integers are divided, the result is an integer, so any fractional part of the result is lost.

TIP

When you work with a program in which you divide integers, you must keep the rules of integer division in mind if you are to avoid serious errors. For example, suppose you write a program for a legislator in which you store survey results from 1,000 voters, and 800 of the voters favor passing a specific law. When you convert the results to percentages, if you divide the integer 800 by the integer 1,000, the result is 0, not .8, because the fractional part of integer division is lost. The legislator to whom you report would be misled as to his or her constituents' wishes.

If either or both of the operands in addition, subtraction, multiplication, or division is a floating-point number (that is, at least one operand is a **float** or a **double)**, then the result is also a floating-point number. For example, the value of the expression $3.2 * 2$ is the floating-point value 6.4 because at least one of the operands is a floating-point number. Similarly, the result of $3.2 / 2$ is 1.6. When at least one of the operands in division is a floating-point value, then the result is floating point, and the fractional part is not lost.

An expression such as $3.2 * 2$ is a **mixed expression**—one in which the operands have different data types. When you mix data types in a binary arithmetic expression, the values on each side of the arithmetic operator are temporarily converted to a **unifying type**—the data type of the value that occupies more memory and to which all the types in the expression are converted. The result is then calculated to be the unifying type. In binary arithmetic expressions, the order of precedence of unifying types from highest to lowest is as follows:

```
long double
double
float
unsigned long
long
unsigned int
int
short
char
```

For example, any binary arithmetic expression that contains a **double** and an **int** results in a **double**, and any binary arithmetic expression that does not contain a **double** but does contain a **float** and an **int** results in a **float**. Figure 2-3 shows some arithmetic examples and explains the computed results that are output in Figure 2-4.

```
    #include<iostream>
// Using arithmetic expressions
// Note that a, b, c, and so on are not very good
// descriptive variable names
// They are used here simply to hold values
using namespace std;
int main()
{
   int a = 2, b = 4, c = 10, intResult;
   double d = 2.0, e = 4.4, f = 12.8, doubleResult;
   float g = 2.0f, h = 4.4f, i = 12.8f, floatResult;
   intResult = a + b;
   cout<<intResult<<endl;
         // result is 6, an int,
         // because both operands are int
   intResult = a * b;
   cout<<intResult<<endl;
         // result is 8, an int,
         // because both operands are int
   intResult = c / a;
   cout<<intResult<<endl;
         // result is 5, an int,
         // because both operands are int
   intResult = c / b;
```

Figure 2-3   The resulting values of some arithmetic expressions

2

```
    cout<<intResult<<endl;
        // result is 2 (losing the decimal fraction),
        // an int, because both operands are int
    floatResult = g / a;
    cout<<floatResult<<endl;
        // result is 1.0, a float,
        // because the operands are int and float
    floatResult = h / g;
    cout<<floatResult<<endl;
        // result is 2.2, a float,
        // because both operands are floats
    doubleResult = a * d;
    cout<<doubleResult<<endl;
        // result is 4.0, a double,
        // because the operands are int and double
        // However, the result displays without the
        // unneeded decimal point and fractional part
    doubleResult = f / a;
    cout<<doubleResult<<endl;
        // result is 6.4, a double,
        // because the operands are int and double
    doubleResult = e + h;
    cout<<doubleResult<<endl;
        // result is 8.8, a double,
        // because operands are float and double
}
```

Figure 2-3   The resulting values of some arithmetic expressions (continued)

Figure 2-4   Output of program in Figure 2-3

TIP   The lowercase f's following the `double` constant values that are assigned to the `float` variables g, h, and i perform an explicit cast, eliminating the warnings that would appear if they were not added. You learned this technique in Chapter 1.

In Figure 2-3, each operation is assigned to a result variable of the correct type. Note that the expression a + b has an integer result because both a and b are integers, *not* because their sum is stored in the `intResult` variable. If the program contained the statement `doubleResult = a + b;` the expression `a + b` would still have an integer value, but the value would be **cast**, or transformed, into a **double** when the sum is assigned to `doubleResult`. Whenever you assign a value to a variable type that is higher in the order of precedence, that value is automatically cast to the unifying type. For example, the declaration `double moneyAmount = 8;` uses the constant integer 8 but actually assigns the value 8.0 to `moneyAmount`.

TIP   The term *cast* means "mold" or "form into," as in *cast iron*.

The automatic cast that occurs when you assign a value of one type to a type with higher precedence is called an **implicit cast**—meaning the cast is performed automatically and without your intervention. However, if you attempt to make an assignment to a variable type with lower precedence, the C++ compiler issues a warning message. For example, when you compile a program containing the following statement, you receive a warning message indicating that you might lose data converting from a **double** to an **int**.

```
int answer = 2.0 * 7;
```

Because 2.0 is a floating-point value, the result of 2.0 * 7 is also a floating-point value. Even though the integer 14 and the floating-point value 14.0 are mathematically identical, they are stored differently in the computer, and C++ warns you of possible misinterpretations. Similarly, the following statement causes the same warning message:

```
int answer = 2.1 * 7;
```

In this case, you actually lose data. The mathematical result of 2.1 * 7 is 14.7, but when the result is assigned to the integer `answer`, the fractional portion, .7, is lost.

You also can perform an **explicit cast**, which is a deliberate cast as opposed to an automatic one. You can perform an explicit cast in one of two ways: by typing `static_cast<data type>` in front of an expression in parentheses, or by using a type name within parentheses in front of an expression. For example, each of the following statements explicitly converts a **double** variable named `doubleVariable` to an **int** before assigning its value to `intResult`.

```
intResult = static_cast<int>(doubleVariable);
intResult = (int)doubleVariable;
```

TIP   Even though the first version of the explicit cast requires more typing, it is the preferred method for explicit casting in C++. The second format was used in C programming.

You can convert a character to its integer equivalent using a cast. For example, if your computer uses the ASCII character set, then `static_cast<int>('A')` is 65 because 'A' is represented by the binary digits with the decimal value 65. Similarly, `static_cast<char>(65)` is 'A'.

TIP

Using Modulus

The modulus operator (%) gives the remainder of integer division; it can be used only with integers. The expression 7 / 3 results in 2 because 3 "goes into" 7 two whole times. The expression 7 % 3 results in 1, because when 3 "goes into" 7 two times, there is 1 remaining. Similarly, the value of 17 % 5 is 2, and the value of 25 % 11 is 3. You can pronounce 7 % 3 as "seven modulus three" or "seven mod three."

The modulus operator proves useful in a variety of situations. For example, if you determine the remainder of dividing by 2, you can determine whether any value is even or odd. Any number with a remainder of 0 when divided by 2 is even, and any number with a remainder of 1 when divided by 2 is odd.

As another example, in time calculations, any integer number of minutes divided by 60 indicates the number of hours, and the result of modulus by 60 indicates the number of minutes left over. In the following code, the value of **hours** is 3 and the value of **extraMinutes** is 7:

```
int minutesOnTheJob = 187;
int hours = minutesOnTheJob / 60;
int extraMinutes = minutesOnTheJob % 60;
```

Similar calculations can be made to determine how many dozens (12), scores (20), or thousands (1,000) are contained in a number, and how many remain.

Using modulus with negative numbers can lead to unexpected results, because there are two ways of thinking about division remainders with negative numbers. For example, –10 % 8 produces –2, but so does –10 % –8.

TIP

When using the decimal numbering system, if you need to know a number's last digit, you can perform modulus by 10. For example, 6,543 % 10 is 3 and 6,789 % 10 is 9. Similarly, you can extract the last two digits from a decimal number by using modulus 100.

When assigning customer, account, or employee ID numbers, many companies use a check digit as part of the number. A **check digit** is a digit added to a number (either at the end or at the beginning) that validates the authenticity of the number. You use a check digit to ensure that input data is correct. Different companies use different algorithms to determine the check digit for numbers they use, but a simple one might work as follows:

1. Assume an account number named **acctNum** is 123454.

2

2. Remove the last digit. You can do this by dividing the number by 10 (`shortAcctNum = acctNum / 10`), giving 12345.

3. Perform modulus on the new number with an arbitrary value, say 7 (`remainder = shortAcctNum % 7`). The remainder is 4.

4. Compare the last digit of the original account number (`lastDigit = acctNum % 10`) with the remainder from the check digit calculation. Because the remainder of 4 equals the last digit in the account number, you have verified that the account number 123454 is a valid combination of digits. Account number 123455 would be invalid because the remainder of the modulus operation on the first five digits, 4, would not equal the last digit, 5.

Just as you can isolate the last digit of a base-10 number by performing modulus with 10, you can find the last two digits by performing modulus with 100, the last three by performing modulus with 1,000, and so on.

PRECEDENCE AND ASSOCIATIVITY OF ARITHMETIC OPERATIONS

When more than one arithmetic operator is included in an expression, then multiplication, division, and modulus operations always occur before addition or subtraction. Multiplication, division, and modulus are said to have higher **arithmetic precedence**—that is, they are performed first in an arithmetic statement with multiple operations. Addition and subtraction operations have lower precedence. When two operations with the same precedence appear in an arithmetic expression, the operations are carried out in order from either left to right or right to left based on their **associativity**—the rule that dictates the order in which an operator works with its operands. The associativity of arithmetic operations (if there are no parentheses in the expression) is from left to right.

Although most operators have left-to-right associativity, some have right-to-left associativity. Appendix C lists all the C++ operators in order of precedence and indicates the associativity of each.

When C++ evaluates a mixed arithmetic expression, the following steps occur:

1. The leftmost operation with the highest precedence (*, /, and %) is evaluated. If the data types of the operands on both sides of the operator are the same data type, the result is the same data type. If the operands are different data types, then C++ performs an implicit cast and the result is the same type as the one that occupies more memory.

2. Each subsequent *, /, or % operation is evaluated in the same manner from left to right.

3. The leftmost operation with the lower precedence (+ and −) is evaluated. If the data types of the operands on both sides of the operator are the same, the result is the same data type. If the operands are different data types, then C++ performs an implicit cast and the result is the same type as the one that occupies more memory.

4. Each subsequent + or − operation is evaluated in the same manner from left to right.

Table 2-1 contains several expressions and explains their evaluation.

Table 2-1   Sample mixed-expression evaluations

Expression	Value	Comments
2 + 3 * 4.0	14.0	3 * 4.0 results in 12.0; then 2 + 12.0 results in 14.0
3 / 4 + 2.2	2.2	The result of integer division 3 / 4 is 0 (not 0.75); then 0 + 2.2 produces 2.2
3.0 / 4 + 2.2	2.95	The result of floating-point division 3.0 / 4 is 0.75; then 0.75 + 2.2 produces 2.95
3.0 * 1.1 / 2	1.65	The multiplication result is 3.3; then the division result is 1.65
3 / 2 * 5 / 2	2	The first integer division, 3 / 2, results in 1 (not 1.5). Then 1 * 5 produces 5. Then 5 / 2 results in 2 (not 2.5)

All precedence rules can be overridden with appropriately placed parentheses. For example, the expression (2 + 3) * 4.0 results in 20.0 (not 14.0) because the expression within the parentheses is evaluated first, and 5 * 4.0 is 20.0.

TIP

The same order of precedence (multiplication and division before addition and subtraction) and associativity (left to right) is used not only in mathematics and C++, but in arithmetic statements in all programming languages.

SHORTCUT ARITHMETIC OPERATORS

In addition to the standard binary arithmetic operators for addition, subtraction, multiplication, division, and modulus, C++ employs several shortcut operators. The two categories of shortcut arithmetic operators are compound assignment operators and increment and decrement operators.

Compound Assignment Operators

When you add two variable values and store the result in a third variable, the expression takes the form `result = firstValue + secondValue`. The two values to the right of the assignment operator are summed, and the result is stored in the variable to the left of the assignment operator. (Unlike the associativity of the arithmetic operators, the associativity of the assignment operator is right to left.) When you use an expression like this, both `firstValue` and `secondValue` retain their original values; only the `result` variable is altered.

When you want to alter the value of a variable by a specific amount–for example, to increase the value of `firstValue` by the amount stored in `secondValue`–the expression takes the form `firstValue = firstValue + secondValue`. This expression results in `firstValue` being increased by the value stored in `secondValue`; `secondValue` remains unchanged, but `firstValue` takes on a new value. For example, if `firstValue` initially holds 5 and `secondValue` initially holds 2, then after the statement `firstValue = firstValue + secondValue` executes, the value of `firstValue` increases to 7.

Because increasing a value by another value is such a common procedure—for example, when accumulating a running total—C++ provides a shortcut **add and assign operator**, +=. The add and assign operator is an example of a **compound assignment operator**–an operator that performs two tasks, one of which is assignment. The statement `firstValue += secondValue` produces results identical to `firstValue = firstValue + secondValue`. Each of these expressions means "Take the value in `secondValue`, add it to `firstValue`, and store the result in `firstValue`," or "Replace the value of `firstValue` with the new value you get when you add `secondValue` to `firstValue`." When you use the += operator, you must *not* insert a space between the + and the =.

Similarly, C++ provides the **subtract and assign operator** (– =) for subtracting one value from another, the **multiply and assign operator** (*=) for multiplying one value by another, the **divide and assign operator** (/=) for dividing one value by another, and the **modulus and assign operator** (%=) for finding the modulus of a value. As with the += operator, you must not insert a space within the subtraction, multiplication, division, or modulus shortcut operators.

The operators +=, –=, *=, /=, and %= are all valid; the operators =+, =–, =*, =/, and =% are not. The assignment operator (=) always appears second in a compound assignment operator.

Be careful when using more complicated expressions to the right of compound assignment operators. The expression on the right is evaluated before the compound assignment operator executes. For example, a *= b + c is equivalent to a = a * (b + c), not a = a * b + c.

Increment and Decrement Operators

Another common programming task is to add 1 to a variable—for example, when keeping count of how many times an event has occurred. C++ provides four ways to add 1 to a variable, shown in the short program in Figure 2-5.

Each of the options shown in Figure 2-5 means "replace the current value of count with the value that is 1 more than count," or simply **increment** count. The expression count = count + 1 uses no shortcuts. The expression count += 1 uses the add and assign operator. The expressions ++count and count++ use the **prefix increment operator** and the **postfix increment operator**, respectively. As you might expect, you can use two minus signs (−−) before or after a variable to **decrement** it, or reduce it by 1.

```
int main()
{
    int count = 0;
    count = count + 1; // count becomes 1
    count += 1; // count becomes 2
    ++count;   //   count becomes 3
       // This ++ is called a prefix increment operator
    count++;   // count becomes 4
       // This ++ is called a postfix increment operator
}
```

Figure 2-5 Some sample selection statements within a C++ program

The prefix and postfix increment and decrement operators are examples of unary operators. **Unary operators** (as opposed to binary operators) are those that require only one operand–that is, they perform an operation on only one side of the operator.

Although the prefix and postfix increment operators each add 1 to a variable, there is a difference in how expressions that use them are evaluated. When an expression includes a prefix operator (as in ++count), the mathematical operation takes place before the expression is evaluated. For example, the following code segment gives count the value 7, which is then assigned to result, so result is also 7.

```
int count = 6;
int result = ++count;
cout<<result;   // result is 7
cout<<count;    // count is 7
```

When an expression includes a postfix operator (as in count++), the mathematical operation takes place after the expression is evaluated. For example, the following code segment gives the result variable the value 6. The value of the variable count is not increased until after it is evaluated, so count is evaluated as 6, 6 is assigned to result, and then count increases to 7.

```
int count = 6;
int result = count++;
cout<<result;   // result is 6
cout<<count;    // count is 7
```

The difference between the results produced by the prefix and postfix operators can be subtle, but the outcome of a program can vary greatly depending on which increment operator you use in an expression. If you use either the prefix or the postfix increment in a stand-alone statement that simply adds 1 to or subtracts 1 from a value, then it does not matter which one you use. However, if the incremented variable is used as part of another expression, then it matters whether the increment is prefix or postfix.

OTHER UNARY OPERATORS

Besides the unary prefix and postfix increment and decrement operators, C++ supports several other unary operators, including +, −, and &.

When you use the + operator with two operands, it performs addition. When used alone in front of an operand, it becomes the **positive value operator**, indicating a positive value—one that is greater than zero. When you use the − operator with two operands, it performs subtraction. When used alone in front of an operand, it becomes the **negative value operator**, indicating a reversal of the sign, for example, turning a positive value to a negative value. The multiple meanings of + and − should not be surprising to you—they have the same multiple meanings in standard arithmetic. You understand which meaning of + or − is appropriate at any time based on the context. For example, you understand 14 − 8 to mean perform subtraction, and −12 to mean a negative number. The diverse meanings of + and − provide an example of polymorphism. In Chapter 1, you learned that object-oriented programs use polymorphism to carry out operations in a customized manner; the operators + and − carry out different processes depending on whether they are used with one or two operands. As you continue reading the book and learning about C++, you will create many polymorphic examples. For now, understand that polymorphism is not a complicated or difficult concept; in fact, you have been using + and − polymorphically since grammar school.

The * operator is also polymorphic, although not in as obvious a manner as + and −. In C++, the * can be used with two operands for multiplication, but can also be used with a single operand to indicate a value stored in a variable that holds a memory address. You will learn about this use of * in Chapter 5.

Unlike + and −, which are used in the same ways in virtually every programming language, the **address operator** (&) is an interesting C++ unary operator that is not available for use in most other programming languages. When you use a variable name in a program, you refer to the contents stored in the memory address with that name. When you use & in front of a variable name, you refer to the memory address of that variable rather than the contents of the variable. For example, although a variable named **x** might hold a value of 50, the memory address of **x** is essentially unpredictable—it is whatever memory address the compiler has assigned to **x**.

For example, Figure 2-6 shows a program in which two integer variables are declared and assigned values. The first **cout** statement displays their values as expected. The second cout statement uses the address operator with each variable to display their memory addresses. Figure 2-7 shows the output.

```cpp
#include<iostream>
using namespace std;
int main()
{
    int x = 5;
    int y = 775;
    cout<<"The value of x is "<<x<<
          " and the value of y is "<<y<<endl;
    cout<<"The address of x is "<<&x<<
          " and the address of y is "<<&y<<endl;
}
```

Figure 2-6   Displaying the values and addresses of two variables

Figure 2-7   Output of program in Figure 2-6

TIP   The addresses in Figure 2-7 are displayed in hexadecimal format. The **hexadecimal numbering system** is a numbering system based on powers of 16. It uses 16 different digits—0 through 9 and A through F—so you see some letters mixed with the digits in the second line of output in Figure 2-7. By convention, programmers use the hexadecimal system to express computer memory address no matter what programming language they are using.

In the first output line in Figure 2-7, you can see the values of x and y. Even though you may not understand the numbering system that is used to display the memory addresses in the second output line in the figure, you can see that the two variables are stored at addresses that are close to each other in value—only the last digit of the addresses differs. At this point in your study of C++, viewing the memory address of a variable is just a curiosity you cannot alter the locations where the variables are declared, and although a program's users are frequently interested in variables' values, they are very rarely interested in the locations of those variables in memory. As you continue to study C++, you will find uses for the address operator, particularly when you study arrays and pointers in Chapter 5 and function parameter passing in Chapter 6.

EVALUATING BOOLEAN EXPRESSIONS

Determining the value of an arithmetic expression such as 2 + 3 * 4 is straightforward. However, C++ also evaluates many other expressions that have nothing to do with arithmetic yet provide a numeric answer.

C++ employs the six binary relational operators listed in Table 2-2. **Relational operators** are those that evaluate the relationship between operands, you use these relational operators to evaluate Boolean expressions. A **Boolean expression** is one that is interpreted to be true or false.

Table 2-2   Relational operators

Relational operator	Description
==	equivalent to
>	greater than
>=	greater than or equal to
<	less than
<=	less than or equal to
!=	not equal to

All false relational expressions are evaluated as 0. Thus, an expression such as 2 > 9 has the value 0. You can prove that 2 > 9 is evaluated as 0 by entering the statement cout<<(2>9); into a C++ program. A 0 appears as output.

All true relational expressions are evaluated as 1. Thus, the expression 9 > 2 has the value 1. You can prove this by entering the statement cout<<(9>2); into a C++ program. A 1 appears as output.

The unary operator ! is the **not operator**; it means "the opposite of," and essentially reverses the true/false value of an expression. For example, cout<<(9>2); displays a 1 because "9 is greater than 2" is true. In contrast, cout<<!(9>2); displays a 0 because the value of !1 ("not one") is 0. The statement "not 9 greater than 2" is grammatically awkward as well as a false statement.

It makes sense that the value of !0 is 1 and that the value of !1 is 0, because the statements "not false is true" and "not true is false" make sense. However, it is less intuitive that !2 is 0, !3 is 0 and !-5 is 0. In fact !anythingExceptZero is always 0—that is, "not any value" is 0, except when the value being negated is 0. You can also apply this concept to the results of arithmetic expressions. So, although the value of the expression 4 + 5 is 9, in a sense it is also true because it is not 0. Additionally, the value of the expression 4 − 4 is 0, but it is also false.

Consider these confusing but true statements:

- The value of 4 − 4 is 0.

- The value of (4 − 4) = = 0 is 1 because it is true that (4 − 4) is equivalent to 0.

- Assume the following assignment has been made: a = 4. Then the value of the expression a = 4 is 4, but the value of the expression a = = 4 is 1 because it is true that a and 4 are equivalent. The value of !a is 0.

- Assume the following assignment has been made: b = 0. Then the value of b = 0 is 0, but the value of b = = 0 is 1 because it is true. The value of !b is 1.

- Assume the following assignment has been made: c = 5. Then the value of c is 5, the value of !c is 0, and the value of !!c is 1.

The relational operator = = deserves special attention. Suppose two variables, q and r, have been declared, and q = 7 and r = 8. The statement cout<<(q==r); produces 0 (false) because the value of q is not equivalent to the value of r. The statement cout<<(q=r);, however, produces 8. The single equal sign does not compare two variables; instead, it assigns the value of the rightmost variable to the variable on the left. Because r is 8, q becomes 8, and the value of the entire expression is 8. In several other programming languages, such as Visual Basic and COBOL, a single equal sign is used as the equals comparison operator, but this is not the case with C++. In other languages–for example, Java– the single equal sign is used for assignment and the double equal sign is used for comparison, just as it is in C++, but the compiler issues an error if you use the assignment operator when making a comparison. In C++, however, the compiler will not warn you if you use the wrong operator. A common C++ programming error is to use the assignment operator (=) when you should use the comparison operator (==). Making this mistake causes a logical error that can be very difficult to locate in your programs.

PERFORMING OPERATIONS ON STRUCT FIELDS

You can perform any operation on a field in a structure that you could perform with its simple data type if it were not part of a structure. For example, if a structure contains a numeric field, you can add to, subtract from, and take the address of the field just as if it were a simple number type. The only difference is that to create these expressions in a program, you must use an object and the dot operator.

Consider a very simple Employee structure that contains only two components: idNumber and hourlySalary. You could define such a structure as shown in Figure 2-8; this is the same structure you examined in Figure 1-15 in Chapter 1.

```
struct Employee
{
    int idNumber;
    double hourlySalary;
};
```

Figure 2-8   A simple `Employee` struct

The `Employee struct` definition shown in Figure 2-8 indicates that an `Employee` has two components: an integer `idNumber` and a `double hourlySalary`. Instead of a structure, you could create an `Employee` class, but conventionally, the data fields would be private and inaccessible with the dot operator. Although you will soon learn to create classes with private data members, for simplicity, a `struct` with default public data is used here. Figure 2-9 shows a program that declares two objects: a `double` and an `Employee`. In this program, you can see that when used with an `Employee` object (`oneStaffMember`), the `Employee struct` field `hourlySalary` is used just like any other arithmetic variable of its type. The program in Figure 2-9 adds a `double` to the structure variable, but whether you add, subtract, multiply, divide, perform modulus, or perform any combination of arithmetic statements, each structure field operates with its object according to the same rules of precedence and associativity as any scalar (or single-value) counterpart that is not associated with any object. Similarly, you can create Boolean expressions using fields, as you can see in the final statement of the program. Figure 2-10 shows the output of the program. The salary has been increased by the raise amount, and the value of `oneStaffMember.hourlySalary > 15` is 0 because it is false.

```
#include<iostream>
using namespace std;
int main()
{
    const double RAISE = 2.77;
    Employee oneStaffMember;
    oneStaffMember.hourlySalary = 10.00;
    oneStaffMember.hourlySalary =
        oneStaffMember.hourlySalary + RAISE;
    cout<<"Salary is "<<oneStaffMember.hourlySalary<<endl;
    cout<<"The value of the employee's salary "<<
        "greater than 15 is "<<
        (oneStaffMember.hourlySalary > 15)<<endl;
}
```

Figure 2-9   A program that uses an Employee's `hourlySalary` field in arithmetic and Boolean expressions

Figure 2-10   Output of program in Figure 2-9

TIP When you create a class instead of a structure, some fields can be used without creating an object. These fields are static fields; you will learn how and why to create them in Chapter 7.

You Do It

Using Arithmetic Operators

In the following steps, you will create a program that demonstrates some arithmetic operators used in C++.

1. Open your C++ editor. Start a new project named **NumberDemo**. Type a line comment that explains that this program demonstrates arithmetic, as well as any other comments that you think are appropriate or that your instructor requests.

2. Type the `include` statement that allows you to use `cout` as well as the `using namespace std` statement.

TIP Also type the `include` statement that supports `getch()` if it is necessary for you to use `getch()` to hold the C++ output on the screen. Then remember to add the `getch()` statement to the end of the program in Step 7. See Appendix B for more details.

```
#include<iostream>
using namespace std;
```

3. Begin the main function by typing its header and the opening curly brace.

```
int main()
{
```

4. Declare some integer and double variables, and then assign values to them.

```
int a,b,c;
double x,y,z;
a = 13;
b = 4;
x = 3.3;
```

```
y = 15.78;
```

5. Type the statement that calculates **c** as the sum of **a** and **b**. Then type the statement that shows the value of **c** on the screen, with an explanation.

```
c = a + b;
cout<<"a + b is "<<c<<endl;
```

6. Perform several more arithmetic calculations and display the results.

```
z = x + y;
cout <<"x + y is "<<z<<endl;
c = a / b;
cout<<"a / b is "<<c<<endl;
c = a % b;
cout<<"a% b is "<<c<<endl;
```

7. Add the closing curly brace for the program.

8. Save the file as NumberDemo.cpp compile it, correct any errors, and execute the program. The results should look like Figure 2-11.

Figure 2-11   Output of NumberDemo application

9. Change the values for the variables within the NumberDemo program. Try to predict the results and then run the program again. Change some of the operations to multiplication and subtraction. Continue to modify and run the program until you are confident you can predict the outcome of every arithmetic operation.

Using Prefix and Postfix Increment and Decrement Operators

In the next steps, you will add increment operator statements to the NumberDemo.cpp program so that you can become comfortable with the differences between prefix and postfix operators.

1. If necessary, open the **NumberDemo.cpp** program that you created in the last set of steps. Copy the contents of NumberDemo into a new project named **NumberDemo2**.

2. Move your insertion point to the beginning of the last executable line of the program, just before the closing curly brace, and press the **Enter** key to start a new line. Type the following statements on their own line to give a new value to **a** and to assign ++a to **c**.

2

```
a = 2;
c = ++a;
```

3. Add a statement to display the results.

```
cout<<"a is "<<a<<" and c is "<<c<<endl;
```

4. Now add statements that are similar, but that use the postfix increment operator with a.

```
a = 2;
c = a++;
cout<<"a is "<<a<<" and c is "<<c<<endl;
```

5. Save the modified program, and compile and run it. The output should look like Figure 2-12. Notice the difference in the last two lines of output. The first of these lines shows that when the prefix increment operator is used with a, the value of a is increased before it is assigned to c. The last line shows that when the postfix increment operator is used, a is assigned to c before the value of a changes.

Figure 2-12   Output of NumberDemo2 application

6. Modify the values for the variables in the program, and continue to run it until you are confident you can predict the values that will be output.

7. Change the instances of the prefix and postfix increment operators (++) to the corresponding decrement operators (--). Try to predict the output, then execute the program to confirm your predictions.

Using Operators with `struct` Fields

In the next steps, you will create a `Student` structure, and then create a program that uses a `Student` object.

1. Open a new file in your C++ compiler. Type the following comment:

```
// Demonstrating a Student struct
```

2. Type the preprocessor directive to include `iostream` so that `cout` and `cin` will work correctly. Also type the `using namespace std;` statement.

```
#include<iostream>
```

```
using namespace std;
```

3. Define a **Student** structure that will contain two public fields: one that holds credit hours, and another that holds the grade point average.

```
struct Student
{
   int creditHours;
   double gradePointAverage;
};
```

4. Next begin the **main( )** function, and declare a **Student** object identified as **oneSophomore**. Also declare a constant that holds the number of credit hours a student must accumulate to be able to graduate, and a scalar integer that holds the number of additional hours this **Student** must complete in order to reach the graduation requirement.

```
int main()
{
   Student oneSophomore;
   const int HOURS_REQUIRED_TO_GRADUATE = 120;
   int hoursRemaining;
```

5. Write the statements that prompt for and allow entry of **Student** data.

```
cout<<"Please enter a student's credit hours ";
cin>>oneSophomore.creditHours;
cout<<"Please enter the student's grade point average ";
cin>>oneSophomore.gradePointAverage;
```

6. Add the statements that echo the data just entered.

```
cout<<"The number of credit hours is " <<
   oneSophomore.creditHours<<endl;
cout<<"The grade point average is "<<
   oneSophomore.gradePointAverage<<endl;
```

7. Compute the number of hours the **Student** needs for graduation by subtracting the student's hours from the graduation requirement. Notice that it is perfectly acceptable to mix structure fields and simple variables in the same arithmetic statement. Display the computed remaining credit hours.

```
hoursRemaining = HOURS_REQUIRED_TO_GRADUATE -
   oneSophomore.creditHours;
cout<<"This student needs "<<hoursRemaining<<
   " more credit hours to graduate"<<endl;
```

8. Add the closing curly brace for the program, and then save the file as **Student.cpp**.

9. Compile the program. When it is error-free, run the program. Depending on the data you use for input, the output should look similar to Figure 2-13.

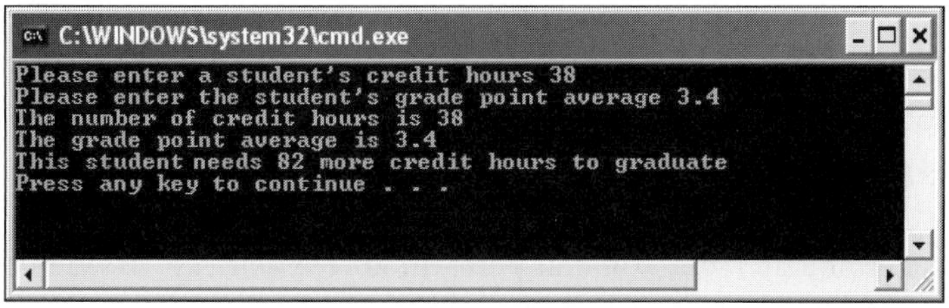

Figure 2-13   Typical execution of Student.cpp program

CHAPTER SUMMARY

- C++ provides five simple binary arithmetic operators for creating arithmetic expressions: addition (+), subtraction (−), multiplication (*), division (/), and modulus (%).

- When you mix data types in a binary arithmetic expression, the result is always the same type as the type that takes the most memory to store.

- C++ employs several shortcut operators for arithmetic, such as +=, prefix ++, and postfix ++.

- A Boolean expression is one that evaluates as true or false. In C++, the value 0 is always interpreted as false; all other values are interpreted as true.

- Fields contained within structures are used in arithmetic and Boolean expressions in the same manner as are primitive variables.

KEY TERMS

The **addition operator** is the + symbol; it is a binary arithmetic operator used to perform addition.

The **subtraction operator** is the − symbol; it is a binary arithmetic operator used to perform subtraction.

The **multiplication operator** is the * symbol; it is a binary arithmetic operator used to perform multiplication.

The **division operator** is the / symbol; it is a binary arithmetic operator used to perform division.

The **modulus operator** is the % symbol; it is a binary arithmetic operator used to perform modulus. The modulus operator gives the remainder of integer division; it can be used only with integers.

An **arithmetic operator** is a symbol that performs arithmetic.

A **binary operator** is an operator that takes two operands, one on each side of the operator.

A **mixed expression** is one in which the operands have different data types.

The **unifying type** is the data type of the value in an arithmetic expression to which all the types in the expression are converted.

To **cast** a value is to transform it to another data type.

An **implicit cast** is the automatic cast, or transformation, that occurs when you assign a value of one type to a type with higher precedence.

An **explicit cast** is a deliberate cast; you can perform an explicit cast in one of two ways: by typing `static_cast<data type>` in front of an expression, or by using a type name within parentheses in front of an expression.

A **check digit** is a digit added to a number (either at the end or at the beginning) that validates the authenticity of the number.

Arithmetic precedence is the set of rules of order of performance of arithmetic operations. Operators with higher precedence are performed first in an arithmetic statement with multiple operations.

Associativity is the rule that dictates the order in which an operator works with its operands.

The **add and assign operator**, +=, adds the right-hand operand to the left-hand operand.

A **compound assignment operator** is an operator that performs two tasks, one of which is assignment.

The **subtract and assign operator** (– =) subtracts the right-hand operand from the left-hand operand.

The **multiply and assign operator** (*=) operator multiplies the left-hand operand by the right-hand operand.

The **divide and assign operator** (/=) divides the operand on the left by the operand on the right.

The **modulus and assign operator** (%=) finds the modulus when you divide the left-hand operand by the right-hand operand, and assigns the result to the left-hand operand.

To **increment** is to increase by one.

The **prefix increment operator** is ++ before a variable.

The **postfix increment operator** is ++ after a variable.

To **decrement** is to reduce by one.

Unary operators are those that require only one operand.

The **positive value operator** (+) is a unary operator that indicates a positive value.

The **negative value operator** (–) is a unary operator that indicates a negative value.

The **address operator** (&) is a unary operator used to refer to the memory address of a variable.

The **hexadecimal numbering system** is a numbering system based on powers of 16.

Relational operators are those that evaluate the relationship between operands.

A **Boolean expression** is one that evaluates as true or false.

The **relational operator** = = means equivalent to.

The **relational operator** > means greater than.
The **relational operator** >= means greater than or equal to.
The **relational operator** < means less than.
The **relational operator** <= means less than or equal to.
The **relational operator** != means not equal to.
The **not operator** (!) reverses the true/false value of an expression.

2

REVIEW QUESTIONS

1. Arithmetic operations, such as addition (+), subtraction (−), multiplication (*), division (/), and modulus (%), that take two arguments use _____ operators.

   a. unary

   b. summary

   c. binary

   d. Boolean

2. Addition, subtraction, multiplication, division, or modulus of any two integers _____.

   a. always results in an integer

   b. usually results in an integer

   c. can result in an integer or floating-point value depending on the arithmetic value of the result

   d. can result in an integer or floating-point value depending on the data type of the result

3. If either or both of the operands in addition, subtraction, multiplication, or division is a floating-point number–that is, a **float** or a **double**–then the result is _____.

   a. always an integer

   b. usually a floating-point number

   c. always a floating-point number

   d. not mathematically defined

4. An expression in which the operands have different data types is _____.

   a. a binary expression

   b. a mixed expression

   c. a disparate expression

   d. illegal in C++

5. If you add a `double`, a `float`, and an `int`, the result is _____.

   a. a `double`

   b. a `float`

   c. an `int`

   d. illegal

6. In C++, what is the result of 5 + 4 * 3 + 2?

   a. 14

   b. 19

   c. 29

   d. 54

7. In C++, what is the result of 19 % 2?

   a. 0

   b. 1

   c. 9

   d. 19

8. If a and b are integers, and a = 10 and b = 30, if you use the statement a += b, what is the resulting value of a?

   a. 10

   b. 20

   c. 30

   d. 40

9. If c is an integer, and c = 34, what is the value of ++c?

   a. 0

   b. 1

   c. 34

   d. 35

10. If c and d are integers, and d = 34, what is the value of c = d++?

   a. 0

   b. 1

   c. 34

   d. 35

11. If e and f are integers, and d = 16 and e = 17, what is the value of d = = --e?

   a. 0

   b. 1

    c. 16

    d. 17

12. An expression that evaluates as true or false is known as a(n) _____ expression.

    a. unary

    b. binary

    c. Boolean

    d. honest

13. In C++, all false relational expressions are evaluated as _____.

    a. 0

    b. 1

    c. negative

    d. positive

14. Multiplication, division, and modulus are said to have _____ than addition and subtraction.

    a. lower arithmetic precedence

    b. higher arithmetic precedence

    c. lower associativity

    d. higher associativity

15. Which of the following does not have the same result as `myValue = myValue + 1`?

    a. `myValue = 1;`

    b. `myValue += 1;`

    c. `++myValue;`

    d. `myValue++;`

16. Assume `k` and `m` are integers, and that `k = 5` and `m = 7`. Which of the following results in a change in the value of `m`?

    a. `m = k + 2;`

    b. `k = m - 2;`

    c. `k = m++;`

    d. `m = 87 % 10;`

17. In C++, the & operator in front of a variable represents _____.

    a. addition

    b. assignment and addition

    c. the address of the variable

    d. a negative value

18. Because + can be used to mean addition as well as a positive value, the + operator is said to be _____.

   a. encapsulated

   b. object-oriented

   c. bilingual

   d. polymorphic

19. In C++, all false relational expressions have the mathematical value _____.

   a. 0

   b. 1

   c. −1

   d. null

20. Consider a structure named Rug that contains two integer fields, length and width. Assume you have declared a Rug named myBedroomCarpet. Which of the following is legal?

   a. Rug.width = 12

   b. Rug.length = Rug.width

   c. myBedroomCarpet = 15

   d. myBedroomCarpet.width = 10;

EXERCISES

1. Assume a, b, and c are integers, and that a = 0, b = 1, and c = 5. What is the value of each of the following? (Do not assume the answers are cumulative; evaluate each expression using the original values for a, b, and c.)

   a. a + b

   b. a > b

   c. 3 + b * c

   d. ++b

   e. b++

   f. b <= c

   g. a > 5

   h. ++a ==b

   i. b != c

   j. b == c

   k. b = c

l. b / c

m. b % c

n. b + c * 4 / 3

o. 22 / (c + 3)

2. Write a C++ program in which you declare a variable that holds an hourly wage. Prompt the user to enter an hourly wage. Multiply the wage by 40 hours and print the standard weekly pay. Save the file as **RegularWorkWeek.cpp**.

3. Write a C++ program in which you declare variables that hold an hourly wage, a number of hours worked, and a withholding percentage. Prompt the user to enter values for each of these fields. Compute and display net weekly pay, which is calculated as hours times rate, minus the percentage of the gross pay that is withholding. Save the file as **NetPay.cpp**.

4. Write a C++ program that prompts the user to enter the number of hours required to install a hardwood floor. Display the number of complete eight-hour workdays required for the job, as well as the remaining hours needed in the last day. Compute and display the total cost of the job at $200 per day plus $40 per hour for any partial day. Save the file as **Floor.cpp**.

5. Write a program that allows the user to enter two values. Display the results of adding the two values, subtracting them from each other, multiplying them, and dividing them. Save the file as **MathExercise.cpp**.

6. a. Write a program for a bank that allows the user to enter an amount of money in cents. Display the number of whole dollars the bank will give the customer in exchange. Save the file as **DollarConversion.cpp**.

   b. Modify the program in 6a so that, in addition to the cents, the user enters the denomination of the coin to which to convert the pennies, such as 5 for nickels or 25 for quarters. Save the file as **ChangeConversion.cpp**.

7. The Universal Product Code (UPC) on most grocery items contains a zero that is printed to the left of the bar code and ten digits that are printed in two groups of five each below the code. The first five digits represent a manufacturer and the second five digits represent a specific product. To the right of the bar code, a check digit is printed. Write a program that allows the user to enter the five-digit manufacturer code, the five-digit product code, and the check digit. Display the result of a Boolean comparison (0 or 1) that shows whether the check digit is correct according to the following algorithm. (*Hint*: Use a combination of modulus, multiplication, and subtraction to separate the digits in the entered code.)

   a. Sum the second and fourth numbers in the manufacturer code.

   b. Sum the first, third, and fifth numbers in the product code.

   c. Sum the results of step a and step b, and multiply the total by 3.

   d. Sum the first, third, and fifth numbers in the manufacturer code.

   e. Sum the second and fourth numbers in the product code.

f. Sum the results of steps d and e, and add to the result from step c.

g. Take the remainder when the result of step f is divided by 10.

h. Subtract the result of step g in 10. Compare this result to the check digit entered by the user. If the result and check digit are equal (if the Boolean value of the comparison is 1), then the UPC is a valid one.

Save the file as **UPC.cpp**. After you write the program, test it using UPC values from several grocery items from your home. (Make sure the digit to the left of the bar code is 0—the 0 indicates that the code follows this algorithm.)

8. On the Web, research the Luhn formula that is used to verify credit card numbers. Write a program that allows the user to enter a sixteen-digit account number in groups of four, and display a 1 or 0 that indicates whether the credit card number is valid or invalid. If you have access to one, test the program with a MasterCard or Visa account number to verify that it works correctly. Save the file as **Luhn.cpp**.

9. Create a `PhoneCall` structure with one public field that contains the number of minutes in a call. Write a `main()` function that instantiates one `PhoneCall` object, such as `myCallToGrandmaOnSunday`. Assign a value to the `minutes` field of this object. Print the value of the `minutes` field. Calculate the cost of the call at 10 cents per minute, and display the results. Save the file as **PhoneCall.cpp**.

10. Create a `Cake` structure. Include two public fields that contain the price of the `Cake` and the calorie count of the `Cake`. Write a `main()` function that declares a `Cake` object. Prompt the user for field values. Echo the values, and then display the cost per calorie. Save the file as **Cake.cpp**.

11. Each of the following files in the Chapter02 folder of your Data Disk contains syntax and/or logical errors. Determine the problem in each case, and fix the program. Save your solutions by adding "Fixed" to the filename, as in **DEBUG2-1Fixed.cpp**.

a. DEBUG2-1.cpp

b. DEBUG2-2.cpp

c. DEBUG2-3.cpp

d. DEBUG2-4.cpp

CASE PROJECT 1

In Chapter 1 you developed a `Fraction` structure for Teacher's Pet Software. The structure contains two public data fields for numerator and denominator. Using the same structure, write a `main()` function in which you create three `Fraction` objects. Prompt the user for values for each field of two of the `Fractions`. Add statements to the `main()` function to do the following:

❏ Display the floating-point equivalent of each `Fraction` object. For example, the floating-point equivalent of 1/4 is 0.25.

❏ Calculate the third **Fraction** to be the sum of the two entered **Fraction**s. To sum fractions, you must find a common denominator. You can do this by multiplying each operand **Fraction**'s numerator and denominator by the denominator of the other **Fraction**, using the common denominators, and adding the numerators. For example, to create a **Fraction** that is the sum of 2/5 plus 1/6, you do the following:

   1. Multiply the numerator and denominator of 2/5 by the denominator of the second **Fraction**, 6, giving 12/30.

   2. Multiply the numerator and denominator of 1/6 by the denominator of the first **Fraction**, 5, giving 5/30.

   3. Add the numerators and use the common denominator, giving 17/30.

❏ Display the result. You do not need to reduce an improper **Fraction** result. For example, when you add 1/2 and 1/4, the result can be displayed as 6/8 instead of being reduced to 3/4.

CASE PROJECT 2

In Chapter 1 you developed a **BankAccount** structure for Parkville Bank. The structure contains two public fields for the integer account number and **double** account balance. Using the same structure, write a **main()** function in which you create two **BankAccount** objects. Add statements to the **main()** function to do the following:

❏ Prompt the user for account numbers and beginning balances for the two **BankAccount**s. When testing your program, use four-digit account numbers, but the program does not have to enforce this rule.

❏ Complete each account number by adding a check digit that is the remainder when the account number is divided by 5.

❏ Prompt the user for a dollar amount to be transferred from the first account to the second account.

❏ Display the full account numbers (including check digits) and starting balances for the two accounts, then display the ending balances after the transfer amount has been deducted from the first account and added to the second.

3

MAKING DECISIONS

In this chapter, you will:

♦ Use the `if` and `if-else` statements
♦ Use nested `if` statements
♦ Avoid common pitfalls with `if` statements
♦ Use the `switch` statement
♦ Use the conditional operator
♦ Use the logical AND and the logical OR
♦ Make decisions with structure fields

Computer programs often seem smart because of their ability to use selections or make decisions. Consider a medical program that diagnoses your ailment based on a group of symptoms, or a program that determines the correct speed and angle for a space-shuttle docking. Some programs make hundreds or thousands of decisions, but no matter how many decisions a program requires, each one is simply a yes-or-no decision. Computer circuitry consists of millions of tiny electronic switches, and the state of each is either on or off. This means that every decision boils down to on or off, yes or no, 1 or 0.

In Chapter 1, you learned that structured programming allows three basic control structures—sequence, selection, and loop. In Chapter 2, you saw many sequences of instructions that evaluated expressions. In this chapter, you will explore the capabilities of the selection structure. In Chapter 4, you will become proficient in using program loops.

C++ lets you perform selections in a number of ways, including using the `if` and `if-else` statements, the `switch` statement, and conditional operators. You can also combine decisions using the logical AND and the logical OR.

USING THE if STATEMENT

The Single-Alternative if

Computer programs use the selection structure to choose one of two possible courses of action (and one of the courses of action might be no action).

The primary C++ selection structure statement used to perform a single-alternative selection is an if statement. One way to use an if is in a **single-alternative selection**—one in which an action takes place only when the result of the decision is true. It takes the form:

Syntax Example

if (*Boolean expression*)
        action if true;

When you write an if statement, you use the keyword if, a Boolean expression within parentheses, and any statement that is the action that occurs if the Boolean expression is true. Figure 3-1 shows a diagram of the logic of the if statement. The diamond holds a true/false question and two paths emerge from the diamond. If the tested expression is true, then the resulting action occurs, but if the tested expression is false, then no action takes place. Either way, when the if statement ends, the program logic continues on the same path.

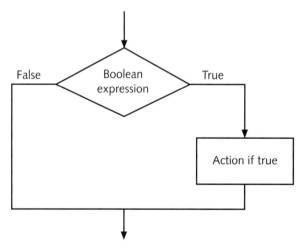

Figure 3-1   Flowchart diagram of an if statement

TIP   Most frequently, you create an if statement's Boolean expression using one of the six relational operators you learned about in Chapter 2. They are:

== equal to

> greater than

< less than

>= greater than or equal to

<= less than or equal to

!= not equal to

Programmers often write the if statement on two lines to visually separate the decision-making condition from its resulting action; however, only one semicolon follows the entire statement.

TIP   The Boolean expression used in an if statement is often a comparison, such as "x greater than y," but in C++ it can also be a number or an arithmetic expression. The value 0 is interpreted as false, and all other values are interpreted as true.

Consider the program shown in Figure 3-2. An insurance policy base premium is set at $75.32. After the program prompts for and receives values for the driver's age and number of traffic tickets, several (shaded) decisions are made.

```
#include<iostream>
using namespace std;

int main()
{
    int driverAge, numTickets;
    double premiumDue = 75.32;
    cout<<"Enter driver's age";
    cin>>driverAge;
    cout<<"Enter traffic tickets issued";
    cin>>numTickets;
    if(driverAge < 26)
        premiumDue += 100;
    if(driverAge > 50)
        premiumDue -= 50;
    if(numTickets == 2)
        premiumDue += 60.25;
    cout<<"Premium due is "<<premiumDue<<endl;
}
```

Figure 3-2   Insurance program containing selection statements

In the application in Figure 3-2, if the expression in the parentheses of any of the if statements is true, then the statement following the if executes. For example, if the `driverAge` is less than 26, then 100 is added to the `premiumDue`. Figure 3-3 shows the output when the driver is under 26 years old and has no tickets. Notice that $100 has been added to the original premium amount because the driver is under 26, not over 50, and does not have two tickets.

Figure 3-3   Output of insurance application when driver is younger than 26 with no tickets

Remember, the parentheses surrounding the evaluated expression in the `if` statement are essential.

TIP

Sometimes you will want to perform multiple tasks when a condition is met. For example, suppose that when a driver is under 26, you want to add $100 to the premium but also display a message. If the execution of more than one statement depends on the selection, then the resulting statements must be blocked with curly braces, as shown in the code segment in Figure 3-4. Figure 3-5 shows a diagram of the logic.

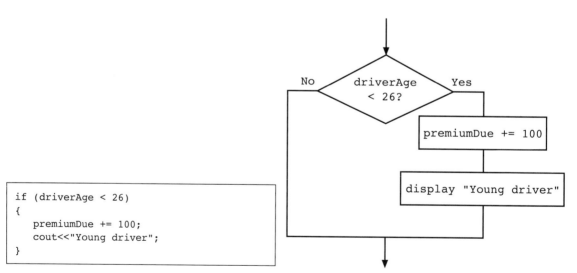

```
if (driverAge < 26)
{
    premiumDue += 100;
    cout<<"Young driver";
}
```

Figure 3-4   Blocking of resulting statements

Figure 3-5   Diagram of logic of `if` statement in Figure 3-4

3

The curly braces in the code segment in Figure 3-4 are very important. If they are removed, then only one statement (the addition statement) depends on the `if`'s Boolean comparison, and the other statement (the output statement) becomes a stand-alone statement. Examine the code segment in Figure 3-6. This code is written without the curly braces. For example, if the **driverAge** is set to 85, then the Boolean expression in the `if` evaluates as false (or 0) and the premium is correctly left alone (not increased). However, the "Young driver" message is displayed on the screen because the output statement is a new statement and not part of the `if` statement. The indentation in Figure 3-6 is misleading because it makes it appear that the execution of the **cout** statement depends on the `if`; however, it does not. (Figure 3-7 contains a diagram of the logic.) The C++ compiler ignores any indentations you make; only curly braces can indicate which statements are performed as a block.

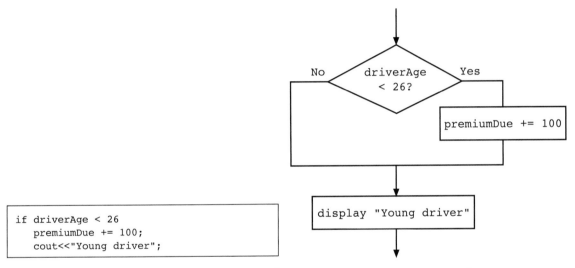

```
if driverAge < 26
    premiumDue += 100;
    cout<<"Young driver";
```

Figure 3-6   An `if` with missing curly braces and misleading indents—only the add and assign statement is dependent on the `if`

Figure 3-7   Diagram of logic of `if` statement in Figure 3-6

TIP   You can surround a single statement after an `if` with curly braces if you want to, but when only one statement should execute, braces are not required.

The Dual-Alternative `if`

The **dual-alternative** `if`, also called the **`if-else`** structure, takes one action when its Boolean expression is evaluated as true, and uses an **`else`** clause to define the actions to take when the expression is evaluated as false. It takes the form:

Syntax Example

if (Boolean expression)
    action if true;
else
    action if false;

For example, Figure 3-8 shows a program that uses an `if-else` structure. In the program, after the user enters a character in the `genderCode` variable, the variable is tested to see if it is equivalent to the character 'F'. If it is, the output is the word "Female"; if it is not, the output is "Male". Figure 3-9 shows a diagram of the logic.

TIP The semicolon that occurs after `cout<<"Female"<<endl` and before the `else` is required, even though the `if-else` statement does not end until after the statement `cout<<"Male"<<endl;`.

```
#include<iostream>
using namespace std;
int main()
{
    char genderCode;
    cout<<"Enter F for female or M for male ";
    cin>>genderCode;
    if(genderCode == 'F')
        cout<<"Female"<<endl;
    else
        cout<<"Male"<<endl;
}
```

Figure 3-8   An `if-else` statement

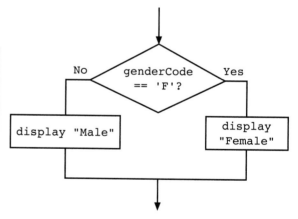

Figure 3-9   Diagram of logic of `if-else` statement in Figure 3-8

TIP An `else` must always be associated with an `if`. You can have an `if` without an `else`, but you can't have an `else` without an `if`.

As with an `if`, you can also block multiple statements in the `else` portion of an `if` statement. Any C++ statements can appear in the block associated with an `if`, and any

C++ statements can appear in the block associated with an else. Those statements can include, but are not limited to, variable declarations, input and output statements, and other if and else pairs.

Using a Nested if

Note that in the program shown in Figure 3-8, the output will be the word "Male" if the user enters any character other than 'F'. The selection tests only whether the genderCode is an 'F', not whether it is an 'M' or any other character. Figure 3-10 shows a program that is slightly more sophisticated than the one in Figure 3-8. This one tests for the character 'M' as well as the character 'F', displaying a default message if the genderCode matches neither value. Figure 3-11 shows a diagram of the logic in the decision.

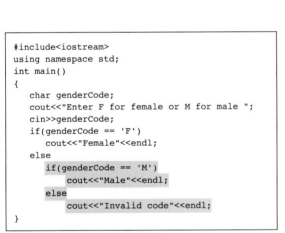

```
#include<iostream>
using namespace std;
int main()
{
    char genderCode;
    cout<<"Enter F for female or M for male ";
    cin>>genderCode;
    if(genderCode == 'F')
        cout<<"Female"<<endl;
    else
        if(genderCode == 'M')
            cout<<"Male"<<endl;
        else
            cout<<"Invalid code"<<endl;
}
```

Figure 3-10   A nested if-else statement

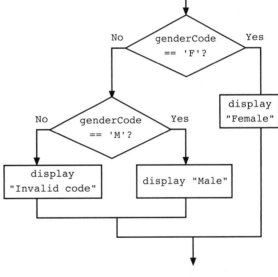

Figure 3-11   Diagram of logic of if-else statement in Figure 3-10

The highlighted code in Figure 3-10 that compares the genderCode to 'M' is known as a **nested if**. In other words, it is an if structure that rests entirely within another if structure—within either the if or the else clause. The entire code segment diagrammed in Figure 3-11 can also be called an **if-else-if**, which is a structure in which a new decision rests within the else clause of another decision. In Figure 3-10, if the genderCode is 'F', one action results. If the genderCode is not an 'F', then another if-else structure executes, testing for genderCode 'M'. The if-else pair that tests for genderCode 'M' occurs within the else portion of the original selection.

AVOIDING COMMON PITFALLS WITH `if` STATEMENTS

Whether you are first learning to use selection statements or are an experienced programmer, it is easy to make several types of mistakes.

- Forgetting that C++ is case sensitive
- Assuming that indentation has a logical purpose
- Adding an unwanted semicolon
- Forgetting curly braces
- Using = instead of ==
- Making unnecessary comparisons
- Creating unreachable code

None of these mistakes involve syntax errors, that is, programs containing these errors will compile without error messages and execute, but each error causes incorrect results or an inefficiently executing program.

Pitfall: Forgetting that C++ is case sensitive

When you compare characters, remember that C++ is case sensitive. When you run the program in Figure 3-10, and enter an 'f' for "female", you might expect the program to display "Female" and be surprised when it displays "Invalid code". The program runs correctly because the code that tests `genderCode == 'F'` checks for only the character specified—an uppercase 'F'. If you want the user to type a lowercase 'f', then the program should test for that character instead. If you want the user to be able to type an uppercase or a lowercase 'f', then you might write a nested `if` statement as shown in Figure 3-12. In this program, if the entered code is 'F', the "Female" message displays. If it is not 'F', but is 'f', the "Female" message also displays.

 Later in this chapter you will learn how to test for two values in the same `if` statement.

TIP

Pitfalls: Assuming that indentation has a logical purpose, adding an unwanted semicolon, and forgetting curly braces

Do not inadvertently insert a semicolon prior to the end of a complete `if` statement. For example, consider the `if` statement in Figure 3-13. The expression `driverAge < 26` is evaluated as true or false. Because the semicolon immediately follows the Boolean expression, the first statement in the code is interpreted as `if driverAge < 26` then do nothing. So, whether the driver's age is less than 26 or not, no resulting action occurs. The next statement, which adds 100 to the `premiumDue`, is a new stand-alone statement and does

```cpp
#include<iostream>
using namespace std;
int main()
{
    char genderCode;
    cout<<"Enter F for female or M for male ";
    cin>>genderCode;
    if(genderCode == 'F')
        cout<<"Female"<<endl;
    else
        if(genderCode == 'f')
            cout<<"Female"<<endl;
        else
            cout<<"Male"<<endl;
}
```

Figure 3-12   A program that tests for both uppercase and lowercase data entry

not depend on the decision regarding the driver's age. All drivers, whether under 26 or not, have 100 added to their premiumDue variable. The example in Figure 3-13 is misleading because the indentation of the addition statement makes it appear as though the addition depends on the if. However, as you first learned in Chapter 1, C++ ignores white spaces, including indentations. In Figure 3-13, the semicolon at the end of the first line indicates that statement's completion. Figure 3-14 shows the logic of the if statement in Figure 3-13. As you can see from the diagram, because of the inserted semicolon, the decision made in the **if** statement has no resulting action. That is, the decision is made, but whether it is true or false, no action is taken. The indentation of the second code line means nothing to the C++ compiler.

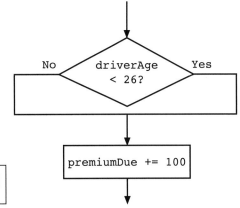

```cpp
if (driverAge < 26); // Notice the incorrect semicolon
    premiumDue += 100;
```

Figure 3-13   A misleading, do-nothing `if` statement

Figure 3-14   Diagram of logic of `if` statement in Figure 3-13

When you insert an unwanted semicolon in a statement, as in the code segment in Figure 3-13, the decision structure ends before you intended. This situation is similar to the one that occurs when you forget necessary curly braces. Recall the program code in Figure 3-6 in which the curly braces were omitted; the two statements intended to depend on the Boolean expression in the `if` statement were not blocked as they should have been. In that case, the `if` decision structure also ends before it should. One resulting statement correctly executes depending on the evaluation of the Boolean expression in the `if`, but the second statement executes either way. Again, C++ ignores the indentation; only the placement of semicolons and curly braces matters in determining where statements and blocks end.

Pitfall: Using = instead of ==

Almost every C++ expression has a numeric value, and any C++ expression can be evaluated as part of an `if` statement. If the expression is evaluated as 0, it is considered false, and the block of statements following the `if` is not executed. If the expression is evaluated as 0 and an `else` exists, then the statements in the `else` block are executed. If the expression in an `if` statement is evaluated as *anything* other than 0, it is considered to be true. In that case, any statement associated with the `if` executes.

Examine the code in Figure 3-15. At first glance, it appears that the output will read, "No vacation days available". However, the programmer has mistakenly used the assignment operator (the single equal sign) in the expression within the highlighted `if` statement. The result is that 0 is assigned to `vacationDays`, the value of the expression is 0, and the expression is determined to be false. Therefore, the `else` portion of the `if-else` selection is the portion that executes, and the message displayed is, "You have vacation days coming".

```cpp
#include<iostream>
using namespace std;
int main()
{
    int vacationDays = 0;
    if(vacationDays = 0)
        cout<<"No vacation days available"<<endl;
    else
        cout<<"You have vacation days coming"<<endl;
}
```

Figure 3-15   An `if` statement that produces an unexpected result because the single equal sign is used

TIP   Any value other than 0, even a negative value, is considered to be true. Thus, the statement `if(-5) cout<<"OK";` would display "OK".

3

The error that occurs when you mistakenly use the single equal sign for comparisons is a particularly hard error to find in your programs. Part of the reason is that the single equal sign "looks" right, especially because the symbol is used for equality comparisons in other programming languages, such as Visual Basic. Another part of the reason the error is so hard to find is that when you read aloud a statement like the highlighted one in Figure 3-15, you tend to say, "If vacation days equal zero…" instead of using the true meaning, which is "If the value of assigning 0 to vacation days results in a non-zero value…" This last statement is very confusing but is always false, and is actually what happens when you use the assignment operator (the single equal sign) in the Boolean expression evaluated in the `if` statement

Pitfall: Making unnecessary comparisons

You should avoid making unnecessary comparisons in your programs. For example, Figure 3-16 shows a program that determines whether the user can vote. The program prompts the user to enter an age. If the user is at least 18, one message is displayed; if the user is under 18, a different message is displayed. The logic is diagrammed in Figure 3-17.

Although the program in Figure 3-16 works correctly, displaying the correct message for each user, it asks an unnecessary question. If a user's age is not greater than or equal to 18, then it must be less than 18. In the program in Figure 3-16, every user's response must go through two decisions, and the second one is unnecessary. In a program that makes one decision about one user, the time taken for this extra decision is negligible, but in a program that makes thousands of decisions for millions of users, program response time could be noticeably affected.

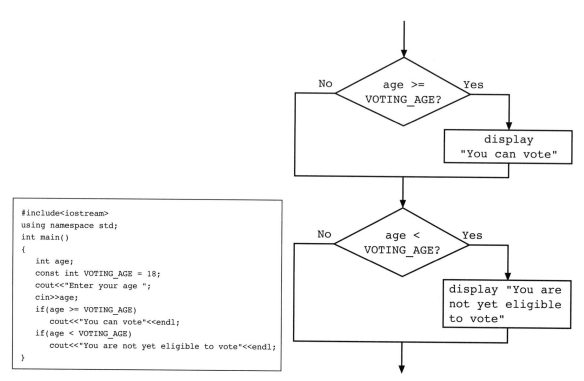

```
#include<iostream>
using namespace std;
int main()
{
    int age;
    const int VOTING_AGE = 18;
    cout<<"Enter your age ";
    cin>>age;
    if(age >= VOTING_AGE)
        cout<<"You can vote"<<endl;
    if(age < VOTING_AGE)
        cout<<"You are not yet eligible to vote"<<endl;
}
```

Figure 3-16 A program containing an unnecessary comparison

Figure 3-17 Diagram of decision-making process in program in Figure 3-16

Figures 3-18 and 3-19 show the code and diagram that correspond to using an `if-else` instead of two separate `if` statements. Each user's data passes through only one decision, which is enough to determine each user's outcome.

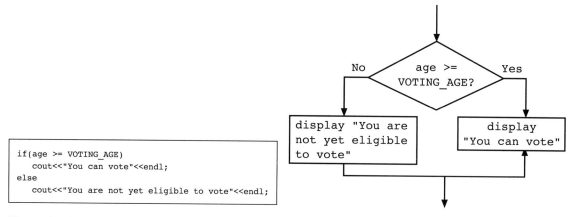

```
if(age >= VOTING_AGE)
    cout<<"You can vote"<<endl;
else
    cout<<"You are not yet eligible to vote"<<endl;
```

Figure 3-18 An `if-else` statement that avoids the unnecessary comparison in Figure 3-16

Figure 3-19 Diagram of decision-making process in program in Figure 3-18

Pitfall: Creating unreachable code

Sometimes when you include an unnecessary decision within a program, extra logical paths are traveled. Other times, you create logical paths that can never be traveled; such paths are sometimes called **dead logical paths**. Consider the application in Figure 3-20; a diagram of its decision-making process appears in Figure 3-21. The program is supposed to display one of three messages as follows:

- "Great job!" if the user's test score is 90 or more

- "You are above average" if the test score is 70 or more but less than 90

- "Below average performance" if the test score is less than 70

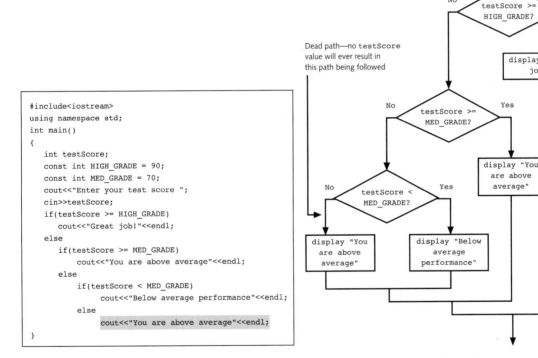

```
#include<iostream>
using namespace std;
int main()
{
    int testScore;
    const int HIGH_GRADE = 90;
    const int MED_GRADE = 70;
    cout<<"Enter your test score ";
    cin>>testScore;
    if(testScore >= HIGH_GRADE)
        cout<<"Great job!"<<endl;
    else
        if(testScore >= MED_GRADE)
            cout<<"You are above average"<<endl;
        else
            if(testScore < MED_GRADE)
                cout<<"Below average performance"<<endl;
            else
                cout<<"You are above average"<<endl;
}
```

Figure 3-20   A program containing a dead logical path

Figure 3-21   Diagram of decision-making process in program in Figure 3-20

The application in Figure 3-20 works correctly. If the user enters a test score of 90 or greater, the "Great job!" message is displayed. If the user enters a test score that is not greater than or equal to 90, then the second question determines if the score is at least 70. If so, "You are above average" is displayed. There is no need to ask whether the test score is less than 70 because if it is not at least 70, then it must be less than 70. The answer to the question testScore < 70? must be Yes; it is impossible for the logic to take the highlighted No path generated by the question. Therefore, the final cout statement can never execute. Figure 3-21 shows a diagram illustrating the dead logical path, which the program will never take.

USING THE switch STATEMENT

When you want to create different outcomes depending on specific values, you can use a series of ifs. For example, the series of nested decisions in Figure 3-22 is used to display an appropriate department name based on the value of a numeric variable that holds the department number.

```
if(department == 1)
   cout<<"Human Resources"<<endl;
else
     if(department == 2)
        cout<<"Sales"<<endl;
     else
         if(department == 3)
             cout<<"Information Systems"<<endl;
         else
             cout<<"No such department"<<endl;
```

Figure 3-22   Nested ifs that display department name based on department number

The series of if statements in Figure 3-22 works correctly. However, as an alternative to the long string of ifs, you can use the **switch statement**. Although not as flexible as the if statement, the switch statement is useful when a single variable must be compared to multiple values. For an example of a switch statement, see Figure 3-23. The logic of the statements in Figure 3-23 is identical to the logic in Figure 3-22.

In Figure 3-23, the keyword **switch** identifies the beginning of the statement. Then the variable in parentheses (**department**) is evaluated. After the opening curly brace, a series of **case** statements separate the actions that should occur when the department equals each case. As soon as a case that equals the value of **department** is found, all statements from that point on execute until either a **break** statement or the final curly brace in the switch is encountered. For example, when the **department** variable holds the value 2, case 1 is ignored; case 2 executes, printing "Sales"; and then the **break** statement executes. The **break** causes the logic to continue with any statements beyond the closing curly brace of the **switch** statement.

```
switch(department)
{
     case 1:
         cout<<"Human Resources"<<endl;
         break;
     case 2:
         cout<<"Sales"<<endl;
         break;
     case 3:
          cout<<"Information Systems"<<endl;
          break;
       default:
           cout<<"No such department"<<endl;
}
```

Figure 3-23   A `switch` statement that displays department name based on department number

If you remove the `break` statements from the code shown in Figure 3-23, then all four
`cout` statements (those that display "Human Resources", "Sales", "Information Systems",
and "No such department") execute when the value of `department` is 1. Similarly, without the `break` statements, the last three `cout` statements execute when the department
is 2, and the last two execute when the department is 3. The `default` option executes
when no cases are equivalent to the value of `department`.

The `switch` statement can contain any number of cases in any order. The values in the
case statements do not have to occur in either ascending or descending order as they do
in Figure 3-23, nor do they have to be consecutive.

The `switch` statement is not as flexible as the `if`; use it only when you have several outcomes that depend on the value of a single variable or expression. The result of the expression must be an integer data type (which includes `int`, `char`, `bool`, `long int`, and
`short int`). In appropriate situations, however, many programmers think the `switch`
statement is easier to read and understand than a long series of nested `if`s.

Each case can be followed by any number of statements to execute. Unlike
with the `if` statement, the statements to be executed do not need to be contained in a block with curly braces.

TIP

USING THE CONDITIONAL OPERATOR

Another alternative to the `if` statement involves the **conditional operator** (also called
the **if operator**), which is represented by a question mark (**?**). The if operator provides
a concise way to express two alternatives. Consider the statements:

```
if(driverAge < 26)
    insurancePremium = 250;
```

```
        else
            insurancePremium = 185;
```

The same logic can be expressed using the conditional operator as follows:

```
        driverAge < 26 ? insurancePremium = 250 : insurancePremium = 185;
```

If the **driverAge** is less than 26, the first assignment takes place; if the **driverAge** is not less than 26, the second assignment occurs. The question mark is necessary after the evaluated expression, and a colon must be included between the two alternatives. The advantage of using the conditional operator is the ability to place a decision and its two possible outcomes in an abbreviated format.

 The conditional operator is an example of a ternary operator, one that takes three operands instead of just one or two. The conditional operator is the only ternary operator used in C++.

 Unlike the **if** statement, you cannot use the conditional operator without designating both true and false results; that is, the conditional operator requires three operands—the Boolean test, the true result, and the false result.

As another example of the usefulness of the conditional operator, consider the following code:

```
        cout<<(a > b ? a : b)<<" is greater"<<endl;
```

In this statement, **a** is compared to **b**, and if **a** is larger, the result is **a**, and if **a** is not larger, the result is **b**. The comparison and the displayed result are handled in a single, concise statement.

 The conditional operator is not used as frequently as many other C++ operators. Many programmers prefer to use **if** statements for all their decisions because they feel the resulting code is easier to understand.

USING THE LOGICAL AND AND THE LOGICAL OR

When you must test multiple conditions before executing a statement, you can always use a series of **if** statements. However, C++ provides convenient shortcuts for testing multiple conditions—the logical AND and the logical OR.

Using the Logical AND

In some programming situations, two or more conditions must be true to initiate an action. For example, you want to display the message "Apply discount" if a customer visits your store more than five times a year *and* spends at least $1,000 during the year.

(Assumes you do not want to provide a discount for infrequent visitors even though they spend a lot, nor do you want to provide a discount for frequent visitors who spend very little.) Assuming the variables are declared and have been assigned reasonable values, you have already learned that the code in Figure 3-24 works correctly using a nested if—that is, one if statement nested within another if statement. (Figure 3-25 shows a diagram of the logic.)

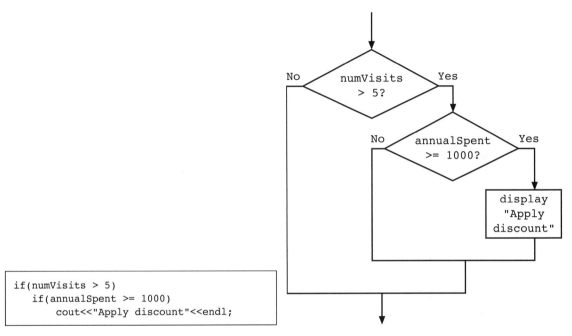

```
if(numVisits > 5)
   if(annualSpent >= 1000)
      cout<<"Apply discount"<<endl;
```

Figure 3-24   Nested if in which two conditions must be true

Figure 3-25   Diagram of logic of if statement in Figure 3-24

If numVisits is not greater than 5, the statement is finished—the second comparison does not even take place. Alternatively, you can use a single if statement that contains a **logical AND**, which you create by typing two ampersands (&&) between two Boolean expressions, as shown in Figure 3-26. You use a logical AND to create a compound Boolean expression in which two conditions must be true for the entire expression to evaluate as true.

```
if(numVisits > 5 && annualSpent >= 1000)
        cout<<"Apply discount"<<endl;
```

Figure 3-26   Selection using a logical AND

TIP

You can also write the logical expression in Figure 3-26 using parentheses to explicitly indicate how the expressions should be evaluated. For example, you can write the following expression using the extra sets of parentheses surrounding the logical expressions:

```
if((numVisits > 5) && (annualSpent >= 1000))
        cout<<"Apply discount"<<endl;
```

This code executes the same way as the version without the extra parentheses, but it makes it clearer to the reader that the value of numVisits > 5 will be determined, then the value of annualSpent >= 1000 will be determined, and finally the logical AND will be evaluated.

TIP

Do not enter a space between the ampersands (&&) in a logical AND.

You read the code in Figure 3-26 as "if numVisits is greater than 5 *and* annualSpent is greater than or equal to 1000, then display 'Apply discount'". The logic of the code in Figure 3-26 is identical to the diagram shown in Figure 3-25. As with the nested ifs, if the first expression (numVisits > 5) is not evaluated as true, then the second expression (annualSpent >= 1000) is not evaluated.

TIP

In many AND selections, if the first expression is evaluated as false, you might not care whether the second expression is evaluated. However, if you write "tricky" code like the following, you might mislead those who read your code:

```
if(++firstNum && ++secondNum)
    cout<<"Some message"<<endl;
```

In this example, if the value of ++firstNum is 0, the second part of the if will never execute and secondNum will neither be increased nor evaluated. Someone reading your code, however, might easily assume secondNum is increased.

When you use the logical AND, you must include a complete Boolean expression on each side of the &&. For example, suppose you want to indicate that a pay rate is valid if it is at least $6.00 but no more than $12.00. You might be tempted to write the following:

```
if(payRate >= 6.00 && <= 12.00)
    cout<<"Valid "<<endl;
```

The code in this example won't compile because the expression to the right of the &&, <= 12.00, is not a complete Boolean expression that can evaluate as 0 or not 0. You must include the **payRate** variable on both sides of the &&, as follows:

```
if(payRate >= 6.00 && payRate <= 12.00)
    cout<<"Valid "<<endl;
```

Table 3-1 shows how an expression using && is evaluated. An entire expression is true only when the expression on each side of the && is true. Either expression can be a "deal killer"— that is, if either expression is false, then the entire comparison is false.

Table 3-1   Truth table for the && (logical AND) operator

Value of expression1	Value of expression2	Value of expression1 && expression2
True	True	True
True	False	False
False	True	False
False	False	False

Using the Logical OR

In certain programming situations, only one of two alternatives must be true for some action to take place. Perhaps a store delivers merchandise if a sale amounts to at least $300, or if the customer lives within the local area code, even if the sale total isn't $300. Two `if` statements could be used to display a "Delivery available" message, as shown in Figure 3-27. (Figure 3-28 shows a diagram of the logic.)

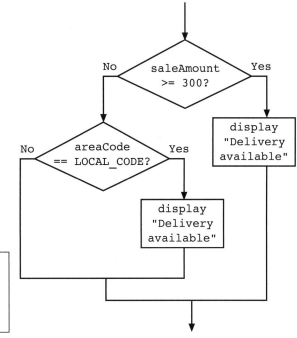

```
if(saleAmount >= 300)
   cout<<"Delivery available"<<endl;
else
  if(areaCode == LOCAL_CODE)
      cout<<"Delivery available"<<endl;
```

Figure 3-27   A nested `if` in which just one of   **Figure 3-28**   Diagram of logic in Figure 3-27
two conditions must be true

If the `saleAmount` is at least $300, the conditions for delivery are established, and the `areaCode` is not evaluated. Only if the `saleAmount` is less than $300 is the `areaCode` evaluated; then delivery might or might not be available. Instead of the nested `if` in Figure 3-27, you could use a logical OR. The **logical OR** is created by typing two pipes (| |) between Boolean expressions. You use a logical OR to create a compound Boolean expression in which at least one of two conditions must be true for the entire expression to evaluate as true, as shown in Figure 3-29.

```
if(saleAmount >= 300 || areaCode == LOCAL_CODE)
     cout<<"Delivery available"<<endl;
```

Figure 3-29   Selection using a logical OR

Do not enter a space between the pipes (ll) in a logical OR.

Read the statement in Figure 3-29 as "if the **saleAmount** is greater than or equal to 300 *or* the **areaCode** is equivalent to the **LOCAL_CODE**, then display 'Delivery available'".

With an AND (&&), if the first Boolean expression to the left of && is false, the second expression is not evaluated. With an OR (ll), if the first expression is true, the second expression is not evaluated; when the first expression is true, the outcome of the second evaluation does not matter.

Table 3-2 shows how C++ evaluates any expression that uses the | | operator. When either **expression1** or **expression2** is true (or both are true), the entire expression is true.

Table 3-2   Truth table for the ll (logical OR) operator

Value of expression1	Value of expression2	Value of expression1 || expression2
True	True	True
True	False	True
False	True	True
False	False	False

Just as with the AND operator, a complete Boolean expression is needed on each side of the OR operator. A particularly tricky error can occur when you ignore this rule while testing for equality. The following code seems to be intended to display "Yes" when the value of **department** is 1 or 2. However, it always displays "Yes" no matter what the value of **department**.

```
if(department == 1 || 2)
     cout<<"Yes";
```

For example, when **department** is 7, the comparison **department == 1** evaluates as false. However, the other side of the OR expression, 2, evaluates as 2. In C++, any non-zero value is a true value, so no matter what the value of **department**, the complete Boolean expression in the **if** evaluates as true and "Yes" displays.

Pitfall: Using OR when you mean AND

Suppose you are told to write a program and are given the following instructions: "The user should enter 1 or 2. If the user doesn't enter 1 or 2, issue an error message." Because the instructions use the word "or," you might be tempted to write a statement like the following:

```
if(userResponse != 1 || userResponse != 2)
    cout<<"Incorrect entry"<<endl;
```

When you execute a program containing this code, every `userResponse`—whether 1, 2, or something else—results in the error message. That's because the expression `userResponse != 1 || userResponse != 2` is always true. When `userResponse` is 1, the first part of the expression is false, but the second part is true. When `userResponse` is 2, 3, or another value, the first part of the expression is true and the second part is not evaluated. To issue the message when the user types something other than 1 or 2, you can use the following:

```
if(userResponse != 1 && userResponse != 2)
    cout<<"Incorrect entry"<<endl;
```

Combining AND and OR Selections

Any number of ANDs can be combined into a single expression. For example, the following expression bases a 20 percent automobile insurance discount on several factors. The driver must possess each trait in order to receive the discount.

```
if(driverAge > 24 && tickets < 1 && accidents == 0 &&
    zipCode == LOWRISK)
        discountRate = 0.20;
```

Similarly, you can combine ORs. In the following example, employees in any one of three selected departments receive a $50 raise.

```
if(dept == 2 || dept == 5 || dept == 13)
    raise = 50.00;
```

When you combine an AND and an OR in the same expression, the AND takes precedence, which means it is evaluated first. For example, suppose the rules in a class you take are as follows: In order to pass the class, you must pass either of two quizzes, and you must pass the final exam. The logic in the code in Figure 3-30 looks correct, but it is not.

```
if(quiz1 == 'P' || quiz2 == 'P' && finalExam == 'P')
    cout<<"Pass"<<endl;
else
    cout<<"Fail"<<endl;
```

Figure 3-30   Incorrect logic for passing a course in which you must pass one quiz and the final exam

Suppose a student passes `quiz1` and `quiz2`, but fails the final exam. According to the rules described, the student should fail the course. However, in the `if` statement in Figure 3-30, the value of `quiz2 == 'P' && finalExam == 'P'` is determined first. The value of this expression is false (or 0) because although the student did not pass the final exam, the student did pass `quiz2`. So the evaluation becomes:

```
if(quiz1 == 'P' || a statement evaluated to be true)
      cout<<"Pass"<<endl;
else
      cout<<"Fail"<<endl;
```

In this evaluation, because the student passed `quiz1`, the entire `if` statement is determined to be true, and "Pass" is displayed—a result that is contrary to the intention.

As you can do with arithmetic expressions, you can override the ordinary precedence of logical expressions by using parentheses. For example, Figure 3-31 shows code that will correctly determine who passes a course in which you must pass one of two quizzes and you must pass the final exam. Because of the parentheses surrounding the OR expression that evaluates the two quiz scores, that result is determined first. If the student has passed at least one of the quizzes, then and only then is the `finalExam` grade evaluated.

```
if((quiz1 == 'P' || quiz2 == 'P') && finalExam == 'P')
      cout<<"Pass"<<endl;
else
      cout<<"Fail"<<endl;
```

Figure 3-31   Correct logic for passing a course in which you must pass one quiz and the final exam

Using parentheses to make your intentions more clear is never wrong. Even when an expression would be evaluated in the desired way without extra parentheses, adding them can help others more easily understand your programs.

MAKING DECISIONS WITH STRUCTURE FIELDS

When you define a structure, and subsequently create objects that are instantiations of the structure, you use the individual structure's fields the same way you use variables of the same type. For example, you can use any numeric structure field in an arithmetic expression, or as part of the conditional test in a selection.

Consider the `BaseballPlayer` structure in Figure 3-32. It contains two public fields: a player number and the number of hits.

```
struct BaseballPlayer
{
        int playerNumber;
        int numberOfHits;
};
```

Figure 3-32   A BaseballPlayer structure with two fields

 TIP Remember that a struct definition always ends with a semicolon following the closing curly brace.

A program that declares a **BaseballPlayer** object named **ourShortStop** is shown in Figure 3-33; a sample execution is shown in Figure 3-34. The program prompts the user for **ourShortStop**'s data, then uses a nested decision to display one of three messages about the player's performance. The program is straightforward; examine it so that you understand that structure object fields are simply variables like any other. Although their identifiers might be long because of the need for the object name, the dot, and the field name, structure object fields can still be used to control decisions the same way that simple variables are.

```
#include<iostream>
using namespace std;
struct BaseballPlayer
{
        int playerNumber;
        int numberOfHits;
};
int main()
{
    BaseballPlayer ourShortStop;
    const int LOW_HITS = 5;
    const int HIGH_HITS = 20;
    cout<<"Enter baseball player's number ";
    cin>>ourShortStop.playerNumber;
    cout<<"Enter number of hits ";
    cin>>ourShortStop.numberOfHits;
    cout<<"Player number #"<<ourShortStop.playerNumber<<
        " with "<<ourShortStop.numberOfHits<<" hits"<<endl;
    if(ourShortStop.numberOfHits <= LOW_HITS)
        cout<<"Player is performing poorly"<<endl;
    else
        if(ourShortStop.numberOfHits <= HIGH_HITS)
            cout<<"Player is doing well"<<endl;
        else
            cout<<"Wow!"<<endl;
}
```

Figure 3-33   A program that declares and uses a BaseballPlayer object

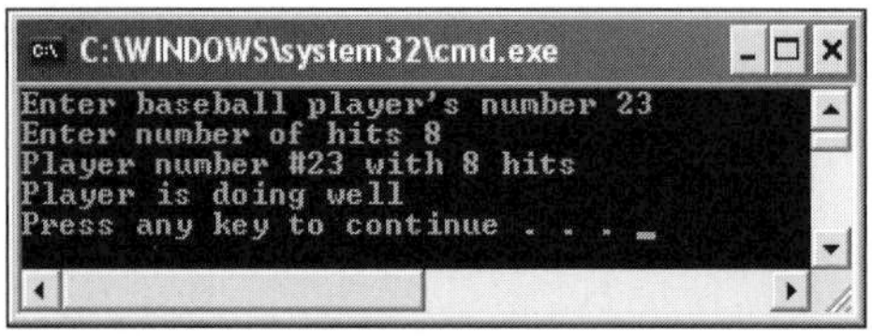

Figure 3-34   A sample execution of the program in Figure 3-33

You Do It

Using a Single-Alternative `if`

In the following steps, you will create a program that demonstrates some of the decision-making capabilities of C++. You will write an interactive program that offers advice on what type of pet to select, based on the potential owner's time away from home and availability and yard size.

1. Open your C++ editor and type identifying comment lines. Then type the following statements:

   ```
   #include<iostream>
   using namespace std;
   ```

2. Begin the `main()` function and declare a variable that will hold the number of hours the user is gone from home on a typical day. Also declare a constant that will serve as the cut-off number of hours gone from home, over which the user should consider owning a cat.

   ```
   int main()
   {
      int hoursGone;
      const int MANY_HOURS = 6;
   ```

3. Ask the user how many hours he or she is gone from home, accept the answer, and if the user is gone more than 6 hours, suggest owning a cat. You will use a simple, single-alternative `if` statement.

   ```
   cout<<"On average, how many hours are you gone from home each day? ";
   cin>>hoursGone;
   if(hoursGone > MANY_HOURS)
      cout<<"You should consider a cat"<<endl;
   ```

4. Add the closing curly brace for the program, then save it as **PetChooserCat.cpp**.

5. Compile and execute the program. When you enter a value that is 7 or more, the program advises you to consider owning a cat. Execute the program again, and when you enter a value of 6 or less, the program just ends, with no output offered.

Using a Dual-Alternative `if`

In the next steps, you will add an `else` clause to the decision in the PetChooserCat application.

1. Open the **PetChooserCat.cpp** application if it is not still open on your screen. Immediately save the file as **PetChooserCatOrDog.cpp**.

2. Add an `else` clause to the `hoursGone` decision. After the output statement that advises owning a cat, add the following:

```
else
     cout<<"You can consider a dog"<<endl;
```

3. Save the application; then compile and execute it. This time, at the prompt, if you enter a value of 6 or less hours gone from home, the application displays the message that you can consider owning a dog. Figure 3-35 shows a sample execution.

```
C:\WINDOWS\system32\cmd.exe                              _ □ ×
On average, how many hours are you gone from home each day? 4
You can consider a dog
Press any key to continue . . .
```

Figure 3-35   Sample execution of PetChooserCatOrDog application

Using a Compound Condition and Nested `ifs`

In the next steps, you will increase the sophistication of the pet-choosing application by providing advice on the specific breed of dog the user can consider owning.

1. Open the **PetChooserCatOrDog.cpp** application if it is not still open on your screen. Immediately save the file as **PetChooser.cpp**.

2. Near the other variables at the top of the file, add a new variable that holds the user's response to a question about a fenced yard, and another variable that holds the size of the yard. Also, add two constants that set the limits for yards considered to be small and large.

```
char haveYard;
int sizeOfYardInSqFeet;
const int SMALL_YARD = 400;
const int LARGE_YARD = 2500;
```

3. Next, you will modify the output of the application by adding another question to the `else` clause of the existing decision, so you can ask more questions before advising the user on a breed of dog. Modify the `else` clause in the current program decision by inserting curly braces around the statement `cout<<"You can consider a dog"<<endl;`. Also, modify this `cout`

statement by inserting a comma and a space after **dog** and before the closing quote, and by removing **<<endl** (but retaining the semicolon). This last modification will allow more output to appear as part of the **<<"You can consider a dog"** statement, on the same line.

4. Within the newly created **else** block of the application, just after the opening curly brace but before the output statement, add a fenced-yard prompt and response as follows:

```
cout<<"Do you have a fenced yard? Y or N ";
cin>>haveYard;
```

5. After the output statement but before the closing curly brace of the **else** clause, add the following new selection that offers advice on the size of the breed.

```
if(haveYard == 'N' || haveYard == 'n')
   cout<<"but a very small breed, such as a Chihuahua"<<endl;
else
{
   cout<<"but you can consider a larger breed"<<endl;
}
```

6. Save, compile, and test the program.

7. Next, you can make the application offer more detailed advice on the larger dog breeds. After the output statement advising a larger breed but before the last three closing curly braces in the program, add another question about yard size. Notice, the user only sees the yard size question if the user has not entered 'N' or 'n' to the question that asks whether there is a yard.

```
cout<<"What is the size of your yard in square feet? ";
cin>>sizeOfYardInSqFeet;
if(sizeOfYardInSqFeet <= SMALL_YARD)
    cout<<"Consider a Schnauzer"<<endl;
else
    if(sizeOfYardInSqFeet <= LARGE_YARD)
       cout<<"Consider a Golden or Labrador Retriever"<<endl;
    else
       cout<<"You can consider a Great Dane"<<endl;
```

8. Save the file, then compile it. (To help you locate any errors, Figure 3-36 shows the entire application.) Execute the program several times using different combinations of responses, and make sure the program's output is correct. For example, Figure 3-37 shows a sample execution when the user is gone only 2 hours a day and has a medium-sized yard.

3

```cpp
#include<iostream>
using namespace std;

int main()
{
   int hoursGone;
   const int MANY_HOURS = 6;
   char haveYard;
   int sizeOfYardInSqFeet;
   const int SMALL_YARD = 400;
   const int LARGE_YARD = 2500;
   cout<<"On average, how many hours are you gone from home each day? ";
   cin>>hoursGone;
   if(hoursGone > MANY_HOURS)
      cout<<"You should consider a cat"<<endl;
   else
   {
      cout<<"Do you have a fenced yard? Y or N ";
      cin>>haveYard;
      cout<<"You can consider a dog, ";
      if(haveYard == 'N' || haveYard == 'n')
         cout<<"but a very small breed, such as a Chihuahua"<<endl;
      else
      {
         cout<<"but you can consider a larger breed"<<endl;
         cout<<"What is the size of your yard in square feet? ";
         cin>>sizeOfYardInSqFeet;
         if(sizeOfYardInSqFeet <= SMALL_YARD)
            cout<<"Consider a Schnauzer"<<endl;
         else
            if(sizeOfYardInSqFeet <= LARGE_YARD)
               cout<<"Consider a Golden or Labrador Retriever"<<endl;
            else
               cout<<"You can consider a Great Dane"<<endl;
      }
   }
}
```

Figure 3-36   The PetChooser application

Figure 3-37   Sample execution of the PetChooser application

CHAPTER SUMMARY

❐ The primary C++ selection structure statement used to perform a single-alternative selection is an **if** statement. A single-alternative selection is one in which one or more actions takes place only when the result of the decision is true.

❐ The dual-alternative **if**, also called the **if-else** structure, takes one action when its Boolean expression is evaluated as true, and uses an **else** clause to define the actions to take when the expression is evaluated as false.

❐ A nested **if** is an **if** structure that rests entirely within another **if** structure.

❐ Whether you are first learning to use selection statements or you are an experienced programmer, it is easy to make several types of mistakes. These include forgetting that C++ is case sensitive, assuming indentation has a logical purpose, adding an unwanted semicolon, forgetting curly braces, using = instead of ==, making unnecessary comparisons, and leaving dead logical paths.

❐ When you want to create different outcomes depending on specific values of a variable, you can use a series of **if**s. However, as an alternative to the long string of **if**s, you can use the **switch** statement.

❐ The conditional operator (also called the **if** operator), is the question mark (**?**). It is used as an alternative to the **if** statement, and it provides a concise way to express two alternatives.

❐ The logical AND is created by typing two ampersands (**&&**). You use a logical AND to create a compound Boolean expression in which two conditions must be true for the entire expression to evaluate as true.

❐ The logical OR is created by typing two pipes (**||**). You use a logical OR to create a compound Boolean expression in which at least one of two conditions must be true for the entire expression to evaluate as true.

❐ When you combine an AND and an OR in the same expression, the AND takes precedence.

❐ When you define a structure, and subsequently create objects that are instantiations of the structure, you use the individual structure's fields the same way you use variables of the same type.

KEY TERMS

A **single-alternative selection** is one in which an action takes place only when the result of the decision is true.

The **dual-alternative if**, also called the **if-else structure**, takes one action when its Boolean expression is evaluated as true, and uses an **else** clause to define the actions to take when the expression is evaluated as false.

A **nested if** is an `if` structure that rests entirely within another `if` structure, within either the `if` or the `else` clause.

An **if-else-if** is a structure in which a new decision rests within the `else` clause of another decision.

A **dead logical path** is one containing unreachable code.

The **switch statement** is an alternative to a series of `if` statements. The keyword `switch` identifies the beginning of the statement. Then the variable or expression in parentheses is evaluated. After the opening curly brace, a series of case statements separate the actions that should occur when the expression equals each case.

The **conditional operator** (also called the **if operator**) is represented by a question mark (?). The `if` operator provides a concise way to express two alternatives.

A **logical AND** is created by typing two ampersands **(&&)** between two Boolean expressions. You use a logical AND to create a compound Boolean expression in which two conditions must be true for the entire expression to evaluate as true.

A **logical OR** is created by typing two pipes (||) between Boolean expressions. You use a logical OR to create a compound Boolean expression in which at least one of two conditions must be true for the entire expression to evaluate as true.

3

REVIEW QUESTIONS

1. A single-alternative selection is one in which an action takes place
   _____.

   a. only when the result of the decision is true

   b. only when the result of the decision is false

   c. when the result of the decision is either true or false

   d. when the result of the decision is both true and false

2. What is the output after executing the following segment of code?

   ```
   int num = 10;
   if (num > 10)
      cout<<"Yes"<<endl;
   else
      cout<<"No"<<endl;
   ```

   a. Yes

   b. No

   c. Yes *and* No

   d. nothing

3. What is the output after executing the following segment of code?

```
int num = 5;
if (num > 10)
    cout<<"Yes"<<endl;
    cout<<"No"<<endl;
```

   a. Yes

   b. No

   c. Yes *and* No

   d. nothing

4. What is the output after executing the following segment of code?

```
int num = 0;
if(num > 1)
    {
        cout<<"Yes"<<endl;
        cout<<"No"<<endl;
    }
```

   a. Yes

   b. No

   c. Yes *and* No

   d. nothing

5. Which of the following is false?

   a. An **if-else** statement can be written on a single line.

   b. You can have an **if** without an **else**.

   c. You can block many actions under the **else** in an **if-else** even though the **if** executes only a single statement.

   d. You could write an **if-else** statement that used no semicolons between the location of the **if** and the location of the **else**.

6. What is the output after executing the following segment of code?

```
int num = 5;
if(num < 4)
        cout<<"Red"<<endl;
else
    if(num < 10)
        cout<<"Yellow"<<endl;
    else
        cout<<"Green"<<endl;
```

   a. Red

   b. Yellow

   c. Green

   d. two of the above

7. What is the output after executing the following segment of code?

```
int num = 15;
if(num > 20)
        cout<<"Red"<<endl;
else
        if(num > 18)
            cout<<"Yellow"<<endl;
        else
            cout<<"Green"<<endl;
```

a. Red

b. Yellow

c. Green

d. two of the above

8. What is the output of this code segment?

```
int age=30;
if(age=40)
        cout<<"Boy that is old!";
else
        cout<<"Some day you will be old too";
```

a. Boy that is old!

b. Some day you will be old too

c. nothing—syntax error

d. prints something—but not choice a or b

9. What is the output of this code segment?

```
int age=40;
if(age)
        cout<<"Boy that is old!";
else
        cout<<"Some day you will be old too";
```

a. Boy that is old!

b. Some day you will be old too

c. nothing—syntax error

d. prints something—but not choice a or b

10. When an `if` statement occurs within either the `if` or the `else` clause of another `if` statement, it is known as a _____ `if`.

a. self-contained

b. nested

c. layered

d. sheltered

3

11. Assume a user runs a program containing the following code segment, and enters 'k' at the prompt. What is the output?

```
char gradeLevel;
const char KINDERGARTEN_CODE = 'K';
cout<<"Enter child's grade level ";
cin>>gradeLevel;
if(gradeLevel == KINDERGARTEN_CODE)
    cout<<"Kindergarten student"<<endl;
else
    cout<<"Older student"<<endl;
```

   a. Kindergarten student

   b. Older student

   c. both of these

   d. none of these

12. You can use the **switch** statement to _____.

   a. compare a single expression to several cases

   b. compare several different expressions to the same case

   c. replace an **if** but not an **if-else**

   d. change a selection statement from an **if** to an **if-else**

13. What is output by the following code segment?

```
int value = 5;
value > 0? cout<<"Yes"<<endl : cout<< "No"<<endl;
```

   a. Yes

   b. No

   c. Yes *and* No

   d. nothing

14. What is output by the following code segment?

```
int value = 12;
value < 0? cout<<"Yes"<<endl : cout<<"No"<<endl;
```

   a. Yes

   b. No

   c. Yes *and* No

   d. nothing

15. You use a _____ to create a compound Boolean expression in which two conditions must be true for the entire expression to evaluate as true.

   a. logical AND

   b. logical OR

   c. **switch** statement

   d. any of the above

16. You use a _____ to create a compound Boolean expression in which only one of two conditions needs to be true for the entire expression to evaluate as true.

    a. logical AND

    b. logical OR

    c. `switch` statement

    d. any of the above

17. What is the output of the following code segment?

```
int x = 3;
int y = 6;
if(x < 0 && y == 2)
    x = 40;
cout<<x<<" "<<y<<endl;
```

    a. 3 6

    b. 40 6

    c. 3 2

    d. 40 2

18. What is the output of the following code segment?

```
int x = 5;
int y = 10;
if(x < 0 || y > 0)
    x = 20;
    y = 35;
cout<<x<<" "<<y<<endl;
```

    a. 5 10

    b. 20 10

    c. 5 35

    d. 20 35

19. What is the output of the following code segment?

```
int x = 20;
int y = 1;
if(x < 0 || x > y && y != 9)
{
    --x;
    --y;
}
cout<<x<<" "<<y<<endl;
```

    a. 20 1

    b. 19 1

    c. 19 0

    d. 20 0

3

20. Assume you have defined a structure named `Invoice`. It contains an integer field named `invoiceNumber` and a `double` field named `amount`. What is the output of the following segment of code?

```
Invoice myInvoice;
myInvoice.invoiceNumber = 2245;
myInvoice.amount = 100.00;
if(myInvoice.invoiceNumber > 1000 || myInvoice.amount >
200.00 &&
    myInvoice.amount < 500.00)
        cout<<"Pay now"<<endl;
else
        cout<<"Pay later"<<endl;
```

a. "Pay now"

b. "Pay later"

c. "Pay now" *and* "Pay later"

d. Nothing

EXERCISES

1. Write a C++ program that allows the user to enter two **double** values. Display one of two messages: "The first number you entered is larger", or "The first number you entered is not larger". Save the file as **LargerOrNot.cpp**.

2. Write a program that allows the user to enter two **double** values. Display one of three messages: "The first number you entered is larger", "The second number you entered is larger", or "The numbers are equal". Save the file as **CompareThree.cpp**.

3. Write a program that allows the user to enter two numeric values. Then let the user enter a single character as the desired operation: 'a' for add, 's' for subtract, 'm' for multiply, or 'd' for divide. Perform the arithmetic operation that the user selects and display the results. Save the file as **ArithmeticChoice.cpp**.

4. Write a program that allows the user to enter two numeric values. Then let the user enter a single character as the desired operation—for example, 'A', 'a', or '+' for add. The user should be able to enter the uppercase initial, lowercase initial, or arithmetic symbol. Perform the arithmetic operation that the user selects and display the results. Save the file as **FlexibleArithmeticChoice.cpp**.

5. Write a program in which you declare variables that will hold an hourly wage and number of hours worked. Prompt the user to enter values for hourly rate and hours worked. Compute and display gross weekly pay, which is calculated as hours times rate for the first 40 hours, plus hours times 1.5 times the rate for any hours over 40. Also display net pay, which is gross pay minus withholding; withholding is calculated as 28 percent of gross pay if gross pay is over $1,000, 21% of gross pay if gross pay is not over $1,000 but is over $600, and 10% of gross pay if gross pay is not over $600. Save the file as **OvertimeAndNet.cpp**.

6. Write a program for a furniture company. Ask the user to choose *P* for pine, *O* for oak, or *M* for mahogany. Show the price of a table manufactured with the chosen wood. Pine tables cost $100, oak tables cost $225, and mahogany tables cost $310. Save the program as **Furniture.cpp**.

7. Write a program for a college admissions office. The user enters a numeric high school grade point average (for example, 3.2), and an admission test score. Print the message "Accept" if the student meets either of the following requirements:

   ❑ A grade point average of 3.0 or above and an admission test score of at least 60

   ❑ A grade point average below 3.0 and an admission test score of at least 80

   If the student does not meet either of the qualification criteria, print "Reject". Save the program as **Admission.cpp**.

8. Write a program that asks the user to type a vowel from the keyboard. If the character entered is a vowel, display "OK"; if it is not a vowel, display an error message. Be sure to allow both uppercase and lowercase vowels. For this exercise, assume *y* is not a vowel. Save the file as **Vowel.cpp**.

9. The Bone Jour Dog Day Care Center charges clients a daily rate that is based on both the size of the dog and the number of days per month in a client's contract. The following table shows the daily rates.

	1 – 10 days per month	11 or more days per month
Under 10 pounds	$12	$10
10 pounds – under 35 pounds	$16	$13
35 pounds and over	$19	$17

   Prompt the user to enter a dog's weight and number of days per month needing care, then calculate and display the daily rate and the total for the month (days times the daily rate). Save the file as **DogDayCare.cpp**.

10. The Carlington Hotel wants a program in which the user enters the type of room that a guest wants (1 for single, 2 for double, 3 for suite), the floor desired (1 through 12), and the number of nights the guest will stay (any number is valid). Compute the nightly rate from the following table, multiply by the number of nights, and then provide a 10% discount on the total if the guest stays 4 or more nights.

	Single	Double	Suite
Floor 1 – 5	45.00	60.00	130.00
Floor 6 – 11	55.00	72.00	215.00
Floor 12	Not available	120.00	350.00

   Display all the input data, the nightly price, and the total price for the guest's stay, or display an error message if a combination is not available or if an invalid room type code or floor is entered. Save the file as **Hotel.cpp**.

11. Create a structure named **Apartment** that contains data fields to hold the number of bedrooms, the number of baths, and the monthly rent for the **Apartment**. Write a program that creates an **Apartment** object and prompts the user for number of bedrooms and baths desired. Determine the rent from the following table, and set the rent field appropriately. If a requested apartment type is not available, set the rent field to 0.

	1 bath	2 baths
1 bedroom	$650	Not available
2 bedrooms	$829	$925
3 bedroom	Not available	$1075

Display all the data, including an error message if the entered data is invalid or if no apartments are available with the requested combination. Save the file as **Apartment.cpp**.

12. Each of the following files in the Chapter03 folder of your Data Disk contains syntax and/or logical errors. Determine the problem in each case and fix the program. Save your solutions by adding "Fixed" to the filename, as in **DEBUG3-1Fixed.cpp**.

   a. DEBUG3-1

   b. DEBUG3-2

   c. DEBUG3-3

   d. DEBUG3-4

CASE PROJECT 1

CASE PROJECTS

In Chapters 1 and 2 you developed a **Fraction** structure for Teacher's Pet Software. The structure contains two public data fields for numerator and denominator. Add a third field that can hold the whole-number portion of a **Fraction**. Write a **main( )** function in which you create three **Fraction** objects. Prompt the user for values for each field of two of the **Fractions**. Add statements to the **main( )** function to do the following:

❑ If the user enters a 0 denominator for a **Fraction**, force it to be 1.

❑ Display each **Fraction**. If the whole-number portion is greater than 1, use it in the output, but if the whole-number portion is 0, just display the fraction portion. For example, a **Fraction** with value 0 1/3 should display as 1/3. If the numerator of a **Fraction** is 0, then just display the whole-number portion; for example, if the user enters 2 0/3, just display 2. If the whole-number portion is 0 and the numerator is 0, as in 0 0/2, then just display 0.

❑ Determine whether the value of the first **Fraction** is greater than, equal to, or less than the value of the second **Fraction**. For example, 1/2 and 3/6 are equal. As another example, 1 1/2 and 0 3/2 are also equal. Display an appropriate message indicating the results.

3

❐ Determine whether each entered **Fraction** is more than 1, and reduce the
Fraction if it is. For example, 7/2 should be reduced to 3 1/2, and 10/4 should
be reduced to 2 2/4 (in other words, you do not need to reduce it to 2 1/2). If the
Fraction is not more than 1, then set the whole-number field to 0. Display the
reduced **Fraction**.

❐ Prompt the user to enter an arithmetic operation: + or *. Calculate the third
Fraction to be the result of applying the requested operation to the two entered
Fractions. Display the result as a whole number, if any, and the fractional part, if
any. For example, adding 1/4 and 1/4 results in 2/4 (you do not need to reduce
2/4 to 1/2) and multiplying 1/3 by 6/1 results in 2. Display the results.

CASE PROJECT 2

**CASE
PROJECTS**

In Chapters 1 and 2 you developed a **BankAccount** structure for Parkville Bank. The
structure contains two public fields for the integer account number and **double** account
balance. Using the same structure, write a **main()** function in which you create two
BankAccount objects. Add statements to the **main()** function to do the following:

❐ Prompt the user for account numbers and beginning balances for the two
BankAccounts. The account number should be between 1000 and 9999; issue an
error message if the user does not enter a valid account number. The balance
should not be negative; issue an error message if it is. Continue with the program
only if the account numbers and balances are valid for both accounts.

❐ Prompt the user for a dollar amount to be transferred from the first account to the
second account.

❐ Issue an error message if the two accounts have the same account number, and do
not carry out the transfer of funds.

❐ Issue an error message if the requested transfer causes the first account to fall below
0, and do not make the transfer.

❐ Issue a warning message if the transfer causes the balance in the first account to
drop below $10, but make the transfer.

❐ Issue a warning message if the transfer causes the balance in the second account to
be greater than $100,000, which is the highest amount that is federally insured.

❐ At the end of the **main()** function, display all account information for both accounts.

4

PERFORMING LOOPS

In this chapter, you will:

♦ Learn about the `while` loop

♦ Write some typical loops

♦ Learn to avoid common pitfalls with loops

♦ Accumulate totals

♦ Learn about the `for` loop

♦ Learn about pretest and posttest loops

♦ Nest loops

♦ Use structure fields in loops

Loops allow you to perform statements repeatedly and, just as importantly, to stop the action when warranted. Frequently, it's decision making that makes computer programs seem smart, but looping makes programs powerful. By using loops, you can write one set of instructions that executes thousands or even millions of times.

In Chapter 1, you learned that structured programming allows three basic control structures—sequence, selection, and loop. In Chapters 2 and 3, you saw many sequences and selections. In this chapter, you will become proficient in using the repetition structure called the loop.

THE WHILE LOOP

In C++, you can use a while loop to repeat actions. The format of the while loop is as follows:

Syntax Example

while(*Boolean expression*)
    action while expression is true;

Figure 4-1 shows a diagram of a while loop. In a **while loop**, a Boolean expression is evaluated. If the expression in the while statement is true, the resulting action, called the **loop body** (which can be a single statement or a block of statements) executes, and the Boolean expression is tested again. If it is false, the loop is over, and program execution continues with the statement that follows the while statement. The cycle of execute-test-execute-test continues as long as the Boolean expression continues to be evaluated as true.

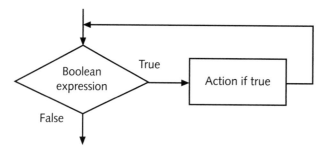

Figure 4-1   Diagram of a while loop structure

TIP

Any C++ expression can be placed inside the required parentheses in the while statement. As with the if statement, if the expression evaluates to false or zero, then the loop body is not entered. If the expression within the parentheses evaluates to true or any non-zero value, the loop body executes. With a while statement, when the expression is evaluated as true, the statements that follow execute repeatedly as long as the expression remains true.

For example, the program shown in Figure 4-2 displays the message "Hello!" five times. Figure 4-3 shows a diagram of the loop in the program.

```
#include<iostream>
using namespace std;

int main()
{
    int count;
    const int NUM_LOOPS = 5;
    count = 0;
    while( count < NUM_LOOPS)
    {
        cout<<"Hello!"<<endl;
        ++count;
    }
}
```

Figure 4-2   Program that displays "Hello!" five times

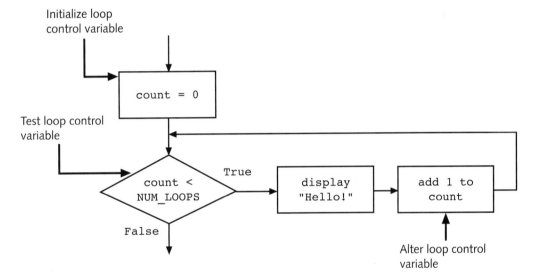

Figure 4-3   Diagram of loop in Figure 4-2

In the program in Figure 4-2, a variable named **count** is declared. This variable will count the number of **iterations** (repetitions) that the program has made through the loop. After declaring a constant to hold the desired number of loops (5), the **count** variable is set to 0. When the program enters the **while** loop, **count** is compared to NUM_LOOPS. Because **count** is 0 and NUM_LOOPS is 5, the Boolean expression is true, and the program executes the loop body (the code between the inner pair of curly braces). The loop body executes two tasks; it displays "Hello!" and then adds 1 to **count**. In other words, the variable named **count** holds 1 after "Hello!" has been displayed exactly one time.

At the end of the first execution of the `while` loop in Figure 4-2, the `count` variable holds the value 1. The Boolean expression in the loop is tested again, and because 1 is less than 5, the loop body executes again. "Hello!" is displayed a second time, and `count` becomes 2.

The "Hello!" message continues to display and `count` continues to increase until `count` eventually holds 5. Then, when `count < NUM_LOOPS` is evaluated, it is found to be false and the loop ends. Figure 4-4 shows the program output.

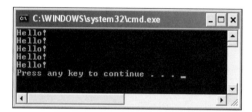

Figure 4-4   Execution of the application in Figure 4-2

In the program in Figure 4-2, the variable named `count` is used as a **loop control variable**, a variable whose value controls the execution of a loop body. When you write a loop, the loop control variable should be used three times:

- The loop control variable must be initialized. In this case, the variable `count` is set to 0.

- The loop control variable is compared to another value. In this case, `count` is compared to `NUM_LOOPS`. A value such as `NUM_LOOPS` that determines when a loop will end is sometimes called a **sentinel value** because a sentinel is a guard, and the sentinel acts like a guard, allowing entrance or denying entrance to the loop body statements. In this example, `NUM_LOOPS` is a named constant, but the sentinel value instead could be a literal constant (such as the number 5) or a variable. It might even be an arithmetic expression.

- The loop control variable must be altered. In this case, `count` is incremented. If the loop control variable was never altered, the result of the loop-controlling Boolean expression would never change, and the loop would never end.

The diagram in Figure 4-3 points out the three times the loop control variable is used. Almost all the loops you write will manipulate a loop control variable in these three ways.

TIP

Technically, a loop control variable can be initialized any time before the loop begins. However, it is usually clearest to those reading a program when you initialize the loop control variable immediately before the start of the loop.

WRITING TYPICAL LOOPS

You use a loop any time you want to repeat actions. In addition to displaying a message multiple times, several programming situations commonly use loops. One situation where a loop is useful is in an interactive program, when you want to force the user to enter specific values, so that you are assured the values are valid before proceeding with the program. Another common situation is one where the user must enter hundreds or thousands of similar records for processing.

A Typical Loop: Input Verification

Suppose a user must make a choice from a limited set of values. For example, if you ask a true/false question, you might require that a user respond with a 'T' or an 'F'. One way to handle this task would be to test the user's response with an if statement, as in the program segment in Figure 4-5.

```
cin>>userResponse;
if(userResponse == 'T')
   cout<<"You responded True"<<endl;
else
   cout<<"You responded False"<<endl;
```

Figure 4-5   Using an if-else that makes a possibly incorrect assumption

The limitation to this approach is that any response other than 'T' is assumed to be false. If the user enters a 't', 'R', 'X', or any other character, the if statement displays "You responded False". In some situations, this might be an acceptable outcome. However, perhaps the user did not intend the response to be "False"; maybe the user made a typographical error. To be more certain of the user's intention, you can force the user to specifically enter a 'T' or an 'F' before proceeding.

One approach would be to use code like that in Figure 4-6. In this example, after the user enters a response, it is tested, and if it is not 'T' or 'F', the user is prompted a second time and given another chance to enter an appropriate response. Then the program continues.

```
cin>>userResponse;
if(userResponse != 'T' && userResponse != 'F')
{
    cout<<"Invalid response. Please enter a T or an F"<<endl;
    cin>>userResponse;
}
if(userResponse == 'T')
    cout<<"You responded True"<<endl;
else
    cout<<"You responded False"<<endl;
```

Figure 4-6   Reprompting a user after an invalid entry; still possibly making an incorrect assumption

The code in Figure 4-6 gives the user a second chance to enter valid input when the first input is not correct. However, what happens if the user enters an invalid response the second time? Using the code in Figure 4-6, the second invalid response would be assumed to be a "False" response. Of course, you could test the user's second response with an `if` statement, and if the response was still not 'T' or 'F', you could prompt the user a third time, but no matter how many "chances to get it right" you include in the program, the user might still enter an invalid response at each opportunity.

To prevent the program from continuing without a valid user response, the superior method is to use a loop like the one shown in Figure 4-7. The `if` statement in the earlier examples has been replaced by a (shaded) `while` statement. In this code segment the user enters a response, and while the response continues to be an invalid one, the user is repeatedly presented with the question and another chance to respond. The program in Figure 4-7 will never progress past the `while` loop until a valid entry is made.

```
cin>>userResponse;
while(userResponse != 'T' && userResponse != 'F')
{
    cout<<"Invalid response. Please enter a T or an F"<<endl;
    cin>>userResponse;
}
if(userResponse == 'T')
    cout<<"You responded True"<<endl;
else
    cout<<"You responded False"<<endl;
```

Figure 4-7   Using a loop to ensure a valid user entry

If you examine the code segment in Figure 4-7, you will find that the data-entry loop contains the three pieces that all loops contain:

■ The loop control variable is initialized. In this case, the loop control variable is userResponse, and it is initialized when the user makes the first entry.

■ The loop control variable is compared to another value. In this case, userResponse is compared to 'T' and 'F'.

■ Within the loop body, the loop control variable is altered. In this case, userResponse is altered by the user's next response.

A Typical Loop: Reading Input Records

Businesses very frequently use computer programs to process hundreds or even millions of records. For example, a credit card company might print several million customer bills each month. Each customer's data is read into memory and processed, following the same set of instructions as all other customers—new charges are added to the bill, payments are subtracted, interest fees are calculated, and so on. Processing credit card bills would be an unbelievably cumbersome task if programs could not loop, using the same instructions to handle each record.

Although credit card bill data is read from stored files, the same types of record-entering loops are needed in many interactive applications. For example, Figure 4-8 shows an application that reads a series of prices, computes a 20 percent discount on each, and displays the results. The application can process any number of items and prices entered by the user until the user enters 0 for the item number. Figure 4-9 shows a typical execution of the application.

TIP

You will learn to write programs that read data from an input file in Chapter 11. The application in Figure 4-8 reads data from a user at the keyboard.

```
#include<iostream>
using namespace std;
 int main()
{
   int itemNumber;
   double price;
   double discountAmount;
   double newPrice;
   const double RATE = 0.20;
   cout<<"Enter the item number or 0 to quit ";
   cin>>itemNumber;
   while(itemNumber != 0)
   {
      cout<<"Enter price for item #"<<itemNumber<<" ";
      cin>>price;
      discountAmount = price * RATE;
      newPrice = price - discountAmount;
      cout<<"Item #"<<itemNumber<<" was $"<<price<<endl;
      cout<<"but with a discount of $"<<discountAmount<<
            ", it is $"<<newPrice<<endl<<end;
      cout<<"Enter another item number or 0 to quit ";
      cin>>itemNumber;
   }
}
```

Figure 4-8   An application that reads records in a loop interactively

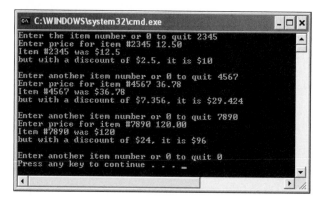

Figure 4-9   A typical execution of the application in Figure 4-8

    The output in Figure 4-9 appears with varying numbers of decimal places depending on the computed value. Although mathematically correct, you might find the output visually unappealing. Appendix D provides techniques for displaying values to a specific number of decimal places.

The program in Figure 4-8 computes discounts on prices as long as the user enters a non-zero item number. In this example, 0 serves as the sentinel that ends the loop. The loop control variable is the `itemNumber`. It is initialized when the user enters the first item number, it is compared to the application-ending sentinel in the `while` statement, and it is altered when the user is prompted for the next item number at the end of the loop body.

TIP The first `itemNumber` input statement in the application in Figure 4-8 is an example of a **priming read**, or **priming input statement**, which is an input statement that initializes a variable before a loop begins. The expression comes from the phrase "priming the pump," which is the action you take with a pump to get it to start producing.

AVOIDING COMMON PITFALLS WITH LOOPS

Whether you are first learning to use repetition statements or you are an experienced programmer, it is easy to make several types of mistakes:

- Adding an unwanted semicolon

- Forgetting curly braces

- Failing to alter a loop control variable

- Failing to initialize a loop control variable

- Making the same types of mistakes you can make with selections, including forgetting that C++ is case sensitive, assuming indentation has a logical purpose, using = instead of ==, and using the AND operator when you intended to use the OR operator

Pitfall: Adding an unwanted semicolon

In C++, you must always remember that a statement is complete when you reach its semicolon. For example, consider the `while` loop in Figure 4-10. The code segment is supposed to display the numbers 1 through 10. However, the programmer has inadvertently included a semicolon at the end of the line containing the `while` statement's Boolean comparison. Figure 4-11 shows the logic that expresses the way the code is written. Because the semicolon immediately follows the Boolean expression, the first statement in the code is interpreted as `if number <= 10,` then do nothing. The entire body of the loop exists after the closing parenthesis of the `while` statement and before the semicolon that immediately follows. The body of the loop is an empty body—that is, one containing no statements. So, although the Boolean expression is true, and although the loop body is entered, no actions are taken because no actions are listed in the body. The Boolean expression is evaluated again and it is still true, so the empty body executes again, and the Boolean expression is evaluated again. This type of loop is an infinite loop; it executes repeatedly forever. In this case, no output displays, but the evaluation occurs infinitely.

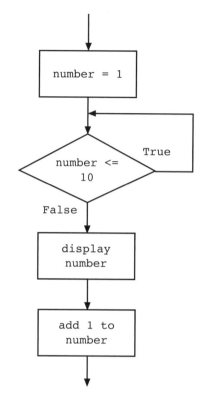

```
number = 1;
while(number <= 10);
{
    cout<<number<<endl;
    ++number;
}
```

Figure 4-10   A misleading, do-nothing
while statement

Figure 4-11   Diagram of logic of while
statement in Figure 4-10

TIP

In most C++ compilers you can stop an infinite loop from executing by pressing the Ctrl + C or Ctrl + Break keys. If a program runs for several seconds and appears to be doing nothing or produces repeated output, you should suspect an infinite loop.

Remember that C++ ignores indentations, so although it appears that the last two statements in the code in Figure 4-10 depend on the evaluation of the Boolean expression, they do not.

Pitfalls: Forgetting curly braces or failing to alter a loop control variable

As you learned with the **if** statement in Chapter 3, the appropriate use of curly braces in C++ is essential to achieving the desired outcome. Consider the loop in Figure 4-12. Just like the example in Figure 4-10, this code is intended to display the values 1 through 10. This example does not include an extraneous semicolon, but the curly braces have been omitted from the block following the `while` statement. Figure 4-13 shows the resulting logic. In the code segment, `number` is initialized to 1. It is compared to 10, so the Boolean expression is true and the number is displayed. The loop ends after that statement, so the comparison is made again, it is still true, and the same number—1—displays again. In this code segment, a series of 1s displays infinitely because the statement that would alter the number is not part of the `while` loop.

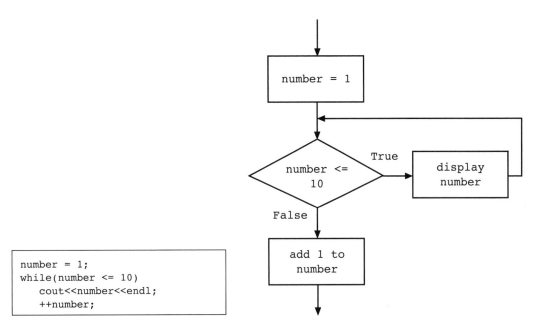

```
number = 1;
while(number <= 10)
   cout<<number<<endl;
   ++number;
```

Figure 4-12   A misleading, infinitely looping `while` statement

Figure 4-13   Diagram of logic of `while` statement in Figure 4-12

In Figure 4-12, the statement that increments `number` appears to be part of the loop because it is indented. However, as you already know, C++ ignores indentation. Only semicolons or curly braces can determine a loop's end.

The error produced by the program in Figure 4-12 is the same type of error that would occur if you failed to alter the loop control variable within the body of the loop. Even if you remembered the braces to block statements after the `while` comparison, no matter how many statements you placed with the loop body, if you did not include any statement that altered the loop control variable, there would be no chance for the `while` comparison to ever be false, and so there would be no chance for the loop to end.

Pitfall: Failing to initialize a loop control variable

In C++, an uninitialized variable has an unknown value; programmers call this unknown value a **garbage value** because it is of no practical use. Failing to initialize a loop control variable produces unpredictable results. For example, Figure 4-14 shows a program that, like several of the previous examples, is intended to display the values 1 through 10. However, the programmer has not assigned any starting value to the loop control variable. When the `while` statement compares the value of `number` to 10, the expression might be true or false. Some compilers will simply use the garbage value of `number`, so if it is, for example, 200, the loop body will never be entered, and the program will produce no output. On the other hand, if it is, for example, -83242, the program will evaluate the Boolean expression as true, print the value, add 1, and print again—for thousands of loop repetitions until `number` increases to 11. Some compilers will simply issue an error message and ask whether you want to stop the program. For example, Visual Studio .NET issues the message shown in Figure 4-15. If you select the option to ignore the warning, the program executes and the output appears as in Figure 4-16.

```cpp
#include<iostream>
using namespace std;
int main()
{
    int number;
    while(number <= 10)
    {
        cout<<number<<endl;
        ++number;
    }
}
```

Figure 4-14   A program containing a loop with an uninitialized loop control variable

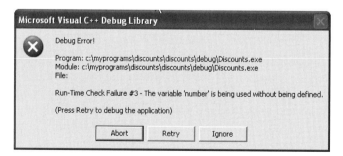

Figure 4-15   Error message displayed in Visual Studio .NET when executing the program in Figure 4-14

If you are using a system other than Visual Studio .NET, you might receive different results.

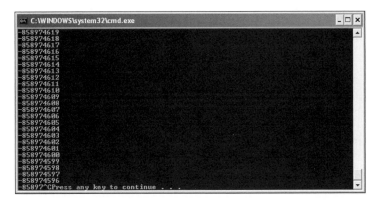

Figure 4-16   Infinite loop that executes when running the application in Figure 4-14

In the output in Figure 4-16, you can see that the loop is doing what it should—adding 1 to a number and displaying the next number. (Notice that the numbers are negative, which is why the value becomes increasingly larger.) This loop would execute for quite a while, until the current value at negative 858 million worked its way up to positive 10. You can see in Figure 4-16 that the user has pressed Ctrl + C to stop the execution.

TIP   Although variables that control a loop must be provided with a usable value before the loop starts, many experienced programmers recommend initializing *every* variable; this technique ensures that no variable ever contains a garbage value. Others feel it is misleading to initialize a variable that will never use the initial value—for example, a variable whose value will be entered by the user. It is up to you to develop a reasonable and consistent style and to use any style guidelines required by your instructors and employers.

ACCUMULATING TOTALS

Many computer programs display totals. When you receive a credit card or telephone service bill, you are usually provided with individual transaction details, but it is the total bill in which you are most interested. Similarly, some programs total the number of credit hours generated by college students, the gross payroll for all employees of a company, or the total accounts receivable value for an organization. These totals are **accumulated**— that is, gathered together and added into a final sum by processing individual records one at a time in a loop.

Figure 4-17 shows an example of an interactive program that accumulates the user's total purchases. The program prompts the user to enter a purchase price, or 0 to quit. While the user continues to enter non-zero values, the amounts are added to a total. With each pass through the loop, the total is calculated to be its current amount plus the new purchase amount. After the user enters the loop-terminating 0, the accumulated total can be displayed. Figure 4-18 shows a typical program execution.

```cpp
#include<iostream>
using namespace std;

int main()
{
    double purchase,
        total = 0;
    cout<<"Enter amount of first purchase ";
    cin>>purchase;
    while(purchase != 0)
    {
        total += purchase;
        cout<<endl<<"Enter amount of next purchase, or 0 to quit ";
        cin>>purchase;
    }
    cout<<endl<<"Your total is $"<<total<<endl;
}
```

Figure 4-17 An application that accumulates total purchases entered by the user

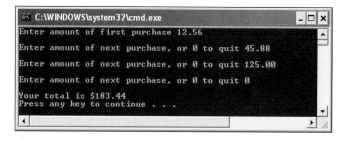

Figure 4-18 Typical execution of the program in Figure 4-17

In the application in Figure 4-17, it is very important that the `total` variable that is used for accumulation is initialized to 0. When it is not, `total` starts with a garbage value and the results are unpredictable. Figure 4-19 shows the results of the same program when the total is not initialized. The odd value that displays for the total is written in scientific notation. The e+061 at the end means that the actual value is one in which the decimal point is 61 places to the right. Because the number is negative, this means that the value is a very small number, nowhere near the actual total of the three purchases.

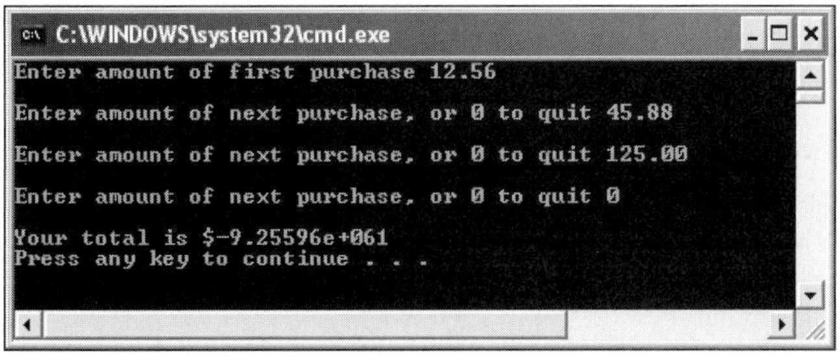

Figure 4-19   Execution of the application in Figure 4-17 in Visual Studio .NET when `total` declaration is altered to leave `total` uninitialized

TIP In the application in Figure 4-17, the `total` variable must be initialized to 0, but the `purchase` variable is uninitialized. Many programmers would say it makes no sense to initialize this variable because no matter what starting value you provide, the value can be changed by the first input statement before the variable is ever used. As a matter of style, this book will not initialize a variable if the initialization value is never used; doing so might mislead you into thinking the starting value had some purpose.

THE for LOOP

The **for statement**, or **for loop**, can be used as an alternative to the `while` statement. It is frequently used in a **definite loop**, or a loop that must execute a definite number of times, but it can be used to replace any `while` loop. The `for` statement takes the following form:

Syntax Example

for(*initialize; evaluate; alter*)
   statement that executes when evaluation is true;

Inside the parentheses of the `for` statement, semicolons separate three expressions—initialize, evaluate, and alter.

Initialize represents any steps you want to take at the beginning of the statement. Most often this includes initializing a loop control variable, but the initialize portion of the statement can consist of any C++ statement or even several C++ statements separated with commas.

TIP Although the initialize portion of a `for` loop can contain multiple statements, some programmers believe the best style is to use only the loop control variable in the `for` statement and to insert other statements before the loop begins.

Evaluate represents any C++ expression that is evaluated as false or true, which in C++ is also expressed as zero or non-zero. Most often the evaluate part of the **for** statement compares the loop control variable with a sentinel or limit, but the evaluate portion of the statement can include any C++ expression. If the value of that expression is true (not 0), any statements in the body of the **for** loop are executed. If the evaluation is false (0), the **for** statement is completed, and program execution continues with the next statement, bypassing the body of the **for** statement.

Alter represents any C++ statements that take place after executing the loop body. If the evaluation of the expression between the semicolons is true, and the statements in the body of the loop are executed, then the final portion of the **for** statement, after the second semicolon, takes place. In the alter part of the loop, most often you use statements that change the value of the loop control variable. However, you can use any C++ statements in the alter part of the **for** loop if you want those statements to execute after the loop body and before the evaluate part executes again.

Any C++ **for** statement can be rewritten as a **while** statement, and vice versa; sometimes one form of the loop suits your needs better than others. For example, Figures 4-20 and 4-21 show loops that produce identical results: the output "1 2 3". Figure 4-20 contains a **while** loop and Figure 4-21 contains a **for** loop. Each program segment initializes the loop control variable, **count**, to 1; compares it to 4; and while the condition is true, displays **count** and increases it.

```
int count;
count = 1;
while(count < 4)
{
    cout<<count<<endl;
    ++count;
}
```

```
int count;
for(count = 1; count < 4; ++count)
    cout<<count<<endl;
```

Figure 4-20   A while loop that displays "1 2 3"   **Figure 4-21**   A for loop that displays "1 2 3"

Although the code used in the **for** loop in Figure 4-21 is more concise than that in the **while** loop in Figure 4-20, the execution is the same. With the **for** statement, you are less likely to make common looping mistakes, such as not initializing the variable that controls the loop, or not changing the value of the loop control variable during loop execution. Those mistakes remain possibilities, however, because C++ allows you to leave empty any of the three items inside the **for** loop parentheses. (The two semicolons are still required, and if you omit the middle portion, the evaluation is considered to be true.) Although you can create a running program using a **for** loop in which one or more of the sections is empty, it is usually clearest to avoid doing so.

The for loop is most frequently used as a **count-controlled loop**, or one whose execution is controlled by counting the number of repetitions. The while loop is used more frequently for repetitions that are not counted.

4

The most common mistake that beginning programmers make when analyzing a for loop is thinking that all three actions (initialize, evaluate, and alter) take place before the body of the loop executes. That is not the case. Another misconception is that all three actions occur on every pass through the loop. That is not the case either. The first portion of the for loop occurs only once, the first time the statement is encountered. Then the middle portion is evaluated, and only if it is true do three things happen: the loop body executes; the third, altering portion of the for statement executes; and the middle evaluation is performed again.

Just as with an if statement or while loop, you can block any number of statements to be executed when the middle portion of the for statement is true. Just as with other C++ statements, the placement of semicolons and curly braces is of the utmost importance.

C++ programmers usually prefer to declare variables at the beginning of a function. This is partly because of tradition (because it was required in the C language that is an ancestor of C++) and also because when all variables are located in one place, it is easier to implement later changes. One common exception to this rule is declaring the variable used to control a for loop. The variable is often declared and initialized inside the for statement, as in the highlighted portion in the following example:

```
for(int count = 1; count < 4; ++count)
    cout<<count<<endl;
```

This form, declaring the loop control variable within the for statement, is most often used when the variable will only be used for the life of the loop. If the variable is one that is needed in other parts of the function, it should be declared along with all the other variables at the start of the function.

As a custom, many programmers use the variable names i and j as **iterators** —that is, variables that are used only to count the executions of a loop.

With some compilers, a variable declared within a for loop is recognized only for the duration of that loop. With others, you can use the variable later in the same function. For portability, you should declare a loop control variable within a for loop if you only intend to use it for the duration of that loop.

TIP

The following code provides an example of a `for` loop that is not a count-controlled loop.

```
int value;
for(cout<<"Enter first value ",cin>>value;
    value != 0;
    cout<<"Enter another value or 0 to quit ", cin>>value)
    cout<<value<<endl;
```

This loop displays the first prompt and accepts the first value; then, in the middle portion, it compares the value to 0. If the value is not 0, the loop body displays the value, and the final part of the `for` loop executes, prompting for and accepting another value. Although this `for` loop works, it is highly unconventional. This type of loop, which relies on user input, would be more clearly expressed as a conventional `while` loop. This book follows the convention of using `for` loops only for count-controlled scenarios.

PRETEST VS. POSTTEST LOOPS

Whether you use a `while` loop or a `for` loop, the loop body might never execute. Both of these loops are **pretest loops**—loops in which the loop control variable is tested before the loop body is executed.

For example, Figure 4-22 shows a program that asks a user to enter an investment amount and a length of time to hold the investment. The application then displays the user's balance at the beginning of every year for the number of years indicated, using a constant interest rate of 4 percent. After the loop ends, the user's final balance is displayed.

Figure 4-23 shows a typical execution of the program, with the user investing $1,000 for five years. However, suppose that when the program in Figure 4-22 is executed, the user enters 0 or a negative number for the years. In those cases, when `count` is compared to `years`, it will not be less or equal; the Boolean expression will be false, the loop body will not execute, and the output will look like that in Figure 4-24. The output in Figure 4-24 is correct—that is, the user's investment amount at the end of the term is correct. However, the user did not receive the data-entry confirming message about the value of the investment at the beginning of the term.

```
#include<iostream>
using namespace std;
int main()
{
   double investment;
   double INTEREST_RATE = 0.04;
   int years;
   int count = 1;
   cout<<"Enter the amount you have to invest ";
   cin>>investment;
   cout<<"Enter the number of years to invest ";
   cin>>years;
   while(count <= years)
   {
     cout<<"At the start of year "<<count<<
        ", you have $"<<investment<<endl;
     investment = investment + investment * INTEREST_RATE;
     ++count;
   }
   cout<<"At the end of the investment period, you have $"<<
      investment<<endl;
}
```

Figure 4-22   A program with a `while` loop that displays a user's increasing investment balance

Figure 4-23   Output of program in Figure 4-22 when user enters 1000.00 and 5

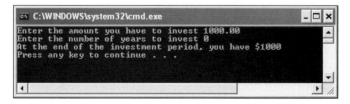

Figure 4-24   Output of program in Figure 4-22 when user enters 1000.00 and 0

Occasionally, you will want to ensure that a loop body executes at least once. One alternative would be to place another copy of the loop body code prior to the loop. That way, the code would definitely execute one time, even if the loop body was never entered. An alternative is to use a **posttest loop**—one in which the loop control variable is tested after the loop body executes. In C++, the **do-while statement** controls a loop that tests the loop-continuing condition at the end, or bottom, of the loop. (With a `while` loop, programmers say that the expression you are testing is evaluated at the top of the loop, or prior to executing any loop body statements.) The `do-while` statement takes the form:

Syntax Example

do

    statement;

while(*Boolean expression*);

For example, suppose you want to write a program that projects sales goals for a salesperson for the next several years. Figure 4-25 shows an application in which the user is prompted for a first year's merchandise sales amount and a number of years to project the goals. For the first year, the salesperson's goal is the current sales amount. After that, sales are projected to grow at a rate of 8 percent per year. Figure 4-26 shows a diagram of the logic of the shaded `do-while` portion of the application.

```cpp
#include<iostream>
using namespace std;
int main()
{
   double sales;
   const double RATE = .08;
   int years;
   int count = 1;
   cout<<"Enter the initial sales amount ";
   cin>>sales;
   cout<<"Enter the number of years to project ";
   cin>>years;
   do
   {
     cout<<"The goal for year "<<count<<" is "<<sales<<endl;
     sales = sales + sales * RATE;
     ++count;
   } while(count <= years);
}
```

Figure 4-25 A program with a `do-while` loop that displays a salesperson's increasing sales goals

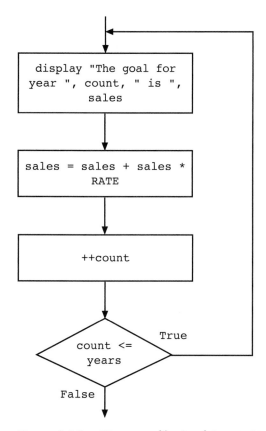

4

Figure 4-26 Diagram of logic of do-while loop in Figure 4-25

In the application in Figure 4-25, after the user enters the original sales figure and the number of years for the projection, the **do-while** loop begins. The goal for year 1 (the original amount) is displayed, and then the sales amount is increased for the next year. The count is increased, and then the first comparison is made. No matter what the outcome of this comparison, the loop body has executed once, ensuring there will always be output. Figure 4-27 shows the projections when a salesperson sells $20,000 worth of merchandise in the current year and asks for a five-year projection. Figure 4-28 shows the output when a salesperson sells $20,000 worth of merchandise but asks for 0 years of projections. Even though the **years** value is 0, the loop executes once, producing some output. After the loop executes, the decision is made that stops the loop from recycling.

Figure 4-27 Output of program in Figure 4-25 when user enters 20000 and 5

Figure 4-28 Output of program in Figure 4-25 when user enters 20000 and 0

NESTED LOOPS

You can place any statements you need within a loop body. When you place another loop within a loop, the loops are **nested loops**. You can nest any type of loop (while, for, or do-while) within any other type. A loop that completely contains another is an **outer loop**. A loop that falls entirely within the body of another is an **inner loop**. Within each pass through an outer loop, the inner loop executes to completion.

For example, the program segment in Figure 4–29 uses two for loops to display interest earned on investments from $1,000 to $10,000, in steps of $1,000, for every interest rate earned from 4 percent through 8 percent, in whole percentages. Figure 4–30 shows a diagram of the loop logic. Figure 4–31 shows the output of a program that contains the loop.

```
for(investment = 1000; investment <= 10000; investment += 1000)
{
    cout<<"$"<<investment<<"    ";
    for(percent = 0.04; percent <= 0.08; percent += 0.01)
        cout<<investment * percent<<"    ";
    cout<<endl;
}
```

Figure 4-29 Loop that displays varying investments at varying rates

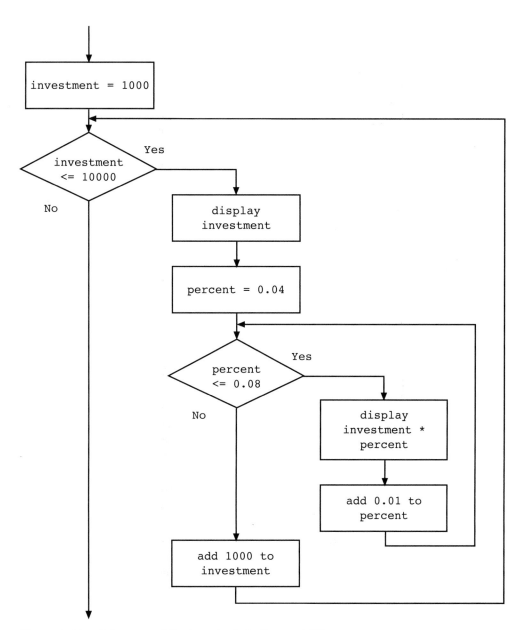

Figure 4-30   Diagram of the loop logic in Figure 4-29

```
C:\WINDOWS\system32\cmd.exe                    _ □ ×
$1000     40    50    60    70    80
$2000     80   100   120   140   160
$3000    120   150   180   210   240
$4000    160   200   240   280   320
$5000    200   250   300   350   400
$6000    240   300   360   420   480
$7000    280   350   420   490   560
$8000    320   400   480   560   640
$9000    360   450   540   630   720
$10000   400   500   600   700   800
Press any key to continue . . .
```

Figure 4-31   Output of the loop in Figure 4-29

TIP   For information on how to align the values in the output in Figure 4-31, see Appendix D.

In the application in Figure 4-29, the outer loop is the first one encountered, the one controlled by the **investment** variable. In the outer loop, the **investment** variable is initialized to 1000; then it is compared to 10000, resulting in a true value, and the loop is entered. The **investment** amount is displayed, and the inner loop is encountered. In the inner loop, **percent** is the loop control variable; it is initialized to 0.04. The **percent** is compared to 0.08, the Boolean expression evaluates as true, and the body of the inner loop executes, displaying the first interest earned—4 percent of $1,000. The last part of the inner **for** statement executes, and the percent variable is increased to 0.05. Because this value is less than or equal to 0.08, the inner loop is entered again, and the value of 5 percent of $1,000 is displayed. The percent is increased to 0.06, displaying a new value; then to 0.07, displaying another number; then to 0.08, displaying another number. Finally the percent is 0.09, and the Boolean expression in the inner **for** loop is false. The loop ends, and the **cout<<endl;** statement executes, forcing any subsequent output to appear on a new line.

After the **endl** statement, the program reaches the closing curly brace for the outer loop. The last portion of the **for** statement that controls the outer loop executes, raising the investment amount by $1,000 to $2,000. The middle, evaluation portion of the outer loop **for** statement executes, the investment is determined to be under $10,000, and the loop body is entered a second time. The new investment amount is displayed at the beginning of the second output line, and the inner loop **for** statement starts again. This loop executes just as if it were being encountered for the first time, so the percent value is initialized to 0.04, compared to 0.08, and the inner loop body is entered again. The inner loop will end up executing five times before the Boolean expression in the middle is false. Then an **endl** will be displayed, ending the second display line, and the outer loop will continue—the investment amount will be increased to $3,000, and the middle comparison will again be true.

In all, the calculations in the inner loop in the application in Figure 4-29 will execute 50 times. The outer loop will execute 10 times—once for every $1,000 increment. And within each execution of the outer loop, the inner loop will execute five times—once for every percentage rate from 4 through 8, inclusive.

The most difficult aspect of working with nested loops is keeping track of the separate loop control variables that direct the program's execution. When you master using nested loops, you can create powerful applications that vary multiple factors to produce useful output.

Using Loops with Structure Fields

Just as you learned with selection statements in Chapter 3, you can use any structure field in a loop in the same way you would use its stand-alone counterpart. In other words, a structure object's field might be a loop control variable, a sentinel value that stops a loop, or a value used within a loop body. In the You Do It exercise, you will use a structure object in a loop.

You Do It

Using a Loop to Validate User Data Entry

In the next set of steps, you will use a `while` loop to ensure that a user is entering an appropriate value for an ID number when the number is required to fall between 111 and 999 inclusive.

1. Open a new file in your C++ editor.

2. Type any comments you want to identify the program, and then type the `include` and `using` statements that you need:

```
#include<iostream>
using namespace std;
```

3. Start the `main()` function by declaring an ID number variable that will hold the user's entry, and two constants that define the high and low valid limits for an ID number.

```
int main()
{
  int idNum;
  const int LOW_NUM = 111;
  const int HIGH_NUM = 999;
```

4. Prompt the user for an ID number and accept the input value.

```
cout<<"Enter an ID number between "<<LOW_NUM<<
      " and "<<HIGH_NUM<<" inclusive ";
cin>> idNum;
```

5. Use a `while` loop that continues while the user entry is out of range. In other words, the loop continues as long as the user enters a value below 111 or over 999.

```
while(idNum < LOW_NUM || idNum > HIGH_NUM)
{
   cout<<"Invalid ID number"<<endl;
   cout<<"Please enter a number from "<<LOW_NUM<<
       " through "<<HIGH_NUM<<" ";
   cin>>idNum;
}
```

6. The program will continue past the `while` loop only when the user enters a valid ID number. To end the application, display the user's valid ID, then type a closing curly brace to end the `main()` function.

```
cout<<"Thank you. Your valid ID is "<<idNum<<endl;
}
```

7. Save the file as **ValidID.cpp**. Then compile and run the program. Confirm that the program continues to loop until your entered response is within the requested range. Figure 4-32 shows a sample run.

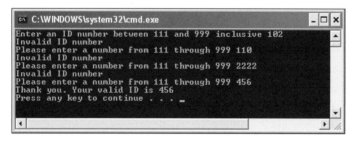

Figure 4-32   Sample execution of the ValidID application

Using a Structure in an Application Containing Several Loops

In the next steps, you will create an application for the Nasty Habit Hypnosis Clinic—a hypnosis clinic that guarantees it can help you lose weight, quit smoking, stop biting your nails, or end any bad habit in four sessions or less. After a potential client is interviewed, the clinic determines how many sessions the client will need. A clerk will use the program you create to enter a client ID number (which must fall between 1000 and 9999 inclusive), the recommended number of sessions (which must not be greater than 4), and the date on which the first session will take place. The program will schedule the next sessions, if any, at one-month intervals after the first session.

To create the hypnosis-clinic application:

1. Open a new file in your C++ editor and enter the first few lines of the application, including the definition of a `Client` structure. The `Client` structure contains all the data gathered about a client.

```
#include<iostream>
using namespace std;
struct Client
{
    int idNum;
    int numSessions;
    int firstSessionMonth;
    int firstSessionDay;
    int firstSessionYear;
};
```

2. Write a `main()` function that declares a `Client` object and the three variables you will use in the loop that schedules a client's future appointments—a loop control variable named `count`, a variable that holds the next month, and a variable that holds the next year if a client's sessions extend into a new year.

```
int main()
{
    Client aClient;
    int count;
    int nextSessionMonth;
    int nextSessionYear;
```

3. Also declare some useful constants, including the high and low limits for client ID numbers, the maximum number of hypnosis sessions that are scheduled, and the number of months in a year.

```
const int LOW_NUM = 1000;
const int HIGH_NUM = 9999;
const int MAX_SESSIONS = 4;
const int MONTHS_IN_YEAR = 12;
```

4. Prompt the user for an ID number that falls between the low and high allowed values (1000 to 9999). Use the named constants in the prompts so that if either the high or the low value ever changes, the prompts will still be correct. Continue to prompt for and accept ID number values until the user enters a valid one.

```
cout<<"Enter an ID number between "<<LOW_NUM<<
        " and "<<HIGH_NUM<<" inclusive ";
cin>> aClient.idNum;
while(aClient.idNum < LOW_NUM || aClient.idNum > HIGH_NUM)
{
    cout<<"Invalid ID number"<<endl;
    cout<<"Please enter a number from "<<LOW_NUM<<
            " through "<<HIGH_NUM<<" ";
    cin>>aClient.idNum;
}
```

5. Prompt the user for a number of client sessions. Continue to prompt until the user enters an acceptable number—no more than four. Use the named constant MAX_SESSIONS in both the comparison and the displayed prompts.

```
cout<<"Enter number of sessions client needs ";
cin>>aClient.numSessions;
while(aClient.numSessions > MAX_SESSIONS)
{
    cout<<"We guarantee that no more than "<<
      MAX_SESSIONS<<" will be necessary."<<endl;
    cout<<"Please re-enter the number of sessions ";
    cin>>aClient.numSessions;
}
```

6. Prompt the user for the month, day, and year of the first session. You will use a loop to ensure that the month entered is correct, but to keep this example short, you will not validate the day of the month or the year.

```
cout<<"Enter the month of the first session ";
cin>>aClient.firstSessionMonth;
while(aClient.firstSessionMonth > MONTHS_IN_YEAR)
{
    cout<<"You must enter a valid month ";
    cin>>aClient.firstSessionMonth;
}
cout<<"Enter the day of the first session ";
cin>>aClient.firstSessionDay;
cout<<"Enter the year of the first session ";
cin>>aClient.firstSessionYear;
```

7. Display the client's ID number and first session date.

```
cout<<"Client #"<<aClient.idNum<<endl;
cout<<"First session is on the following day: "<<
  aClient.firstSessionMonth<<"/"<<aClient.firstSessionDay<<
  "/"<<aClient.firstSessionYear<<endl;
```

8. Next, you will use a for loop to display the next appointment dates. You will use the count variable to count the appointments starting with appointment 2 through the number of appointments scheduled, so in its three sections, the for loop will initialize, compare, and alter the count variable. You can also use the initialize portion of the for loop to set the starting values for nextSessionMonth and nextSessionYear; the three separate statements in the first part of the for statement are separated by commas.

Within the for loop, the nextSessionMonth variable is incremented. If this action brings the month to 13 (greater than MONTHS_IN_YEAR), then subtract 12 from the month value (forcing it to 1) and add 1 to the year value. Then display the details of the next hypnosis session.

```
for(count = 2, nextSessionMonth = aClient.firstSessionMonth,
  nextSessionYear = aClient.firstSessionYear;
  count <= aClient.numSessions; ++count)
{
    nextSessionMonth += 1;
    if(nextSessionMonth > MONTHS_IN_YEAR)
    {
        nextSessionMonth -= MONTHS_IN_YEAR;
        ++nextSessionYear;
    }
    cout<<"Session #"<<count<<
       " is on: "<<nextSessionMonth<<
       "/"<<aClient.firstSessionDay<<
       "/"<<nextSessionYear<<endl;
}
}
```

9. Save the file as **HypnosisCenter.cpp**.

10. Compile and execute the program. Figure 4-33 shows a typical execution. When a four-appointment client begins sessions on 11/7/2006, the next three appointments are on 12/7/2006, 1/7/2007, and 2/7/2007.

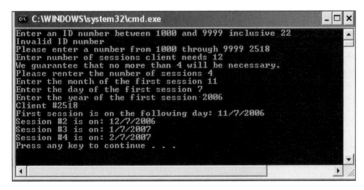

Figure 4-33   Typical execution of the HypnosisCenter application

CHAPTER SUMMARY

❑ In a while loop, a Boolean expression is evaluated. If it is false, the loop is over and program execution continues with the statement that follows the while statement. If the Boolean expression in the while statement is true, the resulting action, called the loop body (which can be a single statement or a block of statements) executes, and the Boolean expression is tested again. The cycle of execute-test-execute-test continues as long as the Boolean expression continues to be evaluated as true.

❑ A loop control variable is a variable that controls the execution of a loop body. When you write a loop, the loop control variable should be used three times: the loop control variable must be initialized, compared to another value, and altered.

❑ You use a loop any time you want to repeat actions. One common situation where a loop is useful is in an interactive program, when you want to force the user to enter specific values, so that you are assured the values are valid before proceeding with the rest of the program. Another very common situation is one where the user must enter hundreds or thousands of similar records for processing.

❑ It is easy to make several types of mistakes with loops: adding an unwanted semicolon, forgetting curly braces, failing to alter a loop control variable, failing to initialize a loop control variable, and making the same types of mistakes you can make with selections, including forgetting that C++ is case sensitive, assuming indentation has a logical purpose, using = instead of ==, and using the AND operator when you intended to use the OR operator.

❑ Totals are accumulated—that is, gathered together and added into a final sum by processing individual records one at a time in a loop.

❑ The `for` statement or `for` loop can be used as an alternative to the `while` statement. It is frequently used in a definite loop, or a loop that must execute a definite number of times, but it can be used to replace any `while` loop inside the parentheses of the `for` statement; semicolons separate three expressions—initialize, evaluate, and alter.

❑ Whether you use a `while` loop or a `for` loop, the loop body might never execute. Both of these loops are pretest loops—loops in which the loop control variable is tested before the loop body is executed. When you want to ensure that a loop body executes at least once, you can use a posttest loop—one in which the loop control variable is tested after the loop body executes. In C++, the `do-while` statement controls a loop that tests the loop-continuing condition at the end, or bottom, of the loop.

❑ You can place any statements you need within a loop body. When you place another loop within a loop, the loops are nested loops. You can nest any type of loop (`while`, `for` or `do-while`) within any other type.

❑ You can use any structure field in a loop in the same way you would use its standalone counterpart.

KEY TERMS

A **`while` loop** is a repetition structure that executes as long as a tested expression is true.

A **loop body** contains the statements that execute within a loop.

Iterations are repetitions.

A **loop control variable** is a variable that controls the execution of a loop body.

A value that determines when a loop will end is sometimes called a **sentinel value**.

A **priming read**, or **priming input statement**, is an input statement that initializes a variable before a loop begins.

In C++, a **garbage value** is an uninitialized variable, which has an unknown value and is of no practical use.

Totals are **accumulated** by processing individual records one at a time in a loop and adding numeric data to a total.

The **for statement**, or **for loop**, can be used as an alternative to the `while` statement; it contains sections that initialize, compare, and alter a loop control variable.

A **definite loop** is one that must execute a definite number of times.

A **count-controlled loop** is one whose execution is controlled by counting the number of repetitions.

Iterators are variables that are used only to count the executions of a loop.

A **pretest loop** is one in which the loop control variable is tested before the loop body is executed.

A **posttest loop** is one in which the loop control variable is tested after the loop body executes.

The **do-while statement** controls a loop that tests the loop-continuing condition at the end, or bottom, of the loop.

When you place another loop within a loop, the loops are **nested loops**.

A loop that completely contains another is an **outer loop**.

A loop that falls entirely within the body of another is an **inner loop**.

REVIEW QUESTIONS

1. In a `while` loop, _____.

   a. a Boolean expression is evaluated; if it is true, the loop is over

   b. the loop body always consists of a single statement

   c. the loop body always executes at least one time

   d. the Boolean expression is always evaluated at least once

2. A variable that determines whether a loop body will execute is the loop _____ variable.

   a. sentinel

   b. power

   c. supervisor

   d. control

3. A loop control variable should almost always be used three times in these ways:

   a. initialize, display, compare

   b. initialize, compare, alter

   c. display, alter, stop

   d. loop, alter, display

4. What is the output produced by the following code?

```
int x = 0;
while(x < 7)
    cout<<x<<" ";
    ++x;
cout<<endl;
```

a. 0 1 2 3 4 5 6

b. 0 1 2 3 4 5 6 7

c. 0 0 0 0 0 . . .

d. nothing

5. What is the output produced by the following code?

```
int x = 0;
while(x < 7);
{
    cout<<x<<" ";
    ++x;
}
cout<<endl;
```

a. 0 1 2 3 4 5 6

b. 0 1 2 3 4 5 6 7

c. 0 0 0 0 0 . . .

d. nothing

6. What is the output produced by the following code?

```
int x = 0;
while(x > 7)
{
    cout<<x<<" ";
    ++x;
}
cout<<endl;
```

a. 0 1 2 3 4 5 6

b. 0 1 2 3 4 5 6 7

c. 0 0 0 0 0 . . .

d. nothing

7. What is the output produced by the following code?

```
int total = 0;
int a = 4;
while(a < 6)
{
    total += a;
    ++a;
}
cout<<total<<endl;
```

a. 4

b. 5

c. 9

d. 15

8. If you know you need to execute a loop exactly 100 times, then it is a(n) _____ loop.

a. certain

b. definite

c. specific

d. explicit

9. Within its parentheses, the **for** loop contains _____ parts that are separated by semicolons.

a. three

b. four

c. five

d. an unknown number of

10. Which of these statements is true?

a. Any **for** statement can be rewritten as a **while** statement.

b. Any **while** statement can be rewritten as a **for** statement.

c. Both a and b are true.

d. Both a and b are false.

11. Which of these statements is true?

a. A **for** statement contains three parts separated by commas.

b. The first part of a **for** statement can be left empty.

c. Any part of a **for** statement can be left empty, but no more than two of the parts can be empty.

d. The body of a **for** statement is written between two semicolons.

4

12. What is the output of the following code segment?

```
int x = 0;
for(x = 3; x < 8; ++x)
    cout<<x<<" ";
cout<<endl;
```

a. 0 1 2 3 4 5 6 7

b. 3 4 5 6 7

c. 4 5 6 7

d. 4 5 6 7 8

13. What is the output of the following code segment?

```
int x = 0;
for(x = 5; x < 8; ++x);
    cout<<x<<" ";
cout<<endl;
```

a. 5 6 7

b. 5

c. 6 7

d. 8

14. Which of the following is a posttest loop?

a. a `while` loop

b. a `for` loop

c. a `do-while` loop

d. all of the above

15. In which type of loop might the loop body never execute?

a. a `while` loop

b. a `for` loop

c. a `do-while` loop

d. a and b, but not c

16. When a loop is contained within another, the loops are _____.

a. nested

b. switched

c. shelled

d. cased

17. Which is true?

    a. An inner loop always repeats more times than an outer loop.

    b. An outer loop always repeats more times than an inner loop.

    c. Both a and b are true.

    d. Both a and b are false.

18. What is the output of this program segment?

```
for(int a = 0; a < 5; ++a)
    for(int b = 3; b < 6; b = b + 2)
        cout<<a<<" "<<b<<" ";
cout<<endl;
```

    a. 0 3 0 5 1 3 1 5 2 3 2 5 3 3 3 5 4 3 4 5

    b. 0 3 0 4 0 5 1 3 1 4 1 5 2 3 2 4 2 5 3 3 3 4 3 5 4 3 4 4 4 5

    c. 1 3 1 5 2 3 2 5 3 3 3 5 4 3 4 5

    d. 1 5 2 5 3 5 4 5 5 5

19. How many times does the loop body in the following code execute?

```
for(int a = 0; a < 4; ++a)
    for(int b = 0; b < 4; ++b)
        cout<<a<<" "<<b<<" ";
cout<<endl;
```

    a. 0

    b. 4

    c. 16

    d. 25

20. How many times does the **cout** statement in the following code execute?

```
int a = 2;
int b = 6;
while(a < 10)
    for(int b = 0; b < 4; ++b)
    {
        cout<<a<<" "<<b<<" ";
        ++a;
    }
cout<<endl;
```

    a. 8

    b. 10

    c. 12

    d. infinitely

4

EXERCISES

1. Write a C++ program that allows the user to enter an integer that represents the number of times a message will display. Display a greeting as many times as requested. Save the file as **MultipleGreetings.cpp**.

2. Write a program that allows the user to enter two integer values. Display every whole number that falls between these values. Save the file as **InBetween.cpp**.

3. Write a program that asks a user to enter an integer between 1 and 10. Continue to prompt the user while the value entered does not fall within this range. When the user is successful, display a congratulatory message. Save the file as **OneToTen.cpp**.

4. Write a program that asks a user to enter an integer between 1 and 10. Continue to prompt the user while the value entered does not fall within this range. When the user is successful, display a congratulatory message the same number of times as the value of the successful number the user entered. Save the file as **OneToTenMessage.cpp**.

5. Write an application that prints all even numbers from 2 to 100 inclusive. Save the file as **EvenNums.cpp**.

6. Write an application that asks a user to type A, B, C, or Q to quit. When the user types Q, the program ends. When the user types A, B, or C, the program displays the message "Good job!" and then asks for another input. When the user types anything else, issue an error message and then ask for another input. Save the file as **ABCInput.cpp**.

7. Write an application that displays every integer value from 1 to 20 along with its squared value. Save the file as **TableOfSquares.cpp**.

8. Write an application that sums the integers from 1 to 50 (that is, 1 + 2 + 3... + 50) and displays the result. Save the file as **Sum50.cpp**.

9. Write an application that shows the sum of 1 to n for every n from 1 to 50. That is, the program prints 1 (the sum of 1 alone), 3 (the sum of 1 and 2), 6 (the sum of 1, 2, and 3), 10 (the sum of 1, 2, 3, and 4), and so on. Save the file as **EverySum.cpp**.

10. Write an application that displays every perfect number from 1 through 1,000. A perfect number is one that equals the sum of all the numbers that divide evenly into it. For example, 6 is perfect because 1, 2, and 3 divide evenly into it, and their sum is 6; however, 12 is not a perfect number because 1, 2, 3, 4, and 6 divide evenly into it, and their sum is greater than 12. Save the file as **Perfect.cpp**.

11. Write an application that calculates the amount of money earned on an investment, based on an 8 percent annual return. Prompt the user to enter an investment amount and the number of years for the investment. Do not allow the user to enter a number of years less than 1 or more than 30. Display the total amount (balance) for each year of the investment. Save the file as **Investment.cpp**.

12. Write an application that creates a quiz that contains at least five questions about a hobby, popular music, astronomy, or any other personal interest. Each question can be multiple choice (for which valid responses are a, b, c, or d) or true/false (for which valid responses are t and f). If the user responds to a question with an invalid character, display an error message and prompt the user again. If the user answers the question with a valid and correct response, display an appropriate message. If the user responds to a question with a valid but incorrect response, display an appropriate message as well as the correct answer. At the end of the quiz, display the number of correct and incorrect answers. Save the file as **Quiz.cpp**.

13. Create a structure named **Purchase**. Each **Purchase** contains an invoice number, amount of sale, and amount of sales tax. Create a **main( )** method that declares a **Purchase** object and prompts the user for purchase details. When you prompt for an invoice number, do not let the user proceed until a number between 1,000 and 8,000 has been entered. When you prompt for a sale amount, do not proceed until the user has entered a non-negative value. Compute the sales tax as 5 percent of the purchase price. After a valid **Purchase** object has been created, display the object's invoice number, sale amount, and sales tax. Save the file as **CreatePurchase.cpp**.

14. Create an **Investment** structure. Include fields for the term of the **Investment** in years, the beginning dollar amount of the **Investment**, and the final value of the **Investment**. Write a **main( )** function in which you declare an **Investment** object. Prompt the user for the term and the initial **Investment** amount for this object. Display the value of the **Investment** after each year of the term, using a simple compound interest rate of 8 percent. At the end of the program, display all of the final field values. Save the file as **Invest.cpp**.

15. Each of the following files in the Chapter04 folder on your Data Disk contains syntax and/or logical errors. Determine the problem in each case, and fix the program. Save your solutions by adding "Fixed" to the file name, as in **DEBUG4-1Fixed.cpp**.

    a. DEBUG4-1.cpp

    b. DEBUG4-2.cpp

    c. DEBUG4-3.cpp

    d. DEBUG4-4.cpp

CASE PROJECT 1

CASE PROJECTS

In earlier chapters, you developed a `Fraction` structure for Teacher's Pet Software. The structure contains three public data fields for whole number, numerator, and denominator. Using the same structure, write a `main()` function in which you create three `Fraction` objects. Prompt the user for values for each field for two of the `Fractions`. Add statements to the `main()` function to do the following:

❑ Do not allow the user to enter a 0 denominator for any `Fraction`; continue to prompt the user until an acceptable denominator is entered.

❑ Reduce each `Fraction` to proper fraction form and display it. For example, the following table shows some user entries and the output you should display.

User Entry			Output	Explanation
Whole number	Numerator	Denominator		
0	1	2	1/2	No whole number needed; no change needed in fraction
0	9	12	3/4	No whole number needed; 9/12 is reduced to 3/4
1	27	12	3 1/4	27/12 is 2 3/12; with the additional whole number portion 1, the result is 3 3/12, and reducing 3/12, the final result is 3 1/4
4	3	3	5	3/3 is 1; adding 1 to 4 is 5; no fraction display necessary

❑ Prompt the user to enter an arithmetic operation: + or *. Calculate the third `Fraction` to be the result of applying the requested operation to the two entered `Fractions`. Display the result as a whole number, if any, and the fractional part, if any. Reduce the result to proper form. For example, adding 1/4 and 1/4 results in 1/2, adding 3/4 and 3/4 results in 1 1/2, subtracting 1/5 from 3/1 results in 2 4/5, and multiplying 1/3 by 6/1 results in 2.

CASE PROJECT 2

In earlier chapters, you developed a `BankAccount` structure for Parkville Bank. The structure contains two fields for the integer account number and `double` account balance. Add a third field that holds an annual interest rate earned on the account. Write a `main()` function in which you create two `BankAccount` objects. Add statements to the `main()` function to do the following:

❏ Prompt the user for account numbers, beginning balances, and interest rates for the two `BankAccounts`. Each account number should be between 1,000 and 9,999; continue to reprompt the user until a valid account number is entered. Additionally, the account number for the second account cannot be the same account number as the first; continue to reprompt the user until an acceptable second account number is entered. The balance of neither account can be negative nor over $100,000; continue to reprompt the user until a valid balance is entered. The interest rate for each account must be between 0 and 0.15; reprompt the user until a valid interest rate is entered.

❏ Prompt the user to enter a term the accounts will be held, from 1 to 10 years; continue to prompt the user until the entry falls between these values. Also prompt the user for an automatic deposit amount per month (in dollars and cents) and an automatic withdrawal amount per month (also in dollars and cents). (Assume the term and the automatic payment will be the same for both accounts.) Then display a table that forecasts the balance every month for the term of each account. Calculate each month's balance as follows:

  ❏ Calculate interest earned on the starting balance; interest earned is 1/12 of the annual interest rate times the starting balance.

  ❏ Add the monthly automatic deposit.

  ❏ Subtract the monthly automatic withdrawal.

  ❏ Display the year number, month number, month-starting balance, and month-ending balance.

See Appendix D if you want your displayed values to align by the decimal point.

TIP

5

UNDERSTANDING ARRAYS, STRINGS, AND POINTERS

In this chapter, you will:

♦ Learn about memory addresses

♦ Learn about arrays

♦ Store values in an array

♦ Access and use array values

♦ Avoid common errors with arrays

♦ Learn techniques to access part of an array

♦ Use parallel arrays

♦ Use arrays of objects

♦ Learn how to use strings

♦ Discover special string-handling problems

♦ Learn about pointers

♦ Use a pointer in place of an array name

C++ is a powerful programming language for many reasons. It lets you examine and manipulate the memory addresses of variables. C++ also allows you to create arrays, or lists, of variables that you can use to store related values efficiently. Once you understand arrays, you can manipulate character strings of data. In this chapter, you will learn to use memory addresses and arrays and learn about their relationship to each other.

UNDERSTANDING MEMORY ADDRESSES

In computer memory, each location where a piece of data can be stored is identified by a **memory address**. A memory address is similar to a street address—just as 345 and 347 identify different houses on a street, different memory locations are labeled with address numbers. Memory address numbers are usually large numbers with many digits because the memory of your computer likely has billions of locations where data can be stored. When you declare a variable with a statement such as int myAge;, the computer chooses an available memory location in which to store your integer, and then associates the name myAge with the memory address of that location. All modern programming languages allow you to use easy-to-remember variable identifiers—like myAge—so that you do not have to remember actual memory addresses.

A variable's memory address is a fixed location; it is a constant. In other words, a variable's address is not changeable; when you declare a variable, it is stored at a specific memory address that cannot be altered. Although you cannot choose a variable's actual memory address, you can examine it. To do so, you use the address operator (&). For example, the program in Figure 5-1 shows both the value and the address of a variable. The output is shown in Figure 5-2. The memory address appears as a **hexadecimal**, or base 16, number.

You first learned about the address operator in Chapter 2.

The value of a variable's memory address is not very useful to you yet; at this point, you can use the address operator merely to view where variables are stored. When you write a C++ program, you are seldom interested in viewing the address of a variable.

```
#include<iostream>
using namespace std;

int main()
{
    int myAge = 21;
    cout<<"The value of myAge is "<<myAge<<endl;
    cout<<"The value of &myAge is "<<&myAge<<endl;
}
```

Figure 5-1   Program that displays the value and address of a variable

Figure 5-2   Output of the program in Figure 5-1

TIP

The hexadecimal numbering system uses the values 0 through 9 and the letters A through F to represent the decimal values 10 through 15. Each column or place in a hexadecimal number is 16 times the value of the column to its right. For example, the hexadecimal number 10 represents 16, the hexadecimal number 11 represents 17, and the hexadecimal number 1A represents 26.

5

UNDERSTANDING ARRAYS

Although the primitive (or scalar) data types—`int`, `char`, `double`, and `float`—suffice to describe the data used in many programs, it is sometimes convenient to create groups of variables that you can manipulate as a unit. A list of individual items that all have the same type is called an **array**. An array can hold multiple variables with the same type in adjacent memory positions. The variables in the array all use the array name and are distinguished from one another by their subscripts. A **subscript** is a number that indicates the position of the particular array element being used. An **element** is a single object in an array. You use a subscript to directly access a particular array element.

Anytime you need many related variables, consider using an array. For example, good candidates for array storage are lists of class grades, daily high or low temperatures, and valid inventory stock numbers. One important feature of arrays is that each array element must be the same type. One reason for this rule is that different data types take up different amounts of memory. Every element within an array is always the same size as all the other elements within the same array, although the size of a particular type of element, such as `int`, can differ from computer system to computer system.

TIP

Remember that you can determine the size of variables in your system with the `sizeof()` operator. (You first learned about this operator in Chapter 1.) For example, to find how much memory an integer uses, you can place the following statement in a program:

```
cout<<"Integer size is "<<sizeof(int)<<
        " on this computer";
```

Output might then be: `Integer size is 4 on this computer`.

In C++, you declare an array by using the form *type arrayName [size]*; where *type* is any simple type, *arrayName* is any legal identifier, and *size* (in the square brackets) represents the number of elements the array contains. For example, the following statement declares an array of five elements, each of which is type **double**:

```
double moneyCollected[5];
```

The elements in an array are numbered from zero to one less than the size of the array. For example, the first variable in the **moneyCollected** array (the first element of the array) is **moneyCollected[0]**. The last element is **moneyCollected[4]**. The number in square brackets, the subscript, should be either an integer constant or variable, or an expression whose value is an integer. Figure 5-3 shows a diagram of how the array looks in memory.

moneyCollected[0]	moneyCollected[1]	moneyCollected[2]	moneyCollected[3]	moneyCollected[4]

Figure 5-3   The **moneyCollected** array in memory

TIP

Beginning C++ programmers often forget that the first element in any array is the element with the 0 subscript. If you assume that the first element is element 1, you commit the error known as the "off by one" error.

An array name actually represents a memory address. When you declare an array, you tell the compiler to use the array name to indicate the beginning address of a series of elements. For example, if you declare an array as **int someNumbers[7];**, you are telling the compiler (which is telling the operating system) to reserve memory locations for seven integers beginning at the memory address that is represented by **someNumbers**. If, for example, integers require four bytes of storage on your system, then the declaration **int someNumbers[7];** reserves exactly 28 bytes of memory. You cannot tell the compiler where you want an array to be stored in memory. You can tell the compiler only the name of an array and how much storage (how many elements) you want to reserve; the compiler chooses the actual memory location.

The subscript that is used to access an element of an array indicates how much is added to the starting address to locate a value. For example, if you declare an array as **int someNumbers[7];**, and if an **int** requires four bytes of storage in your system, when you access the value of **someNumbers[2]**, you access the value exactly two integers, or eight bytes away from the beginning address of the array. Figure 5-4 illustrates how the integer **someNumbers** array looks in memory if it is stored at memory address 3000.

Address:

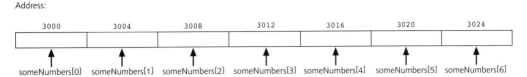

Figure 5-4   The `someNumbers` array stored at memory address 3000

An array subscript must always be an integer. This makes sense when you realize the subscript is used to point to a memory address that is a whole number of bytes away from the beginning of the array.

Many C++ compilers do not issue warnings or errors if a subscript exceeds the size of the array. For example, if you declare an array as `int someNumbers[7]`, and then refer to a location such as `someNumbers[9]`, you might not receive a warning message. Instead, the program simply accesses memory outside the array, with unpredictable results. As the programmer, you are responsible for ensuring that the subscript remains within the intended range.

The array declaration `int someNumbers[7];` declares an array that holds seven integers. The name of the array represents the beginning address of the array. You can view the address of the array with the statement `cout<<someNumbers;`. The statement `cout<<&someNumbers[0];` produces identical output because the name of the array *is* the address of the array's first element. In the first statement, the name of the array represents the beginning address of the array. In the second statement, the address of `someNumbers[0]` is also the beginning address of the array.

Similarly, the following two statements produce the same results:

```
cout<<(someNumbers + 1);
cout<<&someNumbers[1];
```

You can interpret the first statement as displaying the address of `someNumbers` plus one more integer; so if the array is stored at memory address 3000, for example, and integers are four bytes, then the statement displays 3004. You can interpret the second statement as displaying the address of the second element of the `someNumbers` array. As Figure 5-4 shows, that element is at address 3004. These two examples produce the same output because `someNumbers` is the beginning address of the array. Because `someNumbers` is an array of type integer, `someNumbers + 1` is one integer away from the beginning address of the array. That is, the address that is one integer away from the array's beginning address is the address of `someNumbers[1]`.

STORING VALUES IN AN ARRAY

You most often create an array when you want to store a number of related variable elements. For example, assume that you own an apartment building and you charge four different monthly rents depending on whether the apartment is a studio or has one, two, or three bedrooms. You could store the rent figures in four separately named variables such as studioRent, oneRent, twoRent, and threeRent. Alternatively, you can use an array with four elements, like the one shown below. This program segment shows the declaration of a four-element integer array named rent, and also shows how you can assign a rent value to each array element.

```
int rent[4];
rent[0] = 250;
rent[1] = 375;
rent[2] = 460;
rent[3] = 600;
```

When you declare an array like int rent[4];, you set aside enough memory to hold four integers, but you say nothing about the values stored in those four memory locations. The values are unknown—they are whatever was stored in those memory locations before the computer reserved the locations for use by your program. (In Chapter 4, you learned that programmers often say that these memory locations are filled with garbage.) However, after you provide assignment statements such as rent[0] = 250; and rent[1] = 375;, the memory locations have useful values. Figure 5-5 shows how the filled array appears in memory.

250	375	460	600
rent[0]	rent[1]	rent[2]	rent[3]

Figure 5-5   The rent array with assigned values

You are not required to assign array values to elements in sequential order, although it is often logical to do so.

TIP

Just as you can initialize a single variable when you declare it, you can provide values for an array when you declare it. The statement int rent[4] = {250, 375, 460, 600}; provides four values for the array. The four values listed within the curly braces are assigned, in sequence, to rent[0], rent[1], rent[2], and rent[3]. It does not make any difference whether you assign values to an array upon creation, or make assignments later, as long as you assign reasonable values before you try to do anything useful with them.

If you declare an array without a size, but provide initialization values, C++ creates an array with the exact size you need. For example, the following two array declarations create identical arrays:

```
int rent[4] = {250, 375, 460, 600};
int rent[] = {250, 375, 460, 600};
```

Because four values are provided for the second declaration, C++ assumes you want an array large enough to hold four integers.

If you provide one or more values for an array when you first declare it, but do not provide enough values to fill the array, C++ fills any unassigned array elements with zeros. For example, if you declare int rent[20] = {250, 375};, C++ assigns 250 to rent[0] and 375 to rent[1], and then fills the remaining array elements, rent[2] through rent[19], with 0. (Therefore, a convenient way to set all array elements to zero is to declare int rent[20] = {0};.) However, if you declare an array as int rent[20]; (with no assigned values in the declaration) and then make an assignment such as rent[0] = 250;, the remaining 19 array elements continue to hold garbage.

> **TIP**
> If you try to initialize an array with too many values, as in int rent[3] = {22,33,44,55,66};, C++ issues a syntax error message and the program does not compile.

When you declare an array, the size must be a constant. It can be a numeric literal constant, such as 4, or a named constant, declared with a statement such as the following:

```
const int ARRAY_SIZE = 4;
```

After declaring a named constant such as **ARRAY_SIZE**, you can use it in a declaration statement such as:

```
double quarterlyIncome[ARRAY_SIZE];
```

Whether the constant you used is named or literal, an array size cannot be a variable; your program will not compile if you attempt to use a variable name for an array size.

ACCESSING AND USING ARRAY VALUES

Once an array is filled with useful values, you can access and use an individual array value in the same manner you would access and use any single variable of the same type. For example, consider the program shown in Figure 5-6, and the output shown in Figure 5-7. The program contains a single integer variable named **singleInt**, and an array of five integers named **arrayInt**. The single integer and two of the array integers have been initialized. The program demonstrates that you can use **cout**, the prefix increment operator, and the multiplication operator with an array element in the same manner that you use a simple, non-array variable. The same holds true for all other operations you have learned—if you can perform the operation with a single variable, then you also can perform the operation with a single array element of the same type.

```cpp
#include<iostream>
using namespace std;
int main()
{
    const int SIZE = 5;
    int singleInt = 52;
    int arrayInt[SIZE] = {12, 36};
    cout<<"Single int is "<<singleInt<<endl;
    cout<<"First array element is "<<arrayInt[0]<<endl;
    ++singleInt;
    ++arrayInt[0];
    cout<<"After incrementing, single int is "<<
        singleInt<<endl;
    cout<<"After incrementing, first array element is "<<
        arrayInt[0]<<endl;
    singleInt = singleInt * 2;
    arrayInt[0] = arrayInt[0] * 2;
    cout<<"After doubling, single int is "<<singleInt<<endl;
    cout<<"After doubling, first array element is "<<
        arrayInt[0]<<endl;
}
```

Figure 5-6   Program that uses single and array variables

Figure 5-7   Output of the program in Figure 5-6

If you need to access an element in an array, you can use the array name and a constant subscript such as 0 or 1. Alternately, you can use a variable as a subscript. For example, if you declare an integer as `int sub = 0;` and declare an array as `int anArray[7];`, you could display the value of `anArray[0]` with the following statement:

    `cout<<anArray[sub];`

Using a variable as a subscript is particularly useful when you want to access all of the elements in an array. For example, instead of writing five `cout` statements to print the five elements of an array, you can place one **cout** statement in a loop and vary the subscript. Figure 5-8 shows how you can display five array values. The **for** loop displays **arrayInt[0]** through **arrayInt[4]** because **x** starts at 0, is increased by 1 every time through the loop, and continues while it is less than 5.

```
const int SZ_OF_ARRAY = 5;
int arrayInt[SZ_OF_ARRAY] = {34, 56, 12, 3, 99};
for(int x = 0; x < SZ_OF_ARRAY; ++x)
   cout<<arrayInt[x]<<endl;
```

5

Figure 5-8   Displaying five array values in a loop

In a similar fashion, you can fill an array with values that the user enters from the keyboard. Figure 5-9 shows a program in which the user enters 10 **double** values that are then stored in an array. The program displays the values in reverse order from the order in which they were entered. Without an array, this task would be cumbersome. Figure 5-10 shows the output.

```
#include<iostream>
using namespace std;
int main()
{
  const int NUM_PRICES = 10;
  double price[NUM_PRICES];
  int sub;
  for(sub = 0; sub < NUM_PRICES; ++sub)
  {
    cout<<"Enter a price ";
    cin>>price[sub];
  }
  cout<<endl<<"The entered prices, in reverse order:"<<endl;
  for(sub = NUM_PRICES - 1; sub >= 0; --sub)
    cout<<price[sub]<<"   ";
  cout<<endl;
}
```

Figure 5-9   Program that allows a user to enter 10 values, then displays them in reverse-entry order

Figure 5-10   Output of the program in Figure 5-9

When the code in Figure 5-9 executes, the user is prompted 10 times and allowed to enter a floating-point value after each prompt. The 10 values will be stored in `price[0]` through `price[9]`, respectively. Notice that when the 10 values are displayed, the first element displayed is in position 9 (`NUM_PRICES - 1`), because that is the last array position.

> **TIP**
> In the application in Figure 5-9, a single subscript (named `sub`) is used for both loops. This is never a requirement; you could have declared two separate variables to use. Nothing binds a particular variable to an array; the variable simply holds an integer that determines which array element to access.

Avoiding Common Array Errors

Until you become familiar with using arrays, it is easy to make errors when manipulating them. Common errors include forgetting that arrays are zero-based, that is, begin with element 0, and forgetting that the highest legitimate subscript is one less than the array size, that is, accessing locations beyond the limits of the array.

Pitfall: Forgetting that arrays are zero-based

When you work with arrays, it is easy to forget that the first element is 0, partly because people are used to counting beginning with 1. If you remember that when you use a subscript with an array, it indicates how many values "away from" the beginning of the array you are, then it is easier to remember to use 0 for the first element.

Forgetting an array's first element is a particularly likely error when accessing the elements in reverse order. For example, the application in Figure 5-11 is intended to display five part numbers in reverse order. However, the expression `sub > 0` is mistakenly used in the `for` statement (see shading); the program intended to use `sub >= 0`. You can see from the output in Figure 5-12 that the first element in the array (the 0-element) has been left out.

```
#include<iostream>
using namespace std;
int main()
{
  const int SZ = 5;
  int partNum[SZ] = {1000, 2000, 3000, 4000, 5000};
  cout<<endl<<"The part numbers, in reverse order:"<<endl;
  for(int sub = SZ - 1; sub > 0; --sub)
    cout<<partNum[sub]<<"   ";
  cout<<endl;
}
```

Figure 5-11   Program that fails to display an array's first element

Figure 5-12   Output of the program in Figure 5-11

Pitfall: Accessing locations beyond the array

If you forget that the highest array element has a subscript that is one less than the size of the array, you can make the error of "going past" the end of the array, or violating the array bounds. For example, in the program in Figure 5-13, the programmer has accessed an extra element when displaying the array contents. The `for` statement includes a loop when the loop control variable equals the array size (see shading), instead of remaining under the array size. Figure 5-14 shows the output. The first five array elements display correctly, but the last element, `partNum[5]`, is garbage. The last element accessed is not part of the intended array; it is **out of bounds**.

```
#include<iostream>
using namespace std;
int main()
{
  const int SZ = 5;
  int partNum[SZ] = {1000, 2000, 3000, 4000, 5000};
  cout<<endl<<"The part numbers are:"<<endl;
  for(int sub = 0; sub <= SZ; ++sub)
    cout<<partNum[sub]<<"   ";
  cout<<endl;
}
```

Figure 5-13   Program that accesses an element beyond the array

C:\WINDOWS\system32\cmd.exe

```
The part numbers are:
1000   2000   3000   4000   5000   -858993460
Press any key to continue . . . _
```

Figure 5-14   Output of the program in Figure 5-13

TIP In the output in Figure 5-14, the programmer is "fortunate" that the garbage value is so obviously wrong. If the garbage value had been one that looked like a legitimate part number, the programmer would be less likely to notice the mistake.

USING PART OF AN ARRAY

When you want to access a single array element, you use a subscript that indicates the position of the value you want to access. When you want to access all of the elements in an array, a `for` loop is usually convenient. You also might want to access several array elements, but not necessarily all of them. In this case, a `while` loop provides the most convenient structure.

For example, assume you write a program into which a teacher can enter any number of test scores, up to 30. Then the program computes the average test score. You want the program to be flexible enough so that it works whether the teacher has a class of 12, 25, or any other number of students up to 30. You want to create an array that can hold 30 test scores, but in any given execution of the program, the teacher might enter values for only some of the array elements. Figure 5-15 shows a program that allows a teacher to enter any number of test scores (up to 30) into an array. Figure 5-16 shows a typical execution during which the user has entered five scores.

```cpp
#include<iostream>
using namespace std;
int main()
{
   const int TESTS = 30;
   int testScore[TESTS];
   int testNum, a;
   double total = 0;
   double average;
   testNum = 0;
   cout<<"Enter first test score, or 999 to quit ";
   cin>>testScore[testNum];
   while(testNum < TESTS && testScore[testNum] != 999)
     {
         total += testScore[testNum];
         ++testNum;
         if(testNum < TESTS)
         {
             cout<<"Enter next test score or 999 to quit ";
             cin>>testScore[testNum];
         }
     }
   cout<<"The entered test scores are: ";
   for(a = 0; a < testNum; ++a)
     cout<<testScore[a]<<"  ";
   average = total / testNum;
   cout<<endl<<"The average test score is "<<average<<endl;
}
```

Figure 5-15   Program that allows user to enter any number of test scores, to 30

Figure 5-16   Typical execution of the program in Figure 5-15

The program in Figure 5-15 declares an array for 30 integer test scores, and four single variables that serve, respectively, as subscripts, a total, and the average. Although the test scores are integers, the average is a **double** so that the average can be expressed by a floating-point number, such as 82.2. Recall that when you divide an integer by an integer, the result is an integer, so for convenience this program uses type **double** for the **total** instead of type **int**. When you divide the **double total** by the integer number of tests, the resulting average is a **double** by default.

In Chapter 2 you learned that when an arithmetic expression contains more than one data type, an implicit cast converts the values to a unifying type. In the application in Figure 5-13, each integer `testScore` is converted to a `double` when it is added to `total`.

The program in Figure 5-15 does not use a `for` loop for data entry. A `for` loop is usually used when you want to execute a loop a predetermined number of times. Instead, in the application in Figure 5-15, the user sees a prompt for the first test score. A `while` loop controls further data entry. As long as the user does not exceed 30 entries or enter 999, the user's entry is added to `total`, the subscript is incremented, and, unless the user has entered 30 scores, the user is prompted for the next test score. Naturally, you want to choose a sentinel that cannot be a legitimate test score. The loop in Figure 5-15 ends only when the user enters 30 scores or enters 999. (If 999 is a possible test score, you want to choose a different value as the sentinel.)

In Chapter 4, you learned that a loop-ending value such as 999 is commonly called a sentinel value.

In the program in Figure 5-15, every time the user enters a test score, the subscript `testNum` is incremented. After one entry, the `testNum` variable assumes the value 1; after two entries, `testNum` has a value of 2, and so on. Each subsequent data-entry value is stored as the next array element. When the user enters 999, whether two scores or 20 scores have been entered, the value in `testNum` is equivalent to the number of entries made. When the loop ends, the value stored in the `testNum` variable can be used for two purposes. First, it can serve as a sentinel value for the loop that displays all the entered scores. For example, if six scores have been entered, you want to display scores 0 through 5. Second, it can be used as the divisor in the average calculation—an average can be computed by dividing the sum of all the scores by the number of test scores entered.

You cannot use a variable to declare an array's size; you must use a constant. When using an array, you can always use fewer than the number of allocated elements, so if you don't know how many array elements you need, you can overestimate the number.

USING PARALLEL ARRAYS

When you want to access an array element, you use the appropriate subscript. If each array element's position (0, 1, 2, and so on) has a logical connection to the purpose of the array's stored values, then accessing an array value is a straightforward process.

For example, when accessing rent for apartments that have 0, 1, 2, or 3 bedrooms, the number of bedrooms is a logical subscript to use for the `rent` array. Similarly, if employees' health insurance premiums vary when they have 0, 1, 2, 3, 4, 5, or 6 dependents, then the number of dependents can be used as a subscript for a premium array. Bedroom numbers and dependent numbers are conveniently positive, small, whole numbers.

Unfortunately, sometimes the numbers you need to access appropriate array values are not small whole numbers. Consider a company that manufactures parts that have different part numbers and prices, shown in Table 5-1. If you write a program in which you ask the user for a part number so that you can display the price, you cannot use the part number as a subscript to a price array unless you create a price array with at least 456 elements. Creating an array with 456 elements that are needed to store just four prices is cumbersome and inefficient. A better solution is to create two arrays of four elements each—one to hold the four part numbers, and one to hold the four prices that correspond to those part numbers. Such corresponding arrays are called **parallel arrays**.

5

Table 5-1   Part numbers and prices for a manufacturing company

Part Number	Price
210	1.29
312	2.45
367	5.99
456	1.42

Figure 5-17 shows a program that declares two arrays. One stores the four integer part numbers; the other stores the four **double** prices that correspond to those part numbers. After the user enters a needed part, the program loops four times. If the needed part number is equivalent to **partNum[0]**, then **partPrice[0]** is displayed. Alternately, if the needed part number is equivalent to **partNum[1]**, then **partPrice[1]** is displayed. Figure 5-18 shows an execution of the program when the user requests part number 367.

```
#include<iostream>
using namespace std;
int main()
{
   const int NUMPARTS = 4;
   int partNum[NUMPARTS] = {210, 312, 367, 456};
   double partPrice[NUMPARTS] = {1.29, 2.45, 5.99, 1.42};

   int neededPart;
   int x;
   cout<<"Enter the part number you want ";
   cin>>neededPart;
   for(x = 0; x < NUMPARTS; ++x)
   if (neededPart == partNum[x])
       cout<<"The price is "<<partPrice[x]<<endl;
}
```

Figure 5-17   Program that determines part prices

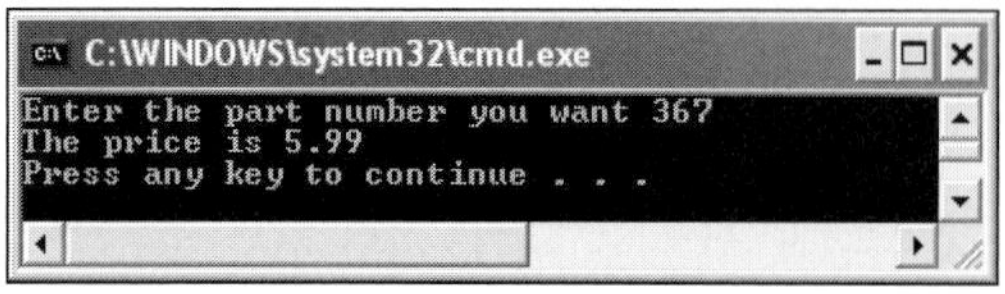

Figure 5-18 Output of the program in Figure 5-17 when user enters 367

The program in Figure 5-17 works correctly as long as the user enters an existing part number. Figure 5-19 shows the output of the program when the user enters a part number not found in the array. The program ends with no output following the user's entry.

Figure 5-19 Output of the program in Figure 5-17 when user enters 200

You can argue that nothing *should* happen, because there is no valid price for part 200. However, a user who thinks there is a part number 200 will be frustrated by the lack of response from the program. To make the program more user-friendly, you can add a flag variable. A **flag variable** is one that you use to mark an occurrence. For example, you can initialize an integer flag variable to 0, and change its value to 1 when a specific event occurs—for example, when an item number is found while searching through the array. At the conclusion of the program, you can check this flag variable's value and determine whether you want to display a message for the user. Figure 5-20 shows the price-finding application with the addition of a flag variable named `isFound`. The changes from the application in Figure 5-17 are shaded in Figure 5-20:

- The flag variable `isFound` is declared and initialized to 0.

- The flag variable is set to 1 if the user's part number request matches a valid part number.

- After the part number array has been searched, if the flag variable has not been changed, the user sees an error message.

Figure 5-21 shows the improved output displayed when a user enters an invalid part number.

```cpp
#include<iostream>
using namespace std;
int main()
{
    const int NUMPARTS = 4;
    int partNum[NUMPARTS] = {210, 312, 367, 456};
    double partPrice[NUMPARTS] = {1.29, 2.45, 5.99, 1.42};
    int isFound = 0;
    int neededPart;
    int x;
    cout<<"Enter the part number you want ";
    cin>>neededPart;
    for(x = 0; x < NUMPARTS; ++x)
        if (neededPart == partNum[x])
        {
        cout<<"The price is "<<partPrice[x]<<endl;
            isFound = 1;
        }
    if(isFound == 0)
        cout<<"Sorry - no such part number"<<endl;
}
```

Figure 5-20   Price-finding program with a variable that flags invalid part numbers

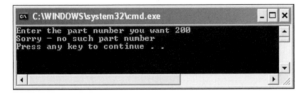

Figure 5-21   Output of the program in Figure 5-20 when user enters 200

When you create parallel arrays, it is important that the values in the same positions in the array correspond to each other. For example, if your company added a new part number to the `partNum` array, it would be important that its price went into the same position in the `partPrice` array; otherwise, the wrong prices would display for some or all of the part numbers. An alternative to creating parallel arrays for the part numbers and their prices is to create a single array of part objects, and allow each part object to hold fields for part number and price. In the next section, you learn to create arrays of structure objects.

In the price-finding program, you might prefer to declare `isFound` to be a `bool` type variable instead of an `int`. A `bool` variable contains one of two values, `true` or `false`.

TIP

CREATING ARRAYS OF STRUCTURE OBJECTS

Just as you can create arrays of simple types such as int and double, you can create arrays of structure objects. For example, consider the Part structure shown in the program in Figure 5-22. Each Part object you create has two public fields: a part number and a price. Instead of needing parallel arrays for part numbers and prices as you did in the program in Figure 5-20, you can create a single array of Part objects because each Part encompasses both needed fields.

You create an object array the same way you create any other array: you use the type name, the array name, and square brackets in which you place an integer value that indicates the number of memory locations to reserve. The program in Figure 5-22 creates an array of four Part objects, prompts the user for data values for them, and then displays them. The changes from the application in Figure 5-20 are shaded. A single array of Part objects is created and initialized with the same part numbers and prices as in the application in Figure 5-20, and the single array is used in the search. Figure 5-23 shows a typical execution.

```
#include<iostream>
using namespace std;
struct Part
{
    int partNum;
    double partPrice;
};
int main()
{
    const int NUMPARTS = 4;
    Part part[NUMPARTS] = {{210, 1.29}, {312, 2.45},
        {367, 5.99}, {456, 1.42}};
    int isFound = 0;
    int neededPart;
    int x;
    cout<<"Enter the part number you want ";
    cin>>neededPart;
    for(x = 0; x < NUMPARTS; ++x)
        if (neededPart == part[x].partNum)
        {
            cout<<"The price is "<<part[x].partPrice<<endl;
            isFound = 1;
        }
        if(isFound == 0)
            cout<<"Sorry - no such part number"<<endl;
}
```

Figure 5-22   Program that creates an array of four Part objects

Figure 5-23   Sample execution of the program in Figure 5-22

To access any individual object field, you use the object's individual name, including its subscript, followed by a dot and the field name. For example, the part number of the first **Part** in the **part** array is **part[0].partNum**. Examine the program in Figure 5-22 to see how all the fields of each **Part** object are accessed and used.

TIP

So far, all the arrays you have encountered have been **one-dimensional arrays**—arrays whose elements are accessed using a single subscript. **Two-dimensional arrays** are accessed using two subscripts; the first represents a row and the second represents a column. Often, you can avoid the complexities of using two-dimensional arrays by grouping related items as a structure (or class, as you will see in the next chapter) and using a single-dimensional array.

USING STRINGS

In C++ a character variable can hold a single character value, such as 'A' or '$'. Single character values are always expressed within single quotation marks. In C++, if you want to express multiple character values as a constant, such as a first name or a book title, you use double quotation marks. A C++ value expressed within double quotation marks is commonly called a **string,** or a **literal string**.

TIP

You can type two characters within single quotation marks, but only when they represent a single character. For example, '\n' represents the newline character. (Remember, the newline character contains the code that moves subsequent output to the next line.) You actually type a backslash and an n within the single quotation marks, but you can do so only because the combination represents one character stored in computer memory.

You already have used literal strings with **cout** statements, as in **cout<<"Hello";**. Just as a value such as 14 is a numeric constant, a value such as "Hello" is referred to as a **string constant**. When you want to store a value such as 14 in a variable, you declare a numeric variable by giving it a type and a name. When you want to store a value such as "Hello", you must create a string variable in one of two ways:

- You can create a string as an array of characters.

- You can create a string using the **string** class defined in the C++ standard library.

Strings Created as Arrays of Characters

In C++ an array of characters and a string can be declared in the same way. You might create an array of characters if you need to store six one-letter department codes, or five one-letter grades that can be assigned on a test. These examples are called character arrays. When you want to store related characters that are used together, such as someone's name, then the characters constitute a string. You also can store the individual characters of a string in an array. However, C++ programmers do not refer to an array of characters as a string unless the last usable character in the string is the null character. The **null character** is represented by the combination '\0' (backslash and zero), or by using the constant NULL that is available if you use the statement `#include<iostream>` at the top of any file you compile.

TIP The constant NULL is defined in several other files in addition to `iostream`. However, if you are including `iostream` because you want to use `cin` and `cout`, then you automatically have access to the NULL constant.

If you want to declare a string named `firstName` and initialize it to "Mary", each of the following statements provides the same result.

```
char firstName[] = "Mary";
char firstName[] = {"Mary"};
char firstName[5] = "Mary";
char firstName[5] = {"Mary"};
char firstName[5] = {'M', 'a', 'r', 'y', '\0'};
```

Each statement reserves five character positions, and stores an 'M' at `firstName[0]`, an 'a' at `firstName[1]`, an 'r' at `firstName[2]`, a 'y' at `firstName[3]`, and a '\0' at `firstName[4]`. (When you store a string, the curly braces are optional, but when you store individual characters, you must include them.)

Assuming the compiler assigns the `firstName` array to memory address 2000, and assuming that character variables occupy one byte of storage in your computer system, Figure 5-24 shows how `firstName` looks in memory.

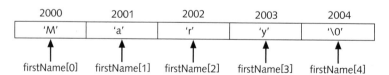

Figure 5-24 How `firstName` appears in computer memory

When you use `cout` to display a string, as in the statement `cout<<firstName;`, `cout` begins to display characters at the memory address `firstName`, and continues to display characters until it encounters a NULL. Whether you write `cout<<firstName;` (output starting at `firstName`) or `cout<<&firstName[0];` (output starting at the address of the first character of `firstName`), the output is the same. Output for each statement starts at the beginning address of the array named `firstName`, and prints characters until the NULL is encountered. If you destroy the NULL at the end of `firstName`, perhaps by making the statement `firstName[4] = 'X';`, then the results of `cout<<firstName;` are unpredictable. The next NULL might be stored at the next byte of memory, or it might be hundreds or thousands of bytes away. C++ prints every character, starting at the beginning address, until it encounters the NULL.

If you create a `firstName` string and initialize it to "Mary", and then use the C++ statement `cout<<firstName[0];`, the output is only the character 'M'. Without using the address operator, each element in the character array is just a character.

If you create a `firstName` string and initialize it to "Mary", and then use the C++ statement `cout<<&firstName[1];`, the output is *ary*. Output begins at the address of `firstName[1]` (the 'a'), and continues until the NULL (the next character after the 'y').

You can easily provide more space than the characters in a string require. For example, you might declare a string to be 15 characters so it can store longer and shorter names at different times. The statement `char firstName[15] = {"Mary"}` assigns 'M' to `firstName[0]`, and so on, just as in the string declared with five characters. The last character assigned is the NULL, which is assigned to `firstName[4]`. The difference is that with this string, positions 5 through 14 are unused. The statement `cout<<firstName;` still displays the four letters of "Mary" and stops at the NULL.

Special String-Handling Problems When Using Character Arrays

When strings are declared as character arrays, using them presents some special handling problems. These problems occur when you:

- try to input a string value that includes whitespace
- try to assign one string to another using the assignment operator
- try to compare strings using the comparison operator
- exceed the bounds of an array

Pitfall: Trying to input a string value including whitespace

When you use the `cin` statement with a string, `cin` stops adding characters to the string when it encounters whitespace. Often, this means that `cin` stops when the user presses the Enter key, but `cin` also stops when the user presses the spacebar or the Tab key. Consider the short program in Figure 5-25 that prompts a user for a name. After the user enters a name, the program echoes it. If the user types *Mary* and then presses the Enter key, the output is *You entered Mary*. However, if the user types *Mary Ann* and then presses the Enter key, the output is also *You entered Mary*, as shown in Figure 5-26.

```
#include<iostream>
using namespace std;
int main()
{
    char name[10];
    cout<<"Enter a name ";
    cin>>name;
    cout<<"You entered "<<name<<endl;
}
```

Figure 5-25   Program that reads a name

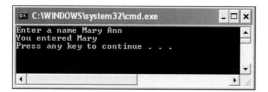

Figure 5-26   Output of the program in Figure 5-25 when user enters *Mary Ann*

When the user types *Mary Ann* in the program in Figure 5-25, the `cin` statement accepts *Mary* into the string and leaves *Ann* as well as a character representing the Enter key waiting in an area called the **input buffer**. If the program contains a subsequent `cin` statement, then *Ann* is accepted and assigned to the string named in the second `cin` statement. So, one way you could accept both *Mary* and *Ann* is to provide two `cin` statements. However, with this change, the program would then be flawed for all the users with one-word names. For those users, the second `cin` would cause the program to appear to "stall"; it would be waiting for the second part of a name that the user did not have.

TIP   Using some compilers, in the application in Figure 5-25, if the user types a space as the first character before typing other letters, the statement would end, ignoring all the characters after the space. The output would appear to indicate that the user entered nothing.

One way to accept multiple word names is to use the C++ **getline() function**. This function reads characters into an array up to a size limit, or until the newline character is encountered, whichever comes first. Figure 5-27 shows a sample program that uses `getline()` to store up to 10 characters in the name array. (See shaded statement.) The characters can include spaces, so, as you can see in Figure 5-28, a name containing a space is read in and stored correctly.

```
#include<iostream>
using namespace std;
int main()
{
    const int SIZE = 10;
    char name[SIZE];
    cout<<"Enter a name ";
    cin.getline(name,SIZE);
    cout<<"You entered "<<name<<endl;
}
```

Figure 5-27 Program that uses the `getline()` function

Figure 5-28 Sample execution of the program in Figure 5-27

TIP You will learn about functions in Chapter 6. For now, you can use `getline()` without understanding how it works internally.

Pitfall: Trying to assign one string to another using the assignment operator

Another string-handling problem occurs when you attempt to assign one string to another. For example, suppose you have a string defined as `char clubPresident[10]` `= {"Eric"};` and another string defined as `char clubVicePresident[10] =` `{"Danielle"};`. If you want to assign the `clubVicePresident` name to the `clubPresident` name, you might suppose a statement like `clubPresident =` `clubVicePresident;` would be appropriate. This statement attempts to use the assignment operator (equal sign) that you use when assigning values to simple data types. The problem is that `clubPresident` and `clubVicePresident` are not simple variables. They are arrays, and array names are addresses. The C++ compiler, not the programmer, decides where program components are located. You cannot change the address of an array, which is what you are attempting to do by assigning a value to `clubPresident`. An array name can never appear on the left side of an assignment operator; it is a constant and cannot be changed by the operator.

To assign the name of the `clubVicePresident` to the `clubPresident` array, you must assign each character value in the `clubVicePresident` name to the corresponding character location in the `clubPresident` name. You can take three approaches to accomplish this. One is to assign each character, one by one, as in:

```
clubPresident[0] = clubVicePresident[0];
clubPresident[1] = clubVicePresident[1];
clubPresident[2] = clubVicePresident[2];
```

... and so on.

Of course, this is a tedious process. A more elegant approach is to provide a loop to assign the characters:

```
for(x = 0; x < 10; ++x)
    clubPresident[x] = clubVicePresident[x];
```

Although the looping solution correctly moves each character from the `clubVicePresident` string to the `clubPresident` string, and is a shorter solution than assigning each character individually, it is still not the easiest solution. Instead, you can use a built-in C++ function. Because programmers often want to store the contents of one string in another string, C++ designers provide a function that copies one string to another, relieving you of the responsibility of writing character-by-character loops each time you want to store one string in another. The function name is `strcpy()`. It takes the following form:

Syntax Example

strcpy(*destinationString, sourceString*);

For example, `strcpy(clubPresident, clubVicePresident);` results in the vice president's name being copied to the `clubPresident` string.

Depending on your compiler, you might have to use the statement `#include<string.h>` at the top of your file to use the `strcpy()` function.

One way to remember the order of the `destinationString` and `sourceString` is that they are in the same order they would be in an assignment statement that uses the equal sign. That is, the receiving string is on the left.

You will learn more about how functions work in Chapter 6. For now, you can just use the `strcpy()` function without understanding its inner workings.

Pitfall: Trying to compare strings using the comparison operator

A related string-handling problem occurs when you try to compare two strings. For example, if you want to determine whether `clubPresident` and `clubVicePresident` have the same value, it might seem natural to write a statement such as:

```
if(clubPresident == clubVicePresident)
    cout<<"They are the same"<<endl;
```

However, if you remember that `clubPresident` and `clubVicePresident` are array names, and therefore addresses, then you realize that the `if` statement is comparing only their memory addresses. Because `clubPresident` and `clubVicePresident` are two separate arrays, their addresses are never equal even though their contents can be, and the result of the comparison will always be false.

You could write instructions to compare two strings by comparing each character of one string to the corresponding character in the other string, such as in the following:

```
if(clubPresident[0] == clubVicePresident[0] &&
clubPresident[1] == clubVicePresident[1]. . .
```

You also can replace this tedious method with the built-in function `strcmp()`. The string compare function `strcmp()` takes the following form:

Syntax Example

strcmp(*firstString, secondString*);

If two strings are equal, then the value of the `strcmp()` function is 0. This might seem wrong, because you know that 0 also means false, and when two strings are equivalent, you would think the `strcmp()` function would have a true value. However, you should interpret the 0 as meaning "no difference" between the strings in question.

The program in Figure 5-29 illustrates how to use the `strcmp()` function. When `firstName` and `secName` each contain the string "Mary", then the result of `strcmp(firstName, secName)` is 0, indicating no difference in the names. When you replace the contents of one string with "Danielle", the result of `strcmp(firstName, secName)` is not 0, indicating a difference.

TIP

Depending on your compiler, you might have to add the preprocessor directive #include<string> or #include<string.h> to the program shown in Figure 5-29 in order to use the `strcmp()` function.

```
#include<iostream>
using namespace std;
int main()
{
   char firstName[10] = {"Mary"};
   char secName[10] = {"Mary"};
   if(strcmp(firstName,secName)==0)
      cout<<firstName<<" and "<<secName<<
        " are the same"<<endl;
   else
      cout<<firstName<<" and "<<secName<<
        " are different"<<endl;
   strcpy(firstName, "Danielle");
   if(strcmp(firstName,secName)==0)
      cout<<firstName<<" and "<<secName<<
        " are the same"<<endl;
   else
      cout<<firstName<<" and "<<secName<<
        " are different"<<endl;
}
```

Figure 5-29   Program that displays values returned by the `strcmp()` function

Figure 5-30   Output of the program in Figure 5-29

TIP   If the first string used in the `strcmp` function is alphabetically greater than the second string, as in `strcmp("Zack", "Alice")`, then the value of `strcmp()` is a positive number. If the value of the first string is alphabetically less than the second string, then the value of the `strcmp()` function is a negative number.

Pitfall: Exceeding an array's bounds

When you work with any type of array, you always run the risk of referencing an address that is out of bounds. This error is particularly easy to make when using character arrays as strings. For example, the application in Figure 5–31 declares two character arrays, displays their contents, and then assigns a very long name to one of the arrays. When the names are displayed the second time, as shown in the output in Figure 5–32, the first name has become corrupted by the overly long second name.

```
#include<iostream>
#include<string>
using namespace std;
int main( )
{
    char name1[ ] = "Mary";
    char name2[ ] = "Diane";
    cout<<"Names are "<<name1<<" and "<<name2<<endl;
    strcpy(name2, "Margaret Veronica");
    cout<<"Names are "<<name1<<" and "<<name2<<endl;
}
```

Figure 5-31   Program that violates array bounds

Figure 5-32   Output of the program in Figure 5-31

TIP   Some compilers can display the two names when you run the program in Figure 5-31. However, the program will end abruptly and an error message will be issued.

Figures 5-33 and 5-34 show how the two names declared in the application look in memory before and after the long name value is assigned to name2. In Figure 5-33, you can see the two names, which, by default, are placed 16 bytes apart, even though both values that are stored are shorter than 16 bytes. (Typically, the computer places the first variable declared at the highest address available for storage, and subsequent declarations at lower addresses, so that the effect appears to be "backwards," or first in at the "bottom.") After "Margaret Veronica" is assigned to name2 in the application, memory looks like Figure 5-34. "Margaret Veronica" has been inserted starting at the beginning address of name2, but has continued to use part of the area assigned to name1. Specifically, the 'a' and the '\0' at the end of the name (shaded) have "fallen into" name1's area. When the application displays name1 in the last line of the program, the display starts at the beginning memory address for name1, and continues to the NULL, displaying only one character, the 'a' that is really the last letter in "Veronica". When the application displays name2, it starts at the beginning address for name2 and continues until encountering a NULL, so the entire name2, "Margaret Veronica", is displayed, even though it goes beyond the locations where name2 should be.

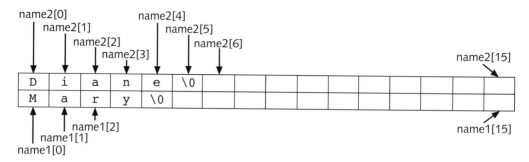

Figure 5-33   View of memory before `strcpy()` in the program in Figure 5-31

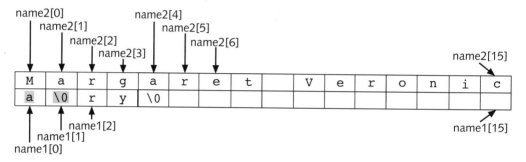

Figure 5-34   View of memory after `strcpy()` in the program in Figure 5-31

An Introduction to the `string` Class

Using character arrays to handle string data is a cumbersome process. You must be aware of the NULL character, learn about special functions to assign and compare string values, and be wary of overrunning the end of the allotted area for the string. These problems are alleviated by using the `string` class.

Figure 5-35 shows an application that uses the `string` class. Notice in the first shaded statement that you must use the statement `#include<string>` to be able to use the `string` class. Next, notice in the second shaded statement that when you declare a `string`, you use it similarly to the way you use any primitive variable type such as `int` or `double`. To declare a `string` variable, you use the data type, an identifier, and an optional initialization value. You can see in the third, fourth, and fifth shaded statements that comparisons and assignments can occur in much the same way they do with the simpler data types.

```cpp
#include<iostream>
#include<string>
using namespace std;
int main()
{
    string oneName = "John";
    string anotherName = "John";
    if(oneName == anotherName)
        cout<<oneName<<" and "<<anotherName<<
            " are equal"<<endl;
    else
        cout<<oneName<<" and "<<anotherName<<
            " are different"<<endl;
    anotherName = "Nicholas";
    if(oneName == anotherName)
        cout<<oneName<<" and "<<anotherName<<
            " are equal"<<endl;
    else
        cout<<oneName<<" and "<<anotherName<<
            " are different"<<endl;
    oneName = anotherName;
    if(oneName == anotherName)
        cout<<oneName<<" and "<<anotherName<<
            " are equal"<<endl;
    else
        cout<<oneName<<" and "<<anotherName<<
            " are different"<<endl;
}
```

5

Figure 5-35   Program that uses the `string` class

Figure 5-36   Output of the program in Figure 5-35

The second line in the application—#include<string>—is required when you use the `string` class.

In C++, it is conventional to begin class names with an uppercase letter. The `string` class is an exception to this rule.

TIP   After you complete Chapter 7, you will understand much more about classes. For now, you can use the string class very much like you would use any other data type.

Using the string class provides you with another benefit—more memory locations are assigned as needed for long values. Compare the application in Figure 5-37 to the one in Figure 5-31. Both declare two strings, display them, and then assign a long name to one of them. In the application in Figure 5-37, however, the other string is not corrupted. Figure 5-38 shows the output; the strings are stored and displayed perfectly.

```
#include<iostream>
#include<string>
using namespace std;
int main()
{
    string name1 = "Mary";
    string name2 = "Diane";
    cout<<"Names are "<<name1<<" and "<<name2<<endl;
    name2 = "Margaret Veronica";
    cout<<"Names are "<<name1<<" and "<<name2<<endl;
}
```

Figure 5-37   Program that assigns a long value to a string

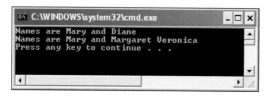

Figure 5-38   Output of the program in Figure 5-37

With so many advantages to using the string class, you might choose never to bother with character arrays for storing string values. However, many C++ programs will use character-array strings (also called **C-style strings**), and understanding them will help you troubleshoot potential programming errors.

USING POINTERS

You can access the value of any variable by using the variable's name. In contrast, inserting an ampersand in front of the variable's name allows you to access its address.

You can also declare variables that can hold memory addresses. These variables are called **pointer variables**, or simply **pointers**. You declare a pointer with a type, just like other variables. A pointer's type indicates the type of variable that has an address the pointer can hold.

To indicate that a variable is a pointer, begin the variable's name with an asterisk. For example, `int *aPointer;` declares an integer pointer variable named `aPointer`. The `aPointer` variable can hold the address of any integer variable. For example, if you declare `int myValue;`, then you can make the assignment, `aPointer = &myValue;`. You then can output the contents of `myValue` in one of two ways:

```
cout<<myValue;
```

or

```
cout<<*aPointer;
```

TIP

When you declare an integer pointer named `aPointer`, you have several options when typing the asterisk. Each of the following statements declares an integer pointer:

```
int *aPointer;
int* aPointer;
int * aPointer;
```

The statement `cout<<myValue;` tells the program to display the value stored at the memory location `myValue`. The statement `cout<<*aPointer;` tells the program to display the value stored at the address held in `aPointer`. Because the address held in `aPointer` is the address of `myValue`, the output from both statements is the same. You interpret `*aPointer` as "the contents at the address pointed to by `aPointer`," or, more simply, as "the contents at `aPointer`."

You can output the memory address of `myValue` in one of two ways:

```
cout<<&myValue;
```

or

```
cout<<aPointer;
```

You read the first statement as "Output the address of the variable `myValue`"; you read the second as "Output the value of `aPointer`, which currently is the address of the `myValue` variable." Of course, you don't frequently have a reason to output a variable's memory address, but in C++, you can.

The major difference between using a pointer name and the address operator with a variable name is that a variable's address is a constant, but a pointer is a variable. That is, a variable's address is fixed permanently when you compile a program, but with a pointer variable, you can assign the address of any variable of the same type to the pointer, and you can also change the address stored in the pointer as many times as you want. For example, if you declare three integers named `x`, `y`, and `z`, and an integer pointer named `aPointer`, then you can make any or all of the following statements:

```
aPointer = &x;
aPointer = &y;
aPointer = &z;
```

The address of a variable, such as &myValue, is a constant. You cannot assign any other value to the address of the myValue variable; its address is fixed and unalterable at the time you compile the program.

Using a Pointer Instead of an Array Name

Advanced C++ programmers use pointers for many purposes. Sometimes they use a pointer as an alternative to an array name. Remember that any array name is actually a memory address, and that pointers hold memory addresses. Therefore, a pointer also can hold an array name, as long as the pointer type and array type are the same.

The program illustrated in Figure 5-39 shows five different ways to access the same seven values. The program declares an integer array with sales figures for seven days for a small business. The program also declares an integer pointer and assigns the address of the first sales figure to that pointer. Then the program displays the same sales figures using five different methods. The five lines of output, all identical, are shown in Figure 5-40.

```cpp
#include<iostream>
using namespace std;
int main()
{
   const int DAYS = 7;
   int sales[DAYS] = {500, 300, 450, 200, 525, 800, 1000};
   int *p = &sales[0];    // int *p = sales;
                          // would produce identical results
   int x;
   for(x = 0; x < DAYS; ++x)
      cout<<"$"<<sales[x]<<"   ";
   cout<<endl;
   for(x = 0; x < DAYS; ++x)
      cout<<"$"<<p[x]<<"   ";
   cout<<endl;
   for(x = 0; x < DAYS; ++x)
      cout<<"$"<<*(sales + x)<<"   ";
   cout<<endl;
   for(x = 0; x < DAYS; ++x)
      cout<<"$"<<*(p + x)<<"   ";
   cout<<endl;
   for(x = 0; x < DAYS; ++x, ++p)
      cout<<"$"<<*p<<"   ";
   cout<<endl;
}
```

Figure 5-39   Program that uses both array and pointer notation

Figure 5-40 Output of the program in Figure 5-39

The first loop shown in Figure 5-39:

```
for(x = 0; x < DAYS; ++x)
    cout<<"$"<<sales[x]<<"   ";
```

shows traditional array and subscript notation. The array name is used with a subscript, **x**, that takes on the sequence of values from 0 through 6. Each of the seven sales figures is output, preceded by a dollar sign and followed by two spaces.

The second loop in the program:

```
for(x = 0; x < DAYS; ++x)
    cout<<"$"<<p[x]<<"   ";
```

shows that the pointer variable **p** can be used in exactly the same manner as the array name **sales**. The array name **sales** is a memory address, or constant pointer, and **p** is a variable pointer that has been initialized to the beginning of the sales array. Both **sales** and **p** hold the same memory address, and either can be used with square brackets and a subscript that indicates which value following the memory address should be accessed. In other words, the subscript simply indicates how far away a value is from the starting address of the array.

The third loop shown in the program in Figure 5-39 is written using more complicated syntax:

```
for(x = 0; x < DAYS; ++x)
    cout<<"$"<<*(sales + x)<<"   ";
```

Although subscript notation is generally easier to understand, the third loop illustrates that if you access the contents (represented by the asterisk) of the address at **sales** (the beginning address of the array) plus **x** more integers (either 0, 1, 2, or so on), the result is that you access each succeeding value in the array.

TIP

The array name **sales** is a constant address; therefore, you cannot alter it with a statement such as ++sales (just as you cannot alter a numeric constant with a statement such as ++9). However, you can refer to the location **sales + 1** as this statement does not attempt to alter **sales**.

The fourth loop:

```
for(x = 0; x < DAYS; ++x)
    cout<<"$"<<*(p + x)<<"    ";
```

is similar to the third one. The fourth loop displays the contents at the memory address p + 0, then the contents at the memory address p + 1, and so on. The calculated address p + 0 is the same as the beginning address of the array. The address p + 1 is the same as the address one integer away from the beginning of the array, also known as &p[1], and in this case, also known as &sales[1].

The last loop in Figure 5-39 displays the contents stored in the pointer p, which was set to be equal to the address of the array at the beginning of the program:

```
for(x = 0; x < DAYS; ++x, ++p)
    cout<<"$"<<*p<<"    ";
cout<<endl;
```

At the end of each loop repetition, p is incremented along with x using the statement ++p;. This last loop demonstrates that p is a variable; it is a pointer variable that holds an address. Figure 5-41 shows how the **sales** array from Figure 5-39 might look in memory, assuming it is stored at address 8000 and assuming that integers are four bytes. When the beginning address of the array is stored in p, p holds 8000, and when *p is displayed, you see the contents at 8000, which is 500. Because the size of an integer is 4, and because p is an integer pointer, ++p increases the value of p by 4. Therefore, on the second cycle through the loop, p holds 8004. The contents there are displayed: 300. When p is incremented again, it holds 8008 and so on.

Address:

8000	8004	8008	8012	8016	8020	8024
500	300	450	200	525	800	1000
sales[0]		sales[2]		sales[4]		sales[6]
	sales[1]		sales[3]		sales[5]	

Figure 5-41   The **sales** array in computer memory

Of course, you do not need to use a pointer to access an array location; you can use a subscript contained in square brackets. However, as you continue to study C++, you will learn that you can store lists of values in nonadjacent locations. In these cases, you need pointers to hold the addresses of subsequent list values. As you become more familiar with C++, you will find many additional uses for pointers. However, because pointers access computer memory locations, using pointers can be dangerous—you might point to and alter memory locations that you had no intention of altering. When you assign one variable to another, as in the statement x = y;, a copy of the value stored in y is assigned to the variable x; each variable holds its own copy of the same value. When you assign one pointer to another, you are not making a copy of the data; instead, you are setting two pointers to point to the same memory location. Later, if you delete the value to which one of the pointers refers, the other pointer is left with a null reference. This condition is known as creating a **dangling reference**. As you gain experience in C++, you will learn how to avoid this dangerous situation.

You Do It

Using an Array

In the following steps, you create an application that can accept, display, and calculate the average of student test scores.

5

1. Open the **TestScores.cpp** file from your Chapter05 folder. Alternatively, you can type the application yourself, as shown in Figure 5-42. The program declares a constant that is used to create an array that can hold 10 student test scores. In a `for` loop, the user enters 10 scores. At the end of the data entry loop, the scores are totaled and displayed, and then their average is calculated and displayed.

```cpp
#include<iostream>
using namespace std;
int main()
{
  const int NUM_SCORES = 10;
  int score[NUM_SCORES];
  int sub;
  double total = 0;
  double average = 0;
  for(sub = 0; sub < NUM_SCORES; ++sub)
  {
    cout<<"Enter score #"<<(sub + 1)<<" ";
    cin>>score[sub];
  }
  cout<<endl<<"The scores are:"<<endl;
  for(sub = 0; sub < NUM_SCORES; ++sub)
  {
    total += score[sub];
    cout<<score[sub]<<"   ";
  }
  cout<<endl;
  average = total / NUM_SCORES;
  cout<<"The average score is "<<average<<endl;
}
```

Figure 5-42   The TestScores.cpp program

2. Run the program. Respond to the prompts with test scores such as **70, 80, 90**, and so on. After you enter all 10 scores, confirm that the output displays them all and that the average is correct. For example, Figure 5-43 shows a typical execution.

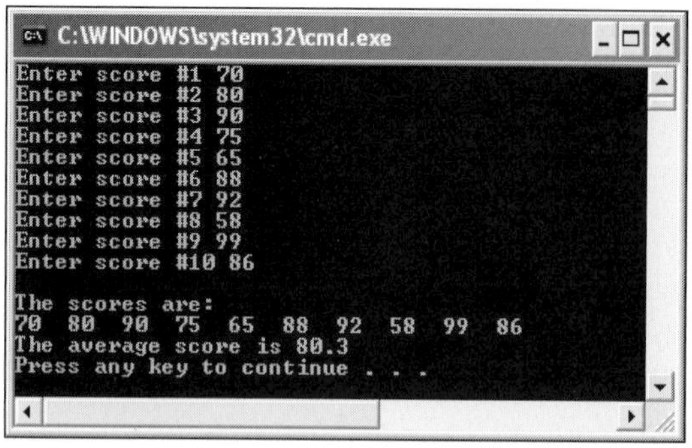

Figure 5-43   Output of the TestScores.cpp program

3. The existing program accepts exactly 10 scores. You can make the program more flexible by allowing fewer scores if the user enters a sentinel value. To allow the user to enter scores until typing 999, make the following changes:

a. Initialize **sub** to 0:

```
int sub = 0;
```

b. Add a new constant to hold the sentinel value:

```
const int END = 999;
```

c. Get the first score and store it in element 0 of the array,

```
cout<<"Enter score #"<<(sub + 1)<<" or "<<END<<" to quit ";
cin>>score[sub];
```

d. Change the data-entry loop so it starts with the second array element (element 1) and continues while two conditions remain true: the last score entered is not the END value, and the subscript remains within range:

```
for(sub = 1; score[sub - 1] != END && sub < NUM_SCORES; ++sub)
```

It is necessary to check **score[sub - 1]** for the sentinel value because after the user enters 999, the last part of the **for** loop will increase **sub**, so the 999 will be located in the previous location.

e. Add an explanation to the prompt the user sees so the user understands the appropriate quitting value:

```
cout<<"Enter score #"<<(sub + 1)<<" or "<<END<<" to quit ";
```

f. The number of scores entered might be fewer than 10, so, with the other variables, declare a variable that can hold the number of items entered:

```
int scoresEntered;
```

g. Immediately after the data entry for the loop's closing curly brace, assign the number of entries, **sub - 1**, to the **scoresEntered** variable:

```
scoresEntered = sub - 1;
```

h. The loop that totals and displays the entered scores should no longer loop until the tenth item. If you do not change the loop, garbage items after the 999 will display. Change the middle portion of the `for` loop to only go as far as the last entered score before the sentinel:

```
for(sub = 0; sub < scoresEntered; ++sub)
```

i. The average score should no longer be calculated by dividing by 10. Change the average calculation to use `scoresEntered`, unless 0 scores were entered, in which case the `average` should be zero.

```
if(scoresEntered == 0)
    average = 0;
else
    average = total / scoresEntered;
```

4. Save the program as **TestScores2.cpp**. Compile and execute the program. You can enter any number of scores, up to 10, and can exit earlier by entering 999. Figure 5-44 shows a typical execution in which the user has entered only two scores.

Figure 5-44   Typical execution of TestScores2.cpp

Understanding Memory Addresses

In the following steps, you experiment with memory addresses in your computer system.

1. Open the **MemoryAddresses.cpp** file from your Chapter05 folder. As shown in Figure 5-45, it declares two integers, prompts you for values, and displays the values. Compile and execute the program and confirm that it works as expected.

```
#include<iostream>
using namespace std;
int main()
{
    int firstNum, secondNum;
    cout<<"Enter first number ";
    cin>>firstNum;
    cout<<"Enter second number ";
    cin>>secondNum;
    cout<<"The numbers are "<<firstNum<<" and "<<secondNum<<endl;
}
```

Figure 5-45   The MemoryAddresses.cpp program

2. Just before the closing curly brace, add a new output statement that displays the memory addresses of the two variables:

   cout<<"The addresses are "<<&firstNum<<" and
   "<<&secondNum<<endl;

3. Save the modified program as **MemoryAddresses2.cpp** and compile and execute the program. Enter any values you like for firstNum and secondNum and observe the output, which should look similar to Figure 5-46. The memory addresses are expressed in hexadecimal, and yours might differ from the values shown in Figure 5-46, but you should be able to recognize that the values are close to each other.

Figure 5-46   Output of MemoryAddresses2.cpp

4. After the declaration of the two integers, add a constant to use as an array size, an integer array declaration, and a single integer declaration as follows:

   const int SIZE = 6;
   int nums[SIZE] = {12,23,34,45,56,67};
   int x;

5. Just before the closing curly brace of the `main()` function, add two loops that in turn display all the array element values, and the addresses of all the array elements.

```
for(x = 0; x < SIZE; ++x)
    cout<<nums[x]<<" ";
cout<<endl;
for(x = 0; x < SIZE; ++x)
    cout<<&nums[x]<<" ";
cout<<endl;
```

6. Save the modified program as **MemoryAddresses3.cpp**, then compile and execute it. Enter any two values you like for the two single integers. When you examine the output, which looks similar to Figure 5-47, you will see the two values you entered, their addresses, the six array values, and their six addresses. Even if you are unfamiliar with the hexadecimal numbering system, by examining the last digits in the displayed addresses you should be able to discern that the array elements are each an equal distance from the next element; in Figure 5-47, they are exactly four bytes apart.

Figure 5-47   Output of MemoryAddresses3.cpp

CHAPTER SUMMARY

❐ In computer memory, each location where a piece of data can be stored is identified by a memory address. A variable's address is a constant. You can use the address operator (&) to examine a variable's memory address.

❐ A list of individual items that all have the same type is called an array. A subscript is a number that indicates the position of the particular array element being used. An array name actually represents a memory address, and the subscript used to access an element of an array indicates how much to add to the starting address to locate a value.

❐ Just as you can initialize a single variable when you declare it, you can provide values for an array when you declare it. If you declare an array without a size, but provide initialization values, C++ creates an array with the exact size you need. If you initialize an array with one or more values but do not provide enough values to fill it, C++ fills any unassigned array elements with zeros.

❐ Once an array is filled with useful values, you can access and use an individual array value in the same manner you would access and use any single variable of the same type. If you need to access an element in an array, you can use the array name and a constant subscript such as 0 or 1. Alternatively, you can use a variable as a subscript.

❐ Until you become familiar with using arrays, it is easy to make errors when manipulating them. Common errors include forgetting that arrays are zero-based, that is, begin with element 0, and forgetting that the highest legitimate subscript is one less than the array size, that is, accessing locations beyond the limits of the array.

❐ When you want to access all of the elements in an array, a `for` loop is usually convenient. You also might want to access several array elements, but not necessarily all of them. In such a case, a `while` loop provides the most convenient structure.

❐ Parallel arrays are those that contain corresponding elements. You might use a flag variable to indicate you have found a value in an array.

❐ Just as you can create arrays of simple types such as `int` and `double`, you can create arrays of structure objects.

❐ A C++ value expressed within double quotation marks is commonly called a string, or a literal string. You can create a string variable in one of two ways: as an array of characters, or using the `string` class defined in the C++ standard library. An array of characters is called a string when the last usable character in the string is the null character. When strings are declared as character arrays, using them presents some special handling problems. These problems occur when you try to input a string value that includes whitespace, try to assign one string to another using the assignment operator, try to compare strings using the comparison operator, or exceed the bounds of an array.

❐ Pointers are variables that can hold memory addresses. You declare a pointer with a type, just like other variables. To indicate that a variable is a pointer, begin the variable's name with an asterisk.

KEY TERMS

A **memory address** identifies each location where a piece of data can be stored.

Hexadecimal is the base 16 numbering system.

An **array** is a list of individual items that all have the same type.

A **subscript** is a number that indicates the position of the particular array element being used.

An **element** is a single object in an array.

Memory locations beyond an array are **out of bounds** for the array.

Parallel arrays are corresponding arrays in which values in the same relative locations are logically related.

A **flag variable** is one that you use to mark an occurrence.

One-dimensional arrays are arrays whose elements are accessed using a single subscript.

Two-dimensional arrays are accessed using two subscripts; the first represents a row and the second represents a column.

A C++ value expressed within double quotation marks is commonly called a **string**, or a **literal string**.

A **string constant** is a value within double quotes.

The **null character** is represented by the combination '\0' (backslash and zero), or by using the constant NULL that is available if you use the statement `#include<iostream>` at the top of any file you compile.

The **input buffer** is a holding area for waiting input.

The **getline() function** reads characters into an array, up to a size limit or until the newline character is encountered, whichever comes first.

Character-array strings are also called **C-style strings**.

Pointer variables, or **pointers**, are variables that can hold memory addresses.

A **dangling reference** occurs when a pointer is left with a null value.

5

REVIEW QUESTIONS

1. C++ uses the _____ as the address operator.

   a. ampersand

   b. dot

   c. asterisk

   d. percent sign

2. If you declare a variable as `int var = 5;` and the compiler stores `var` at memory address 3000, then the value of `&var` is _____.

   a. 5

   b. 3000

   c. 0

   d. unknown

3. A list of individual items that are stored in adjacent memory locations and all have the same type is called a(n) _____.

   a. class

   b. structure

   c. array

   d. constant

4. You use a subscript to _____.

    a. indicate a position within an array

    b. identify empty classes

    c. define classes

    d. locate a variable at a specific, desired memory address

5. If you declare an array as `int numbers[10];`, then `numbers[1]` represents _____.

    a. the first element in the array

    b. the second element in the array

    c. the address of the array

    d. a new array with one element

6. If you declare an array as `double money[4];`, then `&money[2]` represents _____.

    a. the second element in the array

    b. the third element in the array

    c. the address of the array

    d. the address of the third element in the array

7. If you declare an array as `int scores[100];`, then the highest subscript you should use is _____.

    a. 0

    b. 99

    c. 100

    d. 101

8. If integers take four bytes of storage, then `int days[31];` reserves _____ bytes of memory.

    a. 30

    b. 31

    c. 120

    d. 124

9. If you want to store an integer array named `list` at memory location 2000, you make the statement _____.

    a. `int list[] = 2000;`

    b. `&list[] = 2000;`

    c. `2000 = &int list[0];`

    d. You cannot locate an array at a specific address like 2000.

10. If you declare an array as `double prices[10];`, then the expression `&prices[2]` has the same meaning as the expression _____.

    a. `prices + 2`

    b. `double prices[2];`

    c. `prices[2]`

    d. `&prices + &prices`

11. If you declare an array as `int homeRuns[7];`, then the value of `homeRuns[0]` is _____.

    a. 0

    b. 7

    c. unknown

    d. illegal—you cannot access the value `homeRuns[0]`

12. If you declare an array as `int baskets[10] = {2,4,6};`, then the value of `baskets[0]` is _____.

    a. 0

    b. 2

    c. 4

    d. unknown

13. If you declare an array as `int vals[5];`, then you can double the value stored in `vals[2]` with the statement _____.

    a. `vals[5] = vals[5] * 2;`

    b. `vals = vals * 2;`

    c. `vals[2] *= vals[2];`

    d. `vals[2] *= 2;`

14. When you write a program in C++, an advantage of defining a constant to hold an array size is that _____.

    a. if you ever change the size of the array, you change the constant in a single location

    b. you are prevented from ever changing the program to accommodate a larger array size

    c. you can easily access only part of an array, if necessary

    d. you are not required to provide initial values for the array

5

15. A value that you use as input to stop a loop from continuing to execute is commonly called a(n) _____ value.

    a. guard

    b. sentinel

    c. initializer

    d. default

16. If you create a structure named `Dalmatian` that has a public integer field named `numSpots`, then you can create an array of 101 `Dalmatian` objects with the statement _____.

    a. `Dalmatian [101];`

    b. `Dalmatian [101].numSpots;`

    c. `Dalmatian litter[101];`

    d. `Dalmatian [101] litter;`

17. If you create a structure named `Dalmatian` that has a public integer field named `numSpots`, and you create an array of 101 `Dalmatians` named `litter`, then you can display the number of spots belonging to the first `Dalmatian` with the statement _____.

    a. `cout<<Dalmatian[0].numSpots;`

    b. `cout<<litter[0].numSpots;`

    c. `cout<<Dalmatian.numSpots[0];`

    d. `cout<<litter.numSpots[0];`

18. A C++ value expressed within double quotation marks is commonly called a _____.

    a. clone

    b. structure

    c. rope

    d. string

19. If you create a character array using the statement `char name[] = "Paulette";` then the created string ends with a(n) _____.

    a. null character

    b. period

    c. blank character

    d. exclamation point

20. If you declare an integer pointer as `int *pt;` and you declare an integer variable as `int num;` , then which of the following is legal?

    a. `num = &pt;`

    b. `pt = &num;`

    c. `*num = *pt;`

    d. `&num = pt;`

5

EXERCISES

TIP

Although it would be possible to write each of the following programs using a series of selections, the purpose of these exercises is to give you practice using arrays, and your solutions will be more elegant if you do so.

1. Riley Residence Hall charges different rates for semester room and board based on the number of meals per day the student wants. The semester rate with no meals is $300. With one meal per day, the rate is $450. With two meals per day, the rate is $520, and with three meals per day, the rate is $590. Store these rates in an array. Write a program that allows a student to enter the number of meals desired per day. Output the semester room and board rate. Name the file **SemesterMeals.cpp**.

2. Write a program that allows the user to enter seven `double` values representing store sales for each day of one week. After all seven values are entered, echo them to the screen, and display highest and lowest sales values. Name the file **DailySales.cpp**.

3. Write a program that allows the user to enter 12 `double` values representing store sales for each month of one year. After all 12 values are entered, display each month's sales amount and a message indicating whether it is higher, lower, or equal to the average month's sales amount, Name the file **MonthlySales.cpp**.

4. Write a program that allows the user to enter eight integer values. Display the values in the reverse order of the order they were entered. Name the file **ReverseNumbers.cpp**.

5. Audubon High School is holding a fundraiser. Declare an array that can hold contribution amounts for each of the four classes: freshman, sophomore, junior, and senior. Prompt the user for the four total contribution amounts. Display the four amounts, their sum, and their average. Name the file **FundRaiser.cpp**.

6. Addison High School is holding a fundraiser. The freshmen, sophomores, juniors, and seniors hold a competition to see which class contributes the most money. Write a program that allows you to enter two numbers for each contribution as it comes in—the class of the contributor (1, 2, 3, or 4), and the amount contributed in dollars. For example, perhaps a junior contributes $20. The user would enter a 3 and a 20. The program continues to accept data until the user types 999 for the contributor's class. At that point, data entry is completed, so display the four class totals as well as the number of the class (1, 2, 3, or 4) that contributed the most. Name the file **FundRaiser2.cpp**.

7. Lucy Landlord owns five houses. She refers to these houses by the number of their street address. For example, when referring to "601 Pine," she simply says "601." The houses and their monthly rents are:

Address	Rent
128	$500
204	$750
601	$495
609	$800
612	$940

Write a program into which Lucy can type the address number and then have the program display the appropriate rent. Save the file as **Landlord.cpp**.

8. Speedy Overnight Shipping uses four shipping methods: air, truck, rail, and hand delivery. Write a program that allows the user to type in a shipping method code: 'a', 't', 'r', or 'h'. Have the program display the shipping rate according to the following table:

Method	Rate
a	14.95
t	10.25
r	8.75
h	25.99

Save the file as **Shipping.cpp**.

9. Norm's Custom Furniture Shop takes customer requests for dining room tables in oak, cherry, pine, and mahogany. Their prices are $1500, $1700, $800, and $2000, respectively. Write a program that lets the user continue to enter the initial letter of a table order (for example, 'o' for oak). The user continues to enter letters, using 'z' as a sentinel. If the user enters an invalid wood type, display an error message. Otherwise, display the price and ask for another order. When the user has finished entering data, display a count of each code ordered and the total of all the prices. Save the file as **Furniture.cpp**.

10. Carthage Catering charges different meal prices based on the total number of meals ordered, as follows:

Meals	Price each
1-10	14.99
11-20	12.50
21-39	10.75
40 or more	9.45

Write a program in which the user can enter the number of meals desired. Output is the price per meal and the total bill (meals ordered times price per meal). Save the file as **Catering.cpp**.

11. Write a program that accepts your first name into a character array string variable. Display your name with an asterisk between each letter. For example, if your name is Lisa, display L*i*s*a. Save the file as **AsteriskName.cpp**.

12. Write a program that accepts your first name into a character array string variable. Print your name backward. For example, if your name is Lisa, display asiL. Save the file as **BackwardName.cpp**.

13. Write a program that accepts a word into a character array string variable. Display a count of the number of letters in the word. Also display a count of the number of vowels and the number of consonants in the word. Save the file as **WordStatistics.cpp**.

14. Write a program that asks a user to enter a part number to order. The rules for creating a part number are as follows:

    ❑ The first character must be an 'A', 'B', or 'C'.

    ❑ The second and third characters must be numeric; their value when taken as a pair must be between 10 and 49.

    ❑ The fourth character must be a lowercase letter.

    ❑ The fifth and sixth characters must be numeric; their values when taken as a pair must be between 22 and 66.

    Display a message indicating whether the entered part number is or is not valid.

    Save the file as **PartNumber.cpp**.

15. Write a program asking a user to enter a phone number in the following format: (999)999-9999. In other words: an area code in parentheses, a three-digit number, a dash, and a four-digit number.

    ❑ Display a message if the phone number is entered incorrectly.

    ❑ Display the phone number as a series of ten digits, with all other punctuation removed.

    ❑ Assume area code 920 is being changed to 899. If the entered number is in area code 920, redisplay it with the new area code.

    Save the file as **PhoneNumber.cpp**.

16. Write a program that declares an array of ten integers. Write a loop that accepts ten values from the keyboard, and write another loop that displays the ten values. Do not use any subscripts within the two loops; use pointers only. Save the file as **PointerDemo.cpp**.

17. Create a structure named `Employee`. Include data fields to hold the `Employee`'s first name, last name, and hourly pay rate. Create an array of five `Employee` objects. Prompt the user to enter data for each `Employee`. Then prompt the user for the number of an `Employee` to view (1 through 5), and display the corresponding `Employee`'s data. Save the file as **FiveEmployees.cpp**.

18. Create a structure named `Employee`. Include data fields to hold the `Employee`'s ID number, first name, last name, and hourly pay rate. Create an array of five `Employee` objects. Prompt the user to enter data for each `Employee`. Then prompt the user for the ID number of an `Employee` to view. Display an error message if there is no `Employee` with a matching ID number. Continue to prompt and display until the user enters an appropriate sentinel value. Save the file as **FiveEmployeesWithIDs.cpp**.

19. Create a structure named `Employee`. Include data fields to hold the `Employee`'s ID number, first name, last name, and hourly pay rate. Create an array of five `Employee` objects. Prompt the user to enter data for each `Employee`. Do not allow duplicate ID numbers to be entered. Then prompt the user to choose whether to search for an Employee by (1) ID number, (2) last name, or (3) hourly pay. After the user chooses the field on which to search, prompt the user for the search value. Display an error message if there is no `Employee` with matching criteria, otherwise display all the data for every matching `Employee` (more than one `Employee` might have the same last name or pay rate). Save the file as **FiveEmployeesCompleteSearch.cpp**.

20. Each of the following files in your Chapter05 folder contains syntax and/or logical errors. Determine the problem in each case and fix the program. Save your solutions by adding "Fixed" to the filename, as in **DEBUG5-1Fixed.cpp**.

    a. DEBUG5-1.cpp

    b. DEBUG5-2.cpp

    c. DEBUG5-3.cpp

    d. DEBUG5-4.cpp

CASE PROJECT 1

CASE PROJECTS

You are developing a `Fraction` structure for Teacher's Pet Software. The structure contains three public data fields for whole number, numerator, and denominator. Using the same structure, write a `main()` function that declares an array of five `Fraction` objects. Prompt the user for values for each field of each `Fraction`. Do not allow the user to enter a value of 0 for the denominator of any `Fraction`; for each `Fraction`, continue to prompt the user for a denominator value until a non-zero value is entered. After all the objects have been entered:

❑ Display the whole number, numerator, and denominator for each of the five `Fraction` objects entered.

❑ Next, display the five `Fraction` objects all converted to proper form—that is, if the user entered a value such as 2 6/4, now display it as 3 1/2.

❑ Next, display the sum of all the `Fraction`s and the arithmetic average of all the `Fraction`s.

CASE PROJECT 2

You are developing a **BankAccount** structure for Parkville Bank. The structure contains fields for the account number, the account balance, and the annual interest rate earned on the account. Write a **main()** function in which you create an array of five **BankAccount** objects. Prompt the user for values for all the fields in the five **BankAccounts**. Do not allow two or more accounts to have the same account number. After all the objects have been entered:

❏ Display all the data for all five accounts.

❏ Display the total balance in all five accounts and the average balance.

❏ After displaying the statistics, prompt the user for an account number and display the data for the requested account, or display an appropriate message if no such account number exists. Continue to prompt the user for account numbers until an appropriate sentinel value is entered.

5

6

USING C++ FUNCTIONS

In this chapter, you will:

- ◆ Write simple functions
- ◆ Place functions in files
- ◆ Understand procedural abstraction
- ◆ Learn about scope rules
- ◆ Return values from and pass values to functions
- ◆ Learn to avoid common errors when using functions
- ◆ Use objects as arguments to functions and as return types of functions
- ◆ Pass addresses to functions
- ◆ Use reference variables
- ◆ Pass arrays to functions
- ◆ Use inline functions
- ◆ Use default parameters
- ◆ Overload functions

No matter which computer programming language you use, large programs are usually broken down into modules. This strategy allows you to think of the programming task more abstractly—that is, you establish an overview of the major procedures before you determine the detailed steps within them. Creating modules makes it easier to work with programs, allows several programmers to write or modify modules in the same program, and enables you to create reusable program pieces. In C++, modules are known as functions. In this chapter, you will learn to write functions, return values from functions, and pass values into functions. Additionally, you will learn many of the finer points of using C++ functions, including using inline functions, using default function arguments, and overloading.

WRITING SIMPLE FUNCTIONS

Functions are modules that perform a task or group of tasks. (In other programming languages, the counterpart to a function is known as a **subroutine**, **procedure**, or **method**.) Each function can include its own variables and statements. You can write new C++ functions, and you can use functions that other programmers have written. You have already done both: you have written your own C++ `main()` functions, and in Chapter 5, you learned about the `getline()`, `strcpy()`, and `strcmp()` functions, which can be used when you work with strings. All function names are followed by a set of parentheses.

Using C++ functions is not mysterious; any statement allowed in the `main()` function of a C++ program can be used in any other function. In other words, functions contain variable declarations, input and output statements, decisions, loops, and so on.

In C++, every function has a **header**, or introductory line, that includes three parts:

- The type of object or variable that the function returns. Also known as the **function's return type**—or, more simply, the **function's type**—the returned value is sent from the function in question back to its calling function.

- The name or identifier of the function

- In parentheses, the types and names of any variables that are passed to the function

The simplest functions return nothing and require no arguments. For example, the header for a function named `displayLogo()` that returns nothing and requires no arguments is:

```
void displayLogo()
```

This function header begins with the return type `void`, which means the function will not return any value to any function that calls it. Later you will learn to create functions that do return a value, for example a `double` or an `int`. The function name is `displayLogo()`. You can use any legal C++ identifier as a function name. This function identifier includes empty parentheses, which means that no arguments are passed into the function. Later you will learn how to send values into a function. Starting a function identifier with a lowercase letter is not required, but it is conventional in C++. Note that the function header does not end with a semicolon; it is not a C++ statement. You are already familiar with these concepts from using the `main()` function—its header has a return type (`int`), an identifier (`main`), and a set of parentheses, and it does not end with a semicolon.

After the header, every function contains a pair of curly braces. The function body consists of all the statements between the opening and closing brace. For example, Figure 6-1 shows a complete `displayLogo()` function. This function's purpose is to display a company's name and address. This function body consists of three output statements.

```
void displayLogo()
{
    cout<<"Oriented Objects Inc."<<endl;
    cout<<"100 Division Street"<<endl;
    cout<<"Elk Grove Village, IL"<<endl;
}
```

Figure 6-1 The `displayLogo()` function

If you want to use the **displayLogo()** function to display the string "Hello from:" followed by your company logo, you would write the **main()** function shown in Figure 6-2. Figure 6-3 shows the output.

```
int main()
{
    cout<<"Hello from:"<<endl;
    displayLogo();
}
```

Figure 6-2 A `main()` function that uses the `displayLogo()` function

Figure 6-3 Output of application in Figure 6-2

In Figure 6-2, the highlighted statement **displayLogo();** is known as the **call to the function**—or, more simply, the **function call**. When the call is made, control of the program is transferred to the **displayLogo()** function, and statements written within the **displayLogo()** function execute. When the **displayLogo()** function statements are completed, control of the program returns to **main()**, which then proceeds to the next instruction (if any). When you write the **main()** function, you don't need to know what lines of code have been written within the **displayLogo()** function nor how the function works. The function might contain one long **cout** statement containing all the text plus the three **endl** manipulators, or it might contain 40 or 50 **cout** statements that display only one or two characters each; you don't really need to be concerned with the inner workings of the function as long as the logo displays correctly. To use this function, you need to know only the function's name and the fact that it does not require any values within the parentheses; then you call the function simply by using its name. Programmers say a function is like a **black box**—a device that you cannot look into to discover how it works but that works nonetheless.

PLACING FUNCTIONS WITHIN FILES

You can never place a function within another function. You can *call* a function from within a function, but you cannot place a function's header and body within the body of another function. In other words, after any function's header, you must write the opening curly brace, and you cannot start any new function header until after the closing curly brace of the first function.

When you write a `main()` function, you can place any other function (which you might call a **subfunction**) that is used by `main()` in one of three different locations:

- as part of the same file, before the `main()` function
- as part of the same file, after the `main()` function
- in its own file

Placing a Function as Part of the Same File, Before `main()`

You can choose to place a subfunction in the same file as the `main()` function, before `main()` begins. Figure 6-4 shows a file containing a function named `formLetter()` and a `main()` function that uses it. The `formLetter()` function displays a standard letter sent to families that inquire about a time-share property. The `main()` function prompts the user for a family name and a sales representative name, displays a greeting to the family, displays the form letter, and then signs the letter with the sales representative's name. Figure 6-5 shows a typical execution of the program.

```cpp
#include<iostream>
#include<string>

using namespace std;
void formLetter()
{
   cout<<"  Thank you for your interest in our vacation resort. "<<endl<<
        "Enclosed is a color brochure featuring our beautiful time-"<<endl<<
        "share units. I will be in contact in a few days to see "<<endl<<
        "whether you have any questions."<<endl;
}

int main()
{
   string lastName, salesRep;
   cout<<"Enter name of family ";
   cin>>lastName;
   cout<<"Enter name of sales representative ";
   cin>>salesRep;
   cout<<endl<<"Dear "<<lastName<<" Family:"<<endl;
   formLetter();
   cout<<"Sincerely,"<<endl<<salesRep<<endl;
}
```

Figure 6-4   Program that calls the `formLetter()` function, which is placed before

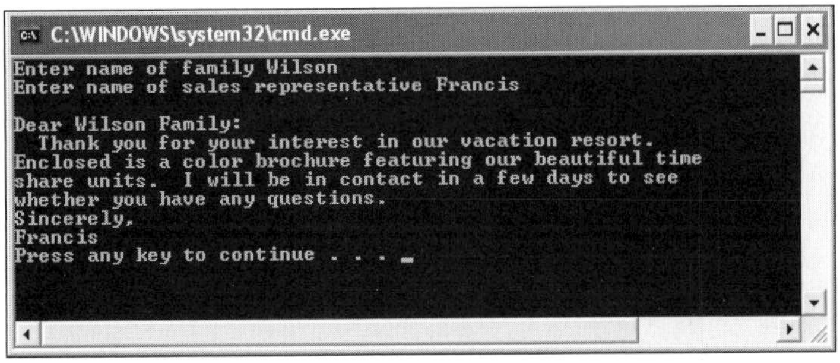

Figure 6-5 Typical execution of program in Figure 6-4

6

In Figure 6-4, notice that the function `formLetter()` is entirely outside of `main()`; its final closing brace occurs before the header of `main()` starts. When this program executes, `main()` begins, the user is prompted for a family name and a sales representative's name, and then the letter greeting to the family is displayed. Then, at the highlighted statement, the `formLetter()` function is called. The program control is transferred to the function, which executes the long `cout` statement that comprises most of the form letter. After the closing curly brace for the `formLetter()` function, control returns to the `main()` function, where "Sincerely," and the sales representative's name are displayed.

Notice in Figure 6-4 that the `formLetter()` function is placed after the `#include<iostream>` and `using namespace std;` statements. If the function was placed before those statements, `cout` and `endl` would not be recognized and compiler error messages would be issued.

Placing a Function as Part of the Same File, After `main()`

You can choose to place a subfunction in the same file as the `main()` function, after `main()` ends. Figure 6-6 shows a file containing a function named `formLetter()` and a `main()` function that uses it. The `formLetter()` function is identical to the one in Figure 6-4, and the `main()` function differs only by the addition of the highlighted statement. The output from the program in Figure 6-6 is identical to the output of the program in Figure 6-4.

The highlighted statement in Figure 6-6 is a **function declaration**, or a **function prototype**; its purpose is to notify the `main()` function that the definition (details) of the named function will come later. Without the function declaration, the `main()` function would not compile, because when the compiler encountered the statement that calls the function, the compiler would not know what to do. In other words, without the function declaration, the `main()` function would "never have heard of" `formLetter()` and would be at a loss as to how to proceed. In Figure 6-4, the `formLetter()` function was defined above `main()`, so the function declaration was not necessary (although it would have been allowed). In Figure 6-6, the function declaration is necessary because the function call comes before the actual function implementation.

```
#include<iostream>
#include<string>

using namespace std;

int main()
{
    string lastName, salesRep;
    void formLetter();
    cout<<"Enter name of family ";
    cin>>lastName;
    cout<<"Enter name of sales representative ";
    cin>>salesRep;
    cout<<endl<<"Dear "<<lastName<<" Family:"<<endl;
    formLetter();
    cout<<"Sincerely,"<<endl<<salesRep<<endl;
}
void formLetter()
{
    cout<<"   Thank you for your interest in our vacation resort. "<<endl<<
        "Enclosed is a color brochure featuring our beautiful time-"<<endl<<
        "share units. I will be in contact in a few days to see "<<endl<<
        "whether you have any questions."<<endl;
}
```

Figure 6-6   Program that calls the `formLetter()` function, which is placed after `main()`

TIP   If you omit the function declaration in the program in Figure 6-6, you receive an error message similar to `'formLetter': identifier not found`. When you call a function that has not been defined, the compiler is unable to use it, even if it appears later in the file.

TIP   Some programmers prefer to declare or prototype functions at the top of the program file, above the `main()` function. Use this format if the standards of your organization or instructor recommend it. Whether the prototype appears before `main()` or within `main()`, it must appear before the function is used.

The highlighted function declaration in Figure 6-6 contains the same parts as the corresponding function header—a return type (**void**) and an identifier (**formLetter()**). This function declaration contains empty parentheses, as does the header of the corresponding function. Later you will learn that if a function requires data between the parentheses in the header, then the function declaration requires data also.

TIP

The header of the `formLetter` function could also be written using `void` between the parentheses, as follows:

`void formLetter(void)`

This format has the same meaning as leaving the parentheses empty. However, you cannot leave the return type `void` off the function header; doing so changes the meaning of the header. With some compilers, the function will not compile without an explicitly named return type; with others, the return type defaults to `int`.

The major difference between the `formLetter()` function header and declaration is that the declaration ends with a semicolon; it is a complete C++ statement and, like all C++ statements, ends with a semicolon. When you declare a variable, for example `int x;`, you use a data type, an identifier, and a semicolon; the same parts are required when you declare a function.

It is possible to avoid creating function declarations by always placing subfunctions prior to any other functions that use them. However, as a C++ programmer, you will encounter function definitions in many programs, so you should recognize and understand them. Additionally, many C++ style guides (you can find many if you search the Web) recommend placing the `main()` function first in a file because it shows the major activities of a program, providing an overview of what the application will accomplish. Anyone reading the program is notified of what the function requires and of what the function returns when it is used later in the program.

Another advantage to including a function's prototype within a program that uses the function is that when you compile the program, the compiler checks to ensure that you are calling the function correctly. If you are not calling the function correctly, you receive an error message from the compiler, and you can correct the error. If you do not prototype a function, the compiler does not detect any error you commit in the way you call the function. You might assume the program is correct, but when you try to run the program (or worse, when someone else tries to run it), a fatal error occurs at execution time. This book will follow the convention of placing `main()` first, at the top of the program file, and including function declarations within `main()`. Subfunctions will follow `main()`, at the bottom of the file.

Placing a Function in Its Own File

You can place any function in its own file, and then include it in an application that needs it. For example, if you write the `formLetter()` function and save it in a file named FormLetter.cpp, you can open another file and write the program shown in Figure 6-7. Along with the iostream file, the FormLetter.cpp file is also included. Because it is included at the top of the file before `main()`, you do not need to declare or prototype the function within `main()` (although you can).

```
#include<iostream>
#include "FormLetter.cpp"
using namespace std;
int main()
{
    string lastName, salesRep;
    cout<<"Enter name of family";
    cin>>lastName;
    cout<<"Enter name of sales representative ";
    cin>>salesRep;
    cout<<"Dear "<<lastName<<" Family: "<<endl;
    formLetter();
    cout<<"Sincerely,"<<endl<<salesRep<<endl;
}
```

Figure 6-7   A main() function file that includes another .cpp file

If you write a program with a main() function, you cannot use #include to include another file that contains its own main() function. Of all the functions included in the final execution of a program, only one can be called main().

In the program in Figure 6-7, if the FormLetter.cpp file does not contain its own #include<iostream> statement, then it is important that iostream is included before FormLetter.cpp is included. Similarly, if the FormLetter.cpp file does not contain a using namespace std; statement, this should also precede the FormLetter.cpp include statement.

Notice that the #include statements used in the program in Figure 6-7 have different formats. When you use the standard files that come with the C++ compiler, angle brackets should surround the header filename. This format tells the compiler to search for the file in the standard folder that holds include files, such as iostream. When working with your own include files, use quotation marks. The compiler then searches in the active folder first. You can also give a full pathname, such as: #include "c:\CIS201\MyProjects\myfile.cpp".

Technically, include statements can be used anywhere in the file as long as they are inserted before their contents need to be accessed. However, it is considered good style to place all include statements at the top of the file. Doing so also prevents side effects that might be caused by "hidden" include statements.

Instead of angle brackets, you can use quotation marks surrounding the standard include filenames, just as you can with your own filenames. Using quotation marks causes the compiler to look for the file in the active folder first, however, and it takes longer to locate the appropriate file. As a result, programmers generally use angle brackets for standard files, and quotation marks for their own files.

When you write C++ programs that employ the input and output objects `cin` and `cout`, you must use `include` files because `cout` and `cin` are defined within the iostream file and cannot be used without it. Similarly, you can create your own `include` files. These files can contain commonly used functions, and might also contain predefined constants. For example, if many programs in your company need to use constant values for `MINIMUM_WAGE`, `STANDARD_WITHHOLDING`, and `UNION_DUES`, then you might want to declare the constants in their own file and use the file within many applications in your organization.

TIP
When you write a function and store it in its own file, you can compile it but you cannot execute it; it does not have a `main()` function. You can only execute applications that contain exactly one `main()` function.

6

When frequently used functions are stored in their own files, they are more easily reusable by different programs. However, the compiler never requires that you place functions in their own files, nor are you required to use a single file. Programmers choose to organize a program's functions in either the same or separate files as they see fit, or as the standards of their organization require.

TIP
You cannot use an `include` statement to include a file containing a function and then use the same name for another function within the file containing your `main()` function. If you do, the compiler issues an error message saying that you have two different bodies for the same function.

TIP
Some programmers write a function such as `displayLogo()` and save it in a file with a .cpp extension. Then they write the prototype and save it in a file with an .h extension, in which the h stands for "header." Finally, they include the .h file in the `main()` function file. This serves to include both the prototype and the function. Because some compiler problems can result when you compile your own files with an .h extension, this book uses .cpp as the extension for all programmer-created files.

Depending on your compiler, you can choose to or are required to use the .h extension for files you create and want to include in other programs. Some programmers prefer using an .h extension for any files that are meant to be included in other programs—in other words, for any files that do not have a `main()` method.

Appendix A explains some special techniques you must use to place functions in their own files when using Microsoft Visual Studio.

UNDERSTANDING PROCEDURAL ABSTRACTION

When you write functions that you include in other programs, you gain several benefits:

- The functions can be written once and subsequently included in any number of programs. For example, a well-written `displayLogo()` function might be used in dozens of programs within an organization.

- When you need to change the contents of the functions you write, you make the change in one location and it is automatically applied in all the programs that use the function. For example, if the company moves to a new location, you change the company address within the `displayLogo()` function. Then the change is automatically executed in every program that uses the function.

- Within a program's `main()` function, you can condense many related actions into a single function call, making the `main()` function easier to write and simpler to read.

- When you use functions that have already been written and tested, you gain an additional benefit: you do not need to worry about how the function works; you simply call it and let it work for you.

Writing a `main()` program function that consists of a series of functional calls means you are using procedural abstraction. **Abstraction** is the process of extracting the relevant attributes of a process or object. It simplifies your concept of the process or object, allowing you to ignore nonessential details.

To some extent, life would be impossible without abstraction. You use all sorts of objects—pencils, keys, forks, and so on—every day, without knowing their molecular structure. You use your telephone, although you might not understand the transmission of voice signals. As a programmer, you have already used objects such as `cin` and `cout` without knowing how each bit of the entered data is stored or displayed.

Using functions is one way to employ procedural abstraction in C++. Writing a to-do list is one way you employ procedural abstraction in everyday life. When you construct a to-do list, you note the main tasks to be accomplished. Figure 6-8 shows a to-do list you might create to remind you of tasks to accomplish during the day.

Write letter to Sunrise Transfer Company

Meeting with Harrison about the museum delivery

Lunch with Gates at 1:00

Figure 6-8   Typical to-do list

When you create a list like the one in Figure 6-8, you don't decide until later whether you'll print the letter to Sunrise Transfer on office letterhead or plain paper, or whether you'll meet with Harrison in your office or in a conference room. You don't even think about what you'll order for lunch let alone how the digestion process works. If you got bogged down in such details, it would take too long to create the list or ever accomplish any of the tasks.

When you write a `main()` function, you can use the names of other functions that perform a variety of tasks. You don't need to worry about the details of the other functions, so the main program is easier to write and easier for others to understand. Anyone reading a payroll program that uses the functions in Figure 6-9 can see the overall purpose of the program. Figure 6-9 shows a `main()` function that does nothing but call other functions. Even without being able to see the implementation of those functions, you can tell what the purpose of the program is.

6

```
int main()
{
    getEmployeeData();
    computeGrossPay();
    computeAndDeductFederalTaxes();
    computeAndDeductLocalTaxes();
    deductInsurancePremium();
    printPaycheck();
}
```

Figure 6-9   A `main()` function employing procedural abstraction

Additionally, you can easily use any of these functions within any other program. By planning your programs with code reusability in mind, you train yourself to think in an object-oriented fashion. When you begin a professional programming career, many of your first assignments require maintaining existing programs—that is, making improvements and modifications to existing systems. Reusing software components is an effective way to facilitate **maintenance programming** and is a hallmark of object-oriented programming.

Whenever possible, you should strive to use functions that have already been written. If a colleague has written, tested, and used a `displayLogo()` function, it is a waste of time for you to reinvent it. If a programmer at another company has written a good `computeAndDeductFederalTaxes()` module, it is probably less expensive to purchase and use it than to develop your own function. Similarly, when you design your own functions, keep the notion of reusability in mind. Future projects will go more smoothly if the functions you write and test now can be reused later.

UNDERSTANDING SCOPE

Some variables can be accessed throughout an entire program, while others can be accessed only in a limited part of the program. The **scope** of a variable defines where it can be accessed in a program. To adequately understand scope, you must be able to distinguish between local and global variables. To avoid conflicts between local and global variables with the same name, you use the scope resolution operator.

Distinguishing between Local and Global Variables

Some named objects in your life are global. At the office, if the conversation turns to Madonna, Oprah, or Cher, you probably assume that your co-workers are talking about the same celebrities that people elsewhere talk about when they use those names. The names are **global** because they are known to people everywhere and always refer to those same celebrities. Similarly, global variables are those that are known to all functions in a program.

Some named objects in your life are **local**; that is, they are known only within a limited scope. When a co-worker speaks of "Jim in Accounting" or "the Taskmaster," you and others in your office understand the reference (and perhaps nod knowingly). People in the company across the street do not recognize these names, however. The references are local, just as some variables are local to a function.

You might have a local co-worker whose name takes precedence over, or **overrides**, a global one. If the sales manager in your company is named Madonna, then co-workers are referring to her, and not the famous performer, when they use the name. Variables work the same way. A variable with a given name inside any function or block overrides any global variable with the same name unless you take special action to specify use of the global variable.

Variables that are declared in a block (that is, between curly braces) are local to that block. They have the following characteristics:

- Local variables are created when they are declared within a block.

- Local variables are known only to that block.

- Local variables cease to exist when their block ends.

You can place pairs of curly braces anywhere within a C++ program, and you always place curly braces at the beginning and end of every function, including `main()`. Therefore, variables declared within a function remain local to that function. Additionally, variables declared within curly braces within any function are local to that block inside that function.

In the program in Figure 6-10, note that the variable **b** comes into existence when it is declared but ceases to exist when the program ends. The variable **c** has a much shorter life; it is only "alive" between the interior, nested braces. In other words, it is **in scope** between the braces. Programmers would also say that **c** is **accessible** only within the braces. After the brace that ends the block in which a variable was declared, the variable is **out of scope**; in other words, it is inaccessible.

```cpp
#include<iostream>
using namespace std;
int main()
{
    int b = 2;   // b comes into existence
    cout<<b;
    {
        int c = 3; // c comes into existence
        cout<<c;
    } // c goes out of scope - you can't use c anymore
    cout<<b;
} // b goes out of scope - you can't use b anymore
```

Figure 6-10   Demonstrating scope

No variable can be accessed outside its scope—that is, beyond the block in which it is declared. You wouldn't try to use a variable before it is declared; similarly, you can't use it after it goes out of scope. Figure 6-11 shows a program that does not compile because it contains several attempts to access a variable outside its scope. Figure 6-11 also shows the use of a global variable named a. Because a is declared outside the `main()` function, a is accessible anywhere in the file.

The program shown in Figure 6-11 demonstrates that you can declare variables prior to or anywhere within a function, but the program does not demonstrate the most preferred technique for declaring variables. C++ programmers usually declare most of their variables inside and at the beginning of the function that uses the variables. That way, anyone reading the program sees all the variables and their types at the beginning of the function's code. A program will compile and run if the variable declarations are scattered throughout the functions, but if the variables are declared in the same place, it is easier to find them and to change their initial values later, if necessary. In addition, when you place the variables together, you can more easily see whether you are inadvertently giving two variables the same name.

Technically, the scope of a variable is the environment in which it is known or visible. The **lifetime** of a variable is the time during which it is defined—from declaration to destruction. Frequently, these periods are the same and the terms are used interchangeably.

```
#include<iostream>
using namespace std;
int a = 1;          // declare a - it is global
int main()
{
    int b = 2;      // declare b
    cout<<b;        // this is OK
    cout<<a;        // so is this
    {
      cout<<c;      // this won't work; c hasn't been declared yet
      int c = 3;    // declare c
      cout<<c;      // c is in scope; this statement is fine
      cout<<b;      // this is fine, too - still inside b's set
                    // of braces
      cout<<a;      // this is fine, too - a is global
    }               // c goes out of scope here
    cout<<b;        // this statement is still fine
                    //   - still within b's braces
    cout<<c;        // this won't work; c is out of scope
    cout<<a;        // this is still fine
}                   // b goes out of scope here
cout<<b;            // won't work - program is over;
                    // b is out of scope
cout<<a;            // won't work - even though a is global
                    // all C++ statements must be in a function
                    // but if you start another function here,
                    // a is still accessible
void anotherFunction()
{
    cout<<a;   // this is OK - a is global to this file
    cout<<b;   // won't work - b does not exist here
}
```

Figure 6-11   An attempted misuse of some variables outside their scope

Every function body is contained within curly braces; every function body is a block. Therefore, all variables that you declare within a function are local to that function. No conflict exists when different functions contain variables with the same identifier, just as few problems exist when different families each have a son named Michael. Figure 6-12 shows an application containing two functions, doArithmetic() and main(). Each contains a variable named num, which is local to the function in which it is declared; each version of num holds its own value. Even though they are declared within the same file, the two num identifiers designate completely different variables stored at separate memory addresses.

```
#include<iostream>
#include<string>

using namespace std;

int main()
{
  void doArithmetic();
  int num = 10;
  cout<<"At the start of main(), num is "<<num<<endl;
  doArithmetic();
  cout<<"At the end of main(), num is "<<num<<endl;
}
void doArithmetic()
{
  int num = 44;
  cout<<"At the start of doArithmetic(), num is "<<num<<endl;
  num = num + 5;
  cout<<"At the end of doArithmetic(), num is "<<num<<endl;
}
```

Figure 6-12   Two functions containing a variable with the same identifier

Figure 6-13   Output of application in Figure 6-12

In the `doArithmetic()` and `main()` functions in Figure 6-12, no conflict arises between the two uses of `num`. Each function can use `num` as a variable name without destroying any values in the other. Just as two people can have the same name, two variables at different memory addresses can have identical names. But just as you develop different names for two Sue's who work in your office (maybe calling one Susie, or perhaps using one's surname), you must not use the same name for two variables if they reside within the same function. A major advantage of using local variables is that many programmers can work on a large program, each writing separate functions, and they can use any variable names inside their own functions. If they happen to choose the same identifiers as other programmers, it doesn't matter.

Using the Scope Resolution Operator

If you choose to create a global variable, and a local variable with the same name exists, the local variable always takes precedence over the global one. For example, the following code acts as the comment indicates; when the `age` variable is displayed, it is the local version that is used.

```
int age = 30;
int main()
{
    int age = 45;
    cout<<age;    // 45 is displayed
}
```

You can use a global variable even when a local variable with the same name exists by using the **scope resolution operator (::)**. Place this operator directly before the variable name to access the global version. Figure 6-14 shows an example of how you can use the scope resolution operator to access a global variable that has the same name as a local variable. Within `main()`, `age` refers to the local value, 45. When you use the scope resolution operator, you access `::age`, which is 30. This situation is analogous to referring to two Sue's in your company as "Sue" and "Sue from Marketing." The scope resolution operator serves to add information to and qualify a global name when the shorter version of that name conflicts with a local name.

```
#include<iostream>
using namespace std;
int age = 30;
int main()
{
    int age = 45;
    cout<<age;    // 45 is displayed
    cout<<::age;  // 30 is displayed
}
```

Figure 6-14   Demonstrating the scope resolution operator

Although you can declare global variables in any file, it is almost always considered better form to use local variables rather than global ones. This strategy represents a preliminary example of **encapsulation**, or data hiding. Think of local variables as being in a capsule, separated from all other functions, which then cannot harm the values stored in the local variables. Beginning programmers often think it is easier to use global variables rather than local ones because global variables are known to all functions. However, using global variables over local variables is actually disadvantageous for the following reasons:

- If variables are global in a file and you reuse any functions in a new program, the variables must be redeclared in the new program. They no longer "come along with" the function.

- Global variables can be altered by any function, leading to errors. In a program with many functions, finding the function that caused an error can prove difficult.

This book will not use global variables in any further examples; always using local variables is better practice. However, using global variables here has shown you one use of the scope resolution operator. The scope resolution operator used here is unary, meaning it takes only one argument—the identifier to its right. You will use the binary scope resolution operator extensively when you start to create classes in Chapter 7.

RETURNING VALUES FROM FUNCTIONS

The type of value that a function returns is also known as the function's type (or the function's return type). Except for `main()`, the functions you have used so far have been type `void`; that is, functions such as the `displayLogo()` function do not return anything to the function that calls them. Sometimes, however, a function should send a value back to the calling module, or **return** a value.

If you write a function that asks users to input their middle initial from the keyboard, you might prototype the function as `char askUserForInitial();`. This prototype indicates that the function returns a character value to the program that calls it. A programmer would say that `askUserForInitial()` is a function of type `char`—or, more simply, that it is a `char` function. Similarly, a function that computes a tax amount might return a `double`. Its prototype might be `double figureTaxes();` and it is a function of type `double`.

Functions used for data entry are typical of the types of functions that return values to a `main()` function or other calling function. For example, the purpose of the function `askUserForInitial()` is to prompt a user for a character entry that the `main()` function needs. The `main()` function shown in Figure 6-15 uses the `askUserForInitial()` function, which is written below the `main()` function. Figure 6-16 shows a typical program execution.

```
#include<iostream>
using namespace std;
// main program
int main()
{
    char usersInitial;
    char askUserForInitial();
    usersInitial = askUserForInitial();
    cout<<"Your initial is "<<usersInitial<<endl;
}
// subfunction
char askUserForInitial()
{
    char letter;
    cout<<"Please type your initial and press Enter "<<endl;
    cin>>letter;
    return letter;
}
```

Figure 6-15 Program that calls `askUserForInitial()`

Figure 6-16 Output of program shown in Figure 6-15

In Figure 6-15, the main program holds two declarations: one for the character variable, usersInitial, and one for the character function, askUserForInitial(). Next, in the shaded statement, the program calls the askUserForInitial() function. The right-most arrow in the figure shows how the function call transfers the logical flow to the sub-function. The function prompts the user for and receives a character. The character is returned from the function with the return statement. As the left arrow in the figure shows, this return value is sent back to the main() function, where it is assigned to the usersInitial variable. Then, the returned value is displayed.

The function askUserForInitial() declares a local variable named letter. At the prompt, the user types a character, which is stored in letter. The variable letter is local to the function; it goes out of existence when the function ends. Before the func-tion ends, however, a copy of the contents of letter is returned to the main() func-tion, where it is assigned to another variable, usersInitial.

TIP

The statement return letter; in Figure 6-15 can be alternatively written with parentheses as return(letter);. Both statements work identically.

TIP

Sometimes you can use a function value directly without assigning it to a vari-able. For example, you might use a numeric function's value in an arithmetic statement. If getAge() is a function that returns an integer, then you can write a subsequent statement such as the following:

```
int ageNextYear = getAge() + 1;
```

It is perfectly legal to call a function that returns a value and then not use the value. For example, the main() function in Figure 6-17 calls askUserForInitial(), but neither displays its return value nor assigns it to any variable. When the main() function calls askUserForInitial(), the prompt appears and the user can enter a character. However, when the program displays its output, usersInitial does not contain the character input by the user; instead, usersInitial contains whatever values were stored in that location by chance when the variable was declared. The programmer surely meant to yet did not assign the return value of askUserForInitial() to the usersInitial variable prior to displaying. There might be other occasions in which you want to execute the statements in a function but are unconcerned with the return value. In those cases, you are free to not use the value.

```
#include<iostream>
using namespace std;
int main()
{
    char usersInitial;
    char askUserForInitial();
    askUserForInitial();
    cout<<"Your initial is "<<usersInitial<<endl;
            // displays garbage
}
```

Figure 6-17   A legal but pointless use of `askUserForInitial()`

Just as any variable in a C++ program can have only one data type, each function in a C++ program can have only a single type (which is its return type), and each time a function executes, it can return only one value. (The value returned might be a simple data type, such as a **char**, but it could be a complex data type, such as a **struct** object.)

If you write a function using a return type, you must use a return statement in the function, and it must return a value of the designated type. The exception to this rule is the **main()** function, which, in many compilers, does not require a return statement even though you declare it to be an **int** function. If you prefer, you can include a statement at the end of every **int main()** function you write. Many programmers use **return 0** to indicate that the **main()** function ended normally.

A function can contain more than one **return** statement, but when that statement executes, it can return only one value. At that point, the function ends, and the function cannot return any additional values. For example, each of the two functions shown in Figures 6-18 and 6-19 returns an integer. The purpose of each function is to return the larger of two values passed to the function (or the second value if the two values are equal).

```
int findLarger()
{
    int x, y;
    cout<<"Enter a value ";
    cin>>x;
    cout<<"Enter another value ";
    cin>>y;
    if(x > y)
        return x;
    else
        return y;
}
```

Figure 6-18   Inferior version of `findLarger()`

```
int findLarger()
{
    int x, y;
    int larger;
    cout<<"Enter a value ";
    cin>>x;
    cout<<"Enter another value ";
    cin>>y;
    if(x > y)
        larger = x;
    else
        larger = y;
    return larger;
}
```

Figure 6-19   Preferred version of `findLarger()`

The version of the `findLarger()` function in Figure 6-18 contains two `return` statements. If the first `return` statement executes, control returns to the calling program immediately and the second `return` never executes. The first version of the function in Figure 6-18 works correctly, but the second version, in Figure 6-19, demonstrates superior style. The second version contains a local variable named `larger`. The variable is assigned the larger of `x` and `y` (or the value of `y` if the two variables are equal), and this value is returned to the calling function via a single `return` statement. The two versions of the function operate identically, and you might see functions written by other programmers that contain multiple `return` statements. However, for clarity and style, many programmers prefer to see a single `return` statement as the last statement in a function body. When you glance at a function, it is clearest to know what is returned when you can see a single `return` statement at the end. If the function contains multiple `return` statements, it is easier to make mistakes over time, as the function is modified and new statements are added, possibly leaving code at the end of the function that never executes (called **dead code**).

TIP   When functions have a single entry and exit point, they reflect a rule of structured programming that says every logical sequence selection and loop should have only one entry and exit point.

TIP   If a function contains several return statements, each must still return a value that is consistent with the function's type.

PASSING VALUES TO FUNCTIONS

Many of the real-world functions you perform require that you provide information. A particular task might always be carried out in the same way, but with specific data. For example, all phone calls are placed in the same manner, but you supply a phone number to the process. All doctor's appointments are made in the same way, but you supply a date and time. Similarly, many C++ functions need specific information from the `main()` or other functions that call them.

Consider a program that computes the amount of sales tax due on an item. After you prompt the user for a price, you want a function named `computeTax()` to calculate and display the tax amount that is due. You can create the `computeTax()` function as a type `void` function, as it does not need to return anything to the `main()` function. It does, however, need to obtain an item's price from the `main()` function. A function that obtains data from another function does so by accepting one or more **parameters** from the sending function. If the price that will be sent into the function is a `double`, then the `computeTax()` function requires a parameter of type `double`.

You can write the definition, or prototype, for the `computeTax()` function that requires a `double` parameter and returns nothing in one of two ways:

```
void computeTax(double);
```

or

```
void computeTax(double price);
```

The prototype's parentheses enclose a list of the variable types that are passed to the function; in this case the `computeTax()` function receives just one type of variable, a `double`. You can choose to list just the type, or you can give the variable a descriptive name, such as `price`. If you use a name such as `price`, you do so to provide **documentation**—that is, to help someone reading the function prototype understand the function's purpose. The name `price` is simply descriptive; it does not have to match any variable name used anywhere else in the program. In a prototype, variable names actually play the same role as comments.

TIP It makes sense that the names in a function definition, if any, need not match anything else. You might call the function multiple times using many different variables, and at most, just one could have the same identifier. In other words, a function that adds two integers should work for any two integers. Thus, `void sumFunction(int a, int b);` can be used with variables named a and b, c and d, `score1` and `score2`, or `januaryTotal` and `februaryTotal`.

You write the function header for the `computeTax()` function as follows:

```
void computeTax(double price)
```

The function header requires a return type (in this case, `void`), an identifier (in this case, `computeTax`), and a parameter list, including a data type and an identifier for each parameter (in this case, `double price`). Unlike with the definition, or prototype, the function header requires an identifier for each parameter.

If more than one argument is to be passed into a function, you provide a list of arguments and separate them with commas. A type must be listed for each variable that is passed, even if two or more variables have the same type. For example, a function that computes the sum of four integers can have the prototype:

```
void computeSumOfFourIntegers(int, int, int, int);
```

or

```
void computeSumOfFourIntegers(int firstVal, int secondVal,
        int thirdVal, int lastVal);
```

Using either of these prototypes, the same function can have either of the following headers. In other words, the identifiers for the arguments do not have to match any identifiers used in the prototype.

```
void computeSumOfFourIntegers(int firstVal, int secondVal,
        int thirdVal, int lastVal)
void computeSumOfFourIntegers(int w, int x, int y, int z)
```

Figure 6-20 shows a complete program that uses the `computeTax()` function, and Figure 6-21 shows the results of a typical execution of the program. After the user enters the `price` in `main()`, the `price` is passed to the `computeTax()` function. You pass a value to a function when you place the value within the parentheses in the function call. In a function call, the passed value is also called an **argument** to the function. As the arrow in Figure 6-20 shows, the value of price is sent to the `computeTax()` function. Within the function, the value of `price` is stored in the function's parameter, which is a local variable named `amount`. After being declared within the `computeTax()` function header, the variable named `amount` is used twice—within a multiplication calculation, and again as part of the output statement.

```cpp
#include<iostream>
using namespace std;
int main()
{
    double price;
    void computeTax(double);
    cout<<"Enter an item's price ";
    cin>>price;
    computeTax(price);
}

void computeTax(double amount)
{
    double tax;
    const double TAX_RATE = 0.07;
    tax = amount * TAX_RATE;
    cout<<"The tax on "<<amount<<" is "<<tax<<endl;
}
```

Figure 6-20   Program using the `computeTax()` function

```
C:\WINDOWS\system32\cmd.exe
Enter an item's price 12.50
The tax on 12.5 is 0.875
Press any key to continue . . .
```

Figure 6-21   Typical execution of program in Figure 6-20

TIP   Besides being referred to as an argument, a parameter used in a function call is known as an **actual parameter** because it holds the value that will actually be used by the function. In the `main()` function in Figure 6-20, when the `price` variable is passed to the `computeTax()` function, `price` is an actual parameter. Any variable listed in a function header is known as a **formal parameter**.

TIP

When you use a function such as `computeTax()`, you do not have to pass a variable. Instead, you could pass a constant, as in the statement `computeTax(22.55);`. The `computeTax()` function must receive a `double`, but it does not matter whether the `double` is a variable or a constant. In fact, if you had a function that returned a `double` (in other words, was type `double`), you could use its call as a function argument. If you wrote a function with the prototype `double getPrice();`, then you could call `computeTax()` with the following statement:

`computeTax(getPrice());`

In this case, `getPrice()` would execute and its returned value would be sent to `computeTax()`.

In the program in Figure 6-20, the value of `price` is passed to the `computeTax()` function, where the variable `amount`, which is local to the function, takes on the value of `price`. The variable `amount` holds a copy of the value of `price`, but `amount` is a separate variable with its own memory address. Within the `computeTax()` function, if you added statements to alter the value of `amount`—for example, assigning a new value to it—the variable `price` in the `main()` method would retain its original value and be completely unaffected.

AVOIDING COMMON ERRORS WHEN USING FUNCTIONS

Beginning programmers often make several types of errors when they declare, call, and write functions. These errors include:

- Neglecting to make sure the function declaration, header, and call agree
- Indicating a parameter type or return type in a function call
- Ignoring the order of parameters
- Assuming that an unused return value has an effect

Pitfall: Neglecting to make sure the function declaration, header, and call agree

A function's declaration must agree with the function header in terms of return type, identifier, and argument list, and any function calls must agree with the declaration. If you attempt to call a function you have not defined, you might receive an error message that refers to an "unresolved external symbol." This means that when the compiler could not find the function you were attempting to call within your file, the compiler looked for a function to use that was external to your file. Still not finding a match, the error message was issued.

Pitfall: Indicating a parameter type in a function call

When you call a function, you do not include the argument type. For example, when you call the `computeTax()` function, you cannot indicate the type for the `price` parameter. In other words, if you have defined `computeTax()` as `void computeTax(double);`, then the following is an illegal function call:

```
computeTax(double price);
```

The function declaration indicates the type expected, and the function header specifies which, if any, types are accepted. Only the variable names or constant values that actually represent data to be sent to the function are needed in the function call.

Pitfall: Indicating a return type in a function call

When you call a function, you do not include the function's return type. For example, when you call the `computeTax()` function, the following is an illegal call:

```
void computeTax(price);
```

The function header and declaration both include the return type, but the call does not.

Pitfall: Ignoring the order of parameters

You can pass any number of arguments to a function, as long as the function is prepared to receive them. You must make sure to use the correct order when you pass arguments to a function. If you do not pass arguments in the correct order, either your program will not compile or, worse, you will cause a difficult-to-locate logical error.

For example, suppose you write a `computeAndDisplayTax()` function that accepts a price of an item and a tax rate. You can write the function declaration as:

```
void computeAndDisplayTax(double price, double taxRate);
```

When you call the `computeAndDisplayTax()` function, you must make sure you pass the price first and the tax rate second. For example, to compute a 5 percent tax on $100.00, you write `computeTax(100.00, .05);`. It is legal to call the new `computeAndDisplayTax()` function with any two `double` arguments, so `computeAndDisplayTax(.05, 100.00);` executes, but you are calculating a 10,000 percent tax on five cents.

In addition to passing arguments in the correct order, make sure that the arguments you pass to a function are the correct type. If you write a function with the following prototype and you call it with arguments that are not the right type in the right order, then your program will not execute correctly:

```
void determineFinalGrade(int quizScore,
    char termPaperGrade, double examPoints);
```

For example, if you use `determineFinalGrade(94.5, 35, 'A');` your final grade results will most likely be inaccurate.

TIP

> In C++, a value you pass to a function will be cast to the correct type if possible. For example, you can pass an integer to a function that expects a double argument because C++ automatically promotes integers to doubles. However, if you send a variable to a function and that variable cannot be automatically cast to the expected argument, data may be lost, incorrect results may be produced, or the program may refuse to run.

Pitfall: Assuming that an unused return value has an effect

6

You are never required to use the value returned from a function. Intending to use the value but failing to do so is a logical error. When you call a function, do not assume that any actions within the function have an effect in `main()`. If a function returns a value and you want to use that value in the calling function, then you must explicitly do so.

USING OBJECTS AS ARGUMENTS TO FUNCTIONS AND AS RETURN TYPES OF FUNCTIONS

A function can contain a variety of combinations of actions. Some functions contain local variables declared within the function body. Some functions return and receive nothing. Others return values, receive values, or both. Functions may receive any number of variables as parameters but may return, at most, only one variable of one type.

Any action you can perform with a simple, scalar variable within a function—such as declaring the variable locally, using it as an argument, or returning it—you can also perform with an object. The program shown in Figure 6-22 shows a `Customer` structure containing two public fields, `custId` and `custName`. A `main()` function declares a `Customer` object and two functions. One function takes no arguments but gets data for a `Customer`, returning a filled `Customer` object to the `main()` function, and one function takes a `Customer` argument and displays its values. The `main()` function itself is very short; after listing the declarations, it simply calls each function once. Figure 6-23 shows a typical execution.

```
#include<iostream>
#include<string>
using namespace std;
struct Customer
{
    int custId;
    string custName;
};
```

Figure 6-22   Using the `Customer` structure with functions

```
int main()
{
    Customer oneCustomer;
    Customer getCustomerData();
    void displayCustomerData(Customer);

    oneCustomer = getCustomerData();
    displayCustomerData(oneCustomer);
}
Customer getCustomerData()
{
    Customer cust;
    cout<<"Enter customer ID number ";
    cin>>cust.custId;
    cout<<"Enter customer's last name ";
    cin>>cust.custName;
    return cust;
}
void displayCustomerData(Customer customer)
{
    cout<<"ID is #"<<customer.custId<<
        " and name is "<<customer.custName<<endl;
}
```

Figure 6-22   Using the `Customer` structure with functions (continued)

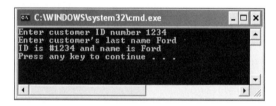

Figure 6-23   Typical execution of program in Figure 6-22

In the `getCustomerData()` function shown in Figure 6-22, a local `Customer` object is created just for purposes of data entry. After the user fills the `custId` and `custName` fields of the local `Customer` object, a copy of the object is returned to `main()`, where it is stored in `main()`'s `oneCustomer` object. This object can then be passed to the `displayCustomerData()` function. This function receives a copy of the `oneCustomer` object and refers to it by the local name `customer`. Within the `displayCustomerData()` function, the fields of the `customer` object are used to display the data.

TIP

Any `struct` field can be passed to or returned from a function, just like its scalar counterpart. For example, a function that accepts an integer argument will accept an integer declared as `int x;` as well as a `struct` object field, such as `oneCustomer.custId`.

Up to this point, you might not have seen much advantage to declaring structures over simple variables, but when you use structures with functions, you get at least two benefits. First, when you group individual fields into a structure, it is easier to pass them all into a function as a unit. Without structures, you would have to pass in each of the individual fields separately. Second, when you return a structure from a function, you can pass back a group of values; because only one value can be returned from a function, there would be no way to return all the field values separately.

When you pass a structure object to a function, the copy made is a **memberwise copy**; that is, if the object contains several fields, the value of each of those members is copied to the formal parameter in the function header.

6

PASSING ADDRESSES TO FUNCTIONS

Like variable values, variable addresses may also be passed to and returned from functions. Passing an address to a function avoids having the function copy the passed object, a process that takes time and memory. Instead, when you pass an address to a function, the function has access to the original variable location. You might also choose to pass addresses to a function if you want a function to change multiple values. (Recall that a function can return only one value—and that value must be the function's type.) If you pass addresses to a function, however, the function can change the contents at those actual memory addresses, eliminating the need to return any values at all.

Recall that you can access any variable's value by using the variable's name. In contrast, inserting an ampersand in front of its name allows you to access a variable's address. Also recall that you can create a pointer variable to hold a memory address; when you declare a pointer, you insert an asterisk in front of the variable name.

Consider a function that determines the result of an integer division, as well as its remainder. You can write two functions to perform the two tasks, making two separate function calls, as shown in Figure 6-24.

The program in Figure 6-24 calls the `getDiv()` function to get the result when the two passed values are divided, and then calls the `getRemainder()` function to get the remainder. To get the two results, both functions are required because each can return only one value.

As an alternative to the program shown in Figure 6-24, you can pass the memory addresses of the variables that hold the results, making a single function call. Figure 6-25 shows a program in which four arguments are passed to a `getResults()` function. Two are the numbers to be divided, and the other two are integer pointers.

```
#include<iostream>
using namespace std;
int main()
{
    int a = 19, b = 7, dividend, modulus;
    int getDiv(int, int);
    int getRemainder(int, int);
    dividend = getDiv(a, b);
    modulus = getRemainder(a, b);
    cout<<"Dividend is "<<dividend<<
            " and modulus is "<<modulus<<endl;
}
int getDiv(int num1, int num2)
{
    int result;
    result = num1 / num2;
    return result;
}
int getRemainder(int num1, int num2)
{
    int result;
    result = num1 % num2;
    return result;
}
```

Figure 6-24   Program that calls two functions to get two results

```
#include<iostream>
using namespace std;
int main()
{
    int a = 19, b = 7, dividend, modulus;
    void getResults(int, int, int*, int*);
    getResults(a, b, &dividend, &modulus);
    cout<<"Dividend is "<<dividend<<" and modulus is "<<
        modulus<<endl;
}
void getResults(int num1, int num2, int *oneAddress,
    int *anotherAddress)
{
    *oneAddress = num1 / num2;
    *anotherAddress = num1 % num2;
}
```

Figure 6-25   Program that calls one function to get two results

In the program shown in Figure 6-25, four items are passed to the `getResults()` function: the value of a, the value of b, the address of `dividend`, and the address of `modulus`. In turn, the `getResults()` function receives four items:

- `num1`, which holds a copy of the value of a

- `num2`, which holds a copy of the value of b

- `oneAddress`, a pointer variable that holds the address of `dividend`

- `anotherAddress`, a pointer variable that holds the address of `modulus`

Within the header of the `getResults()` function in Figure 6-25, the first two parameters are declared as simple integers, but `oneAddress` and `anotherAddress` are declared as pointers, using the asterisk notation. Within the function, when values are stored in `oneAddress` and in `anotherAddress`, you use the asterisk notation with those variables to indicate "the contents at" those addresses. When the arithmetic is performed and the values are stored at `oneAddress` and `anotherAddress`, the values of `dividend` and `modulus` in the `main()` function are also changed because they have the same address. Within the `getResults()` function, the contents pointed to by the `oneAddress` pointer are changed to hold the results of the division operation. Similarly, the contents at the address pointed to by the `anotherAddress` pointer are changed to hold the results of the modulus operation. The `getResults()` function does not need to pass any values back to the `main()` function because the contents of the variables stored at the `dividend` and `modulus` addresses have been altered directly by the `getResults()` function.

Passing an address of a variable to a function has a number of advantages:

- If the function is intended to alter the variable, it alters the actual variable, not a copy of it; therefore, you do not need to return any values.

- You can write the function to alter multiple values. Functions can return only a single value, but they can alter many values if you pass their addresses.

- When you send the address of a variable to a function, the function does not need to make a copy of the variable, a process that takes time (albeit a short time for a single variable).

There are some disadvantages to passing an address of a variable to a function:

- The syntax of using the & and * is awkward and more difficult to understand than using plain variable names.

- Even if a function is not intended to alter a variable, it may do so when it has access to a variable's address.

To take advantage of the benefits of passing addresses to functions, storing them in pointer variables and likewise eliminating the disadvantages, you can use reference variables and constant arguments.

USING REFERENCE VARIABLES WITH FUNCTIONS

A criminal who uses two names is said to have an alias. To create a second name for a variable in a program, you can also generate an **alias**, or an alternative name. In C++, a variable that acts as an alias for another variable is called a **reference variable**, or simply a reference.

Declaring Reference Variables

You declare a reference variable by placing a type and an ampersand in front of a variable name, as in `double &cash;`, and assigning another variable of the same type to the reference variable. For example, suppose you declare a `double` named `someMoney` and a reference named `cash`. When you write the following statements, `someMoney` and `cash` refer to the same variable:

```
double someMoney;
double &cash = someMoney;
```

After these statements, any change to `cash` modifies `someMoney`, and any change to `someMoney` alters `cash`. If you assign a value to either `cash` or `someMoney`, both hold the same value.

TIP You can also declare a reference variable by inserting a space between the ampersand and the reference: `double& dough;`. This format makes sense if you think of dough as "type double reference" or "type double address."

A reference variable is not the same as a pointer. A reference variable refers to the same memory address as does a variable, and a pointer holds the memory address of a variable. There are two major differences between reference variables and pointers:

- Pointers are more flexible.

- Reference variables are easier to use.

Pointers are more flexible because they can store the address of any variable of the correct type. You declare a pointer to a variable by placing an asterisk in front of the pointer's name. You assign a value to a pointer by inserting an ampersand in front of the name of the variable whose address you want to store in the pointer. If you declare an integer pointer named `pnt` and then declare three integers named `x`, `y`, and `z`, you can assign the address of any of the three integers to `pnt`. For example, each statement in Figure 6-26 is a legal statement.

```
int *pnt;
int x = 4, y = 12, z = 35;
pnt = &x;
cout<<*pnt<<endl;     // output is 4
pnt = &y;
cout<<*pnt<<endl;     // output is 12
pnt = &z;
cout<<*pnt<<endl;     // output is 35
```

Figure 6-26   Using a pointer to hold different values

You cannot always substitute reference variables for pointers. Pointers are more flexible. For example, in Chapter 5, you learned that you can perform arithmetic with pointers, referencing successive memory addresses.

Figure 6-26 shows that when you want to use the value stored in the pointer (for example, to display it), you must use the asterisk to **dereference** the pointer, or use the value to which it points instead of the address it holds.

Passing Variable Addresses to Reference Variables

Reference variables are easier to use than pointers because you don't need any extra punctuation to work with their values. You declare a reference variable by placing an ampersand in front of the variable's name. You assign a value to a reference variable by using another variable's name. The value in the reference is then accessed by using the variable's name. For example, Figure 6-27 shows statements that display reference variable values.

```
int x = 4, y = 12, z = 35;
int &ref = x;
cout<<ref<<endl;  // output is 4
ref = y;
cout<<ref<<endl;  // output is 12
ref = z;
cout<<ref<<endl;  // output is 35
```

Figure 6-27   Using a reference

It can be easier to use a reference variable than a pointer when you want to pass the address of a variable to a function, thus allowing the function to alter the variable's memory location and to save the overhead incurred in making a copy. To work with the stored value in a reference variable, you don't need the asterisk notation.

You must assign a value to a reference variable when you declare it. The following is illegal:

```
int &badReference;   // no assignment — illegal
```

Figure 6-28 shows a program that calls a `getResults()` function that serves the same purpose as the function in Figure 6-25. In this program, the `getResults()` function has been rewritten to accept two references for the `dividend` and `modulus` in place of the two pointers in the original version. Notice the following highlighted differences between this version and the one in Figure 6-25:

- In the function prototype, ampersands are used in place of the asterisks.

- In the function call, the variable names are used without address operators.

- In the `getResults()` function header, ampersands are used in place of the asterisks.

- In the assignment statements within the `getResults()` function, no punctuation is necessary with the variables that hold the results.

```cpp
#include<iostream>
using namespace std;
int main()
{
   int a = 19, b = 7, dividend, modulus;
   void getResults(int, int, int&, int&);
   getResults(a, b, dividend, modulus);
   cout<<"Dividend is "<<dividend<<" and modulus is "<<
      modulus<<endl;
}
void getResults(int num1, int num2, int &oneAddress,
   int &anotherAddress)
{
   oneAddress = num1 / num2;
   anotherAddress = num1 % num2;
}
```

Figure 6-28 Using reference variables in a function

When you pass a variable's address to a function, whether with a pointer or with a reference, any changes to the variable made by the function also alter the actual variable in the calling function, eliminating the need to return a value. In addition, the function no longer needs to make a copy of the variable. Passing an address is a double-edged sword, however. A function that receives an address may change the variable—but sometimes you might not want the variable changed. To pass an address (thus eliminating the copy of a variable) and still protect the variable from change, you may pass a reference as a constant.

TIP   Although you may pass a reference to a function as a constant (ensuring that the value will not be altered within the function), programmers do not frequently bother with this added modifier. In the C language, which preceded C++, const was not available as a keyword, so many present-day C++ programmers are not accustomed to using const. Not allowing a function to alter a parameter that should not be altered is following the **principle of least privilege**. This programming principle says you should give a process only the authority it needs to accomplish its job. You should adopt the style your supervisor or instructor prefers.

Figure 6-29 shows a complete program that prototypes and calls a function with a constant reference. The function, named `computeDiscountedPrice()`, computes a 20 percent discount on prices over $100, and a 10 percent discount on prices that are $100 or less. When the `main()` part of the program passes two arguments to the function, both are addresses, but the `price` variable is passed as a constant; it will not be altered by the function. Passing `price`'s address eliminates the necessity of making a copy of the variable, but the function's price is unchangeable, eliminating possible errors. The address of `priceAfterDiscount` is not passed as a constant; its contents should and will be changed by the `computeDiscountedPrice()` function. Figure 6-30 shows a typical execution of the program.

```cpp
#include<iostream>
using namespace std;
int main()
{
    double price, priceAfterDiscount;
    void computeDiscountedPrice(const double&, double&);
    cout<<"Enter the price of the item ";
    cin>>price;
    computeDiscountedPrice(price, priceAfterDiscount);
    cout<<"The original price is $"<<price<<endl;
    cout<<"Your final price after discount is $"<<
        priceAfterDiscount<<endl;
}
void computeDiscountedPrice(const double &itemPrice,
    double &result)
{
    const double CUT_OFF = 100.00;
    const double HIGH_DISCOUNT = 0.80;
    const double LOW_DISCOUNT = 0.90;
    if(itemPrice > CUT_OFF)
        result = itemPrice * HIGH_DISCOUNT;
    else
        result = itemPrice * LOW_DISCOUNT;
}
```

Figure 6-29   Using a constant reference as a function argument

Figure 6-30   Typical execution of program in Figure 6-29

TIP

The time and memory saved by passing a reference to a single variable a single time are minimal. However, if you apply the same techniques when passing many large objects that contain many fields, the time and memory savings are substantial.

In the program in Figure 6-29, if you removed the **const** modifier from both the declaration and header of **computeDiscountedPrice()**, you would not notice any difference in the execution of the program. However, using the **const** modifier for all variables passed to functions when the variable should not change within the function is considered good form. This practice is safe because the compiler checks to ensure that the variable is not changed inadvertently. In addition, this tactic makes your intentions clear to anyone reading your program.

TIP

If a function receives a variable as a constant but then passes the variable to another function that does not receive the variable as a constant, most compilers will not issue an error message. You may inadvertently change a variable that should remain constant; as a programmer, it is your responsibility to declare variables as constants explicitly within any function where you want them to remain constant.

TIP

The program in Figure 6-29 could be rewritten so that the discounted price is not passed in as a reference but rather is returned from the function. When you write programs, you always have many possible ways to accomplish the same results.

PASSING ARRAYS TO FUNCTIONS

An array name actually represents a memory address. Thus, an array name is a pointer. The subscript used to access an element of an array indicates how much to add to the starting address to locate a value.

The array declaration **int nums[15];** declares an array that holds 15 integers. You can view the address of the array with the statement **cout<<nums;** or with the statement **cout<<&nums[0];**. Each statement produces identical output. In the first statement, the name of the array represents the beginning address of the array. In the second statement, the address of **nums[0]** is the beginning address of the array.

Because an array name is a memory address, when you pass an array name to a function, you are actually passing an address. Therefore, any changes made to the array within the function also affect the original array. The program shown in Figure 6-31 shows a `main()` function that declares an array. The program displays the values, sends the array and its size to a function that alters the values, and then displays the values again. Figure 6-32 shows the output. In the output, you can see that the array values have been altered by the function.

```cpp
#include<iostream>
using namespace std;
int main()
{
    const int SIZE = 4;
    int nums[SIZE] = {4, 21, 300, 612};
    void increaseArray(int[], const int);
    int x;
    for(x = 0; x < SIZE; ++x)
      cout<<nums[x]<<" ";
    cout<<endl;
    increaseArray(nums, SIZE);
    for(x = 0; x < SIZE; ++x)
      cout<<nums[x]<<" ";
    cout<<endl;
}
void increaseArray(int values[], const int SZ)
{
    int y;
    for(y = 0; y < SZ; ++y)
        ++values[y];
}
```

Figure 6-31 Program with function that alters array values

Figure 6-32 Execution of program in Figure 6-31

TIP

An array name is a pointer; it holds a memory address. However, unlike other pointers, it is a constant pointer, meaning you cannot alter its contents.

In both the function prototype and the function header in Figure 6-31, the array name is written followed by empty brackets. When an array name is passed to a function, the function identifies the starting address of the array. Therefore, you don't need to indicate a size for the array in the function header. It doesn't matter whether `nums` in the `main()` function consists of four elements or four hundred; the starting address is the same. When you modify the values in the `values` array within the function, you are actually changing `nums` in the main program—`values` holds the same memory address as `nums`. Although the `increaseArray()` function does not return any values to `main()`, each value in the original array is increased when the alternate name for the same location is increased within the function.

TIP

Although passing an array name to a function involves passing an address, passing an array element to a function is no different than passing any single scalar variable of the same type. For example, if you declare `int nums[4];` and you declare a function with the prototype `void someFunction(int x);`, then you can call the function with statements such as `someFunction(nums[0]);` or `someFunction(nums[3]);`. Each call simply passes one integer to the function that is declared to receive a single integer. It does not matter whether the passed integer is a single integer or a part of an array of integers.

USING INLINE FUNCTIONS

Each time you call a function in a C++ program, the computer must do the following:

- Remember where to return when the function eventually ends
- Provide memory for the function's variables
- Provide memory for any value returned by the function
- Pass control to the function
- Pass control back to the calling program

This extra activity constitutes the **overhead**, or cost of doing business, involved in calling a function. When a function contains many lines of code, or when a program calls a function many times, the overhead is relatively small. That's because the cost of calling the function is offset by the fact that you no longer need to write the function's lines of code many times in different locations in the program. If a group of statements is small or is not used many times, however, placing the statements in a function may be convenient but not worth the overhead.

An **inline function** is a small function with no overhead. Overhead is avoided because program control never transfers to the function. Rather, a copy of the function statements is placed directly into the compiled calling program. Figure 6-33 illustrates how to create and use an inline function. As the highlighted portion of the function header shows, you define the function at the top of the file using the keyword `inline` as part of the function header. Whenever you want to use the function later in the file, you call it in the same manner you would call any other function.

```
#include<iostream>
using namespace std;
inline double computeGross(double hours, double rate)
{
    return(hours * rate);
}
int main()
{
    double hrsWorked=37.5, rateOfPay=12.45, gross;
    gross = computeGross(hrsWorked, rateOfPay);
    cout<<endl<<"Gross pay is "<<gross<<endl;
}
```

Figure 6-33   Using an inline function

6

The inline function appears prior to the function that calls it. Placing the inline function first eliminates the need for prototyping in the calling function. When you compile the program, the code for the inline function is placed directly within the calling function. When you run the program, it executes more rapidly than a version with a non-inline function because there is less overhead. However, if you use the inline function many times within the same program, the program could grow dramatically because the function statements are copied at the location of each call. Therefore, you should use an inline function only in the following situations:

- When you want to group statements together so that you can use a function name

- When the number of statements is small (one or two lines in the body of the function)

- When the function is called on few occasions

TIP   When you use an inline function, you make a request to the compiler; however, the compiler does not have to honor this request. This limitation can pose a problem if the function is included in an `include` or header file accessed by two different source files. If the compiler generates a message saying that an inline function has duplicate definitions, put the function in its own source file and include it just once in the compilation.

USING DEFAULT PARAMETERS

When you don't provide enough arguments in a function call, you usually want the compiler to issue a warning message for this error. For example, the program in Figure 6-34 shows an incorrect call to a function that requires three parameters. The code causes the compiler to issue an error message indicating that the function call has the wrong number of arguments.

```
#include<iostream>
using namespace std;
int main()
{
     // function prototype - this function requires 3 arguments
     int compute(int, int, int);
     // function call - one parameter is missing
     cout<<compute(12, 7)<<endl;
}
```

Figure 6-34   Incorrect call to a function

Sometimes it is useful to create a function that supplies a default value for any missing arguments. A **default parameter** to a function is one for which an automatic value is supplied if you do not explicitly use one. For example, you might create a function to calculate either the volume of a cube or the area of a square, such as the function shown in Figure 6-35. Notice the highlighted default value provided for the third function parameter. When you want a cube's area, you pass three arguments to the function: `length`, `width`, and `height`. When you want a square's area, you pass only two parameters, and a default value of 1 is used for the `height`. In this example, the `height` is a default parameter and it is optional; the `length` and `width` are mandatory parameters. The output in Figure 6-36 shows that both function calls work—the one with two arguments as well as the one with three.

```
#include<iostream>
using namespace std;
int main()
{
     int compute(int, int, int = 1);
     cout<<compute(12, 7)<<endl;
     cout<<compute(12, 7, 40)<<endl;
}
int compute(int length, int width, int height)
{
     int result = length * width * height;
     return result;
}
```

Figure 6-35   Program using a function with a default parameter

Figure 6-36   Output of program in Figure 6-35

Two rules apply to using default parameters:

- If you assign a default value to any variable in a function prototype's parameter list, then all parameters to the right of that variable must also have default values.

- If you omit any argument when you call a function that has default parameters, then you must also leave out all arguments to the right of that argument.

For example, examine the program in Figure 6-37 and notice how the default values are applied.

```
#include<iostream>
using namespace std;
int main()
{
    void badFunc(int = 1, int );
            // illegal — if first argument has
            // a default, then second one must too
    void functionWithDefaults(int, int = 2, int = 3);
            // legal
    functionWithDefaults();
        // illegal — in the call, a value for the first variable
        // is mandatory
    functionWithDefaults(4); // legal — output is 423
    functionWithDefaults(4, 5);  // legal — output is 453
    functionWithDefaults(4, 5, 6); // legal — output is 456
}
void functionWithDefaults(int one, int two, int three)
{
    cout<<one<<two<<three;
}
```

Figure 6-37 Examples of legal and illegal use of functions with default parameters

In Figure 6-37, the `functionWithDefaults()` function has one mandatory parameter and two optional, default parameters. Therefore, you must pass at least one—but no more than three—values to the function.

OVERLOADING FUNCTIONS

In many computer programming languages, each variable used in a function must have a unique name, but you learned earlier in this chapter that C++ allows you to employ an alias. Similarly, in many computer programming languages, each function used in a program must have a unique name. For example, if you want a function to display a value's square, you could create a function that squares integers, a function that squares floats, and a function that squares doubles. Figure 6-38 shows three such functions, and each has a unique name.

```
void squareInteger(int x)
{
    cout<<"In integer function "<<x*x<<endl;
}
void squareFloat(float x)
{
    cout<<"In float function "<<x*x<<endl;
}
void squareDouble(double x)
{
    cout<<"In double function "<<x*x<<endl;
}
```

Figure 6-38   Three non-overloaded functions that perform similar tasks

So you don't have to use three names for functions that perform basically the same task, C++ allows you to reuse, or **overload**, function names. When you overload a function, you create multiple functions with the same name but with different argument lists. For example, each function that squares a value can bear the name `squareValue()`. If you want three versions of the function, you must still write three versions of `squareValue()`— one that accepts an `int`, one that accepts a `double`, and one that accepts a `float`. C++ determines which of the three functions to call by reviewing the parameters submitted in your function call. Figure 6–39 shows three overloaded versions of `squareValue()` and a `main()` function that uses them. Figure 6-40 shows the output.

```
#include<iostream>
using namespace std;
void squareValue(int x)
{
    cout<<"In integer function "<<x*x<<endl;
}
void squareValue(float x)
{
    cout<<"In float function "<<x*x<<endl;
}
void squareValue(double x)
{
    cout<<"In double function "<<x*x<<endl;
}
int main()
{
    int i = 5;
    float f = 2.2f;
    double d = 3.3;
    squareValue(i); // output is "In integer function 25"
    squareValue(f); // output is "In float function 4.84"
    squareValue(d); // output is "In double function 10.89"
}
```

Figure 6-39   Using three overloaded functions that perform similar tasks

Figure 6-40   Output of program in Figure 6-39

Whether you use the functions with different names shown in Figure 6-38 or the three that all have the same name in Figure 6-39, you must still write three versions of the function—one for each type of argument you want to support. Overloading a function's name simply allows you to use that name for more than one function. The benefit of overloading derives from your ability to use one easy-to-understand function name without regard to the data types involved. If you create and save the three overloaded functions, then whenever you write programs in which you need to square values, you must remember only the function name `squareValue()`. You don't have to remember three separate function names.

> **TIP**
>
> C++ identifies which version of the overloaded function to call through a process known as **name mangling**. A mangled name contains all the information a compiler needs to distinguish functions for which the programmer has provided identical names.

Avoiding Ambiguity

When you overload a function, you must ensure that the compiler can tell which function to call. You accomplish this by making sure each overloaded function has a different argument list. For example, if you declare two functions as `void someFunction(int a);` and `void someFunction(int b);`, when you make the function call `someFunction(17);`, the compiler does not know which version of `someFunction()` to call. When the compiler cannot tell which version of a function to use, you have created **ambiguity**.

Ambiguity is particularly likely to occur by accident when you provide default values for the arguments to functions. For example, consider the following function declarations:

```
void calculation(int a = 1);
void calculation(char c = 'A');
```

At first glance, these functions appear to have different argument lists; one requires an integer and the other requires a character. As a matter of fact, if you make the function call `calculation(34);` or `calculation('Z');`, there is no ambiguity; the compiler knows which version you want to use. However, because both functions have default arguments, if you call `calculation()` using no arguments, then ambiguity arises. The compiler does not know if you intend to call the function version with the default integer or the version with the default character argument.

You will learn more about ambiguity when you learn to place functions within classes in Chapter 7.

TIP

While functions with the same name need not perform similar tasks, your programs will be clearer if overloaded functions perform essentially the same tasks.

TIP

YOU DO IT

Writing Functions That Return Values

In the next set of steps, you write a program that uses two functions to retrieve from the keyboard a worker's hourly rate and hours worked. The program uses the returned values to calculate and display weekly pay.

1. Open a new file in your C++ editor. Type comments indicating the purpose of this program, which is to demonstrate using functions that return values. Then type the first statements you need:

```
#include<iostream>
using namespace std;
```

2. Begin a `main()` function that declares a `double` variable for `rate` and an integer variable for `hours`. The weekly pay is stored in a `double` variable.

```
int main()
{
     double rate;
     int hours;
     double weekly;
```

3. Add a statement to declare a `getRate()` function that returns a rate, and a `getHours()` function that returns hours worked:

```
     double getRate();
     int getHours();
```

4. The next statements call the functions and store their returned values in variables.

```
     rate = getRate();
     hours = getHours();
```

5. Finish the `main()` function by computing the weekly pay and displaying it. Add a closing curly brace to end `main()`.

```
     weekly = rate * hours;
     cout<<"Weekly pay is $"<<weekly<<endl;
}
```

6. After the closing curly brace of `main()`, you can write the `getRate()` function. This function prompts the user for a rate and returns the value to `main()`. Notice that the function uses a local variable named `rate`, the same name as the variable in the `main()` function. These are separate variables that reside at different memory addresses. Even though they have the same identifier, each is local to its own function.

```
double getRate()
{
    double rate;
    cout<<"Enter your hourly rate in dollars and cents ";
    cin>>rate;
    return rate;
}
```

7. Next, you write the `getHours()` function. This function prompts the user for a number of hours and returns that value to `main()`. Notice that the hours value is stored in a variable named `time`, but when it is returned to `main()`, the same figure will be stored in a variable named `hours`. Just as it was acceptable for the `rate` variable name to have the same name in two functions, the `hours` variable value can have different names in two functions. When `time` is returned from `getHours()`, its value will be assigned to `hours` in the `main()` function.

```
int getHours()
{
    int time;
    cout<<"Please enter the hours you worked"<<endl;
    cout<<"You must enter a whole number ";
    cin>>time;
    return time;
}
```

8. Save the file as **HoursAndRate.cpp** and then compile the program. After you correct any syntax errors, run the program. Depending on the values you supply at the input prompts, the output appears similar to Figure 6-41.

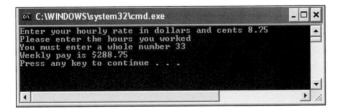

Figure 6-41 Typical execution of the `HoursAndRate` program

Writing a Function That Requires a Parameter

In the next set of steps, you modify the `HoursAndRate` program so that results now display from within a subfunction of `main()`.

1. Open the HoursAndRate.cpp program you wrote earlier if it is not still open on your screen, and immediately save it as **HoursAndRate2.cpp**.

2. Within the `main()` function, delete the line that declares the `weekly` variable. You no longer need this variable because the weekly pay will be calculated in a subfunction.

3. Place the insertion point at the end of the line that declares the `getHours()` function and press the **Enter** key to start a new line. Then, type the declaration for the function that accepts the rate and hours and calculates and displays the weekly pay:

```
void displayWeekly(double, int);
```

4. Place the insertion point after the statement that assigns a value to the `hours` variable and press the **Enter** key to start a new line. Then, type the call to the `displayWeekly()` function:

```
displayWeekly(rate, hours);
```

5. At the bottom of the file, add the `displayWeekly()` function definition. The function takes two arguments representing the rate and the hours, multiplies the arguments, stores the result in a local variable, and then displays the resulting pay value:

```
void displayWeekly(double hourlyWage, int hrs)
{
    double weekPay;
    weekPay = hourlyWage * hrs;
    cout<<"Weekly pay is "<<weekPay<<endl;
}
```

6. In `main()`, delete the following text:

```
weekly = rate * hours;
cout<<"Weekly pay is $"<<weekly<<endl;
```

7. Save the file again, compile, and run the program. The results are the same as when you ran the original `HoursAndRate` program, but now all the action takes place in functions, and the `main()` function itself is very abstract and concise.

CHAPTER SUMMARY

❑ Functions are programming modules. When you call a function, you use its name to transfer control of the program to the function.

❑ You can define a function by writing it above the function that uses it, or by including the function's filename at the top of the file that uses it.

❑ When you write functions, you employ procedural abstraction—the process of extracting the relevant attributes of an object.

❑ Global variables are known to every function and block in a program. Local variables are accessible or in scope only within the block where they are defined. Because local variables override global variables with the same name, you might have to use the scope resolution operator to access such global variables.

❑ The header of a function consists of the return type, the name, and the argument list. A prototype, or function declaration, also contains these parts.

❑ A function can return a value that the calling function can use. The type of value returned is known as the function's type.

❑ You can pass an argument or parameter to a function. When you write a function that takes arguments, you can choose to include documenting names in the prototype. You pass a value to a function when you place the value, called the actual parameter, within the parentheses in the function call. The function makes a copy of the actual parameter and stores it in the formal parameter, which is local to the function.

❑ You can pass class objects to functions and return them from functions in the same way you work with scalar variables.

❑ Passing an address to a function allows you to avoid having the function copy the passed object and allows a function to change multiple values without returning them. However, the syntax of passing an address is awkward, and a function that receives an address can alter a variable even if that is not your intention.

❑ In C++, a variable that acts as an alias for another variable is called a reference variable. You declare a reference variable by placing a type and an ampersand in front of a variable and assigning another variable of the same type to the reference variable. You can pass a variable's address to a reference variable in a function; this makes the syntax of the function less awkward. To protect the variable from change, you may pass a reference as a constant.

❑ Because an array name is a memory address, when you pass an array name to a function, you are actually passing an address. Therefore, any changes made to the array within the function also affect the original array. The array name in a function prototype or header is written with empty brackets.

❑ An inline function is a small function with no overhead. A copy of an inline function's statements is placed directly into the compiled calling program. You should use inline functions when the number of statements is small and when the function is called infrequently.

❑ Default parameters provide values for any parameters that are missing in the function call. If you assign a default value to any variable in a function prototype's parameter list, then all parameters to the right of that variable must also have default values. If you omit any argument when you call a function that has default parameters, then you must leave out all arguments to the right of that argument.

❑ C++ allows you to reuse, or overload, function names. To prevent ambiguity, overloaded functions must have argument lists of different types.

KEY TERMS

Functions are modules that perform a task or group of tasks.

In different programming languages, the counterpart to a function is known as a **subroutine**, **procedure**, or **method**.

In C++, every function has a **header**, or introductory line.

The type of object or variable that the function returns to the function that calls it is the **function's return type**—or, more simply, the **function's type**.

The statement that executes a function is the **call to the function**—or, more simply, the **function call**.

A **black box** is a device that you cannot look into to discover how it works but that works nonetheless.

A **subfunction** is a function used by a `main()` function.

A **function declaration**, or **function prototype**, is a statement that notifies the calling function that the definition (details) of the named function will come later.

Abstraction is the process of extracting the relevant attributes of a process or object; it simplifies your concept of the process or object, allowing you to ignore nonessential details.

Maintenance programming involves making modifications and improvements to existing systems.

The **scope** of a variable defines where it can be accessed in a program.

Global variables are those that are known to all functions in a program.

Local variables are known only in a limited scope.

Overrides means to take precedence over.

A variable is **in scope**, or **accessible**, between the time it is declared and the point at which its block of code ends; usually this is when a variable appears between braces in a program. After the brace that ends the block in which a variable was declared, the variable is **out of scope**; in other words, it is inaccessible.

The **lifetime** of a variable is the time during which it is defined—from declaration to destruction.

The **scope resolution operator (::)** allows you to refer to a global variable when a local one has taken precedence.

Encapsulation, or data hiding, is the principle of containing variables locally in their functions.

A **return** value is a value sent from a subfunction to the function that called it.

Statements that can never execute are called **dead code**.

A function that obtains data from another function accepts one or more **parameters** from the sending function.

Documentation helps readers of program code understand the purpose of the code.

In a function call, the passed value is also called an **argument** to the function.

A parameter used in a function call is known as an **actual parameter** because it holds the value that will actually be used by the function.

Any variable listed in a function header is known as a **formal parameter**.

A **memberwise copy** of an object is one in which the value of each field or member of the object is copied to its counterpart in another object.

An **alias** is an alternative name.

A variable that acts as an alias for another variable is called a **reference variable**, or simply a reference.

When you want to use a value stored in the pointer, you must use the asterisk to **dereference** the pointer, or use the value to which it points.

The **principle of least privilege** is a programming principle that says you should give a process only the authority it needs to accomplish its job.

Overhead is the cost of doing business involved in calling a function.

An **inline function** is a small function with no overhead because program control never transfers to the function. Rather, a copy of the function statements is placed directly into the compiled calling program.

A **default parameter** to a function is one for which an automatic value is supplied if you do not explicitly use one.

Overloading a function name involves creating multiple functions with the same name but different argument lists.

Name mangling is the process by which the compiler creates unique names with all the information a compiler needs to distinguish identically named, overloaded functions.

Ambiguity is a situation in which the compiler cannot tell which version of a function to use.

REVIEW QUESTIONS

1. In different programming languages, program modules are known as all of the following except _____.

   a. functions

   b. procedures

   c. methods

   d. variables

2. In a C++ program, all function names are always followed by a pair of _____.

   a. parentheses

   b. square brackets

   c. angle brackets

   d. curly braces

3. When you use the name of a function where you want it to execute within a program, you are _____ the function.

   a. prototyping

   b. calling

   c. iterating

   d. defining

4. You can define a function by _____.

   a. writing it within the function that uses it

   b. including the function's filename at the top of the file that uses it

   c. inserting a comment that describes the function's purpose

   d. any of the above

5. The process of extracting the relevant attributes of an object is called _____.

   a. codification

   b. object orienting

   c. structuring

   d. abstraction

6. A variable that is known to all functions within a file is said to be _____.

   a. notorious

   b. worldly

   c. global

   d. famous

7. Within a block or function, a local variable _____ a global one.

a. overrides

b. overloads

c. accedes to

d. replaces

8. A local variable is one that _____.

a. is known to functions only within its own file

b. is automatically declared by C++

c. ceases to exist when its block ends

d. has a value that does not change during its life

9. The term C++ programmers use for the extent to which a variable is known is _____.

a. breadth

b. scope

c. scale

d. reach

10. Both a function header and its prototype contain _____.

a. the return type

b. a coded description of what the function does

c. actual parameters

d. square brackets

11. Which of the following is a valid prototype for a function that accepts an integer argument and returns a double value?

a. `int function(double);`

b. `int function(double)`

c. `double function (int);`

d. `double function(int)`

12. Suppose you have a C++ program that contains an integer variable named `yearOfBirth`. To call a function with the prototype `void calculateAge(int);`, you use the statement _____.

a. `void calculateAge();`

b. `calculateAge(int);`

c. `calculateAge(yearOfBirth);`

d. `calculateAge(int yearOfBirth);`

6

13. Which of the following correctly calls a function that has the prototype `void computePrice(int, double, int);`?

 a. `computePrice(5129.95, 8, 36);`

 b. `computePrice(5000, .075, 24);`

 c. `computePrice(10000, .10, 4.5);`

 d. `computePrice(2000, .09);`

14. Which of the following is an advantage of passing an address of a variable to a function?

 a. the function can alter the original variable in the calling function

 b. the function can alter only one value, making it more secure

 c. you need to use no special notation when passing an address

 d. the function automatically makes a copy of the passed variable

15. Which of the following correctly declares a reference for `int myCreditHours;`?

 a. `int &cr = myCreditHours;`

 b. `int *cr = myCreditHours;`

 c. `int cr = &myCreditHours;`

 d. `int *cr = &myCreditHours;`

16. When you pass a reference to a function, the function can alter the variable if the reference is _____.

 a. constant

 b. not constant

 c. absolute

 d. not absolute

17. You should use an inline function when _____.

 a. it is large

 b. it has no arguments

 c. it is called infrequently

 d. it requires arguments that are addresses

18. A program contains the function prototype `void displayData(char [], int = 0);`. Which of the following is a legal function call?

 a. `displayData();`

 b. `displayData("Roberts");`

 c. `displayData("Gonzales", 345);`

 d. two of the above are legal

19. Using the same function name with different argument lists is called
_____ functions.

   a. overriding

   b. overloading

   c. overcompensating

   d. overreacting

20. Which of the following functions could coexist in a program with `void function(double, int);` with no ambiguity possible?

   a. `void function (double);`

   b. `void function(double, int);`

   c. `void function(double = 2.2, int = 3.3);`

   d. all of the above

6

EXERCISES

1. Write a program in which the `main()` function calls a function named `marysLamb()`. Write the `marysLamb()` function, which should display the words to the nursery rhyme "Mary Had a Little Lamb." Save the file as **MarysLamb.cpp**.

2. Write a program in which the `main()` function uses several `cout` statements to display a memo to your boss. Use the company name "C++ Software Developers" at least three times in the memo. Each time you want to display the company name, instead of using a `cout` statement, call a function named `companyName()` that displays the name. Save the file as **Memo.cpp**.

3. Write a program that asks the user to input an integer and then calls a function named `multiplicationTable()`, which displays the results of multiplying the integer by each of the numbers 2 through 10. Save the file as **Multiplication.cpp**.

4. Write a program that asks users for the most expensive and least expensive restaurant bills they anticipate. A function `tipTable()` should calculate and display 15 percent of each whole-dollar amount between the two entered limits. Save the file as **TipCalculator.cpp**.

5. Write a program that asks the user for two integers and a character, 'A', 'S', or 'M'. Call one of three functions that adds, subtracts, or multiplies the user's integers, based on the character input. Save the file as **SimpleCalculator.cpp**.

6. Write a program that includes two functions. The first function should ask a salesperson for the dollar value of daily sales and then return this figure to the main program. The second function should calculate the salesperson's commission based on the following rates:

Sales	Commission
0–999	3%
1,000–2,999	3.5%
3,000–up	4.5%

The dollar value of the calculated commission should be returned to the main program, which then displays it. Save the file as **Commission.cpp**.

7. Write a program that calculates the cost of building a desk. The `main()` function calls four other functions. Pass all variables so that the functions make copies of any variables they receive:

- ❐ A function to accept as input from the keyboard the number of drawers in the desk. This function returns the number of drawers to the main program.

- ❐ A function to accept as input the type of wood—'m' for mahogany, 'o' for oak, or 'p' for pine.

- ❐ A function that receives the drawer number and wood type, and calculates the cost of the desk based on the following:

   Pine desks are $100.

   Oak desks are $140.

   All other woods are $180.

   A $30 surcharge is added for each drawer.

   This function returns the cost to the `main()` function.

- ❐ A function to display the final price.

Save the file as **Desks.cpp**.

8. Rewrite the Desks program from Exercise 7, passing all variables as reference variables and changing all the function return types to **void**. Save the file as **Desks2.cpp**.

9. Write a program that accepts 10 values from the user at the keyboard and stores them in an array. Pass the array and its size to a function that determines and displays the smallest and largest of the 10 values. Save the file as **SmallAndLarge.cpp**.

10. Write a program that prompts the user to enter five integers that you store in an array. Write a function called `quadruple()` that takes a single-integer argument and multiplies it by 4, returning the result to the calling program. Call the function once for each of the five integers, then display the quadrupled results from within the `main()` function. Save the file as **Quadruple.cpp**.

11. Write a program that prompts the user to enter five integers that you store in an array. Write a function called `quadruple()` that takes the array name (or the array address) as an argument and takes the size of the array as a second argument. The function multiplies each value by 4 and returns nothing to the calling program. Display the quadrupled results from within the `main()` function. Save the file as **Quadruple2.cpp**.

12. Write a program that asks students how many tests they have taken so far in a course. The program should accept any number from 1 to 5, but reprompt the user if the entry is invalid. The user can then enter the appropriate number of test scores, which you store in an array. Pass the number of tests and the array of test scores to a function that averages the student's test scores and displays the average. The function should compute a correct average whether the student has taken one, two, three, four, or five tests. Save the file as **StudentAverage.cpp**.

13. Write a program that allows users to enter a dollar amount for their bank account balance at the beginning of the month. Then ask the user to enter dollar amounts for any number of checks written in a month, up to 50. Include an appropriate sentinel value that the user can enter to stop entering checks. Store the amounts in an array and count the entries as the user makes them. Finally, ask the user to enter a monthly interest rate if the account is interest bearing, or a 0 if it is not. If the user enters 0 for the interest rate, then call a function named `balanceAccount()` that accepts the beginning balance, the number of checks, and the array of check amounts as arguments; the function displays the final balance after all the checks have been subtracted from the beginning balance. If the user enters a number other than 0 for the interest rate, then call an overloaded function named `balanceAccount()` that accepts the beginning balance, the number of checks, the array of check amounts, and the interest rate as arguments. This function then computes the final balance by subtracting all the checks from the beginning balance and using the monthly interest rate to increase the final balance before displaying it. Save the file as **BankCalculations.cpp**.

14. Write a function named `customerCreditLimit()` that accepts a `double` as an argument and displays the value as the amount of credit granted to a customer. Provide a default value for the function so that if a program calls the function without an argument, the credit limit displays $500. Write a `main()` function that proves the function works correctly, whether it is called with an argument or without. Save the file as **Credit.cpp**.

15. Write a function that accepts two arguments: a string name of a movie and an integer running time in minutes. Provide a default value for the minutes so that if you call the function without an integer argument, the minutes default to 90. Write a `main()` function that proves you can call the function with a string argument alone as well as with a string and an integer. Save the file as **Movie.cpp**.

16. Create a structure named `Carpet` that has two public data members: `lengthInFeet` and `widthInFeet`. Write a `main()` function that instantiates a `Carpet` object and assigns values to its data fields. Pass the object to a function named `displayArea()` that calculates the `Carpet` area in square feet and displays the results. Save the file as **Carpet.cpp**.

6

17. Create a structure named `Shirt` that has the public data members `collarSize` and `sleeveLength`. Create a structure named `Pants` that has the public data members `waistSize` and `inSeam`. Write a program that declares one object of each type `Shirt` and `Pants` and assigns values to the objects' data fields. Write two overloaded functions named `displayClothingFacts()`. One version of the function takes a `Shirt` object as an argument; the other version takes a `Pants` object. Each version displays the facts about the piece of clothing. Your `main()` function should demonstrate that you can call `displayClothingFacts()` with either type of clothing. Save the file as **Shirt.cpp**.

18. Create a structure named `Dog` with a string field for the `Dog`'s name. Create a structure named `Cat` with a string field for the `Cat`'s name. Write a program that declares one `Dog` and one `Cat`, and assign names to them. Write two overloaded methods named `speak()`. If you pass the `Dog` to `speak()`, the `speak()` method should display the `Dog`'s name and a description of how dogs speak (for example, "Spot says woof"). If you pass the `Cat` to the version of `speak()` that accepts a `Cat` argument, then it should display the `Cat`'s name and a description of how cats speak (for example, "Tiger says meow"). Save the file as **CatDog.cpp**.

19. Each of the following files in your Chapter06 folder contains syntax and/or logical errors. Determine the problem in each case and fix the program. Save your solutions by adding "Fixed" to the filename, as in **DEBUG6-1Fixed.cpp**.

    a. DEBUG6-1.cpp

    b. DEBUG6-2.cpp

    c. DEBUG6-3.cpp

    d. DEBUG6-4.cpp

CASE PROJECT 1

You are developing a `Fraction` structure for Teacher's Pet Software. The structure contains three public data fields for whole number, numerator, and denominator. Using the same structure, write the functions described below:

❐ An `enterFractionValue()` function that declares a local `Fraction` object and prompts the user to enter values for the `Fraction`. Do not allow the user to enter a value of 0 for the denominator of any `Fraction`; continue to prompt the user for a denominator value until a valid one is entered. The function returns a data-filled `Fraction` object to the calling function.

❐ A `reduceFraction()` function that accepts a `Fraction` object and reduces it to proper form, returning the reduced `Fraction`. For example, a `Fraction` entering the function as 0 2/6 would be reduced to 0 1/3, and a `Fraction` entered as 4 18/4 would be reduced to 8 1/2.

- A displayFraction() function that displays any Fraction object passed to it. This function displays a fraction with a slash between the numerator and denominator.

- A main() function that declares a Fraction object and continues to get Fraction values from the user until the user enters a Fraction with value 0 (both the whole number and the numerator are 0). For each Fraction entered, display the Fraction, reduce the Fraction, and display the Fraction again.

CASE PROJECT 2

CASE PROJECTS

You are developing a BankAccount structure for Parkville Bank. The structure contains fields for the account number, the account balance, and the annual interest rate earned on the account. Using the same structure, write the functions below:

- An enterAccountData() function that declares a local BankAccount object and prompts the user for values for each data field. Allow neither a negative balance nor a negative interest rate; continue to prompt the user until valid values are entered. The function returns a data-filled BankAccount object to the calling function.

- A computeInterest() function that accepts a BankAccount argument. Within the function, prompt the user for the number of years the account will earn interest. The function displays the ending balance of the account each year for the number of years entered based on the interest rate attached to the BankAccount.

- A displayAccount() function that displays the details of any BankAccount object passed to it.

- A main() function that declares a BankAccount object and continues to get BankAccount values from the user until the user enters a BankAccount with value 0 for the account number. For each BankAccount entered, display the BankAccount details and a list of future balances based on the term the user requests.

6

7

USING CLASSES

In this chapter, you will:

♦ Create classes

♦ Learn about encapsulating class components

♦ Implement class functions

♦ Use private functions and public data

♦ Use the scope resolution operator with class fields and functions

♦ Use static class members

♦ Learn about the `this` pointer

♦ Understand the advantages of polymorphism

Classes are similar to structures in that both provide a means to group data and behaviors together so you can create objects. So far in this book, you have worked with structures containing `public` data fields. However, structures and classes can contain much more than `public` data fields; they can contain methods that make their objects operate like many concrete objects in the physical world. That is, objects can *do* things as well as *contain* things, and some of their attributes and operations can be hidden from users. By default, `struct` data fields are `public`; that is why you have been using structures instead of classes up to this point in this book—structures are easier to work with. To create objects, most C++ programmers prefer to use classes most of the time, partly because, by default, their data fields are `private`, or hidden, and cannot be altered without the programmer's permission. You needed to learn how to handle functions, including passing parameters to them, before you could learn to use classes in meaningful and conventional ways. This chapter will show you how to add both hidden and visible fields and functions to your classes, and how C++ handles class functions behind the scenes. This chapter will take you into the world of modern object-oriented programming.

CREATING CLASSES

A **class** is a category of objects; it is a new data type you create that is more complex than the basic data types. Classes provide a description of an object—they detail all the data an object has and all the actions the object can perform. Additionally, classes provide a convenient way to group related data and the functions that use the data. One advantage of creating a class is that when you create an object from the class, you automatically create all the related fields. Another advantage is that you gain the ability to pass an object into a function, or receive an object from a function as a returned value, and automatically pass or receive all the individual fields that each object contains. Another advantage to using classes and objects is that you think about them and manipulate them similarly to the way you use real-life classes and objects. For example, you are familiar with the class of objects known as automobiles; you understand what features an automobile has (an engine size, a number of doors, a color) and you understand what an automobile can do (go forward, idle, go in reverse). When you learn that a particular object is an automobile, you know a lot about the object before you even see it. If a friend tells you he is buying an automobile, you know approximately how it looks and works even though you don't know the values of his particular object yet—for example, its engine size, color, or number of doors. Programming classes and objects work similarly: when you define a class you describe what it has and can do; when you create specific objects you supply specific values.

Most C++ compilers contain many built-in classes that are ready for you to use. For example, in Chapter 5 you were introduced to the built-in C++ `string` class. Using this class makes it easier for you to handle strings in your programs.

Consider the `Student` class in Figure 7-1. It contains three data fields: `idNum`, `lastName`, and `gradePointAverage`. C++ programmers would say that the `Student` class shown in the figure is an **abstract data type (ADT)**. This term simply indicates that `Student` is a type you define, as opposed to types like `char` and `int` that are defined by C++. You define a class by using the keyword **class**, the class identifier, and a pair of curly braces. You must include a semicolon following the closing curly brace. Between the curly braces, you define all the data and behaviors that are members of the class.

```
class Student
{
        int idNum;
        string lastName;
        double gradePointAverage;
};
```

Figure 7-1   A `Student` class

The `Student` class in Figure 7-1 contains data fields, but no behaviors or functions. You will learn how to add these later in the chapter.

TIP

A language to which you can add your own data types, such as C++, is an **extensible language**.

TIP

You cannot assign a value to a field in a class definition. For example, in the `Student` class, you cannot write `idNum = 123;`. A class definition is only a description of a type; you cannot assign values to fields until you create an object.

TIP

When you declare a `Student` object, you use the `Student` name just as you use scalar type names. For example, you can declare the following:

        Student aSophomore;

Recall from Chapter 1 that an object is any thing, and that a class is a category of things. An object is a specific item that belongs to a class; it is called an instance of a class. A class defines the characteristics of its objects and the methods that can be applied to its objects.

TIP

Conventionally, class names begin with an uppercase letter and object names begin with a lowercase letter.

TIP

When you refer to `aSophomore`, you are including all the separate attributes that constitute `aSophomore`—an ID number, a name, and a grade point average. However, unlike with a `struct`, you cannot refer to the specific attributes of the class object `aSophomore` by using the object's name, a dot, and the attribute's name. For example, to display the ID number of a declared `Student` named `aSophomore`, you might suppose you could write statements like the following, but you cannot:

        aSophomore.idNum = 7645;
        cout<<aSophomore.idNum;

If you attempt to compile a program containing a statement that accesses a class field such as `aSophomore.idNum`, you receive a message similar to "Cannot access private class member declared in class `Student`". You receive the error message because, by default, all members of a class are **private**, meaning they cannot be accessed using any statements in any functions that are not also part of the class. In other words, private class members cannot be displayed, assigned a value, manipulated arithmetically, or used directly in any other way.

It is possible to declare class data members to be **public** instead of **private**. For example, Figure 7-2 shows a `Student` class in which the keyword **public** and a colon (shaded) have been inserted prior to the declaration of the class fields. In Figure 7-2, the highlighted word `public` is an **access modifier**; it assigns accessibility to the declared variables that follow it. Using the keyword `public` means that the fields are now accessible when they are used with a `Student` object in a `main()` function, just as they would be with a `Student struct`. However, although you could avoid error messages when accessing one of the `Student` fields by using this technique, it would be highly unconventional to do so. Additionally, you would violate the object-oriented principle of encapsulation. Class fields are `private` by default, because that is what they usually *should* be in object-oriented programs.

```
class Student
{
   public:
        int idNum;
        string lastName;
        double gradePointAverage;
};
```

Figure 7-2   An unconventional (and not recommended) version of a `Student` class containing public data fields

TIP

In the class in Figure 7-2, you can use the private access modifier and a colon in place of the shaded public access modifier to clearly identify the fields as private in your program. However, if you use no modifier, the fields are still private by default.

ENCAPSULATING CLASS COMPONENTS

The first step to creating a class involves determining the attributes of an object, and subsequently dealing with the object as a whole. That's what you are doing when you decide on the field types and names for a class like the `Student` class. When you work with a `Student` object, for example, and pass it to a function, you deal with the object as a whole, and do not have to think about its internal fields. You think about the fields only when necessary, such as when you need to assign a value to a `Student`'s `idNum` or when you want to display it. A hallmark of object-oriented programming is that you think about program objects in the same way you think about their real-world counterparts.

For example, when you use a real-world object such as a radio, you usually don't think or care about how it works. Sometimes, however, you change some of the states of the radio's attributes, such as volume level or frequency selection. Just as the internal components of a radio are hidden, when you write a program and create a class name for a group of associated variables, you contain, or **encapsulate**, the individual components. Sometimes you want to change the state or value of some components, but often you want to think about the entity as a whole and not concern yourself with the details. Programmers sometimes refer to encapsulation as an example of using a "black box." A black box is a device that you can use, but cannot look inside to see how it works. When you use a class, you are using a group name without being concerned with the individual components; the details are hidden.

> You first learned the phrase "black box" in Chapter 6 when you learned about functions. Like functions, classes hide their internal components from the outside.
>
> **TIP**

When you work with concrete, real-world objects, you think about more than what components they contain or what states they possess; you also think about what the objects can do. For example, a radio's states or values include its present volume and frequency selection, but a radio also possesses a means for *changing* these states. In other words, radios have methods as well as attributes. When you change the volume or frequency, you use an **interface**, such as a dial or button. The interface intercedes between you and the more complicated inner workings of the radio. When you design C++ classes, you should think about what the class objects will *do* and how programmers will make them do it, as well as what the class objects *contain*. Therefore your classes will contain fields, and functions that often act as interfaces to the class objects. Typically, the fields in your classes will be private, but your interfacing functions will be public.

Designing Classes

You can think of the built-in scalar types of C++ as classes. You do not have to define those classes; the creators of C++ have already done so. For example, when the `int` type was first created, the programmers who designed it had to think of the following:

Q: What shall we call it?

A: `int`.

Q: What are its attributes?

A: An `int` is stored in four bytes (or possibly some other number, depending on your system); it holds whole-number values.

Q: What methods are needed by `int`?

A: A method to assign a value to a variable (for example, `num = 32;`).

Q: Any other methods?

A: A method to perform arithmetic with variables (for example, `num + 6;`).

Q: Any other methods?

A: Of course, there are even more attributes and methods of an `int`, but these are a good start.

Your job in constructing a new class is similar. If you need a class for students, you should ask:

Q: What shall we call it?

A: `Student`.

Q: What are its attributes?

A: It has an integer ID number, a string last name, and a double grade point average.

Q: What methods are needed by `Student`?

A: A method to assign values to a member of this class (for example, one `Student`'s ID number is 3232, her last name is "Walters", and her grade point average is 3.45).

Q: Any other methods?

A: A method to display data in a member of this class (for example, display one `Student`'s data).

Q: Any other methods?

A: Probably, but this is enough to get started.

For most object-oriented classes, then, you declare both fields and functions.

- You declare a field using a data type and an identifier.

- You declare a function by writing its prototype, which serves as the interface to the function.

For example, you might want to create a method for a `Student` class that displays all the details of a `Student`'s data. You could create a function with the prototype `void displayStudentData();` and include it in the `Student` class definition shown in Figure 7-3. In this figure, the three data fields are `private` by default, because no access modifier precedes them. However, the shaded `public` access modifier precedes the `displayStudentData()` function declaration, making the function `public`.

```
class Student
  {
    private:
          int idNum;
          string lastName;
          double gradePointAverage;
    public:
          void displayStudentData();
  };
```

Figure 7-3   `Student` class that includes one function definition

When you declare a class object, you create an instance of the class; you **instantiate** the object. When you declare a class with a function definition such as the one shown in Figure 7-3, and you then instantiate an object of that class, the object possesses more than three fields—it also possesses access to a function. If you declare a `Student` object as `Student aSophomore;`, then you can use the `displayStudentData()` function by referring to `aSophomore.displayStudentData()`. Similarly, another `Student` object, `Student aGraduate;`, could use `aGraduate.displayStudentData()`. Although a `main()` function (or any other function outside the class) cannot use any of the class fields, the `displayStudentData()` function can use them because it belongs to the same class. Other functions, for example a `main()` function, can't use the private data fields directly, but they *are* allowed to use the `displayStudentData()` function because it is `public`, not `private`.

At this point, you might wonder, if you are going to create a public function that accesses private data, why not just make the data public in the first place, avoiding the function? You create the public function so you, the class creator, can control how the data items are used. For example, if your radio provides an interface that allows you to set the volume only as high as 10, then you cannot set it to 11 even though the internal components of your radio might be able to produce that level of sound. Similarly, if you allow access to only public methods for a function that is a user of your class (often called a **class client**), then you control how the user can manipulate the data. For example, if you never want a class client to be able to see the last digit of a `Student` object's ID number, then you simply do not display that digit from within the `displayStudentData()` function. The client must use your public interface to see any data values; the client cannot just code `cout<<aSophomore.idNum;`.

Implementing Class Functions

After you create a class function's prototype, you still must write the actual function. When you construct a class, you create two parts. The first part is a **declaration section**, which contains the class name, variables (attributes), and function prototypes. The second part created is an **implementation section**, which contains the functions themselves. For example, Figure 7-4 shows the Student class that includes a shaded function implementation for `displayStudentData()`.

In the class definition shown in Figure 7-4, the declaration section includes a function prototype, and the implementation section contains the actual function. The `displayStudentData()` function header is preceded by the class name, `Student`, and the scope resolution operator (`::`). You must use both the class name and the scope resolution operator when you implement a class function, because they tie the function to this class and allow every instantiated class object to use the function name. The statements within the function are similar to those in any other function; in this case, they just display the class data fields.

```
// declaration section:
class Student
{
    private:
            int idNum;
            string lastName;
            double gradePointAverage;
    public:
            void displayStudentData();
};
// implementation section:
void Student::displayStudentData()
{
    cout<<"Student #"<<idNum<<"'s last name is "<<
        lastName<<endl;
    cout<<"The grade point average for this student is "<<
        gradePointAverage<<endl;
}
```

Figure 7-4   Student class that includes one function definition and implementation

Instead of prototyping a function in the declaration section of a class and implementing that function later, you can implement it in place of the proto- type. This causes the function to become an inline function. Usually, however, you should keep the function declaration and implementation separate, as in the example in Figure 7-4.

You can refer to the scope resolution operator used in the class function header as a binary scope resolution operator, because it requires two operands: the class name to the left and the function name to the right. In Chapter 6, you learned to use the unary scope resolution operator to access a global variable from within a function that contains a local variable with the same identifier.

Using Public Functions to Alter Private Data

You gain a major advantage when you make a data field private. You might spend a great deal of time creating a class, including writing and debugging all of its member functions. Your carefully crafted methods could be worthless if outside functions over which you have no control could modify or erroneously use the member data of any object in the class. Making data fields private prevents outside manipulation of those fields. When you create and test a class, and store its definition in a file, programs that use the definition can- not use private member data incorrectly. If a private member of your Student class, such as idNum, must be a four-digit number, or if you require that the idNum always be pre- ceded by a pound sign when it is displayed, functions that are not a member of your class can never change those rules (either intentionally or by accident).

TIP   You can choose to make data public if you have a good reason. Frequently, `public` data is also constant, so it can be used, but not altered. For example, a `MathConstants` class might have `public` data members that hold mathematical constants, such as `PI`. Many object-oriented software developers are opposed to making any data `public`, arguing that data should always be `private` and accessed through a `public` interface.

However, if a program can't assign a value to a field because it is private, then the field is not of much use. You keep data private, yet gain the ability to alter it, by creating additional public functions that *can* assign values to a class's private fields. For example, if the offices at your firm are all private and you cannot communicate with the executives in them, the company won't function for long. Usually the receptionists are public, and you can use them to communicate with the private executives. Similarly, you communicate with the private members of a class by sending messages to the public member functions.

Figure 7-5 shows the declaration for a `Student` class that contains three additional functions used to assign values to a `Student`'s data fields. These functions are named `setIdNum()`, `setLastName()`, and `setGradePointAverage()`. Each is used to set the value of one of the fields within the `Student` class.

TIP   Classes can contain many functions with many purposes. Usually the first functions you create for a class are those that provide a means for input and output of the class data fields.

```
class Student
{
   private:
      int idNum;
      string lastName;
      double gradePointAverage;
   public:
      void displayStudentData();
      void setIdNum(int);
      void setLastName(string);
      void setGradePointAverage(double);
};
```

Figure 7-5   `Student` class with set functions for private data

You can place any lines of code you want within these functions when you implement them. If you want the `setLastName()` function to assign a string to the `Student`'s `lastName`, then you can implement the function as shown in Figure 7-6.

```
void Student::setLastName(string name)
{
    lastName = name;
}
```

Figure 7-6   The `setLastName()` function

The `setLastName()` function shown in Figure 7-6 is a member of the `Student` class. You can determine this because the class header contains the `Student` class name and the scope resolution operator. The `setLastName()` function takes a string argument that has the local name `name`. The function assigns the passed name value to the `lastName` field of `Student` object. When you write a program in which you instantiate a `Student` object named `aJunior`, you can assign a last name to the `aJunior` object with a statement such as the following:

```
aJunior.setLastName("Farnsworth");
```

The string "Farnsworth" is passed into the `aJunior` object's `setLastName()` function, where it is copied to the `aJunior` object's `lastName` field.

If `lastName` were a public field within the `Student` class, then you could assign "Farnsworth" to `lastName` with the statement `aJunior.lastName = "Farnsworth";`. That is, you would not have to use the `setLastName()` method. However, making the `lastName` field public would violate one of the canons of object-oriented programming: Whenever possible, data should be kept private, and access to data should be controlled by public functions.

Assume that a student ID number should not be more than four digits in length. When you implement the `setIdNum()` function of the `Student` class, you can assign the ID number argument to the class `idNum` field only if it is a valid ID; otherwise you can force the `idNum` field to 9999. Figure 7-7 shows a `setIdNum()` function that operates in this way.

```
void Student::setIdNum(int num)
{
   const int MAX_NUM = 9999;
   if(num <= MAX_NUM)
        idNum = num;
    else
        idNum = MAX_NUM;
}
```

Figure 7-7   The Student class setIdNum() function

When you use the **setIdNum()** function with an object like **aJunior**, you are assured that **aJunior** receives a valid **idNum** according to the rules you have defined. If the **idNum** field were public, a client could write a program and include a statement that assigned an invalid ID—for example, **aJunior.idNum = 123456;**. However, when the **idNum** is private, you must use the public **setIdNum()** function. If you try to pass in a value with too many digits, such as with the statement **aJunior.setIdNum(123456);** the result is that the **aJunior's idNum** is set to 9999, not 123456.

The **setIdNum()** function in Figure 7-7 allows a negative ID number. You could add more code to further limit the allowed **idNum** values.

TIP

Figure 7-8 shows the entire **Student** class, including the implementation of the **setGradePointAverage()** function that accepts a **double** argument, and assures that the argument value is no more than 4.0 before assigning it to any **Student's** **gradePointAverage** field. Figure 7-8 also includes a short demonstration **main()** function that assigns values for a typical **Student**. (An interactive program would prompt for the values instead.) Figure 7-9 shows the output of the program.

7

```cpp
#include<iostream>
#include<string>
using namespace std;
// declaration section
class Student
{
   private:
       int idNum;
       string lastName;
       double gradePointAverage;
   public:
       void displayStudentData();
       void setIdNum(int);
       void setLastName(string);
       void setGradePointAverage(double);
};
// implementation section
void Student::displayStudentData()
{
  cout<<"Student #"<<idNum<<"'s last name is "<<
      lastName<<endl;
  cout<<"The grade point average for this student is "<<
      gradePointAverage<<endl;
}
void Student::setIdNum(int num)
{
   const int MAX_NUM = 9999;
   if(num <= MAX_NUM)
        idNum = num;
   else
        idNum = MAX_NUM;
}
void Student::setLastName(string name)
{
    lastName = name;
}
void Student::setGradePointAverage(double gpa)
{
    const double MAX_GPA = 4.0;
    if(gpa <= MAX_GPA)
        gradePointAverage = gpa;
    else
        gradePointAverage = 0;
}

int main()
{
    Student aStudent;
    aStudent.setLastName("Smith");
    aStudent.setIdNum(3456);
    aStudent.setGradePointAverage(3.5);
    aStudent.displayStudentData();
}
```

Figure 7-8 The Student class and a demonstration main() function

```
C:\WINDOWS\system32\cmd.exe                              _ □ ×
Student #3456's last name is Smith
The grade point average for this student is 3.5
Press any key to continue . . . _
```

Figure 7-9   Output of the program in Figure 7-8

TIP

You can use the access specifiers `public` and `private` as many times as you want in a class definition—for example, two private members, followed by one public member, followed by two more private members. It's better style, however, to group the private and public members together.

TIP

Many C++ programmers prefer to place the public section before the private section in a class definition. The reasoning is that other programmers then see and use the public interfaces. Use the style you prefer.

In the **Student** class functions in Figure 7-8, notice that the class fields `idNum`, `lastName`, and `gradePointAverage` never need to be passed into the functions as arguments. The functions have direct access to these fields because both the fields and functions belong to the same class. Similarly, the functions that provide values for the class fields never need to return values anywhere; as members of the same class, the functions have direct access to the class fields.

USING PRIVATE FUNCTIONS AND PUBLIC DATA

When you create a class, usually you want to make data items private, to control how they are used, and to make functions public to provide a means to access and manipulate the data. However, if you have a reason to do so, you are free to make particular data items public. Similarly, not all functions are public.

When you think of real-world objects, such as kitchen appliances, there are many functions you control through a public interface: adjusting the temperature on a refrigerator or oven, setting a cycle on a dishwasher, and so on. However, there are other functions that appliances encapsulate: a freezer might defrost itself without your help, and a dishwasher switches from the wash to the rinse cycle. With objects you create, you can choose for functions to be private.

For example, Figure 7-10 shows an **Employee** class containing data fields that store an **Employee's** ID number, birth date, and hire date. The class contains public functions that set each of these fields, and a shaded private function that verifies date accuracy. The `verifyDate()` function is not intended to be used by a client function, such as the `main()` function at the bottom of the figure. Instead, `verifyDate()` is used by the two functions that set class dates. It makes sense to create a single `verifyDate()` function, because all dates follow the same rules, for example, preventing a month value from being greater than 12. By creating a single function that verifies dates, you avoid duplicating a lot of similar code. Because `verifyDate()` is used by class functions and not by outside clients, it can be declared to be `private`. Figure 7-11 shows a typical execution of the `main()` function in which the user enters a valid birth date but an invalid hire date.

TIP

The `verifyDate()` function might be even more useful in a full-blown `Employee` class. For example, besides a birth date and hire date, you might store a date of last promotion, birth dates of dependents, and a termination date. All these dates might be verified using the same basic rules.

```cpp
#include<iostream>
#include<string>
using namespace std;
// declaration section
class Employee
{
   private:
      int idNum;
      int birthDate;
      int hireDate;
      int verifyDate(int);
   public:
      void display();
      void setIdNum(int);
      void setBirthDate(int);
      void setHireDate(int);
};
// implementation section
void Employee::display()
{
   const int YEARFINDER = 10000;
   int bYear = birthDate / YEARFINDER;
   int hYear = hireDate / YEARFINDER;
   cout<<"Employee #"<<idNum<<endl;
   cout<<"Born "<<bYear<<endl;
   cout<<"Hired in: "<<hYear<<endl;
}
void Employee::setIdNum(int num)
{
   idNum = num;
}
void Employee::setBirthDate(int date)
{
   int ok = verifyDate(date);
   if(ok)
      birthDate = date;
```

Figure 7-10   `Employee` class and `main()` demonstration function

```
   else
   {
      birthDate = 0;
      cout<<"Invalid birth date entered"<<endl;
   }
}
void Employee::setHireDate(int date)
{
   int ok = verifyDate(date);
   if(ok)
      hireDate = date;
   else
   {
      hireDate = 0;
      cout<<"Invalid hire date entered"<<endl;
   }
}
int Employee::verifyDate(int date)
{
   const int YEARFINDER = 10000;
   const int MONTHFINDER = 100;
   const int EARLYYEAR = 1900;
   const int LATEYEAR = 1992;
   const int LOWMONTH = 1;
   const int HIGHMONTH = 12;
   int year = date / YEARFINDER;
   int month = date % YEARFINDER / MONTHFINDER;
   int day = date % YEARFINDER % MONTHFINDER;
   int ok = 1;
   if(year < EARLYYEAR || year > LATEYEAR)
       ok = 0;
   if(month < LOWMONTH || month > HIGHMONTH)
       ok = 0;
   return ok;
}
int main()
{
  Employee aWorker;
  int id, birth, hire;
  cout<<"Enter employee ID number ";
  cin>>id;
  cout<<"Enter employee birth date in the format yyyymmdd ";
  cin>>birth;
  cout<<"Enter employee hire date using the same format ";
  cin>>hire;
  aWorker.setIdNum(id);
  aWorker.setBirthDate(birth);
  aWorker.setHireDate(hire);
  aWorker.display();
}
```

Figure 7-10   Employee class and `main()` demonstration function (continued)

```
C:\WINDOWS\system32\cmd.exe                                    _ □ ✕
Enter employee ID number 1236
Enter employee birth date in the format yyyymmdd 19870624
Enter employee hire date using the same format 20050199
Invalid hire date entered
Employee #1236
Born 1987
Hired in: 0
Press any key to continue . . . _
```

Figure 7-11   Typical execution of the application in Figure 7-10

If you choose, you can create the `verifyDate()` function in Figure 7-10 to return a `bool` value of `true` or `false` instead of an `int` 1 or 0.

If you choose, you can make all the class functions public; if you do so in Figure 7-10, then any client that uses your `Employee` class could use any function. You can organize your classes in the way that seems most suitable to you.

You could make the `verifyDate()` function in the `Employee` class more complete by writing code to assure that the day value is not greater than it should be for a specific month. For example, April 31 should not be allowed. The example was kept short here so it would be easier for you to follow.

CONSIDERING SCOPE WHEN DEFINING MEMBER FUNCTIONS

You already know about scope; a local variable is in scope only within the function in which it is declared. The scope resolution operator is a C++ operator that identifies a member function as being in scope within a class. It consists of two colons (::).

For example, the **Customer** class in Figure 7-12 contains two fields (one for the name and another to hold the balance due) and two functions (one that sets the field values and another that displays them). The headers for the functions signal that they are members of the Customer class by using the class name and scope resolution operator in front of the function identifiers (see shading).

```
#include<iostream>
#include<string>
using namespace std;
// declaration section
class Customer
{
   private:
      string name;
      double balance;
   public:
         void display();
         void setFields(string, double);
};
// implementation section
void Customer::display()
{
   cout<<"Customer name: "<<name<<" owes $"<<balance<<endl;
}
void Customer::setFields(string custName, double amtOwed)
{
   name = custName;
   balance = amtOwed;
}
```

Figure 7-12 The Customer class

Within a class function, when you use class field names, you do not need to take any special action; the fields are part of the same class as the function, so the function has access to them. For example, in the setFields() function in Figure 7-12, name and balance refer to the class fields with those names. However, the setFields() function can also be written as shown in Figure 7-13. In this version, the Customer class name and scope resolution operator are used with each class field name.

```
void Customer::setFields(string custName, double amtOwed)
{
   Customer::name = custName;
   Customer::balance = amtOwed;
}
```

Figure 7-13 The setFields() function of the Customer class, using scope resolution with the field names

With the setFields() function in the Customer class, the class name and scope resolution operators are completely optional; the function operates correctly without them because the fields are part of the same class as the function itself. However, the scope resolution operator does no harm, and leaves no doubt as to the origin of the field names; it is equivalent to using your full formal name instead of your nickname. Just as a mother seldom uses the name "Catherine Marie Johnson," opting instead for "Cathy," C++ programmers usually do not bother using the class name and scope resolution operator when referring to field names from within the class.

However, there are circumstances when the scope resolution operator might be used with a class field name. Whenever there is a conflict between local and class variable names, you can use the scope resolution operator to achieve the results you want. Consider the version of the Customer class setFields() function in Figure 7-14. In this version, the variable passed into the function that holds the Customer's name is known locally as name (see shading). Within this version of the function, any use of name refers to the passed argument. To distinguish between the local variable and the class field, the scope resolution operator is used with the class field. If you placed a statement within the setFields() function, such as name = name;, you would simply assign the passed parameter's value to itself, and the class field would never be set. The class variable with the same name as a parameter is hidden if you do not use the scope resolution operator.

```cpp
void Customer::setFields(string name, double balance)
{
    Customer::name = name;
    Customer::balance = balance;
}
```

Figure 7-14   A version of setFields() in which the scope resolution operator is required

Later in this chapter you will learn how to use a this pointer instead of the class name and scope resolution operator when a local variable and a field name conflict.

USING STATIC CLASS MEMBERS

A C++ object is an instantiation of a class that can contain both data members and methods. When you create an object, a block of memory is set aside for the data members. Just as the declaration int x; reserves enough space in your system to hold an integer, the declaration Student oneStudent; reserves enough storage in your system to hold a Student object. For example, if a Student is defined to contain an integer ID number and a double grade point average, then each time a Student object is declared, enough memory for both the integer and the double is reserved.

When it is created, each class object gets its own block of memory for its data members. If you create two Students, you reserve two blocks of memory; if you create an array of 100 objects, 100 blocks of memory are set aside.

Sometimes every instantiation of a class requires the same value. For example, you might want every Student object to contain a data member that holds the student athletic fee—a value that is the same for all Students. If you declare 100 Student objects, all Students need their own ID, name, and grade point average, but not all Students need their own copy of the athletic fee figure. If each Student object contains a copy of the athletic fee, you repeat the same information 100 times, wasting memory. To avoid this, you declare the athletic fee variable as **static**, meaning that only one memory location is allocated, no matter how many class objects you instantiate. In other words, all members of the class share a single storage location for a **static** data member of that same class. A class variable that you declare to be **static** is the same for all objects that are instantiations of the class. Each instantiation of the class *appears* to be storing its own copy of the same value, but each just has access to the same memory location.

TIP

When you create a non-static variable within a function, a new variable is created every time you call that function. The variable might have a different address and different initial value from the previous time you called the function. When you create a static variable, the variable maintains its memory address and previous value for the life of the program.

Defining Static Data Members

Because it uses only one memory location, a **static** data member is defined (given a value) in a single statement outside the class definition. Most often this statement appears just before the class implementation section. Consider the class and program in Figure 7-15. Note that in this example, the small Student class contains just two fields. In this program, every class object that you ever instantiate receives its own copy of the non-static idNum field, but the same static athleticFee value applies to every class member that is ever instantiated. (The first shaded statement in Figure 7-15 shows the declaration of the field.) When the main() function declares two Student objects, aFreshman and aSophomore, they each possess their own idNum value, but they share the athleticFee value. In the output shown in Figure 7-16, each object displays the same athletic fee.

```
#include<iostream>
using namespace std;
// declaration section:
class Student
{
    private:
        int idNum;
    public:
        static double athleticFee;
        void setIdNum(int);
        void displayStudentData();
};
// implementation section:
double Student::athleticFee = 45.25;
void Student::displayStudentData()
{
  cout<<"Student #"<<idNum<<"'s athletic fee is $"
    <<athleticFee<<endl;
}
void Student::setIdNum(int num)
{
    idNum = num;
}
int main()
{
    Student aFreshman, aSophomore;
    aFreshman.setIdNum(1234);
    aSophomore.setIdNum(2345);
    aFreshman.displayStudentData();
    aSophomore.displayStudentData();
    cout<<"The standard student athletic fee is $"<<
        Student::athleticFee<<endl;
}
```

Figure 7-15   A class that contains a static `athleticFee` field

Figure 7-16   Output of application in Figure 7-15

Even though each `Student` declared in the program shown in Figure 7-15 has a unique ID number, all `Student` objects share the athletic fee, which is assigned a value just once (in the second highlighted statement in the figure). You must assign a value to each `static` field outside the class in which it is declared. (You can also change the static field value later, if it is not a constant field.) In Figure 7-15, notice that the keyword `static` is used when the `athleticFee` is declared. The keyword `static` is not used in the assignment statement in which `athleticFee` is assigned a value.

You cannot use the `Student` class `idNum` field unless you have created a `Student` object; no `idNum` exists unless a `Student` exists. However, a `static` class member exists, even when you have not instantiated any objects of the class. For example, when you use the `Student` class, you can access the `Student::athleticFee` even if you have not created any `Student` objects. In the last shaded statement in Figure 7-15, you can see that you can use `athleticFee` with just the class name and the scope resolution operator. Static variables are sometimes called **class variables**, **class fields**, or **class-wide fields** because they don't belong to a specific object; they belong to the class, and you can use them even if you never instantiate an object.

Static fields are frequently defined to be constant, although they do not have to be. For example, a real student athletic fee is most likely a constant that should always have the same value for every student. The field `athleticFee` in Figure 7-15 is not defined as a constant field. You could make it constant in the same way you make other fields constant—by inserting the word `const` in front of its name when you declare it. New programmers frequently confuse the meanings of `static` and constant, but `static` does not mean the same thing as constant. Constant fields are never changeable; static fields hold the same value for every object. *Constant* `static` fields hold the same unchangeable value for every object.

Because the `athleticFee` field in the `Student` class in Figure 7-15 was not declared constant, you could insert a statement like `aFreshman.athleticFee = 139.95;` into the `main()` function. From that point on, every `Student` object (both the `aFreshman` and the `aSophomore`) would have an `athleticFee` of 139.95 instead of 45.25. Alternately, and more logically, you could also make the following statement:

```
Student::athleticFee = 139.95;
```

This statement would also change every `Student`'s `athleticFee` field from that point on. Again, you can see that you do not need to create any objects to use a `static` class variable.

Although you can use static class members with an object name or by using them with the class name, some programmers prefer to use them only with the class name. That's because they perceive static members to truly belong to the class as a whole.

Although static fields are frequently constant, it is not always so. For example, in game programming you might create an `Alien` class. As each `Alien` enters the game, you might want each object to "know" how many of its kind exist because you allow an `Alien` to act more daring if more comrades are in play. You could create a non-constant static field for the class with a value that increased as more `Alien`s entered the game, and to which all `Alien` objects had access.

Using Static Functions

In C++, a static field can be accessed with an object and also without one. (Fields that are not static always need a declared object when you use them.) In the program shown in Figure 7-15, the static athleticFee field is public, which is why you can access it directly, as in the last highlighted output in the figure. If athleticFee were private, and you wanted to access it without using an object, you would have to use a public function to access the value, as you do with any other private variable. Additionally, the function would have to be a static function. A **static function** is one you can use without a declared object.

Non-static functions can access static variables (provided there is an object).
Static functions cannot access non-static variables.

TIP

When an object uses a non-static function, for example as in aFreshman.displayStudentData(), the function receives a pointer to the object. The pointer is known as the this pointer, and you will learn about it in the next section.

Static fields do not need to be associated with an object; they are class-wide fields. When you do not want to declare an object, you can still access a static, class-wide field only by using a function that is also static. In other words, a field that is not associated with an object can be accessed only by a function that is not associated with an object—you need a static function in order to access a static field when you choose not to use an object.

You use a static function by prefixing the function name with the class name and the scope resolution operator. Figure 7-17 shows a modified Student class that holds only one private field—a static athletic fee. Because the field is static, it can be used without an object. The static public functions setFee() and showFee() also need no object; in the shaded statements in main() they are used without objects. Figure 7-18 shows the output.

```
#include<iostream>
using namespace std;
// declaration section:
class Student
{
    private:
      static double athleticFee;
    public:
      static void setFee(double);
      static void showFee();
};
// implementation section:
double Student::athleticFee = 0;
void Student::setFee(double fee)
{
    athleticFee = fee;
}
void Student::showFee()
{
    cout<<"Fee is $"<<athleticFee<<endl;
}

int main()
{
    Student::setFee(87.99);
    Student::showFee();
}
```

Figure 7-17   A Student class containing static fields and functions

Figure 7-18   Output of application in Figure 7-17

The Student class in Figure 7-17 could contain non-static fields and functions as well as the static ones shown. The class was kept small for simplicity. In order to use non-static functions, you would need to instantiate an object.

UNDERSTANDING THE `this` POINTER

When you define a class, you include fields and functions. If the class has two non-static fields and one static field such as the **Employee** class shown in Figure 7-19, and you then declare two **Employee** objects (see shading in **main()** function), you reserve storage for two versions of the non-static fields. However, you store only one version of the static field that every object can use. Figure 7-20 shows how the data fields are stored for the two objects declared in the **main()** function in Figure 7-19. The **clerk** and the **driver** each have their own ID number and **payRate**, but only one **companyIdNum** is stored in memory. Figure 7-21 shows the program output.

```cpp
#include<iostream>
using namespace std;
class Employee
{
    private:
        int employeeIdNum;
        double payRate;
        const static int companyIdNum;
    public:
        void setId(int);
        void setPayRate(double);
        void displayValues();
 };
const int Employee::companyIdNum = 12345;
void Employee::displayValues()
{
  cout<<endl<<"Employee #"<<employeeIdNum<<
    " company #"<<companyIdNum<<endl;
  cout<<"Pay rate is $"<<payRate<<endl;
}
void Employee::setId(int id)
{
    employeeIdNum = id;
}
void Employee::setPayRate(double rate)
{
    payRate = rate;
}
int main()
{
    Employee clerk, driver;
    clerk.setId(777);
    clerk.setPayRate(13.45);
    driver.setId(888);
    driver.setPayRate(18.79);
    clerk.displayValues();
    driver.displayValues();
}
```

Figure 7-19   Employee class and `main()` function that creates two
Employee objects

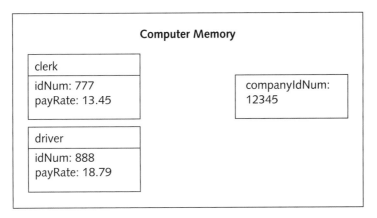

Figure 7-20   How non-static and static fields are stored

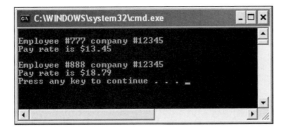

Figure 7-21   Output of program in Figure 7-19

Each Employee needs a unique ID number, so that field is not made **static**. Because all **Employee** objects use the same company ID, it would be wasteful to store multiple copies of the same value. Additionally, if the **static** value required changing (if, for example, the company acquired a new company ID number), then if there was a separate field for each **Employee**, each version associated with each object would have to be updated. As a **static** field, the **companyIdNum** is stored once.

Just as it would be wasteful to store a shared company ID number separately for each declared **Employee**, it would also waste space if you stored the code for the member functions **setId()** and **displayValues()** separately for each **Employee**. The **Employee** class in Figure 7-19 contains only two member functions. Imagine an **Employee** class with 20 member functions, and a program that declares 1,000 **Employee** objects. If the same function code were stored repeatedly for every instance of a class, the storage requirements would be enormous.

Luckily, C++ does not store member functions separately for each instance of a class. Instead, one copy of each member function is stored, and each instance of a class uses the same function code. Whether you make the statement **clerk.displayValues();** or **driver.displayValues();**, you call the same copy of the **displayValues()** function. This does not mean the output results are identical, as you can see from Figure 7-21.

Even though each call to the function uses the same programming instructions, each call to `displayValues()` uses a different memory location to access the appropriate `employeeIdNum`.

Because only one copy of each function exists, when you call a non-static member function, it needs to know which object to use. To ensure that the function uses the correct object, you use the object's name, such as `clerk` or `driver`, with the dot operator. The address of the correct object, `clerk` or `driver`, is then automatically passed to the `displayValues()` function.

Within the `displayValues()` function, the address of the object is stored in a special pointer called the **this pointer**. The `this` pointer holds the memory address of the current object that is using the function; that's why it is named `this`—it refers to "this object" as opposed to any other object. The `this` pointer is automatically supplied every time you call a non-static member function of a class. For example, when you make the function call `clerk.displayValues();`, the actual function call made by the compiler is `displayValues(&clerk);`. Similarly, when you make the function call `driver.displayValues();`, the actual function call is `displayValues (&driver);`. In other words, when you use an object, the dot operator, and a non-static function of the object's class, you actually pass the specific object's address to the function as an unseen argument. The actual argument list used by the compiler for the `displayValues()` function is `displayValues(Employee *this)`. The `displayValues()` function receives a pointer to an `Employee` object; the automatically supplied object address is the means by which the function knows which `Employee`'s data to display.

TIP

Don't explicitly send the address of the object when you call a non-static member function; if you do, the function receives two address values—the one you type and the one automatically sent.

TIP

The `this` pointer is also passed to non-static member functions when they receive additional, explicitly stated arguments. Figure 7-19 shows that the `Employee` class `setId()` function receives an integer argument. In addition, it receives a pointer to the object it manipulates. When you make the statement `clerk.setId(345);`, the actual argument list used by the compiler for `setId()` is `setId(Employee *this, const int id);`. The actual function call used by the compiler is `setId(&clerk, 345);`. When you call a non-static member function using a class object, the first (and sometimes only) argument passed to the function is a pointer that holds the address of the object to which you are referring.

TIP

The `this` pointer is a constant pointer. You cannot modify it, as in the following:
`this = &someOtherObject;   // illegal!`

Using the this Pointer Explicitly

Within any member function, you can prove that the this pointer exists and that it holds the address of the current object. You do so by explicitly using the this pointer to access the object's data fields. In Figure 7-22, displayValues() and setId() have been rewritten to explicitly refer to the this pointer when an object's field is used. Notice in the highlighted sections that the this pointer can precede any field. If you substitute the functions in Figure 7-22 for their counterparts in the original class definition in Figure 7-19, there is no difference in the execution of the program; there would be no difference in any program that uses the Employee class. The versions of the functions shown in Figure 7-22 simply illustrate that the this pointer exists, and that you can refer to the contents stored in the this pointer like you can with any other pointer—by placing an asterisk in front of the pointer's name. (The parentheses are required in (*this).employeeIdNum because only this is a pointer. Without the parentheses, the compiler would treat this.employeeIdNum as a pointer, which it is not—it is an integer, and you cannot dereference it using the asterisk.)

7

```
void Employee::displayValues()
{
   cout<<"Employee #"<<(*this).employeeIdNum<<" company #"
      <<(*this).companyIdNum<<endl;
}
void Employee::setId(const int id)
{
   (*this).employeeIdNum = id;
}
```

Figure 7-22   Member functions explicitly using the this pointer

Using the Pointer-to-Member Operator

Figure 7-23 shows yet another way to use the this pointer. The functions operate like those in Figure 7-22, but they use the C++ **pointer-to-member operator**, which looks like an arrow and is constructed by using a dash followed by a right-angle bracket (or greater-than sign). Any pointer variable that is declared to point to a class object can be used to access individual fields or functions of that class by using the parentheses and the asterisk shown in Figure 7-22. Or, the pointer-to-member operator shown in Figure 7-23 can be used.

```
void Employee::displayValues()
{
  cout<<"Employee #"<<this->employeeIdNum<<" company #"
    <<this->companyIdNum<<endl;
}
void Employee::setId(const int id)
{
   this->employeeIdNum = id;
}
```

Figure 7-23   Explicitly using the `this` pointer with the pointer-to-member operator

Programmers usually do not code their class member functions as shown in Figure 7-22 or Figure 7-23. The functions work fine without typing the `this` references. Often, you do not have to be concerned with the `this` pointer. Although it's helpful to understand how the function knows which object to use, the reference is made automatically, and you don't have to think about it. There are, however, occasions when you might want to use the `this` pointer explicitly within member functions, and other occasions when you will see the `this` pointer used in programs. The most common occurrence is when you want to return the pointer that was sent to a function (for example, `return(*this);`). As another example, you could use the `this` pointer when an argument to a class function has the same identifier as a class field. Then you can use the `this` pointer to identify the class field. In the version of the `Employee` class `setIdNum()` function in Figure 7-24, if you did not include the highlighted `this` pointer, then the value of the local argument `employeeIdNum` would be assigned to itself and the object's `employeeIdNum` would never receive an appropriate value.

```
void Employee::setId(const int employeeIdNum)
{
   this->employeeIdNum =  employeeIdNum;
}
```

Figure 7-24   Using the `this` pointer to differentiate between a class field and a local variable with the same identifier

TIP

The only type of class member function that does not have a `this` pointer is a static member function.

UNDERSTANDING POLYMORPHISM

Polymorphism is the object-oriented program feature that allows the same operation to be carried out differently depending on the object. When you speak English, you use the same instructions with different objects all the time. For example, you interpret a verb differently depending on the object to which it is applied. You catch a ball, but you also catch a cold. You run a computer, a business, a race, or a stocking. The meanings of "catch" and "run" are different in each case, but you can understand each operation because the combination of the verb and the object makes the command clear.

When you write C++ (and other object-oriented) programs, you can send the same message to different objects and different types of objects. Suppose you have two members of the `Employee` class, `clerk` and `driver`. You can display the data of each member with the following statements: `clerk.displayValues();` and `driver.displayValues();`. No confusion arises as to which member's values should be displayed, because the correct pointer is passed as a `this` pointer each time you call the `displayValues()` function.

Similarly, suppose you have three different objects that are members of different classes: a `clerk` who is a member of the `Employee` class, a `shirt` that is a member of the `Inventory` class, and `XYZCompany`, a member of the `Supplier` class. Each object can certainly have different numbers and types of data members. The clerk has an employee `idNumber` and a `salary`. The shirt has a `sleeveLength`, `neckSize`, and `price`. The `XYZCompany` has a `president`, `phoneNumber`, `dateOfLastOrder`, and `annualSalesFigure`. Even though these objects are very different, occasionally you might need to display each of their data members. In such a case, it seems appropriate to call each function `displayValues()`.

C++ allows you to create three very different member functions, one for each of the classes in question, but use the same identifier for each. For example, within an `Employee` class, an `Inventory` class, and a `Supplier` class, you might create the functions shown in Figure 7-25.

7

```
// Within the Employee class
void Employee::displayValues()
{
    cout<<"Employee ID is "<<idNumber;
}

// Within the Inventory class
void Inventory::displayValues()
{
   cout<<"This shirt has a sleeve of "<<sleeveLength;
   cout<<" and a neck size "<<neckSize<<endl;
   cout<<"It sells for $"<<price<<endl;
}

// Within the Supplier class
void Supplier::displayValues()
{
    cout<<"Company president: "<<president<<" at phone "<<
        phoneNumber<<endl;
    cout<<"Last order "<<dateOfLastOrder;
    cout<<" Annual sales "<<annualSalesFigure<<endl;
 }
```

Figure 7-25   Three `displayValues()` functions from three separate classes

The three functions in Figure 7-25 contain different numbers of statements as well as statements with different content, but they all have the name `displayValues()`. Assuming you have declared objects of the appropriate class types, you might make three function calls as follows:

```
clerk.displayValues();
shirt.displayValues();
XYZCompany.displayValues();
```

Each of the preceding functions displays the intended object in a unique, appropriate format. The `this` pointer sends the appropriate address so the function uses the correct object. Because of the object's type (`Employee`, `Inventory`, or `Supplier`), you call the `displayValues()` function that is a member of the appropriate class.

The concept of polymorphism includes far more than using the same function name for different function bodies. As you continue to study C++, you will learn about the role polymorphism plays in inheritance.

TIP

When you can apply the same function name to different objects, your programs become easier to read and make more sense. It takes less time to develop a project; you also can make later changes more rapidly. C++ programmers can often write programs faster than programmers who use non-object-oriented programming languages, and polymorphism is one of the reasons why.

You Do It

Creating and Using a Class

In the next set of steps, you create a class that implements a function. Then you write a short demonstration program to instantiate an object of the class, and use the object's fields and functions.

1. Open a new file. Type a comment identifying the program's purpose, which is to create and demonstrate a class that holds information about a college course. Then type the first statements you need:

```
#include<iostream>
#include<string>
using namespace std;
```

2. Next type the **CollegeCourse** class declaration section. It includes three private fields that hold the three-letter code of the department in which the course is offered, the course number, and the number of seats available for which students can enroll. It also contains the definition for three functions—one that sets the course department and number, one that sets the number of students allowed in the course, and one that displays the course data. Don't forget the class-ending semicolon, which is easy to omit.

```
class CollegeCourse
{
    private:
        string department;
        int courseNum;
        int seats;
    public:
        void setDepartmentAndCourse(string, int);
        void setSeats(int);
        void displayCourseData();
};
```

3. Next, in the implementation section, write the **setDepartmentAndCourse()** function. Notice the class name and scope resolution operator before the function name in the header. The function takes two arguments. The first is the string representing the college department, for example CIS, ENG, or SOC. The second is the course number, for example 101 or 200. The two are assigned to the class fields without any validation, although in a more sophisticated program you might want to ensure that the department was an existing department in the college, or that the course number fell between specific values.

```
void CollegeCourse::setDepartmentAndCourse(string dept, int num)
{
    department = dept;
    courseNum = num;
}
```

7

4. The `setSeats()` function accepts a number of students allowed to enroll in a course. The function assures that the number is not negative, assigning 0 if it is. The function assigns the local seats variable to the class member variable. Notice that because the function parameter and the class field have the same identifier, the `this` pointer must be used with the class member to distinguish it.

```
void CollegeCourse::setSeats(int seats)
{
    if(seats < 0)
        seats = 0;
    this->seats = seats;
}
```

5. The `displayCourseData()` function that is a member of the `CollegeCourse` class contains a single statement that displays the values of the `CollegeCourse`'s data fields.

```
void CollegeCourse::displayCourseData()
{
    cout<<department<<courseNum<<" accommodates "<<
        seats<<" students"<<endl;
}
```

6. Start a `main()` function that declares a `CollegeCourse` object and prompts the user for values. Notice how the second two prompts make use of the data the user has already entered, to make the prompts more personalized.

```
int main()
{
    CollegeCourse myMondayClass;
    string dept;
    int num;
    int students;
    cout<<"Enter the department that hosts the
        class,"<<endl;
    cout<<"for example 'CIS'>> ";
    cin>>dept;
    cout<<"Enter the course number, for example, for "<<
        dept<<"101, enter 101>> ";
    cin>>num;
    cout<<"Enter the number of students that are
        allowed"<<endl;
    cout<<"to enroll in "<<dept<<num<<">> ";
    cin>>students;
```

7. Add the code to assign the user-entered values to the declared `CollegeCourse` object and then display the results. End the `main()` function with a closing curly brace.

```
myMondayClass.setDepartmentAndCourse(dept, num);
myMondayClass.setSeats(students);
myMondayClass.displayCourseData();
}
```

8. Save the file as **CollegeCourse.cpp**. Compile and run the program. The output should look like Figure 7-26.

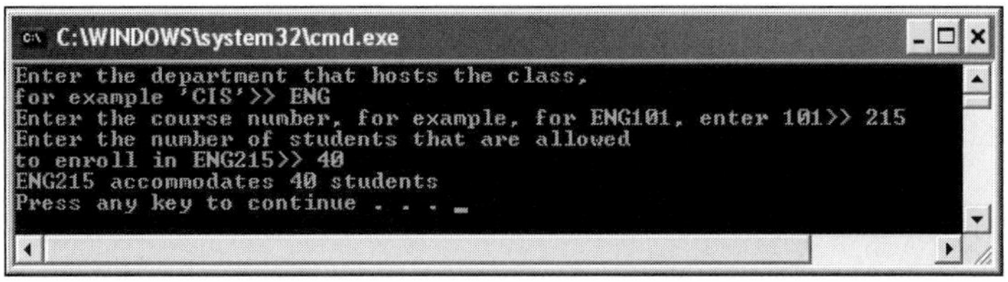

Figure 7-26   Output of the `CollegeCourse` application

Using a `static` Field

In the following set of steps, you use a **private static** class variable to keep track of how many objects have been initialized. You will use a **public static** function to display the **private static** variable.

1. Open a new file in your C++ editor. Type the necessary **include** and **using** statements, and begin a class that holds information about business letters you write. For simplicity, this class contains just three **private** fields: the title and last name of the recipient and a count of how many letters have been sent. (A real-life class might also include the recipient's mailing address data.)

```
#include<iostream>
#include<string>
using namespace std;
class Letter
{
   private:
     string title;
     string recipient;
     static int count;
```

2. Include three functions in the public section of the class—one to set the recipient data, one to display the letter greeting, and one to display the count of letters that have been sent. The `displayCount()` function is **static** because it will be used without an object to display the **static** class field.

```
   public:
     void setRecipient(string, string);
     void displayGreeting();
     static void displayCount();
};
```

3. Initialize the `Letter` count to zero. This statement is placed outside the body of the class definition.

```
int Letter::count = 0;
```

4. Write the `setRecipient()` function. This function is a member of the `Letter` class, so you use the class name and scope resolution operator in the function heading. The function sets the title and name of the `Letter` recipient with parameter values that are passed into it. Because the identifier for the name argument is the same as a field in the class, the `this` pointer is used to refer to the class field. The `setRecipient()` function also adds 1 to the count of letters sent.

```
void Letter::setRecipient(string title, string name)
{
        this->title = title;
        recipient = name;
        ++count;
}
```

5. Write the `displayGreeting()` function that displays a full letter salutation including a title, name, and comma—for example, "Dear Mr. Johnson,".

```
void Letter::displayGreeting()
{
        cout <<"Dear "<<title<<". "<<recipient<<","<<endl;
}
```

6. The `displayCount()` function displays the count of the number of `Letter` objects that have been created.

```
void Letter::displayCount()
{
        cout<<"Current count is "<<count<<endl<<endl;
}
```

7. Next, begin a `main()` function that declares a `Letter` object as well as two strings into which the user can enter a title and name. Also prototype a `displayLetter()` funtion to which you will pass a `Letter` recipient.

```
int main()
{
   Letter aLetter;
   string title;
   string name;
   void displayLetter(Letter);
```

8. Next, declare a loop control variable named `more`. The variable is initialized to 'y'. A loop continues while the value of `more` is not 'n'. At the end of the loop, the user provides a new value for `more`, perhaps entering 'n' to stop the loop's execution. Within the loop, prompt the user for a title and name, then use these values

to set the `Letter`'s values. Pass the `Letter` to the `displayLetter()` function before displaying the count of the number of letters created and before asking the user whether more letters should be created. The `displayCount()` function is not used with an object (although it could be); instead, it is used without an object which can be done because it is `static`. Include a closing curly brace for the while loop and a closing brace for the `main()` function.

```cpp
char more = 'y';
while(more != 'n')
{
  cout<<"Enter title for recipient, for example 'Mr' or 'Ms' >> ";
  cin>>title;
  cout<< "Enter last name of recipient>> ";
  cin>>name;
  aLetter.setRecipient(title, name);
  displayLetter(aLetter);
  Letter::displayCount();
  cout<<"Do you want to send another - y or n? ";
  cin>>more;
}
}
```

9. Finally, write the `displayLetter()` function. This function is not a member of the `Letter` class; it is a function called by `main()`. The `Letter` that contains the recipient data is passed to this function in which a business letter is created. The function uses the `displayGreeting()` function that is part of the `Letter` class to display a greeting, then displays the letter body.

```cpp
void displayLetter(Letter letter)
{
  letter.displayGreeting();
  cout<<"Thank you for your recent order. We look"<<endl<<
        "forward to serving you again soon."<<endl<<
        "                    Sincerely,"<<endl<<
        "                    ABC Company"<<endl<<endl;
}
```

10. Save the program as **Letter.cpp**, and compile and run the program. A typical run is shown in Figure 7-27. Notice how each `Letter` passed to the `displayLetter()` function has a unique greeting. Also notice that the `static count` continues to increase as each new `Letter` is created; this is possible because all `Letter` objects share the same `count` field.

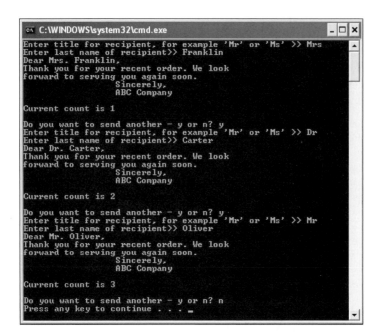

Figure 7-27   Typical execution of the `Letter` application

Understanding How `static` and Non-`static` Fields are Stored

When you create an object that contains non-`static` data fields, the fields are stored together in adjacent memory locations. However, `static` fields do not belong to any one object; they belong to the class as a whole. Therefore, it makes sense that any `static` data fields are not stored with any one object. In the next steps, you will prove this for yourself by adding a function to the `Letter` class that displays the memory locations of an object's fields.

1. If it is not still open, open the **Letter.cpp** file in your text editor.

2. In the public section of the `Letter` class, add a declaration for the function that will display the memory locations of the class fields:

   ```
   void showMemoryLocations();
   ```

3. Below the `displayCount()` function but above `main()`, add the implementation of the `showMemoryLocations()` function. The function uses the address operator (&) to display the memory address of each field in a `Letter` object.

   ```
   void Letter::showMemoryLocations()
   {
        cout<<"Memory addresses:"<<endl;
        cout<<"title:      "<<&title<<endl;
        cout<<"recipient   "<<&recipient<<endl;
        cout<<"count       "<<&count<<endl;
   }
   ```

4. In the `while` loop within the `main()` function, just after the call to the `displayCount()` function, add a call to the `showMemoryLocations()` function as follows:

```
aLetter.showMemoryLocations();
```

5. Save the modified file as **Letter2.cpp**, then compile and execute the program. Figure 7-28 shows the start of a typical execution. After the user enters a title and name, the letter and the count display. The function that displays the field memory addresses executes. From the output, you can see that the memory addresses of the title and recipient fields are very close to each other, but the static `count` field is in a very different memory location. It makes sense that an object's fields are stored adjacently; it also makes sense that a static field is not stored with any individual object.

Figure 7-28   Execution of the `Letter2` application

CHAPTER SUMMARY

❑ A class is a category of objects; it provides a convenient way to group related data and functions. By default, all members of a class are `private`, meaning they cannot be accessed using any statements in any functions that are not also part of the class.

❑ When you write a program and create a class name for a group of associated variables, you hide, or encapsulate, the individual components. When you design C++ classes, you think about what the class objects will *do* and how programmers will make them do it, as well as what the class objects *contain*. Therefore your classes will contain fields, and functions that often act as interfaces to the class objects. Typically, the fields in your classes will be private, but your interfacing functions will be public.

❑ When you construct a class, you create two parts. The first part is a declaration section, which contains the class name, variables (attributes), and function prototypes. The second part created is an implementation section, which contains the functions themselves.

❐ When you create a class, usually you want to make data items private, to control how they are used, and to make functions public, to provide a means to access and manipulate the data. However, if you have a reason to do so, you are free to make particular data items public. Similarly, not all functions are public; some are private.

❐ The scope resolution operator is a C++ operator that identifies a member function as being in scope within a class. It consists of two colons (::).

❐ When it is created, each class object gets its own block of memory for its data members. When you declare a field as static only one memory location is allocated, no matter how many class objects you instantiate. In other words, all members of the class share a single storage location for a static data member of that same class. Because it uses only one memory location, a static data member is defined (given a value) in a single statement outside the class definition. Static fields are frequently defined to be constant, although they do not have to be.

❐ When you do not want to declare an object, you still can access a **static**, class-wide field only by using a function that is also **static**.

❐ One copy of each class member function is stored no matter how many objects exist, and each instance of a class uses the same function code. When you call a member function, it knows which object to use because you use the object's name, such as **clerk** or **driver**, with the dot operator. The address of the correct object is stored in the **this** pointer and automatically passed to the function.

❐ Within any member function, you can explicitly use the **this** pointer to access the object's data fields. You can also use the C++ pointer-to-member operator, which looks like an arrow and is constructed by using a dash followed by a right angle bracket (or greater-than sign).

❐ Polymorphism is the object-oriented program feature that allows the same operation to be carried out differently depending on the object. When you can apply the same function name to different objects, your programs become easier to read and make more sense. It takes less time to develop a project; you can also make later changes more rapidly.

KEY TERMS

A **class** is a category of objects; it is a new data type you create that is more complex than the basic data types.

An **abstract data type (ADT)** is a type you define, as opposed to types that are defined by C++.

An **extensible language** is a language to which you can add your own data types.

An **access modifier** assigns accessibility to the declared variables that follow it.

The access modifier **private** means a class member cannot be accessed using any statements in any functions that are not also part of the class.

To **encapsulate** components is to contain them.

An **interface** intercedes between you and the inner workings of an object.

To **instantiate** an object is to declare or create it.

A function that is a user of your class is a **class client**.

The **declaration section** of a class contains the class name, variables (attributes), and function prototypes.

The **implementation section** of a class contains the functions.

When a class field is **static**, only one memory location is allocated, no matter how many class objects you instantiate. All members of the class share a single storage location for a **static** data member of that same class.

Static variables are sometimes called **class variables**, **class fields**, or **class-wide fields** because they don't belong to a specific object; they belong to the class, and you can use them even if you never instantiate an object.

A **static function** is one you can use without a declared object.

The **this pointer** holds the memory address of the current object that is using a class function. It is automatically supplied every time you call a non-static member function of a class.

The **pointer-to-member operator** looks like an arrow and is used between an object's pointer and an object's field. It is constructed by using a dash followed by a right angle bracket (or greater-than sign).

7

REVIEW QUESTIONS

1. C++ programmers refer to a type you define as an ADT, or an _____.

   a. abstract data type

   b. alternative data theory

   c. adaptable data type

   d. anonymous default test

2. You have defined a class named `Invoice` that contains two non-static private fields, `invoiceNumber` and `amount`. When you write a `main()` function and declare one `Invoice` object named `anInvoice`, you can display the object's `amount` field with the statement _____.

   a. `cout<<anInvoice(amount);`

   b. `cout<<Invoice.amount;`

   c. `cout<<anInvoice.amount;`

   d. None of the above

3. You have defined a class named `Invoice` that contains two non-static private fields, `invoiceNumber` and `amount`. The class also contains a non-static public function that displays the amount; the function's prototype is `void showAmount();`. When you write a `main()` function and declare one `Invoice` object named `anInvoice`, you can display the object's amount field with the statement _____.

a. `cout<<Invoice::showAmount();`

b. `cout<<Invoice.showAmount();`

c. `cout<<anInvoice.showAmount();`

d. None of the above

4. When you encapsulate class components, you _____ them.

a. destroy

b. hide

c. display

d. format

5. The word interface is most closely associated with _____.

a. public class functions

b. private class variables

c. class descriptions

d. function implementations

6. You create a class in two sections called _____.

a. declaration and implementation

b. typical and atypical

c. common and protected

d. abstract and concrete

7. A class named `Apartment` contains a non-static public function named `showRent()` that neither takes nor receives arguments. The correct function header for the `showRent()` function is _____.

a. `showRent()`

b. `Apartment::showRent()`

c. `void Apartment::showRent()`

d. `void Apartment.showRent()`

8. The operator you use in a function header that ties a function name to a class is the
   _____ operator.

   a. pointer-to-member

   b. `this`

   c. scope resolution

   d. binary

9. A technique that programmers use to provide object encapsulation is to usually
   make objects' data _____.

   a. `private`

   b. polymorphic

   c. accessible

   d. `static`

10. The most common arrangement for a class is that _____.

    a. data members are `static` and functions are not

    b. data members are not `static` and functions are

    c. data members are `public` and functions are not

    d. data members are not `public` and functions are

11. You control how data is stored in classes by using _____.

    a. polymorphism

    b. well-written public functions

    c. anonymous classes

    d. private methods that clients cannot access

12. Which is true?

    a. All class functions are private.

    b. Most class functions are private.

    c. Most class functions are public.

    d. Most classes contain no functions.

13. A program that uses a class is known as the class's _____.

    a. patient

    b. superclass

    c. consumer

    d. client

14. You create a class named `Car` with private non–static data fields named `year`, `make`, and `price`. The `Car` class contains a public non-static function named `setYear()` whose header is `void Car::setYear(int year)`. Within this function, which statement correctly sets the class field to the value of the argument?

    a. `year = year;`

    b. `Car::year = year;`

    c. `year = Car::year;`

    d. Two of the above are correct.

15. You create a class named `Car` with private non-static data fields named `year`, `make`, and `price`. The `Car` class contains a public non-static function named `setMake()` whose header is `void Car::setMake(string carMake)`. Within this function, which statement correctly sets the class field to the value of the argument?

    a. `make = carMake;`

    b. `this->make = carMake;`

    c. `carMake = make;`

    d. Two of the above are correct.

16. To create just one memory location for a field no matter how many objects you instantiate, you should declare the field to be _____.

    a. private

    b. anonymous

    c. static

    d. stagnant

17. A function that you use to display a static variable without creating an object must be _____.

    a. private

    b. anonymous

    c. static

    d. stagnant

18. The pointer that is automatically supplied when you call a non-static class member function is the _____ pointer.

    a. public

    b. this

    c. implicit

    d. reference

19. When you call a public static class function from outside the class, you
    _____ .

    a. can use an object

    b. must use an object

    c. must not use an object

    d. Static functions cannot be called from outside the class.

20. The feature in object-oriented programs that allows the same operation to be car-
    ried out differently, depending on the object, is _____ .

    a. encapsulation

    b. inheritance

    c. pointer creation

    d. polymorphism

7

EXERCISES

1. Define a class named **Movie**. Include private fields for the title, year, and
   name of the director. Include three public functions with the prototypes
   void Movie::setTitle(cstring);, **void Movie::setYear(int);**,
   and **void Movie::setDirector(string);**. Include another function that
   displays all the information about a **Movie**. Write a **main()** function that
   declares a movie object named **myFavoriteMovie**. Set and display the
   object's fields. Save the file as **Movie.cpp**.

2. a. Define a class named **Customer** that holds private fields for a customer ID
      number, last name, first name, and credit limit. Include four public functions that
      each set one of the four fields. Do not allow any credit limit over $10,000.
      Include a public function that displays a **Customer**'s data. Write a **main()** func-
      tion in which you declare a **Customer**, set the **Customer**'s fields, and display
      the results. Save the file as **Customer.cpp**.

   b. Write a **main()** function that declares an array of five **Customer** objects.
      Prompt the user for values for each **Customer**, and display all five **Customer**
      objects. Save the file as **Customer2.cpp**.

3. a. Define a class named **GroceryItem**. Include private fields that hold an item's
      stock number, price, quantity in stock, and total value. Write a public function
      named **dataEntry()** that calls four private functions. Three of the private
      functions prompt the user for keyboard input for a value for one of the data
      fields stock number, price, and quantity in stock. The function that sets the stock
      number requires the user to enter a value between 1000 and 9999 inclusive; con-

tinue to prompt the user until a valid stock number is entered. The functions that set the price and quantity in stock require non-negative values; continue to prompt the user until valid values are entered. Include a fourth private function that calculates the GroceryItem's total value field (price times quantity in stock). Write a public function that displays a GroceryItem's values. Finally, write a main() function that declares a GroceryItem object, assigns values to its fields, and uses the display function. Save the file as **Grocery.cpp**.

b. Write a main() function that declares an array of 10 GroceryItem objects. Assign values to all 10 items and display them. Save the file as **Grocery2.cpp**.

4. Write the class definition for a Dog. Private data fields include name, breed, and age, and a constant static field for the license fee, which is $12.25. Create public member functions to set and display the data. Write a main() function that demonstrates the class operates correctly. Save the file as **Dog.cpp**.

5. a. Write a class definition for an Order class for a nightclub that contains a table number, a server's name, and the number of patrons at the table. Include a private static data member for the table minimum charge, which is $4.75. Write a main() function that declares no Order objects, but that uses a static member function to display the table minimum charge. Save the file as **Order.cpp**.

b. Using the same Order class, write a main() function that declares an Order object, assigns appropriate values, and displays the Order data, including the minimum charge for the table (the minimum charge times the number of patrons at the table). Save the file as **Order2.cpp**.

6. a. Write the class definition for a Date class that contains three private integer data members: month, day, and year. Create a static member to hold a slash. Create two public member functions, setDate() and showDate(). You will use the static slash in the showDate() function. The setDate() function accepts three integer arguments and passes them on to three private functions—setMonth(), setDay(), and setYear(). If a month is greater than 12, then set it to 12. If a day is greater than 31, then set it to 31. Write a main() function that instantiates several objects of the Date class and tests the class functions. Save the file as **Date.cpp**.

b. Improve the setDay() function by ensuring the day is not higher than allowed for a month—31 for January, March, May, July, August, October, or December; 30 for April, June, September, or November; and 28 or 29 for February. February usually contains 28 days. If a year is evenly divisible by 4, but not by 100, February contains 29 days. (For example, February has only 28 days in 1900 and 2100.) However, if a year is evenly divisible by 400, then February has 29 days (as in the year 2000). Write a main() function that instantiates several objects of the Date class and tests the class functions. Save the file as **Date2.cpp**.

c. Add a public function named increaseDay() to the Date class. Its purpose is to add 1 to the day field of a Date object. When the day is increased to more than the highest day number allowed for a month, the month increases by 1 and the day is set to 1. Write a `main()` function that declares several `Date` objects that will thoroughly test all the functions; in other words, make sure some are close to the end of a month. Loop to call the `increaseDay()` function five times for each `Date`, displaying each version of the `Date` as soon as it is increased. Write a `main()` function that instantiates several objects of the `Date` class and tests the class functions. Save the file as **Date3.cpp**.

d. Add instructions to the `increaseDay()` function so that when the month becomes more than 12, the year increases by 1, and the month and day are set to 1. Write a `main()` function that declares a `Date` object. Set the `Date` to 12/29/2007 and call the `increaseDay()` function 400 times, displaying each version of the `Date` as soon as it is increased. Examine the output to make sure each month and year changes correctly. Save the file as **Date4.cpp**.

7. a. Define a class named `CoffeeOrder`. Declare a private static field that holds the price of a cup of coffee as $1.25. Include private integer fields that you set to a flag value of 1 or 0 to indicate whether the order should have any of the following: cream, milk, sugar, or artificial sweetener. Include a public function that takes a user's order from the keyboard and sets the values of the four fields in response to four prompts. If the user indicates both milk and cream, turn off the milk flag to allow only cream. If the user indicates both sugar and artificial sweetener, turn off the artificial sweetener flag, allowing only sugar. Include another function that displays the user's completed order. Write a `main()` function that declares a `CoffeeOrder` object and calls the data entry and display methods. Save the file as **Coffee.cpp**.

b. Using the `CoffeeOrder` class, write a `main()` function that continues to ask a user for an order in a loop until the user indicates the order is complete or 10 orders have been placed, whichever comes first. After the user indicates that ordering is complete, display a recap of all the coffee orders, including the cream, milk, sugar, and sweetener status of each, as well as a count of the number of coffees ordered and the total price. Save the file as **Coffee2.cpp**.

8. a. Define a class named `TaxReturn` that contains a tax ID number, last name, first name, annual income, number of dependents, and amount of tax owed for a taxpayer. Include constant static fields that hold the tax rates for the situations shown in the following table.

Income	0 dependents	1 dependent	2 or more dependents
0–10,000	0.10	0.08	0.07
10,001–30,000	0.12	0.11	0.09
30,001–60,000	0.18	0.15	0.13
60,001 and up	0.25	0.22	0.19

7

Include a static function that displays the tax table. Write a **main()** function that contains a single statement that displays the tax table. Save the file as **TaxReturn.cpp**.

b. Add two public functions to the **TaxReturn** class: **setAll()**, which can set the field values; and **display()**, which can display them. The **setAll()** function accepts arguments for the tax ID number, last and first names, annual income, and number of dependents. The **setAll()** function should then call a private function that computes the tax owed. Create an array of 10 **TaxReturn** objects. In a loop, prompt the user for ID number, first and last name, annual income, and number of dependents, then use these values to set a **TaxReturn**'s fields. At the end of the loop, display all the values for all 10 **TaxReturn** objects, including the tax owed. Save the file as **TaxReturn2.cpp**.

9. Each of the following files in your Chapter07 folder contains syntax and/or logical errors. Determine the problem in each case and fix the program. Save your solutions by adding "Fixed" to the file name, as in **DEBUG7-1Fixed.cpp**.

a. DEBUG7-1.cpp

b. DEBUG7-2.cpp

c. DEBUG7-3.cpp

d. DEBUG7-4.cpp

CASE PROJECT 1

CASE PROJECTS

In previous chapters, you have been developing a **Fraction** structure for Teacher's Pet Software. Now you will develop a class that contains the fields and functions that a **Fraction** needs. Create a **Fraction** class with three private data fields for whole number, numerator, and denominator. Also create a constant static public field to hold the symbol that separates a numerator and denominator when a **Fraction** is displayed—the slash. Create three public member functions for the class, as follows:

❐ An **enterFractionValue()** function that prompts the user to enter values for the **Fraction**. Do not allow the user to enter a value of 0 for the denominator of any **Fraction**; continue to prompt the user for a denominator value until a valid one is entered.

❐ A **reduceFraction()** function that reduces a **Fraction** to proper form. For example, a **Fraction** with the value 0 2/6 would be reduced to 0 1/3 and a **Fraction** with the value 4 18/4 would be reduced to 8 1/2.

❐ A **displayFraction()** function that displays the **Fraction** whole number, numerator, slash, and denominator.

Add any other functions to the `Fraction` class that will be useful to you. Create a `main()` function that declares a `Fraction` object, and continues to get `Fraction` values from the user until the user enters a `Fraction` with value 0 (both the whole number and numerator are 0). For each `Fraction` entered, display the `Fraction`, reduce the `Fraction`, and display the `Fraction` again.

CASE PROJECT 2

**CASE
PROJECTS**

In previous chapters, you have been developing a `BankAccount` structure for Parkville Bank. Now you will develop a class that contains the fields and functions that a `BankAccount` needs. Create a class containing private fields that hold the account number and the account balance. Include a constant static field that holds the annual interest rate (3 percent) earned on accounts at Parkville Bank. Create three public member functions for the class, as follows:

7

- An `enterAccountData()` function that prompts the user for values for the account number and balance. Allow neither a negative account number nor one less than 1000, and do not allow a negative balance; continue to prompt the user until valid values are entered.

- A `computeInterest()` function that accepts an integer argument that represents the number of years the account will earn interest. The function displays the account number, then displays the ending balance of the account each year, based on the interest rate attached to the `BankAccount`.

- A `displayAccount()` function that displays the details of the `BankAccount`.

Create a `main()` function that declares an array of 10 `BankAccount` objects. After the first `BankAccount` object is entered, ask the user if he or she wants to continue. Prompt the user for `BankAccount` values until the user wants to quit or enters 10 `BankAccount` objects, whichever comes first. For each `BankAccount` entered, display the `BankAccount` details. Then prompt the user for a term with a value between 1 and 40 inclusive. Continue to prompt the user until a valid value is entered. Then pass the array of `BankAccount` objects, the count of valid objects in the array, and the desired term to a function that calculates and displays the values of each of the `BankAccounts` after the given number of years at the standard interest rate.

CHAPTER

8

CLASS FEATURES AND DESIGN ISSUES

In this chapter, you will:

♦ Classify the roles of member functions
♦ Understand constructors
♦ Write constructors both with and without arguments
♦ Overload constructors
♦ Create destructors
♦ Understand composition
♦ Learn how, why, and when to use the preprocessor directives `#ifndef`, `#define`, and `#endif`
♦ Master techniques for improving classes and their functions

The ability to create classes provides a major advantage to object-oriented programming. Classes let you encapsulate data and functions, and therefore allow you to think of programming objects as you do their real-world counterparts. You have started to learn about classes; this chapter provides information about useful class features and capabilities, and offers advice on creating easy-to-use and reusable classes.

CLASSIFYING THE ROLES OF MEMBER FUNCTIONS

You can create an infinite number of classes and write an infinite number of functions within those classes. You use the data members of a class to describe the state of an object, and you use the member functions to work with those data members. So far, you have learned about functions that assign values to data and then display those values. Eventually, you want to add many other specialized functions to your classes. The roles of member functions can be classified into four basic groups:

- **Inspector functions**, also called **access functions**. These functions return information about an object's state, or display some or all of an object's attributes. An inspector function typically has a name such as `getName()` or `displayValues()`. A subcategory of access functions is **predicate functions**. These functions test the truth of some condition, such as `isdigit()` (which determines if a character is a digit) and `isupper()` (which determines if a character is uppercase).

- **Mutator functions**, also known as **implementors**. These functions change an object's state or attributes. A mutator function often has a name such as `setData()`, which obtains values from an input device and assigns those values to an object's data members, or a name such as `computeValue()`, which calculates a data member based on values in other data members.

- **Auxiliary functions**, also known as **facilitators**. These functions perform some action or service, such as sorting data or searching for data. A typical name for an auxiliary function is `sortAscending()` or `findLowestValue()`.

- **Manager functions**, which create and destroy objects for you. They perform initialization and cleanup. Called constructors and destructors, these functions have special properties that you need to understand to have full command of class capabilities.

In Chapter 7 you created classes containing inspector functions that retrieved private data from within a class object and mutator functions that set the values for the private data. You also wrote some auxiliary functions that performed a service for a class, such as verifying a date. In this chapter, you will concentrate on manager functions—those that are used to create and destroy objects.

UNDERSTANDING CONSTRUCTORS

A **constructor** is a function that is called automatically each time an object is created. You have been using constructors all along in your programs, even if you haven't realized it. When you declare a simple scalar variable, such as `int someNumber;`, C++ calls an internal constructor function that reserves a memory location of the correct size for an integer, and attaches the name `someNumber` to that location. The value at the `someNumber` location might be anything; in other words, C++ does not automatically initialize the variable, and its contents are garbage.

The definition `int someNumber = 23;` calls a different constructor that reserves memory, attaches a name, and assigns a value. This definition sends the constant value 23 to the constructor function. The preceding definition does not look like it contains a function call; the following one does:

```
int someNumber(23);
```

This definition does exactly the same things as the one that uses the assignment operator—it allocates memory, attaches the name `someNumber`, and assigns a value. You can use these two definition statements interchangeably.

In the same way, if you have defined a class named `Employee`, then `Employee clerk;` reserves memory and assigns a name, but does not initialize the values of any data members of `clerk`. If the `clerk` object contains an ID number and a pay rate, both fields will hold garbage. If the statement `Employee clerk;` compiles successfully, you know that either the programmer has written no constructor for the `Employee` class, or that the programmer has written a default constructor. A **default constructor** is one that does not require any arguments.

With some `Employee` classes you define, you also may be able to make the following statement:

```
Employee clerk(23);
```

If this statement compiles without error, it means the `Employee` class contains a constructor that accepts an integer argument; in other words, the `Employee` class contains a **non-default constructor**. The statement `Employee clerk(23);` reserves enough memory for an `Employee`—the precise amount of memory depends on the size of an `Employee` object. It then attaches a name to that memory location (`clerk`), and passes a value (23), to the `clerk` `Employee`. Possibly, the 23 is used as an `Employee` ID number, pay rate, or age. You can't tell what the 23 is used for by looking at the statement `Employee clerk(23);`. However, assuming the statement compiles, you do know that an `Employee` can be constructed with an initial value in the same way that an integer can.

Because an integer is a scalar variable, `someNumber` occupies one memory location and only that location can assume the assigned value. When you write `int someNumber(23);`, you know where the integer constructor is assigning the 23—to the `someNumber` variable. In contrast, because `Employee` is a class, it may have many data members. When you write `Employee clerk(23);`, you don't know which data member, if any, will receive the 23 unless you can look at the code within the body of the constructor.

8

WRITING CONSTRUCTORS WITHOUT ARGUMENTS

Until now, when you created class objects, you let C++ provide its own default constructor for the objects. For example, Figure 8-1 shows an `Employee` class similar to other classes you have seen. The class contains two data fields and two public functions. In the `main()` function, an `Employee` object is created using the automatically supplied default constructor. When its contents are displayed just after creation, the object's fields hold garbage, as shown in the first two lines of output in Figure 8-2. After reasonable values are assigned to the `Employee` object using the class's `setValues()` function, the object holds valid values, as shown in the last two output lines in the same figure.

```cpp
#include<iostream>
using namespace std;
class Employee
{
    private:
        int idNum;
        double hourlyRate;
    public:
        void setValues(const int, const double);
        void displayValues();
};
void Employee::displayValues()
{
    cout<<"Employee #"<<idNum<<" rate $"<<hourlyRate<<
        " per hour"<<endl;
}
void Employee::setValues(const int id, const double hourly)
{
    idNum = id;
    hourlyRate = hourly;
}
int main()
{
    Employee assistant;
    cout<<"Before setting values with setValues()"<<endl;
    assistant.displayValues();
    assistant.setValues(4321, 12.75);
    cout<<"After setting values with setValues()"<<endl;
    assistant.displayValues();
}
```

Figure 8-1   `Employee` class that uses automatically supplied constructor

Figure 8-2 Output of program in Figure 8-1

Instead of using the automatically supplied constructor, you can write your own default version. You write your own constructors for classes any time you want specific tasks performed when an object is instantiated. Although you can write virtually any C++ statement in a constructor, most often you write a constructor because you want to properly define or initialize all data members in an object when it is created.

TIP The automatically supplied constructor that executes when you do not explicitly write a constructor is a default constructor. (In other words, it takes no arguments.) Programmers sometimes erroneously refer to the automatically supplied constructor as *the* default constructor, implying that this is the *only* type of constructor that is a default constructor. Actually, any constructor that requires no arguments is a default constructor, so if you write a constructor that does not require any arguments, it is a default constructor. The automatically supplied constructor is simply *an example of* a default constructor.

TIP Each class can have, at most, one default constructor.

TIP You might have a compiler that initializes each data member to a non-garbage value. However, it is still best to initialize data so that your programs run correctly on other compilers.

Constructor functions differ from other member functions in two ways:

- You must give a constructor function the same name as the class for which it is a constructor.

- You cannot give a constructor function a return type (it's not necessary because constructors always return an object of the class to which they belong).

A constructor must have the same name as its class because the constructor is called automatically when an object is created. If you named a constructor something other than its class name, C++ would not know it was a constructor. In other words, without the same name as the class, C++ would not know the constructor was the correct function to call when an object was created.

Constructor functions are not coded with a return type. This format doesn't mean the return type is **void**. Because it is a type, you should not use the term **void** when you code a constructor; constructors are always written without a return type.

Consider the `Employee` class in Figure 8-3. The `Employee` is similar to the version in Figure 8-1, but a (shaded) prototype for a constructor has been added. You can place the constructor prototype at any position within the list of `public` class members; many programmers place it first because it is the first function used by the class.

```
class Employee
{
    private:
        int idNum;
        double hourlyRate;
    public:
        Employee();
        void setValues(const int, const double);
        void displayValues();
};
```

Figure 8-3   Definition of an `Employee` class with a constructor

It is possible to create a non-public constructor, but you would do so only under very unusual circumstances. In this book, all constructors will be public.

TIP

Rather than define objects of class `Employee` to have meaningless values, you can, for example, use the constructor to assign default values 9999 to `idNum`, and 5.65 to `hourlyRate`. Figure 8-4 shows the constructor definition. You place this function in the implementation section of the class file, along with the other functions the class defines. You must remember to include the class name and the scope resolution operator in the constructor header—for example, `Employee::Employee()`—to show the constructor is a member of the class just like other member functions.

```
Employee::Employee()
{
    idNum = 9999;
    hourlyRate = 5.65;
}
```

Figure 8-4   Implementation of `Employee` constructor

The constructor `Employee()` shown in Figure 8-4 is a default constructor because it does not require any arguments. The data members in an `Employee` object will be set automatically, by default. Any subsequent object instantiation, such as `Employee assistant;`, results in an object with an `idNum` of 9999 and an `hourlyRate` of 5.65. Of course, you can change these values later using the `setValues()` function. Figure 8-5 shows a `main()` function that uses the `Employee` class, and Figure 8-6 shows the output. The first two lines of output show the default values set from within the constructor. The second pair of lines of output shows the values after using the setValues() function to assign 4321 and 12.75 to the assistant's data fields.

The default constructor provided by the compiler when you do not write your own version initializes each class member variable using its respective default constructor. For example, because an integer is created to hold garbage by default, integer field members of classes also hold garbage by default.

TIP

You usually should provide initial values for the data members in your objects. Even if you simply set all numeric attributes to zeros and all character attributes to spaces, the results are better than the random, meaningless data that happen to be held in the memory locations where your objects are instantiated.

TIP

```cpp
#include<iostream>
using namespace std;
class Employee
{
    private:
        int idNum;
        double hourlyRate;
    public:
        Employee();
        void setValues(const int, const double);
        void displayValues();
};
Employee::Employee()
{
    idNum = 9999;
    hourlyRate = 5.65;
}
void Employee::displayValues()
{
    cout<<"Employee #"<<idNum<<" rate $"<<hourlyRate<<
        " per hour"<<endl;
}
void Employee::setValues(const int id, const double hourly)
{
    idNum = id;
    hourlyRate = hourly;
}
int main()
{
    Employee assistant;
    cout<<"Before setting values with setValues()"<<endl;
    assistant.displayValues();
    assistant.setValues(4321, 12.75);
    cout<<"After setting values with setValues()"<<endl;
    assistant.displayValues();
}
```

Figure 8-5   Employee class and main() function that instantiates an Employee

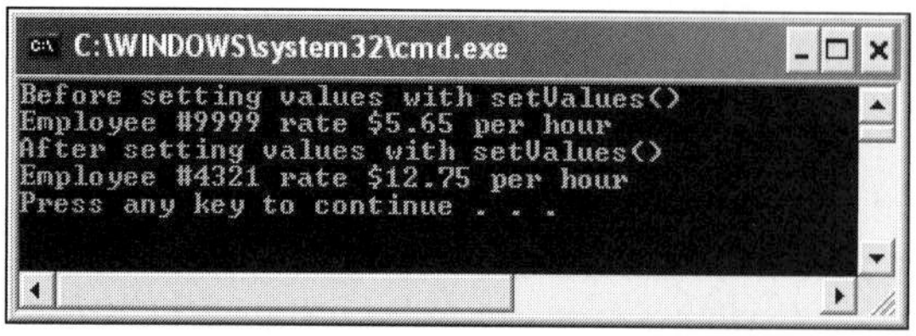

Figure 8-6 Output of program in Figure 8-5

WRITING CONSTRUCTORS WITH ARGUMENTS

Like other functions, a constructor header can contain an argument list. For example, the following **Employee** class constructor prototype requires two arguments:

```
Employee(int, double);
```

This constructor might be implemented using the code in Figure 8-7. In this example, the two arguments to the constructor are used to set the class fields **idNum** and **hourlyRate**. In a slightly more complicated constructor, the code might perform other tasks, for example, checking to assure the parameters were within specific ranges before assigning them to the fields and issuing an error message or assigning default values if either one of them is not within range.

```
Employee::Employee(int id, double hourly)
{
    idNum = id;
    hourlyRate = hourly;
}
```

Figure 8-7 Employee constructor with two required arguments

The constructor in Figure 8-7 is a non-default constructor; that is, it requires parameters. If the only constructor in a class is non-default, and if you write a function that attempts to instantiate an **Employee** with a statement such as **Employee assistant;**, you will receive an error message that indicates there is no appropriate default constructor. Instead you must declare an **Employee** with a statement that includes two arguments. For example, you might declare the following:

```
Employee buyer(2345, 16.75);
```

Alternately, if you have declared an integer named **num** and a **double** named **money**, and assigned appropriate values to them, then you can declare an **Employee** with a statement such as the following:

```
Employee bookkeeper(num, money);
```

TIP As soon as you write a constructor for a class, whether you write one with an argument list or with no arguments, you no longer have the automatically supplied version available to use.

In Chapter 6, you learned to use default arguments with functions. You also can create constructors that have default values for one or more of the arguments. Just as with ordinary functions, once you provide a default value for one of the arguments in a constructor's argument list, then you must provide default values for all the remaining arguments to the right. So, for example, you can create the following constructor prototype:

```
Employee(int, double, int = 3, char = 'A');
```

This constructor would execute with any of the following instantiations:

```
Employee firstEmp(111, 7.77, 5, 'C');
Employee secondEmp(222, 8.88, 6);
Employee thirdEmp(333, 9.9);
```

In other words, with this constructor prototype, an integer and **double** are required when an object is created. Optionally, you also can provide a second integer as the third argument, or a second integer and a character, as the third and fourth arguments. If you provide only two of the arguments, default values are used for the final two parameters, and if you provide three arguments, a default value is used for the last (**char**) parameter.

You also can create a default constructor that contains arguments by providing default values for all the parameters. Figure 8-8 shows the complete class definition for the **Employee** class that uses this format for its constructor. The shaded constructor prototype provides default values for all its arguments. If you use this **Employee** class with the **main()** function shown following the class, you can see from the output in Figure 8-9 that when you provide no arguments upon object creation, both default parameter values are used. When you provide one argument, one of the default values is used, and when you provide two arguments, neither of the default values is used.

```
#include<iostream>
using namespace std;
class Employee
{
   private:
        int idNum;
        double hourlyRate;
   public:
        Employee(int = 9999, double = 0);
        void setValues(const int, const double);
        void displayValues();
};
```

Figure 8-8 Employee class with constructor that uses default arguments

```
Employee::Employee(int id, double rate)
{
   idNum = id;
   hourlyRate = rate;
}
void Employee::displayValues()
{
    cout<<"Employee #"<<idNum<<" rate $"<<hourlyRate<<
        " per hour"<<endl;
}
void Employee::setValues(const int id, const double hourly)
{
    idNum = id;
    hourlyRate = hourly;
}
int main()
{
    Employee one;
    Employee two(345);
    Employee three(678, 15.44);
    one.displayValues();
    two.displayValues();
    three.displayValues();
}
```

Figure 8-8   Employee class with constructor that uses default arguments (continued)

Figure 8-9   Output of program in Figure 8-8

A constructor in the format shown in Figure 8-8, including parameters with default values, is a default constructor. The constructor in Figure 8-3, which takes no arguments, is also a default constructor. A constructor that *requires* no arguments is a default constructor, regardless of whether the constructor *has* an argument list and can accept arguments.

TIP   Some C++ compilers allow you to provide argument default values in the function header instead of in the prototype. Most C++ programmers prefer providing constructor default values in the prototype. Using this style makes the programmers' intentions clear to anyone looking at the prototype.

Pitfall: Using Parentheses When Instantiating an Object with a Default Constructor

In the `main()` function in Figure 8-8, the `Employee` that uses all the constructor default parameters is defined as follows:

```
Employee one;
```

This is the same format you would use if you had not written a constructor at all. Do not make the mistake of using the following to attempt to instantiate an `Employee` that uses no arguments:

```
Employee one();
```

The C++ compiler treats this statement as if you are prototyping a function named `one()` that takes no arguments and returns an `Employee` object. Although this is a legal function definition, and you might want to write such a function, it is not your intention if you are trying to define an `Employee` object named `one`. The correct way to define an `Employee` that uses all the default values of the constructor is `Employee one;`, with no parentheses.

8

OVERLOADING CONSTRUCTORS

Just like other C++ functions, constructors can be overloaded. Recall that overloading a function name allows you to use the same name for separate functions that have different argument lists. Constructor functions for a given class must all have the same name as their class. Therefore, if you provide two or more constructors for the same class, they are overloaded by definition. As with other overloaded functions, two constructor functions used in the same program must have different argument lists so that the compiler can tell them apart.

Suppose you create a `Writer` class, such as for applications used by a library or bookstore, and you want to be able to instantiate some `Writer` objects with first, middle, and last names, but be able to instantiate others with first and last names only. If you used the middle name as a third argument in the constructor argument list, you could just provide a default value for it, and create some `Writer`s with and some without the middle name. However, supplying the middle name as the last argument in the list might not seem natural to you. Instead, you can choose to create two constructors so that your class client functions can use whichever version is more appropriate at the time.

Figure 8-10 shows a usable `Writer` class definition. Notice the two shaded constructors: One requires two arguments; the other requires three.

```
class Writer
{
   private:
       string firstName;
       string middleName;
       string lastName;
       // other data members go here
   public:
       Writer(string, string, string);
       Writer(string, string);
       void displayValues();
       // other functions go here
};
```

Figure 8-10 A `Writer` class definition containing overloaded constructors

In Figure 8-10, the `Writer` constructor that requires three arguments is implemented to use the arguments as the first, middle, and last name. The constructor that requires only two arguments uses them as the first and last name and sets the middle name to an empty string. Figure 8-11 shows a `Writer` class containing the implemented functions and a brief `main()` method that uses each constructor version. Figure 8-12 shows how the output correctly displays a `Writer` that is instantiated with three arguments as well as one that uses only two.

```
#include<iostream>
#include<string>
using namespace std;
class Writer
{
   private:
       string firstName;
       string middleName;
       string lastName;
       // other data members go here
   public:
       Writer(string, string, string);
       Writer(string, string);
       void displayValues();
       // other functions go here
};
Writer::Writer(string first, string middle, string last)
{
   firstName = first;
   middleName = middle;
   lastName = last;
}
```

Figure 8-11 Program that uses the `Writer` class

```
Writer::Writer(string first, string last)
{
   firstName = first;
   middleName = "";
   lastName = last;
}
void Writer::displayValues()
{
   cout<<"Name is "<<firstName<<" ";
   if(middleName != "")
       cout<<middleName<<" ";
   cout<<lastName<<endl;
}
int main()
{
   Writer oneWriter("Edgar", "Allan", "Poe");
   Writer anotherWriter("Ernest", "Hemingway");
   oneWriter.displayValues();
   anotherWriter.displayValues();
}
```

8

Figure 8-11   Program that uses the `Writer` class (continued)

Figure 8-12   Output of the program in Figure 8-11

TIP   Although you might create several constructors for a class, most often you use only a single version of a constructor within an application. You usually create a class with several overloaded constructors so that those who use your class can choose how they instantiate objects, but your class's clients each might choose to use just one constructor version.

TIP   Just as you can create ambiguous situations with functions, you can do the same with constructors. For example, if you create any two or more of the following constructors, you will create ambiguity when you try to instantiate an object using no arguments because the compiler cannot determine which constructor to use:
```
Employee();
Employee(int = 100);
Employee(int = 100, double = 0);
Employee(double = 5.15, int = 999);
```

USING DESTRUCTORS

A **destructor** is a function that is called automatically each time an object is destroyed. An object is destroyed when it goes out of scope. For example, local variables are destroyed at the end of their function. Just as with constructors, you have been using destructors in your programs whether you realized it or not. When you declare a simple scalar variable, such as `int aNumber;`, the variable `aNumber` goes out of scope at the end of the block in which you declare it, and a destructor is called automatically. Similarly, when you declare an object such as `Employee clerk;`, the `clerk` object ceases to exist at the end of the block in which you declared it, and an automatically supplied destructor function executes. Just as with constructors, C++ provides a destructor if you don't declare one.

 You can think of the default destructor that is automatically provided with a class as "empty." However, that does not mean it does not do anything. A destructor destroys each class member using the member's destructor. For example, if a class contains another class object, then the destructor of the containing class calls the destructor of the contained class. In the next section, you learn to create a class that contains another class object.

The rules for creating destructor function prototypes are similar to the rules for constructor function prototypes:

- As with constructors, you must give a destructor function the same name as its class (and therefore the same name as any constructor for that class). Unlike constructors, you must precede the destructor name with a tilde (~).

- As with constructors, you cannot give a destructor function a return type (it's not necessary because destructors never return anything).

- Unlike constructors, you *cannot* pass any values to a destructor.

A destructor must have the same name as its class (plus the tilde) because it is called automatically when an object is destroyed. As with the constructor, it makes sense that an automatically called function has a standardized identifier, and that you cannot choose any identifier you want.

 It makes sense that the tilde is the symbol used to distinguish a constructor from the destructor. In C++ the tilde is also used as the **one's complement operator**—the operator that makes every bit become its opposite. When you apply the one's complement operator to a byte, every bit that is 1 becomes a 0 and every 0 becomes a 1. The one's complement operator is also called the **bitwise complement operator**. Because a destructor is "the opposite of" a constructor, using the tilde with the destructor name makes sense.

Unlike constructors, only one destructor can exist for each class. In other words, you cannot overload destructor functions. Because destructors cannot accept arguments, C++ would have no way to distinguish between multiple destructors.

TIP   Destructor functions have *no* return type. That doesn't mean the return type is void; void is a type.

 TIP   Programmers usually do not need to perform as many tasks in destructor functions as they do in constructor functions. Typically, you need code in a destructor when an object contains a pointer to a member. You don't want to retain a pointer that holds the address of an object that has been destroyed. In Chapter 9, you will write destructors that handle pointer issues. Additionally, when your programs write data to disk files, you often want to close those files in a destructor function.

 TIP   Every C++ class object automatically has four special member functions: a default constructor, a default destructor, an assignment operator, and a copy constructor. The default assignment operator allows you to assign one object to another, as in object1 = object2. The **copy constructor** executes when you pass an object to a function, making a local copy.

The House class in Figure 8-13 contains one field, a constructor, and a destructor. The constructor and destructor functions have the same name as the class, but the destructor function name is preceded by the tilde (~). The main() function in the figure contains a single line of code—it creates a House object. When you run the program in Figure 8-13, you get the output shown in Figure 8-14. A message displays when the House object is created, and another message displays a moment later when the object goes out of scope and is destroyed.

```
#include<iostream>
using namespace std;
class House
{
   private:
        int squareFeet;
   public:
        House();
        ~House();
};
House::House()
{
   squareFeet = 1000;
   cout<<"House created."<<endl;
}
House::~House()
{
   cout<<"House destroyed!"<<endl;
}
int main()
{
   House aHouse;
}
```

Figure 8-13   Program that creates a House

Figure 8-14 Output of program in Figure 8-13

TIP

If you are using a compiler that dismisses the output screen immediately, you may have been using a statement such as getch(); to hold the output screen at the end of the program. However, if you run the program shown in Figure 8-13, if you add a getch(); statement within and at the end of the main() function, the program is held before the object goes out of scope, so you don't see the "House destroyed!" message. To be able to see the message, you can place the House declaration within its own block (in a set of curly braces) within main(), and then place the getch(); statement outside that block. The object will go out of scope, the destructor will be called, you can read the message, then enter a character to end the main() function.

Figure 8-15 shows a main() function that creates six House objects. The output in Figure 8-16 shows that when you create an array of objects, each is created as well as destroyed separately and automatically. All six objects are created, the message "End of program" displays, and at the end of main(), all six objects are destroyed.

```
int main()
{
    House aHouse[6];
    cout<<"End of program"<<endl;
}
```

Figure 8-15 A main() function that uses an array of objects

Figure 8-16 Output of program in Figure 8-15

TIP

If you want to create an array of class objects such as House aHouse[3], the class must have a default constructor. If every constructor for the class requires one or more arguments (for example, House(int x);), then the declaration takes the form House aHouse[3] = {House(1000), House(2000), House(3000)};. This assigns the values 1000, 2000, and 3000 to the first, second, and third elements of the aHouse array, respectively.

Contrast the program in Figure 8-15 with the one in Figure 8-17. In Figure 8-17, a createHouse() function is called six times. Within the function, a House is instantiated, an "End of function" message displays, and, when the function ends, the House is destroyed. In this example's output, shown in Figure 8-18, you can see that the constructor and destructor are called in sequence—once for each new House that is created with each new call to the createHouse() function.

```
int main()
{
  void createHouse();
  int x;
  for(x = 0; x < 6; ++x)
     createHouse();
}
void createHouse()
{
    House aHouse;
    cout<<"End of function"<<endl;
}
```

Figure 8-17 A main() function that calls a House-creating function six times

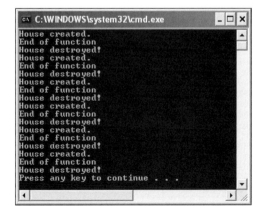

Figure 8-18 Output of program in Figure 8-17

8

Examine the differences in the output shown in Figures 8-16 and 8-18. In Figure 8-16, you can see that all six objects are created, and then, at the end of the function, all the objects are destroyed. In Figure 8-18, each time the `createHouse()` function is called, an object is created, and then almost immediately destroyed. Examining these two figures and the functions that generated them will help you to understand when constructors and destructors are called.

UNDERSTANDING COMPOSITION

On many occasions you might want to use a class object within another class. Just as you build any complex real-life item, such as an automobile, from other well-designed parts, complex classes are easier to create if you use previously written, well-designed classes as components. Using a class object within another class object is known as **composition**.

For example, Figure 8-19 shows a simple `InventoryItem` class that a store could use to hold stock numbers and prices of items for sale. It contains just three methods—one that sets the stock number, one that sets the price, and one that displays the item. You have written many classes like this one, and you have written many `main()` functions that instantiate objects that are similar to an `InventoryItem` object.

```
class InventoryItem
{
   private:
      int stockNum;
      double price;
   public:
      void setNum(int);
      void setPrice(double);
      void displayItem();
};
void InventoryItem::setNum(int stkNum)
{
   stockNum = stkNum;
}
void InventoryItem::setPrice(double pr)
{
   price = pr;
}
void InventoryItem::displayItem()
{
   cout<<"Item #"<<stockNum<<" costs $"<<price<<endl;
}
```

Figure 8-19 The `InventoryItem` class

Figure 8-20 shows a `Salesperson` class. It, too, is similar to many classes you have created and used.

```
class Salesperson
{
    private:
        int idNum;
        string name;
    public:
        void setId(int);
        void setName(string);
        void displayPerson();
};
void Salesperson::setId(int id)
{
    idNum = id;
}
void Salesperson::setName(string lastName)
{
    name = lastName;
}
void Salesperson::displayPerson()
{
    cout<<"Salesperson #"<<idNum<<" "<<name<<endl;
}
```

Figure 8-20   The `Salesperson` class

Figure 8-21 shows a `Transaction` class. To represent a sales transaction, you want to include a transaction number as well as information about the item sold and the salesperson who sold it. You could write a transaction class that contained individual fields with item and salesperson data—such as item stock number and price, and salesperson ID number and name—but it is more efficient to reuse the `InventoryItem` and `Salesperson` classes that are already created and tested. When you create class objects within another class object, you can call the contained objects **member-objects**. A benefit of object-oriented programming is that you can reuse well-crafted components as member-objects, instead of starting from scratch each time you create a class.

 TIP   An emerging field in the software industry is RAD—rapid application development. Its focus is on delivering useable software products to clients in less time. One of the techniques that supports RAD is the reuse of well-designed components.

```
class Transaction
{
   private:
      int transNum;
      InventoryItem itemSold;
      Salesperson seller;
   public:
      Transaction(int, int, double, int, string);
      void displayTransactionInfo();
};
Transaction::Transaction(int num, int item, double pr,
   int salesId, string name)
{
   transNum = num;
   itemSold.setNum(item);
   itemSold.setPrice(pr);
   seller.setId(salesId);
   seller.setName(name);
}
void Transaction::displayTransactionInfo()
{
   cout<<"Data for transaction #"<<transNum<<endl;
   itemSold.displayItem();
   seller.displayPerson();
}
```

Figure 8-21 The `Transaction` class

In the `Transaction` class in Figure 8-21, the data members include a transaction number and two more complicated members—an `InventoryItem` and a `Salesperson`. The `Transaction` class is composed of objects of these other types. The composition relationship is called a **"has–a" relationship** because you can make statements such as "A `Transaction` has an `InventoryItem`," and "A `Transaction` has a `Salesperson`." Figure 8-22 shows the relationship between the `Transaction` class and the objects it contains.

Figure 8-22 The `Transaction` class containing an `InventoryItem` and a `Salesperson`

TIP   If you are designing a class that contains another class and you cannot make a reasonable sentence describing the relationship between the classes that uses the phrase "has a," then you probably should not be using composition. For example, because you would reasonably say "An Automobile has an Engine," then the `Automobile` class reasonably can contain a member field of type `Engine`. If the phrase "is a" seems more appropriate, then you might want to consider using inheritance. For example, you would not say, "An Automobile has a Convertible." Instead, you would say, "A Convertible is an Automobile." You will learn about inheritance in Chapter 10.

The `Transaction` constructor in Figure 8-21 takes five arguments. The first is used to set the transaction number, and the other four are used as arguments to the set functions for the `InventoryItem` and `Salesperson` objects that are part of a `Transaction`. Notice in the shaded statements in Figure 8-21 that the `itemSold` and `seller` members of the `Transaction` class have access to their own class methods. When you create the `Transaction` class, you do not have to start from scratch creating all the methods that belong to the `InventoryItem` and `Salesperson` classes; instead, you build the `Transaction` class from pre-existing, working components.

Figure 8-23 shows a `main()` method that instantiates a `Transaction` object, and Figure 8-24 shows the output. Each argument sent to the `Transaction` constructor is sent correctly to the fields of the `Transaction`'s members.

```
int main()
{
    Transaction aSale(1533, 988, 22.95, 312, "Patterson");
    aSale.displayTransactionInfo();
}
```

Figure 8-23   A `main()` function that instantiates a `Transaction` object

Figure 8-24   Output of program in Figure 8-23

Using Composition When Member Classes Contain Non-Default Constructors

When you instantiate a `Transaction` object using the class in Figure 8-21, you actually instantiate three objects—an `InventoryItem`, a `Salesperson`, and a `Transaction`, in that order. The two member-objects are instantiated in the order they are declared in the containing class, and then the `Transaction` class object is instantiated. In this example, the member-objects (the `InventoryItem` and `Salesperson` objects) are created using their built-in default constructors because neither of those classes contains a programmer-written non-default constructor.

TIP   You could prove to yourself the order in which the constructors for the three classes that compose the `Transaction` class are called by placing a default constructor within each class and displaying a different message within each constructor.

When the classes used within a containing class have only non-default constructors—that is, constructors that require arguments—the syntax you must use to instantiate an object is more complicated. When one class contains others that have only non-default constructors, then the constructor of the containing class must provide whatever its members' constructors need.

Figure 8-25 shows revised `InventoryItem` and `Salesperson` classes that contain non-default constructors. (The functions that set values after construction have been removed from these classes to simplify the example.) The `Transaction` class contains the same fields as it did in Figure 8-21, but its constructor header has been revised. In the shaded header you can see that the set of parentheses that contains the argument list is followed by a single colon. The part of the constructor header to the right of the colon is an **initialization list**; it provides constructor-required values for the member-objects. Each of the member-object names is listed after the colon, and each has parentheses in which its constructor's arguments are listed. The values of `item` and `pr` (taken from the `Transaction` parameter list) are passed to the `InventoryItem` constructor for the `itemSold` object, and the values of `salesId` and `name` are passed to the `Salesperson` constructor for the `seller` object. Figure 8-26 shows the output when the `main()` method in Figure 8-25 executes.

```
#include<iostream>
#include<string>
using namespace std;
class InventoryItem
{
   private:
      int stockNum;
      double price;
   public:
      InventoryItem(int, double);
      void displayItem();
};
```

Figure 8-25   Program that uses `Transaction` class whose members require constructor arguments

```
InventoryItem::InventoryItem(int num, double pr)
{
   stockNum = num;
   price = pr;
}
void InventoryItem::displayItem()
{
   cout<<"Item #"<<stockNum<<" costs $"<<price<<endl;
}
class Salesperson
{
    private:
       int idNum;
       string name;
    public:
       Salesperson(int, string);
       void displayPerson();
};
Salesperson::Salesperson(int num, string name)
{
   idNum = num;
   this->name = name;
}
void Salesperson::displayPerson()
{
   cout<<"Salesperson #"<<idNum<<" "<<name<<endl;
}
class Transaction
{
   private:
      int transNum;
      InventoryItem itemSold;
      Salesperson seller;
   public:
      Transaction(int, int, double, int, string);
      void displayTransactionInfo();
 };
Transaction::Transaction(int num, int item, double pr,
     int salesId, string name):itemSold(item, pr),
     seller(salesId, name)
{
     transNum = num;
}
void Transaction::displayTransactionInfo()
{
   cout<<"Data for transaction #"<<transNum<<endl;
   itemSold.displayItem();
   seller.displayPerson();
}
int main()
{
   Transaction aSale(8787, 577, 456.78, 812, "Reynolds");
   aSale.displayTransactionInfo();
}
```

Figure 8-25 Program that uses `Transaction` class whose members require
            constructor arguments (continued)

Figure 8-26   Output of program in Figure 8-25

In the **Transaction** class constructor in Figure 8-25, the only statement within the constructor assigns the transaction number. All the other constructor arguments are passed on to member-object constructors. Just because the **Transaction** class contains member-objects, you are not required to write the **Transaction** constructor to accept arguments for all of them. Instead, you could use constants for some or all of the member-object constructors. For example, if you wanted item and salesperson numbers to be initialized to 999, the item price to be initialized to 0.00, and the salesperson name to be initialized to "ZZZ", then the following would be a useable constructor header for a **Transaction** class that uses the **InventoryItem** and **Salesperson** classes in Figure 8-25:

```
Transaction::Transaction() :  itemSold(999, 0.00),
     seller(999, "ZZZ")
```

Then you would include a default Transaction constructor implementation containing an empty body.

If a member-object class contains overloaded constructors, then any of the constructors can be the one used in the containing class's constructor header initialization list. If one of the member-object class constructors is a default constructor, then you do not need to initialize the member-object in the constructor header.

TIP

When one class inherits from another, you also might need a constructor initialization list. You will learn how to create initialization lists for classes that inherit in Chapter 10.

TIP

Using #ifndef, #define, and #endif

Reusability is a major focus of object-oriented thinking. Developing a class such as **InventoryItem** or **Salesperson** and storing it in its own file for later use in other, more comprehensive, classes is a good example of planning for reuse. Additionally, creating self-contained components such as **InventoryItem** that you include in other classes makes program maintenance easier. **Program maintenance** is the upkeep of professional programs over time.

More than half of most programmers' time on the job (and almost all of new programmers' time) is spent maintaining or changing existing programs. For example, an administrator might decide that an **InventoryItem** needs a new data field or method. If the **InventoryItem** class file is written as part of the code of many separate programs, then someone must change all those programs. The more places a change must be made, the more time it takes, the more likely an error will occur when that change is made, and the greater the chance that one of the necessary changes is overlooked. It makes sense to store a class such as `InventoryItem` in one location, make changes there, and use the `#include` statement so the new file definition is part of every program that needs it.

After you have created a collection of useful classes, often called a **library**, you might find that many class files contain the same `#include` statements. For example, if the `InventoryItem` and `Salesperson` classes each contain `cout` statements, then each contains an `#include<iostream>` statement.

Suppose your organization develops the following classes and stores each in its own file:

- `Transaction`—This class, shown in Figure 8-25, contains `InventoryItem` and `Salesperson` objects.

- `PayCheck`—This class includes a `Salesperson` object and an array of `Transactions` generated by that `Salesperson`.

- `YearEndReport`—This class contains arrays of `InventoryItem`, `Transaction`, and `PayCheck` objects, from which year-end statistics are generated.

When you write an application in which you use a `YearEndReport` object and include its file, you will be including the `Salesperson` file twice—with the `Transaction` class and the `Paycheck` class; you will be including the `InventoryItem` file three times— once to use it within the `YearEndReport` class directly, and twice more with the `Transaction` class and the `Paycheck` class. If you compile such a program, you will receive error messages such as "Multiple declaration for `Salesperson`" or "Multiple declaration for `InventoryItem`" and "Body has already been defined for…" for each of the `Salesperson` and `InventoryItem` class functions.

To resolve this problem, you can give each class a **#define name**, which is simply an internal name for the group of statements that make up the definition of the class. In Chapter 1, you learned that a statement that begins with a pound sign is a preprocessor directive, or a statement that gives instructions to the compiler. You have been using the `#include` preprocessor directive in every C++ program you have written.

For example, to use `#define` within the `Salesperson` class, you can insert the directive `#define SALESPERSON_CPP` at the top of the `Salesperson` file. You can use any name you want, but it is conventional to use the filename with an underscore replacing the usual position of the dot in the filename. You do not have to use all uppercase letters in the name of the preprocessor `#define` directive, but it is conventional to do so.

Using the `#define` directive alone does not provide much benefit. Instead, it is usually coupled with two other directives: `#ifndef` and `#endif`. The C++ directive **#ifndef** allows you to test whether a class has already been defined in a project; it means "if not defined." If you place an `#ifndef` directive at the beginning of a class and the class has not been defined, then the `#define` directive will be implemented. If the class has already been defined, everything up to the `#endif` directive will be ignored. The **#endif** directive means that you have reached the end of the block of code that you are defining.

The shaded statements in Figure 8-27 show how the `#ifndef`, `#define`, and `#endif` directives should appear within the Salesperson.cpp class file. The statement they make is "If SALESPERSON_CPP has not been defined in this project, define all the following code, up to the `#endif`, as SALESPERSON_CPP." When you write a program that includes the `Salesperson` class multiple times, the first inclusion causes the `Salesperson` code to be named SALESPERSON_CPP and imported into the final project. At the second inclusion, SALESPERSON_CPP already has been defined, the answer to `#ifndef` is false, and the code isn't included a second time.

```
#ifndef SALESPERSON_CPP
#define SALESPERSON_CPP
class Salesperson
{
    private:
        int idNum;
        string name;
    public:
        Salesperson(int, string);
        void displayPerson();
  };
Salesperson::Salesperson(int num, string name)
{
    idNum = num;
    this->name = name;
}
void Salesperson::displayPerson()
{
    cout<<"Salesperson #"<<idNum<<" "<<name<<endl;
}
#endif
```

Figure 8-27   `Salesperson` class definition with `#ifndef`, `#define`, and `#endif` directives

IMPROVING CLASSES AND THEIR FUNCTIONS

As you write larger and more complicated programs, be sure to spend time on planning and design. Think of an application you use, such as a word processor or spreadsheet. The number and variety of user options are staggering. It is impossible for a single programmer to write such an application, so thorough planning and design are essential for the components to work together properly. Each class you design must be well thought out. A final product is great only if each component is well designed—just ask anyone with a $30,000 car that leaks oil.

The following sections describe how to improve your functions by selecting member data and meaningful function names, reducing coupling between functions, and increasing cohesion within a function.

Selecting Member Data and Function Names

Usually, it is easier to select the data members you want in a class than it is to select the member functions. When you define an `Employee` class, for example, you realize that the `Employee` has a first name, last name, Social Security number, and so on. You might not predict all the different tasks you want to perform, though. Are any special functions required when the `Employee` is hired? Do you need a method to decide on raises or promotions? Are there complicated insurance or tax calculations to be performed? Must any special procedures be completed when the `Employee` is terminated? When you begin to design a class and select its member functions, you need to consider the following questions:

- Will special initialization tasks be necessary? Must you guarantee that class data members begin with specific values? If so, you should explicitly declare a constructor function.

- Will any special clean-up tasks be carried out when a class object goes out of scope? Must you ensure that a pointer is not left pointing to nothing? Must you free any memory that has been explicitly allocated during the life of the class object? If clean-up tasks are needed, you should explicitly declare a destructor function.

- Will class data members be assigned values after their construction? Will class data values need to be displayed? Will class data members need operations (such as arithmetic, sorting, or capitalization) performed on them? These tasks are performed by your inspector, mutator, and auxiliary member functions.

When you know what data members and functions you need, you can give them legal C++ identifiers. An often-overlooked element in class design is the selection of good data-member and function names. Of course, C++ identifiers must not include spaces and cannot begin with a number, but you also must apply other general guidelines:

- **Use meaningful names.** A data member named `someData` or a function named `firstFunction()` makes a program cryptic. You will forget the purpose of these identifiers, even in your own programs. All programmers occasionally use short, nondescriptive names, such as `x` or `val`, in a short program written to test a function. In a professional class design, however, names should be meaningful.

- **Use pronounceable names.** A data name like `zbq` is neither pronounceable nor meaningful. Sometimes a name looks meaningful when you write it, but `goout()` might mean "go out" to you and mean "goot" to others. However, standard abbreviations do not always have to be pronounceable. For example, anyone in business probably interprets `ssn` as a Social Security number.

- **Be judicious in your use of abbreviations.** You might save a few keystrokes if you create a class function called `getStat()`, but is its purpose to output static variables, determine the status of flags, or print statistics?

8

- **Avoid using digits in a name.** Zero (0) can be confused with the letter "O" and "1" (one) can be misread as a lowercase L ("l"). In a short test program, it is sometimes convenient to name variables `var1` and `var2`, but a final professional class design should use clearer names. The name `budgetFor2008`, however, probably will not be misinterpreted and is therefore acceptable.

- **Use capitalization freely in multiword names.** Recall that the `goout()` function is better written as `goOut()`. A function name such as `initializeintegervalues()` is far more readable when it is changed to `initializeIntegerValues()`. Some C++ programmers prefer to use underscores to separate words, as in `initialize_integer_values()`, but it is more common to use camel casing, running the words together and capitalizing each new word.

- **Include a form of "to be," such as "is" or "are," in names for variables that hold a status.** For example, whether the `isOverdrawn` variable is of type integer or boolean (a C++ type that holds true or false), the intent of the name is clearer than if the variable is simply called `overdrawn`.

- **Often a verb–noun provides a good combination for a function.** Names such as `computeBalance()` or `displayTotal()` are descriptive.

TIP   Some unprofessional programmers name functions or data members after their dogs or favorite vacation spots. Not only does this approach make their programs more difficult to understand, but it also marks them as amateurs.

When you begin to design a class, the process of determining which data members and functions you need and what names they should receive can seem overwhelming. The design process is crucial, however. When you are given your first programming assignment, the design process might very well have been completed already. Most likely, your first assignment will be to write or modify one small member function in a much larger class. The better the original design, the easier your job will be.

When you design your own classes as a professional, you should make all identifiers as clear as possible so that you can assign the individual functions to other programmers for writing and, eventually, for maintenance. When you design your own classes as a student, you still need to make all identifiers clear so that you can keep track of your work. You want to identify what needs to be done, choose names for those processes, and then write the code that makes up those processes.

Luckily, you do not have to write a C++ class or program completely before you can see whether the overall plan works. Most programmers use stubs during the initial phases of a project. **Stubs** are simple routines that do nothing (or very little); you incorporate them into a program as placeholders. For example, if you need to write a calculateInsurancePremium() function that consists of many decisions and numeric calculations, you might write an empty version such as the following:

```
double calculateInsurancePremium()
{
    return 0.0;
}
```

Once you have written this stub function, you can call it from the appropriate places within a program you are creating. This allows you to test the order of operations in the main() function. After the main() function works correctly, you can return to the stub function and begin to code the complicated logic that belongs in it.

Reducing Coupling Between Functions

Coupling is a measure of the strength of the connection between two functions; it expresses the extent to which information is exchanged by functions. Coupling is either **tight coupling** or **loose coupling**, depending on how much one function depends on information from another. Tight coupling, which features much dependence between functions, makes programs more prone to errors; there are many data paths to manage, many chances for bad data to pass from one function to another, and many chances for one function to alter information needed by another. Loose coupling occurs when functions do not depend on others. In general, you want to reduce coupling as much as possible because connections between functions make them more difficult to write, maintain, and reuse.

You can evaluate whether coupling between functions is loose or tight by looking at several characteristics:

- *The intimacy between functions.* The least intimate situation is one in which functions have access to the same global structures or variables; these functions have tight coupling. The most intimate way to share data is by passing parameters by value—that is, passing a copy of the variable from one function to another.

- *The number of parameters that are passed between functions.* The loosest (best) functions pass single parameters rather than entire structures, if possible.

- *The visibility of accessed data in a function prototype.* When you define a function, if you can state how it receives and returns values, it is highly visible and, therefore, loosely coupled. If a function alters global values, you do not see those values in a prototype, and the function is not loosely coupled.

Increasing Cohesion Within a Function

Analyzing coupling allows you to see how functions connect externally with other functions. You also want to analyze how well the internal statements of a function accomplish the purposes of the function. **Cohesion** refers to how well the operations in a function relate to one another. In highly cohesive functions, all operations are related. Such functions

8

are usually more reliable than those with low cohesion. Highly cohesive functions are considered stronger, and make programs easier to write, read, and maintain.

Functional cohesion occurs when all of the function operations contribute to the performance of only one task. It is the highest level of cohesion; you should strive for functional cohesion in all functions you write. For example, consider the following `square()` function definition:

```
double square(double number)
{
        return (number * number);
}
```

TIP

If you can write a sentence describing what a function does and use only two words, such as "Cube value" or "Print answer," the function is probably functionally cohesive.

The function `square()` is highly cohesive; it performs one simple task, squaring a number. It is easiest to imagine mathematical functions as functionally cohesive because they often perform one simple task, such as adding two values or finding a square root. However, a function also would have high functional cohesion if the task was initializing the data members of a class or displaying a message. Because functionally cohesive functions perform a single task, they tend to be short. The issue is not size, however. If it takes 20 statements to perform one task in a function, then the function is still cohesive.

TIP

You might work in a programming environment with rules such as "No function, when printed, will be longer than one page" or "No function will have more than 30 lines of code." The rule-maker is trying to achieve more cohesion, but such rules represent an arbitrary way of doing so. It's possible for a two-line function to have low cohesion, and, although less likely, a 40-line function might also possess high cohesion.

There is a time and a place for shortcuts. If you need a result from spreadsheet data in a hurry, you can type in two values and take a sum rather than creating a formula with proper cell references. If a memo must go out in five minutes, you don't have time to change fonts or add clip art with your word processor. If you need a quick programming result, you might use cryptic variable names, create tight coupling, and forego thinking about cohesion. When you create a professional application, however, you should keep professional guidelines in mind. Even when writing small pieces of code, most professional programmers find that following sound practices is so useful that it becomes second nature.

You Do It

Creating a Class with a Constructor

In the following set of steps, you create a class named `Pizza`. A constructor sets the default `Pizza` to cheese topping, a 12-inch diameter, and a price of $8.99. When a `Pizza` is instantiated, the user can override these default values in response to prompts.

1. Open a new file in your C++ editor and type the statements that include the header files you need.

```cpp
#include<iostream>
#include<string>
using namespace std;
```

2. Define the `Pizza` class to contain three variable fields (the topping, diameter, and price of the `Pizza`), and three constant fields (the standard topping, diameter, and price for `Pizza` objects). The class also contains three functions—a constructor, `setValues()`, and `displayValues()`. The constructor contains default values for each field within its argument list.

```cpp
class Pizza
{
   private:
      string topping;
      int diameter;
      double price;
      const static string STDTOP;
      const static int STDSIZE;
      const static double STDPRICE;
   public:
      Pizza(const string = STDTOP, const int = STDSIZE,
              const double = STDPRICE);
      void setValues();
      void displayValues();
};
```

3. After the class definition, provide values for the three class constants.

```cpp
const string Pizza::STDTOP = "cheese";
const int Pizza::STDSIZE = 12;
const double Pizza::STDPRICE = 8.99;
```

8

4. Write the `Pizza` constructor, which assigns each constructor argument to the appropriate class field. (Note that because the argument name for `price` was chosen to be the same as the field name, it is necessary to use the `this` pointer with the field.)

```
Pizza::Pizza(const string top, const int size,
     const double price)
{
   topping = top;
   diameter = size;
   this->price = price;
}
```

5. Write the `displayValues()` function, which produces a single line of output.

```
void Pizza::displayValues()
{
   cout<<"a "<<diameter<<" inch "<<topping<<
      " pizza. Price $"<<price<<endl;
}
```

6. Write the `setValues()` function, which prompts the user for a topping and a size. Any topping other than cheese increases the `Pizza` price to $9.99. Any `Pizza` diameter greater than 12 increases the `Pizza` price by $1.50.

```
void Pizza::setValues()
{
   const double TOPPINGPREMIUM = 1.00;
   const double SIZEPREMIUM = 1.50;
   cout<<"Enter topping ";
   cin>>topping;
   if(topping != STDTOP)
      price = STDPRICE + TOPPINGPREMIUM;
   cout<<"Enter size ";
   cin>>diameter;
   if(diameter > STDSIZE)
      price += SIZEPREMIUM;
}
```

7. Write a `main()` function that tests the `Pizza` class. Create a `Pizza` object and display it to show the default values. (You can create a `Pizza` object using no constructor arguments because default values have been provided for each one.) Then prompt the user to accept or reject these default values. If the user does not respond with 'y' for "yes," use the `setValues()` function to assign new

values to the `Pizza`'s data fields. Finally, use the `displayValues()` function a second time to show the user the complete order, including the price.

```cpp
int main()
{
    Pizza aPizza;
    char standard;
    cout<<"The standard pizza is: ";
    aPizza.displayValues();
    cout<<"Let me take your order"<<endl;
    cout<<"Do you want the standard pizza - y or n? ";
    cin>>standard;
    if(standard != 'y')
        aPizza.setValues();
    cout<<"Your order is ";
    aPizza.displayValues();
}
```

8. Save the file as **Pizza.cpp** in your Chapter08 folder. Compile and run the program. When you choose the standard `Pizza`, the output looks like Figure 8-28. When you choose to alter the default values, the output might look like Figure 8-29.

Figure 8-28   Output of the `Pizza` program when the user accepts the default values

Figure 8-29   Output of the `Pizza` program when the user rejects the default values

Using Constructor Parameters

In the following set of steps, you write a `main()` function that instantiates several objects of the `Pizza` class that you defined earlier. You also create objects that use all, some, and none of the constructor default values.

1. Open the **Pizza.cpp** file if it is not still open. Immediately save the file as **Pizza2.cpp** in your Chapter08 folder.

2. Delete the `main()` function in the Pizza2 file, and replace it with the following `main()` function that declares four `Pizza` objects. Declare a standard `Pizza` that uses all three constructor default values. Declare three other `Pizza` objects that use two, one, and no default values, respectively.

```
int main()
{
  Pizza stdPizza;
  Pizza special("pineapple");
  Pizza deluxeSpecial("sausage", 16);
  Pizza veryDeluxeSpecial("lobster", 20, 17.99);
```

3. Add statements to display each `Pizza`, then add a closing curly brace for the `main()` function.

```
    cout<<"The standard pizza is: ";
    stdPizza.displayValues();
    cout<<"Today's special is ";
    special.displayValues();
    cout<<"The deluxe special is ";
    deluxeSpecial.displayValues();
    cout<<"And the very deluxe special is ";
    veryDeluxeSpecial.displayValues();
}
```

4. Save the program again, then compile and run it. The output looks like Figure 8-30, and shows that each `Pizza` object uses any arguments passed to it upon construction. The output also shows that each `Pizza` object uses default values for any arguments not passed.

Figure 8-30   Output of the `Pizza2` program

Understanding Composition

In the next steps, you will take advantage of existing `Name` and `CreditData` classes to build a `Customer` class that contains objects of `Name` and `CreditData` type.

1. Open a new file in your C++ editor and type the following:

```
#include<iostream>
#include<string>
using namespace std;
```

2. Open the **Name.cpp** file in your Chapter08 folder. Figure 8-31 shows the contents. Copy the class and paste it into your newly started file. The file contains a `Name` class that has three private fields that hold a first, middle, and last name. The constructor requires values for all three fields. A `displayFullName()` function displays the `Name` values.

```cpp
class Name
{
  private:
    string first;
    string middle;
    string last;
  public:
    Name(string, string, string);
    void displayFullName();
};
Name::Name(string first, string middle, string last)
{
  this->first = first;
  this->middle = middle;
  this->last = last;
}
void Name::displayFullName()
{
  cout<<first<<" "<<middle<<" "<<last<<endl;
}
```

Figure 8-31   The `Name` class

3. Open the **CreditData.cpp** file in your Chapter08 folder. Figure 8-32 shows the contents. Paste the `CreditData` class into your editor below the `Name` class. The `CreditData` class holds private fields for a current balance and a maximum balance. The constructor has been created to assign a current balance argument to the `currentBalance` field, and to assign a maximum balance to the `maxBalance` field only if the maximum balance is not less than the current balance. If the maximum balance is less than the current balance, then the maximum balance is increased to be equal to the current balance. The `displayCreditData()` function displays the field values as well as the difference between the maximum balance and the current balance.

```
class CreditData
{
  private:
    double currentBalance;
    double maxBalance;
  public:
    CreditData(double, double = 0);
    void displayCreditData();
};
CreditData::CreditData(double currBal, double maxBal)
{
    currentBalance = currBal;
    if(maxBal < currBal)
       maxBalance = currBal;
    else
       maxBalance = maxBal;
}
void CreditData::displayCreditData()
{
    double creditLeft = maxBalance - currentBalance;
    cout<<"Current balance: $"<<currentBalance<<
       "\nMaximum balance $"<<maxBalance<<"\nCredit left: $"<<
       creditLeft<<endl;
}
```

Figure 8-32   The CreditData class

4. Next, you will create a **Customer** class that uses the pre-existing classes. Enter the class as follows, so it contains a name, some credit data, and a phone number. Include a prototype for the class constructor and a function that displays Customer data.

```
class Customer
{
  private:
    Name name;
    CreditData credit;
    string phoneNumber;
  public:
    Customer(string, string, string, double, double, string);
       void showCustomer();
};
```

5. Enter the constructor function as follows. Most of the work is done in the constructor header. The first, middle, and last names are passed to the object-member name, and the balance and maximum are passed to the object-member `credit`. A single statement in the constructor body assigns the phone number argument.

```
Customer::Customer(string firstName, string middleName,
    string lastName, double bal, double max, string phone) :
    name(firstName, middleName, lastName), credit(bal, max)
{
    phoneNumber = phone;
}
```

6. The `showCustomer()` function uses the already-created display functions from the `Name` and `CreditData` classes to display those parts of the data.

```
void Customer::showCustomer()
{
    cout<<"Customer data:"<<endl;
    name.displayFullName();
    cout<<phoneNumber<<endl;
    credit.displayCreditData();
}
```

7. Add a `main()` function to demonstrate the class. The `main()` function loops two times (although you can adjust the value of the `TIMES` constant to perform additional loops). At each iteration, the function prompts you for customer data, creates a `Customer` object, and displays it.

```
int main()
{
    int x;
    const int TIMES = 2;
    string first, middle, last, phone;
    double bal, lim;
    for(x = 0; x < TIMES; ++x)
    {
        cout<<endl<<"Please enter first name for customer #"<<
            (x + 1)<<" ";
        cin>>first;
        cout<<"Please enter middle name ";
        cin>>middle;
        cout<<"Please enter last name ";
        cin>>last;
        cout<<"Enter current balance ";
        cin>>bal;
        cout<<"Enter credit limit ";
        cin>>lim;
        cout<<"Enter phone number ";
        cin>>phone;
        Customer cust(first, middle, last, bal, lim, phone);
        cust.showCustomer();
    }
}
```

8

8. Save the file as **Customer.cpp**. Compile and execute the program. The pre-existing `Name` and `CreditData` classes perform as expected, as you can see from the output in Figure 8-33. In the first loop, the `Customer` has a maximum that is greater than the balance, so both are set using the input value. In the second loop, the maximum did not exceed the balance, so the maximum was reset to the current balance. When you created the `Customer` class, you did not have to perform these decisions and calculations because the member-object classes already contained them.

Figure 8-33 Output of the `Customer` program

CHAPTER SUMMARY

❏ You can classify the roles of member functions into four basic groups: inspector functions that return information about an object, mutator functions that change an object, auxiliary functions that perform some action or service, and manager functions, which create and destroy objects for you.

❏ A constructor is a function that is called automatically each time an object is created. A default constructor is one that does not require any arguments; a non-default constructor requires at least one argument.

❏ You write your own constructors for classes any time you want specific tasks performed when an object is instantiated. You must give a constructor function the same name as the class for which it is a constructor and you cannot give a constructor function a return type.

❐ Like other functions, a constructor header can contain an argument list. If the only constructor in a class is non-default, you must provide appropriate arguments when you instantiate an object. You can create constructors that have default values for one or more of the arguments. Just as with ordinary functions, once you provide a value for one of the arguments in a constructor's argument list, then you must provide default values for all the remaining arguments listed to the right.

❐ Constructors can be overloaded. If you provide two or more constructors for the same class, they are overloaded by definition. As with other overloaded functions, two constructor functions used in the same program must have different argument lists so that the compiler can tell them apart.

❐ A destructor is a function that is called automatically each time an object is destroyed. As with constructors, you must give a destructor function the same name as its class (and therefore the same name as any constructor for that class). Unlike constructors, you must precede the destructor name with a tilde (~). As with constructors, you cannot give a destructor function a return type (it's not necessary because destructors never return anything). Unlike constructors, you *cannot* pass any values to a destructor. You cannot overload destructor functions.

❐ Using a class object within another class object is known as composition. When you create class objects within another class object, you can call the contained objects member-objects. A benefit of object-oriented programming is that you can reuse well-crafted components as member-objects, instead of starting from scratch each time you create a class. The composition relationship is called a "has-a" relationship. When one class contains others that have only non-default constructors, then the constructor of the containing class must provide values for its members' constructors by using an initialization list.

❐ Reusability is a major focus of object-oriented thinking. After you have created a collection of useful classes, often called a library, you might find that many class files contain the same `#include` statements. To resolve conflicts, you can give each class a `#define` name, which is simply an internal name for the group of statements that make up the definition of the class. The `#define` statement is usually coupled with `#ifndef` and `#endif`. The C++ directive `#ifndef` allows you to test whether a class has already been defined in a project; if the class has already been defined, everything up to the `#endif` directive will be ignored.

❐ As you write larger and more complicated programs, be sure to spend time on planning and design. When you know what data members and functions you need, you can give them legal, clear, and appropriate C++ identifiers. When developing a system, you can use stubs—simple routines that do nothing (or very little) that you incorporate into a program as placeholders. When developing functions, consider coupling, which is a measure of the strength of the connection between two functions, and cohesion, which refers to how well the operations in a function relate to one another.

KEY TERMS

Inspector functions, also called **access functions**, are functions that return information about an object's state, or display some or all of an object's attributes.

Predicate functions are functions that test the truth of some condition.

Mutator functions, also known as **implementors**, are functions that change an object's state or attributes.

Auxiliary functions, also known as **facilitators**, are functions that perform some action or service, such as sorting data or searching for data.

Manager functions create and destroy objects for you.

A **constructor** is a function that is called automatically each time an object is created; it has the same name as its class.

A **default constructor** is one that does not require any arguments.

A **non-default constructor** is one that requires at least one argument.

A **destructor** is a function that is called automatically each time an object is destroyed; it has the same name as its class, preceded with a tilde.

The **one's complement operator** (~) is the operator that makes every bit become its opposite. It is also called the **bitwise complement operator**.

A **copy constructor** executes when you pass an object to a function, making a local copy.

Using a class object within another class object is known as **composition**.

Member-objects are objects contained within another class.

The composition relationship is called a **"has-a" relationship**.

An **initialization list** provides constructor-required values for the member-objects; it is the part of the constructor header to the right of the colon.

Program maintenance is the upkeep of professional programs over time.

A **library** is a collection of useful classes.

A `#define` **name** is an internal name for the group of statements that make up the definition of a class.

The C++ directive `#ifndef` allows you to test whether a class has already been defined in a project; it means "if not defined."

The `#endif` directive means that you have reached the end of the block of code that you are defining.

Stubs are simple routines that do nothing (or very little); you incorporate them into a program as placeholders.

Coupling is a measure of the strength of the connection between two functions; it expresses the extent to which information is exchanged by functions.

Coupling is either **tight coupling** or **loose coupling**, depending on how much one function depends on information from another.

Cohesion refers to how well the operations in a function relate to one another. In highly cohesive functions, all operations are related.

Functional cohesion occurs when all of the function operations contribute to the performance of only one task.

REVIEW QUESTIONS

1. Which of the following is not a classification of class member functions?

   a. inspector functions

   b. detective functions

   c. mutator functions

   d. auxiliary functions

2. A _____ is called automatically each time an object is created.

   a. compiler

   b. builder

   c. constructor

   d. destructor

3. Which of the following is equivalent to `double money = 4.56;`?

   a. `double 4.56 = money;`

   b. `money double = 4.56;`

   c. `double money(4.56);`

   d. `float money = 4.56;`

4. A class named `Carpet` contains three data fields: `int length, int width,` and `double price.` A program declares `Carpet myRug(129.95);`. You know that _____.

   a. the length is 129.95

   b. the width is 129.95

   c. the price is 129.95

   d. You do not know any of the above.

5. The most common use of constructors is to _____.

   a. initialize data fields

   b. perform mathematical calculations

   c. call mutator functions

   d. deallocate memory

6. Which of the following is a legal constructor definition for a class named `Table`?

   a. `Table();`

   b. `void Table();`

   c. `TableConstructor();`

   d. All of the above are legal constructor definitions.

8

7. A constructor that requires no arguments is an example of a _____ constructor.

   a. no fault

   b. default

   c. faultless

   d. static

8. A constructor is defined as `LightBulb(int = 60);`. The parameter is assigned to a field named `watts`. When you define an object as `LightBulb oneBulb(90);`, the watts variable will be set to _____.

   a. 0

   b. 60

   c. 90

   d. 150

9. A constructor is defined as `Computer(int = 512, int = 2, double = 1000.00);`. Which of the following is a legal statement that uses the constructor?

   a. `Computer myMachine(128);`

   b. `Computer myMachine(1234.56);`

   c. `Computer myMachine(256, 899.99);`

   d. All of the above are legal.

10. When you want to override one of four constructor default values for an object you are instantiating, you also must _____.

   a. override all parameters to the right of the one you want to override

   b. override all parameters to the left of the one you want to override

   c. override all parameters in the constructor

   d. not override any other parameters in the constructor

11. A constructor has been defined as `Painting(string = "oil", int = 0);`. The first argument is used to set the `Painting`'s medium and the second sets the price. Which of the following can you use to declare an oil `Painting` valued at $2000?

   a. `Painting myArtWork(2000);`

   b. `Painting myArtWork("oil", 2000);`

   c. `Painting myArtwork;`

   d. Two of the above

12. A constructor has been defined as `Painting(string = "oil",   int = 0);`.
Which of the following can you use to declare an oil `Painting` valued at $0?

    a. `Painting myArtWork;`

    b. `Painting myArtWork();`

    c. `Painting myArtwork(0, "oil");`

    d. Two of the above

13. Whenever a class contains two constructors, the constructors are _____.

    a. default constructors

    b. destructors

    c. overloaded

    d. static

14. A constructor has been defined as `FlowerSeed(int = 7);`. Which of the following constructors could coexist with the defined constructor without any possible
ambiguity?

    a. `FlowerSeed(int);`

    b. `FlowerSeed();`

    c. `FlowerSeed(int = 10, int = 18);`

    d. `FlowerSeed(int, double);`

15. When an object goes out of scope, a(n) _____ is called automatically.

    a. destructor

    b. constructor

    c. overloaded function

    d. operating system error message

16. Which is a legal destructor for the `Game` class?

    a. `Game();`

    b. `~Game();`

    c. `void ~Game();`

    d. Two of the above are legal destructors for the `Game` class.

17. The primary reason you want to use `#define`, `#ifndef`, and `#endif` is to
_____.

    a. provide names for class constructors and destructors

    b. save memory

    c. avoid declaring a class twice

    d. ensure a class has been declared before using it

8

18. A function must calculate federal withholding tax for each employee's paycheck. According to the general guidelines mentioned in this chapter, the best function name is _____.

    a. `fwt()` for federal withholding tax, because it is short, saving typing

    b. `governmentTakesTooMuch()` because it makes a political statement and amuses your co-workers

    c. `calculatefederalwithholdingforeachemployee()` because it is very descriptive

    d. `calculateWithholdingTax()` because it is descriptive and capitalizes each new word

19. The measure of the strength of the connection between two functions is called _____.

    a. coupling

    b. cohesion

    c. pathological

    d. blending

20. The best functions have _____.

    a. low cohesion and loose coupling

    b. low cohesion and tight coupling

    c. high cohesion and loose coupling

    d. high cohesion and tight coupling

EXERCISES

1. Perform the following tasks:

   a. Create a class named `TestClass` that holds a single private integer field and a public constructor. The only statement in the constructor is one that displays the message "Constructing". Write a `main()` function that instantiates one object of the `TestClass`. Save the file as **TestClass.cpp** in the Chapter08 folder. Run the program and observe the results.

   b. Write another `main()` function that instantiates an array of ten `TestClass` objects. Save the file as **TestClassArray.cpp**. Run this program and observe the results.

2. Write the class definition for a `Date` class that contains three integer data members: month, day, and year. Include a default constructor that assigns the date 1/1/2000 to any new object that does not receive arguments. Also include a function that displays the `Date` object. Write a `main()` function in which you instantiate two `Date` objects—one that you create using the default constructor values, and one that you create using three arguments—and display its values. Save the file as **Date.cpp**. You will use the `Date` class in other exercises in this chapter.

3. Create a **Person** class that includes fields for last name, first name, and zip code. Include a default constructor that initializes last name, first name, and zip code to "X" if no arguments are supplied. Also include a display function. Write a **main()** function that instantiates and displays two **Person** objects: one that uses the default values, and one for which you supply your own values. Save the file as **Person.cpp**. You will use the **Person** class in other exercises in this chapter.

4. Create a class named **Time** that contains integer fields for hours and minutes. Store the hours in military time, that is, 0 through 23. Add a function that displays the fields, using a colon to separate hours and minutes. (Make sure the minutes display as two digits. For example, 3 o'clock should display as 3:00, not 3:0.) Add another function that takes an argument that represents minutes to add to the time. The function updates the time based on the number of minutes added. For example, 12:30 plus 15 is 12:45, 14:50 plus 20 is 15:10, and 23:59 plus 2 is 0:01. The **Time** constructor requires an argument for hours. The argument for minutes is optional; the value defaults to 0 if no argument is supplied. The constructor ensures that the hours field is not greater than 23 and that the minutes field is not greater than 59; default to these maximum values if the arguments to the constructor are out of range. Create a **main()** function that instantiates an array of at least four **Time** objects and demonstrates that they display correctly both before and after varying amounts of time have been added to them. Save the file as **Time.cpp**. You will use the **Time** class in another exercise in this chapter.

5. Create a class named **SavingsAccount**. Provide fields for the customer (use the **Person** class from Exercise 3), account number, balance, and interest rate. Provide two constructors. One requires a customer and sets each numeric field to 0; the other requires a customer and an account number and sets the account's opening balance to $100 at 3% interest. Include a function that displays an account's data fields. Write a **main()** function that instantiates one **SavingsAccount** object of each type and displays their values. Save the file as **SavingsAccount.cpp**.

6. Create a class named **RealtorCommission**. Fields include the sale price of a house, the sales commission rate, and the commission. Create two constructors. Each constructor requires the sales price (expressed as a double) and the commission rate. One constructor requires the commission rate to be a double, such as .06. The other requires the sale price and the commission rate expressed as a whole number, such as 6. Each constructor calculates the commission value based on the price of the house multiplied by the commission rate. The difference is that the constructor that accepts the whole number must convert it to a percentage by dividing by 100. Also include a display function for the fields contained in the **RealtorCommission** class. Write a **main()** function that instantiates at least two **RealtorCommission** objects—one that uses a decimal and one that uses a whole number as the commission rate. Display the **RealtorCommission** object values. Save the file as **RealtorCommission.cpp**.

8

7. Create a class named `StudentGrade`. Include fields for a student ID number, student name (use the `Person` class from Exercise 3), numeric test score, possible points, and letter grade. Create a constructor that requires the student ID, name, and test score, and allows a fourth parameter that holds possible test points. If a value for possible points is not passed to the constructor, the possible points value defaults to 100. (If a 0 value is passed for possible points, force possible points to 1 so that you do not divide by 0 when calculating a grade.) The constructor calculates the student's percentage (divides score by possible points) and assigns a letter grade based on the following: 90% and above (A), 80% (B), 70% (C), and 60% (D). Create a main() function that instantiates and displays enough `StudentGrade` objects to test a variety of scores and possible point values. Save the file as **StudentGrade.cpp**.

8. Create a class named `Car`. The Car class contains a static integer field named count. Create a constructor that adds 1 to the count and displays the count each time a `Car` is created. Create a destructor that subtracts 1 from the count and displays the count each time a `Car` goes out of scope. Write a **main()** function that declares an array of five `Car` objects. Output consists of five constructor messages and five destructor messages, each displaying the current count, similar to the output in Figure 8-34. Save the file as **Car.cpp**.

Figure 8-34 Output of `Car` program

9. Create a class named `MagazineSubscription`. Include fields for the subscriber (use the `Person` class you created in Exercise 3) and the subscription's start and expiration dates (use the `Date` class you created in Exercise 2). Include a constructor that takes three arguments—a `Person` and two `Dates`. Also include a display function that displays `MagazineSubscription` fields by calling the `Person` and `Date` display functions. Write a main() function in which you instantiate a `Person` object and two `Date` objects. Use these as arguments to the constructor that instantiates a `MagazineSubscription` object. Display the `MagazineSubscription` object. Save the file as **MagazineSubscription.cpp**.

10. Create a class named `DentalAppointment`. Include fields for a patient's data (use the `Person` class from Exercise 3), the date (using the `Date` class from Exercise 2), the time (use the `Time` class from Exercise 4), and the duration of the appointment in minutes. Also include a field that contains the ending time of the appointment; this field will be calculated based on the start time and the duration using the `Time`

class function that adds minutes to a `Time` object. The `DentalAppointment` constructor requires a first and last name, and a month, day, year, hour, and minute for the appointment. Allow a `DentalAppointment` to be constructed with or without an additional argument for appointment duration, and force the duration to 30 minutes when no argument is supplied. The constructor does not allow any appointment over 240 minutes. The constructor calculates the appointment ending time based on the start time and the duration. Also include a display function for the `DentalAppointment` class. Write a `main()` function that loops at least three times, prompting the user for `DentalAppointment` data and displaying all the information. (Note, if you use the `Person` class display function, the zip code will be "X"; this is acceptable.) Figure 8-35 shows the output after a typical patient has been entered. Save the file as **DentalAppointment.cpp**.

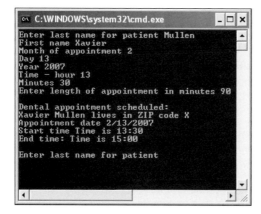

Figure 8-35   Typical execution of `DentalAppointment`

11. Create a class named `IceCreamCone` with fields for flavor, number of scoops, type of cone, and price. Unless arguments are supplied, flavor defaults to "Vanilla", number of scoops defaults to 1, and cone type defaults to "Sugar". The constructor calculates the price based on 75 cents per scoop, with an additional 40 cents for a waffle cone. Write a `main()` function demonstrating that the class works correctly. Save the file as **IceCreamCone.cpp**.

12. Create a class named `Instructor`. It contains a first and last name and an office number, and its only constructor requires all three as arguments. Create a class named `Classroom`. It contains a building and a room number, and its only constructor requires both as arguments. Create a class named `CollegeCourse`. A `CollegeCourse` contains an `Instructor`, a `Classroom`, and a number of credits. Its constructor requires a first and last name of an instructor, the instructor's office number, a `Classroom` building and room number, and a number of credits. Each of these classes contains a function that displays an object's values. Write a `main()` function that instantiates at least two `CollegeCourse` objects and displays their values. Save the file as **CollegeCourse.cpp**.

13. Each of the following files in your Chapter08 folder contains syntax and/or logical errors. Determine the problem in each case, and fix the program. Save your solutions by adding "Fixed" to the filename, as in **DEBUG8-1Fixed.cpp**.

   a. DEBUG8-1.cpp

   b. DEBUG8-2.cpp

   c. DEBUG8-3.cpp

   d. DEBUG8-4.cpp

CASE PROJECT 1

CASE PROJECTS

a. You have been developing a **Fraction** class for Teacher's Pet Software that contains several fields and functions.

Add two constructors to the class. The first accepts two integer values representing the numerator and denominator. If a single integer is passed to the constructor, use it as the numerator, and use a default value of 1 for the denominator. If no values are passed to the constructor, use a default value of 0 for the numerator and 1 for the denominator. When any **Fraction** is constructed with a 0 argument for the denominator, force the denominator value to 1.

The second constructor requires three arguments: a whole number portion for a **Fraction**, a numerator, and a denominator. This constructor executes when any **Fraction** object is instantiated using three integer arguments. As with the other constructor, when any **Fraction** is constructed with a 0 argument for the denominator, force the denominator value to 1.

Whenever a **Fraction** object is constructed, automatically reduce the **Fraction** to the proper format. For example, a **Fraction** created using 0, 2, and 4 as arguments should be reduced to 1/2, and a **Fraction** created as 3 10/2 should be reduced to 8 0/1.

Write a **main()** function that declares several **Fraction** objects, and confirm that the class works correctly.

Save the file as **Fraction.cpp**.

b. Create a **MathProblem** class that contains four **Fraction** objects: the first **Fraction** operand in a problem, the second **Fraction** operand in a problem, the user's **Fraction** answer to a problem, and the correct **Fraction** answer to a problem. The **MathProblem** class also contains a character field that stores an operator (for now, assume the operator will be either + or *) and contains an integer or **bool** field named **isAnswerCorrect**, indicating whether the user correctly answered the problem. For example, a **MathProblem** object containing 1/2, 1/4, and + for the operands and operators; 3/4 for the correct answer; and 3/8 for the user's answer would contain a 0 or false in the **isAnswerCorrect** field because the correct answer and user's answer do not match. Set the **isAnswerCorrect** field to true if the user's answer is equivalent to the correct answer; for example, if 3/4 is the correct answer, then 3/4, 6/8, and 9/12 are all correct.

Include a function named **setProblem()** that sets a **MathProblem**'s values with arguments that include two **Fraction** operands and an operation. This function calculates and stores the correct answer, assigns 0 to the user's answer, and sets **isAnswerCorrect** to 0 or false. Include a **displayProblem()** function that displays the math problem as a question, and an **askUserForAnswer()** function that accepts the user's answer from the keyboard and assigns an appropriate value to **isAnswerCorrect**.

Include any other **MathProblem** functions you feel are useful and appropriate.

Write a **main()** function that declares five **MathProblem** objects you can use to test a student's fraction arithmetic skills. Assign values to the **MathProblem**s. Display the problems and accept the answers. When the five problems are completed, display each of the problems, along with the student's answer, the correct answer, and a message indicating whether the student is right or wrong. Finally, show the student a score indicating the percentage of problems answered correctly.

Save the file as **MathProblem.cpp**.

8

CASE PROJECT 2

a. You have been developing a **BankAccount** class for Parkville Bank that contains several fields and functions. In previous chapters, you declared the interest rate to be static and constant; remove those modifiers as well as the definition of the interest rate as 0.03.

Add a constructor to the class that accepts arguments for the account number, balance, and interest rate. The account number is required, but both the balance and interest rate default to 0 if no argument is supplied to the constructor. If the account number is not between 1000 and 9999 inclusive, force it to zero.

Modify the display function, if necessary, so that all **BankAccount** fields are displayed.

Write a **main()** function that declares several **BankAccount** objects and confirm that the class works correctly.

Save the file as **BankAccount.cpp**.

b. Parkville Investment Consulting keeps track of clients' asset portfolios. Create a class named **Portfolio** that contains a client number and two **BankAccount** objects—one for checking and one for savings. Include two other **double** fields for stock market holdings total value and real estate holdings total value. The **Portfolio** constructor requires the client number, checking account data (account number and balance), savings account data (account number, balance, and interest rate), and the value of stock market and real estate holdings. The constructor calls a function named **balancePortfolio()** that determines the relative percentage of the client's holdings in each of the four investment types. If any investment type's value is more than 40% of the client's total holdings, an appropriate message displays warning that the client's portfolio might be out of balance. Also create a display function for the `Portfolio` class to display all the details. Add any additional functions you need to the classes.

Write a `main()` function that continues to prompt a user for `Portfolio` data until zero is entered for the client account number. Create each `Portfolio` object and display its values, including the possible out-of-balance warning message.

Save the file as **Portfolio.cpp**.

9

UNDERSTANDING FRIENDS AND OVERLOADING OPERATORS

In this chapter, you will:

♦ Learn what a friend is
♦ Declare a friend function
♦ Examine the benefits of polymorphism and overloading
♦ Use a friend function to access data from two classes
♦ Learn the rules that apply to operator overloading
♦ Overload an arithmetic operator
♦ Overload operators to work with a class object and a primitive type
♦ Chain multiple mathematical operations in a statement
♦ Overload the insertion operator (<<) for output
♦ Overload the extraction operator (>>) for input
♦ Overload the prefix and postfix ++ and -- operators
♦ Overload the == operator
♦ Overload the = operator
♦ Overload the subscript and parentheses operators

Creating classes that contain private data and public interfaces to the data is a hallmark of object-oriented programming, in part because the technique allows objects to resemble their real-world counterparts. However, you occasionally may want to allow some outside functions to have access to private data so that you can add "natural" language features. Using objects with features, like arithmetic operators and insertion and extraction operators, adds to the "naturalness" of object-orientation. This chapter expands your mastery of object-oriented programming in C++ by familiarizing you with `friend` functions and overloaded operator functions. These features allow you to create classes that clients can use in an intuitive manner.

WHAT ARE FRIENDS?

Encapsulation and data hiding are two primary features of object-oriented programs. You use encapsulation when you place data and functions together in a capsule as objects. You use data hiding when you create `private` class members; they remain inaccessible to functions that are not part of the class. In the classes you have written, you took advantage of data hiding: Once you create a class, including writing and debugging all of its member functions, no outside function could ever modify or use the `private` member data in your class. Only the functions that are part of a class can access the class's `private` data. This approach ensures that all data members are used correctly and appropriately.

Sometimes, however, it is convenient to allow an outside, nonmember function to have access to a `private` data member. For example, you might have two objects that belong to different classes, and you want a single function to use data members from each object. If the function is a member of the first class, it doesn't have access to the data in the second class; if the function is a member of the second class, it doesn't have access to the data in the first. One solution to this dilemma is to create special functions called `friend` functions.

A **friend function** is a function that can access the non-`public` members of a class, even though the function itself is not a member of the class. A `friend` function is a normal function with special access privileges.

> In addition to `friend` functions, you can create `friend` classes. A **friend class** is a class in which every function can access non-`public` members of another class; in other words, every function in a `friend` class is a `friend` function.

In your own relationships, when you bestow friendship on someone, you often give your friend access to private information you don't want the outside world to know. For example, you might give a friend a key to your house, tell a friend your salary, or provide your friend with embarrassing details of your high school days. In a similar way, a C++ function or class that is a `friend` has access to the private information in a class.

> Non-`public` members of a class include all `private` and `protected` data fields and functions. You will learn about the `protected` access specifier in Chapter 10.

A `friend` function can access `private` data from a class of which it is not a member, but a `friend` function cannot be a `friend` on its own. That is, when you create a function, you cannot simply call it a `friend` function and declare it to be the `friend` of a class, thus allowing access to the `private` data in the class. Instead, when you create a class, you must declare the names of the functions you will allow to be `friends` of your class. You must specifically name all functions that will have access to a class's `private` data.

The C++ **friend** relationship is always one-sided. A class declaration must state which functions will be its friends; functions cannot declare that they are friends of a class. You can think of a class as *bestowing* friendship on or *granting* friendship to a function. When you think about the principles of data hiding and encapsulation, this idea makes sense. You use data hiding to make data members in a class **private** so that you can control access to them. Making data members **private** would serve no purpose if any function could declare itself to be a friend of your class and then alter the private data within your class objects. When creating a class, you must consciously decide whether any outside functions will have access to your private data, and you must explicitly bestow friendship on those functions.

Because **friend** functions can access private data, and the data members are **private** for a reason, **friend** functions should be used only when absolutely necessary. Use **friend** functions only when it makes sense that a nonmember function should be able to use a **private** piece of data. Don't write **friend** functions simply to overcome data encapsulation—that approach violates the spirit of object-oriented programming. Instead, most of the time, you should provide access to **private** data using **public** functions that return data values.

Some programmers disapprove of the use of **friend** functions because they weaken the object-oriented concept of hiding data. However, others think of **friend** functions the same way they think of any **public** functions—as interfaces to the class. On a few occasions, being able to grant **friend** status to a function is helpful. Later in this chapter, you will learn about overloading operators, in which friendship sometimes plays a useful part.

9

HOW TO DECLARE A FUNCTION AS A FRIEND

Figure 9-1 shows a class named **Customer** that can be used by a business to hold a customer number and the balance owed. The class contains three functions; two are members of the class. The default constructor for the **Customer** class supplies values for the data fields if none are provided when a **Customer** object is instantiated. The **displayCustomer()** function displays the values stored in a **Customer** object. The third function (whose prototype and implementation are shaded in Figure 9-1) is named **displayAsAFriend()**; it is not a member of the **Customer** class; instead it is a **friend**.

As shown in the **Customer** class in Figure 9-1, the member function **displayCustomer()** is similar to many functions you have seen. As a member of the **Customer** class, the **displayCustomer()** function has access to the private fields **custNum** and **balanceDue**. The function meets the following conditions:

- It requires the class name **Customer** and the scope resolution operator in the function header.

- It must be declared in the **public** section of the **Customer** class definition, so that a **main()** function (or any other client function) can use it.

- It does not use the keyword **friend** in its declaration.

```
class Customer
{
   friend void displayAsAFriend(Customer);
   private:
      int custNum;
      double balanceDue;
   public:
      Customer(int = 0, double = 0.0);
      void displayCustomer();
};
Customer::Customer(int num, double balance)
{
   custNum = num;
   balanceDue = balance;
}
void Customer::displayCustomer()
{
    cout<<"In the member function"<<endl;
    cout<<"Customer #"<<custNum<<" has a balance of $"
        <<balanceDue<<endl;
}
void displayAsAFriend(Customer cust)
{
    cout<<"In the friend function:"<<endl;
    cout<<"Customer #"<<cust.custNum<<" has a balance of $"<<
        cust.balanceDue<<endl;
}
```

Figure 9-1 The `Customer` class and a `friend` function

The function `displayAsAFriend()` is not a `Customer` member function. As a non-member function that has access to the **private** data members `custNum` and `balanceDue`:

- It cannot use the class name `Customer` and the scope resolution operator in the function header.

- It need not be declared in the **public** section of the class definition.

- It must use the C++ keyword **friend** in its declaration.

As a nonmember function, `displayAsAFriend()` can be declared in the **public** section of the `Customer` class, the **private** section, or first in the class as it is here (which is actually a **private** section by default). Because the `displayAsAFriend()` function is neither **public** nor **private**, you can prototype it in any portion of the class declaration you want. Some programmers place **friend** function prototypes first in a class declaration, to separate them from member functions. Other programmers place **friend** function prototypes wherever most of the other function prototypes are stored, which is usually the **public** section. (Also, because a **friend** function is simply a nonmember function, it acts more like a **public** member than a **private** one, so placing the **friend** function's declaration within the **public** section might make sense to you.)

A function that displays private data from a single class should be a member function of that class. The displayAsAFriend() function only displays data from the Customer class, so there really is no need for it to be a friend function. It is created as a friend in Figure 9-1 for discussion purposes, and to contrast the syntax of friends with that of member functions.

TIP

You are not required to use the word friend within the function name of a friend function. The name displayAsAFriend() is used here to remind you that the function is a friend. A more typical name for this function would be display() or displayValues().

TIP

An individual function can be declared to be a friend by any number of classes.

TIP

The prototypes of displayCustomer() and displayAsAFriend() exhibit the differences between class functions and friend functions. The prototype void displayCustomer(); shows that the displayCustomer() function takes no arguments. In reality, the function does take one argument—the this pointer. All member functions receive a this pointer that contains a reference to the object using the function. The function can display a Customer idNum and balanceDue because the function is a member of the Customer class, and receives a this pointer to a Customer object that contains those fields.

On the other hand, the void displayAsAFriend(Customer); prototype shows that displayAsAFriend() receives a Customer object as an argument. Because displayAsAFriend() does not receive a this pointer, it must receive a copy of the object whose idNum and balanceDue it will use.

Ordinarily, a nonmember function could not use a statement like cout<<cust.idNum; because idNum is a private field. Instead, an ordinary function would have to use a public Customer function (perhaps with a name like getID()) to access the private data. However, displayAsAFriend() is allowed to use cust.idNum and cust.balanceDue directly, because it is a friend to the Customer class.

When any function tries to access an object's private member, the compiler examines the list of function prototypes in the class declaration, and one of three things happens:

- The function is found to be a member function of the same class as the object, and access is approved.

- The function is found to be a friend function of the class of the object, and access is approved.

- The function is not found to be a member or a friend of the class of the object, and access is denied; you receive an error message.

9

Figure 9-2 shows a short demonstration program that uses both the member and friend display functions within the **Customer** class. The program declares a **Customer** named **onePatron**. You can access the member function by using the object name, the dot operator, and the member function's name. You access the **friend** function by using the function's name and passing **onePatron** to the function as an argument. You can't use an object and dot in front of the **friend** function name because the **friend** function is not a **Customer** class member. You must pass the **Customer** object to the **friend** function because it does not receive a **this** pointer. Figure 9-3 shows the output.

```
int main()
{
    Customer onePatron(3815, 259.25);
    onePatron.displayCustomer();
    displayAsAFriend(onePatron);
}
```

Figure 9-2   A main() function that uses a Customer member function and friend function

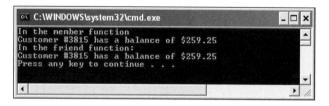

Figure 9-3   Output of program in Figure 9-2

A class can have any number of **friend** functions; you simply list the **friend** function prototypes as you do the member function prototypes. The only difference is that the **friend** function prototypes are preceded by the keyword **friend**.

Overloaded functions can be friends, but each must be explicitly designated as a **friend** function.

TIP

The occasions on which you need to use **friend** functions are limited. If a class contains public functions that return values in its fields, then you can always use those functions instead of creating a function that is a friend. The most noteworthy occasion in which **friend** functions are useful is when you overload input and output operators for a class.

UNDERSTANDING THE BENEFITS OF OVERLOADING AND POLYMORPHISM

You are already familiar with overloading:

- You overload the word "open" in your vocabulary when you distinguish between opening a door, opening a bank account, opening your eyes, and opening a computer file. You interpret the meaning of "open" based on the context.

- You overload ordinary C++ functions when you give two functions the same name, but different argument lists. For example, you might create multiple versions of an **add()** function that can accept two, three, or four integer arguments.

- You overload C++ constructors by creating two or more constructors for the same class. Constructors, by definition, must have the same name. Therefore, when a class contains multiple constructors, they are overloaded; they simply have different argument lists.

In English, having multiple meanings for the same word is useful. In C++, having more than one function with the same name is beneficial because you can use one easy-to-understand function name without paying attention to the data types involved.

You already are familiar with the concept of polymorphism, meaning "many forms." (You first read about polymorphism in Chapter 1.) Polymorphism allows the same operation to be carried out differently, depending on the object. When you overload a verb such as open, the verb is said to be polymorphic; when you overload a function, the function name is polymorphic.

TIP

Purists find a subtle difference between overloading and polymorphism. Some reserve the term polymorphism (or **pure polymorphism**) for situations in which one function body is used with a variety of arguments. For example, a single function that can be used with either a `Person` object, or a more specific `Student` object is polymorphic. (You create such functions in the next chapters as you learn about inheritance and templates.) The term "overloading" is applied to situations where you define multiple functions with a single name (for example, three functions all named `display()` that display an integer, a double, and a `Person` object). Certainly, the two terms are related; both refer to the ability to use a single name to communicate multiple meanings. For now, think of overloading as a primitive type of polymorphism. You will be able to distinguish between overloading and polymorphism more precisely after completing this book.

TIP

The use of functions that are distinguished by their number or types of arguments is sometimes called **parametric overloading**.

C++ operators are the symbols you use to perform operations on objects. You have used many operators, including arithmetic operators, logical operators, and the insertion and extraction operators. Separate actions can result from what seems to be the same operation or command. This occurs frequently in all computer programming languages, not just object-oriented languages. For example, in most programming languages and applications such as spreadsheets and databases, the + operator has a variety of meanings. A few of them include:

- Alone before a value (called unary form), + indicates a positive value, as in the expression +7.

- Between two integers (called binary form), + indicates integer addition, as in the expression 5 + 9.

- Between two floating-point numbers (also called binary form), + indicates floating-point addition, as in the expression 6.4 + 2.1.

Expressing a value as positive is different from using the + operator to perform arithmetic, so the + is polymorphic in that it can take one or two arguments and have a different meaning in each case. This reflects how people are used to thinking about the + sign. The code generated by the computer differs when you use the + in its unary form, rather than binary form. In addition, although most people don't realize it, the machine language code generated by the compiler for integer addition often differs dramatically from the code created for floating-point addition, so the + is overloaded; that is, distinct procedures are carried out, based on the arguments. Even though the two types of addition force the computer to perform two separate procedures, spreadsheet and database users (as well as programmers) do not concern themselves with the multiple machine-language code routines. They think of the binary + operation as a single operation—addition. The creators of C++, and most other programming languages and applications, have encapsulated the precise + operations so the programmers or users can concentrate on the higher-level processes of their jobs.

TIP In addition to overloading, compilers often need to perform coercion or casting when the + symbol is used with mixed arithmetic. In C++, when an integer and floating-point number are added, the integer is coerced into a floating-point number before the appropriate addition code executes.

Although it is convenient that the + symbol between two numbers means addition whether the two numbers are integers, doubles, or floats, the creators of C++ (and other programming languages) were not *required* to overload the + symbol. Overloading the + would be unnecessary if separate symbols—perhaps # and @ or I+ and F+—were used for integer addition and floating-point addition. However, if programmers had to use separate symbols for integer and floating-point addition, their written expressions would look confusing and unnatural, and it would take longer to learn a programming language. Separate symbols also would be needed for integer and floating-point subtraction, multiplication, and division, not to mention many other operations, such as using the comparisons greater-than and less-than.

Just as other people can understand "open" correctly when you provide the context of "door" or "eyes," the + sign is understood in context by the compiler. Of course, overhead (time and memory) is involved when the compiler must determine which type of action to initiate when it encounters a +. Nevertheless, using the computer's time and memory to perform this task is preferable to using the programmer's time and memory to keep track of unnatural symbols.

Just as it is convenient to use a + between both integers and doubles to add them, it also can be convenient to use a + between objects, such as `Students`, `BankAccounts`, or `Fractions`, to add them. To be able to use arithmetic symbols with your own objects, you must overload the symbols.

USING A FRIEND FUNCTION TO ACCESS DATA FROM TWO CLASSES

Figure 9-4 shows the definition section of a `Transaction` class. You might create a `Transaction` object for each customer transaction, such as a purchase of an item, payment on an account, or return of an item. The `Transaction` has an identification number and contains a field that identifies the customer who made the payment, purchase, or return. A field also holds the amount of the transaction. Periodically, you might want to update a customer's record (a `Customer` class object) with transaction information. For example, a customer might start the month with a $200 balance and make a payment of $150. After updating, the customer's record should show a $50 balance.

```
class Transaction
{
   private:
      int transactionNum;
      int custNum;
      double amount;
   public:
      Transaction(int = 0, int = 0, double = 0.0);
};
```

Figure 9-4   Definition section of the Transaction class

In a program that updates customer accounts, you typically match transactions to the appropriate customer, and then update the customer's balance owed using the transaction amount. In other words, a `payment` from the `Transaction` class is applied to the `balanceDue` from the `Customer` class.

You might design a `Transaction` class so that purchases and returns are stored as positive numbers, and payments are stored as negative numbers. Alternatively, each `Transaction` can be stored with a code that indicates the type of transaction it is. This example uses the first approach; payments are stored as negative values.

If you create a function that performs the payment application operation, you might consider five approaches (although four of these are either unusable or inferior choices):

- If you make both the `balanceDue` field in the `Customer` class and the `amount` field in the `Transaction` class public, then any function can use and modify them. However, this violates a basic principle of object-oriented programming.

- If you create a payment application function that is not a member of either the `Customer` or the `Transaction` class, the function will not have access to the private data fields of either class.

- If you make the payment application function a member of the `Customer` class, the function has access to `balanceDue`, but not to `amount`, which is private within the `Transaction` class.

- If you make the payment application function a member of the `Transaction` class, the function has access to `amount`, but not to `balanceDue`, which is private within the `Customer` class.

- If you make the payment application function a `friend` of both classes, it can use data from each class.

 TIP   A sixth approach is to create functions for both the `Customer` and `Transaction` classes that allow you to alter their private data fields. So that you can learn about `friend` functions, this example assumes you cannot or do not want to do that.

Figure 9-5 shows a function named `applyTransaction()` that you can use as a `friend` function. It takes two arguments, a `Customer` and a `Transaction`. The `friend` function also displays data from the `Customer` object, applies the payment `amount` of the `Transaction` object to the `balanceDue` of the `Customer` object, and displays `Transaction` data. If `applyTransaction()` was a `Customer` member function, it would not have access to `Transaction` data, and vice versa. As a `friend` to both classes, the `applyTransaction()` function has access to all the data it needs.

```
void applyTransaction(Customer cust, Transaction trans)
{
   cout<<"Customer #"<<cust.custNum<<
       " original balance of $"<<cust.balanceDue<<endl;
   cust.balanceDue += trans.amount;
   cout<<"After transaction #"<<trans.transactionNum<<
       " for "<<trans.amount<<
       " the new balance is $"<<cust.balanceDue<<endl;
}
```

Figure 9-5   The `applyTransaction()` function

Using a Forward Reference

To use the `applyTransaction()` function as a `friend` to both the `Customer` and the `Transaction` class, you must declare the function as a `friend` within each class. Then you can place the `Customer` and `Transaction` classes and the `applyTransaction()` function in the same file with a `main()` function that uses them, or you can place each in its own file and use `#include` statements in the file with the `main()` function. Whichever approach you choose, however, when you try to compile a `main()` function that uses both classes, error messages indicate that some data members are inaccessible.

The declaration of the `applyTransaction()` function is:

```
friend void applyTransaction(Customer, Transaction);
```

The declaration refers to both the `Customer` and the `Transaction` class as arguments. If you place the `Customer` class definition first in the file, and then declare the applyTransaction() `friend` function within the `Customer` class definition, the class `Transaction` has not yet been defined. If you place the `Transaction` definition first, and then declare the `applyTransaction()` `friend` function within the `Transaction` definition, the class `Customer` has not yet been defined. Either way, one of the class definitions makes reference to an undefined class.

You already know that you must declare a variable before using it. You also must declare, or prototype, a function before you use it. Similarly, a class must be declared before you use it. The most common solution to this dilemma is to make a forward reference to one of the classes. A **forward reference** is a statement that lets the compiler know that the class exists, and that the details will come later. You make a forward reference by using the keyword `class`, naming the referenced `class`, and ending the statement with a semicolon. The first shaded statement in Figure 9-6 is a forward reference that allows the `applyTransaction()` function to be a friend to both `Customer` and `Transaction`. The forward declaration of `Transaction` allows the `Customer` class to refer to the `Transaction` class without causing a compiler error. Alternatively, you could use a forward reference to declare the `Customer` class, and then define the `Transaction` class and the `Customer` class. The last two shaded statements in Figure 9-6 show the `friend` function declarations in the classes. The output from the program in Figure 9-6 is shown in Figure 9-7. The `main()` function creates a customer with a $200 balance, and applies a $150 payment.

```
#include<iostream>
using namespace std;
class Transaction;
class Customer
{
   friend void applyTransaction(Customer, Transaction);
   private:
      int custNum;
      double balanceDue;
```

Figure 9-6   Using a forward reference and a `friend` function with two classes

```
  public:
    Customer(int = 0, double = 0.0);
};
Customer::Customer(int num, double balance)
{
    custNum = num;
    balanceDue = balance;
}
class Transaction
{
    friend void applyTransaction(Customer, Transaction);
    private:
      int transactionNum;
      int custNum;
      double amount;
    public:
    Transaction(int = 0, int = 0, double = 0.0);
};
Transaction::Transaction(int trans, int cust, double amt)
{
    transactionNum = trans;
    custNum = cust;
    amount = amt;
}
void applyTransaction(Customer cust, Transaction trans)
{
    cout<<"Customer #"<<cust.custNum<<
        " original balance of $"<<cust.balanceDue<<endl;
    cust.balanceDue += trans.amount;
    cout<<"After transaction #"<<trans.transactionNum<<
        " for "<<trans.amount<<
        " the new balance is $"<<cust.balanceDue<<endl;
}
int main()
{
    Transaction oneTrans(111, 888, -150.00);
    Customer oneCust(888, 200.00);
    applyTransaction(oneCust, oneTrans);
}
```

Figure 9-6 Using a forward reference and a `friend` function with two classes (continued)

Figure 9-7 Output of program in Figure 9-6

When two classes refer to each other, you can choose to forward declare either one, and then define the other class first. The same principle holds true if three, four, or more classes share a `friend` function that makes a reference to all the classes. In this case you:

- Forward declare all the classes except one.

- Define the class you did not forward declare, and include the `friend` function prototype in the class definition.

- Define all classes that you did forward declare. The forward-declared classes will contain the same friend function prototype as the first class you defined.

- Define the `friend` function itself.

OVERLOADING OPERATORS—THE RULES

Operator overloading is the process by which you apply operators to your own abstract data types. The +, -, *, and / symbols make it easy to work with built-in data types such as `int` and `double`. Because programmers already understand how these symbols operate with simple data types, it is convenient to use the same symbols with your classes. For example, if you create a `Student` class and instantiate two objects, `firstStudent` and `secondStudent`, then adding the `Student`s with the expression `firstStudent + secondStudent` is natural.

When you add two integer values, as in 6 + 3, it is clear what should be added. Classes, however, contain a variety of data members. As a result, if you want the compiler to perform arithmetic with two class objects, you must tell the compiler what you mean. When you add two `Student`s using the + operator, you might intend to add their tuition bills, their credit hours, or their library fines. You might intend that when you add two `Student`s, you add each of the preceding fields. Whatever your intention is regarding the `Student`s, you can invoke the appropriate operations only when you properly overload the + operator within the `Student` class.

Although you can overload the + operator to have any meaning, good programming style dictates that you endow the operator with a reasonable meaning. For example, an `Employee` class might contain a name, department number, and salary. You would never need to add two employees' names or department numbers, but you might want to add their salaries. Similarly, if you have 100 instances of `Employee`, you might want to obtain a total salary figure.

TIP In addition to overloading an operator to add two `Student`s or two `Employee`s, you also can overload an operator to work with diverse types. You might have a `Salesperson` class that contains a data member for annual sales, and a `Client` class that contains a data member for annual revenue. You might want to perform division with these two dissimilar classes to determine a particular `Client`'s percentage contribution to a particular `Salesperson`'s annual sales total. Overloading the / operator would be a good choice for such an operation.

9

You overload an operator by making it a function; subsequently, you can use it just like any other function. However, in the same way that the modulus operator (%) is not defined for use with floating-point values, you don't overload every available operator for each defined class. Rather, you choose the operators that you need and which make sense for your class.

C++ operators are classified as unary or binary, depending on whether they take one or two arguments, respectively. Table 9-1 lists the unary C++ operators that can be overloaded; Table 9-2 lists the binary operators that can be overloaded. If an operator is normally defined to be unary only, then you cannot overload it to be binary, and vice versa. If an operator such as + is either binary or unary, you can overload it in either one or both contexts.

TIP   If a unary operator can be placed only in front of objects with built-in C++ types, then the same holds true for your classes when you overload the operator. In other words, the expression !Employee is allowed; the expression Employee! is not.

Table 9-1   Unary operators that can be overloaded

Operator	Usual Use	Associativity
->	member	left to right
->*	indirect pointer to member	left to right
!	not	right to left
&	address of	right to left
*	indirection (dereference)	right to left
+	positive value	right to left
-	negative value	right to left
++	increment	right to left
--	decrement	right to left
~	complement	right to left

Table 9-2   Binary operators that can be overloaded

Operator	Usual, Built-in Use	Associativity
*	multiplication	left to right
/	division	left to right
%	remainder (modulus)	left to right
+	addition	left to right
-	subtraction	left to right
<<	shift bits to left	left to right
>>	shift bits to right	left to right

Table 9-2   Binary operators that can be overloaded (continued)

Operator	Usual, Built-in Use	Associativity
>	greater than	left to right
<	less than	left to right
>=	greater than or equal to	left to right
<=	less than or equal to	left to right
==	equal to	left to right
!=	not equal to	left to right
&&	logical AND	left to right
||	logical OR	left to right
&	bitwise AND	left to right
|	bitwise inclusive OR	left to right
^	bitwise exclusive OR	left to right
=	assignment	right to left
+=	add and assign	right to left
-=	subtract and assign	right to left
*=	multiply and assign	right to left
/=	divide and assign	right to left
%=	modulus and assign	right to left
&=	bitwise AND and assign	right to left
|=	bitwise OR and assign	right to left
^=	bitwise OR and assign	right to left
<<=	shift left and assign	right to left
>>=	shift right and assign	right to left
()	function call	left to right
[ ]	array element subscript	left to right
->	member pointer	left to right
new	allocate memory	right to left
delete	deallocate memory	right to left
,	comma	left to right

Tables 9-1 and 9-2 list the usual, built-in use for each operator that can be overloaded. When you overload any of these operators to use with your classes, C++ does not require that you use the operator for its usual purpose. For example, you can legally overload the + symbol to mean subtraction, although it obviously would be poor programming practice.

In addition, Tables 9-1 and 9-2 list the normal associativity for each operator. **Associativity** refers to the order in which actions within an expression are carried out. You cannot change associativity when you overload operators. For example, the assignment operation takes place from right to left, as in the statement int x = 8;. You cannot change assignment for your classes so that it takes place from left to right. For example, even if you overload the = operator to work with an **Employee** class, you can never use a statement such as 2376 = myEmployee;.

You also cannot change the normal precedence of any operator. Table 9-3 lists operators in order of precedence. Those at the top of the list have the highest precedence; that means they execute first. (Operators in the same cell of the table have equal precedence.) For example, you cannot cause addition to occur before multiplication in an expression that uses simple variables such as **x + y * z;**. If you overload the addition and multiplication operators for a class and create three objects, the same rules apply—multiplication occurs before addition.

Table 9-3   Precedence of operators

Operator	Description
::	scope resolution
. (dot operator)	member
->	member pointer
[ ]	array element subscript
( )	function call
++	postfix increment
--	postfix decrement
++	prefix increment
--	prefix decrement
!	not
+	positive value
-	negative value
*	dereference
&	address
new	allocate memory
delete	deallocate memory
*	multiply
/	divide
%	modulus
+	addition
-	subtraction
<<	insertion
>>	extraction
<	less than
>	greater than
<=	less than or equal
>=	greater than or equal

Table 9-3   Precedence of operators (continued)

Operator	Description
==	equal to
!=	not equal to
&&	logical AND
||	logical OR
=	assignment
+=	add and assign
-=	subtract and assign
*=	multiply and assign
/=	divide and assign
%=	modulus and assign

Five operators cannot be overloaded; they are listed in Table 9-4. In addition to the prohibited operators, you cannot overload operators that you invent. For example, because C++ does not include a $ operator, you may not define this symbol as an overloaded operator.

Table 9-4   Operators that cannot be overloaded

Operator	Usual Use
. (dot operator)	member
*	pointer to member
::	scope resolution
?:	conditional
sizeof	size of

> **TIP**   Operators cannot be overloaded for the C++ built-in types; these types can be overloaded only for classes. For example, you cannot change the meaning of the binary + operator to mean anything other than addition when you use it with two integers.

OVERLOADING AN ARITHMETIC OPERATOR

When you code an expression such as 4 + 7, C++ understands that you intend to carry out binary integer addition because of the context of the + symbol; that is, you surrounded the operator with integers, defining the operation. When you code an expression such as `regularSal + bonus`, if C++ can recognize `regularSal` and `bonus` as declared `double` variables, then floating-point addition takes place. Similarly, when you code `aClerk + aSecretary`, if C++ can recognize `aClerk` and `aSecretary` as two instances of a class, then C++ tries to find an overloaded operator function you have written for the + symbol for that class. The name of the function that overloads the + symbol is **operator+() function**.

Assume that you have an `Employee` class with two data members—`idNum` and `salary`—and a constructor as well as a member function that adds two `Employees`' salaries. The class definition is shown in Figure 9-8. The syntax of the `addTwo()` function contains nothing new; this member function takes an `Employee` object argument and returns a `double`. Within the function, the `salary` for the `this` `Employee` and the `salary` for the argument `Employee` are summed, and the result is returned to the calling function. If you write a `main()` function that declares a `double` named `sum` and two objects of `Employee` type—`clerk` and `driver`, for example—you could use either of the shaded statements in Figure 9-8 to sum the salaries of the two `Employee` objects. In other words, you can use the `clerk`'s `addTwo()` function and pass the `driver` to it, or use the `driver`'s `addTwo()` function and pass the `clerk` to it. Either way, the result is the sum of the two salaries. Figure 9-9 shows the output.

```cpp
#include<iostream>
using namespace std;
class Employee
{
    private:
        int idNum;
        double salary;
    public:
        Employee(int, double);
        double addTwo(Employee);
};
Employee::Employee(int id, double sal)
{
    idNum = id;
    salary = sal;
}
double Employee::addTwo(Employee emp)
{
    double total;
    total = salary + emp.salary;
    return total;
}
int main()
{
    Employee clerk(1234, 400.00);
    Employee driver(3456, 650.00);
    double sum;
    sum = clerk.addTwo(driver);
    cout<<"Adding driver to clerk - Sum is $"<<sum<<endl;
    sum = driver.addTwo(clerk);
    cout<<"Adding clerk to driver - Sum is $"<<sum<<endl;
}
```

Figure 9-8   Employee class with an `addTwo()` function

Figure 9-9   Output of program in Figure 9-8

TIP   It's also a logical choice for you to create the summing function in the `Employee` class to return an `Employee` summary object instead of a `double` value. In other words, when you add an `Employee` to an `Employee`, perhaps you get a different `Employee`. You will learn how to accomplish this later in this chapter. You can design your class functions in any way that makes sense to you; a `double` is used here for simplicity.

Figure 9-10 shows a revised `Employee` class containing an `operator+()` function. When you examine the code in the function body for the `addTwo()` function in Figure 9-8 and the `operator+()` function in Figure 9-10, you see that the only difference between the prototype and function header (which are the first two shaded lines in Figure 9-10) is the function name; the return types, argument lists, and bodies of the `addTwo()` and `operator+()` functions are identical. As with the `addTwo()` function, you can use any `Employee` object to control the `operator+()` function, and any `Employee` object as a function argument. The third shaded statement in Figure 9-10 is `clerk.operator+(driver);`, but you could achieve the same result using `driver.operator+(clerk);`.

If the `operator+()` function works exactly like the `addTwo()` function, why not just use the `addTwo()` function? The answer is that, instead of the awkward `sum = clerk.operator+(driver);`, the `operator+()` function allows you to omit the word `operator` in the function name and just use the + sign, as shown in the last shaded statement in the `main()` function in Figure 9-10. Figure 9-11 shows the output.

```
#include<iostream>
using namespace std;
class Employee
{
   private:
      int idNum;
      double salary;
   public:
      Employee(int, double);
      double operator+(Employee);
};
```

Figure 9-10   Employee class with an `operator+()` function

```
Employee::Employee(int id, double sal)
{
    idNum = id;
    salary = sal;
}
double Employee::operator+(Employee emp)
{
    double total;
    total = salary + emp.salary;
    return total;
}
int main()
{
    Employee clerk(1234, 400.00);
    Employee driver(3456, 650.00);
    double sum;
    sum = clerk.operator+(driver);
    cout<<"Using operator+() function - Sum is $"<<sum<<endl;
    sum = clerk + driver;
    cout<<"Using + operator - Sum is $"<<sum<<endl;
}
```

Figure 9-10   Employee class with an `operator+()` function (continued)

Figure 9-11   Output of program in Figure 9-10

The syntax involved in using the + operator alone is intuitively understood by anyone who has added simple numeric variables: you use an operand, an operator, and another operand. The results are the same when you use a function with a name like **addTwo()**, or use the full name of the **operator+()** function, but the syntax used with the stand-alone + is simpler, more natural, and easier to remember.

Paying Attention to the Order of the Operands

You can choose to overload any of the arithmetic operators for any classes you develop. Then you can use the corresponding operator symbol in a natural way with class objects. For example, Figure 9-12 shows how you might overload the − operator to subtract two **Employee** objects from each other, thus subtracting their salaries.

```
double Employee::operator-(Employee emp)
{
    double difference;
    difference = salary - emp.salary;
    return difference;
}
```

Figure 9-12   The `operator-()` function for the `Employee` class

When you use the `operator-()` function in Figure 9-12, you must use the two `Employee` objects you want to subtract in the correct order. Just as integer subtraction produces different results when you reverse the operands (8 – 2 is different from 2 – 8), so does overloaded operator subtraction. When you use a subtraction statement such as `diff = clerk - driver;` in a C++ program, the `clerk` object is the object that calls the `operator-()` function. Within the function in Figure 9-12, the reference to `salary` is a reference to `this.salary`, or the `clerk`'s salary. The second operand in the expression `clerk - driver` is the `driver`; it is the `driver` who becomes the passed argument `emp` in the function header, and who requires the object name and dot operator within the function body. Because of the way the `Employee::operator-()` is written, subtraction takes place in the usual and expected order.

OVERLOADING AN OPERATOR TO WORK WITH A CLASS OBJECT AND A PRIMITIVE TYPE

When you add two objects using the + operator (or use any binary operator), the objects do not have to be the same type on both sides of the operator. For example, you can add an integer and a double with an expression such as `5 + 7.84`. If you want to add a class object and a primitive object, you can, but you must overload the + operator appropriately. Figure 9-13 shows an overloaded `operator+()` `Employee` class function that adds a `double` to an `Employee`; more specifically, it adds a `double` to an `Employee`'s salary. The function takes a `double` argument, and declares a temporary `Employee` object. The `this` pointer within the function contains the object that called the function (the one to the left of the + operator); that object contains an `idNum` and a `salary`. You use the existing `idNum` for the temporary object, but use a `salary` that is increased by the value of `raise`.

```
Employee Employee::operator+(double raise)
{
    Employee temp;
    temp.idNum = idNum;
    temp.salary = salary + raise;
    return temp;
}
```

Figure 9-13   The `operator+()` function that adds an `Employee` and a `double`

When you add the `operator+( )` function from Figure 9-8 to the `Employee` class and declare an `Employee` object named `aClerk`, then you can write a statement such as `aClerk = aClerk + 50.00;`. This statement increases the `aClerk`'s salary by $50. Alternatively, the statement `anotherClerk = aClerk + 50.00;` retains the `aClerk` salary at its original value. Within the `operator+( )` function, the temporary `Employee` object is assigned the `aClerk`'s `idNum` and `salary` plus $50.00. The temporary object is returned to the calling function, where it is assigned to `anotherClerk`. In other words, the addition statement sets `anotherClerk`'s `idNum` to `aClerk`'s `idNum`, and `anotherClerk`'s `salary` to $50.00 more than `aClerk`'s `salary`. The `aClerk` object on the left side of the + in each expression is the `this` object within the `operator+( )` function. You can think of the `aClerk` object to the left of the + as "driving" the function. When the function returns the `temp Employee` object, then an `Employee` with an increased salary is returned to the calling function.

When you write an operator function, you define the operator to mean whatever it should in your applications. For example, you might write an `Employee` class `operator+( )` function to increase the `idNum` instead of the `salary`, or you might write it to increase the values in both fields.

You cannot overload operators that use only C++'s built-in data types. For example, you cannot overload the + that works with two doubles to make it do anything but add two doubles. However, you can overload operators whose first operand is an object that is a built-in type and whose second operand is a class object. For example, you can write a function that allows you to code `aClerk = 50.00 + aClerk;`, where the `double` is the driving operand in front of the + operator, but because you cannot modify the built-in data type's operations, you must make the operator function a `friend` function.

For example, Figure 9-14 shows an `Employee` class that includes a `friend operator+( )` function; the shaded prototype shows that it accepts a `double` and an `Employee` as arguments and returns a `double`. The shaded function implementation shows how the `double` argument and the `salary` field of the `Employee` argument are added to produce a sum, which is the return value. In the `main( )` function at the bottom of the figure, a `double` is added to an `Employee`. Figure 9-15 shows the output: the result is the sum of the `double` and the `Employee`'s salary.

The Employee class in Figure 9-14 could contain both overloaded operators—the class member and the friend. Additionally, the class could contain any number of operator+() functions as long as their argument lists differed.

At least one argument of an overloaded operator function must be an object or a reference to a user-defined data type.

```
#include<iostream>
#include<string>
using namespace std;
class Employee
{
    friend double operator+(double, Employee);
    private:
        int idNum;
        double salary;
    public:
        Employee(int, double);
};
Employee::Employee(int id, double sal)
{
    idNum = id;
    salary = sal;
}
double operator+(double raise, Employee emp)
{
    double newSalary = raise + emp.salary;
    return newSalary;
}

int main()
{
    Employee oneEmp(1234, 14.55);
    double newSalary = 2.33 + oneEmp;
    cout<<"New salary will be $"<<newSalary<<endl;
}
```

Figure 9-14   Employee class containing a `friend operator+()` function

Figure 9-15   Output of program in Figure 9-14

USING MULTIPLE OPERATIONS IN A STATEMENT

Most modern programming languages allow you to **chain operations**, that is, they allow several operators to be used within the same statement. For example, to add three values in C++, you write a statement like `total = a + b + c;`. Because one purpose of operator overloading is to create class operators that work "naturally" like built-in operators, you should consider creating operators for your own classes to have the same capability. This means that, for many operations, you will want the return type to be a class object.

TIP If you want to sum three values in an older programming language such as assembler or RPG, you first must add two values, producing a temporary total. Then, in a separate statement, you add the third value to that total. Older languages more closely reflected how the computer operated. Even though modern languages allow multiple operations in a statement, the computer actually performs just one operation at a time.

When you write a statement using integers or doubles, such as `total = a + b + c;`, first `a` and `b` are added, creating a temporary value. Then, `c` is added to the temporary value, and the final result is stored in `total`. The same rules of operation apply when you want to create class objects that can use multiple operations in a statement.

Figure 9-16 shows a `Sale` class that includes an overloaded `operator+()` function. Suppose that when a store makes a sale, a `Sale` object is created, storing the receipt number and the amount of the sale. The overloaded `operator+()` function is written to allow the addition of multiple `Sale` objects in sequence, for example: `aShirt + aTie + pants` (as in the shaded statement in the `main()` function). The function assigns 999 as a dummy `Sale` number to any summed object, to distinguish it from a regular `Sale`. Figure 9-17 shows the output of the `main()` function in Figure 9-16.

```
class Sale
{
    private:
      int receiptNum;
      double saleAmount;
    public:
      Sale(int, double);   //constructor
      Sale operator+(Sale);
      void showSale();
};
Sale::Sale(int num, double sale)
{
    receiptNum = num;
    saleAmount = sale;
}
Sale Sale::operator+(Sale transaction)
{
    Sale temp(999,0);
    temp.saleAmount = saleAmount + transaction.saleAmount;
    return temp;
}
void Sale::showSale()
{
    cout<<"Sale #"<<receiptNum<<" for $"<<saleAmount<<endl;
}
```

Figure 9-16   The `Sale` class and a `main()` function that uses it

```
int main()
{
    Sale aShirt(1567, 39.95);
    Sale aTie(1568, 33.55);
    Sale pants(1569, 49.99);
    Sale total(0,0);
    total = aShirt + aTie + pants;
    aShirt.showSale();
    aTie.showSale();
    pants.showSale();
    cout<<endl<<"Total:"<<endl;
    total.showSale();
}
```

Figure 9-16   The Sale class and a main() function that uses it (continued)

Figure 9-17   Output of program in Figure 9-16

If you write the overloaded operator+() function in the Sale class in Figure 9-16 to return a double instead of a Sale, then you cannot use a statement that adds multiple Sale objects in sequence. If the operator+() function returns a double, then when you try to add three objects, you receive an error message similar to "Illegal structure operation." Because the associativity of addition occurs from left to right, the attempt to execute the addition shaded in Figure 9-16 would follow this sequence:

1. The leftmost + operator is encountered, and C++ recognizes a Sale on each side of the + symbol. The overloaded operator+() function is called, and saleAmounts for aShirt and aTie are added. A double is returned.

2. The next + operator is encountered. A Sale object is found as the operand to the right of the +, but a double value is used as the operand to the left. You have not created a function that can handle this situation (your function adds Sale + Sale), and there is no built-in + operation that can handle this situation (although there is one for other operations such as double + double and double + int). The result is an error message.

When the Sale class operator+() function does not return a double, but instead returns an object of Sale type (as shown in Figure 9-16), the chained addition works correctly. The sequence of events now occurs as follows:

1. The leftmost + operator is encountered, and C++ recognizes a Sale object on each side of the + symbol. The overloaded operator+() function is

called, and `saleAmounts` for `aShirt` and `aTie` are added. A temporary `Sale` object with the total sale ($73.50 so far) is returned.

2. The next + operator is encountered. A `Sale` object is now found on each side of the + (the temporary object returned by the first addition, and the `pants` object). The overloaded `operator+()` function is called again. The `saleAmounts` for the temporary object and the pants are added, and a new temporary `Sale` object with the total sale (123.49) is returned.

3. The new temporary object is assigned to the `total Sale` object.

TIP

C++ forces you to use the built-in precedence rules for your class operators. Therefore, if you define both `operator*()` and `operator+()`, and then code a statement such as `aShirt + aTie * pants`, then the usual precedence rules are followed. That is, the multiplication takes place before the addition.

TIP

If you want to be able to add either a `double` or a `Sale` object to a `Sale` object, then simply write both versions of the overloaded operator for the class. As with any other function, you can overload an operator function as many times as you like.

OVERLOADING OUTPUT

You already know that C++ automatically overloads several of its operators. For example, in unary context the + operator is understood differently than when it is used in binary context; the * might mean multiplication or be used to dereference a pointer. The << operator also is overloaded by C++. It is both a bitwise left–shift operator and an output operator; it is called the insertion operator when used for output.

The << operator acts as an output operator only when `cout` (or another output stream object) appears on the left side. Therefore, `cout` becomes the driving object and the `this` object in the overloaded **operator<<() function**.

TIP

You do not need to understand the use of << as a bitwise left-shift operator to understand that it is overloaded, or understand how to use it with `cout`. If you're curious, however, bitwise left-shift simply means that each bit in a given byte takes the value of the bit to the right. Thus, 00010100 becomes 00101000. The leftmost bit is lost, and the new rightmost bit becomes a 0. Incidentally, the binary number 00010100 is decimal value 20, and 00101000 is decimal 40; left-shifting is actually just a tricky way of multiplying by 2 (as long as the leftmost bit, which represents the sign, doesn't change).

When you use `cout` in a program, you must include a file that defines the `cout` object, usually with a statement such as `#include<iostream>`. The `cout` object is a member of a class named `ostream`. The `iostream` file overloads << with functions that output each of C++'s built-in data types. For example, the following overloaded `operator<<()` function prototypes are the ones used to output an `int`, a `double`, and a `float`:

```
ostream& operator<<(ostream &, int);
ostream& operator<<(ostream &, double);
ostream& operator<<(ostream &, float);
```

The preceding functions, called `operator<<()`, each return a reference to `ostream`. They accept two arguments: a reference to `ostream` and the appropriate data type. In other words, these functions receive both an address where output will go and a value to output; the functions return the address where the next output will go. Recall how the overloaded + operator in the `Sale` class in Figure 9-16 returns a `Sale` object, so that more than one addition operation can be carried out within the same statement. Similarly, `cout`'s `operator<<()` function returns the next address for output, ensuring that a chained output statement with multiple arguments like `cout<<22<<33;` will work. The statement `cout<<22` returns a reference to an object (an `ostream` reference) that `33` can use (just as it would use the `cout` object directly.).

Programmers sometimes refer to the use of multiple calls to the same operator function (for example, `cout<<22<<33;`) as **stacking**.

The reason that the `cout` overloaded << operator needs to receive a reference to `ostream` is because `operator<<()` is a `friend` function, which—you will recall from the beginning of this chapter—has no `this` pointer (unlike a member function).

C++ overloads the << operator to work with the built-in data types so that you can easily display their values; you also may overload the << operator to work with your own classes. Instead of a `showSale()` function for a `Sale` object named `total` that requires the statement `total.showSale();` (as in Figure 9-16), you might prefer a more natural form:

```
cout<<total;
```

To overload the << operator so it can work with a `Sale` object, you must add the overloaded `operator<<()` function to the Sale class. The prototype is:

```
friend ostream& operator<<(ostream &, const Sale &);
```

The `operator<<()` function is a `friend` to the `Sale` class. It receives a reference to an `ostream` object and a reference to a `Sale`. The `Sale` reference can be defined as `const` because the output should not alter the `Sale`'s data. The contents of the function body can display a `Sale` with any desired text and in any format you want. For example, Figure 9-18 shows a usable `operator<<()` function for the `Sale` class.

```
ostream& operator<<(ostream &out, const Sale &aSale)
{
     out<<"Sale #"<<aSale.receiptNum
         <<" for $"<<aSale.saleAmount<<endl;
     return out;
}
```

Figure 9-18   Overloaded `operator<<()` function for the `Sale` class

In Figure 9-18, the function name is not `Sale::operator<<()`. The class name `Sale` and the scope resolution operator do not appear in the function header. The `operator<<()` function is not a member of the `Sale` class. Instead, it is a nonmember `friend` function so that the operator can access the private members of the `ostream` class and the `Sale` class, and then operate like the built-in versions of `<<`. Because `operator<<()` is not a member of the `Sale` class, you cannot output the values `receiptNum` and `saleAmount` without using a `Sale` object and a dot operator. Because it is not a `Sale` class member, the `operator<<()` function does not receive a `this` pointer. Therefore, it cannot directly refer to any controlling object's data by just using a field name. The data that displays is the data that belongs to the argument named `aSale`, which is the argument that appears to the right of `<<` in a `cout` statement.

TIP   The "out" in the `operator<<()` definition in Figure 9-18 is not a keyword. It is a programmer-chosen local name for the reference to `ostream`, just as `aSale` is a local name for the `Sale` object. You can use any legal C++ variable name you choose.

After you include the overloaded `operator<<()` function in the `Sale` class, any function that includes a `Sale` object declaration such as `Sale aShirt;` can subsequently use a statement such as `cout<<aShirt;` to display the `aShirt` object's data. The statement that uses `cout` is only a few characters shorter than `aShirt.showSale();`, but the statement makes `Sale` appear to be a built-in data type. Using the overloaded `<<` operator allows the use of simpler program statements.

Figure 9-19 shows a `Sale` class and a `main()` function that declares a `Sale` object. (To save space here, the overloaded + operator function has been removed from the class.) The first shaded statement is the prototype for the `friend` function. As a nonmember function, it could have been declared anywhere within the class. The second shaded line is the `operator<<()` function header. The body of the function displays the `Sale` object details in whatever form the programmer decides is useful. The third shaded line in Figure 9-19 shows how the overloaded insertion operator is used with a `Sale` object. Figure 9-20 shows the output.

```
#include<iostream>
using namespace std;
class Sale
{
   friend ostream& operator<<(ostream&, const Sale&);
   private:
      int receiptNum;
      double saleAmount;
    public:
      Sale(int, double);  //constructor
};
Sale::Sale(int num, double sale)
{
   receiptNum = num;
   saleAmount = sale;
}
ostream& operator<<(ostream &out, const Sale &aSale)
{
    out<<"Sale #"<<aSale.receiptNum
        <<" for $"<<aSale.saleAmount<<endl;
    return out;
}
int main()
{
    Sale aShirt(1567, 39.95);
    cout<<aShirt;
}
```

Figure 9-19   The `Sale` class including an overloaded insertion operator

Figure 9-20   Output of program in Figure 9-19

OVERLOADING INPUT

If the insertion operator (<<) can be overloaded for output, it makes sense that the extraction operator (>>) operator can also be overloaded for input using the **operator>>()** **function**. The advantage of overloading operators such as >> is that the resulting programs look cleaner and are easier to read.

Consider the `Sale` class that contains a `receiptNum` and a `saleAmount`. You can create an extraction operator, or **operator>>()** function, that uses the `istream` class (which is defined in the `iostream` file along with `ostream`) by using a prototype as follows:

```
friend istream& operator>>(istream&, Sale&);
```

Within the preceding function, it is appropriate to code statements that retrieve `Sale` values from an input device. For example, you might choose to create prompts and data entry statements that allow a user to enter values for any or all of a `Sale`'s data fields. The arguments to the `operator>>()` function are an `istream` object and a `Sale` object. Unlike the `operator<<()` function, the `Sale` object that receives data values cannot be passed to this function as a constant. That's because this function needs to change `Sale`'s data values through keyboard data entry. Figure 9-21 shows the implementation of the `operator>>()` function for the `Sale` class.

```
istream& operator>>(istream &in, Sale &aSale)
{
   cout<<endl;    // to clear the buffer
   cout<<"Enter receipt number ";
   in>>aSale.receiptNum;
   cout<<"Enter the amount of the sale ";
   in>>aSale.saleAmount;
   cout<<endl<<"     Thank you!"<<endl;
   return in;
}
```

Figure 9-21   Overloaded `operator>>()` function for the `Sale` class

TIP

The first statement in the `operator>>()` function in Figure 9-21 sends a newline to output. Although this step would not be required in all applications, sending the newline to output ensures that no intended output from earlier in an application is left waiting in the buffer—and thus undisplayed—before data entry from this function begins.

In the function in Figure 9-21, the local name for the `istream` object is `in`. By creating the function to return this object, you allow chaining of input items, as in `cin>>a>>b>>c;`. In addition to displaying prompts, the overloaded extraction operator function also displays "Thank you!" when the user has entered the requested data. You could improve the `operator>>()` function shown in Figure 9-21 by adding code that verifies valid receipt numbers and sale amounts to be within specific ranges. No matter how many instructions you place within the `operator>>()` function, however, when you write a program that uses a `Sale` class member such as `aShirt`, you need only the following code: `cin>>aShirt;`. That simple input statement generates all the prompts and verifications you need to fill a `Sale` object with appropriate data. Figure 9-22 shows a `Sale` class containing both extraction and insertion operators. The shaded statements are the additions required to overload and use the extraction operator. Figure 9-23 shows the output generated during a typical execution of the program.

```cpp
#include<iostream>
using namespace std;
class Sale
{
    friend ostream& operator<<(ostream&, const Sale&);
    friend istream& operator>>(istream&, Sale&);
    private:
        int receiptNum;
        double saleAmount;
     public:
        Sale(int, double);   //constructor
};
Sale::Sale(int num, double sale)
{
    receiptNum = num;
    saleAmount = sale;
}
ostream& operator<<(ostream &out, const Sale &aSale)
{
    out<<"Sale #"<<aSale.receiptNum
        <<" for $"<<aSale.saleAmount<<endl;
    return out;
}
istream& operator>>(istream &in, Sale &aSale)
{
    cout<<endl;    // to clear the buffer
    cout<<"Enter receipt number ";
    in>>aSale.receiptNum;
    cout<<"Enter the amount of the sale ";
    in>>aSale.saleAmount;
    cout<<endl<<"     Thank you!"<<endl;
    return in;
}

int main()
{
    Sale aShirt(0,0);
    cin>>aShirt;
    cout<<aShirt;
}
```

Figure 9-22   The `Sale` class including an overloaded extraction operator

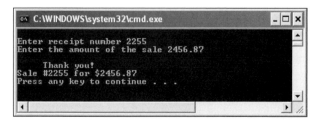

Figure 9-23   Typical execution of program in Figure 9-22

Overloading the Prefix ++ and − −

With C++, you use ++ to increment variables, and -- to decrement variables. It's important to notice the difference in how expressions are evaluated when the ++ or -- is placed before a variable, rather than after the variable.

When a prefix operator such as ++ is used in an expression, the mathematical operation takes place before the expression is evaluated. When the postfix operator is used, the expression is evaluated before the mathematical operation takes place. Figure 9-24 illustrates the difference in how the prefix and postfix ++ operators work.

```
int num, result;
num = 3;
result = ++num;
cout<<result;      // displays 4
cout<<num;         // displays 4
// reinitialize num
num = 3;
result = num++;
cout<<result;      // displays 3
cout<<num;         // displays 4
```

Figure 9-24   Using the prefix and postfix ++ operators with an integer

Figure 9-24 shows that when you use the prefix ++ operator on the num variable, first the variable increases, then it is evaluated and assigned to the result variable. In other words, num increases to 4, then result takes on the value 4.

When num is reset to 3 and then assigned to result using the postfix ++ operator, however, the num variable evaluates as a 3, then is assigned to result, and finally num increases. So, result holds the original value of num—3—even though at the end of the operation, num itself holds the value 4.

You can overload the prefix ++ or -- operators to use with your own class objects, just as you can overload other operators; the function names are **operator++()** and **operator--()**. When you use ++ or -- with class objects, the same prefix/postfix rules apply as they do with simple built-in types.

Consider an **Inventory** class definition with data members for a stock number and a quantity sold. Its three functions are a constructor, an overloaded **operator<<()** function for output, and an overloaded **operator++()** function for incrementing the quantity sold each time a sale occurs. Figure 9-25 shows the class.

```
class Inventory
{
   friend ostream& operator<<(ostream&, const Inventory&);
   private:
     int stockNum;
     int numSold;
   public:
     Inventory(int, int);
     Inventory& operator++();
};
Inventory::Inventory(int stknum, int sold)
{
   stockNum = stknum;
   numSold = sold;
}
ostream& operator<<(ostream &out, const Inventory &item)
{
   out<<"Item #"<<item.stockNum<<" Quantity: "<<
    item.numSold<<endl;
   return out;
}
Inventory& Inventory::operator++()
{
    ++numSold;
    return *this;
}
```

Figure 9-25   The `Inventory` class

9

Within the `operator++()` function in the `Inventory` class, you can define ++ however you feel is appropriate for your class. For example, when an Inventory item is incremented, perhaps your intention is to increment the stock number, the number sold, or both. Suppose you decide that incrementing an `Inventory` object will increase the number sold. Within the operator function, you can write the statement that increases `numSold` in several different ways. The statements `numSold++;`, `numSold = numSold + 1;`, and `numSold += 1;` all would work. However, since you are using the prefix ++ operator with the class, it makes sense to be consistent and use the same operator with the field, so this example uses `++numSold`.

Within the `operator++()` function in the `Inventory` class in Figure 9-25, the `numSold` variable that belongs to the `this` object is increased. Then the newly altered `this` object with its increased `numSold` field is returned to the calling function, where it is assigned to the object that was preceded with ++. This last assignment occurs automatically because that's how ++ is defined in C++. When you write a program that instantiates an `Inventory` object using the class in Figure 9-25, the object's `numSold` value increases when you place ++ in front of the object's name. Figure 9-26 illustrates a `main()` function that declares an `Inventory` object that is initialized with 475 items sold. The `main()` function increments the object twice, and displays the result after each operation. The results of the program are shown in Figure 9-27.

```
int main()
{
  Inventory anItem(101, 475);
  cout<<anItem;
  ++anItem;
  cout<<anItem;
  ++anItem;
  cout<<anItem;
}
```

Figure 9-26 Program using the `Inventory` class

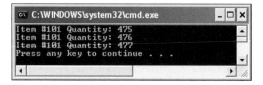

Figure 9-27 Output of program in Figure 9-26

The ++ operator is a unary operator; that is, it takes only one argument. Because the function is a member function of the `Inventory` class, it receives a `this` pointer to the object that calls it; therefore, no other information need be passed to the `operator++()` function. The reference to the `Inventory` object returned is a reference to the `this` object—that is, a reference to the newly incremented object that was automatically passed to the function.

Overloading -- is similar to overloading ++. To overload a prefix decrement operator, you simply prototype the function as `Inventory& operator--();` and place appropriate statements within the function body.

USING POSTFIX INCREMENT AND DECREMENT OPERATORS

A problem arises if you want to use a postfix ++ operator as well as a prefix ++ operator with a class. You cannot use the prototype `Inventory& operator++();` for the postfix increment operator because, as with all overloaded functions, C++ needs a method to distinguish between two functions with the same name. When you overload any C++ function, you must supply different argument lists; for the postfix ++ operator, you use an integer argument. The `Inventory` class postfix `operator++()` function prototype is:

```
Inventory& operator++(int);
```

The `int` argument to the `Inventory` class `operator++()` function is a **dummy argument**; that is, it is an argument that is not used within the function but exists only to provide a different function prototype. You do not actually pass an integer to the `operator++()` function when you want to use the postfix ++. The `int` is present only to help C++ tell the difference between the prefix and postfix operators, and subsequently distinguish the two functions. In other words, if you call the prefix ++ operator function with a statement such as `++item;`, the function *without* the dummy argument executes; if you call the postfix operator function with a statement such as `item++;`, the function *with* the dummy argument executes.

TIP

You can give the dummy integer argument a name if you want. For example, you can code the `Inventory operator++()` function header as:

`Inventory& Inventory::operator++(int x)`

If you use x within the function, you will see that it contains a 0. There is no purpose in giving the variable a name, however, and it is considered unconventional programming to do so.

TIP

A function's prototype is also called its **signature**. For example, you would say that the prefix and postfix increment operator functions have different signatures.

9

OVERLOADING THE == OPERATOR

After you have learned to overload several arithmetic operators, writing an `operator==()` function should be an easy task. You simply decide what will constitute equality in class members. When you create your own classes, you choose whether equivalency means that every data field must be equivalent, or only specific data members. The `operator==()` function usually returns either an integer value representing 0 or 1 or a Boolean variable representing true or false. Figure 9-28 shows two versions of an overloaded `operator==()` function for the `Inventory` class. Each of these functions considers two `Inventory` objects to be equal if their stock numbers are equal. The first version returns a 0 when the `stockNum` of the `this` object and the argument object are different; it returns 1 if the stock numbers are the same. The second version returns a `bool`. In Chapter 1, you learned that a variable of type `bool` can hold one of two values: `true` or `false`. Some older C++ compilers do not support the `bool` type; with those compilers you would use the first version of `operator==()` that returns an integer. Either of the functions shown in Figure 9-28 allows `Inventory` objects to be compared using ==, as in the statement:

```
if(itemA == itemB)
   cout<<"The stock numbers are the same"<<endl;
```

```
// Version that returns an int
int Inventory::operator==(const Inventory& item)
{
    int truth = 0;
    if(stockNum == item.stockNum)
      truth = 1;
    return truth;
}
// Alternate version that returns a bool
bool Inventory::operator==(const Inventory& item)
{
    bool truth = false;
    if(stockNum == item.stockNum)
        truth = true;
    return truth;
}
```

Figure 9-28   Usable overloaded `operator==()` functions for the `Inventory` class

OVERLOADING THE = OPERATOR

Like +, -, ++, --, and all the other operators, the assignment operator (=) can be overloaded for use with your own classes. Unlike the other operators, if you don't define the = operator, C++ provides a definition for you. In an example earlier in this chapter (see Figure 9-16), you saw that when you properly overload the + operator for the `Sale` class, you can create four `Sale` objects and use the statement `total = aShirt + aTie + pants;`. The assignment operator (the equal sign) correctly assigned an object to the `total Sale` object; the assigned object was the temporary object that was the sum of all the objects in the chained addition operation. Similarly, if you write `aShirt = aTie;` you assign all the values of all the fields of `aTie` to the `aShirt` object without having to write a function to overload the = operator. Ordinarily, if you intend to use the = operator to assign the value of every field of the class object on the right of the = operator to each corresponding field of the class object on the = operator's left, then you do not need to write an overloaded = operator.

If you want the = operator to do something other than assign each member, then you must create a custom **operator=() function**. In addition, if the class contains data fields that are pointers, you should create a custom function.

If a class contains a pointer and you create two objects from the class and assign one object to the other, then the two objects will contain pointers to the same memory. This overlap might not pose a problem unless one of the objects is deleted or goes out of scope. When the destructor function is called for the first object, the memory to which that object points is released. Now the second object contains a pointer to **deallocated memory**, memory that is no longer assigned to anything in the application.

Consider a class that holds classroom data as shown in Figure 9-29. This `Classroom` class has data fields that hold the number of students in a class and the grade level. The class also contains a string pointer for student names. The `student` field is declared as a pointer because any number of students might be held in a `Classroom`. Instead of using a pointer, the `Classroom` class could be designed to hold an array of strings to accommodate the student names. However, the class creator would have to arbitrarily decide on a number of array elements. For example, if 20 were chosen, then a `Classroom` with 21 or more students could not be accommodated, but a `Classroom` with 19 or fewer students would contain some wasted memory. Instead, the `Classroom` class is designed to prompt the user for the number of students in a class and, in the first shaded statement, allocates just enough memory to hold the needed students' first names. When you declare any data field, you **allocate memory** for that field—that is, you allot storage for it and assign a name to the location. Most memory allocation is accomplished when you compile a program. When you allocate memory later, during the execution of a program (as opposed to when the program is compiled) you **dynamically allocate memory**. When you dynamically allocate memory, you use a pointer variable so you can assign the starting address of the new block of memory to it.

In C++ you use the **new operator** to dynamically allocate memory. In the constructor for the `Classroom` class in Figure 9-29, the user is prompted for a grade level and number of students in a `Classroom`. Then the `numStudents` value is used to allocate as many strings as there are students. The **new** operator reserves the requested amount of memory and stores the starting address in the pointer variable named `student`.

TIP   In the `Classroom` class in Figure 9-29, in addition to allocating enough memory for student first names, you might also want to allocate memory for just enough student ID numbers, last names, addresses, phone numbers, and so on. This example uses only first names to keep the example short.

TIP   When you allocate memory using the new operator, it's still possible that not enough new memory is available; perhaps other elements in your application have already used up the computer's resources. You will learn how to handle this problem when you study C++ exception handling.

When you declare variables and objects causing memory to be automatically allocated for them, then that memory is also automatically released when your variables and objects go out of scope. Whenever you dynamically allocate memory with the new operator, the memory is not automatically released. Therefore, it is a good practice to delete the reserved memory when the object using it goes out of scope. Because a class's destructor is called when an object goes out of scope, it is good practice to use the destructor to free memory. If you fail to do so, you are tying up computer resources that could be used by another application. Because the `student` pointer refers to a segment of memory allocated with the **new** operator, the `Classroom` destructor function shown in Figure 9-29 uses the **delete operator** to free the previously allocated memory.

```
class Classroom
{
  private:
    string *student;
    int numStudents;
    int gradeLevel;
  public:
    Classroom();
    ~Classroom();
    void display();
};
Classroom::Classroom()
{
  int x;
  cout<<"What grade level is this class? ";
  cin>>gradeLevel;
  cout<<"How any students in this class? ";
  cin>>numStudents;
  student = new string[numStudents];
  for(x = 0; x < numStudents; ++x)
  {
      cout<<"Please enter the student's name ";
          cin>>student[x];
  }
}
Classroom::~Classroom()
{
  delete [] student;
}
void Classroom::display()
{
  int x;
  cout<<"Grade "<<gradeLevel<<" class list:"<<endl;
  for(x = 0; x < numStudents; ++x)
      cout<<student[x]<<endl;
}
```

Figure 9-29   The Classroom class

Recall that destructor names always begin with a tilde (~).

TIP

Figure 9-30 shows a program that declares two Classroom objects. This sample program uses unconventional blocking to illustrate the potential error situation. The program instantiates a Classroom named oneClass, then, within a new block, instantiates another Classroom named anotherclass. The two classes can be constructed as shown in the sample run in Figure 9-31, in which oneClass is created for a third-grade classroom with two students and anotherClass is created for a fourth-grade classroom with two students.

When the built-in = operator is used in the shaded statement, each field of **anotherClass** is copied to **oneClass**; both **Classroom** objects contain **student** pointer variables that point to the same list of students. The first call to the **display()** function after the assignment confirms that the copy is successful.

```
int main()
{
 Classroom oneClass;
 {
    Classroom anotherClass;
    cout<<endl<<
        "The original classroom before assignment:"<<endl;
    oneClass.display();
    cout<<endl<<"The second classroom ";
     anotherClass.display();
    oneClass = anotherClass;
    cout<<endl<<
         "The original classroom after assignment:"<<endl;
    oneClass.display();
 }
 cout<<endl<<
     "After the second class has gone out of scope:"<<endl;
 oneClass.display();
}
```

Figure 9-30 Program that uses assignment operator in the **Classroom** class

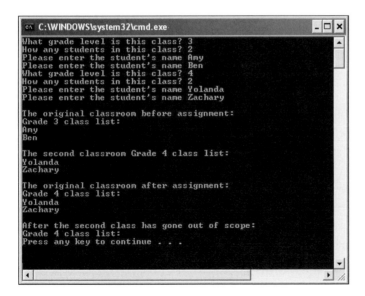

Figure 9-31 Typical execution of program in Figure 9-30 using **Classroom** class without an **operator=()**

At the first closing curly brace in the program in Figure 9-30, the **anotherClass** object goes out of scope and the memory reserved for the **oneClass** object's student list is released by the **Classroom** destructor function. That means the student pointer in the **oneClass** object is pointing to deallocated memory. When you use the **display()** function with the **oneClass** object for the second time (in the second shaded statement in Figure 9-30, at the end of the **main()** function), the student list is not printable. Most compilers issue an error message, and the result, as shown in Figure 9-31, is an empty, invalid list of students.

You can avoid the preceding problem by overloading the = operator so the two **Classroom** objects' student list pointers don't point to the same memory when an assignment is made. As shown in the shaded function in Figure 9-32, when a **Classroom** is copied to another using the = operator, you deallocate the memory that holds the first object's student list, allocate new memory for the list, and then copy the second object's list to the first. Additionally, you copy the integer variables that hold the grade level and number of students. When you insert the overloaded **operator=()** function (and its prototype) into the **Classroom** class, the output of the **main()** program looks like Figure 9-33. Notice that the copied list of student names is correct in the final output for the first object, after the second object has been destroyed.

```
#include<iostream>
#include<string>
using namespace std;
class Classroom
{
  private:
    string *student;
    int numStudents;
    int gradeLevel;
  public:
    Classroom();
    ~Classroom();
    void display();
    Classroom& operator=(Classroom&);
};
Classroom::Classroom()
{
  int x;
  cout<<"What grade level is this class? ";
  cin>>gradeLevel;
  cout<<"How any students in this class? ";
  cin>>numStudents;
  student = new string[numStudents];
  for(x = 0; x < numStudents; ++x)
  {
      cout<<"Please enter the student's name ";
      cin>>student[x];
  }
}
```

Figure 9-32   **Classroom** class with overloaded **operator=()** and program that demonstrates it

```
Classroom::~Classroom()
{
  delete [] student;
}
void Classroom::display()
{
  int x;
  cout<<"Grade "<<gradeLevel<<" class list:"<<endl;
  for(x = 0; x < numStudents; ++x)
      cout<<student[x]<<endl;
}
Classroom& Classroom::operator =(Classroom &aClassroom)
{
  int x;
  gradeLevel = aClassroom.gradeLevel;
  numStudents = aClassroom.numStudents;
  delete [] student;
  student = new string[numStudents];
  for(x = 0; x < aClassroom.numStudents; ++x)
  {
      student[x] = aClassroom.student[x];
  }
  return *this;
}
int main()
{
    Classroom oneClass;
    {
      Classroom anotherClass;
      cout<<endl<<
        "The original classroom before assignment:"<<endl;
      oneClass.display();
      cout<<endl<<"The second classroom ";
      anotherClass.display();
      oneClass = anotherClass;
      cout<<endl<<
          "The original classroom after assignment:"<<endl;
      oneClass.display();
    }
    cout<<endl<<
      "After the second class has gone out of scope:"<<endl;
    oneClass.display();
}
```

9

Figure 9-32   `Classroom` class with overloaded `operator=()` and program that demonstrates it (continued)

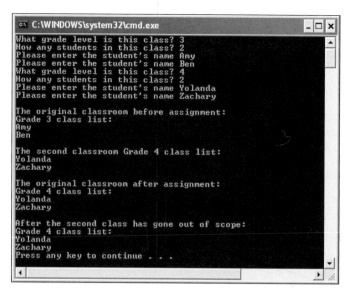

Figure 9-33   Output of program in Figure 9-32

OVERLOADING [ ] AND ( )

C++ provides two special operators, the subscript operator and the parentheses operator, that can be used as adjuncts to the more conventional operators.

The **subscript operator**, `operator[ ]`, is declared like any other function, but called in a manner similar to accessing an array element. As with every other operator, you can include any instructions you want within an `operator[ ]` function. Typically, you might use this function to access an element of a class, or to perform a task that both requires an argument and does not quite fit into another operator's usual meaning.

TIP

When you overload the `operator[]()` function for a class, the argument is not required to be an integer, as it is when you access an array with a subscript; you can create the operator to use any data type you need.

For example, suppose you have overloaded the `Classroom` class `operator=()` to accept a `Classroom` argument, as shown in Figure 9-32, so you can assign one `Classroom` to another. You might also choose to overload the same operator to accept an integer argument so you can use the assignment operator to change a `Classroom`'s grade level with a statement such as the following:

```
oneClass = 7;
```

Figure 9-34 shows a usable function that makes such an assignment possible. The function changes the grade level, but everything else remains the same.

```
Classroom& Classroom::operator=(int grade)
{
    gradeLevel = grade;
    return *this;
}
```

Figure 9-34   Overloaded `operator=( )` function that accepts an integer

Now, suppose you wanted to create a third overloaded `operator=( )` function that also accepts an integer. Perhaps you want to use this function to change the number of students in a class, or, in a class with more data, to change some other value. You cannot create two functions with the same signature; they would be ambiguous. In a case like this, you can choose to use the `operator[ ]( )` function.

Figure 9-35 shows an overloaded `operator[ ]( )` function that accepts an integer argument that changes the number of students in a class. If the number of students is greater than the existing number of students, the function creates a temporary string pointer and assigns enough memory to it to hold names for all the existing students as well as the new students in the class. The existing students are copied to the temporary area, then the remainder of the area is filled with new student names entered by the user. The existing student memory is deleted and a new block of memory that is large enough for all the students is allocated. Then the student names in the temporary block of memory are copied to the **student** class field, and the temporary memory is released. Finally, the number of students in the **Classroom** is updated and the revised object is returned.

```
Classroom& Classroom::operator[](int num)
{
    int x;
    string *temp;
    if(num > numStudents)
    {
        temp = new string[num];
        for(x = 0; x < numStudents; ++x)
            temp[x] = student[x];
        for(x = numStudents; x < num; ++x)
        {
            cout<<"Please enter the student's name ";
            cin>>temp[x];
        }
        delete [] student;
        student = new string[num];
        for(x = 0; x < num; ++x)
            student[x] = temp[x];
        delete [] temp;
    }
    numStudents = num;
    return *this;
}
```

Figure 9-35   An overloaded `operator[ ]( )` function for the `Classroom` class

TIP

If the number of students assigned using the [] operator in Figure 9-35 is less than the existing number of students, the extra students simply will not be displayed. A more sophisticated function would probably prompt the user for guidance on which students to remove. This example is kept short so you can more easily follow its logic.

The instructions written in the overloaded `operator[]()` function could have performed any set of tasks. If an overloaded operator function that accepts an integer argument to change the grade level did not already exist, then writing an overloaded `operator=()` function to change the number of students would make more sense than writing the [] version.

Figure 9-36 shows a `main()` function that uses both the overloaded = function that accepts an integer and the overloaded [] function that accepts an integer. Figure 9-37 shows a typical execution in which a `Classroom` is created for grade 7 with three students. The grade level is changed to 8 in the first shaded statement, and the `Classroom` is displayed again. Then the class size is changed to 5 in the second shaded statement. The overloaded `operator[]()` function adjusts the size of the class and prompts the user for the new student names. Then the adjusted `Classroom` is displayed a final time.

```
int main()
{
    Classroom oneClass;
    oneClass.display();
    cout<<endl;
    oneClass = 8;
    oneClass.display();
    cout<<endl;
    oneClass[5];
    oneClass.display();
}
```

Figure 9-36   A `main()` function that uses overloaded = and [] operators that each accept an integer argument

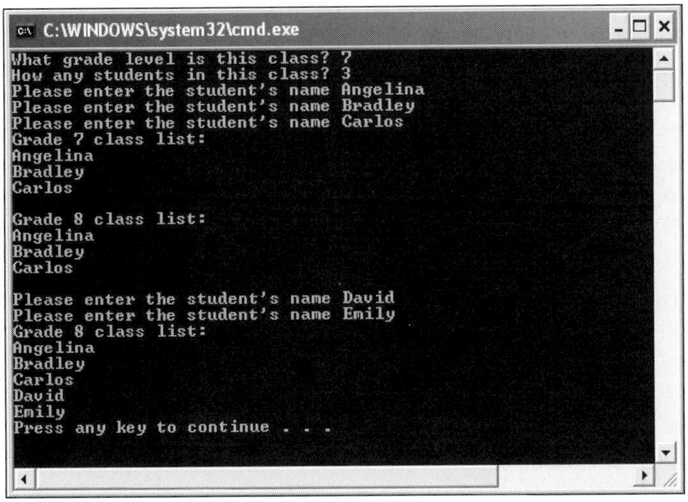

Figure 9-37   Typical execution of function in Figure 9-36

Like the subscript operator, you can use the **parentheses operator**, `operator()`, to make multiple assignments within a class. You write this function in the same way you write any other overloaded operator function. Usually, you use this function only when you want it for a logical purpose that is already being used by another operator.

YOU DO IT

Overloading an Arithmetic Operator

In the following set of steps, you create a class for a `SalesOffice`. The class will include an overloaded division operator (`operator/`) so you can divide one office's sales by another's to determine the ratio of their sales.

1. Open a new file in your C++ editor and type the first statements you need.

```
#include<iostream>
#include<string>
using namespace std;
```

2. Create the `SalesOffice` class definition. Each `SalesOffice` will have a name and a sales figure. You provide a constructor that initializes the `SalesOffice` data fields with supplied arguments. You also overload the division operator so you can divide one `SalesOffice`'s sales figure by another's to determine the ratio of their sales.

```
class SalesOffice
{
    private:
      string officeName;
      double sales;
    public:
      SalesOffice(string, double);
      double operator/(SalesOffice);
};
```

3. The constructor simply assigns provided values to the `SalesOffice`'s fields.

```
SalesOffice::SalesOffice(string office, double salesAmt)
{
    officeName = office;
    sales = salesAmt;
}
```

4. The `operator/()` function divides the sales figure from one `SalesOffice` by the sales figure from another `SalesOffice`. The ratio is a `double`, so the return type for `operator/()` is a double. It is important that the sales figure for the `this` object is divided by the sales figure for the argument object so division works as expected.

```
double SalesOffice::operator/(SalesOffice office)
{
    double ratio;
    ratio = sales / office.sales;
    return ratio;
}
```

TIP   As you improve the `SalesOffice` class, you might add code that ensures that the value for `office.sales` is not 0 (zero) before attempting to divide the `sales` figure by it.

5. Add a `main()` function that declares two `SalesOffice` objects—north and south—and compares their sales. The `main()` function will display the ratio times 100, and express the percentage as a whole number.

```
int main()
{
    SalesOffice north("North", 2454.88);
    SalesOffice south("South", 2830.92);
    double ratio;
    ratio = north / south;
    cout<<"The North Office has "<<(ratio * 100)<<
          "% of the sales of South Office"<<endl;
}
```

6. Save the program as **SalesOffice.cpp**, then compile and run the program. The output looks like Figure 9-38; the ratio of the sales of the two `SalesOffices` is expressed as a percentage.

Figure 9-38   Output of the `SalesOffice` program

Overloading an Output Operator

Next, you overload an insertion operator for the `SalesOffice` class so that output can be achieved in a natural fashion.

1. Open the **SalesOffice.cpp** file if it is not still open on your screen, and immediately save it as **SalesOffice2.cpp**.

2. Just after the opening curly brace of the `SalesOffice` class, insert the following prototype for the overloaded `operator<<()` function:

   ```
   friend ostream& operator<<(ostream&, const SalesOffice&);
   ```

3. After the complete `operator/()` function and just before the `main()` function, insert the implementation of the `operator<<()` function:

   ```
   ostream& operator<<(ostream& out,
       const SalesOffice &anOffice)
   {
       out<<"The "<<anOffice.officeName<<
           " Office sold $"<<anOffice.sales<<endl;
       return out;
   }
   ```

4. Within the `main()` function, just after the statement that computes the ratio between north and south, and just before the statement that begins: `cout<<"The North Office has"`, insert two `cout` statements that display the details of the north and south `SalesOffice`s, respectively:

   ```
   cout<<north;
   cout<<south;
   ```

5. Save the modified program and compile and run it. Your output should look like Figure 9-39.

Figure 9-39   Output of SalesOffice2.cpp

CHAPTER SUMMARY

❑ A `friend` function is a function that can access the non-`public` members of a class, even though the function itself is not a member of the class. A class declaration must state which functions or classes will be its friends.

❑ A `friend` function does not use the class name and the scope resolution operator in the function header. A `friend` function need not be declared in the `public` section of the class definition, and it must use the C++ keyword `friend` in its declaration. When any function tries to access an object's `private` member, the compiler examines the list of function prototypes in the class declaration, and access is approved only if the function is found to be a class member or a `friend`.

❑ Polymorphism allows the same operation to be carried out differently, depending on the object. Expressing a value as positive is different from using the + operator to perform arithmetic, so the + is polymorphic in that it can take one or two arguments and have a different meaning in each case. To be able to use arithmetic symbols with your own objects, you must overload the symbols.

❑ If you make a function a `friend` of multiple classes, it can use data from each class. When classes refer to each other, you must create a forward reference—a statement that lets the compiler know that the class exists, and that the details will come later.

❑ Operator overloading is the process by which you apply operators to your own abstract data types. Although you can overload an operator to have any meaning, good programming style dictates that you endow the operator with a reasonable meaning. You overload an operator by making it a function; subsequently, you can use it just like any other function. If an operator is normally defined to be unary only, then you cannot overload it to be binary, and vice versa. If an operator such as + is either binary or unary, you can overload it in either one or both contexts. Associativity refers to the order in which actions within an expression are carried out; you cannot change associativity when you overload operators. You also cannot change the normal precedence of any operator.

❑ The name of the operator function that overloads the + symbol is `operator+()`. The syntax involved in using the + operator alone is intuitively understood by anyone who has added simple numeric variables: you use an operand, an operator, and another operand. You can choose to overload any of the arithmetic operators for any classes you develop; with some operators you must be certain to pay attention to the order of the operands.

❑ When you create an overloaded operator, the objects on both sides of the operator can be different types. You cannot overload operators whose only operands are built-in data types.

❑ Most modern programming languages allow you to chain operations, that is, they allow several operators to be used within the same statement. Because one purpose of operator overloading is to create class operators that work "naturally" like built-in operators, you should consider creating operators for your own classes to have the same capability. This means that, for many operations, you will want the return type to be a class object.

❑ The << operator is overloaded by C++; it is called the insertion operator when used for output. The << operator acts as an output operator only when `cout` (or another output stream object) appears on the left side. Therefore, `cout` becomes the driving object and the `this` object in the overloaded `operator<<()` function. You can overload the << operator to work with your own classes. The `operator<<()` function is a nonmember `friend` function so that the operator can access the private members of the `ostream` class and the class being displayed.

❑ The extraction operator (>>) operator can also be overloaded for input. The advantage of overloading operators such as >> is that the resulting programs look cleaner and are easier to read.

❑ With C++, you use ++ to increment variables, and -- to decrement variables. You can overload the prefix ++ or -- operators to use with your own class objects, just like you can overload other operators. When you use ++ or -- with class objects, the same prefix/postfix rules apply as they do with simple built-in types.

❑ If you want to use a postfix ++ operator with a class, you use a dummy integer argument. This argument distinguishes the postfix ++ operator from the prefix version.

❑ When you write an overloaded `operator==()` function for a class, you must decide what will constitute equality in class members. The `operator==()` function usually returns either an integer value representing 0 or 1 or a Boolean variable representing true or false.

❑ Unlike the other operators, if you don't define the = operator, C++ provides a definition for you. However, if you want the = operator to do something other than assign each member, then you must create a custom `operator=()` function. In addition, if the class contains data fields that are pointers, you should create a custom function. When you dynamically allocate memory using the new operator, it is a good practice to delete the reserved memory when the object using it goes out of scope.

❑ C++ provides two special operators, the subscript operator and the parentheses operator, that can be used as adjuncts to the more conventional operators.

9

KEY TERMS

A **friend function** is a function that can access the non-`public` members of a class, even though the function itself is not a member of the class.

A **friend class** is a class in which all functions can access the non-**public** members of another class.

Pure polymorphism is the situation in which one function body is used with a variety of arguments.

The use of functions that are distinguished by their number or types of arguments is sometimes called **parametric overloading**.

A **forward reference** is a statement that lets the compiler know that the class exists, and that the details will come later.

Operator overloading is the process by which you apply operators to your own abstract data types.

Associativity refers to the order in which actions within an expression are carried out.

The name of the function that overloads the + symbol is the **operator+() function**.

To **chain operations** is to allow several operators to be used within the same statement.

The **operator>>() function** overloads the insertion operator.

Multiple calls to the same operator function is called **stacking**.

The **operator>>()** function overloads the extraction operator.

The **operator++()** function overloads the increment operator.

The **operator--()** function overloads the decrement operator.

A **dummy argument** is one that is not used within the function but exists only to provide a different function prototype.

A function's prototype is also called its **signature**.

The **operator=() function** overloads the assignment operator.

Deallocated memory is memory that is no longer assigned to anything in an application.

To **allocate memory** for a field is to allot storage for and assign a name to it.

When you allocate memory during the execution of a program (as opposed to when the program is compiled) you **dynamically allocate memory**.

In C++ you use the **new operator** to dynamically allocate memory.

The **delete operator** frees previously allocated memory.

The **subscript operator**, **operator[]**, is declared like any other function, but is called in a manner similar to accessing an array element.

You can use the **parentheses operator**, **operator()**, to make multiple assignments within a class.

REVIEW QUESTIONS

1. Which of the following statements is true?

   a. A `friend` function can declare itself to be a friend of a class.

   b. A `friend` function can declare itself to be a friend of another function.

   c. Both of the above are true.

   d. None of the above are true.

2. A function that has been declared to be a friend of a class has access to the _____ data in the class.

   a. public

   b. private

   c. both of the above

   d. none of the above

3. Which of the following is a legal example of the way overloading is used in C++?

   a. creating any two functions for a class

   b. creating two constructors for a class

   c. creating two destructors for a class

   d. all of the above

4. The primary advantage to overloading functions is _____.

   a. you can use one function name for every operation you want to perform with a class

   b. you can use one class name for many types of items

   c. you can use one function name for similar operations, regardless of the data types involved

   d. you do not have to write separate code for the bodies of functions that perform similar tasks

5. The built-in * operator is _____.

   a. polymorphic

   b. recursive

   c. retroactive

   d. all of the above

6. Applying operators to your own abstract data types is called _____ overloading.

   a. abstract

   b. parametric

   c. data

   d. operator

9

7. Which of the following is true?

   a. You overload an operator by making it an argument to a function.

   b. You should overload every C++ operator for each new class you create.

   c. To avoid confusion, you should not overload operators to carry out tasks that are similar in meaning to the built-in version of the operator.

   d. Operators that are normally defined to be only unary must remain unary when you overload them.

8. Which of the following operators can be overloaded to be binary?

   a. >

   b. ->

   c. ++

   d. !

9. _____ refers to the order in which actions within an expression are carried out.

   a. Overloading

   b. Associativity

   c. Communicativity

   d. Operating

10. Which of the following operators can be overloaded?

   a. .

   b. &

   c. ::

   d. ?:

11. If you have correctly overloaded the * operator to multiply two members of the Furniture class, and you have declared two Furniture objects, aDesk and aChair, then which of the following is a legal expression?

   a. Furniture * Furniture

   b. aDesk * aChair

   c. Furniture * aChair

   d. all of the above

12. If you have correctly overloaded the * operator to multiply two members of the Furniture class, and you have declared two Furniture objects, aDesk and aChair, then which of the following is a legal expression?

   a. aChair.operator*(aDesk)

   b. aChair * aChair

   c. aChair * aDesk

   d. all of the above

13. The `Shipment` class holds information about a shipment, including its weight. An overloaded division operator divides a `Shipment`'s `totalWeight` field into the number of packages in the `Shipment` to determine the average package weight. The function header is `int Shipment::operator/(int packages)`. Which of the following statements is correct within the function?

   a. `int numPackages = Shipment / packages;`

   b. `int numPackages = totalWeight / packages;`

   c. `int numPackages = packages.totalWeight / packages;`

   d. `int numPackages = packages.totalWeight / totalWeight;`

14. An overloaded subtraction operator subtracts two `Shipment` objects from each other, returning an integer that represents the difference in their `totalWeight` variables. The subtraction operator works as expected, with the object to the right of the minus sign being subtracted from the object to the left. The function header is `int Shipment::operator-(Shipment ship);`. Within the function, which of the following is correct?

   a. `int difference = ship - totalWeight;`

   b. `int difference = totalWeight - ship;`

   c. `int difference = ship.totalWeight - totalWeight;`

   d. `int difference = totalWeight - ship.totalWeight;`

15. The `Student` class contains an overloaded addition operator which allows a number of credits to be added to a `Student`'s `totalCredits`. The function header is `Student Student::operator+(int newCredits)`. The `=` operator has not been overloaded. Which of the following is correct in a program that declares a `Student` object named `aStudent`?

   a. `aStudent = 3 + aStudent;`

   b. `aStudent = aStudent + 3;`

   c. both of the above

   d. none of the above

16. To be able to add three or more objects in sequence, as in `x + y + z`, you must overload the + operator to _____.

   a. accept multiple arguments

   b. accept no arguments

   c. return an object of the same type as the arguments

   d. return a primitive type

9

17. When you overload the << operator to work with a class object, you must
_____.

   a. make the operator function a **friend** function

   b. make the operator function a member function

   c. return an object of the same type as the class

   d. return a simple built-in type

18. The primary advantage to overloading >> and << to use with class objects is
_____.

   a. you write less code than with standard input and output functions

   b. the << and >> functions, being member functions of the class, have access to private class data

   c. the program code that uses the functions contains syntax that is easy to understand

   d. all of the above

19. The difference between the function prototypes for the overloaded prefix and postfix ++ for any class is the _____.

   a. return type

   b. function name

   c. argument list

   d. all of the above

20. If you do not overload an = operator for a class _____.

   a. C++ provides you with a built-in version

   b. you must write a regular member function to copy one object to another

   c. you cannot use the class objects in mathematical expressions

   d. you cannot use = with class objects

EXERCISES

1. Create two classes. The first holds customer data—specifically, a customer number and zip code. The second, a class for cities, holds the city name, state, and zip code. Additionally, each class contains a constructor that takes arguments to set the field values. Create a **friend** function that displays a customer number and the customer's city, state, and zip code. Write a brief **main()** function to test the classes and **friend** function. Save the file as **Customer.cpp**.

2. a. Create two classes. The first, named **Sale**, holds data for a sales transaction. Its private data members include the day of the month, amount of the sale, and the salesperson's ID number. The second class, named **Salesperson**, holds data for a salesperson, and its private data members include each salesperson's ID number and last name. Each class includes a constructor to which you can pass the field values. Create a **friend** function named **display()** that is a

friend of both classes and displays the date of sale, the amount, and the sales-person ID and name. Write a short `main()` demonstration program to test your classes and `friend` function. Save the file as **Sales.cpp**.

b. Add a function to both the `Sale` and `Salesperson` classes that returns the private salesperson ID number. Write a `main()` function that contains an array of five `Salesperson` objects and store appropriate data in it. Then, continue to prompt the user for `Sale` data until the user enters an appropriate sentinel value. For each `Sale` transaction entered, determine whether the salesperson's ID number is valid. Either display an error message, or use the `friend display()` function to display all the data. Save the file as **Sales2.cpp**.

TIP If you want to create an array of class objects for a class without a default constructor, you must call the constructor for each array element and provide arguments. For example, if you have a `Salesperson` class whose constructor requires an integer and a string, then you can declare an array of two `Salesperson` objects as follows:

```
Salesperson sp[2] = {Salesperson(103,"Woods"),
    Salesperson(104, "Martin"),};
```

9

3. Create a class named `WeatherReport` that holds a daily weather report with data members such as `dayOfMonth`, `highTemp`, `lowTemp`, `amountRain`, and `amountSnow`. The constructor initializes the fields with default values: 99 for `dayOfMonth`, 9999 for `highTemp`, -9999 for `lowTemp`, and 0 for `amountRain` and `amountSnow`. Include a function that prompts the user and sets values for each field so that you can override the default values. Instantiate 30 `WeatherReport` objects and, in a loop, prompt the user for a month's data.

At the end of the month, a month-end `WeatherReport` object is created. Initialize the object with default values; then use a `friend` function to store the high temperature, low temperature, and rain and snow totals for the month in the object. The `friend` function takes two `WeatherReport` objects—the summary object and one day's object—and it returns an updated summary object. If the day's high temperature is higher than the summary object's high, then replace the summary high. If the day's low temperature is lower than the summary object's low, then replace the summary low. Accumulate rain and snow in the summary object. Write a `main()` function that creates a month-end weather report from the 30 daily reports. Save the file as **WeatherReport.cpp**.

4. Complete the following tasks:

a. Design a `Job` class with three data fields—Job number, time in hours to complete the Job, and per-hour rate charged for the Job.

b. Include overloaded extraction and insertion operators that get and display a `Job`'s values.

c. Include overloaded + and − operators that return integers that indicate the total time for two Jobs, and indicate the difference in time between two Jobs, respectively.

d. Write a `main()` function demonstrating that all the functions work correctly. Save the file as **Jobs.cpp**.

5. Complete the following tasks:

a. Design a class to hold a `JobBid`. Each `JobBid` contains a bid number and a quoted price. Each `JobBid` also contains overloaded extraction and insertion operators.

b. Include an overloaded `operator<()` function. A `JobBid` is considered lower than another `JobBid` when the quoted price is lower.

c. Write a `main()` function that declares an array of four `JobBid` objects. Find and display the lowest `JobBid`. Save the file as **JobBid.cpp**.

6. Complete the following tasks:

a. Design a `PhoneCall` class that holds a phone number to which a call is placed, the length of the call in minutes, and the rate charged per minute. Overload extraction and insertion operators for the class.

b. Overload the == operator to compare two `PhoneCalls`. Consider one `PhoneCall` to be equal to another if both calls are placed to the same number.

c. Create a `main()` function that allows you to enter 10 `PhoneCalls` into an array. If a `PhoneCall` has already been placed to a number, do not allow a second `PhoneCall` to the same number. Save the file as **PhoneCall.cpp**.

7. Complete the following tasks:

a. Design a `SoccerPlayer` class that includes three integer fields: a player's jersey number, number of goals, and number of assists. Overload extraction and insertion operators for the class.

b. Include an `operator>()` function for the class. One `SoccerPlayer` is considered greater than another if the sum of goals plus assists is greater.

c. Create an array of 11 `SoccerPlayers`, then use the > operator to find the player who has the greatest total of goals plus assists. Save the file as **SoccerPlayer.cpp**.

8. Complete the following tasks:

a. Design a `Dog` class that includes fields for a breed (for example, "Labrador") and eye color. Include extraction and insertion operators.

b. Overload an `operator*()` function for the `Dog` class. When you multiply two `Dogs`, the result is a `Dog`. If the two operand `Dogs` are the same breed, then the resulting `Dog` is that breed; if the two operand `Dogs` have different breeds, then the resulting `Dog` is "Mixed" breed. Obtain a random number of 0 or 1 for the resulting `Dog`'s eye color. (See Appendix E for instructions on creating random numbers.) When the random number chosen is 0, use the eye color from the first operand `Dog` for the resulting `Dog`'s eye color; when the random number is 1, use the eye color of the second `Dog` for the result `Dog`.

c. Write a `main()` function in which you declare four parent Dogs. When you execute the program, make sure you assign the same breed to two Dogs, and different breeds to each of the other two Dogs. (You will have a total of three breeds for the four Dogs.) Also assign a variety of eye colors. In a loop, multiply each pair eight times, and display the results. Save the file as **Dog.cpp**.

9. Complete the following tasks:

a. Design a `Meal` class with two fields—one that holds the name of the entrée, the other that holds a calorie count integer. Include a constructor that sets a `Meal`'s fields with arguments, or uses default values when no arguments are provided.

b. Include an overloaded insertion operator function that displays a `Meal`'s values.

c. Include an overloaded extraction operator that prompts a user for an entrée name and calorie count for a meal.

d. Include an overloaded `operator+()` function that allows you to add two or more `Meal` objects. Adding two `Meal` objects means adding their calorie values and creating a summary `Meal` object in which you store "Daily Total" in the entrée field.

e. Write a `main()` function that declares four `Meal` objects named `breakfast`, `lunch`, `dinner`, and `total`. Provide values for the `breakfast`, `lunch`, and `dinner` objects. Include the statement `total = breakfast + lunch + dinner;` in your program, then display values for the four `Meal` objects. Save the file as **Meal.cpp**.

f. Write a `main()` function that declares an array of 21 `Meal` objects. Allow a user to enter values for 21 `Meal`s for the week. Total these meals and display the calorie total for the end of the week. (*Hint:* You might find it useful to create a constructor for the `Meal` class.) Save the file as **Meal2.cpp**.

10. Complete the following tasks:

a. Create a `PhoneBook` class. Fields include first name, last name, area code, and phone number.

b. Include an extraction operator that prompts the user for values for each field. Also include an insertion operator that displays the values of each field.

c. Overload the `operator[]()` function to change a `PhoneBook` object's phone number (but not area code).

d. Overload the `operator()()` function to change the area code and phone number.

e. Write a `main()` function in which you declare an array of five `PhoneBook` objects and assign data to each. Using a loop, display numbers 1 through 5, along with each object's data. Prompt the user to select a number 1 through 5 to modify a `PhoneBook` entry. When the user has chosen an entry, ask whether the user wants to alter an entire entry, alter the entire phone number including the area code, or alter just the phone number and not the area code. Accept new data values accordingly. If the user wants to modify an entire entry, create a temporary object, assign values, and use the built-in = operator to assign the temporary object to the correct location in the array. If the user wants to change the area code and phone number, or change the phone number only, prompt for values, then use either the [] or () operator to assign the new values to the proper existing object within the array. After the update has taken effect, redisplay the five `PhoneBook` entries. Save the file as **PhoneBook.cpp**.

11. Complete the following tasks:

   a. Design a `ScoreKeeper` class that tracks the scores a student receives in a course. Include fields for the name of the course, an integer that holds the number of different scores a student is assigned during the course, and an integer pointer that points to a list of the student's scores on tests and assignments in a class. Include a constructor that accepts the course name and number of scored items and then prompts the user for the individual scores. Each score must be a value from 0 to 100; if the score is too high or too low, reprompt the user for a valid score.

   b. Overload an insertion operator that displays an object's values.

   c. Overload an = operator that assigns one `ScoreKeeper` to another.

   d Write a `main()` function that demonstrates the class works correctly when two objects are created, one object is assigned to another, and, subsequently, the object that was assigned goes out of scope. Save the file as **ScoreKeeper.cpp**.

12. Complete the following tasks:

   a. Design a `CollegeDepartment` class. Include fields for the department name (for example "Mathematics"), the department chair's name (for example, "Lewis"), an integer that holds the number of classes offered by a department (for example, 10), and a string pointer that points to the individual courses offered by the department (for example, "MAT101"). Create two constructors. The default constructor assigns appropriate default values to the fields. The other constructor accepts arguments for the department name, department chair's name, and number of courses and assigns them to their respective fields, and also prompts the user for the names of all the courses offered.

   b. Overload an insertion operator for the class.

   c. Overload > and < operators that compare `CollegeDepartment`s based on number of courses offered.

   d. Overload an = operator to assign one `CollegeDepartment` to another.

   e. Write a `main()` function that declares an array of four `CollegeDepartment` objects. In a loop, prompt the user for a department name, chair name, and number of courses, then pass those arguments to the constructor to create a temporary `CollegeDepartment`. (The constructor then gets the individual course names from the user). Assign each entered department to a spot in the array. After all the `CollegeDepartment` objects have been entered, display them in a loop. Save the file as **CollegeDepartment.cpp**.

   f. Modify the `main()` function to also display the `CollegeDepartment` objects with the most and fewest number of courses. Save the file as **CollegeDepartment2.cpp**.

13. Each of the following files in your Chapter09 folder contains syntax and/or logical errors. Determine the problem in each case, and fix the program. Save your
solutions by adding "Fixed" to the filename, as in **DEBUG9-1Fixed.cpp**.

a. DEBUG9-1

b. DEBUG9-2

c. DEBUG9-3

d. DEBUG9-4

CASE PROJECT 1

**CASE
PROJECTS**

You have been developing a `Fraction` class for Teacher's Pet Software that contains
several fields and functions.

a. Add four arithmetic operators, +, -, *, and /. Remember that to add or subtract
two `Fraction`s, you first must convert them to `Fraction`s with a common
denominator. You multiply two `Fraction`s by multiplying the numerators and
multiplying the denominators. You divide two `Fraction`s by inverting the second
`Fraction`, then multiplying. After any arithmetic operation, be sure the
`Fraction` is in proper format; for example, 1/2 * 2/3 results in 1/3, not 2/6.

b. Add an `operator==()` function that compares the value of two `Fraction`s.

c. Add `operator>()` and `operator<()` functions that compare the values of two
`Fraction`s.

d. Add extraction and insertion operators for the `Fraction` class.

e. Write a `main()` program that declares an array of 10 randomly generated
`Fraction` values, for which each numerator is a random value between 1 and 5
inclusive. (Instructions on generating random numbers appear in Appendix E.)
Assign the value 10 to the denominator of each `Fraction`. Reduce each of the
ten randomly generated `Fraction`s to its proper form (for example, 2/10 is 1/5)
and display them. Save the file as **FractionPartE.cpp**.

f. Remove the statements from `main()` that display the ten `Fraction` objects. Add
statements to the `main()` function that prompt the user to choose between four
operations for an arithmetic drill—addition, subtraction, multiplication, or division. After the user has selected an operation, generate five problems using five
pairs of `Fraction`s from the 10-element array. (If the user selects the subtraction
option, make sure the first operand in the problem is not smaller than the second
so that the correct answer is not negative.) Display a problem (for example, if the
user chooses addition, the problem might be "1/10 + 3/10") and allow the user
to enter an answer from the keyboard. After each keyboard answer, notify the user
whether the answer was correct. Save the file as **FractionPartF.cpp**.

g. Add code to the `main()` function that allows the user up to three attempts to
correctly answer each problem. Save the file as **FractionPartG.cpp**.

9

h. Add code to the `main()` function that keeps score. At the end of the program, display a message similar to "You got 3 correct out of 5 problems". Save the file as **FractionPartH.cpp**.

i. Alter the `main()` function to generate random numbers between 6 and 10 inclusive for the denominators. Save the file as **FractionPartI.cpp**.

CASE PROJECT 2

CASE PROJECTS

You have been developing a `BankAccount` class for Parkville Bank that contains several fields and functions.

a. Add arithmetic operators that operate as follows:

◘ The `+=` operator takes a **double** argument, which can represent a deposit (or credit) to be added to the `BankAccount` balance. (If the argument is negative, it will represent a withdrawal or debit from the account.)

Because the `+=` operator alters the object with which it is used, it should return `*this`.

TIP

◘ The `+` operator takes an integer argument that increases the account number, returning a new `BankAccount` object with the new account number.

b. Include `<` and `>` operators that determine whether one account is less than or greater than another. These comparisons are based on balances. Include an `==` operator that makes a comparison based on account numbers.

c. Include extraction and insertion operators for the class.

d. If you do not already have one, create a default constructor that assigns 0 to all the class fields.

e. Write a `main()` function that declares an array of five `BankAccount` objects. (Use the default constructor, so all the data fields will be initialized to 0s.) For each account, prompt the user for a series of transactions. The user enters a positive number for each deposit, a negative number for each withdrawal, and a 0 to quit entering transactions for an account. After the user has entered transactions for all five accounts, display the resulting details for each `BankAccount`. Save the file as **BankAccountPartE.cpp**.

f. Alter the `main()` function so that the user is prompted for starting account data instead of accepting the default 0 values. Save the file as **BankAccountPartF.cpp**.

g. Modify the `main()` function so that no two accounts are allowed with the same account number. Reprompt the user for a new account number when a duplicate occurs. Save the file as **BankAccountPartG.cpp**.

h. Modify the `main()` function to display the data for the accounts with the highest and lowest balances after all the data has been entered. Save the file as **BankAccountPartH.cpp**.

CHAPTER 10

UNDERSTANDING INHERITANCE

> **In this chapter, you will:**
>
> ♦ Learn about inheritance and its benefits
>
> ♦ Create a derived class
>
> ♦ Learn about restrictions imposed with inheritance
>
> ♦ Choose a class access specifier
>
> ♦ Override inherited access
>
> ♦ Override and overload parent class functions within a child class
>
> ♦ Provide for a base class constructor within a derived class
>
> ♦ Use multiple inheritance
>
> ♦ Learn about the special problems posed by multiple inheritance
>
> ♦ Use virtual inheritance

Inheritance is based on the principle that knowledge of a general category can be applied to more specific objects. Specifically, inheritance in C++ means you can create classes that derive their attributes from existing classes; in other words, a newly created class can absorb all the data fields and functions of a class already being used. Inheritance saves you time because you don't have to start from scratch every time you want to create a class. Instead, when you use inheritance to create a class, you expand on an existing class.

In this chapter, you learn about various types of inheritance and their advantages and disadvantages.

UNDERSTANDING INHERITANCE

You are familiar with the concept of inheritance from situations unrelated to programming. When you hear the term "inheritance," you might think of genetics. You know that your hair and eye color have been inherited. You may have selected a family pet or a variety of plants for your garden on the basis of its genetic traits. With genetic inheritance, you often think about hierarchies of classifications—your Siamese is a member of the cat family, which is a mammal, which is an animal, and so on.

With any subject matter, your knowledge of existing hierarchies makes it easier to understand new information. If a friend tells you he's getting an item that belongs to the "Carmello" category, you might be uncertain what he means. If he tells you that the item is a variety of tomato, you understand many of a Carmello's traits without ever having seen one—that is, you know a Carmello tomato has the general traits of a tomato (but possibly different traits than a "Beefsteak" tomato). If you had not heard of the tomato category, your friend could explain that a tomato is a member of the fruit category, and you would at least have an idea that a Carmello must grow, have seeds, and probably be edible.

When you organize a hard disk, you set up your files using inheritance concepts. Your C drive probably contains a number of folders, each of which contains folders that contain more specific material. For example, your CollegeCourses folder might contain a MathCourses folder that contains a CollegeAlgebra folder. You organize your files this way because CollegeAlgebra is one of the MathCourses and the MathCourses are CollegeCourses. You can consider class inheritance in a similar manner.

Objects used in computer programs are also easier to understand if you can place them within a hierarchy of inheritance. Suppose you have written several programs with a class named `Student`. You have learned the names of the data fields, and you understand what the various member functions do. If you need to write a program using a new class named `FirstYearStudent`, the job is easier if `FirstYearStudent` is inherited from a class named `Student`. The `FirstYearStudent` class may require some additional data members and functions that other `Student` objects do not require (perhaps an `applicationFee` field or an `orientation()` method), but `FirstYearStudent` also will have the more general `Student` members with which you are already familiar. You need to master only the differences contained in the new members.

The `FirstYearStudent` class inherits from the `Student` class, or is **derived** from it. The `Student` class is called a **parent class**, **base class**, **superclass**, or **ancestor**; the `FirstYearStudent` class is called a **child class**, **derived class**, **subclass**, or **descendant**.

TIP Don't confuse a child class with an object; an object is a very specific instance of a class. For example, `Animal`, `Horse`, and `Stallion` are all classes, listed in descending order of inheritance. An object (with an exaggeratedly long name) might be `theBlackStallionInStallSixteen`.

TIP Generally, inheritance terms for base and derived classes are used in pairs. That is, if one programmer calls the base class a "parent" class, then he probably uses the term "child class" for the descendant. Similarly, "superclass" and "subclass" go together, as do "ancestor" and "descendant."

In many real-life cases, a derived class might not possess all of its parents' traits. For example, you may be the only redhead in your family. Another example is that some fruits should not be eaten. Similarly, child class members might not possess all the traits of their parents' class. For example, members of the `FirstYearStudent` class might require a different display format than members of the `Student` class. Thus, a useful feature of C++ inheritance is that the descendant class can override inappropriate attributes from the parent. When you **override** a function, you substitute one version of the function for another.

TIP Object-oriented programmers say that inheritance supports **generalization and specialization**. That is, base classes are more general, and derived classes are more specialized cases of their base classes.

10

UNDERSTANDING THE ADVANTAGES PROVIDED BY INHERITANCE

Inheritance is considered a basic building block of object-oriented programming. To be truly "object-oriented," a programming language must allow inheritance. One major feature of object-oriented programming is its ability to create classes from ones that already exist. Programs in which you derive new classes from existing classes offer several advantages:

- You save time because much of the code needed for your class is already written.

- You save additional time because the existing code has already been tested—that is, you know it works correctly; it is **reliable**.

- You save even more time because you already understand how the base class works, and you can concentrate on the complexity added as a result of your extensions to the class.

- In a derived class, you can extend and revise a parent class without corrupting the existing parent class features. In other words, you don't have to modify a parent class to get it to work correctly with your new category of objects; you leave the original class alone.

- If other classes have been derived from the parent class, the parent class is even more reliable—the more its code has been used, the more likely it is that logical errors have already been found and fixed.

TIP In some object-oriented programming languages, such as Java and Smalltalk, every new class must inherit from an existing class that is built into the language. (In both languages, the ultimate base class is named `Object`.) C++ is sometimes called a hybrid object-oriented programming language because you can create original base classes without deriving them from some other class. You have been creating classes without inheritance throughout this text.

Despite its advantages, inheritance is not used as often as it could be. In many companies, a program is needed quickly to solve a particular problem. Developing good, general-purpose software from which more specific classes can be inherited is more difficult and time-consuming than writing a "quick and dirty" program to solve an immediate problem. Because the benefits of creating a good, reusable base class are usually not realized in one project, programmers often have little incentive to design software from which derived classes can be created in the future. If programmers take the time to develop reliable base classes, however, future programming projects will go much more smoothly.

TIP With C++, you cannot inherit regular functions and variables, only classes.

Creating a Derived Class

Consider a class originally developed by a company to hold an individual's data, such as an ID number and name. The class, named **Person**, is shown in Figure 10-1. It contains three fields and two member functions, which set and display the data field values.

TIP A fully developed `Person` class most likely would contain street address information, a phone number, and other personal data. Additionally, you might include a constructor and destructor. For simplicity, this `Person` class is short.

The company that uses the **Person** class soon realizes that the class can be used for all kinds of individuals; customers, full-time employees, part-time employees, and suppliers all have names and numbers as well. The **Person** class appears to be a good candidate to be inherited by new classes.

```
class Person
{
    private:
       int idNum;
       string lastName;
       string firstName;
    public:
       void setFields(int, string, string);
       void outputData();
};
void Person::setFields(int num, string last, string first)
{
    idNum = num;
    lastName = last;
    firstName = first;
}
void Person::outputData()
{
    cout<<"ID #"<<idNum<<" Name: "<<firstName<<" "<<
        lastName<<endl;
}
```

Figure 10-1   The `Person` class

10

TIP

Often, you can distinguish child and parent classes by the order in which you would most commonly use the terms—you use the child class first and the base class last. For example, `Dog` represents a category of animals, and `Poodle` is more specific. You might refer to a "Poodle Dog" but not a "Dog Poodle", because a `Poodle` is a more specific example that describes a type of `Dog`. Similarly, a `Customer Person` is a more specific example of a `Person`.

To create a derived class, you include the following elements in the order listed:

- keyword **class**
- derived class name
- colon
- class access specifier—either **public**, **private**, or **protected**
- base class name
- opening brace
- class definition statements
- closing brace
- semicolon

For example, Figure 10-2 shows the shell, or outline, of a `Customer` class that inherits the members of the `Person` class. This class uses `public` inheritance, which is most common; you will learn more about the use of `public` in the derived class header later in this chapter.

```
class Customer : public Person
{
     // other statements go here
};
```

Figure 10-2 The `Customer` class shell

TIP A common programmer error is to place two colons after the derived class name in the class header line. C++ will then issue an error message, because two colons indicate class scope and the class has yet to be completely declared. Declaring a derived class requires using a single colon after the new class name.

The `Customer` class shown in Figure 10-2 contains all the members of `Person` because it inherits them. In other words, every `Customer` object has an `idNum`, `lastName`, and `firstName`, just as a `Person` object does. A `Customer` object can also use the `setFields()` and `outputData()` functions defined in the `Person` class. Additionally, you can add new, more specific fields for the `Customer` class. For example, you can include an additional data member, `balanceDue`, and two more functions: `setBalDue()` and `outputBalDue()`. A complete `Customer` definition is shown in Figure 10-3.

TIP You can say every child class object "is a" parent class object. For example, every `Customer` "is a" `Person`, not vice versa. In Chapter 8 you learned about composition; those relationships are "has a" relationships.

After you define the `Customer` class, you can write a function that declares a `Customer`, such as the one in Figure 10-4; the output appears in Figure 10-5. Notice in the shaded statements that a `Customer` can use methods from its parent's class definition. Because the `Customer` class is a child of the `Person` class, then a `Customer` object can use the functions that belong to its own class, as well as those of its parent.

Of course, a `Customer` object can use its own class's member functions, `setBalDue()` and `outputBalDue()`. Additionally, it can use the `Person` functions, `setFields()` and `outputData()`, just as a `Person` object could.

```
class Customer : public Person
{
    private:
        double balanceDue;
    public:
        void setBalDue(double);
        void outputBalDue();
};
void Customer::setBalDue(double bal)
{
    balanceDue = bal;
}
void Customer::outputBalDue()
{
    cout<<"Balance due $"<<balanceDue<<endl;
}
```

Figure 10-3   The Customer class

```
int main()
{
    Customer cust;
    // the next two functions are defined
    // in the base class Person
    cust.setFields(215,"Santini","Linda");
    cust.outputData();
    // the next two functions are defined
    // in the derived class Customer
    cust.setBalDue(147.95);
    cust.outputBalDue();
}
```

10

Figure 10-4   Function that uses a Customer object

Figure 10-5   Output of function in Figure 10-4

UNDERSTANDING INHERITANCE RESTRICTIONS

Figure 10-6 shows a modified version of the `Customer` class `outputBalDue()` function, originally presented in Figure 10-3. The improvement lies in the shaded area where the `Customer` ID number has been added to the explanation of the output. It makes sense that because a `Customer` has an `idNum` (as well as a `lastName` and `firstName`) inherited from the `Person` class, the `Customer` class `outputBalDue()` function should be able to access it. However, if you replace the original `outputBalDue()` function with the one shown in Figure 10-6, programs that use the function no longer run. The error message generated states that the `private Person` field `idNum` is **inaccessible**; that is, the `Customer` class function has no access to it and cannot use it.

```
void Customer::outputBalDue()
{
    cout<<"ID #"<<idNum<<" Balance due $"<<balanceDue<<endl;
}
```

Figure 10-6   Modified `outputBalDue()` function that does not work with the `Person` definition from Figure 10-1

When a class serves as a base class to other classes, all of its members are included when you create an object from a derived class. However, the members of the base class that are `private` are not directly accessible from within the child class functions. That's why `idNum` is not accessible within the function `outputBalDue()`. When you think about data hiding and encapsulation, this restriction makes sense. You purposely make class data members `private` so they cannot be accessed or altered by nonmember functions. If anyone could access your `private` data members by simply extending your class through inheritance, then using the `private` keyword would be pointless. You create `private` data to require that users of your class access the data only through the `public` functions you have written.

Locking your house is a good idea, but when relatives show up unexpectedly while you are at the store, it might be inconvenient. Similarly, while having `private` class members is a good idea so you can control how they are used, it often is inconvenient. There are times when you want a child class object to be able to access `private` data members that it owns, but that originated with the parent, but, at the same time, you do not want outside classes or functions to have access.

Fortunately, C++ provides an alternative and intermediate security level to using `private` and `public` specifiers. The `protected` access specifier allows members to be used by class member functions and by derived classes, but not by other parts of a program. The access specifiers follow these rules:

- **private** data and functions can be accessed only within a class
- **protected** data and functions can be accessed only by class functions, or by functions in child classes
- **public** data and functions can be accessed anywhere

Thus, the rewritten **Person** class definition in Figure 10-7 represents a possible candidate for an inheritable base class. The shaded keyword **protected** has been substituted for **private**. It means that not only can **Person** class functions refer to the listed members that follow, but so can any member of a class that is a child of **Person**. With the substitution of **protected** for **private** in the **Person** class definition, the **Customer** class's **outputBalDue()** function in Figure 10-6 works correctly.

```
class Person
{
    protected:
        int idNum;
        string lastName;
        string firstName;
    public:
        void setFields(int, string, string);
        void outputData();
};
```

Figure 10-7   The **Person** class with protected data

You are never required to define data as **protected** rather than **private** simply because a class is a base class. You use **protected** access as a convenience, so that derived classes can use the base class data fields without having to go through the base class's **public** functions. If you want a child class to access data only through **public** parent class functions, then continue to declare the parent class fields as **private**. Some programmers argue that you are observing the spirit of object-oriented programming only when you make all data **private**, and that using the **protected** access specifier for data members is somewhat "lazy."

TIP   If a base class contains a function through which a field is modified, it generally is considered good practice to use that function from within a derived class, even though the derived class has direct access to the field. That way, if the base class function enforces restrictions on a field's values, the same restrictions will automatically be enforced in the derived class.

TIP Although many programmers oppose creating `protected` and `public` data fields in a base class, they might approve of creating `protected` functions. A `protected` function is appropriate for a function that provides a service to a class and its descendants, but not to outside methods.

For example, Figure 10-8 shows a modified `Person` class in which all the data fields are declared as `private`. This class contains a `public getId()` function (shaded) that returns the `private` ID number. The child class, `Customer`, uses this `public` function to access the ID number (in the shaded statement in the `outputBalDue()` function) just as any nonmember function would. Just as the programmer who creates the `Person` class can choose for any members to be public or private, the programmer also can decide whether limited-access members will be private and accessed only through `public` functions, or will be `protected` and freely accessible by child classes. You must decide, with guidance from your instructors and employers, which techniques to use when creating your own classes.

```
class Person
{
    private:
      int idNum;
      string lastName;
      string firstName;
    public:
      void setFields(int num, string last, string first);
      void outputData();
      int getId();
};
void Person::setFields(int num, string last, string first)
{
    idNum = num;
    lastName = last;
    firstName = first;
}
void Person::outputData()
{
    cout<<"ID #"<<idNum<<" Name: "<<firstName<<" "<<
        lastName<<endl;
}
int Person::getId()
{
    return idNum;
}
```

Figure 10-8   `Person` class containing private data and a public function to access it, and `Customer` child class

```
class Customer : public Person
{
    private:
        double balanceDue;
    public:
        void setBalDue(double bal);
        void outputBalDue(void);
};
void Customer::setBalDue(double bal)
{
    balanceDue = bal;
}
void Customer::outputBalDue()
{
```

Figure 10-8   `Person` class containing private data and a public function to access it, and `Customer` child class (continued)

Besides being unable to directly access `private` members of a parent class, there are several other restrictions on derived classes. For example, a child class function cannot use its parent class's constructor. The following are never inherited:

- constructors

- destructors

- `friend` functions

- overloaded `new` operators

- overloaded = operators

If a derived class requires any of the preceding items, the item must be explicitly defined within the derived class definition.

TIP

Not only are `friend` functions not inherited; class friendship also is not inherited.

CHOOSING THE CLASS ACCESS SPECIFIER

When you define a derived class, you can insert one of the three class access specifiers (`public`, `private`, or `protected`) just prior to the base class name. For example, you can write any of the following to indicate that a `Customer` is a `Person`:

```
class Customer : public Person

class Customer : protected Person

class Customer : private Person
```

C++ programmers usually use the `public` access specifier for inheritance. If a derived class uses the `public` access specifier for inheritance, then the following statements are true:

- Base class members that are `public` remain `public` in the derived class.

- Base class members that are `protected` remain `protected` in the derived class.

- Base class members that are `private` are inaccessible in the derived class.

For example, if a `Customer` inherits publicly from `Person`, and `Person` contains a `protected idNum` field, then this field is also `protected` in the `Customer` class. That is, outside functions do not have access to it, but `Customer` class functions, and functions in classes that inherit from `Customer`, do have access to it.

If a derived class uses the `protected` access specifier for inheritance, then the following statements are true:

- Base class members that are `public` become `protected` in the derived class.

- Base class members that are `protected` remain `protected` in the derived class.

- Base class members that are `private` are inaccessible in the derived class.

If a derived class uses the `private` access specifier for inheritance, then the following statements are true:

- Base class members that are `public` become `private` in the derived class.

- Base class members that are `protected` become `private` in the derived class.

- Base class members that are `private` are inaccessible in the derived class.

TIP   No matter which access specifier you use when creating a child class, access to parent class members never becomes more lenient than originally coded.

In other words, `private` base class members are always inaccessible in any classes derived from them. With `private` inheritance, both `public` and `protected` base class members become `private`. With `protected` inheritance, both `public` and `protected` base class members become `protected`. With `public` inheritance, both `public` and `protected` base class members retain their original access status. Table 10-1 summarizes this discussion.

Table 10-1 The effect of inheritance access specifiers on derived class members

If inheritance access specifier is → If base class member is ↓	private	protected	public
private	inaccessible	inaccessible	inaccessible
protected	private	protected	protected
public	private	protected	public

If you do not use an access specifier when you create a derived class, access is `private` by default.

To phrase the relationships differently, if a class has `private` data members, they can be used only by member functions of that class. If a class has `protected` data members, they can be used by member functions of that class and by member functions of derived classes. If a class has `public` data members, they can be used by member functions of that class, by member functions of derived classes, and by any other functions, including the `main()` function of a program.

10

The important points to remember include:

- A class's `private` data can be accessed only by a class's member functions (or `friend` functions), and not by any functions in derived classes. If a class serves as a base class, most often its data members are `protected`, or the data members are `private` and `public` functions are provided to retrieve the values.

- The inheritance access specifier in derived classes is most often `public`, so that the derived class can refer to all nonprivate data and functions of the base class, and the nonprivate base class members retain their original accessibility level in the derived classes.

- When a class is derived from another derived class, the newly derived class never has any more liberal access to a base class member than does its immediate predecessor.

OVERRIDING INHERITED ACCESS

Nine inheritance access specifier combinations are possible: Base class members that are `private`, `protected`, or `public` can be inherited with `private`, `protected`, or `public` access. In addition, you can override the class access specifier for any specific class members. You override the class access specifier when it does not suit your needs for some members of a class. For example, consider the `InsurancePolicy` base class in

Figure 10-9. For illustration purposes, it contains data field members of each of the three types—one field, `policyNumber`, is `private`; another, `policyHolder`, is `protected`; and the third field, `annualRate`, is `public`. The `setPolicy()` and `showPolicy()` functions are also `public`.

```cpp
class InsurancePolicy
{
    private:
        int policyNumber;
    protected:
        string policyHolder;
    public:
        double annualRate;
        void setPolicy(int, string, double);
        void showPolicy();
};
void InsurancePolicy::setPolicy(int num, string name,
    double rate)
{
    policyNumber = num;
    policyHolder = name;
    annualRate = rate;
}
void InsurancePolicy::showPolicy()
{
    cout<<"Policy #"<<policyNumber<<
        "   Name: "<<policyHolder<<
        "   Annual premium : "<<annualRate<<endl;
}
```

Figure 10-9   The `InsurancePolicy` class

In the `InsurancePolicy` class in Figure 10-9, the `showPolicy()` function can refer to `policyNumber`, `policyHolder`, and `annualRate`. The function has access to all three data fields by virtue of being a member of the same class. Because the `showPolicy()` function is `public`, a `main()` function (or any other nonmember function) that uses the `InsurancePolicy` class can use `showPolicy()` to access any of the three data members.

Although it is unusual to make a class data member `public`, the field `annualRate` is `public` in the `InsurancePolicy` class. A `main()` function (or other nonmember function) can refer to `annualRate` directly, without using a class member function. For example, if you declare an `InsurancePolicy` object named `aPolicy`, then the statement `cout<<aPolicy.annualRate;` works correctly.

```
int main()
{
    InsurancePolicy aPolicy;
    aPolicy.setPolicy(17171, "Johnson", 299.95);
    cout<<"Directly from the main() function, annual rate is "
          <<aPolicy.annualRate<<endl;
    /* cout<<"Directly from the main() function, policy holder is "
          <<aPolicy.policyHolder<<endl; */
    /* cout<<"Directly from the main() function, policy number is "
          <<aPolicy.policyNumber<<endl; */
}
```

Figure 10-10   Program using the `InsurancePolicy` class

The two shaded and commented `cout` statements in Figure 10-10 are not correct. If you remove the comment designation from either of these statements, the program does not compile, and you receive an error message indicating that you cannot access `protected` or `private` members of the class. The `InsurancePolicy` class fields `policyNumber` and `policyHolder` are not accessible from within the `main()` function because they are not `public`.

If a derived class, `AutomobileInsurancePolicy`, uses the `protected` access specifier when inheriting from `InsurancePolicy`, then the following statements hold true:

- The field named `policyNumber`, which is `private` in `InsurancePolicy`, is inaccessible in the derived class.

- The field named `policyHolder`, which is `protected` in the base class, remains `protected` in the derived class.

- The field named `annualRate`, which is `public` in the base class, becomes `protected` in the derived class.

- The functions `setPolicy()` and `showPolicy()`, which are `public` in `InsurancePolicy`, become `protected` in the derived class.

In other words, with a `protected` inheritance specifier, all `public` and `protected` members of the base class become `protected` in the child class, and all `private` members of the base class remain inaccessible to the child class.

Suppose you want three of the `protected` and `public` members of the base class (`policyHolder`, `annualRate`, and `setPolicy()`) to remain `protected` in the `AutomobileInsurancePolicy` class, but you want only the `showPolicy()` function to become `public`. You can still can derive `AutomobileInsurancePolicy` with `protected` access, but you can also can override the `protected` inheritance access specifier for only the `showPolicy()` function. In the `AutomobileInsurancePolicy` class definition, you could add the code shown in Figure 10-11. The shaded statement

10

shows that access for the `showPolicy()` function is `public` within `AutomobileInsurancePolicy`, even though all other `public` members of `InsurancePolicy` are `protected` within the child, `AutomobileInsurancePolicy`. Notice that you do not use parentheses after the name of the `showPolicy()` function in the statement that alters its access. If you do, the C++ compiler attempts to declare the same function multiple times.

```
class AutomobileInsurancePolicy : protected InsurancePolicy
     // inheritance is still protected
{
     public:
          InsurancePolicy::showPolicy;
          // showPolicy() is public in the
          // AutomobileInsurancePolicy class
};
```

Figure 10-11   `AutomobileInsurancePolicy` class with one function's access overriding the class access specifier

For the `showPolicy()` function to become `public` within the `AutomobileInsurancePolicy` subclass, the shaded statement in Figure 10-11 must appear in the `public` section of the `AutomobileInsurancePolicy` class. Additionally, the `InsurancePolicy` class name and scope resolution operator must appear before the `showPolicy()` function name. Finally, and most oddly, no parentheses appear after the `showPolicy()` function name within the child class. The use of `showPolicy` indicates neither a function definition nor a function call, and you must omit the parentheses to compile the program without errors.

The `showPolicy()` function that is `public` within the `InsurancePolicy` class is also `public` in the `AutomobileInsurancePolicy` class, even though `protected` inheritance was used. The `showPolicy()` function can be used in a `main()` function (or other function) with any `InsurancePolicy` or `AutomobileInsurancePolicy` object. If `showPolicy()` remained `protected` in the child class, only functions that were members of `InsurancePolicy` or `AutomobileInsurancePolicy` (or their future descendants) could use it.

TIP   Within the `AutomobileInsurancePolicy` class, the `protected` access specifier is overridden for the `showPolicy()` function. In this example, `showPolicy()` is allowed more liberal access than are other inherited class members, but the function does not have more liberal access than it originally had in `InsurancePolicy`. You can never override a function's original access specifier in a parent class to make it more liberal in the child. However, you can override the inherited access to make an individual member's access more conservative.

Remember: For most C++ classes, data is `private` or `protected`, and most functions are `public`. Most inheritance is activated with `public` access so that child class members retain the same access that's available in the parent class. However, you can achieve a variety of effects by inheriting with any of the three access specifiers, and overriding the access specifier for particular child class members.

OVERRIDING AND OVERLOADING PARENT CLASS FUNCTIONS

When a new class is derived from an existing class, the derived class has access to non-private member functions in the base class. The new class also can have its own member functions. Those functions can have names that are identical to the function names in the base class. Any child class function with the same name and argument list as the parent overrides the parent function; any child class function with the same name as the parent, yet with an argument list that differs from the parent's, overloads the parent function.

TIP   When a child class function overrides a parent class function, you can say you have redefined the function.

10

Recall the `Person` class from Figure 10-8, and repeated for your convenience in Figure 10-12. (In this example, the data fields have been declared `protected` so a child class can access them directly.) It contains three fields (`idNum`, `lastName`, and `firstName`) and three functions (`setFields()`, `outputData()`, and `getId()`).

```
class Person
{
    protected:
        int idNum;
        string lastName;
        string firstName;
    public:
        void setFields(int, string, string);
        void outputData();
        int getId();
};
void Person::setFields(int num, string last, string first)
{
    idNum = num;
    lastName = last;
    firstName = first;
}
```

Figure 10-12   The `Person` class

```
void Person::outputData()
{
    cout<<"ID #"<<idNum<<" Name: "<<firstName<<" "<<
        lastName<<endl;
}
int Person::getId()
{
    return idNum;
}
```

Figure 10-12   The `Person` class (continued)

Suppose you create a class named `Employee` that derives from `Person`. The `Employee` class inherits the members of `Person`, so every `Employee` has an `idNum`, `lastName`, and `firstName`; additionally, `Employee` includes a department number and an hourly pay rate. The `Employee` class also includes a new `setFields()` function because it has additional data members—a department number and pay rate—that must be accommodated. Figure 10-13 shows the definition of the `Employee` class. The shaded `setFields()` function has the same name as the `setFields()` function in the parent `Person` class, but has an extended argument list so that values can be assigned for department number and pay.

```
class Employee : public Person
{
    private:
        int dept;
        double hourlyRate;
    public:
        void setFields(int, string, string, int, double);
};
```

Figure 10-13   The `Employee` class definition

The `Employee setFields()` function in Figure 10-13 receives values that are intended for fields that are defined in the parent `Person` class, as well as for fields defined within the `Employee` class. The `Employee::setFields()` function could directly assign values to `idNum`, `lastName`, and `firstName`, as shown in Figure 10-14. The shaded lines of code in Figure 10-14 are identical to lines of code in the parent class version of `setFields()`, so you can also rewrite the `Employee` class `setFields()` function to call `Person`'s `setFields()` function. This version appears in Figure 10-15. You can use either version of `Employee::setFields()`—the one shown in Figure 10-14 or Figure 10-15—but the one in Figure 10-15 requires less work on your part and takes advantage of code reusability.

```
void Employee:: setFields(int num, string last,
    string first, int dep, double sal);
{
    idNum = num;
    lastName = last;
    firstName = first;
    dept = dep;
    hourlyRate = sal;
}
```

Figure 10-14   `Employee::setFields()` directly assigning values for parent class fields

```
void Employee:: setFields(int num, string last,
    string first, int dep, double sal)
{
    Person::setFields(num, last, first);
    dept = dep;
    hourlyRate = sal;
}
```

Figure 10-15   Improved `Employee::setFields()` that calls `Person::setFields()`

TIP

The version of the `Employee::setFields()` function in Figure 10-15 could be used even if the data fields in the **Person** class were declared to be private rather than `protected`.

In the shaded statement in the `setFields()` function in Figure 10-15, the values for `num`, `last`, and `first` are passed to the parent class function, where they are assigned to the appropriate fields. It's important to use the parent class name (**Person**) and the scope resolution operator when calling `setFields()`. Without them, the `Employee::setFields()` function attempts to call itself, which is incorrect.

When you use the `Employee` class defined in Figure 10-13 to instantiate an `Employee` object with a statement such as `Employee Worker;`, then the call to `Worker.setFields();` uses the child class function with the name `setFields()`. When used with a child class object, the child class function overloads the parent class version because it uses a different number of arguments. On the other hand, the statement `Worker.outputData();` uses the parent class function because no child class function has the name `outputData()`. Figure 10-16 shows both complete classes and a `main()` function that creates two objects—a `Person` object and an `Employee` object. Each object uses a unique `setFields()` function, but uses the same `outputData()` function. The output is shown in Figure 10-17.

```cpp
#include<iostream>
#include<string>
using namespace std;
class Person
{
  private:
    int idNum;
    string lastName;
    string firstName;
  public:
    void setFields(int num, string last, string first);
    void outputData();
    int getId();
};
void Person::setFields(int num, string last, string first)
{
    idNum = num;
    lastName = last;
    firstName = first;
}
void Person::outputData()
{
    cout<<"ID #"<<idNum<<" Name: "<<firstName<<" "<<
        lastName<<endl;
}
int Person::getId()
{
    return idNum;
}
```

Figure 10-16 Program using a `Person` and an `Employee`

```
class Employee : public Person
{
   private:
      int dept;
      double hourlyRate;
   public:
      void setFields(int, string, string, int, double);
};
void Employee::setFields(int num, string last, string first,
   int dep, double sal)
{
   Person::setFields(num, last, first);
   dept = dep;
   hourlyRate = sal;
}
int main()
{
   Person aPerson;
   aPerson.setFields(123, "Kroening", "Ginny");
   aPerson.outputData();
   cout<<endl;
   Employee worker;
   worker.setFields(987, "Lewis", "Kathy", 6, 23.55);
   worker.outputData();
   cout<<endl;
}
```

10

Figure 10-16   Program using a `Person` and an `Employee` (continued)

Figure 10-17   Output of program in Figure 10-16

The output in Figure 10-17 shows that even though you set fields for a `Person` and an `Employee` by using separate functions that require separate argument lists, you use the same `outputData()` function that exists only within the parent class for both a `Person` and an `Employee`. If you want the `Employee` class to contain its own `outputData()` function, you can override the parent version of that function as well. Figure 10-18 shows possible `Person` and `Employee` class versions of `outputData()`. If you add the `Employee::outputData()` function to the class (and add a prototype for the function in the class definition), then when you run the same `main()` function shown in Figure 10-18, the new output looks like Figure 10-19.

```
void Person::outputData()
{
    cout<<"ID #"<<idNum<<" Name: "<<firstName<<" "<<
        lastName<<endl;
}
void Employee::outputData()
{
    cout<<"A valued employee:"<<endl;
    Person::outputData();
    cout<<"Department #"<<dept<<" Pay rate $"<<
        hourlyRate<<endl;
}
```

Figure 10-18   Person and Employee class versions of outputData()

Figure 10-19   Output of program in Figure 10-16 when Employee::outputData() function in Figure 10-18 is added to the Employee class

Within the Employee::outputData() function, it's important to use the class name Person and the scope resolution operator in the statement Person:: outputData(); (see shading). If the Person class name is not used, the Employee:: outputData() function calls itself. That call results in another call to itself, and an infinite loop executes.

The different output formats in Figure 10-19 verify that the outputData() function called using the Person object differs from the outputData() function called using the Employee object. Any Person object calls the Person functions. If a class derived from Person has functions with the same names as the Person class functions, the new class functions override the base class functions. The exception occurs when you use a class specifier with a function name, as in one of the following:

```
worker.Person::setFields(id,last,first);
```

```
worker.Person::outputData();
```

Using the class name Person indicates precisely which version of setFields() or outputData() should be called. Thus, a child class object can use its own functions or its parent's (as long as the parent functions are not private). The opposite is not true— a parent object cannot use its child's functions. In other words, an Employee is a Person and can do all the things a Person can do. However, every Person is not an Employee; therefore, a Person cannot use Employee functions.

A derived class object can be assigned to a base class object, as in `aPerson = worker;`. The assignment causes each data member to be copied from `worker` to `aPerson`, and leaves off any data for which the base class doesn't have members. The reverse assignment cannot take place without writing a specialized function.

Because each child is a more specific instance of a parent, you can create an array of parent class objects, and store either parent or child class objects in each element of the array. If you do this, the child class objects become members of the parent class, losing any more specific child class data.

The `outputData()` function used by members of the `Employee` class remain separate from the version used by members of the `Person` class. These functions are not overloaded. Overloaded functions, you will recall, require different parameter lists, and the `outputData()` functions in `Person` and `Employee` have identical parameter lists. Instead, `Employee`'s `outputData()` function *overrides* the `outputData()` function defined in `Person`.

If a base class contains a function that the derived class should not have, you can create a dummy, or empty, function with the same name in the derived class. If a derived class object uses this function name, no statements are executed.

10

In summary, when any class member function is called, the following steps take place:

1. The compiler looks for a matching function (name and argument list) in the class of the object using the function name (also called the class of the object **invoking the method**).

2. If no match is found in this class, the compiler looks for a matching function in the parent class.

3. If no match is found in the parent class, the compiler continues up the inheritance hierarchy, looking at the parent of the parent, until the base class is reached.

4. If no match is found in any class, an error message is issued.

Overriding a base class member function with a derived member function demonstrates the concept of polymorphism. (In Chapter 9, you learned that this type of polymorphism is sometimes referred to as pure polymorphism.) Recall that polymorphism permits the same function name to take many forms. When you inherit functions and then override them with identically named functions that have identical argument lists in a subclass, the same message can be carried out appropriately by different objects. Just as the command "play" invokes different responses in a CD player and a baseball player, a program command with a name such as `setFields()`, `outputData()`, giveInstructions(), or any other name can invoke different responses in different objects. This process models the way things work in the real world, and is a basic feature—and advantage—of object-oriented programming.

PROVIDING FOR BASE CLASS CONSTRUCTION

When you instantiate an object in a C++ program, you automatically call its constructor function. This pattern holds true whether you write a custom constructor or use a default constructor. When you instantiate a class object that has been derived from another class, a constructor for the base class is called first, followed by the derived class constructor. This format is followed even if the base and derived classes both have only default constructors. If a base class does not contain a default constructor—that is, if the base class contains only constructors that require arguments—then you must provide a constructor for every derived class, even if the derived class does not need a constructor for any other reason.

For example, consider a class developed for all items sold by a pet store. As shown in Figure 10-20, the PetStoreItem class might contain data members for stock number and price. The constructor accepts values for the arguments and assigns them.

```
class PetStoreItem
{
    protected:
        int stockNum;
        double price;
    public:
        PetStoreItem(int, double);
};
PetStoreItem::PetStoreItem(int stock, double pr)
{
    stockNum = stock;
    price = pr;
}
```

Figure 10-20   The PetStoreItem class

The management personnel of a pet store might want to create several derived classes from PetStoreItem. For example, a specialized class would be appropriate for animals in the store; other specialized classes might support food items, pet accessories, books, training classes, and so on. You can create a derived PetStoreAnimal class that contains all members of PetStoreItem, plus a data field for the age of the pet and its own constructor. Figure 10-21 shows the class definition for PetStoreAnimal.

```
class PetStoreAnimal : public PetStoreItem
{
   protected:
      int petAge;
   public:
      PetStoreAnimal(int);
};
```

Figure 10-21 The `PetStoreAnimal` class with incomplete constructor

If the `PetStoreAnimal` class were merely a noninheriting or base class, its constructor could have the following implementation:

```
PetStoreAnimal::PetStoreAnimal(int age)
{
   petAge = age;
}
```

If `PetStoreAnimal` were a simple base class, the `PetStoreAnimal` class constructor could require just an integer argument that would be assigned to the `petAge` field. However, because `PetStoreAnimal` is derived from `PetStoreItem`, when a child class object is instantiated, a `PetStoreItem` object is constructed first, and the `PetStoreItem` class constructor is called. The `PetStoreItem` constructor requires arguments for `stockNum` and `price`, so those arguments have to be provided to the constructor.

TIP If you fail to call a needed base class constructor for a derived class object, you will receive an error message such as, "No appropriate default constructor available" to initialize the base class.

The `PetStoreAnimal` class constructor must provide values for all the arguments it needs as well as all the arguments its parent needs. In other words, the `PetStoreAnimal` class needs values for the stock number and price so that `PetStoreItem` can be constructed. The values can be constant or variable. For example, one possible `PetStoreAnimal` constructor implementation might be the following:

```
PetStoreAnimal::PetStoreAnimal(int age) :
   PetStoreItem(1234, 69.95)
{
   petAge = age;
}
```

In this example, two constant values—1234 and 69.95—are provided for the parent constructor. Another possibility is to revise the `PetStoreAnimal` constructor prototype so it accepts three arguments, as follows:

```
PetStoreAnimal::PetStoreAnimal(int, double, int);
```

10

With this definition, the constructor accepts three arguments: a stock number and a price as well as an age. Then the constructor implementation might be the following:

```
PetStoreAnimal::PetStoreAnimal(int stock, double price,
   int age) : PetStoreItem(stock, price)
{
   petAge = age;
}
```

In this example, the constructor takes three arguments and passes two of them on to the parent class constructor.

Figure 10-22 shows complete, functional `PetStoreItem` and `PetStoreAnimal` classes as well as a `main()` function that does nothing but initialize one `PetStoreAnimal` object.

```
#include<iostream>
using namespace std;
class PetStoreItem
{
   protected:
      int stockNum;
      double price;
   public:
      PetStoreItem(int, double);
};
PetStoreItem::PetStoreItem(int stock, double pr)
{
   stockNum = stock;
   price = pr;
}
class PetStoreAnimal : public PetStoreItem
{
   protected:
      int petAge;
   public:
      PetStoreAnimal(int, double, int);
};
PetStoreAnimal::PetStoreAnimal(int stock, double price, int age) :
   PetStoreItem(stock, price)
{
   petAge = age;
}
int main()
{
   PetStoreAnimal aKitten(111, 45.00, 1);
}
```

Figure 10-22 `PetStoreItem` and `PetStoreAnimal` classes, and a `main()` function

When you construct a derived class object, the base class constructor is called first. When a derived class object is destroyed, the opposite order prevails: The child class destructor is called first and the base class destructor is called last.

TIP

Although it is not required, if you list child class constructor arguments in the same order as you list the parent class constructor arguments, your programs will be easier to follow and maintain.

TIP

Figure 10-23 shows one more option for coding the `PetStoreAnimal` class. This example uses an initialization list in the prototype for the constructor. (See shaded statement.) The constructor takes three arguments. After the colon, two arguments (`stock` and `price`) are passed to the parent class constructor, and the third argument (`age`) is assigned to the child class data field. Using this technique, you do not need to write a function body for the constructor; the assignments are made from within the prototype. The advantage to using this format is that it is more concise, and it reflects the immediate purpose of `stock`, `price`, and `age`—they are initialization values.

In Chapter 8, you learned to use an initialization list when you create a class that contains a class object as one of its members, and the contained class has a nondefault constructor.

TIP

10

```
class PetStoreAnimal : public PetStoreItem
{
   protected:
      int petAge;
   public:
      PetStoreAnimal(int stock, double price, int age) :
         PetStoreItem(stock,price), petAge(age){};
};
```

Figure 10-23   Alternate code for the `PetStoreAnimal` class

If a default base class constructor exists, then no compiler error arises if you omit the call to the base class constructor when deriving a class. It is perfectly okay to use the default base class constructor with a derived class if that suits your purpose.

TIP

You do not have to pass a variable to a base class constructor that requires an argument; you can pass a constant of the same type. For example, if you want all `PetStoreAnimal` objects to cost $99.95, then you might create a `PetStoreAnimal` constructor such as:

```
PetStoreAnimal(int stock, int age) :
PetStoreItem(stock, 99.95), petAge(age){};
```

TIP

USING MULTIPLE INHERITANCE

A base class may have many derived classes. For example, a company might create an `Employee` base class, and derive `SalariedEmployee`, `HourlyEmployee`, and `ContractEmployee` classes from it. An `InsurancePolicy` class might be the basis for `AutomobileInsurancePolicy`, `HomeOwnersInsurancePolicy`, `HealthInsurancePolicy`, and `LifeInsurancePolicy` classes. When a child class derives from a single parent, you are using **single inheritance**.

A child class can also derive from more than one base class; this type of inheritance is called **multiple inheritance**. For example, suppose you work for a financial services company and have already developed two classes of objects on which you make loans: the classes are named `Vehicle` and `Dwelling`. The `Vehicle` class contains data members such as a vehicle identification number, make, and number of miles the vehicle can travel on a gallon of gas. The `Dwelling` class contains data members such as number of bedrooms and area in square feet. The two classes are defined in Figures 10-24 and 10-25.

```
class Vehicle
{
   protected:
     int idNumber;
     string make;
     double milesPerGallon;
   public:
     Vehicle(int, string, double);
     void display();
};
Vehicle::Vehicle(int id, string make, double mpg)
{
     idNumber = id;
     this->make = make;
     milesPerGallon = mpg;
}
void Vehicle::display()
{
     cout<<"ID #"<<idNumber<<"  Make: "<<make<<
         " gets "<<milesPerGallon<<" miles per gallon"<<endl;
}
```

Figure 10-24   The `Vehicle` class

```
class Dwelling
{
    protected:
       int numberOfBedrooms;
       int squareFeet;
    public:
       Dwelling(int, int);
       void display();
};
Dwelling::Dwelling(int bedrooms, int sqFeet)
{
    numberOfBedrooms = bedrooms;
    squareFeet = sqFeet;
}
void Dwelling::display()
{
    cout<<numberOfBedrooms<<" bedrooms and "<<
       squareFeet<<" square feet"<<endl;
}
```

Figure 10-25   The `Dwelling` class

Next, suppose a client applies for a loan on a recreational vehicle—a vehicle that "is a" `Vehicle` (you drive it; it runs on gas), but also "is a" `Dwelling` (you sleep, cook, and live in it, at least during road trips). You might choose to create a new class named `RV` that inherits from both `Vehicle` and `Dwelling`. Figure 10-26 shows a simple version of the class.

```
class RV : public Vehicle, public Dwelling
{
    public:
         RV(int, string, double, int, int);
         void display();
};
RV::RV(int id, string make, double mpg, int bedrooms, int sqFt) :
    Vehicle(id, make, mpg), Dwelling(bedrooms, sqFt)
{
}
void RV::display()
{
    cout<<"A recreational vehicle: "<<endl;
    Vehicle::display();
    Dwelling::display();
}
```

Figure 10-26   The `RV` class

The `RV` class in Figure 10-26 inherits from both `Vehicle` and `Dwelling`, so both classes are listed after the colon in the class header, separated by a comma. (The class access specifier for each is `public`; you could also choose `private` or `protected`.) The RV class in Figure 10-26 includes all of the data members of each of its parents' classes. In this case, the child class contains no new data fields, but it could. The RV class also has access to its parents' functions, and adds two of its own: a constructor and a `display()` function.

Five arguments are required in the header for the RV class constructor; three are passed to the `Vehicle` constructor and the other two are passed to the `Dwelling` constructor. Additional arguments could have been required and used within the RV constructor. However, in this example, because the RV class declares no new fields of its own, the constructor body is empty.

You can place any statements you like within the RV class `display()` function. In this case, because the parent classes already contained useable `display()` functions, those functions are simply called from the child. The scope resolution operators are necessary with the two calls to the parent `display()` functions, both to distinguish them from the child class function with the same name, and to distinguish them from each other. (If the child class function was not named `display()` and only one parent class contained a `display()` function, then no scope resolution operator would be necessary to use the function.)

Figure 10-27 shows a `main()` function that creates and displays an RV object, and Figure 10-28 shows the output.

```
int main()
{
    RV aRecreationalVehicle(2345, "Winnebago", 12, 2, 110);
    aRecreationalVehicle.display();
}
```

Figure 10-27   A `main()` function instantiating an RV object

Figure 10-28   Output of program in Figure 10-27

 You already use multiple inheritance each time you include `iostream` in a program. Each `cin` and `cout` object is derived from other classes. (Chapter 11 provides more details on this example of multiple inheritance.)

TIP

Multiple inheritance made developing the RV class quicker than it would have been without the technique. Fields for identification number, make of vehicle, miles per gallon, number of bedrooms, and square feet did not have to be redefined in the RV class, because their definitions were already handled by the parent classes. Writing the details of the `display()` function was streamlined because much of the output had already been formatted in the parent class versions of the function. Of course, this example is short to help you follow the logic, but in a class with dozens or even hundreds of members, you can imagine that the time saved by inheriting from already developed classes would be even greater.

DISADVANTAGES OF USING MULTIPLE INHERITANCE

Some programmers are vehemently opposed to using multiple inheritance. They may even insist that when multiple inheritance is needed, you should suspect a bad class design. Multiple inheritance is never required to solve a programming problem; the same results always can be achieved through single inheritance. For example, the RV class could be written to inherit from the Vehicle class alone, but could contain a Dwelling object as a data member instead of inheriting from two classes. (If your vision of an RV is that it "is a" Vehicle that contains a Dwelling, then this would be a superior approach. If your vision of an RV is that is "is a" Vehicle *as well as* a Dwelling, then multiple inheritance is more logical.)

10

One problem with multiple inheritance is that if two parent classes contain members with the same name (as with the `display()` function in the Vehicle and Dwelling classes), then you must use the resolution operator when working with those members. Even though the dilemma of identically named functions in two parent classes is resolved fairly easily, many programmers avoid multiple inheritance because of this type of problem.

You have learned that a derived class must often call its parent class constructor with an initialization list. A derived class with more than one parent must provide for the constructors of all parents, so the syntax can become quite long. The definition of a class that inherits from a single parent is almost always easier to understand and less prone to error than the definition of a class that inherits from two or more base classes.

TIP
As proof that multiple inheritance is never required, consider that the widely used object-oriented programming languages Smalltalk and Java both allow only single inheritance, and manage quite nicely.

As you advance in your programming career, you will have to decide when using multiple inheritance is appropriate. If you work as a programmer for an organization, there might be policies prohibiting or discouraging its use. However, in your own programs, if you need a class that truly "is a" member of two existing classes, you might be able to save a lot of development time by using multiple inheritance.

USING VIRTUAL BASE CLASSES

You already know that a base class may have many descendants through single inheritance. A college might use a **Person** base class, for example, and create child classes **Student**, **Employee**, and **Alumnus**. You also know that a class may inherit from two other classes through multiple inheritance. For example, a **StudentEmployee** class might inherit from both **Student** and **Employee**, as a **StudentEmployee** object might take advantage of already developed functions in each of its parent classes. The class definition for **StudentEmployee** would begin as follows:

```
class StudentEmployee : public Student, public Employee
```

Figure 10-29 shows the relationship that occurs when **StudentEmployee** inherits from both **Student** and **Employee**, and both **Student** and **Employee** inherit from **Person**. The **StudentEmployee** class ends up being a descendant of **Person** two times; without intervention, **StudentEmployee** would end up with two copies of each member of **Person**.

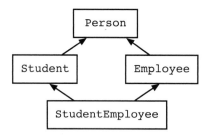

Figure 10-29 Diagram of the family tree of the **StudentEmployee** class

To avoid this duplicate inheritance, you use the keyword **virtual** when you define each of the child classes. The word **virtual** indicates that the base class should be used only once. The headers of the classes become:

```
class Student : virtual public Person
```
and
```
class Employee : virtual public Person
```
Now when **StudentEmployee** is defined as

```
class StudentEmployee : public Student, public Employee
```
the members of **Person** are included just once in **StudentEmployee**.

Alternately, you could define **StudentEmployee** using the keyword **virtual** in *its* class definition, as follows:

```
class StudentEmployee : virtual public Student, virtual
public Employee
```

By adding `virtual` to the `StudentEmployee` inheritance definition, you forestall problems when new classes are created based on `StudentEmployee` and another of the classes in its family tree.

Handling the constructor functions when a class is derived from two classes with a common ancestor can be complicated. When a `StudentEmployee` object is constructed, it needs to construct its base classes. If its base classes, `Student` and `Employee`, both are constructed as usual (without using the keyword `virtual`), then `Person` would be constructed twice. Therefore, when you write the `StudentEmployee` class constructor, it must handle the construction needs of `Student`, `Employee`, and `Person`.

For example, if `Person` requires values for ID number and name, `Student` requires a grade point average, `Employee` requires an hourly rate, and `StudentEmployee` requires a limit on the number of hours allowed to work per week, then the `StudentEmployee` constructor might take the following form:

```
StudentEmployee (int idNum, string name, double gradePoint,
    double hourlyRate, int workHoursLimit) :
    StudentEmployee (workHoursLimit), Person(idNum, name),
    Student(gradePoint), Employee(hourlyRate) { };
```

If the `Student` and `Employee` classes did not use the word `virtual`, each would construct a `Person`. Because the `virtual` keyword is used when `Student` and `Employee` inherit from `Person`, the construction of `Student` and `Employee` does not prompt the construction of `Person`. Instead, `StudentEmployee` must construct all of its ancestors; that is, `StudentEmployee` must construct `Person`, `Student`, and `Employee`.

 Many of the constructor complications that occur when inheriting from multiple classes are minimized if you always include a default constructor for every class.

TIP

You Do It

Creating a Base Class

In the next sets of steps, you create two classes: `Car` and `Convertible`. The `Car` class serves as a base class and includes features common to all cars—an ignition that is off or on, and a current speed. The `Convertible` class extends the `Car` class so that a `Convertible` possesses the added feature of a top that lowers and raises. These steps create and test the `Car` class.

    1. Open a new file in your C++ editor, and type the statements you need to create the `Car` class.

10

```
#include<iostream>
using namespace std;
```

2. The `Car` class contains two fields. One is a `bool` flag indicating whether the ignition is on; the other holds the `Car`'s current speed in miles per hour. There are four member functions: two functions that turn the ignition on and off, a function that sets the `Car`'s speed, and a function that displays the `Car`'s status. (If your compiler does not support type `bool`, you can use `int` as the type for `isIgnitionOn`, setting it to 0 when the ignition is off, and 1 when it is on.)

```
class Car
{
   private:
       bool isIgnitionOn;
       int speed;
   public:
       void turnIgnitionOn();
       void turnIgnitionOff();
       void setSpeed(int);
       void showCar();
};
```

TIP

To keep this example short, the `Car` class contains no constructor. However, in a fully functional class you might consider instantiating every `Car` object with the ignition off and a speed of 0.

3. The function that displays the values of a `Car`'s fields uses the value of the `isIgnitionOn` flag to determine whether the `Car` is running. It also displays the current speed of the `Car`.

```
void Car::showCar()
{
   if(isIgnitionOn)
        cout<<"Ignition is on. ";
   else
        cout<<"Ignition is off. ";
   cout<<"Speed is "<<speed<<endl;
}
```

4. The two functions named `turnIgnitionOn()` and `turnIgnitionOff()` are similar; each sets the value of the `isIgnitionOn` flag, making it `true` or `false`. Additionally, when you turn the ignition off, it makes sense to set the `Car`'s speed to 0.

```
void Car::turnIgnitionOn()
{
    isIgnitionOn = true;
}
void Car::turnIgnitionOff()
{
    speed = 0;
    isIgnitionOn = false;
}
```

5. The `setSpeed()` function takes an integer argument and uses it to set the value of the `speed` field. However, no `Car` is allowed a speed greater than 65 miles per hour, and no `Car` is allowed any speed other than 0 if the ignition is off.

```
void Car::setSpeed(int mph)
{
    const int STD_LIMIT = 65;
    if(isIgnitionOn)
        if (mph <= STD_LIMIT)
            speed = mph;
        else
            speed = STD_LIMIT;
    else
        cout<<"Can't set speed - ignition is off!"<<endl;
}
```

10

TIP

When developing a complete `Car` class, you might consider rejecting negative speeds as well as those over the standard speed limit.

6. Add a `main()` function that demonstrates the class functions at work. The `main()` function declares a `Car` object, turns the `Car` on and sets a speed, shows the `Car` values, and so on.

```
int main()
{
    Car myCar;
    myCar.turnIgnitionOn();
    myCar.setSpeed(35);
    myCar.showCar();
    myCar.setSpeed(70);
    myCar.showCar();
    myCar.turnIgnitionOff();
    myCar.showCar();
}
```

7. Save the file as **Car.cpp**. Compile and run the program. The output appears in Figure 10-30. Notice that even though the `main()` function attempts to set the `Car`'s speed at 70 miles per hour at one point, the `setSpeed()` function enforces a limit of 65 miles per hour.

Figure 10-30   Output of Car.cpp program

Creating a Child Class

The `Car` class doesn't contain anything unusual; you have already created many classes like it. You could create a similar class from scratch to use for a `Convertible`, but it is more convenient to create a child class derived from `Car`. You create the `Convertible` class and a demonstration program in the next set of steps.

1. Remove the entire `main()` function from the Car.cpp file, and save the abbreviated file as **Convertible.cpp**. You will create the `Convertible` class within this new file.

TIP

As an alternative to creating the `Convertible` class in the same file as the `Car` class, you could save the `Car` class in a file by itself and include it (by using a `#include` statement) in a new file named Convertible.cpp.

2. At the bottom of the file, after the existing `Car` class code, define the `Convertible` class as an extension of the `Car` class. The `Convertible` class contains one new data member named `isTopUp` that holds the status of the `Convertible`'s top. Three functions work with this data field: one puts the top up, another puts it down, and the third displays the `Convertible`'s status, including the state of its top.

```
class Convertible: public Car
{
  private:
    bool isTopUp;
  public:
    void putTopUp();
    void putTopDown();
    void showCar();
};
```

3. The functions `putTopUp()` and `putTopDown()` set the `isTopUp` field to `true` and `false` respectively.

```
void Convertible::putTopUp()
{
    isTopUp = true;
}
```

```cpp
void Convertible::putTopDown()
{
    isTopUp = false;
}
```

4. The showCar() function overrides the parent class function with the same name. It calls the parent class function to display the status of the ignition and speed, then also displays an appropriate message based on the status of the isTopUp field.

```cpp
void Convertible::showCar()
{
    Car::showCar();
    if(isTopUp)
        cout<<"Top is up."<<endl;
    else
        cout<<"Top is down."<<endl;
}
```

5. Finally, create a main() function that declares a Convertible object and uses the functions to start the Convertible, set the speed, put the top down and up, and so on.

```cpp
int main()
{
    Convertible myCar;
    myCar.turnIgnitionOn();
    myCar.setSpeed(35);
    myCar.putTopDown();
    myCar.showCar();
    myCar.setSpeed(70);
    myCar.showCar();
    myCar.putTopUp();
    myCar.turnIgnitionOff();
    myCar.showCar();
}
```

6. Save the file again as **Convertible.cpp**. Compile and run the program. The output looks like Figure 10-31. Notice that the Convertible object has access to all the Car functions as well as its own more specific functions.

10

Ignition is on. Speed is 35
Top is down.
Ignition is on. Speed is 65
Top is down.
Ignition is off. Speed is 0
Top is up.
Press any key to continue . . .

Figure 10-31   Output of Convertible.cpp program

Creating Another Child Class

In the next set of steps, you create a RaceCar class as a child of the Car class you created earlier. A RaceCar has all the attributes of a Car, but its maximum allowed speed is higher.

1. Open the **Car.cpp** file. Remove the main() function and save the modified file as **RaceCar.cpp**.

2. Change the Car class private access specifier to protected so that when you extend the Car class, its child can use the Car data fields directly.

3. At the bottom of the file, define the RaceCar class to extend Car and include one new setSpeed() function that overrides the Car class setSpeed() function.

```
class RaceCar : public Car
{
   public:
   void setSpeed(int mph);
};
```

4. Implement the RaceCar::setSpeed() function so that it sets the RaceCar speed to the value passed into the function, as long as the speed is not more than 200 miles per hour. Recall that the Car speed limit is only 65 miles per hour.

```
void RaceCar::setSpeed(int mph)
{
   const int MAX_SPEED = 200;
   if(isIgnitionOn)
      if (mph <= MAX_SPEED)
         speed = mph;
      else
         speed = MAX_SPEED;
   else
      cout<<"Can't set speed - ignition is off!"<<endl;
}
```

5. Write a main() function that instantiates a Car and a RaceCar. Use the setSpeed() function to attempt to set the speed of each object to 80, and then display the results.

```
int main()
{
   Car aCar;
   RaceCar aRaceCar;
   aCar.turnIgnitionOn();
   aCar.setSpeed(80);
   cout<<"Car at 80 mph: ";
   aCar.showCar();
```

```
    aRaceCar.turnIgnitionOn();
    aRaceCar.setSpeed(80);
    cout<<"Race car at 80 mph: ";
    aRaceCar.showCar();
}
```

6. Save the file as **RaceCar.cpp** and compile it. Execute the program. The results appear in Figure 10-32. When you attempt to set the `Car` speed to 80, it is reduced to 65. However, 80 is an acceptable speed for a `RaceCar`. Each object uses its own class's version of the `setSpeed()` function.

Figure 10-32   Output of RaceCar.cpp program

7. Change the speed values for the `Car` and the `RaceCar`, then compile and run the program again to ensure that the functions work correctly, whether the set speed is higher or lower than the cutoff values of 65 and 200.

Using Multiple Inheritance

In the next set of steps, you create a new class `ConvertibleRaceCar` that inherits from both `Convertible` and `RaceCar`.

1. Either paste the definitions of the three classes `Car`, `Convertible`, and `RaceCar` into the same file, or start a new file and use `#include` statements to include these files in a new file.

2. Create the `ConvertibleRaceCar` class which contains no new data members or functions of its own.

```
class ConvertibleRaceCar : public Convertible,
    public RaceCar
{
};
```

3. Add a `main()` function that instantiates a `ConvertibleRaceCar` and tests all the functions that originated with the parent classes—attempting to set various speeds and lowering and raising the top.

```
int main()
{
    ConvertibleRaceCar aCar;
    aCar.turnIgnitionOn();
    aCar.setSpeed(30);
    cout<<"Car at 30 mph: ";
    aCar.showCar();
    aCar.putTopDown();
    aCar.setSpeed(80);
    cout<<"Car at 80 mph with top down: ";
    aCar.showCar();
    aCar.putTopUp();
    aCar.setSpeed(210);
    cout<<"Car at 210 mph with top up: ";
    aCar.showCar();
}
```

4. Save the file as **ConvertibleRaceCar.cpp** and compile the program. You should receive error messages that indicate functions such as `turnIgnitionOn()` are ambiguous because they exist in both parent classes. To rectify this, add the keyword `virtual` to the class headers of the `Convertible` and `RaceCar` classes as shown in the shaded sections here:

```
class Convertible : virtual public Car
class RaceCar : virtual public Car
```

Adding the `virtual` keyword insures that the members of the original base class, `Car`, are inherited only once.

5. Save the file, compile, and execute it again. The output appears in Figure 10-33. Even though the `ConvertibleRaceCar` class has no members of its own, it has access to all the nonprivate data fields and functions of its ancestors.

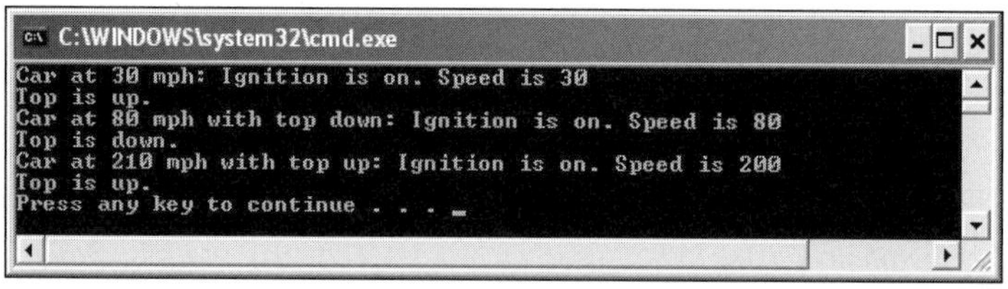

Figure 10-33   Output of ConvertibleRaceCar.cpp program

Chapter Summary

❐ Inheritance in C++ means you can create classes that derive their attributes from existing classes; in other words, a newly created class can absorb all the data fields and functions of a class already being used. When one class is derived from another, the original class is the parent class, base class, superclass, or ancestor; the derived class is a child class, subclass, or descendant.

❐ To be truly "object-oriented," a programming language must allow inheritance. Programs in which you derive new classes from existing classes offer several advantages; much of the code needed for your class is already written and tested.

❐ To create a derived class, you include the keyword `class`, the derived class name, a colon, a class access specifier (either `public`, `private`, or `protected`), the base class name, an opening brace, class definition statements, a closing brace, and a semicolon.

❐ When a class serves as a base class to other classes, all of its members are included when you create an object from a derived class. However, the members of the base class that are `private` are not directly accessible from within the child class functions. The access specifiers follow these rules: `private` data and functions can be accessed only within a class, `protected` data and functions can be accessed only by class functions or by functions in child classes, and `public` data and functions can be accessed anywhere. The following are never inherited: constructors, destructors, `friend` functions, static data members, static member functions, overloaded `new` operators, and overloaded = operators.

❐ When you define a derived class, you can insert one of the three class access specifiers (`public`, `private`, or `protected`) just prior to the base class name. C++ programmers usually use the `public` access specifier for inheritance. A class's `private` data can be accessed only by a class's member functions (or `friend` functions), and not by any functions in derived classes. If a class serves as a base class, most often its data members are `protected`—or the data members are `private` and `public` functions are provided to retrieve the values. The inheritance access specifier in derived classes is most often `public`, so that the derived class can refer to all nonprivate data and functions of the base class, and the nonprivate base class members retain their original accessibility level in the derived classes. When a class is derived from another derived class, the newly derived class never has any more liberal access to a base class member than does its immediate predecessor.

❐ Nine inheritance access specifier combinations are possible: base class members that are `private`, `protected`, or `public` can be inherited with `private`,

10

protected, or public access. In addition, you can override the class access specifier for any derived class member. For most C++ classes, data is private or protected, and most functions are public. Most inheritance is activated with public access so that child class members retain the same access that's available in the parent class. However, you can achieve a variety of effects by inheriting with any of the three access specifiers, and overriding the access specifier for particular child class members.

❑ Any child class function with the same name and argument list as the parent overrides the parent function; any child class function with the same name as the parent, yet with an argument that differs from the parent's, overloads the parent function. When any class member function is called, the compiler looks for a matching function in the class of the object using the function name. If no match is found in this class, the compiler looks for a matching function in the parent class, and then in its parent. If no match is found in any class, an error message is issued. Overriding a base class member function with a derived member function demonstrates the concept of polymorphism.

❑ When you instantiate a class object that has been derived from another class, a constructor for the base class is called first, followed by the derived class constructor. If a base class does not contain a default constructor—that is, if the base class contains only constructors that require arguments—then you must provide a constructor for every derived class, even if the derived class does not need a constructor for any other reason.

❑ A base class may have many derived classes. A child class can also derive from more than one base class; this type of inheritance is called multiple inheritance.

❑ Some programmers are vehemently opposed to using multiple inheritance. Multiple inheritance is never required to solve a programming problem; the same results can always be achieved through single inheritance.

❑ When a class descends from two classes that both descend from the same base class, you need to prevent duplicate inheritance of the base class. The word **virtual** in a child class definition indicates that the base class should be used only once.

KEY TERMS

Inheritance is based on the principle that knowledge of a general category can be applied to more specific objects. Specifically, inheritance in C++ means you can create classes that derive their attributes from existing classes.

A **derived** class is called a **child class**, **derived class**, **subclass**, or **descendant**.

A class from which another is derived is a **parent class**, **base class**, **superclass**, or **ancestor**.

When you **override** a function, you substitute one version of the function for another.

Inheritance supports **generalization and specialization**. That is, base classes are more general, and derived classes are more specialized cases of their base classes.

A **reliable** class is one that is already known to work correctly.

An **inaccessible** class member is one that cannot be used from the current location.

The **protected** access specifier allows members to be used by class member functions and by derived classes, but not by other parts of a program.

When you call a function, you **invoke the method**.

When a child class derives from a single parent, you are using **single inheritance**.

A child class can derive from more than one base class; this type of inheritance is called **multiple inheritance**.

The keyword **virtual** indicates that a base class should be used only once, even though more than one of its children is also being used as a base to another class.

10

REVIEW QUESTIONS

1. The principle that knowledge of a general category can be applied to more specific objects is _____.

   a. inheritance

   b. polymorphism

   c. object-oriented

   d. overriding

2. A derived class can also be called a _____ class.

   a. super

   b. base

   c. child

   d. parent

3. Parent class is to child class as _____.

   a. subclass is to superclass

   b. base class is to derived class

   c. derived class is to driven class

   d. child class is to superclass

4. Which of the following is not an advantage of inheritance?

   a. You save time because much of the code needed for your class is already written.

   b. You save time because the existing code has already been tested.

   c. You save time because you already understand how the base class works.

   d. You save time because parent classes always provide more detail than child classes.

5. Which of the following pairs of class names is most likely to represent a parent/child relationship?

   a. `Army/Military`

   b. `Dollar/Currency`

   c. `Song/Lullaby`

   d. `Cat/Dog`

6. The most commonly used inheritance access specifier is _____.

   a. `private`

   b. `protected`

   c. `public`

   d. `promoted`

7. To indicate that class `X` is a child of class `Y`, and that inheritance is `public`, the class definition is _____.

   a. `class X :: public class Y`

   b. `class X : public class Y`

   c. `class Y :: public class X`

   d. `class Y : public class X`

8. If a field named `someField` is `private` in the parent class, and a child class inherits with `public` access, then within the child class `someField` is _____.

   a. `private`

   b. `protected`

   c. `public`

   d. inaccessible

9. If a field named `someField` is `public` in the parent class, and a child class inherits with `protected` access, then within the child class `someField` is _____.

   a. `private`

   b. `protected`

   c. `public`

   d. inaccessible

10. If a field named `someField` is `public` in the parent class, and a child class inherits with `private` access, then within the child class `someField` is _____.

    a. `private`
    b. `protected`
    c. `public`
    d. inaccessible

11. If a member of a base class named `Base` is `protected`, then it can be used by functions that are _____.

    a. members of `Base`
    b. members of children of `Base`
    c. both of the above
    d. none of the above

12. Within a class that serves as a parent class, _____.

    a. all data fields must be `protected`
    b. no data fields can be `private`
    c. all functions must be `public`
    d. none of the above

13. Which of the following are inherited?

    a. constructor functions
    b. `void` functions
    c. `friend` functions
    d. `operator=()` functions

14. Class `A` has a protected field named `fieldA`. When a class `B` is derived from class `A`, and `C` is derived from class `B`, then you know that class `C` _____.

    a. has more liberal access to `fieldA` than class `B` does
    b. does not have more liberal access to `fieldA` than class `B` does
    c. has access to `fieldA`
    d. does not have access to `fieldA`

10

15. Class A contains a nonstatic `void public` function named `functionA()` that requires an integer argument. Class B derives from class A, and also contains a nonstatic `void public` function named `functionA()` that requires an integer argument. An object of class A can use _____.

    a. the class A version of the function

    b. the class B version of the function

    c. both of the above

    d. none of the above

16. Class A contains a nonstatic `void public` function named `functionA()` that requires an integer argument. Class B derives from class A, and also contains a nonstatic `void public` function named `functionA()` that requires an integer argument. An object of class B can use _____.

    a. the class A version of the function

    b. the class B version of the function

    c. both of the above

    d. none of the above

17. An initialization list used in the prototype for a constructor provides _____.

    a. a summary of overloaded versions allowed for a constructor

    b. the types and names of arguments required by a constructor

    c. the types and names of arguments overridden by a constructor

    d. values for class fields in the same statement as the definition of the constructor

18. Class A serves as a base class to class B, and B is a parent to class C. When you instantiate a class B object, the first constructor called belongs to class _____.

    a. A

    b. B

    c. C

    d. none of the above

19. A parent class named `Parent` contains a protected member named `parentField`. A class named `Child` derives from `Parent` with `public` access. Which is true?

    a. You can override the `public` access so `parentField` is `private` within `Child`.

    b. You can override the `public` access so `parentField` is `public` within `Child`.

    c. Both of the above are true.

    d. None of the above are true.

20. Which statement is true in C++?

    a. A child class can have multiple parents.

    b. A parent class can have multiple children.

    c. Both of the above are true.

    d. None of the above are true.

EXERCISES

1. Complete the following tasks:

    a. Create a base class named `Rectangle` that includes data members for the length and width of a `Rectangle`, as well as functions to assign and display those values. Derive a class named `Block` that contains an additional data member to store height, and contains functions to assign and display the height. Write a `main()` function that demonstrates the classes by instantiating and displaying the values for both a `Rectangle` and a `Block`. Save the file as **RectangleAndBlock.cpp**.

    b. Add a member function to the `Rectangle` class that computes the area of a `Rectangle` (length multiplied by width). Add a member function to `Block` that has the same name, but overrides the computation with a volume calculation (length by width by height). Write a `main()` function that demonstrates the classes. Save the file as **RectangleAndBlock2.cpp**.

2. Create a base class named `Book`. Data fields include those for title and author; functions include those that can set and display the fields. Derive two classes from the `Book` class: `Fiction`, which also contains a numeric grade reading level, and `NonFiction`, which contains a variable to hold the number of pages. The functions that set and display data field values for the subclasses should call the appropriate parent class functions to set and display the common fields, and include specific code pertaining to the new subclass fields. Write a `main()` function that demonstrates the use of the classes and their functions. Save the file as **Books.cpp**.

3. Create a class named `MusicalComposition` that contains fields for title, composer, and year written. Include a constructor that requires all three values and an appropriate display function. The child class `NationalAnthem` contains an additional field that holds the name of the anthem's nation. The child class constructor requires a value for this additional field. The child class also contains a display function. Write a `main()` function that instantiates objects of each class and demonstrates that the functions work correctly. Save the file as **Compositions.cpp**.

4. A `CollegeCourse` class includes fields representing department, course number, credit hours, and tuition. Its child, `LabCourse`, includes one more field that holds a lab fee charged in addition to the tuition. Create appropriate functions for these classes, and write a `main()` function that instantiates and uses objects of each class. Save the file as **Courses.cpp**.

10

5. Create a `RestaurantMeal` class that holds the name and price of a food item served by a restaurant. Its constructor requires arguments for each field. Create a `HotelService` class that holds the name of the service, the service fee, and the room number to which the service was supplied. Its constructor also requires arguments for each field. Create a `RoomServiceMeal` class that inherits from both `RestaurantMeal` and `HotelService`. Whenever you create a `RoomServiceMeal` object, the constructor assigns the string "room service" to the name of the service field, and $4.00 is assigned to the service fee inherited from `HotelService`. Include a `RoomServiceMeal` function that displays all of the fields in a `RoomServiceMeal` by calling display functions from the two parent classes. Additionally, the display function should display the total of the meals plus the room service fee. In a `main()` function, instantiate a `RoomServiceMeal` object that inherits from both classes. For example, a "steak dinner" costing $19.99 is a "room service" provided to room 1202 for a $4.00 fee. Save the file as **RoomService.cpp**.

6. Create a `Painting` class that holds the painting title, artist name, and value. All `Paintings` are valued at $400 unless they are `FamousPaintings`. Include a display function that displays all fields. The `FamousPainting` subclass overrides the `Painting` value and sets each `Painting`'s value to $25,000. Write a `main()` function that declares an array of 10 `Painting` objects. Prompt the user to enter the title and artist for each of the 10 `Paintings`. Consider the `Painting` to be a `FamousPainting` if the artist is one of the following: Degas, Monet, Picasso, or Rembrandt. Display the 10 `Paintings`. Save the file as **Paintings.cpp**.

7. Create an `Investment` class that contains fields to hold the initial value of an investment, the current value, the profit (calculated as the difference between current value and initial value), and the percent profit (the profit divided by the initial value). Include a constructor that requires initial and current values and a display function. Create a `House` class that includes fields for street address and square feet, a constructor that requires values for both fields, and a display function. Create a `HouseThatIsAnInvestment` class that inherits from `Investment` and `House`. It includes a constructor and a display function that calls the display functions of the parents. Write a `main()` function that declares a `HouseThatIsAnInvestment` and displays its values. Save the file as **HouseInvestment.cpp**.

8. Use the `Car` and `RaceCar` classes you created in the You Do It section of this chapter, or create them now. Make the following changes:

   a. Add fields to the `Car` class to hold a `Car` identification number and the number of miles the `Car` has traveled.

   b. Add a function to set the `Car` number. Add a function to increase the miles a `Car` has traveled in the last hour. The function adds the current speed (in miles per hour) to the number of miles traveled. Add a function to return the miles a `Car` has traveled so you can display the value.

   c. Alter the `turnIgnitionOn()` function to initialize miles traveled to zero. Alter the `showCar()` function to display the newly added `Car` number and miles traveled in addition to the other `Car` data.

d. Write a `main()` function that declares a `Car` and a `RaceCar`. Set a constant distance for the length of a race—for example, 500 miles. Assign numbers to the cars, start them, and while they have not traveled more than the race distance, select a random number under 200 to use to set the speed of both cars, and then increase the number of miles each car has traveled. (Because the `Car` and `RaceCar` have different maximum speeds, during some hours they will travel at different speeds. Appendix E contains instructions on producing random numbers.) After one of the cars exceeds the race distance, display the winner. Save the file as **Race.cpp**.

e. Alter the `main()` function so that different random speeds are used for each car. Save the file as **Race2.cpp**.

f. Alter the `main()` function so that both cars are `RaceCars`. Save the file as **Race3.cpp**.

g. Alter the `main()` function so it becomes a game. Start the user with $100 cash and ask the user to bet an amount of money on which `RaceCar` will win the race. After the race, if the user is correct, add the bet to the user's cash, otherwise, subtract it. Display the user's total winnings. Continue to run races as long as the user places a bet greater than 0. When the user is done, display the final cash value. Save the file as **Race4.cpp**.

10

9. Each of the following files in your Chapter10 folder on your Data Disk contains syntax and/or logical errors. Determine the problem in each case, and fix the program. Save your solutions by adding "Fixed" to the filename, as in **DEBUG10–1Fixed.cpp**.

a. DEBUG10–1.cpp

b. DEBUG10–2.cpp

c. DEBUG10–3.cpp

d. DEBUG10–4.cpp

CASE PROJECT 1

CASE PROJECTS

You have been developing a `Fraction` class for Teacher's Pet Software. Each `Fraction` contains a numerator, denominator, a whole number portion, and access to several functions you have developed, including overloaded operators.

a. Create a `MathProblem` class that holds fields for four `Fraction` objects: the first `Fraction` operand in a problem, the second `Fraction` operand in a problem, the user's answer to a problem, and the correct answer; to a problem. The `MathProblem` class also contains a character field that stores an operator (such as +), and contains an integer or `bool` field named `isAnswerCorrect`, indicating whether the user correctly answered the problem. For example, a `MathProblem` object containing 1/2, +, and 1/4 for the operands and operator;

3/4 for the correct answer; and 3/8 for the user's answer would contain a 0 or `false` in the `isAnswerCorrect` field. However, if the user's answer was 3/4, `isAnswerCorrect` would be `true`.

b. Include a function named `setProblem()` that sets a `MathProblem`'s values with arguments that include two `Fraction` operands and an operation. This function calculates and stores the correct answer, assigns 0 to the user's answer, and sets `isAnswerCorrect` to `false`. Include a `displayProblem()` function that displays the math problem as a question, and an `askUserForAnswer()` function that accepts the user's answer from the keyboard and assigns an appropriate value to `isAnswerCorrect`.

c. Include any other `MathProblem` functions you feel are useful and appropriate.

d. Write a `main()` function that declares five `MathProblem` objects you can use to test a student's fraction arithmetic skills. Assign random `Fraction` values to the `MathProblems`, choosing any appropriate limits for the numerators and denominators. (See Appendix E for information on creating random numbers.) In a loop, display the problems using an operation of your choice (for example, the problems might all be addition problems) and accept the answers. When the five problems are completed, display the problems, along with the student's answer, the correct answer, and a message indicating whether the student is right or wrong. Finally, show the student a score indicating the percentage of problems answered correctly. Save the file as **MathProblems.cpp**.

e. Create a class named `DoublingMathProblem` that derives from `MathProblem`. The `DoublingMathProblem` class includes a `setProblem()` function that overrides its parent's `setProblem()` function. This version requires a single `Fraction` argument; this argument is used as both the first and second operand in a problem. The operator for a doubling problem is always +. In other words, each `DoublingMathProblem` is a problem such as 1/3 + 1/3 where a `Fraction` value is doubled.

f. Write a `main()` function that declares five `DoublingMathProblem` objects you can use to test a student's fraction arithmetic skills. In a loop, display the problems and accept the answers. When the five problems are completed, display the problems, along with the student's answer, the correct answer, and a message indicating whether the student is right or wrong. Finally, show the student a score indicating the percentage of problems answered correctly. Save the file as **DoublingMathProblems.cpp**.

CASE PROJECT 2

You have been developing a **BankAccount** class for Parkville Bank that contains several fields and functions, including overloaded operators.

   a. Remove the annual rate field and all references to it so that a **BankAccount** contains only an account number and a balance. Also remove the **computeInterest()** function if it is still part of your class.

   b. Create a class named **SavingsAccount** that descends from **BankAccount**. Include an interest rate field that is initialized to 3 percent when a **SavingsAccount** is constructed. Create an overloaded insertion operator that displays all of the data for a **SavingsAccount**.

   c. Create a class named **CheckingAccount** that descends from **BankAccount**. Include two new fields including a monthly fee and the number of checks allowed per month; both are entered from prompts within the constructor. Create an overloaded insertion operator that displays all the data for a **CheckingAccount**.

   d. Write a **main()** function to demonstrate the **SavingsAccount** and **CheckingAccount** classes. Save the file as **CheckingAndSavings.cpp**.

   e. Add a constructor for the **SavingsAccount** class that requires a **double** argument that is used to set the interest rate. Create a class named **CheckingWithInterest** that descends from both **SavingsAccount** and **CheckingAccount**. This class provides for special interest-bearing checking accounts. When you create a **CheckingWithInterest** object, force the interest rate to .02, but continue to prompt for values for all the other fields. Create an array of five **CheckingWithInterest** accounts, prompt the user for values for each, and display the accounts. Save the file as **CheckingWithInterest.cpp**.

10

11

USING TEMPLATES

In this chapter, you will:

♦ Learn about the usefulness of function templates
♦ Learn about the structure of function templates
♦ Overload function templates
♦ Create function templates with multiple data types
♦ Create function templates with multiple parameterized types
♦ Override a function template's implicit type
♦ Use multiple explicit types when you call a function template
♦ Learn about the usefulness of class templates
♦ Learn about container classes and how to create them

Object-oriented programming provides many benefits compared to traditional procedural programming. You have already used concepts such as inheritance and polymorphism that make a programmer's task easier. In this chapter, you learn to create function templates and container classes. Understanding these concepts also makes your future programming tasks easier by providing new techniques that promote code reusability.

Understanding the Usefulness of Function Templates

The concepts involved in the use of variables are basic to all programming languages, and the use of variable names makes programming manageable. If a program should process 1,000 employee records, you don't need 1,000 different variable names to hold the salaries. When you can label a computer memory location with a variable name such as employeeSalary, the variable can contain any number of unique values, one at a time, during each execution of the program that declares it.

Similarly, creating functions within programs is a helpful feature because functions can operate on any values passed to them (as long as the values are of the correct type). A function that has the header void compute(int aNum) can receive any integer value, whether it is a constant (such as 15 or –2) or a value stored in another integer variable in the calling function. You can call the compute() function dozens of times from various locations in a program, and it can receive dozens of different integer values. Each integer value, however, will have the name aNum within the compute() function.

In your C++ programs, you have created many functions with a variety of types in their argument lists. Not only have you used scalar types such as int, double, and char in function argument lists, but you also have passed programmer-created class objects, such as Students or InventoryItems, to functions. In each case, the C++ compiler determined the function's argument types when the function was created and compiled. Once the function was created, the argument types remained fixed.

You have learned that you can overload a function to accept different argument lists. Overloading involves writing two or more functions with the same name but different argument lists. It allows you to employ polymorphism, using a consistent message that acts appropriately with different objects. For example, you might want to create several functions named reverse(). A reverse() function might change the sign of a number if a numeric variable is passed to it, reverse the order of characters in a string if a string is passed to it, set a code to make a PhoneCall object a collect call if a PhoneCall is passed to it, or issue a refund to a customer if a Customer class object is passed to it. Because "reverse" makes sense in each of these instances, and because such diverse tasks are needed for the four cases of reverse(), overloading is a useful and appropriate tool. When the function name is the same, but the program logic is different depending on the argument, the ability to overload functions is a valuable asset.

Sometimes the tasks required are not so diverse, however, and overloading requires a lot of unnecessary, tedious coding. When the programming logic is the same, writing multiple overloaded functions becomes wearisome. For example, assume you need a simple function named reverse() that reverses the sign of a number. Figure 11-1 shows three overloaded versions of the reverse() function. Each has a different argument list so the function can work with integers, doubles, or floats.

```
int reverse(int x)
{
    return -x;
}
double reverse(double x)
{
    return -x;
}
float reverse(float x)
{
    return -x;
}
```

Figure 11-1   Three overloaded versions of `reverse()`

The three function bodies in Figure 11-1 are identical. Because these functions differ only in the argument and return types involved, it would be convenient to write just one function with a variable name standing in for the type, as in Figure 11-2. The code in Figure 11-2 shows a shaded `variableType` where the type belongs, as both the argument type and the return type. Although it demonstrates a good idea, this function doesn't quite work in C++. You need to create a template definition.

```
variableType reverse(variableType x)
{
    return -x;
}
```

Figure 11-2   Proposed, but incomplete, variable type function

11

CREATING FUNCTION TEMPLATES

In C++, you can create functions that use variable types. These **function templates** serve as an outline or pattern for a group of functions that differ in the types of parameters they use. A group of functions that generates from the same template is often called a **family of functions**.

In a function template, at least one argument is **generic**, or **parameterized**, meaning that one argument can stand for any number of C++ types. If you write a function template for `reverse()`, for example, a user can invoke the function using any type for the parameter, as long as negating the value with a unary minus sign makes sense and is defined for that type. Thus, if a positive integer argument is passed to `reverse()`, it will return a negative integer, and if a positive `double` argument is passed, the function will return a negative `double`. If you have overloaded the negative (minus sign) operator to reverse the charges for a `PhoneCall` object, then if a `PhoneCall` is passed to `reverse()`, the charges will be reversed.

C++ also allows you to define macros, which permit generic substitution. Macros are seldom recommended, however, because no type-checking is performed (unlike with a template). Object-oriented C++ programmers rarely use macros.

TIP

Programmers often use the terms "function template" and **"template function"** interchangeably. Technically, you write a function template and it generates one or more template functions.

TIP

Before you code a function template, you must include a template definition with the following information:

- the keyword `template`
- a left angle bracket (<)
- a list of generic types, separated with commas if more than one type is needed
- a right angle bracket (>)

Each generic type in the list of generic types has two parts:

- the keyword `class`
- an identifier that represents the generic type

For example, the template definition for the `reverse()` function can be written as shown in Figure 11-3. The first line of code uses the `template` and `class` keywords to identify `T` as the generic class name. Although any legal C++ identifier can be used for the type in the function template, many programmers prefer `T` (for Template).

```
template <class T>
// T stands for any type — simple or programmer-defined
T reverse(T x)
{
    return -x;
}
```

Figure 11-3   The `reverse()` function template

Using the keyword `class` in the template definition does not necessarily mean that `T` stands for a programmer-created class type, but it may. Despite the `class` keyword, `T` can represent a simple scalar type such as `int`. `T` is simply a placeholder for the type that will be used at each location in the function definition where `T` appears.

For clarity, many newer C++ compilers also allow you to replace `class` with `typename` in the template definition. This substitution makes sense because the template is creating a name for a type, whether it stands for a programmer-defined class type or a built-in type.

TIP

When you call the `reverse()` function template, as in the following code, the compiler determines the type of the actual argument passed to the function (in this case, a `double`).

```
double amount = -9.86;
amount = reverse(amount);
```

The compiler substitutes the argument type (a `double` in this example) for the generic type in the function template, creating a generated function that uses the appropriate type. The designation of the parameterized type is **implicit**; that is, it is determined not by naming the type, but by the compiler's ability to determine the argument type. The compiler generates code for as many different functions as it needs, depending on the function calls that are made. In this case, the generated function is:

```
double reverse(double x)
{
    return -x;
}
```

TIP   If you have trouble deciding where to use the generic type when you write a function template, first write and test the function using a built-in type such as `int` or `double`. When your function works correctly with the built-in type, replace the appropriate type names with the generic type.

You can place function templates at the start of a program file, in the global area above the `main()` function. Alternatively, you can place them in a separate file, and include that file in your program with an `#include` statement. In either case, the definition of the class template (the statement that contains the word `template` and the angle brackets holding the class name) and the function template itself must reside in the same source file. When you create a function template, you can't place the template definition and the function code in separate files because the function can't be compiled into object format without knowing the types, and the function won't "know" that it needs to recognize the types without the template definition.

11

USING MULTIPLE ARGUMENTS TO FUNCTION TEMPLATES

Function templates can support multiple parameters. You might, for example, write a function that compares three arguments and returns the largest of the three. Figure 11-4 shows the function template named `findLargest()`, which accomplishes this task.

```
template<class T>
T findLargest(T x, T y, T z)
{
    T big;
    if (x > y)
        big = x;
    else
        big = y;
      if (z > big)
            big = z;
    return big;
}
```

Figure 11-4   The `findLargest()` function template

The `findLargest()` function in Figure 11-4 receives three parameters. Within this function, a temporary variable named `big` is declared. The `big` variable is the same type as the function arguments. That is, if three `int`s are passed to the function, `big` is also an `int`, but if three `double`s are passed, then `big` is a `double`. If the first parameter, `x`, passed to `findLargest()` is larger than the second parameter, `y`, then `x` is assigned to `big`; otherwise `y` is assigned to `big`. Then, if the third parameter, `z`, is larger than `big`, `z` is assigned to `big`. Finally, the value of `big` is returned. The variables `x`, `y`, `z`, and `big` may be of any type for which the greater than operator (>) and the assignment operator (=) have been defined, but `x`, `y`, `z`, and `big` all must be of the same type because they are all defined to be the same type, named `T`.

The assignment operator is automatically defined for classes you create, but you can also overload it.

TIP

The `findLargest()` function takes three arguments of type `T` (whatever type `T` is). Because all three arguments are the same type, the compiler can create object code for `findLargest(int, int, int)` and `findLargest(double, double, double)`, but it will not compile `findLargest(int, double, double)` or `findLargest(double, int, int)`, or any other combination in which the parameter types are not the same. For example, `findLargest(3, 5, 9);` returns 9, and `findLargest(12.3, 5.7, 2.1);` returns 12.3. However, `findLargest(3, 5.7, 9);` produces a compiler error because the argument types do not match. Wherever `T` occurs in the function template, `T` must stand for the same type.

Figure 11-5 shows the `findLargest()` template function and a `PhoneCall` class that includes an overloaded insertion operator as well as an overloaded > operator that determines whether a `PhoneCall` is larger than another, based on the time of the call in minutes. The `main()` method calls `findLargest()` using three integers, then using three `double`s, and finally using three `PhoneCall` objects. The output, in Figure 11-6, shows that in each case, the largest of the three arguments has correctly been determined.

```
#include<iostream>
#include<string>
using namespace std;
template<class T>
T findLargest(T x, T y)
{
    T big;
    if (x > y)
        big = x;
    else
        big = y;
    return big;
}
class PhoneCall
{
  friend ostream& operator<<(ostream&, PhoneCall);
  private:
    int minutes;
  public:
    PhoneCall(int = 0);
    bool operator>(PhoneCall);
};
PhoneCall::PhoneCall(int min)
{
    minutes = min;
}
ostream& operator<<(ostream& out, PhoneCall call)
{
    out<<"Phone call that lasted "<<
        call.minutes<<" minutes"<<endl;
    return out;
}
bool PhoneCall::operator>(PhoneCall call)
{
    bool isTrue = false;
    if(minutes > call.minutes)
        isTrue = true;
    return isTrue;
}

int main()
{
    int a;
    double b;
    PhoneCall oneCall(4);
    PhoneCall anotherCall(6);
    PhoneCall c(0);
    a = findLargest(3, 5);
    b = findLargest(12.3, 5.7);
    c = findLargest(oneCall, anotherCall);
    cout<<"The largest ones are"<<endl<<a<<
        endl<<b<<endl<<c<<endl;
}
```

Figure 11-5   Program that finds the larger of two integers, two `doubles`, and two `PhoneCalls`

11

```
C:\WINDOWS\system32\cmd.exe                    _ □ ×
The largest ones are
5
12.3
Phone call that lasted 6 minutes

Press any key to continue . . .
```

Figure 11-6 Output of program in Figure 11-5

TIP

It is unlikely that you would need to write an application in which you find the largest of such diverse types as integers, doubles, and PhoneCalls. The advantage to using the function template is that you can use one easy-to-remember function name no matter what type of arguments you need.

OVERLOADING FUNCTION TEMPLATES

You overload functions when you create functions with the same name but with different argument lists. You can overload function templates only when each version of the function takes a different argument list, allowing the compiler to distinguish between the functions. For example, you can create an invert() function template that swaps the values of its parameters if it receives two parameters, but reverses the sign if it receives only one parameter. Figure 11-7 shows the two versions of the function. The first version receives two reference arguments, locally called x and y. The variable named temp holds x; y is assigned to x, and temp is assigned to y. The result is that the values of x and y are switched. Because the function receives the addresses of the parameters, the values of the variables are switched in the calling program. The second version of invert() receives the address of a single argument. When you use this version, the sign is reversed for the parameter.

Notice in the shaded lines of code in Figure 11-7 that you must repeat the template definition template<class T> for each version of the function. Different versions of overloaded function templates do not need to use the same identifier to stand in for the variable type or class. For example, one version of the invert() function in Figure 11-7 could use T, while the other might use U. The class name is used locally in much the same way that variable names are used locally.

```
template<class T>
void invert(T &x, T &y)
{
    T temp;
    temp = x;
    x = y;
    y = temp;
}
template<class T>
void invert(T &x)
{
    x = -x;
}
```

Figure 11-7   The overloaded `invert()` function template

Figure 11-8 shows the two template functions and a `main()` function that uses the `invert()` function four times. Figure 11-9 shows the output of this program. When you call `invert()` with two integers or two `doubles`, it swaps their values. When you call `invert()` with a single argument, the version of the function that executes is the one that reverses the sign of the argument.

```
#include<iostream>
#include<string>
using namespace std;
template<class T>
void invert(T &x, T &y)
{
    T temp;
    temp = x;
    x = y;
    y = temp;
}
template<class T>
void invert(T &x)
{
    x = -x;
}
```

Figure 11-8   Program that uses the overloaded `invert()` function template

11

```
int main()
{
    int oneInt = -10, twoInt = -20;
    double oneDouble = 11.11, twoDouble = 22.22;
    cout<<"Using invert() with "<<oneInt<<
        " and "<<twoInt;
    invert(oneInt, twoInt);
    cout<<"   results are: "<<oneInt<<" and "
        <<twoInt<<endl;
    cout<<"Using invert() with "<<oneDouble<<" and "
        <<twoDouble;
    invert(oneDouble, twoDouble);
    cout<<"   results are: "<<oneDouble<<" and "
        <<twoDouble<<endl;
    cout<<"Using invert() with "<<oneInt;
    invert(oneInt);
    cout<<"   result is: "<<oneInt<<endl;
    cout<<"Using invert() with "<<oneDouble;
    invert(oneDouble);
    cout<<"   result is: "<<oneDouble<<endl;
}
```

Figure 11-8 Program that uses the overloaded `invert()` function template (continued)

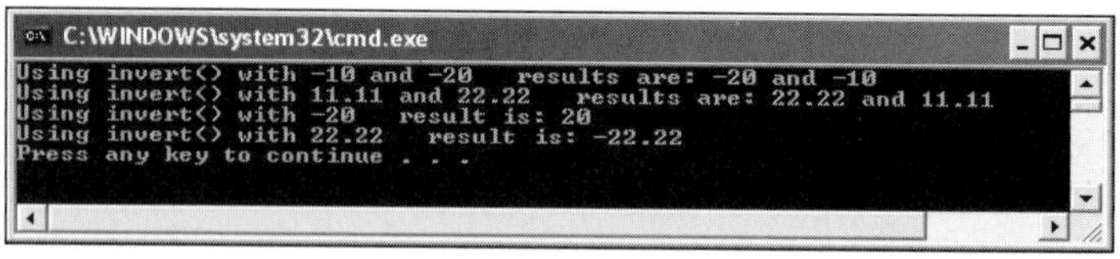

Figure 11-9 Output of program in Figure 11-8

Using More than One Type in a Function Template

Like other functions, function templates can use variables of multiple types. For example, a function might receive an integer and return a **double**, or another function might receive a character and a **double** and return an integer. In addition to containing a parameterized variable, function templates can also contain multiple arguments and internal variables that are not generic.

Suppose you want to create a function template that displays a particular value a given number of times. The value could be any type, but the number of times to repeat the value is an integer. It is perfectly legal to include some nonparameterized types in the function argument list, along with the parameterized ones. Figure 11-10 shows a `repeatValue()` function. The parameterized argument value, **val**, appears with a pound sign and a counter as many times as is indicated by the second, nonparameterized parameter, **times**. The **val** argument type is generic; the **times** argument type is not.

TIP

Figure 11-10 also contains a Store class; a Store contains a store number, a street address, and a manager's name. The Store class has an overloaded insertion operator.

When you run the program in Figure 11-10, the output looks like Figure 11-11—the integer displays three times, the **double** displays four times, the **character** displays five times, the **string** displays six times, and the Store displays three times. Any type of object can be displayed the specified number of times as long as the << operator is defined for the object's data type.

```cpp
#include<iostream>
#include<string>
using namespace std;
template <class T>
void repeatValue(T val, int times)
{
    int x;
    for(x = 0; x < times; ++x)
      cout<<"#"<<(x+1)<<" "<<val<<endl;
}
class Store
{
      friend ostream& operator<<(ostream&, Store);
      private:
        int storeNumber;
        string streetAddress;
        string manager;
      public:
        Store(int = 0, string = "", string = "");
};
Store::Store(int num, string add, string mgr)
{
      storeNumber = num;
      streetAddress = add;
      manager = mgr;
}
ostream& operator<<(ostream& out, Store store)
{
      out<<"Store #"<<store.storeNumber<<"  Address: "<<
        store.streetAddress<<"  Manager name: "<<
        store.manager;
      return out;
}
```

Figure 11-10   Program that demonstrates the repeatValue() function

```
int main()
{
    int a = 7;
    double b = 4.5;
    char c = 'C';
    string name = "Alice";
    Store store(718, "47 Pine Avenue", "Julia Winters");
    repeatValue(a,3);
    repeatValue(b,4);
    repeatValue(c,5);
    repeatValue(name,6);
    repeatValue(store,3);
}
```

Figure 11-10   Program that demonstrates the `repeatValue()` function (continued)

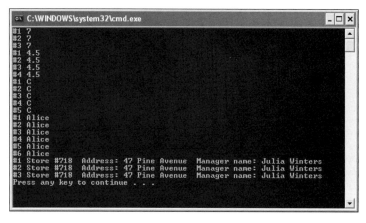

Figure 11-11   Output of program in Figure 11-10

 TIP   Most likely, you would not want to display such diverse data types varying numbers of times, as in the application in Figure 11-10. Usually, you would store a function such as `repeatValue()` in a library and use it with different data types in different applications.

USING MORE THAN ONE PARAMETERIZED TYPE IN A FUNCTION TEMPLATE

To create a function template that employs multiple generic types, you simply use a unique type identifier for each type. For example, suppose you want to create a `displayAndCompare()` function that displays two values, compares them, and displays a message indicating which is larger. The function works when any two parameters are passed, whether or not the two parameters are of the same type, as long as > and == are defined correctly for the parameters. The function template for `displayAndCompare()`

is shown in Figure 11-12. Two generic types, T and U, are defined in the shaded line of code. The first parameterized type, T, can stand for any type. The second type, U, can stand for the same type or any other type. Figure 11-12 includes a PhoneCall class that is similar to the one in Figure 11-10, but to which comparison operators have been added that compare a PhoneCall to an integer as well as to another PhoneCall. The demonstration main() function in Figure 11-12 passes a variety of arguments to displayAndCompare(). Figure 11-13 shows the results.

```cpp
#include<iostream>
#include<string>
using namespace std;
template <class T, class U>
void displayAndCompare(T val1, U val2)
{
    cout<<"First is "<<val1<<" Second is "<<val2<<"   ";
    if (val1 > val2)
        cout<<" First is larger"<<endl;
    else
        if(val1 == val2)
                cout<<" First and second are equal"<<endl;
        else
                cout<<" Second is larger"<<endl;
}
class PhoneCall
{
  friend ostream& operator<<(ostream&, PhoneCall);
  private:
     int minutes;
  public:
     PhoneCall(int = 0);
     bool operator>(PhoneCall);
     bool operator>(int);
     bool operator==(PhoneCall);
     bool operator==(int);
};
PhoneCall::PhoneCall(int min)
{
    minutes = min;
}
ostream& operator<<(ostream& out, PhoneCall call)
{
    out<<"PhoneCall time "<<call.minutes<<" min";
    return out;
}
bool PhoneCall::operator>(PhoneCall call)
{
    bool isTrue = false;
    if(minutes > call.minutes)
        isTrue = true;
    return isTrue;
}
```

11

Figure 11-12   The displayAndCompare() function and main() function

```
bool PhoneCall::operator>(int min)
{
    bool isTrue = false;
    if(minutes > min)
        isTrue = true;
    return isTrue;
}
bool PhoneCall::operator==(PhoneCall call)
{
    bool isTrue = false;
    if(minutes == call.minutes)
        isTrue = true;
    return isTrue;
}
bool PhoneCall::operator==(int min)
{
    bool isTrue = false;
    if(minutes == min)
        isTrue = true;
    return isTrue;
}
int main()
{
    int a = 68, b = 20;
    double c = 68.5;
    char d = 'D';
    PhoneCall oneCall(3), anotherCall(5);
    displayAndCompare(a, b);
    displayAndCompare(a, 68);
    displayAndCompare(a, c);
    displayAndCompare(a, d);
    displayAndCompare(c, d);
    displayAndCompare(oneCall, a);
    displayAndCompare(oneCall, 3);
    displayAndCompare(oneCall, anotherCall);
}
```

Figure 11-12 The `displayAndCompare()` function and `main()` function (continued)

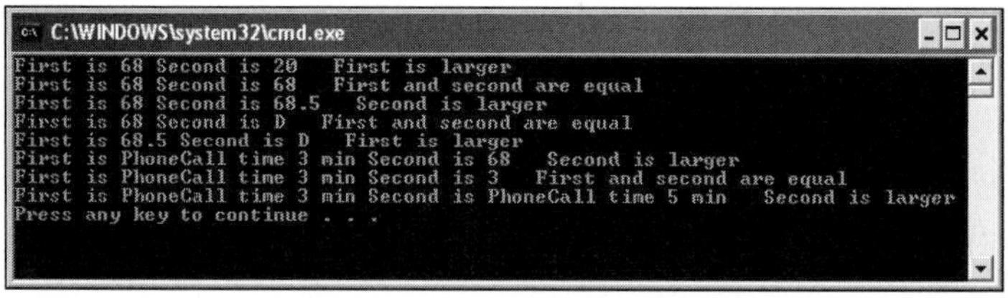

Figure 11-13 Output of program in Figure 11-12

You can see from the program in Figure 11-12 and the output in Figure 11-13 that the function works correctly in recognizing the types of the two parameters, whether or not they are the same. The program successfully compares two integers, an integer and a `double`, an integer and a character, a character and a `double`, a `PhoneCall` and an integer, and two `PhoneCalls`. The only requirement for the arguments to `displayAndCompare()` is that `T` and `U` are types for which the greater than comparison (>) and the equivalency comparison (==) are valid.

TIP

The value of the character 'D' in ASCII is 68, so when 'D' is compared to the integer 68 in Figure 11-12, they are considered equal. When 'D' is compared to the `double` 68.5, the `double` is larger.

TIP

The option of using multiple types in a function template is not available on some older C++ compilers.

EXPLICITLY SPECIFYING THE TYPE IN A FUNCTION TEMPLATE

When you call a template function, the arguments to the function dictate the types to be used. In other words, the compiler deduces the correct types to use within the function template, based on what types the programmer uses in the function call. The determination of the types is implicit, that is, automatic and unspoken. To override a deduced type, when you call a function template you can explicitly, or purposefully, code a type name within angle brackets immediately following the function name in the function call. For example, the function call `someFunction<char>(someArgument);` specifies that `someFunction`'s parameterized type (for example, `T`) will be `char`, no matter what type `someArgument` is.

Explicitly specifying a type for the parameterized type is particularly useful when at least one of the types you need to generate within the function is not an argument to the function. Because the compiler can deduce function template types only by using the values passed to the function, if the return type of a function must vary independently from the arguments, the compiler cannot deduce this requirement. In this case, you must specify the type within angle brackets.

For example, Figure 11-14 shows a function template named `doubleVal()`, which accepts an argument, multiplies it by 2, and returns it. The return value is the same type as the original argument.

11

```
template <class T>
T doubleVal(T val)
{
   val *= 2;
   return val;
}
```

Figure 11-14 The doubleVal() function template

The main() function in Figure 11-15 calls the doubleVal() function template three times, using an integer, a double, and a double converted to an integer, respectively. When you examine the output in Figure 11-16, you can see that when the int 5 is doubled, the result is an int, 10, and when the double 6.7 is doubled, the result is a double, 13.4. In the shaded statement, when the double 6.7 is passed to the function and the function parameter type is explicitly converted to int, then 6.7 is received by the function as 6, and the result is 12 instead of 13.4.

```
int main()
{
   int a = 5;
   double b = 6.7;
   cout<<"Using an integer "<<a<<" double is "
        <<doubleVal(a)<<endl;
   cout<<"Using a double "<<b<<" double is "
        <<doubleVal(b)<<endl;
   cout<<"Using a double "<<b<<
        " converted to an int, double is "
        <<doubleVal<int>(b)<<endl;
}
```

Figure 11-15 Function that uses an explicit type for a function's parameterized type

Figure 11-16 Output of function in Figure 11-15

 You can code empty angle brackets after the function name in a function call to indicate that the types should be deduced and not overridden. For example, in Figure 11-15, you might write doubleVal<>(a) instead of doubleVal(a). Using the empty brackets provides clear documentation to anyone reading the program that you intend the type to be deduced from the argument. However, using no angle brackets at all achieves the same result.

Using Multiple Explicit Types in a Function Template

You can use multiple explicit types when you call a template function. If sometimes you want the return value of a template function to be the same type as the argument, and sometimes you want it to be a different type, write the function template with two parameterized types. When you use the template function, the two parameterized types, for example T and U, can both stand for the same type, or they can stand for different types. Additionally, you can exercise the option to explicitly name one or both types. For example, Figure 11-17 shows a tripleVal() function that uses two generic types, T and U. The first type, T, must be explicitly coded, because it might or might not be different from the single argument. The second type, U, can be implicitly deduced from the function argument, or explicitly coded. The main() function in Figure 11-17 uses the function in several ways:

- Explicitly codes int for the T type and passes an integer to implicitly assign the U type

- Explicitly codes int for the T type and passes a double to implicitly assign the U type

- Explicitly codes int for the T type and explicitly codes a double for the U type

- Explicitly codes int for both T and U

```
#include<iostream>
using namespace std;
template <class T, class U>
T tripleVal(U val)
{
    T temp = val * 3;
    return temp ;
}
int main()
{
    int a = 22;
    double d = 8.88;
    cout<<"Explicit int; int argument: "
        <<tripleVal<int>(a)<<endl;
    cout<<"Explicit int; double argument: "
        <<tripleVal<int>(d)<<endl;
    cout<<"Explicit int, double; double argument: "
        <<tripleVal<int, double>(d)<<endl;
    cout<<"Explicit int, int; double argument: "
        <<tripleVal<int, int>(d)<<endl;
}
```

Figure 11-17   The tripleVal() function and a main() function that uses it four ways

Figure 11-18 shows the output of the program in Figure 11-17. The explanation of the output is as follows:

- When `tripleVal()` receives the integer 22 as an argument, triples it, and returns the integer result, the output is 66.

- When `tripleVal()` receives the `double` 8.88 as an argument, triples it to 26.64, stores the result in an integer, and returns the integer result, the output is the truncated result, 26. This is true whether `tripleVal()` receives 8.88 as a `double` implicitly or explicitly.

- When 8.88 is explicitly received as an integer, the function receives an 8. The output tripled value is 24.

```
C:\WINDOWS\system32\cmd.exe
Explicit int; int argument: 66
Explicit int; double argument: 26
Explicit int, double; double argument: 26
Explicit int, int; double argument: 24
Press any key to continue . . .
```

Figure 11-18   Output of program in Figure 11-17

When you explicitly code multiple types in a template function call, as in `tripleVal<int, double>(d)`, the order is important. The types are assigned in the same order as the generic classes are defined.

TIP

USING CLASS TEMPLATES

Function templates allow you to create generic functions that have the same bodies but can take different data types as parameters. Likewise, in some situations classes are similar and you want to perform very similar operations with them. If you need to create several similar classes, you might consider developing a **class template** to generate a class in which at least one type is generic or parameterized. The class template provides the outline for a family of similar classes.

Programmers often use the terms "class template" and "**template class**" interchangeably. Technically, you write a class template and it generates a template class.

TIP

To create a class template, you begin with the template definition, just as you do with a function template. Then you write the class definition using the generic type or types in each instance for which a substitution should take place.

For example, consider a very simple `Number` class that has one data member which can hold any number, a constructor that takes an argument, and a `displayNumber()` function. The class template definition is shown in Figure 11-19.

```
template<class T>
class Number
{
    private:
        T theNumber;
    public:
        Number(T n);
        void displayNumber();
};
// function implementations go here
// - more about this in the next section
```

Figure 11-19   The `Number` class definition

The class in Figure 11-19 is named `Number`. Its `private` data member, `theNumber`, may be of any type; in other words, `theNumber` is parameterized. If `T` stands for `double`—that is, if `theNumber` becomes a `double`—then the `Number()` constructor takes a `double` argument. If `T` stands for `int`, then `theNumber` is an `int` and `Number()` takes an integer. If you have developed a class for a more complicated number, for example a `Fraction` class, then `theNumber` can become a `Fraction` and the constructor requires a `Fraction`.

Within a program, you can instantiate objects that possess the class template type. You add the desired type to the current class instantiation by placing the type's name between angle brackets following the generic class name. For example, if you want an object named `myValue` to be of type `Number`, and you want `myValue` to hold an integer with value 25 (that is, you want to pass 25 to the constructor), your declaration is:

```
Number<int> myValue(25);
```

To use the `Number` class member `displayNumber()` function with the `myValue` object, you add the dot operator, just as you would with an instantiation of any other class:

```
myValue.displayNumber();
```

If you instantiate another `Number` object with a `double`, the `displayNumber()` function is called in exactly the same way:

```
Number<double> yourValue(3.46);
yourValue.displayNumber();
```

An object of type `Number` might "really" be an `int`, `double`, or any other type behind the scenes. The advantage of using a class template to work with these values lies in your ability to use the `Number` class functions with data of any type. When you need to write similar functions to display or use data of several different types, it makes sense to create a class template.

11

CREATING A COMPLETE CLASS TEMPLATE

Figure 11-20 shows the class definition for the Number class, along with the implementation of the Number class functions. As shown in the shaded lines, the code that identifies the parameterized data type, template<class T>, must appear immediately before the class definition and all function implementations—including the constructor function implementation and the member function displayNumber() implementation. Each of the three must recognize T and understand that it represents a type.

```
template<class T>
class Number
{
    private:
       T theNumber;
    public:
       Number(T n);
       void displayNumber();
};
template<class T>
Number<T>::Number(T n)
{
    theNumber = n;
}
template<class T>
void Number<T>::displayNumber()
{
    cout<<"Number # ";
    cout<<theNumber<<endl;
}
```

Figure 11-20 The Number class

The header for the constructor in Figure 11-20 indicates that the Number constructor belongs to the Number<T> class (whatever T turns out to be), and that its name is Number(). Like all other constructors, the Number constructor shares its class name. This constructor takes an argument of type T, although you could also write a constructor that takes no arguments or other types of arguments. In this example, the constructor body simply sets the value of Number's data member, theNumber, to the value of the argument n.

You can see in Figure 11-20 that the definition template<class T> is also required before the definition of the displayNumber() function, so as to identify the T in the class name, Number<T>. In this example, the displayNumber() function always displays "Number #" just before the value of theNumber. Even though T does not happen to be used within the body of this function, Number<T> is required in the function header to identify the function as a member of the Number<T> class. Remember that for displayNumber() to work correctly, the insertion operator must be defined for the class or type represented by T.

Figure 11-21 contains a `main()` function that declares three `Number` objects constructed using `int`, `double`, and `char` arguments, respectively. Figure 11-22 shows that the `displayNumber()` function can handle each argument and display it in the `Number` class format. Notice, in the last two displayed statements, that the class can even accommodate displaying a character as an integer (the ASCII value for 'K' is 75) and an integer as a character (65 is the ASCII value for 'A').

```
int main()
{
    Number<int> anInt(65);
    Number<double> aDouble(3.46);
    Number<char> aChar('K');
    Number<int> aCharAsAnInt('K');
    Number<char> anIntAsAChar(65);
    anInt.displayNumber();
    aDouble.displayNumber();
    aChar.displayNumber();
    aCharAsAnInt.displayNumber();
    anIntAsAChar.displayNumber();
}
```

Figure 11-21   A `main()` function instantiating three `Numbers`

11

Figure 11-22   Output of function in Figure 11-21

The `Number` class has been created here to help you understand how to create and use class templates. However, it is a stretch to imagine that a business would create the `Number` class as it stands. If you simply want to construct and display integers, `double`s, and characters (and even your own class objects) preceded by "Number #", a generic class is unnecessary, and it is too much trouble to create it. After all, each operation (construction and displaying) is already defined for these types, and it is simple to display "Number #" as part of a program. In this instance, creating the class template merely adds a layer of complexity to an otherwise simple task.

However, if extensive formatting was applied prior to displaying any object, then creating a class template might be worth the effort. Imagine, for example, that a company name and address, followed by a logo, always needs to be printed before data, whether the data belongs to the class used for `Employee`s, `Customer`s, or `Supplier`s. In such a case, it might make sense to create a template class that handles the formatted printing for each of the different type objects. Programmers commonly use template classes for even more generic applications, such as linked lists, stacks, and queues. Such generic classes are called container classes.

In programming, a **queue** is a data structure in which elements are removed in the same order they were entered, often referred to as FIFO (first in, first out). In contrast, a **stack** is a data structure in which elements are removed in the reverse order from which they were entered, referred to as LIFO (last in, first out). You will learn more about these structures as you continue to study computer programming, but for now, understand that the elements in these structures might be any data type.

Linked lists provide a method of organizing stored data in a computer's memory or on a storage medium based on the logical order of the data and not the physical order. Linked lists are discussed in the next section.

Understanding the Usefulness of Container Classes

Many C++ compilers come with class libraries called container classes. A **container class** is a template class that has been written to perform common class tasks; the purpose of container classes is to manage groups of other classes. Of course, you can always write your own container classes, but the creators of C++ have already done much of the work for you.

In Java and Smalltalk, all objects derive from the same container class, called `Object`. This consistently ensures that every object has at least some standard functionality.

Using container classes is a complicated topic, usually reserved for higher level programming classes. This discussion is meant only to be an introduction to the topic so you appreciate the usefulness of templates and containers.

For example, a common programming task that is used in a variety of applications is the construction of a linked list. A **linked list** is a chain of objects, each of which consists of at least two parts—the usual components of the object itself and a pointer to another object.

For example, a school might create a `Student` object with data fields for first name, last name, and grade point average. The school also might want to place `Student` objects in a linked list based on their registration dates. The first `Student` in the list would represent the first student to register. This first link in the chain of `Student` objects would contain the first `Student`'s data as well as a pointer that is able to hold the memory address of the second `Student` to register. When a second `Student` registers, additional memory is allocated to accommodate this `Student` and a pointer to the newly allocated memory is stored with the first `Student`. In other words, the second `Student` object's memory address is stored in the pointer that belongs to the first `Student`. The second element in the linked list chain holds the second `Student` object and a pointer to the address of a third `Student`, and so on. The last `Student`'s pointer typically holds a dummy value, such as a null character, to indicate the end of the list.

The diagram in Figure 11-23 illustrates a linked list of `Students`. The first `Student`, Ewa Shannon, is stored at memory address 2000. Besides her `Student` data, the linked list object holds a pointer to address 2500, where George Thoma's `Student` data is stored. The last `Student` link, Don Anderson, holds null in the linking pointer, because there is no one else in the list.

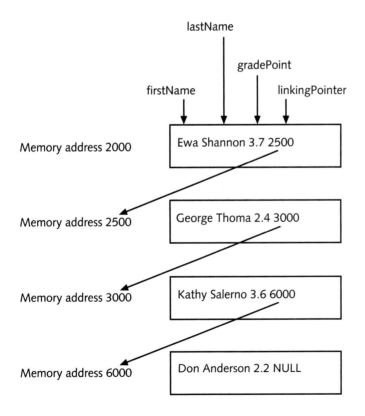

Figure 11-23 A linked list of `Students`

The school that uses the linked list to link `Students` in order of registration might want to link `Employee` objects by Social Security number, `InventorySupply` objects by item number, and `Alumnus` objects by a combination of major, year of graduation, and student ID number. Although each of the diverse objects `Student`, `Employee`, and `Alumnus` has a different size, different data members, and different functions, the procedures involved in creating the linked lists are basically the same.

TIP   Many linked lists provide more than a pointer to the next logical object. For example, they might contain another pointer to the previous object, enabling the list to be traversed backward as well as forward. Providing this extra link adds complexity to the programming task, but adds functionality to the linked list.

No matter what types of objects are linked, procedures must be developed to establish links between objects and to insert new member objects into appropriate spots within the linked list. The procedures include assigning the correct linking pointer values to the new list members. Other common procedures are deleting a member from the list, reordering a list, and retrieving and displaying the objects from a list. You also might want functions that count the number of items in a list or functions that search through a list for a certain object and pinpoint its position. Each of these functions may prove useful in a linked list, regardless of what type of object is being linked.

A generic class that holds an object and a link, and holds all linked list functions that handle the list's chores, is a useful tool when working with lists, whether they link students, employees, supplies, or alumni. Because a generic class of this type is so useful, the developers of C++ have already created such a container class. Its name is `list`, and it contains functions such as `merge()` and `reverse()`. The `list` container class is a template class because the programmers who designed your compiler could not have predicted the exact characteristics of all classes you might create. Even if they could, it would be pointless to develop an `Employee` linked list class, a `Student` linked list class, and an `InventorySupply` linked list class when the "linking" aspects are identical in each case. If you use the `list` container class, you never have to write your own linked list class, and you can use this tool with any class you create.

TIP   In Microsoft C++ .NET, the `list` class begins with a lowercase letter. In older compilers, the class was named `List`.

TIP   Teaching you to use all the built-in container classes that are part of the standard libraries of common compilers is beyond the scope of this book. Standard containers have names such as `vector`, `deque`, and `list`. (The C++ class name deque is awkward; programmers more naturally want to call it "queue" or "dequeue", but the C++ container name is `deque`.)

Different compilers include different built-in container classes. Indeed, some compilers may not offer any. The more container classes your compiler supplies, the less often you will need to write your own template classes. Nevertheless, it is still beneficial to understand how you would create your own container class if you found a need to.

CREATING AN ARRAY TEMPLATE CLASS

When you create an array, you create a list of same-type objects at adjacent memory locations. You perform many standard operations on array data, no matter what type is involved. For example, whether you are working with integers, characters, or **Employee**s, you often want to perform generic tasks such as storing the data into array locations, displaying the array, and displaying only the first element of the array. Class templates offer the perfect way to create generic functions that accomplish these tasks for any type of array.

You can create a generic **Array** class with two private data members: a pointer to the beginning of the array, and an integer representing the size of the array. The public functions include a constructor and member functions that show every element in the **Array**, and show the first **Array** element only. Figure 11-24 contains the **Array** class definition.

```
template<class T>
class Array
{
    private:
        T *data;    // T is the type of the array
        int size;
    public:
        Array(T *d, int s);
        void showList();
        void showFirst();
};
template<class T>
Array<T>::Array(T *d, int s)
{
    data = d;
    size = s;
}
template<class T>
void Array<T>::showList()
{
    cout<<"Entire list:"<<endl;
    for(int x = 0; x < size; ++x)
        cout<<data[x]<<endl;
    cout<<"--------------------"<<endl;
}
template<class T>
void Array<T>::showFirst()
{
    cout<<"First element is ";
    cout<<data[0]<<endl;
}
```

Figure 11-24 The Array class

11

The `Array` class constructor assigns the argument's array address to the `Array` class array address, and assigns the argument's array size to the `Array` class member size. For example, if an array of three integers is sent to the constructor, then the `data` pointer holds the address of the integer array, and the `size` variable holds 3.

The `showList()` function displays each element of the `Array`, from element 0 up through 1 less than `size`. The last `cout` statement in the `showList()` function displays a dashed line that serves as a separator that shows where the list ends. This statement is part of the function for cosmetic reasons—when you display several lists in a row, the dashed line makes it easy to see where one list ends and another begins.

 Remember that the subscript for any array can hold a value of 0 through 1 less than the array's size. For example, a 10-element array uses subscripts 0 through 9.

TIP

The `showFirst()` function is even simpler than the `showList()` function—it simply shows element 0 of the `Array`.

When you create an `Array` object, you must supply the beginning address of the array and the size of the array. Assuming you have declared an array such as `int nums[4];`, then you can call the constructor for an `arrayOfIntegers` with the statement `Array<int> arrayOfIntegers(nums,4);`. The two arguments to the `Array` object are the name of the `nums` array and the number of elements it contains.

Instead of hard-coding the size of the array with a constant such as 4, you can calculate the array size. If you divide the size of an array in bytes by the size of one element of the array in bytes, the result is the number of elements in the array. For example, the following statement serves to calculate the `arraySize` by dividing the size of `nums` (the array) by the size of `nums[0]` (one element of the array).

```
int arraySize = sizeof(nums)/sizeof(nums[0]);
```

You can use the calculated value `arraySize` in the declaration of `arrayOfIntegers`, as in the following:

```
Array<int> arrayOfIntegers(nums, arraySize);
```

Using a calculated array size means that if you change the size of the array later, this argument to the `Array` constructor will not have to be changed; its value will automatically be recalculated.

The `Array` class can be used with arrays of `int`s, `double`s, `char`s, or any other data type. For example, Figures 11-25 and 11-26 show a `Book` class and a `Client` class, respectively. Neither contains anything unusual; you have created many similar classes. Each contains some private data, a function that sets values, and an overloaded insertion operator. (Any type of object that will be stored in the `Array` class must be able to be displayed using `<<` if either the `showList()` or `showFirst()` function will be used.) Arrays of these objects can be used with the `Array` class as well as the simpler data types can.

```
class Book
{
    friend ostream& operator<<(ostream&, const Book &);
    private:
        string title;
        double price;
    public:
        void setBook(string, double);
};
void Book::setBook(string bookTitle, double pr)
{
    title = bookTitle;
    price = pr;
}
ostream& operator<<(ostream& out, const Book &aBook)
{
    out<<aBook.title<<" sells for $"<<aBook.price;
    return out;
}
```

Figure 11-25   The Book class

```
class Client
{
    friend ostream& operator<<(ostream&, const Client &);
    private:
        string name;
        double balDue;
    public:
        void setClient(string, double);
};
void Client::setClient(string clientName, double pr)
{
    name = clientName;
    balDue = pr;
}
ostream& operator<<(ostream& out, const Client &aClient)
{
    out<<aClient.name<<" owes  $"<<aClient.balDue;
    return out;
}
```

Figure 11-26   The Client class

Figure 11-27 shows a main() function that contains several types of arrays. The program in Figure 11-27 is divided into four parts. First, four arrays are created:

- An array named someInts is initialized with three integers.

- An array named someDoubles is initialized with four doubles.

11

- A two-element **Book** array uses the **Book** class shown in Figure 11-25. The two **Book** objects receive values through the **setBook()** function.

- A four-element **Client** array uses the **Client** class shown in Figure 11-26. The **Client** objects receive values through the **setClient()** function.

Second, a size is calculated for each type of array, then an **Array** container object is created using each of the four array types and a correct size value. Third, the **Array** container class function **showList()** is called with each **Array** type. The first part of Figure 11-28 shows each **Array** is displayed correctly—three integers, four **doubles**, two **Books**, and four **Clients**. Finally, in the last part of the output in Figure 11-28, the **Array** function **showFirst()** is called with each **Array** type.

```
int main()
{
    int arraySize;
// Declare and assign values to four kinds of arrays
    int someInts[] = {12,34,55};
    double someDoubles[] = {11.11, 23.44, 44.55, 123.66};
    Book someBooks[2];
    someBooks[0].setBook("The Shining",12.99);
    someBooks[1].setBook("Carrie",6.89);
    Client someClients[4];
    someClients[0].setClient("Harris",123.55);
    someClients[1].setClient("Baker",2155.77);
    someClients[2].setClient("Howard",33.88);
    someClients[3].setClient("Silvers",5123.99);
// Calculate size and create Array objects
    arraySize = sizeof(someInts)/sizeof(someInts[0]);
    Array<int> arrayOfIntegers(someInts, arraySize);
    arraySize = sizeof(someDoubles)/sizeof(someDoubles[0]);
    Array<double> arrayOfDoubles(someDoubles, arraySize);
    arraySize = sizeof(someBooks)/sizeof(someBooks[0]);
    Array<Book> arrayOfBooks(someBooks, arraySize);
    arraySize = sizeof(someClients)/sizeof(someClients[0]);
    Array<Client> arrayOfClients(someClients, arraySize);
// Use showList() with each Array
    arrayOfIntegers.showList();
    arrayOfDoubles.showList();
    arrayOfBooks.showList();
    arrayOfClients.showList();
// Use showFirst() with each Array
    arrayOfIntegers.showFirst();
    arrayOfDoubles.showFirst();
    arrayOfBooks.showFirst();
    arrayOfClients.showFirst();
}
```

Figure 11-27   Program using the **Array** container class

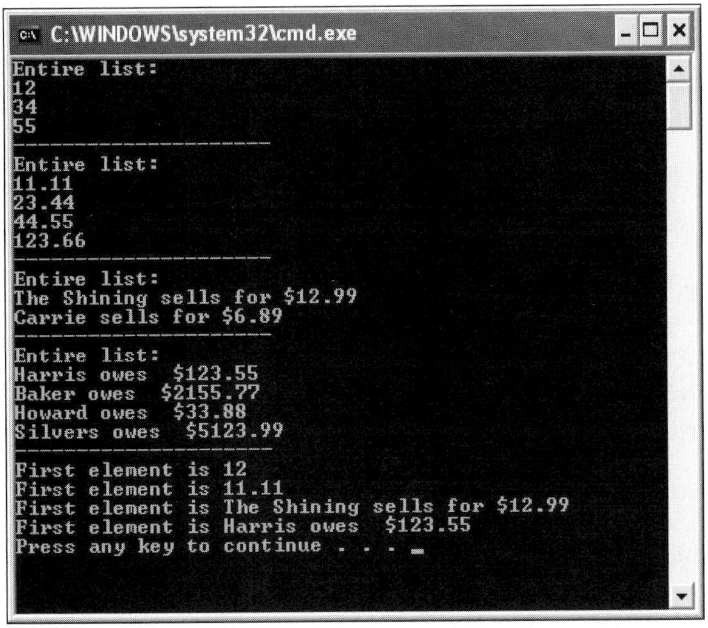

Figure 11-28   Output of program in Figure 11-27

You can see from Figure 11-28 that when you use the showList() function, each list appears correctly no matter how many elements the array contains. With both showList() and showFirst(), each element of each array appears in the proper format, integers and doubles appear in the usual way that they appear within C++, and Books and Clients appear as their overloaded insertion operators were programmed.

Understand that you usually would not create an application that displayed such diverse types as integers, doubles, Books, and Clients. Instead, you would most often use the Array class with integers in one application, Books in another, and so on. The beauty of having the container class at your disposal is that you don't have to recreate similar code every time you want to display an array of a different type of object. Instead, you can use one set of easy-to-remember function names to display any type of array.

If the Array class is carefully constructed, and new member functions are added as needed by various applications, you can handle any type of array. You might find it useful to add functions to the Array class such as any of the following:

- a function that displays the last element in an array

- a function that displays an element in a specified position in an array

- a function that reverses the order of elements in an array

- a function that sorts the elements in an array in ascending or descending order

- a function that removes duplicate elements from an array

In future applications, whether you create arrays of people, equipment, college courses, or any other items, you will have tried-and-true methods for performing common tasks with the arrays. For example, you have probably already written code that, by mistake, failed to display the first or last element in an array. By using the already written and tested **Array** class, you don't have to worry about that potential error—the **Array** class display function will have already been tested. Creating useful container class templates takes time, but the subsequent program development process goes more smoothly and is less error-prone.

YOU DO IT

Creating a Template Function

In the next set of steps, you define a function that increases any object by a specified integer.

1. Open a new file in your C++ editor, and enter the first statements you need for your file.

```
#include<iostream>
using namespace std;
```

2. Write the template definition to use the generic name **T**.

```
template <class T>
```

3. Write the **increase()** function. This function takes two arguments; the first is parameterized, and the second is an integer. The integer is added to the generic object and the newly increased object is returned.

```
T increase(T item, int byValue)
{
    item = item + byValue;
    return item;
}
```

4. Write a **main()** function demonstrating that the function template works whether the argument is an integer, **double**, or character. Declare three variables (one of each type), and display their values. Then pass each variable to the **increase()** function with an integer variable that contains a 2. Display each variable again.

```
int main()
{
    int anInteger = 12;
    double aDouble = 13.5;
    char aChar = 'F';
    int byValue = 2;
    cout<<anInteger<<endl<<aDouble<<endl<<aChar<<endl;
    anInteger = increase(anInteger, byValue);
```

```
        aDouble = increase(aDouble, byValue);
        aChar = increase(aChar, byValue);
        cout<<anInteger<<endl<<aDouble<<endl<<aChar<<endl;
}
```

5. Save the file as **Increase.cpp**. Compile and run the program. The output in Figure 11-29 shows the original value of each variable, and its value after it has been increased by 2. Notice that the character 'F' has become an 'H' because the ASCII value of 'H' is two more than 'F'.

Figure 11-29   Output of Increase.cpp

Proving the Template Function Works with Class Objects

In the next set of steps, you create two classes so you can use them with the `increase()` template function.

1. If it is not still open, open the **Increase.cpp** file. Immediately save the file as **Increase2.cpp**.

2. Add the include statement for the `string` class at the top of the file, just after the include statement for the `iostream` class:

   ```
   #include<string>
   ```

3. Place your insertion point after the function template definition and press Enter to start a new line where you will add new classes. First, create a class named `Classroom` that holds a teacher's name and the number of students in the `Classroom`. The class contains an overloaded insertion operator that displays the class values, a constructor, and an overloaded + operator that adds an integer to a `Classroom`. Adding an integer to a `Classroom` increases the number of students in the `Classroom`.

   ```
   class Classroom
   {
       friend ostream& operator<<(ostream&, Classroom);
       private:
           string teacher;
           int numStudents;
   ```

```
public:
    Classroom(string, int);
    Classroom operator+(int);
};
```

4. Create the `Classroom` constructor. Its arguments are assigned to the corresponding data fields.

```
Classroom::Classroom(string teacherName, int students)
{
    teacher = teacherName;
    numStudents = students;
}
```

5. Create the overloaded + operator for the class. The operator adds an integer to the number of students in a `Classroom`.

```
Classroom Classroom::operator+(int val)
{
    numStudents += val;
    return *this;
}
```

6. Create the insertion operator that displays the `Classroom` data.

```
ostream& operator<<(ostream &out, Classroom c)
{
    out<<c.teacher<<"'s classroom has "<<c.numStudents<<
        " students"<<endl;
    return out;
}
```

7. Next, create a new class named `DinnerReservation`. This class contains the number of guests that will eat dinner, the last name of the person in whose name the reservation was made, and the starting time for the reservation. The class contains a constructor, an overloaded + operator, and an insertion operator.

```
class DinnerReservation
{
    friend ostream& operator<<(ostream&, DinnerReservation);
    private:
        int numGuests;
        string lastName;
        string time;
    public:
        DinnerReservation(int, string, string);
        DinnerReservation operator+(int);
};
```

8. Create the function implementations. The constructor assigns field values, the + operator adds an integer to the number of dinner guests, and the insertion operator displays all the class fields.

```
DinnerReservation::DinnerReservation(int guests,
    string last, string resTime)
{
   numGuests = guests;
   lastName = last;
   time = resTime;
}
DinnerReservation DinnerReservation::operator+(int val)
{
   numGuests += val;
   return *this;
}
ostream& operator<<(ostream &out, DinnerReservation res)
{
   out<<"The dinner reservation for the "<<
      res.lastName<<" party at "<<
      res.time<<" is for "<<res.numGuests<<
      " dinner guests"<<endl;
   return out;
}
```

9. Replace the existing main() function with a new version that declares a Classroom and a DinnerReservation, supplying them with starting values. Also declare an integer named byValue that is assigned 2. Display the two objects, call the increase() function using each, and display the objects again.

```
int main()
{
   Classroom aClassroom("Miss Gleason", 28);
   DinnerReservation aDinnerReservation(4, "Parker", "7:30");
   int byValue = 2;
   cout<<aClassroom<<aDinnerReservation<<endl;
   aClassroom = increase(aClassroom, byValue);
   aDinnerReservation = increase(aDinnerReservation, byValue);
   cout<<aClassroom<<aDinnerReservation<<endl;
}
```

10. Save the file, compile it, and execute the program. Figure 11-30 shows the objects before and after the increase. The Classroom that had 28 students now has 30, and the DinnerReservation for 4 guests now has 6. Just as the increase() function worked correctly with an int, double, and char, it also works as it should with Classroom and DinnerReservation objects.

11

Figure 11-30   Output of the Increase2 application

CHAPTER SUMMARY

❏ Sometimes the tasks required by overloaded functions are so similar that you create a lot of repetitious code. To avoid this you can create a template definition.

❏ Function templates serve as an outline or pattern for a group of functions that differ in the types of parameters they use. A group of functions that generates from the same template is often called a family of functions. In a function template, at least one argument is generic, or parameterized, meaning that one argument can stand for any number of C++ types.

❏ Function templates can support multiple parameters.

❏ You can overload function templates, as long as each version of the function takes a different argument list, allowing the compiler to distinguish between them.

❏ Like other functions, function templates can use variables of multiple types. In addition to containing a parameterized variable, function templates can also contain multiple arguments and internal variables that are not generic.

❏ To create a function template that employs multiple generic types, you simply use a unique type identifier for each type.

❏ When you call a template function, the arguments to the function dictate the types to be used. To override a deduced type, when you call a function template you can explicitly code a type name within angle brackets immediately following the function name in the function call.

❏ You can use multiple explicit types when you call a template function. When you use a template function with multiple types, they can stand for the same type, or they can stand for different types. Additionally, you can exercise the option to explicitly name one or both types.

❏ If you need to create several similar classes, you might consider developing a template class, a class in which at least one type is generic or parameterized. The template class provides the outline for a family of similar classes. To create a template class, you begin with the template definition, just as you do with a function template. Then you write the class definition using the generic type or types in each instance for which a substitution should take place.

❐ The code identifying the parameterized class must appear immediately before the class definition and every function implementation.

❐ A container class is a template class that has been written to perform common class tasks; the purpose of container classes is to manage groups of other classes. You can write your own container classes, but many come packaged in C++ compiler libraries. For example, a common programming task that is used in a variety of applications is the construction of a linked list. A linked list is a chain of objects, each of which consists of at least two parts—the usual components of the object itself and a pointer to another object. A generic class that holds an object and a link, and holds all linked list functions that handle the list's chores, is a useful tool when working with lists, no matter what data types are linked. Different compilers include different built-in container classes.

❐ Class templates offer the perfect way to create generic functions that accomplish similar tasks. Although container classes can handle diverse types, you most often use the template class with one type per application. The beauty of having the container class at your disposal is that you don't have to recreate similar code every time you want to work with a different type of object. Creating useful container class templates takes time, but the subsequent program development process goes more smoothly and is less error-prone.

KEY TERMS

11

Function templates are functions that use variable data types.

A group of functions that generates from the same template is often called a **family of functions**.

A **generic**, or **parameterized**, argument is one that can stand for any number of C++ types.

A **template function** is one that is generated by a function template. The terms are often used interchangeably.

The keyword `typename` can replace `class` in a template definition in some C++ compilers.

The designation of the parameterized type is **implicit**; that is, it is determined not by naming the type, but by the compiler's ability to determine the argument type.

A **class template** is a class in which at least one type is generic or parameterized.

A **template class** is one that is generated by a class template. The terms are often used interchangeably.

A **queue** is a data structure in which elements are removed in the same order they were entered, often referred to as FIFO (first in, first out).

A **stack** is a data structure in which elements are removed in the reverse order from which they were entered, referred to as LIFO (last in, first out).

A **container class** is a template class that has been written to perform common class tasks; the purpose of container classes is to manage groups of other classes.

A **linked list** is a chain of objects, each of which consists of at least two parts—the usual components of the object itself and a pointer to another object.

REVIEW QUESTIONS

1. Writing two or more functions with the same name, but with different argument lists, is known as _____.
   a. inheritance
   b. overloading
   c. orienting
   d. creating a template

2. Creating a function template is most appropriate when _____.
   a. you want a function to take multiple arguments
   b. you are writing several functions that take different argument types, but use the same logic
   c. you need several functions with the same name, but the logic is different depending on the arguments
   d. you want only one version of a function to exist so as to avoid confusion

3. A group of functions that generates from the same template is often called _____.
   a. a family of functions
   b. a class
   c. a polymorphic template
   d. an assembly

4. Another term for parameterized is _____.
   a. polymorphic
   b. template
   c. object-oriented
   d. generic

5. In the template definition `template<class D>`, D stands for _____.
   a. double
   b. any programmer-created class
   c. any built-in type
   d. any class or type

6. The compiler determines the parameterized type in a function template _____.
   a. implicitly
   b. explicitly
   c. duplicitly
   d. polymorphically

7. Template functions can receive _____.

    a. only one parameter

    b. one or two parameters

    c. any number of parameters

    d. no parameters

8. Function templates _____.

    a. are overloaded automatically

    b. can be overloaded

    c. are never overloaded

    d. can be overloaded, but seldom are in common programming practice

9. A function template argument list can contain _____.

    a. only parameterized types

    b. only nonparameterized types

    c. either parameterized or nonparameterized types, but not both in the same argument list

    d. any combination of parameterized and nonparameterized types

10. You explicitly name a type in a function template call _____.

    a. always

    b. never

    c. to override an implicit type

    d. to overload the function

11. When a function template has two parameterized types, one as the return value, and one as an argument, then _____.

    a. the first type must be explicitly coded

    b. the first type must not be explicitly coded

    c. the second type must be explicitly coded

    d. both types must be explicitly coded

12. When you use a class object with a function template, you must _____.

    a. supply a default constructor for the class

    b. not use scalar types with the function

    c. define within the class any operation used within the function template

    d. overload the function template

11

13. A template class is a class in which _____.

    a. at least one type is parameterized

    b. at least one field is not generic

    c. no fields are generic

    d. all types are parameterized

14. Which of the following is a template definition?

    a. `template<T>`

    b. `template<class T>`

    c. `template class <T>`

    d. `<template class T>`

15. To create an `Order` template class object named `backOrder` and assign 0 as the argument to the constructor, the proper syntax is _____.

    a. `Order backOrder = 0;`

    b. `Order<int> backOrder = 0;`

    c. `Order<int> backOrder(0);`

    d. `Order backOrder<int>(0);`

16. When you create a template class, _____.

    a. each of its functions must be overloaded

    b. its functions can receive only a single argument

    c. the list of types the template can use to replace the generic type must be specified in the class header

    d. none of the above

17. A template class that has been written to perform common class tasks, such as linking lists or sorting, is a(n) _____ class.

    a. container

    b. bottle

    c. overloaded

    d. parameter

18. Each link in a linked list is usually made up of _____.

    a. two or more objects

    b. an object and a pointer

    c. an object and a function

    d. an object, a function, and a pointer

19. A container class named `SortedObjects` can sort a list of any type of object in ascending order. Therefore, which of the following must be true?

    a. The `SortedObjects` class must use the > operator.

    b. Objects passed to the `SortedObjects` class must have an overloaded > operator.

    c. Objects passed to the `SortedObjects` class must not have any overloaded operators.

    d. None of the above

20. The advantage to creating container classes is that _____.

    a. you don't have to instantiate objects within a `main()` function

    b. development time for future classes is reduced

    c. container class code is typically more concise than code for other classes

    d. unlike other class files, container class files can be included in programs using the `#include` statement

EXERCISES

1. Create a function template named `circleArea()`. The function receives a parameterized argument representing the radius of a circle, and returns a `double` representing the circle's area. (The area is computed as 3.14 multiplied by the radius squared.) Write a `main()` function that demonstrates that the function works correctly with either an integer or a `double` argument. Save the file as **CircleArea.cpp**.

11

2. Complete the following tasks:

    a. Create a function template to display a value that is both preceded and followed by 10 asterisks on a line. Write a `main()` function that tests the function with character, integer, `double`, and `string` arguments. Save the file as **Asterisks.cpp**.

    b. Create an `Employee` class that contains three data fields of your choice. Include a constructor to set the data values and an overloaded insertion operator that displays the data fields. Write a `main()` function that demonstrates the template that displays the preceding and trailing asterisks and also works with an `Employee` argument. Save the file as **Asterisks2.cpp**.

3. Complete the following tasks:

    a. Create a `Homework` class with fields for the class name, the assignment (for example, "read chapter 11"), and the number of minutes predicted it will take to complete the assignment. Include functions to set the values for the `Homework` fields, to provide output, and to overload the + operator to add `Homework` objects' minutes. The result of the addition is a summary `Homework` object.

    b. Create a function template that adds two values and returns their sum.

    c. Write a `main()` function that tests the function template with integer, `double`, and `Homework` objects. Save the file as **AddTwoObjects.cpp**.

4. Complete the following tasks:

   a. Create a `calcDistance()` function template that accepts two parameters representing two distances from a given point. The function returns the total distance as an integer.

   b. Create a `City` class with fields for the city name and for the distance from Chicago, the hub city for Amalgamated Airlines. Overload the + operator to sum the distances to produce a `City` result in which the city name contains the two operand city names (for example, "New York to Los Angeles") and the distance contains the total distance.

   c. Create a `Planet` class with fields for the planet name and distance from Earth, the hub planet for the new Amalgamated Galactic Travel Corporation. Overload the + operator to sum the distances to produce a `Planet` result in which the planet name contains the two operand planet names (for example, "Venus to Mars") and the distance contains the total distance.

   d. Write a `main()` function that declares several integer, `double`, and `City` and `Planet` objects, and uses the `calcDistance()` function to compute the distance for several pairs. Save the file as **Distance.cpp**.

5. Complete the following tasks:

   a. Create a function template named `average()`. It accepts two arguments of the same type and computes their arithmetic average. The average is returned as a `double`.

   b. Overload the `average()` function to work correctly with three arguments.

   c. Create a class named `CollegeCourse` with fields for the course ID (for example, 'ENG 101'), your grade (for example, 'A'), and the credits earned for the `CollegeCourse` (for example, 3). The `CollegeCourse` constructor accepts values for these fields as arguments, and calculates a fourth field named `honorPoints`. Calculate `honorPoints` as the product of the grade points (4 for an A, 3 for a B, 2 for a C, and 1 for a D) and the credits. Overload the + operator so that honor points for courses can be summed to create a summary `CollegeCourse` object. Overload the / operator so that a `CollegeCourse` object's `honorPoints` can be divided by an integer. Overload the << operator to display the details of a `CollegeCourse`.

   d. Write a `main()` function that declares several integers, `doubles`, and `CollegeCourses`, and demonstrates that both versions of `average()` work correctly with different arguments. Save the file as **Averages.cpp**.

   e. Design a class of your choice where averaging objects makes sense. Include any necessary member functions so the class can be demonstrated using the `average()` template functions. and write a `main()` function that provides the demonstration. Save the file as **Averages2.cpp**.

6. Create a class template for a class that holds an object. The template should provide a standard data input function that begins with a generic warning message to enter data carefully. The template should also include a standard output function that issues a generic "Here's the data you requested" message. Write a **main()** function that tests your template class with an integer and two programmer-designed classes. Save the file as **StandardizedInAndOut.cpp**.

7. Create a class template for a class that holds an object and the number of data elements in the object. For example, if an **Employee** class has two data elements, an ID number and a salary, then the class template holds the number 2 and an **Employee** object; if a **Student** class contains 12 data elements, then the class template holds 12 and a **Student**. Code a standard input function for the object that displays a message on the screen—"You will be asked to enter X items"—where X is the number of data elements. Write a **main()** function that tests your template class with an integer and two programmer-designed classes. Save the file as **NumberOfFields.cpp**.

8. Using the **Array** class in Figure 11-24, add functions that perform the following tasks:

   ❑ display the last element in an array

   ❑ display an element in a specified position in an array (the argument specifies the position)

   ❑ reverse the order of elements in an array

   ❑ sort the elements in an array in ascending order

   ❑ sort the elements in an array in descending order

   ❑ sum the elements in an array

   (As a starting point, you can copy the **Array** class code from the figure, or, more conveniently, open the file named **CodeForFig11-24.cpp** in the Chapter 11 folder on your data disk.)

   Create at least two programmer-defined classes that you can use with the container class. Write a **main()** function that demonstrates your container class works with at least two built-in types and two programmer-defined types. Save the file as **ArrayContainer.cpp**.

9. Each of the following files in your Chapter 11 folder contains syntax and/or logical errors. Determine the problem in each case, and fix the program. Save your solutions by adding "Fixed" to the filename, as in **DEBUG11-1Fixed.cpp**.

   a. DEBUG11-1.cpp

   b. DEBUG11-2.cpp

   c. DEBUG11-3.cpp

   d. DEBUG11-4.cpp

11

CASE PROJECT 1

You have been developing a **Fraction** class for Teacher's Pet Software. Each **Fraction** contains a numerator, denominator, a whole-number portion, and access to several functions you have developed, including overloaded operators. Complete these tasks:

a. Create a function template named **problem()** that accepts three arguments. The first and third arguments are generic values representing values a student will use as an arithmetic drill problem. The middle argument is a character representing a mathematical operation such as '+' or '-'. The **problem()** function displays the first argument, the operation sign, and the second argument on the screen, and allows the student to input an answer. The function returns the student answer to the calling program; the answer is the same data type as the first and third function arguments.

b. Create another function template named **solution()** that accepts three arguments. The first and third arguments are generic values representing values, and the middle argument is a character representing a mathematical operation such as '+' or '-'. The **solution()** function returns the correct answer to the problem.

c. Create a third function template named **congrats()** that accepts a correct answer. It displays the correct answer and a congratulatory message when a student enters the correct answer to a problem. Display the answer and the message 10 times on the screen, cascading to the right. For example, if the correct answer is 27, then the output is:

```
27 Congratulations! Correct Answer!
   27 Congratulations! Correct Answer!
      27 Congratulations! Correct Answer!
```

...and so on, until it appears 10 times.

The function will be used whether the problem needs an integer, **double**, character, or **Fraction** answer.

d. Write a **main()** function that presents a student with at least three integer or **double** arithmetic problems. Display the problems using the **problem()** function, and compute the correct answer with the **solution()** function. If a solution is incorrect, display a brief message, but pass any correct student solutions to the **congrats()** function.

e. Add three multiple-choice problems to the student drill. The answers are characters—'a', 'b', or 'c'. Display the questions and answer choices with **cout** statements. If a solution is incorrect, display a brief message, but pass any correct student solutions to the **congrats()** function.

f. Add three true/false questions to the student drill. The answers are characters—'t' or 'f'. Display the questions and answer choices with **cout** statements. If a solution is incorrect, display a brief message, but pass any correct student solutions to the **congrats()** function.

g. Add three `Fraction` problems to the student drill. Display the problems using the `problem()` function, and compute the correct answer with the `solution()` function. If a solution is incorrect, display a brief message, but pass any correct student solutions to the `congrats()` function.

Save the final program as **FractionTemplateFunctions.cpp**.

CASE PROJECT 2

**CASE
PROJECTS**

You have been developing a `BankAccount` class for Parkville Bank that contains several fields and functions, including overloaded operators. You have also created child classes derived from the `BankAccount` class: `CheckingAccount`, `SavingsAccount`, and `CheckingAccountWithInterest`. Complete these tasks:

a. Create a function template named `produceReport()` that accepts three arguments as follows:

❑ a string value for the report title

❑ a parameterized array that contains the elements in the report

❑ an integer indicating the number of table rows

The `produceReport()` function displays the table heading and each element of the array separated by a dashed line. The dashed line varies in size based on the size of the array element passed in as the parameterized value. For example, because integers are four bytes, the integers in the report are separated by a four-dash line. The report ends with an "End of report" message.

b. Write a `main()` function in which, in turn, you pass an array of at least five of each of the following types to the `produceReport()` function:

❑ `CheckingAccountWithInterest`

❑ `CheckingAccount`

❑ `SavingsAccount`

❑ integer

❑ string

Save the file as **ProduceReport.cpp**.

11

12

HANDLING EXCEPTIONS

In this chapter, you will:

♦ Learn about the limitations of traditional error-handling methods

♦ Throw exceptions

♦ Use `try` blocks

♦ Catch exceptions

♦ Use multiple `throw` statements and multiple `catch` blocks

♦ Throw objects

♦ Use the default exception handler

♦ Use exception specifications

♦ Learn about unwinding the stack

♦ Handle memory-allocation exceptions

Most beginning programmers assume that their programs will work as expected. Experienced programmers, on the other hand, know that things often go awry. If you issue a command to read a file from a disk, the file might not exist. If you want to write to a disk, the disk might be full or unformatted. If the program asks for user input, users might enter invalid data. Such errors that occur during execution of object-oriented programs are called **exceptions**—so-named because, presumably, they are not usual occurrences. The object-oriented techniques to manage such errors comprise the group of methods known as **exception handling**. You learn these techniques in this chapter.

Understanding the Limitations of Traditional Error Handling

From the time the first computer programs were written, programmers have had to deal with error conditions; errors occurred during the execution of programs long before object-oriented methods emerged. Probably the most popular traditional response to errors was to terminate the program. For example, many older C++ programs contain code similar to the code in Figure 12-1. The function uses the shaded **exit() function**, which forces the program to end.

```
int dataEntryRoutine()
{
    int userEntry;
    cout<<"Enter a positive number ";
    cin>>userEntry;
    if(userEntry <= 0)
        exit(1);
    // rest of function goes here
}
```

Figure 12-1   Using the exit() function

In the shaded statement in the program segment in Figure 12-1, if the **userEntry** is a negative value, the program in which the code appears is terminated. The **exit()** function requires an integer argument. It is traditional to use a 0 argument to indicate a program exited normally, and a non-zero argument to indicate an error.

TIP   As an alternative to 1 and 0, many compilers allow you to use the defined constants EXIT_FAILURE and EXIT_SUCCESS as arguments to the exit() function. They are defined as 1 and 0, respectively.

When you use the **exit()** function, the program ends abruptly. If the program is a spreadsheet or a game, the user might become annoyed that the program has prematurely stopped working. However, if the program monitors a patient's blood pressure during surgery or guides an airplane in flight, the results could be far more serious. Either way, the user has no idea what caused the program to end.

A slightly better alternative to **exit()** involves using the **atexit()** function. The **atexit() function** requires a function name as its argument; this function is then registered with **atexit()**, which means the named function is called automatically whenever the **exit()** function executes. Figure 12-2 shows a program that uses the `atexit()` function to call the `displayFinalMessage()` function, and Figure 12-3 shows two typical executions of the program. When you use `atexit()` to register a function to execute when `exit()` is called, the program still ends, but the named function can perform any necessary clean-up tasks. In the program in Figure 12-2, the user is provided with a message. In other applications, you might want to perform tasks such as freeing allocated memory and closing any open data files. Notice in the shaded call to `atexit()` in Figure 12-2 that the function name used as an argument is not followed with parentheses.

TIP

Although it would be easier to read the function name if the function name were `atExit()`, that isn't the function name. The name `atexit()` contains all lowercase letters.

```cpp
#include<iostream>
#include<string>
using namespace std;
int dataEntryRoutine()
{
    int userEntry;
    cout<<"Enter a positive number ";
    cin>>userEntry;
    if(userEntry <= 0)
        exit(1);
    cout<<"Thanks!"<<endl;
    return userEntry;
}
void displayFinalMessage()
{
    cout<<"Program terminated."<<endl;
}
int main()
{
    int dataEntryRoutine();
    void displayFinalMessage();
    atexit(displayFinalMessage);
    int entry = 999;
    entry = dataEntryRoutine();
    cout<<"You entered "<<entry<<endl;
}
```

Figure 12-2   Program using `atexit()`

12

Figure 12-3 Two executions of the application in Figure 12-2

TIP

Functions registered with the `atexit()`function (such as `displayFinalMessage()`) must be type `void` and take no arguments.

TIP

If you register multiple functions with `atexit()` within a program, each function will execute in reverse of the registration order. For example, if the `main()` function in Figure 12-2 contained two `atexit()` statements, the function named in the last one would execute first.

TIP

The `main()` function in Figure 12-2 would execute correctly without containing the prototypes for `dataEntryRoutine()` and `displayFinalMessage()`, because these functions are implemented before `main()`.

Notice in the output in Figure 12-3 that the function named in the `atexit()` call executes when the program ends, whether the program came to a natural end or the end was forced by a data entry error.

Although the program in Figure 12-2 works as expected and terminates when the user enters an inappropriate value for `userEntry`, the program remains somewhat inflexible. An invalid entry results in a message and program termination. When you write a different application in which invalid data should result in providing the user with an attempt to reenter the data, you must create a new and different version of the data entry function. Later, in a new application, you might need to assign a default value and continue with the program when the user enters invalid data. Then, you will have to write a new, third version of the data entry function.

A general rule of modular programming is that a function should be able to determine an error situation, but not necessarily take action on it. If the `dataEntryRoutine()` function is useful and well-written, it will be used by many programmers in many situations. Some of these programs (and programmers) might not want to cause such a sudden exit to the program when the user enters an invalid value. Other programs might require that additional tasks be accomplished before the program actually ends. A better alternative to the function version in Figure 12-2 is to let a function discover an error, and then notify the calling function of the error so the calling function can then decide what to do about it. This approach provides flexibility by letting the calling function decide whether to carry on or terminate when the invalid data entry occurs. This approach promotes function reusability—the `dataEntryRoutine()` function can be used no matter what actions are needed after invalid data is entered.

For example, the function in Figure 12-4 returns a 1 if the `dataEntryRoutine()` function detects an error, and a 0 if it does not. In the shaded decision in Figure 12-4, the calling `main()` function checks the return value of the function and takes appropriate action, printing an error message or not. A different application could use the same function and, based on the return value, continue to loop and call the function until a valid entry is made. A third application might assign a default value if the data entry was invalid.

```cpp
#include<iostream>
#include<string>
using namespace std;
int dataEntryRoutine()
{
     int userEntry;
     int errorCode = 0;
     const int ERROR_CODE = 1;
     cout<<"Enter a positive number ";
     cin>>userEntry;
     if(userEntry < 0)
          errorCode = ERROR_CODE;
     cout<<"Thanks!"<<endl;
     return errorCode;
}
void displayErrorMessage()
{
     cout<<"You entered a negative number. ";
     cout<<"Program terminated."<<endl;
}
int main()
{
     const int GOOD_CODE = 0;
     int code;
     int dataEntryRoutine();
     void displayErrorMessage();
     code = dataEntryRoutine();
     if(code == GOOD_CODE)
     {
          cout<<"You entered a valid number"<<endl;
          // other actions that occur when entered
          //   number is valid can go here
     }
     else
          displayErrorMessage();
}
```

Figure 12-4   Program using `dataEntryRoutine()` that returns an error code

Although the error-handling technique demonstrated in Figure 12-4 works to identify negative entered values, it has at least two drawbacks based on the following limitations:

- A function can return, at most, only one value.

- When a function returns a value, it must return only the type indicated as its return type.

First, because a function can return only one value, and the scope of a local variable ends at the end of the block in which it is declared, the `userEntry` value is lost when the `dataEntryRoutine()` function in Figure 12-4 ends. The function can return the code that indicates the error status, but if it does, then it can't return the `userEntry` value as well. (Or, you can rewrite the `dataEntryRoutine()` so it returns the `userEntry`, but then the error code is not returned and so its value is lost.)

Although a function can return just one value, that value might be an object containing multiple fields.

In the example in Figure 12-4, you could work around the problem of losing one of the values by rewriting the `dataEntryRoutine()` function so that sometimes it returns the `userEntry`, and sometimes it returns the error code. For example, the function could return the `userEntry` if it is not negative, and return an arbitrary error code value such as -1 when the `userEntry` is negative. However, if you wanted to return the value of `userEntry` even if it was invalid (negative), you would have no way to indicate the error situation.

As another remedy, you could write the `dataEntryRoutine()` function so that it accepts the address of the `userEntry` variable from `main()`. Then the `dataEntryRoutine()` could alter the actual entry variable instead of a copy of it, and still return an error code. However, allowing functions to access and alter passed variable values violates the general principle of encapsulation, and increases the data coupling of the function.

Second, any error code returned by a function must be the same type as the function's return type. In this case, the data entry is an integer and the error code is an integer, so you could write the `dataEntryRoutine()` function to make the decision to return either the valid entry or an error code. However, when you have other functions with a return type of, for example, a `double`, an array of integers, or a class object, then any error code returned must be the same type, and it simply is not intuitive to think of an error code this way. Of course, the error code could be stored globally, avoiding the return issue. In that case, however, any function could change the error code, and the "feel" of encapsulation and object-orientedness would be lost, and, again, data coupling would be increased.

Fortunately, object-oriented programming languages provide you with techniques that circumvent the problems of traditional error handling. The name for this group of error-handling techniques is exception handling; the actions you take with exceptions involve trying, throwing, and catching them. You **try** a function; if it **throws** an exception, you **catch** and handle it.

THROWING EXCEPTIONS

A function can contain code to check for errors, and then send a message when it detects an error. In object-oriented terminology, an **exception** is an object that contains information that is passed from the place where a problem occurs to another place that will handle the problem. This exception object can be of any type, including a scalar or class type, and a variety of exception objects of different types can be sent from the same function, regardless of the function's return type. In addition, true to object-oriented style, exception handling acknowledges inheritance and can be overridden by the programmer.

TIP

In object-oriented terminology, you pass a **message** to tell another object what to do. Every function call is a message, and exceptions that are thrown are also messages.

The general principle underlying good object-oriented error handling is that any called function should check for errors, but should not be required to handle an error if one is found. You find this form of error handling convenient in real life. For example, suppose you call your hair stylist to make a 1 o'clock appointment on Thursday, and suppose the stylist has no openings then. Rather than have the stylist make a decision that, instead, you will come in on Thursday at 3 o'clock, you want to be notified of the error situations. Sometimes you will choose to handle the exception by rescheduling for Thursday at 3 o'clock, but other times you will choose a different time, different day, or perhaps a different stylist.

With the `dataEntryRoutine()` function, when an exception occurs, it might need to be handled differently, depending on the purpose of the calling function. For example, one program that uses the function might need to terminate if the user enters a negative value. Another program might simply want the user to reenter the data. Maximum flexibility is achieved when the calling function is responsible for handling the error detected by the called function.

When an object-oriented program detects an error within a function, the function should send an error object to the calling function, or **throw an exception**. A `throw` resembles a return statement in a function, except that the execution of the program does not continue from where the function was called.

You throw an exception by using the keyword `throw` followed by any C++ object, including an object that is a built-in scalar type, such as an `int` or a `double`; a nonscalar type, such as a `string` or numeric array; or even a programmer-defined object such as an `Employee` or a `Student`. For example, if you write a `dataEntryRoutine()` function in which a negative `userEntry` value represents an error condition, then you can throw an error message exception that is a string, as shown in Figure 12-5.

12

```
int dataEntryRoutine()
{
    int userEntry;
    const string MSG = "Invalid entry";
    cout<<"Enter a positive value ";
    cin>>userEntry;
    if(userEntry < 0)
        throw(MSG);
    return userEntry;
}
```

Figure 12-5   Function that throws an exception

In the **dataEntryRoutine()** function in Figure 12-5, if **userEntry** is invalid, then a string is thrown (in the shaded statement) and the execution of the function is finished. Therefore, only valid (that is, nonnegative) entries cause the function to continue to execute all the way through the **return** statement. The string that is thrown is not "returned" from the **dataEntryRoutine()** function; the function has an **int** return type and so can return only an **int**. The **dataEntryRoutine()** function concludes in one of two ways: either the error message **string** is thrown or the **userEntry** integer is returned.

A function can make more than one **throw**. Assume, for example, that you need one error message if a value is negative, but a different error message if a value is greater than 9. The function in Figure 12-6 throws two different error messages, based on a **userEntry**.

```
int getPositiveSingleDigit()
{
    int userEntry;
    const int LOW = 0;
    const int HIGH = 9;
    const string MSG1 = "Value is negative";
    const string MSG2 = "Value is too high";
    cout<<"Enter a single-digit positive value   ";
    cin>>userEntry;
    if(userEntry < LOW)
        throw(MSG1);
    if(userEntry > HIGH)
        throw(MSG2);
    return userEntry ;
}
```

Figure 12-6   Function that throws one of two exceptions

The shaded statements in Figure 12-6 throw strings—one if the value entered is too low and a different one if it is too high. Not only can a function make multiple throws, but it also can make throws of different types. Assume you need a function that throws an error message if **userEntry** is negative, but throws the actual value entered if the user enters a number greater than 9. The `getPositiveSingleDigit()` function in Figure 12-7 accomplishes this goal. One shaded `throw` statement throws a `string`; the other throws an integer.

```
int getPositiveSingleDigit()
{
    int userEntry;
    const int LOW = 0;
    const int HIGH = 9;
    const string ERROR_MSG = "Negative number";
    cout<<"Enter a single-digit positive value  ";
    cin>>userEntry;
    if(userEntry < LOW)
        throw(ERROR_MSG);
    if(userEntry >HIGH)
        throw(userEntry);
    return userEntry;
}
```

Figure 12-7   Function that throws one of two exceptions of different types

When you use the version of the `getPositiveSingleDigit()` function shown in Figure 12-7, if the user enters a value between 0 and 9 inclusive, the actual value is returned to the calling function when the function ends. If the user enters a negative number, the string message "Negative number" is thrown. If the user entry is greater than 9, the actual number that the user entered is thrown. This does not mean that the number is returned to the calling function; only values between 0 and 9 are returned to the calling function, which presumably continues using the value and processing. Instead, any value that is 10 or greater is thrown, or sent, to a different function where it can be caught.

12

USING try BLOCKS

When a function might cause an exception, and therefore includes a `throw` statement to handle errors, the call to the potentially offending function should be placed within a `try` block. A **try block** consists of one or more statements that the program attempts to execute, but which might result in thrown exceptions. You want to place a function call in a `try` block when the function might throw an exception, because placing it in a `try` block allows you to handle, or "take care of," the problem that caused the exception.

A `try` block includes the following components:

- the keyword `try`
- an opening curly brace
- the statements that are tried
- a closing curly brace

For example, a `main()` function that calls any of the data entry functions created so far in this chapter would place the call to the data entry function within a `try` block. Figure 12-8 shows a `main()` function that calls the `dataEntryRoutine()` function from Figure 12-5. In this case, the function call is contained in the only statement within the shaded `try` block, but any number of statements could be placed within the block. When an `if`, `for`, or `while` block contains just one statement, curly braces are not required around the contained statement. With a `try` block, however, you must include the curly braces, even if only one statement is tried.

```
int main()
{
    int value;
    try
    {
        value = dataEntryRoutine();
    }
    cout<<"Data entry value is "<<value<<endl;
    // rest of the program goes here
}
```

Figure 12-8 Incomplete `main()` function containing a `try` block

In Figure 12-8, the call to the `dataEntryRoutine()` function occurs within the shaded `try` block. When the function executes, if the `userEntry` is valid, then no exception is thrown, and `main()` executes to the end, using the valid value returned by the `dataEntryRoutine()` function.

Programmers refer to the scenario where no errors occur and hence no exceptions are thrown as the "sunny day" case.

The `main()` function in Figure 12-8 is incomplete, however. If the `dataEntryRoutine()` function throws an exception, you want to be able to handle the exception; you handle a thrown exception by catching it.

If a function throws an exception, but the function call has not been placed in a `try` block, then the program terminates.

CATCHING EXCEPTIONS

To handle a thrown object, you include one or more **catch** blocks in your program immediately following a **try** block. A **catch** block contains statements that execute when an exception is thrown and includes the following components:

- the keyword **catch**
- a single argument in parentheses
- an opening curly brace
- one or more statements that describe the exception action to be taken
- a closing curly brace

For example, Figure 12-9 shows the **dataEntryRoutine()** function from Figure 12-5, along with a **main()** function that uses it. The **main()** function calls **dataEntryRoutine()** in a **try** block. The **dataEntryRoutine()** function throws a string error message if the user enters a negative number. If the user enters a nonnegative number during the execution of **dataEntryRoutine()**, control returns to the **main()** function where the entered value is displayed, then the **catch** block is bypassed and the "End of program" message displays. Figure 12-10 shows the execution of the program when the user enters a nonnegative value.

```cpp
#include<iostream>
#include<string>
using namespace std;
int dataEntryRoutine()
{
    int userEntry;
    const string MSG = "Invalid entry";
    cout<<"Enter a positive value ";
    cin>>userEntry;
    if(userEntry < 0)
        throw(MSG);
    return userEntry;
}
int main()
{
    int returnedValue;
    try
    {
        returnedValue = dataEntryRoutine();
        cout<<"Data entry value is "<<returnedValue<<endl;
    }
    catch(string message)
    {
        cout<<"There was an error!"<<endl;
        cout<<message<<endl;
    }
    cout<<"End of program"<<endl;
}
```

Figure 12-9   A main() function that tries dataEntryRoutine() and catches the thrown exception

Figure 12-10 Output of program in Figure 12-9 when user enters a nonnegative number

TIP

As with a `try` block, a `catch` block must contain curly braces, even if they surround only one statement.

TIP

The `catch` block in Figure 12-9 could alternately be coded to accept a `const string` argument.

If the user enters a negative number during the execution of `dataEntryRoutine()` in the program shown in Figure 12-9, then the `dataEntryRoutine()` function is abandoned, the rest of the `try` block (the statement that displays the entered number) is bypassed, and the shaded `catch` block executes. For example, Figure 12-11 shows the execution of the same program when the user enters a negative number. In this case, the `catch` block executes, catching the thrown string message. The `catch` block displays two strings: the first ("There was an error!") is coded within the `catch` block, and the second (locally called `message`) was thrown by the `dataEntryRoutine()` function. After executing the `catch` block, the `main()` function continues and displays "End of program".

Figure 12-11 Output of program in Figure 12-9 when user enters a negative number

If you want a `catch` block to execute, it must `catch` the correct type of argument thrown from a `try` block. If an argument is thrown and no `catch` block has a matching argument type, then the program terminates. However, a `catch` block is not required to display, or to use in any way, what is thrown. For example, the `catch` block in the program in Figure 12-9 is not required to display the `message` argument. Instead, the `catch` block could display only its own message, assign a default value to `returnedValue`, or contain any number of valid C++ statements, including those that call other functions. The `catch` block could even contain no statements at all.

TIP

Calling functions from within `catch` blocks can be dangerous, especially if you call the function that caused the thrown exception in the first place.

USING MULTIPLE throw STATEMENTS AND MULTIPLE catch BLOCKS

Often, several types of exceptions can occur within a function. You can write a function to throw any number of exceptions, and you can provide multiple `catch` blocks to react appropriately to each type of exception that is thrown.

```cpp
#include<iostream>
#include<string>
using namespace std;
int dataEntry()
{
   const int MAX = 100;
   const string MSG = "Value is negative";
   int userEntry;
   cout<<"Enter a positive value less than "<<MAX<<" ";
   cin>>userEntry;
   if(userEntry < 0)
        throw(MSG);
   if (userEntry >= MAX)
        throw(userEntry);
   return userEntry;
}
int main()
{
    int value = 0;
    try
    {
        value = dataEntry();
    }
    catch(string msg)
    {
        cout<<msg<<endl;
    }
    catch(int badValue)
    {
        const int REDUCTION = 100;
        value = badValue % REDUCTION;
        cout<<"The number you entered, "<<badValue<<
            ", is too large."<<endl;
        cout<<"So it is being reduced to "<<value<<endl;
    }
    cout<<"The value at the end of the program is "
        <<value<<endl;
}
```

Figure 12-12 A `dataEntry()` function that throws two types of exceptions

For example, you can create a `dataEntry()` function that throws a string message when the user enters a negative number, but throws an invalid value when the user enters a number that is greater than 100. In the example in Figure 12-12, the `dataEntry()` function throws two types of exceptions—a string and an integer. When a function throws more than one type of exception, then you can write multiple `catch` blocks as shown in the `main()` function. Figure 12-12 shows that if the `string MSG` is thrown, it is caught by the first `catch` block; if the integer is `thrown`, it is caught by the second `catch` block; and that if the function ends normally and the `userEntry` is returned, it is assigned to the `value` variable in the `main()` function.

When you run the program in Figure 12-12, if no exception is thrown, the program bypasses both `catch` blocks and prints the valid value, as shown in Figure 12-13. If the user enters a negative number, as shown in Figure 12-14, then a string is thrown. In this case, the first `catch` block executes, and the second `catch` block is bypassed. If the user enters a number greater than or equal to 100, as in Figure 12-15, then an integer is thrown. In this case, the first `catch` block is bypassed, and the second `catch` block executes. In this `catch` block, the remainder that results when the number is divided by 100 is used as the value; the value of `badValue % 100` always produces a number no larger than 99. In Figure 12-12, whether the `dataEntry()` function ends normally (with the `return` statement) or throws an exception, the program ends with the `cout` statement that follows the last `catch` block.

Figure 12-13 Output of program in Figure 12-12 when user enters a value between 0 and 99 inclusive

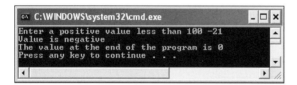

Figure 12-14 Output of program in Figure 12-12 when user enters a negative value

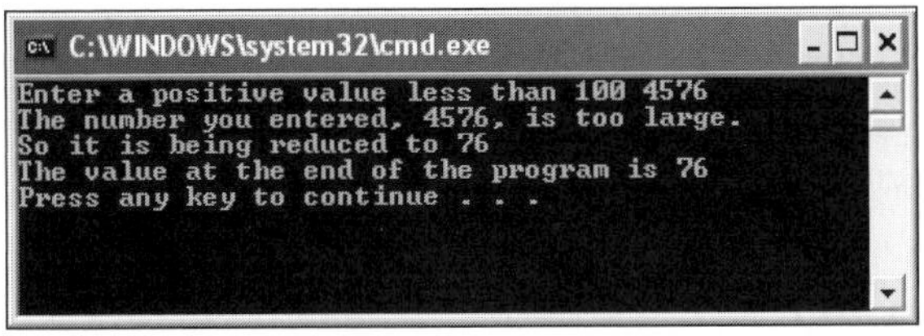

Figure 12-15   Output of program in Figure 12-12 when user enters a value that is 100 or greater

Remember, if an exception is thrown, and no catch block matches the type of the thrown parameter, then the program terminates.

TIP

THROWING OBJECTS

Just as simple variables such as doubles, ints, and strings can be thrown via exception-handling techniques, programmer-defined class objects can also be thrown. This approach is particularly useful in two types of situations:

- If a class object contains errors, you may want to throw the entire object, rather than just one data member or a string message.

- Whenever you want to throw two or more values, you can encapsulate them into a class object so that they can be thrown together.

12

Throwing Standard Class Objects

Figure 12-16 shows an Employee class containing two data fields, empNum and hourlyRate. The insertion operator is overloaded in the same way you have seen it coded in many other classes, but in this Employee class, the extraction operator has been overloaded to throw an exception. As you can see in the shaded if statement, if either the Employee empNum or the Employee hourlyRate is too high or too low, the entire Employee object is thrown.

```
class Employee
{
   friend ostream& operator<<(ostream&, Employee&);
   friend istream& operator>>(istream&, Employee&);
   private:
      int empNum;
      double hourlyRate;
};
```

Figure 12-16   The Employee class

```
ostream& operator<<(ostream &out, Employee &emp)
{
   out<<"Employee "<<emp.empNum<<" Rate $"<<
      emp.hourlyRate<<" per hour";
   return out;
}
istream& operator>>(istream &in, Employee &emp)
{
   const int LOWNUM = 100;
   const int HIGHNUM = 999;
   const double LOWPAY = 5.65;
   const double HIGHPAY = 39.99;
   cout<<"Enter employee number ";
   in>>emp.empNum;
   cout<<"Enter hourly rate ";
   in>>emp.hourlyRate;
   if(emp.empNum < LOWNUM || emp.empNum > HIGHNUM ||
      emp.hourlyRate < LOWPAY || emp.hourlyRate > HIGHPAY)
        throw(emp);
   return in;
}
```

Figure 12-16   The `Employee` class (continued)

Any program that uses the **Employee** class can catch the thrown **Employee** object and handle it appropriately for the application. A few possibilities include:

- A program might assign default values to any **Employee** whose data entry resulted in an exception.

- A program that tests the accuracy of data entry operators might store caught exceptions just as they are entered and count them.

- A program that is used when hiring **Employee**s for a special assignment that pays more than the usual maximum might ignore the high-end salary violations.

- A program might refuse to accept an **Employee** with an exception, and force the user to reenter the values, as in the **main( )** function shown in Figure 12-17.

```
int main()
{
   const int NUM_EMPLOYEES = 3;
   Employee aWorker[NUM_EMPLOYEES];
   int x;
   for(x = 0; x < NUM_EMPLOYEES; ++x)
   {
      try
      {
         cout<<"Employee #"<<(x+1)<<"   ";
         cin>>aWorker[x];
      }
```

Figure 12-17   A `main( )` function that instantiates three `Employee` objects

```
        catch(Employee emp)
        {
            cout<<"Bad data! "<<emp<<endl<<
                "Please re-enter"<<endl;
            --x;
        }
    }
    cout<<endl<<"Employees:"<<endl;
    for(x = 0; x < NUM_EMPLOYEES; ++x)
    cout<<aWorker[x]<<endl;
}
    cout<<endl<<"Employees:"<<endl;
    for(x = 0; x < NUM_EMPLOYEES; ++x)
        cout<<aWorker[x]<<endl;
}
```

Figure 12-17   A `main()` function that instantiates three `Employee` objects (continued)

The program in Figure 12-17 declares an array of three `Employee` objects. Within a `for` loop, a `count` is displayed, and the data entry occurs within a `try` block. If the `Employee` class insertion operator throws an exception, the user is notified that the data entry attempt was invalid, the subscript is decremented so that the user will enter new data in the same array position as the invalid data, and the data entry is tried again. Figure 12-18 shows a typical run of the program. The data entry is tried repeatedly until three valid `Employee`s, have been entered; only then are the three valid `Employee`s shown.

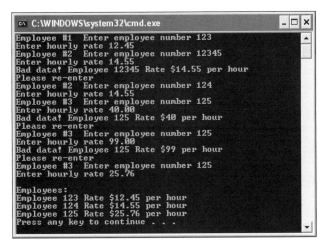

Figure 12-18   Typical execution of the `main()` function in Figure 12-17

TIP   Although this chapter uses data entry functions as typical examples of functions that generate exceptions, you should understand that any function might cause an exception that you choose to handle.

Throwing Multiple Object Types

When you include multiple `catch` blocks in a program, the first `catch` block that is able to accept a thrown object is the one that will execute. When you create a function that throws several types, such as an integer and an `Employee`, it doesn't matter which `catch` block you place first. If an `Employee` object is thrown, the appropriate `catch` block executes whether it is written before or after the integer `catch` block. Similarly, if you develop an `Inventory` class, and a function throws both an `Employee` and an `Inventory` object, it does not matter which `catch` block is placed first.

However, if you need to throw both a base class object and an object that is a member of its derived class from the same function, and you want to carry out different operations when they are caught, then you must code the `catch` for the derived object first. For example, if you create an `Employee` class and a child `PartTimeEmployee` class, and either might be thrown from a function, then you must code the `catch` block for the `PartTimeEmployee` object first. If you code the `Employee` `catch` block first, the derived `PartTimeEmployee` object that is thrown will incorrectly match the first catch block because, as a child of `Employee`, a `PartTimeEmployee` "is an" `Employee`. If the `Employee` `catch` block precedes the `PartTimeEmployee` `catch` block, no object can ever reach the second `catch` block.

Throwing Exception Objects

You can create a class that represents an exception. For instance, you might create a class that contains both bad data and a message concerning that data. The class is instantiated only when an exception occurs; each object of such a class is an **exception object**.

Figure 12-19 shows a `Customer` class that is similar to many classes you already have worked with. Each `Customer` holds data fields for a customer number and a balance due, and has access to overloaded extraction and insertion operators that you can use for input and output. The overloaded extraction operator prompts the user for values for the data fields. It allows any `Customer` number, but checks the entered `balanceDue` against a `HIGH_CREDIT_LIMIT` constant that has been set to $1,000. The shaded `if` statement shows that when the `Customer` balance exceeds the credit limit, a new object of type `CustomerException` is created. The `CustomerException` object has the local name `e`, and its constructor takes two arguments—the `Customer` object and a warning string. The newly created `CustomerException` object is then thrown from the overloaded `operator>>( )` function. Any program that creates a `Customer` object and uses the `operator>>( )` function within a `try` block can choose to `catch` the encapsulated `CustomerException` object, and use the `Customer` data, the message, both, or neither as the programmer deems appropriate for the application.

```
class Customer
{
   friend ostream& operator<<(ostream&, Customer&);
   friend istream& operator>>(istream&, Customer&);
   private:
       int custNum;
       double balanceDue;
};
ostream& operator<<(ostream &out, Customer &cust)
{
    out<<"Customer "<<cust.custNum<<" Balance $"<<
       cust.balanceDue;
    return out;
}
istream& operator>>(istream &in, Customer &cust)
{
   const double HIGH_CREDIT_LIMIT = 1000;
   cout<<"Enter Customer number ";
   in>>cust.custNum;
   cout<<"Enter balance due ";
   in>>cust.balanceDue;
   if(cust.balanceDue > HIGH_CREDIT_LIMIT)
   {
      const string WARNING = "Balance due exceeds limit!";
      CustomerException e(cust, WARNING);
      throw(e);
   }
   return in;
}
```

Figure 12-19 The Customer class

Figure 12-20 shows the CustomerException class. Its data members include a Customer object and a string message, and its constructor requires values for both. The CustomerException class also contains a showMsg() function that displays the details of the Customer object (using the Customer class overloaded insertion operator) and the string message.

TIP Some C++ programmers often give names that begin with a lowercase x (for exception) to classes that are created specifically to handle exceptions, although this violates the general guideline that class names should begin with an uppercase character.

```
class CustomerException
{
   private:
       Customer cust;
       string errorMessage;
   public:
       CustomerException(Customer, string);
       void showMsg();
};
CustomerException::CustomerException(Customer aCust,
     string msg)
{
     cust = aCust;
     errorMessage = msg;
}
void CustomerException::showMsg()
{
     cout<<cust<<endl<<errorMessage<<endl;
}
```

Figure 12-20   The CustomerException class

Figure 12-21 shows a **main( )** function that declares an array of four **Customer** objects. In this program, a loop contains four calls to the overloaded **operator>>( )** function. Because each of the data entry functions is within a **try** block, the **catch** block can accept a **CustomerException** object if the balance entered by the user exceeds the $1,000 credit limit. The program in Figure 12-21 accepts the **Customer** data into the array whether the balance is high or not, but displays the warning message that is part of the thrown **CustomerException** object for those **Customers** with a balance exceeding $1,000. Figure 12-22 shows the output of a typical execution of the program, in which some of the **Customers** exceed the credit limit and others do not.

The application in Figure 12-21 could have been written to handle the thrown exception in any number of ways. For example, instead of allowing a high balance and displaying a warning, the **catch** block could have forced the balance to a lower figure, forced reentry of the data, stored the amount over the high balance limit in a variable for later processing, or simply accepted the balance without warning, even though it exceeded the limit. When you use exception-handling techniques, the application that uses a function that might throw an exception controls how the exception is handled.

```
int main()
{
    const int NUM_CUSTS = 4;
    Customer aCust[NUM_CUSTS];
    int x;
    for(x = 0; x < NUM_CUSTS; ++x)
    {
        try
        {
            cout<<"Enter data for customer #"<<(x+1)<<"  ";
            cin>>aCust[x];
        }
        catch(CustomerException error)
        {
            error.showMsg();
            cout<<endl;
        }
    }
    cout<<endl<<"Customer list:"<<endl;
    for(x = 0; x < NUM_CUSTS; ++x)
        cout<<aCust[x]<<endl;
}
```

Figure 12-21   Program that instantiates four `Customer`s, some with high balances

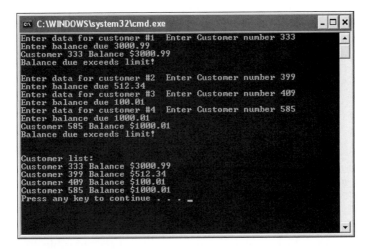

Figure 12-22   Typical execution of program in Figure 12-21

TIP

When creating a class to hold an exception, make sure that the instantiation of your exception class does not result in the same problem as the original error did. For example, if the original error was caused by insufficient memory, it's probably a poor idea to have the exception class constructor allocate more memory.

USING THE DEFAULT EXCEPTION HANDLER

When any object is thrown with a `throw` statement, then a subsequent `catch` block has a usable match if one of the following conditions is true:

- The type of the thrown object and the type of the `catch` argument are identical (for example, `int` and `int` or `EmployeeException` and `EmployeeException`).

- The type of the thrown object and the type of the `catch` argument are the same, except the `catch` contains the `const` qualifier, a reference qualifier, or both (for example, `int` can be caught by `const int`, `int&`, or `const int&`).

- The `catch` argument type is a parent class of the thrown argument. For example, if `PartTimeEmployee` derives from `Employee`, a `catch` block with an `Employee` argument can catch both.

If you throw an argument and no `catch` block exists with an acceptable argument type, then the program terminates. To avoid termination, you can code a **default exception handler** that catches any type of object not previously caught. You create a default exception handler by creating a `catch` block with an ellipsis (…) as its argument. If you use a default `catch` block, it must be the last `catch` block listed after a `try`. The default `catch` block will catch any type of thrown object that has not been caught by an earlier `catch` block.

TIP Besides avoiding unexpected program termination, you might want to code a default `catch` block when you need to handle several exception types the same way. For example, if a function might throw an `int`, `double`, or `string` and you want to handle the `int` exception one way but the other types in the same way, then you need only two `catch` blocks—one for the `int` and the other one that is a default `catch` block.

USING EXCEPTION SPECIFICATIONS

Any C++ function might throw any type of object. You might not realize how many different types of objects a function throws if you fail to carefully examine the code. You can explicitly indicate the exceptions that a function can possibly throw by writing an **exception specification**, which is a declaration of a function's possible `throw` types. Creating an exception specification provides documentation for later users of the function by indicating what types of errors might possibly be thrown. The user then can plan appropriate `catch` blocks. If a function throws an error whose type was not listed in its exception specification, then it will produce a run-time error, and abort the program.

You write an exception specification in both a function's prototype and in a function's header immediately after the list of function arguments. Simply write the keyword `throw` followed by a list of argument types in parentheses. For example, for a `dataEntry( )` function that takes no arguments and returns an integer—and that might throw a character, a `double`, or an `Employee` object—you could code the function header as follows:

```
int dataEntry() throw(char, double, Employee)
```

Besides throwing a character, `double`, or `Employee`, the function `int dataEntry() throw(char, double, Employee)` could also throw any object of a class derived from the `Employee` class.

If you write an exception specification with empty parentheses following `throw`, you declare that the function will not throw any exceptions. For example, the following `dataEntry( )` function will not throw any exceptions:

```
int dataEntry() throw()
```

Remember that function headers and prototypes that do not include an exception specification list can throw anything (or might throw nothing). You have seen many such functions throughout this chapter. In other words, if you do not specify the exceptions, then any type of exception might be thrown. But once you do specify the exceptions for a function, then only those types listed should be thrown. In some compilers, if you use a `throw` specification clause with a function, and then `throw` a type that is not listed, an error will occur and the program will stop prematurely.

If you include an exception specification list with a function, and code a throw type that is not listed, the program will compile and execute if the unlisted type is never actually thrown. For example, if a function specification list does not include type `double`, but the function throws a `double` as the result of a negative data entry, and if no user ever enters a negative value, the function will still run correctly. However, if a user does enter a negative value and the `double` is thrown, then the program will end because `double` was not included in the specification list.

Be careful when writing an exception specification using a function template because any type might eventually be instantiated. If you can't predict what type the function might throw, it is safer to omit the specification list.

Visual C++ departs from the ANSI standard in its implementation of exception specifications. In Visual C++ .NET, you receive a warning that the exception specification is ignored. However, including an exception specification for documentation purposes is still a good idea.

In Java, the exception specification list is written using "`throws`" instead of "`throw`", and makes more sense grammatically.

UNWINDING THE STACK

When you write a function, you can **try** a function call and, if the function you call throws an exception, you can catch the exception. However, if your function that calls the exception-throwing function doesn't catch the exception, then a function that calls your function can still catch the exception. A simpler way to say this is that if function A calls function B, function B calls function C, and function C throws an exception, then if B does not catch the exception, function A can. If no function catches the exception, then the program terminates. This process is called **unwinding the stack**, because each time you call a function, the address of the place to which the logic should return at the end of the function is stored in a memory location called the stack. Each time you return from a function, the correct return-to destination is retrieved from the stack.

You can picture the stack as a stack of plates, as shown in Figure 12-23. When you stack plates on top of each other, and later want to dismantle the stack, you must remove the last plate stacked before you can remove the previous one. Similarly, when a **main()** function calls **functionA()**, the computer "remembers" where to return at the end of the function by placing the return location (memory address) that resides in **main()** at the bottom of the stack. When **functionA()** calls **functionB()**, the return location within **functionA()** is placed "on top of" the **main()** address in the stack. When **functionB()** ends, the top address in the stack (the one that returns to **functionA()**) is retrieved from the stack and the logic continues within **functionA()**. When **functionA()** ends, the next address in the stack (the one that returns to **main()**) is retrieved, and the logic continues with the rest of the **main()** function.

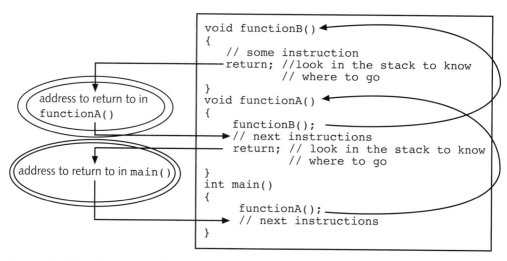

Figure 12-23   Unwinding the stack

Consider a simple Dog class like the one shown in Figure 12-24. It holds a Dog's name and age, and supports overloaded insertion and extraction operators. In this example, the overloaded extraction operator that provides data entry uses the shaded if statement to throw the Dog object if the Dog's age is higher than the specified limit.

```
class Dog
{
    friend ostream& operator<<(ostream&, Dog&);
    friend istream& operator>>(istream&, Dog&) throw(Dog);
    private:
        string name;
        int age;
};
ostream& operator<<(ostream &out, Dog &dog)
{
    out<<dog.name<<" Age: "<<dog.age<<" years old";
    return out;
}
istream& operator>>(istream &in, Dog &dog) throw(Dog)
{
    const int HIGH_AGE = 20;
    cout<<"Enter dog's name ";
    in>>dog.name;
    cout<<"Enter age ";
    in>>dog.age;
    if(dog.age > HIGH_AGE)
        throw(dog);
    return in;
}
```

Figure 12-24   The Dog class

Figure 12-25 shows a KennelReservation class that holds information about boarding a Dog. Each KennelReservation includes a kennel number, a month and day for the reservation, and a Dog. The extraction operator implementation includes an exception specification (which is shaded) indicating that the extraction operator might throw a Dog object. If you examine the operator>>( ) function code, you cannot find a throw statement. The throw is hidden within the Dog class overloaded operator>>( ) function. If the Dog class input function throws an exception, it will be passed to the KennelReservation input function. Since the KennelReservation input function does not catch the exception, the exception will be passed on to any function that uses the KennelReservation operator>>( ) function.

12

```
class KennelReservation
{
    friend ostream& operator<<(ostream&, KennelReservation);
    friend istream& operator>>(istream&, KennelReservation&)
        throw (Dog);
    private:
        int kennelNumber;
        Dog dog;
        int month;
        int day;
};
ostream& operator<<(ostream &out, KennelReservation res)
{
    out<<"Reservation for "<<res.dog<<" for "<<res.month
        <<"/"<<res.day<<" for kennel #"<<res.kennelNumber;
    return out;
}
istream& operator>>(istream &in, KennelReservation &res)
    throw(Dog)
{
    cout<<"Enter kennel # ";
    in>>res.kennelNumber;
    cout<<"Enter month ";
    in>>res.month;
    cout<<"Enter day ";
    in>>res.day;
    in>>res.dog;   // call to Dog operator>>()
    return in;
}
```

Figure 12-25   The KennelReservation class

Within the KennelReservation function in Figure 12-25, both shaded exception spec-ifications could be deleted, and the class would still function properly. However, they provide useful documentation. Without the exception specifications, a client who uses the KennelReservation class might be unaware or forget that the Dog class throws an exception. Using the exception specification clause in the KennelReservation input function prototype and header provides a reminder to users that they might want to place the KennelReservation operator>>( ) call within a try block, and they might want to catch any potentially thrown Dog object.

Figure 12-26 shows a main( ) function that instantiates a KennelReservation object, and Figure 12-27 shows a typical execution. When the user enters KennelReservation data, Dog data also is entered. When the user's data causes an exception, the Dog input function throws an exception to the KennelReservation input function, which throws the exception to main( ), which in turn catches it and displays a message. In this main( ) function, the Dog is allowed to have a high age, but a warning message is issued. Other client programs that use the KennelReservation class might use a default age or require the user to reenter the age.

```
int main()
 {
     KennelReservation aRes;
     try
     {
        cin>>aRes;
     }
     catch(Dog aDog)
     {
        cout<<"Please call the owner and verify the age."<<
             endl;
     }
     cout<<aRes<<endl;
 }
```

Figure 12-26   A main() function that instantiates a KennelReservation

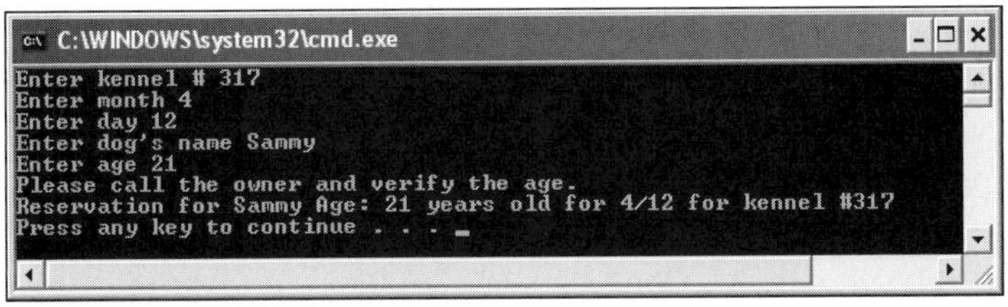

Figure 12-27   Typical execution of program in Figure 12-26

12

HANDLING MEMORY ALLOCATION EXCEPTIONS

Recall from Chapter 9 that you can use the operator **new** to allocate new memory dynamically while a program is running. For example, a common place to allocate memory is when you want to create an array whose size is not determined until a program executes.

When you allocate memory, enough memory might not be available on your computer. If the **new** operator fails, the program ends abruptly. Because an out-of-memory condition causes a problem in any application, the creators of C++ created an out-of-memory exception handler. The **set_new_handler() function** was created to solve the universal problem of insufficient memory. To use it, you insert #include<new> at the top of your program file.

You use the set_new_handler() function by creating a function to handle the error, then passing that error-handling function's name (which is a pointer to the function) to the set_new_handler() function. The function you create to handle the error cannot return any values; it must be type void. You must call set_new_handler() within your program with a statement that takes the following form:

```
set_new_handler(nameOfYourErrorHandlingFunction);
```

TIP

Notice that when you pass the error-handling function's name to the `set_new_handler()` function that you do not include the parentheses that you normally associate with a function name.

For example, Figure 12-28 shows a shaded `handleMemoryDepletion()` function that simply displays a message and exits the application. The `main()` function that calls it passes the name of the `handleMemoryDepletion()` function to the `set_new_handler()` function (in the shaded statement within `main()`). Then the `main()` function attempts to allocate 30 arrays that each hold ten million doubles. The loop control variable is displayed for two reasons: (1) the program takes so long to execute that displaying a count of the number of loops helps to assure you that the program is actually running, and (2) you can see how many loops execute before the computer runs out of memory for the application. Figure 12-29 shows the output of a typical execution of the program. In the output, you see from the displayed messages that the `handleMemoryDepletion()` function is executed after the memory–allocation loop has executed 19 times.

TIP

If you execute the program in Figure 12-28 on your own computer, you might not run out of memory at the same spot. You might even have to increase the number of loops to be able to recreate the out-of-memory situation.

TIP

If you execute the program in Figure 12-28 on your own computer, it might take several minutes to execute.

```
#include<iostream>
#include <new>
using namespace std;
void handleMemoryDepletion()
{
    cout<<"Out of memory!"<<endl;
    exit(1);
}
int main( )
{
    int NUM = 10000000;
    set_new_handler(handleMemoryDepletion);
    const int LIMIT = 30;
    for(int x = 0; x < LIMIT; ++x)
    {
        double *a = new double[NUM];
        cout<<"x is "<<x<<endl;
    }
}
```

Figure 12-28   Program that attempts to allocate a significant amount of memory

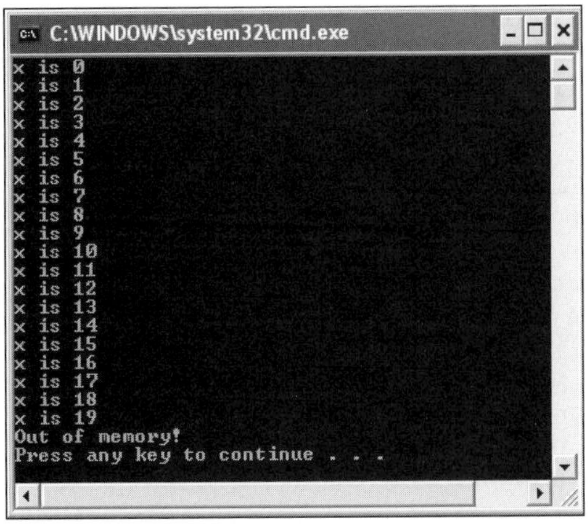

Figure 12-29   Output of program in Figure 12-28

YOU DO IT

Throwing an Exception

In the next set of steps, you create a `passwordEntry()` function that asks a user to supply a password. The function takes an integer argument that indicates the maximum legal password size so that any function that calls `passwordEntry()` can specify its own appropriate size; the function throws the password when the entered password exceeds the size limit. If the password is valid (not too long), then the password is returned to the calling function.

The function could limit password character entry to eight characters by requiring the user to enter one character at a time and counting the characters. However, by allowing even longer passwords to be entered and throwing an exception when the password is too long, the calling function gains control over how the `passwordEntry()` function is used. For example, a calling function might be written to display an error message, to use only the valid portion of the entered password, or to replace the invalid password with a default value.

1. Open a new file in your C++ editor. Type the first statements you will need in this program. You include the `string` class so that you can display a string, and you include the `cstring` file because it contains a function that calculates a string's length.

```
#include<iostream>
#include<string>
#include<cstring>
using namespace std;
```

2. The `passwordEntry()` function takes a constant unsigned integer argument that indicates the maximum password length and returns a character pointer that contains the address of the user's password string. The function allows passwords up to 300 characters and checks to ensure the calling function does not attempt to exceed this limit.

```cpp
char* passwordEntry(unsigned int allowedSize)
{
    const unsigned int MAX_SIZE = 300;
    char password[MAX_SIZE];
    if(allowedSize > MAX_SIZE)
        allowedSize = MAX_SIZE;
```

3. Once a valid password size is established, prompt the user for and accept the password. The `strlen()` function returns the length of a string; use it to compare the length of the entered password to the maximum size as requested by any client of the `passwordEntry()` function. Throw the password if it exceeds the maximum size as requested by the calling function. If the entered password has a valid size, then return the password.

```cpp
    cout<<"Enter your password. ";
    cin>>password;
    if(strlen(password) > allowedSize)
        throw(password);
    return(password);
}
```

4. Next, write a `main()` function that declares a constant for the maximum password length allowed in this application and declares a string to hold a password. In a `try` block, call the `passwordEntry()` function using the desired maximum length as the argument.

```cpp
int main()
{
    const unsigned int LEGAL_PASSWORD_SIZE = 8;
    string password;
    try
    {
        password = passwordEntry(LEGAL_PASSWORD_SIZE);
    }
```

5. If an exception is thrown, catch it, display an error message, and use a default value of all asterisks for the password. Finally, display the password whether it was valid or invalid and close the `main()` function with a curly brace.

```cpp
    catch(char *pswrd)
    {
        cout<<"Password is invalid"<<endl;
        password = "********";
    }
    cout<<"Password entered is stored as "<<password<<endl;
}
```

6. Save the program as **Password1.cpp**, then compile and execute the program, entering a valid password of eight characters or less. The output is similar to Figure 12-30. Execute the program entering an invalid password (over eight characters). The output is similar to Figure 12-31.

TIP   When you run or compile the Password1.cpp program, your compiler might issue one or two warnings. For example, some compilers issue a warning because the pswrd variable named in the `catch` block is never used. You can ignore these warnings.

Figure 12-30   Output of Password1.cpp when a valid password is entered

Figure 12-31   Output of Password1.cpp when an invalid password is entered

12

Throwing Multiple Exceptions

In the next set of steps, you modify the Password program so that it throws two types—a string and an integer.

1. Open the **Password1.cpp** file if it is not still open. Immediately save it as **Password2.cpp** in the same location.

2. Currently, within the `passwordEntry()` function, if the function argument `allowedSize` is greater than 300, you simply force `allowedSize` to 300. Now, you will throw an exception instead. Remove the statement

```
if(allowedSize > MAX_SIZE)
      allowedSize = MAX_SIZE;
```

and replace it with the following statement:

```
if(allowedSize > MAX_SIZE)
      throw(allowedSize);
```

3. To demonstrate that the throw works when a calling function requests that the allowed password size should exceed 300, change the value for the `LEGAL_PASSWORD_SIZE` in the `main()` function from 8 to any value over 300—for example, **350**.

4. Within the `main()` function, insert a new `catch` block just after the closing brace of the existing `catch` block, and just before the `cout` statement that displays "Password entered is stored as ". The new `catch` block catches an integer, and sets the password to four X's.

```
catch(const unsigned int size)
{
    password = "XXXX";
}
```

5. Save the program again (as **Password2.cpp**). Compile and execute the program. The output looks like Figure 12-32. Because the `main()` function requested a password that is too large, the `passwordEntry()` function throws the size, and the `main()` function uses "XXXX" as the password value. Any other program that uses the `passwordEntry()` function and requests a size of 300 or less will work as before—either the password will be entered correctly and be stored as the user enters it, or the password entered will exceed the requested limit and eight asterisks will be stored.

When you compile the Password2.cpp program, your compiler might issue one or two warnings. You can ignore these warnings.

Figure 12-32   Execution of Password2.cpp

Using a Default `catch` Block

In the next set of steps, you demonstrate that a default `catch` block works as expected to catch any exceptions not listed in previous `catch` blocks. You will create an `Order` class whose data entry function accepts several values for a customer order and throws a variety of exception types. You decide to handle two types of exceptions with specific actions, and the other types of exceptions with a default action.

1. Open a new file in your C++ editor and enter the include statements you need for this program.

```
#include<iostream>
#include<string>
using namespace std;
```

2. Create the definition for an `Order` class that contains fields for an order number, quantity ordered, price of each item, and order total. Two overloaded operators provide means for input and output. An additional public function is available to set an `Order`'s data fields to zeros.

```
class Order
{
    friend ostream& operator<<(ostream&, const Order&);
    friend istream& operator>>(istream&, Order&);
    private:
        int orderNum;
        int quantity;
        double priceEach;
        double total;
    public:
        void zeroAll();
};
```

3. The `zeroAll()` function sets each `Order` field to zero.

```
void Order::zeroAll()
{
    orderNum = 0;
    quantity = 0;
    priceEach = 0;
    total = 0;
}
```

4. Add the overloaded `operator<<()` function that displays an `Order`'s details.

```
ostream& operator<<(ostream &out, const Order &order)
{
    out<<"Order "<<order.orderNum<<" for "<<order.quantity
        <<" items  at $"<<order.priceEach<<"  Total due $"
        <<order.total;
    return out;
}
```

5. The overloaded `operator>>()` function holds declarations for the `Order` constants and prompts the user for `Order` values. After the `Order` values have been entered, an `Order` total is calculated by multiplying quantity ordered by price for each item ordered. Begin the overloaded extraction operator implementation as follows:

```
istream& operator>>(istream &in, Order &order)
{
    const int HIGH_ORDER_NUM = 9999;
    const string ORDER_MSG = "Order number is too high.";
    const int HIGH_QUANTITY = 50;
    const double HIGH_PRICE_EACH = 39.95;
    const double HIGH_TOTAL = 1000.00;
    cout<<"Enter order number - no higher than "<<
        HIGH_ORDER_NUM<<" ";
```

12

```
in>>order.orderNum;
cout<<"Enter quantity ";
in>>order.quantity;
cout<<"Enter price per item ";
in>>order.priceEach;
order.total = order.quantity * order.priceEach;
```

6. Continue the overloaded `operator>>()` function with a series of statements that test the validity of each entered value. When the order number is too high, throw a `string` message. When the quantity or price of an item in an `Order` is too high, throw the offending field. When a calculated total is too high, throw the entire `Order` object. Finally, if no error is detected and nothing is thrown, return from the function.

```
    if(order.orderNum > HIGH_ORDER_NUM)
        throw(ORDER_MSG);
    if(order.quantity > HIGH_QUANTITY)
        throw(order.quantity);
    if(order.priceEach > HIGH_PRICE_EACH)
        throw(order.priceEach);
    if(order.total > HIGH_TOTAL)
        throw(order);
    return in;
}
```

7. Next, write a `main()` function that begins by declaring five `Order` objects and trying data entry for each one.

```
int main()
{
    const int NUM_ORDERS = 5;
    Order anOrder[NUM_ORDERS];
    int x;
    for(x = 0; x < NUM_ORDERS; ++x)
    {
        try
        {
            cout<<"Order #"<<(x+1)<<"   ";
            cin>>anOrder[x];
        }
```

8. Still within the data-entry `for` loop, add several `catch` blocks so that you can handle each error type in a specific way for the current application. Suppose that in this application you want to do the following:

- Force the user to reenter an `Order` when the order number is incorrect and a `string` is thrown

- Issue a warning message when a total is high and an `Order` is thrown

- Set each field in an `Order` to 0 if any other errors are detected, and either an integer or `double` is thrown

Enter the three appropriate `catch` blocks as follows, ending with the closing curly brace for the `for` loop:

```
catch(string msg)
{
   cout<<msg<<" Please re-enter"<<endl;
   --x;
}
catch(Order orderWithHighTotal)
{
   cout<<"Order accepted -";
   cout<<"but check credit limit before shipping"<<
      endl;
}
catch(...)
{
   cout<<"Either the quantity or price is too high. "
      <<"Setting all values to 0."<<endl;
   anOrder[x].zeroAll();
}
}
```

9. After data entry is complete, display the five `Order`s and add the closing brace for the program.

```
cout<<"Order list:"<<endl;
for(x = 0; x < NUM_ORDERS; ++x)
   cout<<anOrder[x]<<endl;
}
```

10. Save the file as **OrderExceptions.cpp**. Compile and run the program, sometimes choosing input values that reflect each of the possible exception situations. Figure 12-33 shows a typical program execution. At the first `Order` entry prompt, the user enters an order number that is too high, so a string message is thrown. When it is caught, the user is prompted to reenter the order and the subscript for the `Order` array is decremented (so the next entry will occupy the position of the `Order` with the too-high order number). After entering the first order correctly, the user enters the second order with a quantity that exceeds the allowed value. When this error is detected, an integer is thrown. Because the first two `catch` blocks in `main()` are coded to accept a `string` and an `Order` object respectively, the first two `catch` blocks are bypassed, and the default `catch` block executes and sets all the fields in the order to 0.

When the third `Order` is entered, the quantity and the price are within acceptable limits, but their product (the total price) exceeds $1,000. An `Order` is thrown and the `catch` block displays a warning message but accepts the `Order`. For the fourth `Order`, the order number and quantity are acceptable, but the price of the item is too high. The thrown price is a `double`, so when it is thrown the `catch` blocks that accept a `string` and an `Order` are bypassed. As with the integer, the thrown **double** causes the default **catch** block to execute, setting the **Order**'s fields to zeros. In the last **Order**, all the data is acceptable. Finally, the output shows a summary of the five **Order**s.

Figure 12-33   Typical execution of **OrderExceptions** application

---

CHAPTER SUMMARY

- A popular traditional way to handle error situations was to terminate the program. A superior alternative to traditional error-handling techniques is called exception handling. The actions you take with exceptions involve trying, throwing, and catching them.

- The general principle underlying good object-oriented error handling is that any function that is called should check for errors, but should not be required to handle an error if it finds one. When an object-oriented program detects an error within a function, the function should send an error message to the calling function, or throw an exception. You throw an exception by using the keyword **throw** followed by any C++ object. Functions can make multiple throws, and a function can make throws of different types.

- When a function might cause an exception, and therefore includes a **throw** statement to handle errors, the call to the potentially offending function should be placed within a **try** block.

- To handle a thrown object, you include one or more **catch** blocks in your program immediately following a **try** block. If you want a **catch** block to execute, it must catch the correct type of argument thrown from a **try** block. If an argument is thrown and no **catch** block exists with a matching argument type, then the program terminates.

❐ You can write a function to throw any number of exceptions, and you can provide multiple `catch` blocks to react appropriately to each type of exception that is thrown.

❐ Just as simple variables such as `double`s, integers, and `string`s can be thrown via exception-handling techniques, so can programmer-defined class objects. You can throw standard class objects, or create exception classes as a way of encapsulating objects and messages. When you write `catch` blocks for parent and child classes, code the catch for the derived object first.

❐ You can create a class that represents an exception. Usually, the class is instantiated only when an exception occurs.

❐ If you throw an argument and no `catch` block exists with an acceptable argument type, then the program terminates. To avoid termination, you can code a default exception handler that catches any type of object not previously caught. You create a default exception handler by creating a `catch` block with an ellipsis (…) as its argument, and place the `catch` block as the last one listed after a `try`.

❐ You can explicitly indicate the exceptions that a function can possibly throw by writing an exception specification, which is a declaration of a function's possible throw types.

❐ When you allocate memory, it is always possible that there is not enough memory available, so the creators of C++ created an out-of-memory exception handler called `set_new_handler()`. You use `set_new_handler()` by creating a function to handle the error, then passing the function's name to the `set_new_handler()` function.

12

KEY TERMS

Exceptions are errors that occur during execution of object-oriented programs, so-named because, presumably, they are not usual occurrences.

Exception handling is the set of object-oriented techniques used to manage execution-time errors.

The **exit() function** forces a program to end.

The **atexit() function** requires a function name as its argument; this function is then registered with `atexit()`, which means the named function is called automatically whenever the `exit()` function executes.

An **exception** is an object that contains information that is passed from the place where a problem occurs to another place that will handle the problem.

A **message** is a passed object that contains information.

When an object-oriented program detects an error within a function, the function should send an error object to the calling function, or **throw an exception**. A `throw` resembles a return statement in a function, except that the execution of the program does not continue from where the function was called.

A **try block** consists of one or more statements that the program attempts to execute, but which might result in thrown exceptions.

To handle a thrown object, you include one or more **catch** blocks in your program immediately following a **try** block. A **catch block** contains statements that execute when an exception is thrown.

An **exception object** is created when an exception occurs and contains information about the exception.

A **default exception handler** catches any type of object not previously caught; you create a default exception handler by creating a **catch** block with an ellipsis (...) as its argument.

An **exception specification** is a declaration of a function's possible **throw** types.

Unwinding the stack is the process of, in turn, returning from each called function to the one that called it.

The **set_new_handler()** **function** handles the problem of insufficient memory.

REVIEW QUESTIONS

1. Errors that occur during a program's execution are called _____.

    a. faults

    b. omissions

    c. exceptions

    d. exclusions

2. Traditionally, computer program error-handling techniques most often resulted in _____.

    a. displaying multiple, confusing error messages

    b. recompiling the program

    c. terminating the program

    d. terminating the programmer

3. A general principle of object-oriented error handling is that a function that might cause an exception should _____.

    a. detect an exception but not handle it

    b. handle an exception but not detect it

    c. both detect and handle exceptions

    d. not allow exceptions to occur

4. When a function sends an error message to the calling function, the function is said to _____ an exception.

    a. **try**

    b. **throw**

    c. **catch**

    d. create

5. A throw most closely resembles _____.

  a. an `exit`

  b. a `catch`

  c. an output statement

  d. a `return`

6. You can throw objects that are _____ type.

  a. `int` and `double`

  b. any built-in

  c. any class

  d. any

7. Which of the following is true?

  a. A single function can throw two different data types.

  b. A single `throw` statement can throw two different data types.

  c. A single `catch` block can catch two different (and named) data types.

  d. All of the above are true.

8. Which of the following is true?

  a. You cannot have a `try` without a `catch`.

  b. You cannot have a `throw` without a `catch`.

  c. You cannot have a `catch` without a `try`.

  d. You cannot have a function without a `throw`.

9. A program _____ `throw` an exception from a function named within a `try` block.

  a. might

  b. must

  c. cannot

  d. must be compiled twice in order to

10. A `catch` block can contain _____ argument(s).

  a. no

  b. exactly one

  c. exactly two

  d. any number of

11. A `catch` block _____.

  a. must not contain an argument

  b. must use any argument it receives

  c. can use any argument it receives

  d. cannot use any argument it receives

12

12. If an argument is thrown and no `catch` block exists with a matching argument type, then the program _____.

    a. terminates

    b. continues without problem

    c. displays a warning and continues

    d. uses an automatically-supplied default `catch` block

13. Which of the following is true when you `try` a function that throws three different types of exceptions?

    a. The program will not compile.

    b. You must provide exactly three `catch` blocks to react appropriately to each type of exception that is thrown.

    c. You can provide up to three `catch` blocks to react appropriately to each type of exception that is thrown.

    d. You must provide one `catch` block with three arguments to react appropriately to each type of exception that is thrown.

14. When a `try` block contains a function that might throw an exception, but no exception is thrown, then the program _____.

    a. terminates

    b. issues a warning, but continues with statements beyond any `catch` blocks

    c. continues without incident

    d. uses a default `catch` block

15. When you include multiple `catch` blocks in a program, and a thrown object can be accepted by two of them, _____.

    a. the program will not compile

    b. the first `catch` block will execute

    c. the last `catch` block will execute

    d. you cannot predict which `catch` block will execute

16. A primary reason you might create an exception class is to _____.

    a. avoid exception situations

    b. improve program documentation

    c. avoid having to throw and catch objects

    d. encapsulate an object with appropriate error messages

17. A default exception handler catches _____.

    a. any type of object not previously caught

    b. all objects

    c. the first object thrown from a function

    d. the last object thrown from a function

18. The primary reason you use an exception specification is _____.

   a. to allow multiple exceptions to be thrown

   b. as a substitute for `catch` blocks

   c. to avoid having to use the default `catch` block

   d. for documentation

19. Functions that contain no exception specification list _____.

   a. can throw string messages

   b. can throw anything

   c. might throw nothing

   d. all of the above

20. The purpose of the `set_new_handler()` function is to _____.

   a. exit a program with insufficient memory

   b. recognize out-of-memory situations, and call a function you specify

   c. allocate new memory for dynamically created arrays

   d. throw memory-exception messages to predefined functions

EXERCISES

1. Create a class named `RealEstate` that has data members to hold the price of a house, the number of bedrooms, and the number of baths. Member functions include overloaded insertion and extraction operators. Write a `main()` function that instantiates a `RealEstate` object, allows the user to enter data, and displays the data members entered. The `main()` function should display an appropriate thrown error message if negative values are entered for any of the data members. Save the file as **RealEstate.cpp**.

2. Create a class named `Television` that has data members to hold the model number of a television, the screen size in inches, and the price. Member functions include overloaded insertion and extraction operators. If more than four digits are entered for the model number, if the screen size is smaller than 12 or greater than 70 inches, or if the price is negative or over $5,000, then throw an integer. Write a `main()` function that instantiates a `Television` object, allows the user to enter data, and displays the data members. If an exception is caught, replace all the data member values with zero values. Save the file as **Television.cpp**.

3. Create an `Inventory` class with data members for stock number, quantity, and price, and overloaded data entry and output operators. The data entry operator function should throw:

   ❏ An error message, if the stock number is negative or higher than 999

   ❏ The quantity, if it is less than 0

   ❏ The price, if it is over $100.00

12

Then perform the following tasks:

a. Write a `main()` function that instantiates an array of five `Inventory` objects, and accepts data for each. Display an appropriate error message for each exception situation. When an exception is detected, replace all data fields with zeros. At the end of the program, display data fields for all five objects. Save the file as **Inventory.cpp**.

b. Write a `main()` function that instantiates an array of five `Inventory` objects and accepts data for each. If an exception is thrown because of an invalid stock number, force the user to reenter the stock number for the `Inventory` object. If the quantity is invalid, do nothing. If the price is in error, then set the price to 99.99. (Add a `setPrice()` function to the `Inventory` class to accomplish this.) At the end of the program, display data fields for all five objects. Save the file as **Inventory2.cpp**.

c. Write a `main()` function that instantiates an array of five `Inventory` objects and accepts data for each. If an exception is thrown because of an invalid stock number, force the stock number to 999; otherwise, do nothing. (Add any needed functions to the `Inventory` class.) At the end of the program, display data fields for all five objects. Save the file as **Inventory3.cpp**.

4. Create a class named `Student` that holds a student ID and a grade point average, and contains functions for construction, insertion, and extraction. The constructor function should accept arguments for the ID number and grade point average, and throw a `Student` object if the ID is larger than four digits or the grade point average is negative or greater than 4.0. The extraction operator should prompt the user for field values and throw a `Student` object under the same error conditions. Write a `main()` function that, first, tries to instantiate a `Student` with invalid data, and second, tries to input data for a `Student`. In each case, `catch` any exception and handle each in a unique manner that you choose. For example, when the constructor fails, you might choose to display a message, but when the extraction operator fails, you might choose to reset the `Student` fields to default values. Save the file as **Student.cpp**.

5. Complete the following tasks:

a. Create a `Meal` class. Data fields include a `string` entrée name and a `double` price. Include a data entry function that prompts for and accepts values for both data fields, and that throws an exception if the price is less than $5.00 or more than $29.99. Include a public function that returns the `Meal` price so that you can use it in a calculation in the `Party` class that you will create in part c of this problem. Also include an overloaded insertion operator to display a `Meal`'s data values.

b. Create an `EntertainmentAct` class. Data fields include a `string` phone number for the contact person for the act and a `double` fee for the entertainment act. Include a data entry function that prompts for and accepts values for both data fields, and that throws an exception if the price is less than $50.00 or more than $3,000. Include a public function that returns the `EntertainmentAct` price so that you can use it in a calculation in the `Party` class that you will create in part c of this problem. Also include an overloaded insertion operator to display an `EntertainmentAct` object's data values.

c. Create a **Party** class for a party-planning organization. A **Party** contains a **Meal**, an **EntertainmentAct**, an integer number of guests invited to the party, and a total cost for the party. The **Party** data entry function prompts the user for **Meal**, **EntertainmentAct**, and guest number values. The function also calculates the **Party** cost, based on the **Meal**'s price times the number of guests, plus the price of the **EntertainmentAct**.

d. Write a **main( )** function that instantiates at least five **Party** objects and accepts data for each. When you run the program, provide data that tests that each type of exception is being recognized. The **main( )** function should catch the exceptions and display an appropriate error message about each. Save the file as **Party.cpp**.

6. Create a **Job** class that holds a **Job** ID number and the cost of the **Job**. Include insertion and extraction operators. Create a **JobException** class that holds a **Job** and an error message. When the user enters **Job** data, if the **Job** fee is below $250, then create a **JobException** object and throw it. Write a **main( )** function that declares an array of eight **Job** objects. If a **JobException** object is thrown during the data entry for any **Job**, require the user to enter data for a new **Job**, and replace the invalid **Job**. Save the file as **Job.cpp**.

7. Create a **Book** class that holds a **Book** ID number, title, author, number of pages, and price. The book title and author are character pointers. Include a constructor that allocates 80 characters of new memory for each. Include insertion and extraction operators. Create a **BookException** class that holds a **Book** and an error message. When manufacturing a **Book**, the number of pages should be evenly divisible by four; if it is not, then create a **BookException** object and throw it. The price should be between $5.00 and $250.00 inclusive; if it is not, create a **BookException** object and throw it. Write a **main( )** function that declares an array of five **Book** objects. If a **BookException** object is thrown during the data entry for any **Book**, require the user to enter data for a new **Book** to replace the invalid **Book**. Save the file as **Book.cpp**.

8. Complete the following tasks:

a. Create a class named **Teacher** that holds a **Teacher**'s first and last names and the grade level the **Teacher** teaches. Include a constructor function that uses default first and last names, such as "ZZZZZZ" and a default grade level, such as 0, when no arguments are provided.

b. Create a class named **Student** that holds a **Student**'s first and last names. Include a constructor function that uses default first and last names, such as "ZZZZZZ," when no names are provided.

c. Create a class named **Classroom**. A **Classroom** holds a **Teacher** and an array of 35 **Student** objects.

d. Create a class named **School**. A **School** contains an array of 100 **Classroom** objects. (This class is designed to be a very large class, to more quickly demonstrate running out of memory.)

12

e. In a `main()` demonstration function, declare a pointer to an array of 500 `School` objects and include code to handle any memory allocation errors that occur. In a loop, declare 500 array objects at a time, continuing to rewrite the `main()` function if necessary until you create enough `School` objects to cause a memory allocation exception. (*Hint:* You might want to display a count periodically to assure yourself that the `School` objects are being created.) When memory is exhausted, display an appropriate message and terminate the application. Save the file as **School.cpp**.

9. Each of the following files in the Chapter12 folder contains syntax and/or logical errors. Determine the problem in each case, and fix the program. Save your solutions by adding "Fixed" to the filename, as in **DEBUG12-1Fixed.cpp**.

   a. DEBUG12-1.cpp

   b. DEBUG12-2.cpp

   c. DEBUG12-3.cpp

   d. DEBUG12-4.cpp

CASE PROJECT 1

CASE PROJECTS

You have been developing a `Fraction` class for Teacher's Pet Software. Each `Fraction` contains a numerator, denominator, a whole number portion, and has access to several functions you have developed, including overloaded operators. Complete these tasks:

a. Create a `FractionException` class. The class contains a `Fraction` object and a string message explaining the reason for the exception. Include a constructor that requires values for the `Fraction` and the message. Also include a function that displays the message.

b. Modify each `Fraction` class constructor and data entry function so that it throws a `FractionException` whenever a client attempts to instantiate a `Fraction` with a zero denominator.

c. Write a `main()` function that asks the user to enter values for four `Fraction`s. If the user attempts to create a `Fraction` with a zero denominator, catch the exception, display a message, and force the `Fraction` to 0 / 1. Display the four `Fraction` objects. Save the file as **FractionException1.cpp**.

d. Write a `main()` function that asks the user to enter values for four `Fraction`s. If the user attempts to create a `Fraction` with a zero denominator, catch the exception, display a message, and force the user to reenter the `Fraction` values. Display the four `Fraction` objects. Save the file as **FractionException2.cpp**.

e. Write a `main()` function that asks the user to enter values for four `Fraction`s. If the user attempts to create a `Fraction` with a zero denominator, catch the exception, display a message, and terminate the program. Save the file as **FractionException3.cpp**.

CASE PROJECT 2

You have been developing a **BankAccount** class for Parkville Bank that contains several fields and functions, including overloaded operators. You have also created child classes derived from the **BankAccount** class: **CheckingAccount**, **SavingsAccount**, and **CheckingWithInterest**. Complete these tasks:

a. Create a **BankAccountException** class. The class contains a **BankAccount** object and a string message explaining the reason for the exception. Include a constructor that requires values for the **BankAccount** and the message. Also include a function that displays the message.

b. Modify each **BankAccount** class constructor and data entry function so that it throws an exception whenever a client attempts to instantiate a **BankAccount** with an account number that is less than 1000 or greater than 9999.

c. Write a **main()** function that asks the user to enter values for four **BankAccounts**. If the user attempts to create a **BankAccount** with an invalid account number, catch the exception, display a message, and force the account number and balance to 0. Display the four **BankAccount** objects. Save the file as **BankException1.cpp**.

d. Write a **main()** function that declares an array of four **CheckingAccounts**. (The **CheckingAccount** constructor calls the **BankAccount** data entry function, so an exception might be thrown.) If the user attempts to create a **CheckingAccount** with an invalid account number, catch the exception, and, before ending the program, display two messages. The first message is the string message contained in the **BankAccountException** object. The second indicates which **CheckingAccount** (1, 2, 3, or 4) caused the early termination. If all four **CheckingAccounts** are valid, then display them. Save the file as **BankException2.cpp**.

e. Alter the **SavingsAccount** constructor to make sure an exception is thrown when the account number is invalid (based on the same rules for a **BankAccount** account number) and also when the interest rate is negative. (Make sure the messages are different.) Write a **main()** function that declares an array of four **SavingsAccounts**. If the user attempts to create a **SavingsAccount** with an invalid account number or a negative interest rate, catch the exception, display the appropriate message, and display which account caused the early termination (1, 2, 3, or 4). If all four **SavingsAccounts** are valid, then display them. Save the file as **BankException3.cpp**.

12

13

ADVANCED INPUT AND OUTPUT

In this chapter, you will:

♦ Discover how `cout` and `cin` possess the same traits as other C++ objects
♦ Use `istream` member functions
♦ Use `ostream` member functions
♦ Use manipulators
♦ Create your own manipulators
♦ Learn about computer files and the data hierarchy
♦ Perform file output
♦ Read a file from within a program
♦ Read and write objects

From the first time you wrote a line of code in C++, you used **cout** to display data; shortly thereafter, you used **cin** for input. You could use the **cin** and **cout** objects long before you knew anything about object-oriented programming, and before you even knew that **cin** and **cout** were objects, in part because **cout** and **cin** resemble real-world objects (your screen and your keyboard), and real-world objects are easy to understand. In this chapter, what you have learned about object-oriented programming in general will help you gain a deeper understanding of input and output.

Throughout your C++ programming experiences, you have written functions. Now that you understand how your own classes and member functions work, you can take advantage of one of the most powerful aspects of modern programming languages—using the classes and functions that other programmers have already created for you.

Understanding `cin` and `cout` as Class Objects

You can think of `cout` and `cin` as real-world objects. Like other C++ objects you have created, `cout` and `cin` are members of a class. Their class is derived from another class (which is derived from yet another class), so they use inheritance. The `cout` and `cin` objects can take advantage of overloaded operators such as << and >> (which are used for shifting bits in other contexts). The `cout` and `cin` objects also use polymorphism—they can generate different machine instructions when placed with different types of variables (with integers rather than characters, for example). In other words, `cout` and `cin` have all the characteristics of any class objects you have created throughout this book.

 You don't have to understand objects or classes to use `cin` or `cout`. That's part of the appeal of object-oriented programming. Just as you can use a microwave oven without knowing how it works, you can use well-designed C++ objects without knowledge of the implementation details.

 You will learn about using << and >> for shifting bits in Chapter 14.

Almost all (if not all) the C++ programs you have written have included the directive `#include<iostream>`. The name `iostream` is short for "input and output" stream. When you include `iostream` in a program using the `#include` statement, you are including a file that contains the definition for a derived template named `basic_iostream`.

 You first learned about templates in Chapter 11.

In C++, a **stream** is a sequence of bytes used in an input or output operation. In an input operation, the stream flows from an input device—for example, a keyboard—to computer memory. In an output operation, the stream flows from memory to an output device—for example, a monitor.

 It is convenient to think of bytes flowing in an input or output stream as characters that can be displayed, such as 'A' and 'B'. However, instead of characters, they might be parts of graphic images or sound or other unprintable bytes.

C++ provides both low-level and high-level input/output (I/O) capabilities. **Low-level I/O** is unformatted; that is, bytes are transferred into and out from memory without regard to the type of data they represent. This type of unformatted I/O is best suited for high-volume processing where speed is very important. **High-level I/O** is formatted; that is, bytes are grouped into meaningful units such as integers, **doubles**, and class object types. This form of I/O is useful to programmers most of the time.

In older versions of C++, the stream libraries available in C++ enabled the input and output of single bytes, which could contain a **char**. Because it is only one byte in size, a **char** can contain only 256 different values, including the ASCII character set, which includes values such as 'A', 'B', '1', and '2'. However, many languages contain more characters than one byte can hold, so **Unicode** was developed as an extended, international encoding system. In Unicode, you can represent characters from Latin, Hebrew, Ancient Greek, and dozens of other languages. Unicode provides a unique code for every character no matter what language or operating system is used. The standard stream libraries in newer versions of C++ enable programmers to perform I/O operations with Unicode characters using a new data type named **wchar_t**. Newer versions of C++ contain class templates with specializations for processing both **char** and **wchar_t** data types.

You first learned about the ASCII character set in Chapter 1. To learn more about Unicode, visit *www.unicode.org*.

TIP

The grandparent base class from which **basic_iostream** is derived is named **basic_ios**. The **basic_istream** and **basic_ostream** classes are both derived from **basic_ios**, and so they are parents to **basic_iostream**. The **basic_istream** class handles input, and includes a definition of the extraction operator >>. The **basic_ostream** class handles output, and includes a definition of the insertion operator <<. The **basic_iostream** class is derived from both **basic_istream** and **basic_ostream**, so **basic_iostream** inherits all the properties of both parent classes, including the >> and << operators. In other words, the **basic_iostream** class is a working example of multiple inheritance. Figure 13-1 illustrates the relationships among **basic_ios**, **basic_istream**, **basic_ostream**, and **basic_iostream**.

13

Technically, templates are not inherited, However, the template specializations that enable **char** I/O are classes and so they can be inherited.

TIP

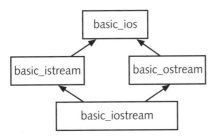

Figure 13-1   The family tree of **basic_iostream**

Within the `iostream` library, the creators of C++ have used `typedef`s to provide aliases for the template names that begin with basic and the underscore. A **typedef** is a C++ statement that provides a synonym for an identifier in a C++ program; it is a way to create a shorter, easier-to-remember nickname for an unwieldy identifier. The `typedef`s `istream`, `ostream`, and `iostream` are used for character input and output; this book will use these shorter terms throughout this chapter.

USING `istream` MEMBER FUNCTIONS

In C++, the easiest way to read a character is to use `cin` with the extraction operator, for example, `cin>>someVariable;`. The extraction operator is actually an overloaded function named `operator>>()`. You can overload the `>>` operator to work with your own class objects. If you create a class named `Person` and declare a `Person` named `someOne`, the extraction operator can be overloaded, and then you can write `cin>>someOne;`. Similarly, the creators of C++ have also overloaded `>>` to work to input all built-in data types, so you can make statements such as `cin>>someInteger;` and `cin>>someDouble;`. When you make these statements, the compiler determines the data type of the object to input and selects the correct version of the overloaded extraction function. When you include `iostream` at the top of your program files, you gain access to these functions.

TIP

You learned to overload insertion and extraction operators to work with your own classes in Chapter 9.

Besides the overloaded extraction operator, including `iostream` provides several other functions related to input.

Using the `get()` Function

Another member function of the `istream` class is `get()`. The **get()** function takes a character argument and returns a reference to the object that invoked the `get()` function; therefore multiple `get()` function calls can be chained in a statement. Its prototype has the following form:

```
istream& get(char &);
```

The `get()` function takes a reference to a character as an argument, and returns a reference to the `istream` class which is the address of the `cin` object that is used in the function call. You use the `get()` function with the `cin` object just like you use other member functions with an object—you use the object name, the dot operator, and the function name. For example, the following code segment uses two statements to accept three characters from the keyboard:

```
char first, middle, last;
cin.get(first);
cin.get(middle).get(last);
```

TIP

The `cin.get()` statement can retrieve any character, including letters, numbers, punctuation, and white space such as the character generated by pressing the Enter key.

Most compilers overload `get()` so that, in addition to taking a character reference as an argument, it can also take no argument. The following version of the `get()` function returns the character being read as an integer. Its prototype is:

```
int get();
```

The preceding form of the function often is used when it doesn't matter which character is extracted, and you do not need to store the character. For example, the following statements allow a program to wait for the user to press a key; there is no need to store the value of the key.

```
cout<<"Press any key to continue";
cin.get();
```

TIP

You also can use the `getch()` function to accept a keyboard character.

13

The `istream` class `get()` function is also overloaded so that it can take two or three arguments. The prototype is as follows:

```
istream& get(char *str, int len, char c = '\n');
```

This form of `get()` allows you to input a string of characters. The first argument is a pointer that holds the address of the string. The second argument is the number of characters that will be stored. The third argument is the character that terminates the entry, often called the **delimiter character**. The default value to stop data entry, as you can see from the prototype, is the Enter key, which is coded as '\n'. If you don't supply an alternative third argument, the Enter key automatically becomes the signal to end data entry.

TIP

Recall that a character pointer or the name of a character array can be used as a string address.

The second argument of the `get()` function—the number of characters to be stored—is very important. Without the second argument, a user could destroy memory by entering a string of characters that was longer than the area prepared to receive it. Figure 13-2 contains a program in which a 10-character limit is applied to the entry for **userName**. Because the length of the string is limited to 10 in the **cin.get()** statement, if a user enters a name longer than nine characters, only the first nine characters and a string-ending null character will be stored. If no provision was made to limit the user's entry, a long entry could be stored starting at the address of the **userName** array, but when the entry continued past the end of the array, it would destroy other values stored in memory beyond the locations reserved for **userName**. Figure 13-3 shows the output of the program when the entered name is short enough to fit in the allocated area. Figure 13-4 shows the output when the entered name is too long.

```cpp
#include<iostream>
using namespace std;
int main()
{
    const int SIZE = 10;
    char userName[SIZE];
    cout<<"Enter your name ";
    cin.get(userName, SIZE);
    cout<<"Hello, "<<userName<<endl;
}
```

Figure 13-2   Program using the get() function

Figure 13-3   Typical execution of program in Figure 13-2

Figure 13-4   Another execution of program in Figure 13-2

In Figure 13-4, nine characters are shown—7 in Barbara, a space, and a J. The tenth character in the accepted string is the NULL character, which terminates all strings.

TIP

The output in Figure 13-4 illustrates a benefit of using the get() function instead of the extraction operator (>>) with cin for keyboard data entry. Using cin with the operator>>() function will bypass all white space characters (blanks, tabs, and newline characters) and stop accepting characters when white space is entered, but the get() function accepts white space characters into the variable arguments. If the program used the extraction operator, the output in Figure 13-4 would use only the name "Barbara".

TIP

Programmers refer to the character for which each bit holds a 0 as a null character. The C++ constant that represents this value is called NULL. In C++, strings end with NULL.

One unfortunate side effect of the get() function is that it leaves unused characters in the input stream. A subsequent call to get() retrieves the next (unused) character, whether or not that retrieval was intended. For example, when you modify the program in Figure 13-2 with the shaded additions shown in Figure 13-5, you'll receive the output shown in Figure 13-6. When you execute the program, you can't enter the class grade; the program seems to fly past the statement that gets the letter grade. The first cin.get() statement accepts the name from the keyboard, specifically "Barbara J" and appends a NULL character to the name string. The remaining characters entered at the keyboard ("ean") remain in the input stream. The second cin.get() statement is intended to retrieve the user's letter grade, but instead accepts the 'e', the next character waiting for input. As shown in Figure 13-6, the program doesn't stop to obtain the grade, because the second call to get() has already been satisfied with the waiting 'e' character.

13

```
#include<iostream>
using namespace std;
int main()
{
    const int SIZE = 10;
    char userName[SIZE];
    char grade;
    cout<<"Enter your name ";
    cin.get(userName, SIZE);
    cout<<"Hello, "<<userName<<endl;
    cout<<"Enter your grade in this class ";
    cin.get(grade);
    cout<<"Your grade is "<<grade<<endl;
}
```

Figure 13-5   Program that attempts to accept data after using the get() function

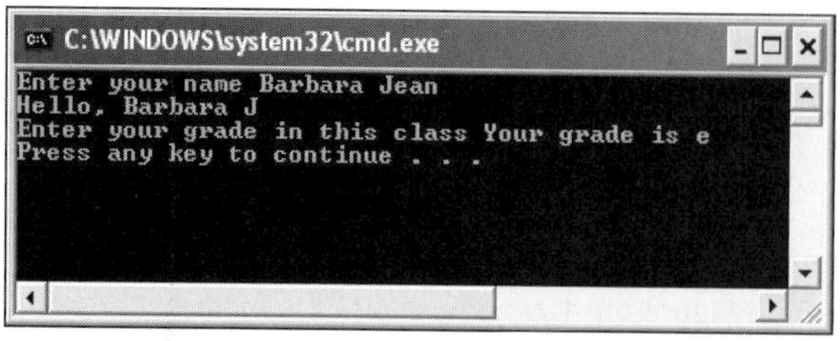

Figure 13-6   Typical execution of program in Figure 13-5

The program output shown in Figure 13-6 includes the first name and a waiting character (instead of an entered grade) for the letter grade. To allow the user to enter a grade, you could add `cin.get( )` statements to the program until the name was consumed before attempting to get the letter grade, but, because a user might enter a name of any length, including a short one that does not require any additional `get( )` statements, you cannot predict how many extra `get( )` statements to add, if any.

Using the `ignore( )` Function

It is impossible to guess how many `cin.get( )` statements are needed to consume all the potential additional letters of a name if you use the program in Figure 13-5. A superior alternative is to use the **`ignore( )`** function to ignore or skip any additional characters left in the input stream.

The prototype of the `ignore( )` function is:

```
istream& ignore(int length = 1, char c = '\n');
```

where *length* indicates the maximum number of characters to ignore, and the character argument indicates the consumed character that stops the `ignore( )` function. The prototype indicates that if you leave off the delimiting character argument, then the newline character is used by default. Additionally, if you leave off the length, then 1 is used by default. Typically, programmers use the `ignore( )` function as shown in the shaded statement in Figure 13-7. A high number (such as 100) is used for the length to ensure that even the longest name is accommodated. The output in Figures 13-8 and 13-9 show that whether the entered name is short or long, all characters that should not be part of the name are consumed, and the grade entry can proceed as intended. Unlike with the `get( )` function, the delimiting character ('\n' in the program in Figure 13-7) is absorbed when you use `ignore( )`.

```
#include<iostream>
using namespace std;
int main()
{
    const int SIZE = 10;
    char userName[SIZE];
    char grade;
    cout<<"Enter your name ";
    cin.get(userName, SIZE);
    cout<<"Hello, "<<userName<<endl;
    cin.ignore(100, '\n');
    cout<<"Enter your grade in this class ";
    cin.get(grade);
    cout<<"Your grade is "<<grade<<endl;
}
```

Figure 13-7   Program that uses the ignore() function

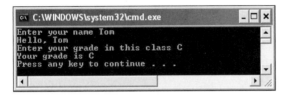

Figure 13-8   Execution of program in Figure 13-7 using a short name

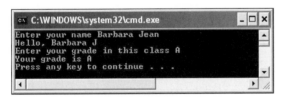

Figure 13-9   Execution of program in Figure 13-7 using a long name

13

Using the getline() Function

As an alternative to using an extra call to get() to absorb the Enter key after character data entry, or using the ignore() function to absorb any number of characters, you can include another istream member, getline(). Its prototype is:

```
istream& getline(char *str, int len, char  c = '\n');
```

You first learned about the getline() function in Chapter 5.

TIP

The **getline( ) function** reads a line of text at the address represented by **str**. It reads text until it reaches either the length used as the second argument or the character used as the third argument. (If you don't supply a third argument, the line-ending character becomes '\n' by default.) Like the **ignore( )** function, **getline( )** discards the newline character, so any additional data entry begins fresh. The program in Figure 13-10, and the output in Figure 13-11, show how the **getline( )** function correctly accepts characters up to and including the default newline delimiter. The **getline( )** function absorbs the newline character, so the subsequent prompt for and echo of the **listedStatus** character variable operates as intended.

```cpp
#include<iostream>
using namespace std;
int main()
{
    const int PHONE_SZ = 16;
    char phoneNumber[PHONE_SZ];
    char listedStatus;
    cout<<"Enter your phone number ";
    cin.getline(phoneNumber, PHONE_SZ);
    cout<<"Your number is "<<phoneNumber<<endl;
    cout<<"Enter an L if you are listed in the phone book,"<<endl;
    cout<<" O if listed with the operator only, ";
    cout<<" or N if not listed ";
    cin.get(listedStatus);
    cout<<"Listed status is "<<listedStatus<<endl;
}
```

Figure 13-10   Program that uses the **getline( )** function to get a phone number

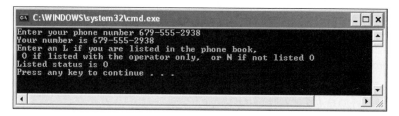

Figure 13-11   Typical execution of program in Figure 13-10

TIP

When you use a delimiter other than '\n' with **getline( )**, the **getline( )** function consumes the delimiter but leaves the subsequent Enter key in the input stream, so you still must account for it, perhaps by using an extra **get( )** statement. The difference between **get( )** and **getline( )** is the way each handles the delimiter character. The **getline( )** function consumes the delimiter character; the **get( )** function does not.

Some compilers contain a bug that requires you to press Enter twice after using the getline() function.

Other istream Member Functions

Most compilers support other istream member functions with names such as eof( ), bad( ), and good( ). For now, the point is that the istream class is not mysterious. It is just a class, not unlike many you have created, and cin is just an object that already has been instantiated for you. As an object, cin—like objects of most other classes—contains member functions. You use those member functions with the dot operator and the function name.

USING ostream MEMBER FUNCTIONS

The concepts you have learned while studying the cin object apply to the cout object as well. It is a member of a class (the ostream class), which supports member functions and overloaded operators just like the istream class—or any other class, for that matter. (You already know how to use one overloaded ostream class operator function—the operator<<( ) function.) Besides member functions, and just like other class objects, the cout object also has data members, or states.

Using stream member functions is just one method of formatting C++ output. See Appendix D for other useful formatting methods.

Using Format Flags with setf( ) and unsetf( )

Many of the states of the cout object are contained in a single long integer field, in which each bit represents some condition of the object. For example, the bit that represents "show positive sign" might be turned on. If so, any positive value subsequently sent through the output stream will be preceded by a plus sign (+) when that value is shown.

C++ actually instantiates three ostream objects. Besides cout, which is associated with the standard output device (usually a monitor), C++ includes cerr and clog, which are used for error conditions.

The arguments that determine the state of the cout object are called **format flags** or **state flags**. All format flags begin with ios::. As you know from your work with classes,

`::` is the scope resolution operator, and its use indicates that format flags are members of the `ios` base class. Some commonly used format flags are:

- `ios::left`—left-justifies output within the field size, which may be set by the `width( )` function (described in a following section)

- `ios::right`—right-justifies output within the field size

- `ios::dec`—formats numbers in decimal (base 10)

- `ios::showpos`—inserts a + before positive numbers

- `ios::showpoint`—displays the decimal point and six decimal positions for all floating-point numbers, including those for which the decimal part is 0

One member function of the `ios` class, the **setf( )** function, takes arguments that set the bits of `cout`; that is, the arguments turn the bits in the format flag on. Like any member function, `setf( )` is called by using an object's name, followed by a dot, followed by the function name. For example, the statement `cout.setf(ios::showpos);` turns on the bit that forces the display of the plus sign with positive numbers. Subsequent output will show the + with positive values. Another member, the **unsetf( )** function, can be used to deselect the bit. For example, you can call `cout.unsetf(ios::showpos);`.

TIP
You will probably prefer using manipulators rather than using `ostream` member functions as described here. However, it's important that you understand how `ostream` member functions work so you can write your own manipulators. (Manipulators are discussed later in this chapter.)

Using the `setf( )` function, you also can combine format flags using the bitwise OR operator (|). The following statements, when placed together, produce output that is signed, in base 10 format, and with six significant digits—the output appears as +4.00000.

```
cout.setf(ios::showpos | ios::dec | ios::showpoint);
cout<<4.0;
```

Using the `width( )` Function

You can change the output field width with the `iostream` member **width( )** function. This function defines the size of the output field in which the next output will be displayed. By default, the argument will be right-aligned in this field. Of course, you can use the `ios::left` format flag to change the default alignment. For example, the following pair of statements produces three blanks followed by 13, for a total output of five characters.

```
cout.width(5);
cout<<13;
```

The `width( )` function applies only to the first subsequent field to be output. As a result, you must call it each time you want a width specification to take effect. For example, the program in Figure 13-12 produces the output shown in Figure 13-13. The width is set to 10 before an output loop begins, then the constant value 22 displays in a loop. The width setting applies only to the first instance of 22; the remaining 22s are not assigned a field width. In the second loop in the program in Figure 13-12, the `width()` function appears within the loop, so it is called again before each time 33 is displayed, and the 33 is right-aligned in a 10-space field each time it appears.

```cpp
#include<iostream>
using namespace std;
int main()
{
    int x;
    const int TIMES = 3;
    const int WIDTH = 10;
    cout.width(WIDTH);
    for(x = 0; x < TIMES; ++x)
        cout<<22<<endl;
    for(x = 0; x < TIMES; ++x)
    {
        cout.width(WIDTH);
        cout<<33<<endl;
    }
}
```

Figure 13-12   Program that demonstrates the `width()` function

Figure 13-13   Output of program in Figure 13-12

TIP   The `width()` function is particularly useful when displaying lists of numbers. You almost always want to view numeric values right-aligned.

TIP   When you display a number left-aligned in a field, it is difficult to tell whether the width function is working correctly unless you produce output after the value. For example, the following produces 78, three spaces (completing the field width of 5), and an X. Without the X, you would not realize the output field was so wide.

```cpp
cout.setf(ios::left);
cout.width(5);
cout<<78<<"X"<<endl;
```

13

If the value you provide for the `width()` function is not large enough to include all of the displayed value, then the width designation is disregarded. For example, the following statements display 5555 on the screen, not 55 as you might expect; the width designation is simply ignored.

```
cout.width(2);
cout<<(5555);
```

The creators of C++ assumed that seeing an accurate value is more important than having the value properly aligned.

Using the `precision()` Function

You can use the **precision() function** to control the number of significant digits you see in the output. For example, the constant 12.54321 contains seven digits. To display just four digits, giving the output as 12.54, you can use the following statements:

```
cout.precision(4);
cout<<12.54321;
```

Unlike the `width()` function, which must be called again prior to subsequent output, the `precision()` function applies to all subsequent output fields until the precision is reset by another call to it.

USING MANIPULATORS

If you want to control the number of positions shown to the right of the decimal point (instead of simply the number of significant positions visible), you must use a manipulator. A **manipulator** (or a **manipulator function**) is used to manipulate, or change, the state of the `cout` object. When you use a standard function with `cout`, you use the dot operator and parentheses. When you use a manipulator, you use the insertion operator with the `cout` object.

The **fixed manipulator** allows you to output a specified number of decimal places. When you combine `cout<<fixed;` with a call to the `precision()` function, the value used as the argument to the `precision()` function becomes the number of decimal places shown, instead of the precision. For example, the following code segment produces 12.5432 (but not the 1), displaying four decimal places instead of four digits in total as it would without using `fixed`:

```
cout.precision(4);
cout<<fixed;
cout<<12.54321<<endl;
```

TIP

No matter how many decimal positions a number contains, C++ will display six positions if you do not explicitly set a precision for output.

Many manipulators have been coded and placed in libraries included with your C++ compiler. You have already used the **endl** manipulator to output a newline character and flush the output stream. It is easy to use **endl** because you can chain it with the insertion operator (<<) within the same statements as other output. For example, you have written statements similar to the following in your C++ programs:

```
cout<<"Hello"<<endl<<"How are you?"<<endl;
```

In addition to endl, C++ provides a flush operator to flush the stream without sending a newline character, and also provides an ends operator to send a null (or space) character rather than a newline.

Even though manipulators are functions, this book refers to many that do not need arguments without the parentheses that usually follow function names. For example, this book refers to endl, not endl( ). If a manipulator requires parentheses when you call it, then this book uses parentheses when referring to it.

Using the `setprecision()` Manipulator

You use the **setprecision() manipulator** to specify the number of decimals that will display. The **setprecision()** manipulator works like the **precision()** function—it specifies the number of significant digits to display. However, it is considered a manipulator instead of a member function because you chain a call to **setprecision()** along with other output and the insertion operator, rather than using an object and a dot operator, as you do with **cout.precision()**.

Any C++ manipulator, such as **setprecision()**, that takes an argument requires the inclusion of the **iomanip** file in your program. Any manipulator, such as **endl**, that does not take an argument does not require the inclusion of **iomanip**.

The program in Figure 13-14 produces the output in Figure 13-15. The program uses the **setprecision()** manipulator in a loop, and increases the value of its argument from 0 through 6. When the precision is set to 0, the output shows four decimal places, which is the minimum that can be shown while still expressing the value. When the precision is set to 1, one decimal place is shown; the value .8888 becomes .9 when set to display a single decimal place. When the **setprecision()** argument is not 0, but smaller than the number of digits in the output value, rounding takes place. When the argument to the **setprecision()** manipulator is greater than or equal to the number of digits in the value to be output, then the full value is shown.

13

```
#include<iostream>
#include<iomanip>
using namespace std;
int main()
{
    int x;
    const int TIMES = 7;
    for(x = 0; x < TIMES; ++x)
        cout<<"precision "<<x<<"   "<<
             setprecision(x)<<0.8888<<endl;
}
```

Figure 13-14   Program using the `setprecision()` manipulator

Figure 13-15   Output of program in Figure 13-14

The `setprecision()` manipulator doesn't perform any tasks that the `cout.precision()` member function can't accomplish, but the `cout` statement that actually outputs the data includes the precision, and the intention is clearer.

Using the `setw()` Manipulator

The **`setw()` manipulator** allows you to set the width of a field for output. Use of the `setw()` manipulator requires inclusion of the `iomanip` file, because `setw()` requires an argument that represents the width of the output field. The `setw()` manipulator works like the `width()` member function you can use with the `cout` object; the advantage of using `setw()` is its chaining capability in a `cout` statement. As with the `width()` function, output is right-justified in the field, and if the parameter sent to `setw()` is too small to support the displayed value, then the width is simply ignored. Also like the `width()` function, you must repeat `setw()` for each new output, even if you write just one `cout` statement. For example, the following statement produces two spaces followed by 123 (because 123 is shown in a field of 5), followed immediately by 456. The 456 does not have a width of 5:

```
cout<<setw(5)<<123<<456<<endl;
```

On the other hand, because of the extra shaded call to `setw()`, the following statement produces two spaces, 123, two more spaces, and 456:

```
cout<<setw(5)<<123<<setw(5)<<456<<endl;
```

Using the `setiosflags()` and `resetiosflags()` Manipulators

Two additional manipulators, `setiosflags()` and `resetiosflags()`, each perform several manipulations, depending on the flags (such as `ios::left` or `ios::showpoint`) they receive as arguments. The **setiosflags()** manipulator turns on bit codes for the attributes named as arguments; the **resetiosflags()** manipulator turns off those bit codes. As with other manipulators, the advantage of using `setiosflags()` and `resetiosflags()` relates to their ability to be placed in a `cout` statement chain, as opposed to using a `cout.setf()` member function call prior to actual data output. As with `setf()`, the bitwise OR operator (`|`) can be used with `setiosflags()` or `resetiosflags()`, as in the following:

```
cout<<setw(7)<<setiosflags( ios::showpos | ios::left)<<
    12<<"X"<<endl;
```

The preceding code displays 12 with a positive sign left–aligned in a field of size seven.

Using the oct, hex, and `showbase` manipulators

You can output integral values in octal (base 8) or hexadecimal (base 16) using the **oct** and **hex** manipulators. For example, the following displays 1f, which is 31 in base 16:

```
cout<<hex<<31<<endl;
```

Including the **showbase manipulator** in the chain of output displays octal numbers with a leading 0 and hexadecimal numbers with a leading 0x so you do not mistake them for base 10 (decimal) numbers. For example, the following displays 0x1f:

```
cout<<showbase<<hex<<31<<endl;
```

TIP

Programmers use hexadecimal numbers to represent computer memory addresses. For business programming, you almost always want to display numbers in the default decimal format.

Many additional manipulators have been created for you. Table 13-1 lists just some of them.

Table 13-1 Some useful manipulators

Manipulator	Purpose
boolalpha	Insert or extract bool objects as their names (true or false) instead of numeric values
dec	Insert or extract values in decimal (base 10) format
fixed	Insert floating-point values in fixed format
hex	Insert or extract values in hexadecimal (base 16) format
noboolalpha	Insert or extract bool objects as their numeric values (1 or 0)
noshowpoint	Do not prefix a value with its base
noshowpos	Do not insert a plus sign for nonnegative numbers
oct	Insert or extract values in octal (base 8) format
scientific	Insert floating-point values in scientific format
showbase	Prefix value with its base
showpoint	Show decimal point in floating-point values
showpos	Insert + before nonnegative values

CREATING MANIPULATOR FUNCTIONS

The code to produce output in the desired format using the **ostream** member functions can become quite tedious to write. For example, if you need to display a variable named **amountMoney** in currency format with a dollar sign in a field size of twelve, you might write the code shown in Figure 13-16. You need several statements before you can output the actual dollar figure you want to be shown:

```
cout<<'$';
cout<<setprecision(2);
cout<<fixed;
cout.width(12);
cout<<amountMoney<<endl;
```

Figure 13-16 Displaying a variable in currency format

The statements in Figure 13-16 would correctly display the **amountMoney** variable with a dollar sign and two decimal points, right-aligned in a field of twelve spaces. If you needed to display more money values in the same format, then at least the first statement, **cout<<'$';**, and the last statement, **cout.width(12);**, would have to be executed again before you could display the next figure. When you use the **iostream** member functions, not only are many statements needed to obtain the correct format, but nothing in the final **cout** statement (**cout<<amountMoney<<endl;**) indicates the format you are using. If the program is revised (and almost all programs are revised eventually) and new statements are added between the several **cout** calls, it becomes difficult for someone reading the program code to see how **amountMoney** will look on output.

When you create a manipulator function, the desired results become much clearer. Any output manipulator function you create should take as an argument an instance of `ostream` as a reference. It also should return the same reference. This approach allows manipulators to be chained or stacked with other calls to the `cout` insertion operator.

TIP You can code manipulators for `cin` as well as `cout`, but you are less likely to need to do so.

For example, you could write a manipulator to format output as currency, as shown in Figure 13-17. Creating the function requires you to write the statements that display the dollar sign and so on, but when the statements are packaged as a function that receives and returns a reference to `ostream`, you can code `cout<<currency<<amountMoney;` to display the value with the proper formatting. The results are not different, but the code is clearer and concise. In the `main()` function in Figure 13-17, the shaded call to the `currency` manipulator is chained in the statement that displays the `amountMoney` value. Figure 13-18 shows the output.

```
#include<iostream>
#include<iomanip>
using namespace std;
ostream& currency(ostream &s)
{
    s<<'$';
    s<<setprecision(2);
    s<<fixed;
    s.width(12);
    return s;
}
int main()
{
    double amountMoney = 123.455;
    cout<<"Formatted money:"<<endl;
    cout<<currency<<amountMoney<<endl;
}
```

Figure 13-17   The currency manipulator function and a `main()` function that uses it

Figure 13-18   Output of program in Figure 13-17

In the function shown in Figure 13-17, a reference to `ostream` is passed into the function as a parameter, locally named `s`. When you write `cout<<currency<<amountMoney;`, the `currency` function receives the current `ostream` reference. This reference is updated within the function four times—when the '$' displays, and when `setprecision()`, `fixed`, and `width()` are called. The new address is returned to the calling program where `amountMoney` is the next value passes to `ostream`. As with other functions, you can place any C++ statements within the body of a manipulator function. As long as you receive an `ostream` reference and return the reference, you can use the manipulator in a calling function by using the insertion operator and the `cout` object.

Many programmers find that it's convenient to create a library of manipulator functions they can use to create formats they frequently need.

You can create a manipulator that takes an argument (called a **parameterized manipulator**) but the technique varies among compilers. Consult your compiler's documentation if you want to create a parameterized manipulator.

As with other functions, the programmer of a manipulator has to code as many statements as he or she would have to in order to display a value without the manipulator. The advantage to creating the manipulator is its reusability—in future programs you need only insert the manipulator name to achieve desired results.

UNDERSTANDING COMPUTER FILES

When you store data items in a computer system, you use a **persistent storage device**, such as a disk or a CD. The term **permanent storage device** is also used to describe disks and similar devices, but "permanent" is misleading; a permanent storage device does not store data forever—data can be erased or replaced with new data. Instead, the terms persistent and permanent refer to storage that is retained when power is turned off or lost. The terms are used to contrast this type of data storage with the **temporary data storage** that exists in computer memory. Data items typically exist in memory for only a short time. For example, when you register for a college class, information about the class you want to take is kept in memory for a few moments while your registration is processed. As soon as you complete the registration transaction, your student data is stored on a persistent device such as a disk. This "permanent" data is accessed again when the college bills you, prints class lists for your instructors, prints a final grade, and someday, mails you a letter asking for contributions to the alumni fund.

You can store data on a disk (or other persistent storage device) as a simple stream of characters. However, it is common practice to store data in a **data hierarchy**, which represents the relationships between the sizes of data units that business professionals most often use.

The smallest unit of data that concerns businesspeople is usually the field. A **data field** represents one piece of data, such as a first or last name, phone or Social Security number, or salary. Data fields are created from smaller units of data—for example, a first name might contain 10 characters. However, from a business point of view, individual characters in a name are not as important as the name itself. (Characters are also made of smaller units, called **bits**. Each bit represents a 1 or 0 in memory. However, from a businessperson's perspective, bits are usually unimportant.)

A **data record** consists of a number of data fields that are logically connected because they pertain to the same entity. For example, your first name, last name, Social Security number, and salary constitute the fields of your record, and your coworkers' records are constructed from the same fields. In C++, a data record is created as a `struct` or as a `class`.

A **data file** contains records that are logically related. For example, the company you work for maintains an employee data file that contains hundreds of records—each one containing all the data fields that pertain to each employee.

TIP   A file that is stored on a disk is not necessarily a data file. You have already created many program files when you wrote your C++ programs. Programmers usually reserve the term "data file" for files that contain data, rather than program instructions.

Often, records within a data file are stored with a space or other **delimiting character** between fields, and a newline between each record. The contents of a typical data file, along with labels for the file's components, are shown in Figure 13-19. All the data in the figure represents the data file, each row represents a record, and each column represents a field.

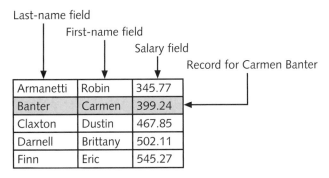

Figure 13-19   A data file containing employee data

Organizations use many files in which to store their data. A group of related files often is stored in a **database**. In a database, frequently a field in each record in a file corresponds to a field in another file. For example, a customer order might contain a file for the product number of the item ordered, and an inventory file might contain the same product number in one record, along with product information such as the product's name and price.

13

SIMPLE FILE OUTPUT

You have used a descendant of the `basic_ios` class—`basic_ostream`—and its descendant `basic_iostream` to produce all sorts of screen output. In C++, when you write to a disk file rather than to the screen, you use a class named `basic_fstream`, which, like `basic_ostream`, is ultimately derived from `basic_ios`. Figure 13-20 shows the relationship between `basic_fstream` and some other input and output classes.

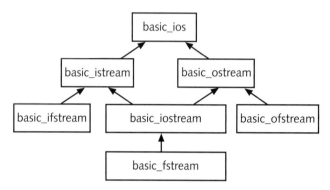

Figure 13-20 The family tree of `basic_fstream`

To perform file processing in C++, the `<iostream>` and `<fstream>` header files must be included in your program file. The `fstream` file contains definitions for the **stream** class templates `basic_ifstream` (for file input), `basic_ofstream` (for file output, and `basic_fstream` (for file input and output). Each of the templates has a specialization that enables char I/O. Just as with the `iostream` library, the `fstream` library contains a number of **typedefs** that provide aliases for the template specializations in the class; `ifstream`, `ofstream`, and `fstream` are the shorter aliases that represent the specializations that enable char input to and output from files. Figure 13-20 shows that `basic_fstream` inherits from `basic_iostream` and its ancestors.

> Because of inheritance, all the functions and manipulators that work with `basic_iostream` that you learned about earlier in this chapter also work with file streams.
>
> **TIP**

When you want to perform standard screen output, you use the **cout** object, a member of the **ostream** class that has already been instantiated. To perform file output, you must instantiate your own member of the **fstream** or **ofstream** class. The object has not already been instantiated for you because, although programs use only one standard output device, they frequently use multiple output files. Therefore, you must create an object with a unique name for each file that your program uses.

You instantiate an `fstream` or `ofstream` output file object as you do any other object—by giving it a type, a name, and optionally, passing arguments to its constructor. When you call an `fstream` or `ofstream` constructor, you can use a filename as an argument; the constructor then will open the file. For example, the following statement instantiates an object named `outFile` that is a member of the `ofstream` class:

```
ofstream outFile("Data.txt");
```

> The `ofstream`, `ifstream`, and `fstream` constructors require a literal string or a variable of type `char` pointer as a filename. The same is true for the `open()` functions that correspond to these types.

TIP

The filename "Data.txt" is passed to the `ofstream` constructor, which then opens the file on the disk. In C++, you do not need to use a special "open file" statement, as required by many other programming languages (although an `open()` function exists and is discussed in a few paragraphs).

If a file with the given name does not exist when the `ofstream` constructor is called, the file is created. If a file with the given name already exists, it is overwritten. The programmer-assigned object name `outFile` is used within the program whenever you want to refer to the file. Your program's internal name for the file object, such as `outFile`, is not stored on the disk; the disk file is recognized only by the filename passed to your object's constructor.

If you use a filename without a path, the file must exist (or be created) in the same folder as the program that opens the file. If the file is located elsewhere, you can use a complete pathname in the `outFile` constructor (or with the `open()` function discussed in the next paragraph). Because the backslash character is also the escape character in C++, you should use two backslashes in any pathnames, for example, `"c:\\DataFolder\\Data.txt"`.

Similarly to how you can declare a variable and later assign it a value, if you don't provide a filename as an argument when you instantiate an `fstream` or `ofstream` object, and then you create the object, no file is opened. However, you can explicitly open the file later with the **open() function**, as in the following pair of statements:

```
ofstream outFile;
outFile.open("Data.txt");
```

The `fstream` and `ofstream` constructors and the `open()` function are overloaded to accept a second argument you can use if you want to indicate a file mode. Using a **file mode** tells C++ how to open the file. For example:

- `ios_base::out` means open the file for output. When you open an `ostream` object and do not provide a mode, `ios_base::out` is the mode by default.

- `ios_base::app` means append the file (rather than re-create it)

- `ios_base::in` means the file is open for input

In Chapter 6 you learned to supply default parameters for functions, so when you learn that the second argument to the `ofstream` constructor is `ios_base::out` by default, you understand that this value is assigned to the second parameter in the constructor declaration.

Depending on your compiler, you might be able to use the simpler versions of the file mode names: `ios::out`, `ios::app`, and `ios::in`.

When you open an `ofstream` object, the mode can be either `out` or `app`.

An `open()` operation (whether explicit or through the constructor) can fail for several reasons. For example, you might attempt to open an existing file using the wrong path, you might attempt to create a file on a storage device that is full, or you might attempt to open a file using an invalid mode. To check whether an `open()` has failed, you can try several methods, using the `out` object itself or its `good()` or `bad()` function. For example, the code segment in Figure 13-21 attempts to open a file named Customers.dat for input, and will display an appropriate message, when the file does not exist and therefore cannot be opened.

```
#include<iostream>
#include<fstream>
#include<iomanip>
using namespace std;
int main()
{
    fstream myFile;
    myFile.open("Customers.dat", ios_base::in);
    if(myFile.good())
      cout<<"File opened!"<<endl;
    else
      cout<<"File could not be opened"<<endl;
}
```

Figure 13-21   Program that checks whether file is opened

In an object-oriented program, you might prefer to throw an exception when a file fails to open. Chapter 12 provides instruction on exception throwing.

You can see from Figure 13-21 that the programmer chose the name **myFile** for the **fstream** object. The value of **myFile.good()** is nonzero (or true) if the file was opened successfully. You can also use the function call `myFile.fail( )`; its value is nonzero (true) if the file is not opened successfully.

 Instead of coding the filename explicitly within the file definition statement (as in `fstream myFile("Customers.dat");`), you also can store the filename in a `char` pointer-defined variable.

Because you can use the overloaded insertion operator within the `fstream` and `ofstream` classes, once the file is open, you can write to it with a statement such as the following:

```
myFile<<"This is going to the disk";
```

After you have written to a file, you do not need to explicitly execute any sort of "close file" statement when using C++, as you do in many other programming languages. Instead, as with any other object, whenever an `fstream` or `ofstream` object goes out of scope, a destructor is called that closes the file for you. If you want to close a file before the file object goes out of scope, however, you can use the `close( )` function, as in `myFile.close();`. As an alternative, you can explicitly call the file object's destructor with a statement such as `myFile.~ofstream();`. The destructor closes the file.

 Although a file is closed when its destructor is called, for clarity, you may choose to explicitly call the `close( )` function. Closing the file explicitly can improve program performance in an application that continues with other tasks after a file is no longer needed.

To create a data file, you typically want to send a series of fields that constitute a record to an output file. For example, suppose you want to send student ID numbers, last names, and grade point averages to a data file. Figure 13-22 shows an interactive application that accomplishes this. After the file is opened successfully, the user is prompted to enter an ID number, name, and grade point average, or, if finished, an end-of-file indicator. The first shaded statement in the figure shows that while data continues to be entered, the data is sent to the output file, separated by a space between each field. The statement that appears in the `while` loop (`cin>>stuId>>name>>gpa`) continues to retrieve one field for each identifier until it reaches the end of file. At the end of file, the statement is evaluated as false, and the `while` loop ends.

Figure 13-23 shows a typical execution of the program. Figure 13-24 shows how the data looks when the output file is opened using Notepad. Each record contains three fields separated by a space, because spaces were used in the output statement using `outFile` (in the second shaded statement). Each record occupies its own line because the `endl` manipulator was used at the end of the `outFile` statement.

13

```
#include<iostream>
#include<fstream>
#include<string>
using namespace std;
int main()
{
   int stuId;
   string name;
   double gpa;
   ofstream outFile;
   outFile.open("Students.txt");
   if(!outFile.good())
     cout<<"File could not be opened"<<endl;
   else
   {
      cout<<"Enter ID, name, and grade point average"<<
         endl;
      cout<<"Enter end-of-file key combination to end ";
      while (cin>>stuId>>name>>gpa)
      {
         outFile<<stuId<<" "<<name<<" "<<gpa<<endl;
         cout<<"Enter ID, name, and grade point average"<<
            endl;
         cout<<"Enter end-of-file key combination to end ";
      }
   }
   outFile.close();
}
```

Figure 13-22   Interactive program that creates a Students.txt file

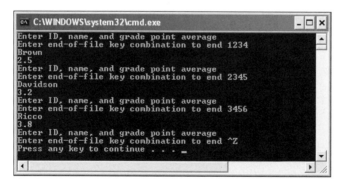

Figure 13-23   Typical execution of program in Figure 13-22

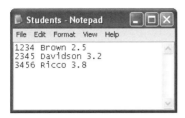

Figure 13-24   Student file created by typical execution shown in Figure 13-23

In Figure 13-23, the **while** loop ends when the user enters **Ctrl-z** to indicate end-of-file. The **end-of-file indicator** is a key combination that indicates completion of data entry. The keys you use to indicate end-of-file vary in different computer systems. Table 13-2 shows the keys needed to indicate end-of-file in commonly used systems.

In Figure 13-23, the user held down the Ctrl key and pressed the letter "z". The key combination is displayed as the carat (^) and an uppercase "Z".

TIP

Table 13-2   End-of-file key combinations

Operating system	Key combination for end-of-file
Unix	Ctrl+d
IBM PC and compatibles	Ctrl+z (Sometimes followed by the Enter key)
Macintosh	Ctrl+d
VAX (VMS)	Ctrl+z

13

SIMPLE FILE INPUT

To read a file from within a program, you can create an object that is an instantiation of the **ifstream** class. As with **ofstream**, when you declare an **ifstream** object, you pass a filename to the object's constructor and the file opens—for example, **ifstream someData("Data.txt");**.

Objects of type **ifstream** and **ofstream** are used in many similar ways. Like the **ofstream** class, the name of the **ifstream** object you instantiate can be any legal C++ identifier; the name has no relationship to the name of the file being opened. The file is identified by the filename used as a parameter to the **ifstream** object's constructor, not by the name of the **ifstream** object. The **open( )** and **close( )** functions work with **ifstream** class objects, and appropriate file modes can be used as arguments to the **ifstream** constructor or to **open( )** statements, just as they are with **ofstream** objects.

Figure 13-25 shows an application that reads a data file that contains an `int`, `string`, and `double` representing a student ID number, name, and grade point average. After the file is successfully opened, two heading lines display on the screen. The statement that displays the column headings uses a constant, `COL_SZ`, to evenly space the displayed columns. Then, in a `while` loop (shaded), the three fields are read from the data file using the `inFile` object. The `while` loop continues as long as the end-of-file indicator is not encountered in the data file. As each record is read, it is displayed on the screen, left-aligned in columns that are 10 spaces wide. Figure 13-26 shows the output when the data file in Figure 13-24 is used.

```
#include<iostream>
#include<fstream>
#include<string>
#include<iomanip>
using namespace std;
int main()
{
    int stuId;
    string name;
    double gpa;
    const int COL_SZ = 10;
    ifstream inFile;
    inFile.open("Students.txt");
    if(!inFile.good())
        cout<<"File could not be opened"<<endl;
    else
    {
        cout<<left;
        cout<<"Student records:"<<endl;
        cout<<setw(COL_SZ)<<"ID"<<setw(COL_SZ)<<
           "Name"<<setw(COL_SZ)<<"Grade point average"<<endl;
        while (inFile>>stuId>>name>>gpa)
        {
            cout<<setw(COL_SZ)<<stuId<<setw(COL_SZ)<<name<<
                 setw(COL_SZ)<<gpa<<endl;
        }
    }
    inFile.close();
}
```

Figure 13-25   Program that reads records from a data file and displays them on the screen

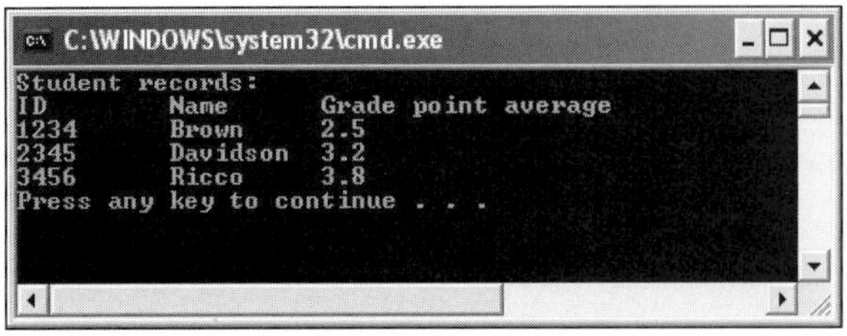

Figure 13-26 Output of program in Figure 13-25 using data file shown in Figure 13-24

TIP
As with `ofstream` objects, when an `ifstream` object goes out of scope, the file is closed automatically. However, you can always call the `close()` function for clarity or to free resources when the file is no longer needed.

TIP
In the program in Figure 13-25, if the last record is incomplete (for example, if it contains only a student ID, but no name or grade point average), then the incomplete record is ignored.

WRITING AND READING OBJECTS

It is simple and intuitive to use the `ofstream` class's overloaded insertion operator to write data items such as `int`s, `double`s, and `string`s to files. It makes sense, however, that in object-oriented programs you should also be able to write objects to disk files.

Figure 13-27 shows a `Student` class that contains three data members and two friend functions that enable data entry and display. It is similar to dozens of classes you have previously worked with. Because `fstream`, `ifstream`, and `ofstream` are all descendents of `istream` and `ostream`, the `friend` functions that read data from the keyboard with `cin` and write data to the screen with `cout` can also be used with `fstream` objects to read from and write to files.

13

```
class Student
{
    friend ostream& operator<<(ostream&, Student);
    friend istream& operator>>(istream&, Student&);
    private:
        int stuId;
        string name;
        double gpa;
};
ostream& operator<<(ostream &out, Student stu)
{
    out<<stu.stuId<<" "<<stu.name<<" "<<stu.gpa<<endl;
    return out;
}
istream& operator>>(istream &in, Student &stu)
{
    in>>stu.stuId>>stu.name>>stu.gpa;
    return in;
}
```

Figure 13-27 A Student class

Figure 13-28 shows a function that writes objects to an output file. In the first shaded statement, outFile is declared as an **ofstream** object. The user is prompted, and the overloaded extraction operator for the **Student** class is used in a while loop that continues until the user types the end-of-file key combination. Within the loop, the **Student** object that was read from the keyboard is written to the **outFile** object (see the third shaded statement). Then the user is prompted again for data entry. Figure 13-29 shows a typical execution, and Figure 13-30 shows the resulting data file when viewed in a text editor.

```
#include<iostream>
#include<fstream>
#include<string>
#include<iomanip>
using namespace std;
int main()
{
    Student aStudent;
    ofstream outFile;
    outFile.open("Students2.txt");
    cout<<"Enter ID, name, and grade point average"<<endl;
    cout<<"Enter end-of-file key combination to end ";
    while (cin>>aStudent)
    {
        outFile<<aStudent<<endl;
        cout<<"Enter ID, name, and grade point average"<<
            endl;
        cout<<"Enter end-of-file key combination to end ";
    }
    outFile.close();
}
```

Figure 13-28   Program that writes objects to an output file

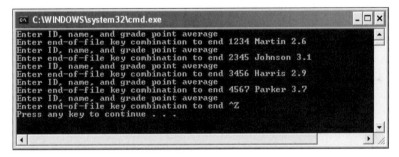

Figure 13-29   Typical execution of program in Figure 13-28

13

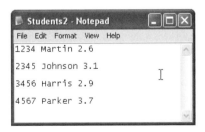

Figure 13-30   Data file created by execution of program shown in Figure 13-29

TIP

Whenever you open a file, it is a good idea to check whether the file has actually been opened, and to notify the user if it has not. However, in some of the programs in this book, the check step is left out to keep the examples short.

You can read an object from a file as easily as you can write one—as long as the object's class contains an overloaded extraction operator. Figure 13-31 shows an application that reads a file containing **Student** objects. The shaded **while** statement continues to read objects from the **ifstream** file until the end-of-file is encountered. In this application, as each **Student** is read, the word "Student" is displayed followed by the **Student** data. Figure 13-32 shows the output when the file that was created in the execution in Figure 13-29 is used.

```
#include<iostream>
#include<fstream>
#include<string>
#include<iomanip>
using namespace std;
int main()
{
    Student aStudent;
    ifstream inFile;
    inFile.open("Students2.txt");
    cout<<endl<<"Output from disk:"<<endl;
    while (inFile>>aStudent)
    {
        cout<<"Student: "<<aStudent;
    }
    inFile.close();
}
```

Figure 13-31 Reading **Student** records from a file

Figure 13-32 Execution of program in Figure 13-31 using the data file created in Figure 13-29

You Do It

Using `stream` Functions and Manipulators

In the next set of steps, you declare an array of doubles, assign values with different numbers of significant digits, and then display all the values several times, experimenting with width, precision, and the fixed manipulator.

1. Open a new file in your C++ editor. Enter the statements to include the files you need, start the `main()` function, and declare the variables and constants you will use. You will use a field size of 10 for display, and an array size of 5 to hold five double values.

```cpp
#include<iostream>
#include<iomanip>
using namespace std;
int main()
{
    int x;
    const int FIELD_SIZE = 10;
    const int ARRAY_SIZE = 5;
    double values[ARRAY_SIZE];
```

2. Set the first array element to a number with three positions, one of which is to the right of the decimal point. Then, in a loop, set each subsequent array element to one-tenth of the previous one. This stores the values 23.4, 2.34, 0.234, 0.0234, and 0.00234 in the array.

```cpp
values [0] = 23.4;
for (x = 0; x < (ARRAY_SIZE - 1); ++x)
    values[x+1] = values[x] * 0.10;
```

3. To confirm that the array values are what you expect, display each in a field of size 10. You must use the `width()` function to reset the field width for each output.

```cpp
for(x = 0; x < ARRAY_SIZE; ++x)
{
    cout.width(FIELD_SIZE);
    cout<<values[x]<<endl;
}
```

4. Set the precision with a call to the `precision()` function, then display an explanation and, in a loop, display the array values a second time.

```cpp
cout.precision(2);
cout<<"After precision(2) call"<<endl;
for(x = 0; x < ARRAY_SIZE; ++x)
{
    cout.width(FIELD_SIZE);
    cout<<values[x]<<endl;
}
```

13

5. Use the `fixed` manipulator with the `cout` object. Display an explanation and then display the values again. The precision remains set at 2 from the earlier statement. Add the closing curly brace for the function.

```
cout<<fixed;
cout<<"After fixed is added"<<endl;
for(x = 0; x < ARRAY_SIZE; ++x)
{
    cout.width(FIELD_SIZE);
    cout<<values[x]<<endl;
}
}
```

6. Save the file as **DemoPrecision.cpp**. Compile and run the program. The output appears in Figure 13-33. The first loop execution shows the calculated values stored in the array. In the second loop, each array element is shown with a precision of 2. In other words, each line shows the two most significant digits, 2 and 3, in their proper position relative to the decimal point. In the third loop, after the `fixed` manipulator has been called, each value is shown with two significant digits to the right of the decimal point.

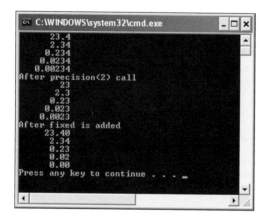

Figure 13-33   Output of DemoPrecision.cpp

Creating a Manipulator

In the next set of steps, you create a manipulator that formats student grade point averages so they all display to three decimal places in a field that is seven characters wide.

1. Open a new file in your C++ editor. Type the first statements you need as follows:

```
#include<iostream>
#include<iomanip>
using namespace std;
```

2. Create the function that actually does the work of creating a properly formatted grade point average. The function takes an `ostream` reference as an argument and uses it to set the precision and display grade point averages in a seven-character field.

```
ostream& gpa(ostream &s)
{
    s<<setprecision(3);
    s<<fixed;
    s.width(7);
    return s;
}
```

3. Begin a `main()` function that declares a constant to use as an array size and declares an array that can hold grade point averages. Also declare an integer that will be used to loop through the array.

```
int main()
{
    const int NUM = 10;
    double gradePoints[NUM];
    int x;
```

4. Write a `for` loop that prompts the user for grade point averages and loads them into the array. Displaying the value of the loop control variable plus 1 allows the user to keep track of his progress.

```
for(x = 0; x < NUM; ++x)
{
    cout<<"Enter grade point average for student "<<
        (x + 1)<<" ";
    cin>>gradePoints[x];
}
```

5. Display an explanation, then use another `for` loop to display the entered grade point averages. In the `cout` statement, you use the `gpa` manipulator to ensure that each grade point average displays using the same format. Include a closing curly brace for the `main()` function.

```
    cout<<endl<<"Grade point averages are "<<endl;
    for(x = 0; x < NUM; ++x)
        cout<<gpa<<gradePoints[x]<<endl;
}
```

6. Save the program as **GPAManipulator.cpp**. Compile and run the program. When you are prompted for grade point averages, enter some without decimal parts, and others with varying numbers of digits to the right of the decimal point. Figure 13-34 shows a typical execution in which the user has entered grade point averages that are all displayed with three decimal places and right-aligned in their fields.

13

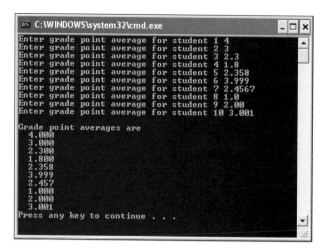

Figure 13-34 Typical execution of GPAManipulator program

Writing to and Reading from a File

In the next set of steps, you open a file for output, write some friends' names to it, close it, reopen the file for input, and read and display the names.

1. Open a new file in your C++ editor and enter the `include` and `using` statements you need.

   ```
   #include<iostream>
   #include<fstream>
   #include<string>
   #include<iomanip>
   using namespace std;
   ```

2. Start the `main()` function by declaring a string variable to hold friends' names, an integer to count the names, and a constant character pointer to hold the filename. You must use a constant `char` pointer instead of a `string` because that is the data type required by the `ifstream` and `ofstream` constructors. Use the filename in the output file constructor. Also define an input file, but do not open it yet.

   ```
   int main()
   {
       string name;
       int count;
       const char* FILENAME = "MyFriends.txt";
       ofstream writingFile(FILENAME);
       ifstream readingFile;
   ```

TIP
Instead of storing the data file in the default folder in your program, you might prefer to use a full path as the filename, for example:

```
const char* FILENAME = "c:\\temp\\MyFriends.txt";
```

3. Test whether the output file was opened successfully; if not, display a message. The rest of the program statements execute in the `else` clause, that is, only if the file was opened successfully. Otherwise, prompt the user for the name of a friend and, while the user does not indicate end-of-file, write the name to the output file and prompt for a new name.

```
if(!writingFile.good())
   cout<<"File could not be opened for writing"<<endl;
else
{
    cout<<"Enter a name or end-of-file to quit ";
    while(cin>>name)
    {
       writingFile<<name<<endl;
       cout<<"Enter a name or end-of-file to quit ";
    }
}
```

4. Close the output file and then open it for input. Set the count to 0.

```
writingFile.close();
readingFile.open(FILENAME);
count = 0;
```

5. Test whether the file was opened successfully and issue a message if it was not. Otherwise, read the names in a loop. Add 1 to the `count` variable each time a record is read, and display the count and the name. At the end of the list of names, display the final count.

```
if(!readingFile.good())
   cout<<"File could not be opened for reading"<<endl;
else
{
    while(readingFile>>name)
    {
       ++count;
       cout<<"Friend #"<<count<<" "<<name<<endl;
    }
    cout<<endl<<"Total number of friends is "<<
       count<<endl;
}
}
```

13

6. Save the file as **FriendsFile.cpp**. Compile and run the program. Enter any number of friends' names. A typical execution looks like Figure 13-35.

```
C:\WINDOWS\system32\cmd.exe                          [ - ][ □ ][ x ]
Enter a name or end-of-file to quit Inez
Enter a name or end-of-file to quit Jason
Enter a name or end-of-file to quit Miranda
Enter a name or end-of-file to quit Sarah
Enter a name or end-of-file to quit Lilly
Enter a name or end-of-file to quit Eduardo
Enter a name or end-of-file to quit Benny
Enter a name or end-of-file to quit ^Z
Friend #1 Inez
Friend #2 Jason
Friend #3 Miranda
Friend #4 Sarah
Friend #5 Lilly
Friend #6 Eduardo
Friend #7 Benny

Total number of friends is 7
Press any key to continue . . . _
```

Figure 13-35   Typical execution of FriendsFile.cpp

7. Open a text editor such as NotePad. Open the **MyFriends.txt** file in the editor and confirm that the list of names appears in the output file.

> **TIP**
> Some operating systems do not distinguish between uppercase and lowercase in a filename. Even though you use the name MyFriends.txt within your program, your operating system might refer to the file as myfriends.txt.

CHAPTER SUMMARY

❑ Like other C++ objects you have created, **cout** and **cin** are members of a class. They use inheritance and polymorphism, and they have all the characteristics of other class objects. They are class members of **ostream**. In C++, a stream is a sequence of bytes used in an input or output operation. C++ provides both low-level and high-level input/output (I/O) capabilities.

❑ The creators of C++ have overloaded >> to work to input all built-in data types. When you include **iostream** at the top of your program files, you gain access to these functions as well as the **get()**, **ignore()**, **getline()** and other input functions.

❑ Besides the overloaded insertion operator, the **ostream** class provides other useful output functions including **setf()**, **unsetf()**, **width()**, and **precision()**.

❑ A manipulator (or a manipulator function) is used to manipulate, or change, the state of the **cout** object. When you use a manipulator, you use the insertion operator with the **cout** object. The **fixed** manipulator allows you to output a specified number of decimal places. Many other manipulators have been coded and placed in libraries included with your C++ compiler; you can use the **endl**, **setprecision()**, **setw()**, **setiosflags()**, **resetiosflags**, **oct**, **hex**, and **showbase** manipulators.

❑ When you create a manipulator function, the desired results become much clearer. Any output manipulator function you create should take as an argument an instance of `ostream` as a reference. It should also return the same reference. This approach allows manipulators to be chained or stacked with other calls to the `cout` insertion operator.

❑ When you store data items in a computer system, you use a persistent storage device, such as a disk or a CD. The term "permanent storage device" also is used to describe disks and similar devices. Temporary data storage exists in computer memory. You can store data on a disk (or other persistent storage device) as a simple stream of characters. However, it is common practice to store data in a data hierarchy, which represents the relationships between the sizes of data units that business professionals most often use. A data field represents one piece of data, such as a first or last name. A data record consists of a number of data fields that are logically connected because they pertain to the same entity. A data file contains records that are logically related.

❑ To perform file output, you must instantiate your own member of the `fstream` or `ofstream` class. When you call an `fstream` or `ofstream` constructor, you can use a filename as an argument; the constructor then will open the file. If you don't provide a filename as an argument when you instantiate an `fstream` or `ofstream` object, and then you create the object, no file is opened. However, you can explicitly open the file later with the `open()` member function. The end-of-file indicator is a key combination that indicates completion of data entry.

❑ To read a file from within a program, you can create an object that is an instantiation of the `ifstream` class.

❑ Besides simple data fields, in object-oriented programs you can write objects to disk files. Because `fstream`, `ifstream`, and `ofstream` are all descendents of `ostream`, a class's friend functions that read data from the keyboard with `cin` and write data to the screen with `cout` also can be used to read from and write to files.

13

KEY TERMS

A **stream** is a sequence of bytes used in an input or output operation.

Low-level I/O is unformatted; that is, bytes are transferred into and out from memory without regard to the type of data they represent.

High-level I/O is formatted; that is, bytes are grouped into meaningful units such as integers, doubles, and class object types.

Unicode is an extended, international coding system.

A **typedef** is a C++ statement that provides a synonym for an identifier in a C++ program; it is a way to create a shorter, easier-to-remember nickname for an unwieldy identifier.

The **get() function** takes a character argument and returns a reference to the object that invoked the `get()` function.

The **delimiter character** is the character that terminates data entry.

The **ignore( ) function** skips any additional characters left in the input stream after data is accepted.

The **getline( ) function** reads a line of text into the string that is the first argument to the function until it reaches either the length used as the second argument or the character used as the third argument.

Format flags or **state flags** are the arguments that determine the state of the cout object.

The **setf( ) function** takes arguments that set the bits of cout; that is, the arguments turn the bits in the format flag on

The **unsetf( ) function** can be used to deselect a bit in the format flag.

The **width( ) function** defines the size of the output field in which the next output will be displayed.

The **precision( ) function** controls the number of significant digits you see in the output.

A **manipulator** (or a **manipulator function**) is used to manipulate, or change, the state of the cout object.

The **fixed manipulator** allows you to output a specified number of decimal places.

The **setprecision( ) manipulator** specifies the number of significant digits displayed; combined with the fixed manipulator, you control the number of decimals that display.

The **setw( ) manipulator** allows you to set the width of a field for output.

The **setiosflags( ) manipulator** turns on bit codes for the attributes named as arguments.

The **resetiosflags( ) manipulator** turns off bit codes for the attributes named as arguments.

The **oct manipulator** displays values in octal form.

The **hex manipulator** displays numbers in hexadecimal form.

The **showbase manipulator** displays octal numbers with a leading 0 and hexadecimal numbers with a leading 0x so you do not mistake them for base 10 (decimal) numbers.

A **parameterized manipulator** is a manipulator that takes an argument.

A **persistent storage device**, such as a disk or a CD, retains data when power is lost.

The term **permanent storage device** is also used to describe disks and similar devices.

Temporary data storage exists in computer memory; it is lost when power is lost.

A **data hierarchy** represents the relationships between the sizes of data units that business professionals most often use.

A **data field** represents one piece of data, such as a first or last name, phone or Social Security number, or salary.

Characters are made of smaller units, called **bits**. Each bit represents a 1 or 0 in memory.

A **data record** consists of a number of data fields that are logically connected because they pertain to the same entity.

A **data file** contains records that are logically related.

A **delimiting character** separates data fields.

A group of related files is often stored in a **database**.

The **open()** **function** opens a data file.

A **file mode** indicates how a file is opened—for example, for input or output.

The **end-of-file indicator** is a key combination that indicates completion of data entry.

REVIEW QUESTIONS

1. In C++, **cout** and **cin** are _____.

   a. classes

   b. functions

   c. objects

   d. overloaded

2. A sequence of bytes used to perform input and output operations is a _____.

   a. string

   b. stream

   c. flow

   d. parameter

3. The C++ operator used for input with **cin** is called the _____ operator.

   a. insertion

   b. extraction

   c. inclusion

   d. withdrawal

4. The **get()** function _____.

   a. takes a reference to a **char** as an argument and returns a reference to the **istream** class

   b. takes a reference to a **char** as an argument and returns a reference to a **char**

   c. takes a reference to the **istream** class as an argument and returns a reference to the **istream** class

   d. takes a reference to the **istream** class as an argument and returns a reference to a **char**

5. A character that terminates data entry is called the _____ character.

   a. delimiter

   b. dummy

   c. parameter

   d. Enter

13

6. The data entry function that leaves unused characters in the input stream is _____.

    a. `format()`

    b. `ignore()`

    c. `getline()`

    d. `get()`

7. You use the `ignore()` function to _____.

    a. discard whitespace characters entered by the user

    b. skip any characters entered after the user presses the Enter key

    c. skip any characters left in the input stream after a call to `get()`

    d. read and discard characters when it doesn't matter which character is used

8. The `getline()` function reads a line of text until it reaches _____.

    a. the length used as the second argument

    b. the character used as the third argument

    c. both of the above, that is, whichever occurs last

    d. either a or b, that is, whichever occurs first

9. The arguments such, as `ios::showpoint`, that determine the state of the `cout` object are called _____.

    a. state terminators

    b. delimiters

    c. format flags

    d. final parameters

10. You can combine the arguments to the `setf()` function using _____.

    a. the bitwise AND operator

    b. the logical AND operator

    c. the bitwise OR operator

    d. the logical OR operator

11. What is the output of the following?

```
int main()
{
    cout<<"X";
    cout.width(4);
    cout<<11;
    cout<<22<<"X";
}
```

    a. X1122X   c. X 11 22X

    b. X 1122X   d. X 11 22 X

12. What is the output of the following?

```
int main()
{
    cout.precision(3);
    cout<<9.8765;
}
```

a. 9.9

b. 9.87

c. 9.88

d. 9.876

13. A function that changes the state of the cout object is _____.

a. a manipulator

b. an operator

c. a format flag

d. an overloaded function

14. Which of the following is a manipulator?

a. >>

b. ++

c. endl

d. cout

15. Which of the following is *not* a manipulator?

a. setw

b. setprecision

c. flush

d. width

16. What is the output of the following?

```
int main()
{
    cout<<setw(2)<<5678;
}
```

a. 56

b. 78

c. 57

d. 5678

13

17. Which is the correct order from largest to smallest?

   a. field, record, file

   b. file, record, field

   c. record, field, file

   d. field, file, record

18. When you call an `ofstream` constructor and use a filename as an argument, then _____.

   a. the constructor creates the file

   b. the constructor opens the file

   c. the constructor creates and opens the file

   d. you receive an error message

19. When you create an object with the following statement, then what is the output file object within the program?

```
ofstream oFile("a:\\data\\document");
```

   a. `ofstream`

   b. `oFile`

   c. `data`

   d. `document`

20. If a file named `someFile` is opened successfully, which of the following is evaluated as true?

   a. `someFile.open()`

   b. `someFile.fail()`

   c. `someFile.good()`

   d. `!someFile`

EXERCISES

1. Write a program that allows a user to use the keyboard to input the first and last names of 40 friends, up to 50 characters each. Display the names 15 at a time, pausing to let the user press a key before the list continues. Save the file as **Friends40.cpp**.

2. Write a program that allows a user to enter 10 floating-point values into an array, and then displays each value to an accuracy of three positions. Save the file as **Accuracy3.cpp**.

3. Write a program that allows a user to enter 10 floating-point values into an array. Then, in a loop, the program should prompt the user for a desired precision and subsequently display each value to the correct precision. The loop continues prompting for a precision and displaying the 10 values until the user enters a negative value for the precision. Save the file as **PrecisionRequest.cpp**.

4. Write a program that allows a user to enter 10 item stock numbers, prices, and quantities in stock into three parallel arrays. Display all the data in report form— that is, aligned correctly in columns. Save the file as **ItemArrayReport.cpp**.

5. Create an `Item` class that contains fields for a stock number, price, and quantity in stock, and functions to set and display each field. Write a program that declares an array of 10 `Item` objects. Display all the data in report form—that is, aligned correctly in columns. Save the file as **ItemClassReport.cpp**.

6. a. Write a program that lets a user enter a five-line limerick and save it in a file. Save the file as **SaveLimerick.cpp**.

   b. Write another program that reads the file and displays the limerick on the screen. Save the file as **DisplayLimerick.cpp**.

7. Complete the following tasks:

   a. Create a class named `InsurancePolicy` for a life insurance company. Data members include a policy number, last name of the policy holder, value of the policy, and annual premium. Member functions include overloaded insertion and extraction operators. Continue to prompt the user for data for `InsurancePolicy` objects and write each `InsurancePolicy` to a data file until the end-of-file is entered. Save the file as **CreateInsPolicyFile.cpp**.

   b. Write a program that reads the insurance file from Exercise 7a and displays the policy data on the screen. Save the file as **DisplayInsPolicyData.cpp**.

   c. Add a function to the `InsurancePolicy` class that returns the policy value. Write a program that prompts the user for a minimum policy amount. Read the `InsurancePolicy` file and display only those records for which the policy value equals or exceeds the entered amount. Save the file as **DisplaySelectedPolicyData.cpp**.

   d. Add a function to the `InsurancePolicy` class that displays policy information in a formatted line suitable for a report, including appropriately spaced columns and dollar signs, and decimal points for the monetary values. Modify the `DisplaySelectedPolicyData` application created in part c of this exercise so that the selected records are displayed using the report-creating function. Save the file as **DisplaySelectedPolicyDataReport.cpp**.

13

8. Complete the following tasks:

   a. Create a class named **Employee**. Data members include the Employee's ID number, first and last names, and hourly pay rate. Member functions include overloaded insertion and extraction operators. Continue to prompt the user for data for **Employee**s and write each **Employee** to a data file until the end-of-file is entered. Save the file as **CreateEmployeeDataFile.cpp**.

   b. Write a program that reads the **Employee** file from Exercise 8a and displays **Employee** data on the screen. Save the file as **DisplayEmployeeData.cpp**.

   c. Revise the **CreateEmployeeFile** application so the user is prompted for a filename for the output file. Execute the program twice, using the names **North.txt** and **South.txt** to represent files of **Employee** data from the North and South divisions of the company. Save the file as **RequestEmployeeFileName.cpp**.

   d. Add an overloaded **operator>()** function to the **Employee** class. The **operator>()** function compares **Employee** ID numbers and is used to sort **Employee** objects. Write an application that reads the North and South division files created in part c of this exercise. As each record is read, display it and load it into an array of **Employee** objects. Then sort the array by **Employee** ID number and display the newly merged and sorted records. Save the file as **MergeEmployeeRecords.cpp**.

9. Each of the following files in the Chapter13 folder contains syntax and/or logical errors. Determine the problem in each case, and fix the program. Save your solutions by adding "Fixed" to the filename, as in **DEBUG13-1Fixed.cpp**.

   a. DEBUG13-1.cpp

   b. DEBUG13-2.cpp

   c. DEBUG13-3.cpp

   d. DEBUG13-4.cpp

CASE PROJECT 1

You have been developing a **Fraction** class for Teacher's Pet Software. Each **Fraction** contains a numerator, denominator, a whole-number portion, and access to several functions you have developed, including overloaded operators. Complete these tasks:

a. Create a manipulator that formats floating-point values to display with three decimal places right-aligned in a field of 10 spaces. Write a **main()** function that instantiates an array of at least 10 **Fraction** objects, prompts the user for their values, and displays their floating-point values using the manipulator. Save the file as **FractionManipulator.cpp**.

b. Modify the `Fraction` class so that the insertion and extraction operators write and read the three parts of a `Fraction` (whole number, numerator, and denominator) separated by spaces. Use these operators when writing to and reading from a file. Make sure the `Fraction` class also contains data entry and display functions that allow user-friendly display on the screen (for example, with a slash between numerator and denominator) and data entry from the keyboard (with appropriate prompts). As a `Fraction` drill, write a program that prompts a student user to enter five `Fraction` objects for which each `Fraction` value is less than 1/2. Create a disk file that contains the `Fraction`s the student creates. Save the file as **FractionFile.cpp**.

c. Write a program a teacher can use to review a student's progress. The program reads the `Fraction` objects previously created by the student and saved to disk. The program compares each `Fraction` to 1/2 and displays the `Fraction` answers that are incorrect (1/2 or more). At the end of the file, display a percent-correct score for the five student answers. Save the file as **FractionGrader.cpp**.

d. Teachers using the `FractionFile` and `FractionGrader` programs have discovered that students are "cheating" by learning one Fraction value that is less than 1/2, for example 1/3, and typing it for all five entries in the `FractionFile` program. Modify the program so that no duplicates are accepted and that five unique values are written to the data file. Save the file as **FractionFileNoRepeats.cpp**.

Case Project 2

CASE PROJECTS

You have been developing a `BankAccount` class for Parkville Bank that contains several fields and functions, including overloaded operators. You have also created child classes derived from the `BankAccount` class: `CheckingAccount`, `SavingsAccount`, and `CheckingWithInterest`. Complete these tasks:

13

a. Create a manipulator that displays with the words "Account number" and a pound sign (#) before any `BankAccount` account number. Create another manipulator that displays every interest rate to two decimal places. Write a `main()` function that instantiates an array of at least 10 `CheckingWithInterest` objects, prompts the user for their values, and displays their values using the manipulators. Save the file as **AccountManipulators.cpp**.

b. Modify the `CheckingWithInterest` classes so that the insertion and extraction operators write and read the parts of a `CheckingWithInterest` separated by spaces. Use these operators when writing to and reading from a file. Make sure the class also contains data entry and display functions that allow user-friendly display on the screen and data entry from the keyboard (with appropriate prompts). Write a program that asks a user to enter five `CheckingWithInterest` objects. Create a disk file that contains the `CheckingWithInterest` objects the user creates. Save the file as **AccountFile.cpp**.

c. Write a program that reads the `CheckingWithInterest` objects previously created by the user and saved to disk. Display each on the screen. Save the file as **ReadAccountFile.cpp**.

d. Write a program that reads the `CheckingWithInterest` objects previously created by the user and saved to disk. The program allows a user to enter a value for a minimum required balance, then compares each `CheckingWithInterest` to the minimum balance and displays any accounts that fall below the minimum. At the end of the file, display a count of the number of accounts displayed. Save the file as **AccountsBelowMinimum.cpp**.

e. Modify the `AccountFile` application so that the user is prompted for the appropriate bank branch to use as a filename for the entered accounts. Execute the application twice, creating a file for the Eastside and Westside branches. Save the file as **RequestAccountFileName.cpp**.

f. Read the data files created in part e, store them in an array, and sort them in descending order by balance. Display the sorted accounts. Save the file as **MergeAndSortAccounts.cpp**.

14

ADVANCED TOPICS

In this chapter, you will:

- ♦ Use enumerations
- ♦ Examine the binary system and why computers use it
- ♦ Use individual bits to store data
- ♦ Convert a group of bit fields to an integer value
- ♦ Use the bitwise AND operator with a mask
- ♦ Use the bitwise inclusive OR operator
- ♦ Explore how and why to shift bits
- ♦ Learn about recursion
- ♦ Use a recursive function to sort a list

The most valuable commodity in a programming environment is the programmers' time. Programmers are paid well to ensure that their systems operate as expected. They concern themselves with two other commodities—computer memory and program run time. In the past, programmers tried to save memory because it was an expensive resource. Over time, the cost of storage has been greatly reduced, but reducing the size of objects is still important, especially when objects are sent over data communication lines. Additionally, speed of operation is important in programs that use many instructions to operate on large quantities of data. This chapter discusses features of the C++ language that allow programmers to save time and memory within their programs—creating enumerations, manipulating bits, and using recursion.

Using Enumerations

A data type is a set of values and the operations that can be performed on those values. For example, the `int` data type represents all the values from approximately −2,000,000,000 to +2,000,000,000. When you declare a variable or constant to be an `int`, you also declare the set of operations you can perform with it, for example + and *. In this book, you have worked with many built-in C++ data types including `int`, `double`, and `bool`.

TIP
You first learned about data types and the values that can be represented by an `int` in Chapter 1.

In C++ you also can create your own data types. You have created both structures and classes throughout this book and defined operations that can be performed with them by creating functions and overloading operators. For example, you can create a `Student` class and define the greater than (>) operator to compare the grade point averages of two `Student` objects.

An enumeration type is an additional type you can create in C++. An **enumeration** is a programmer-defined set of integer constants represented by identifiers. The named constants are called **enumerators**. In C++ programs, you might want to create an enumeration when you have a list of values that can carry useful identifiers. For example, if seven values represent the days of the week in an application, it might be convenient for you to refer to 0 as `SUN` and 1 as `MON`.

You create an enumeration using the keyword `enum` followed by a type name, and, in curly braces, a list of identifiers that represent numeric values. For example, the following enumeration gives the values 0 through 6 to the identifiers `SUN`, `MON`, and so on:

```
enum Days {SUN, MON, TUE, WED, THU, FRI, SAT};
```

The values of enumeration constants start at 0 by default, but you can assign a different starting value. For example, because users typically think of January as month 1 and not month 0, you can create a `Months` enumeration as follows:

```
enum Months {JAN = 1, FEB, MAR, APR, MAY, JUN, JUL,
        AUG, SEP, OCT, NOV, DEC};
```

In this case, each month identifier is represented by its "natural" value—for example, `OCT` is 10.

Whether they begin with 0 or some other value, by default each subsequent value in an enumeration is one larger than the previous one. (However, you can assign different values.) Thus, in the `Months` enumerator above, you could assign 2 to `FEB`, 3 to `MAR`, and so on, but, if the months are listed in order, there is no need to make any explicit assignments after `JAN`.

The identifiers in an **enum** must be unique within a block. For example, the following is illegal because two identifiers in the same block are named **MAR**.

```
{
    enum Winter {JAN, FEB, MAR};
    enum Spring {MAR, APR, MAY};
}
```

Separate enumerators can have the same value. The following **enum** definition is fine; both **LA** and **SAN_FRANCISCO** can have the value 2:

```
enum Cities {NYC = 0, CHICAGO = 1, LA = 2, SAN_FRANCISCO = 2};
```

TIP   Although not required by C++, by convention, a user-defined type begins with an uppercase letter. You have followed this convention when naming structs and classes throughout this book. Also, by convention, the defined constant identifiers are created using all uppercase letters.

You could always use separate constant declarations instead of enumerations to achieve similar results. As with unenumerated named constants, using enumerations rather than hard-coded numbers makes programs easier to read and maintain. Using enumerations simply provides a convenient shorthand for naming a series of values.

For example, Figure 14-1 contains a shaded enumeration that supplies numeric values for the days of the week. The shaded for loop varies **x** from **SUN** to **SAT**. The loop could have been written to vary **x** from 0 to 6; it's just that the intent is clearer using the day names. Figure 14-2 shows a typical execution of the program.

```
#include<iostream>
using namespace std;
int main()
{
    enum Days {SUN, MON, TUE, WED, THU, FRI, SAT};
    int x;
    double hours;
    double total = 0;
    for(x = SUN; x <= SAT; ++x)
    {
        cout<<"Enter hours worked on day "<<(x + 1)<<" ";
        cin>>hours;
        total += hours;
    }
    cout<<"Total hours worked for week is "<<total<<endl;
}
```

Figure 14-1   Program using an enumeration for days of the week

14

Figure 14-2   Typical execution of program in Figure 14-1

As with any constant, after an enumeration constant has been defined, you cannot assign a different value to it.

TIP

The enum keyword is required to declare a variable of type *enumeration* in C. In C++, the enum keyword can be omitted in the declaration statement, but it is clearer to include it.

TIP

When an organization maintains a set of enumerations that will be used in a variety of applications, such as department name codes, the enumerations are frequently stored in their own file and included by individual programmers using an #include directive.

TIP

In GUI environments, enumerations are often used for attributes that are implemented across many applications. For example, colors that can be used to change the image of buttons, text, and other GUI objects are often enumerated. It is easier for programmers to remember WHITE or BLUE than the numeric values of those constants.

TIP

You can declare a variable to be an enumeration type. For example, you might want to declare the following:

        Days dayOff;

Then, you could make an assignment such as the following:

        dayOff = FRI;

However, only values of the enumeration type can be assigned to the variable. You cannot increment or decrement enumeration type variables.

UNDERSTANDING THE BINARY SYSTEM

Every piece of data on every computer in the world is stored as a series of 0s and 1s. This system of storage, called the **binary system**, has been used since the earliest computers were created because it is the cheapest way to store data electronically. Any circuit can be only off or on; therefore, any circuit can be represented by a 0 or 1. The prefix "bi" means two.

The numbers you are accustomed to using are organized in the decimal system. The **decimal system** is so named because the prefix "dec" means 10 and the decimal system uses 10 digits: 0 through 9. When you use the decimal system and you want to express a value greater than 9, you do not use an additional, unique symbol for each subsequent value. (For example, perhaps you could use an asterisk for 10, an exclamation point for 11, a smiley face for 12, and so on.) Numbers would be too difficult to use if you had to learn thousands of separate symbols, one for each possible value; instead, to create values larger than 9, you use additional columns that each contain one of the existing 10 symbols.

The binary numbering system uses only two digits: 0 and 1. When you use the binary system and you want to express a value greater than 1, you do not use symbols other than 0 or 1. Instead, you combine two or more of the existing two symbols, displaying them in multiple columns.

When you first learned how to construct large values using the decimal system, a teacher probably told you to think of a value such as 321 as having three columns—a hundreds column with a 3, a tens column with a 2, and a ones column with a 1. You can express the value of 321 as 3 times 100, plus 2 times 10, plus 1 times 1. The column values 100, 10, and 1 also can be expressed as 10^2, 10^1, and 10^0. You also learned that for larger numbers in the decimal system, each successive column added on the left is worth 10 times the previous column. In other words, when you analyze a multidigit value, the sequence of column values from right to left is 1, 10, 100, 1000, 10000, 100000, and so on. Table 14-1 shows a few examples of four-digit numbers and how you analyze their values. The columns with leading zeros are shaded because you don't usually use them when expressing a value—for example, you say "14", not "0014". However, you understand that you could use 0s in the hundreds and thousands positions without altering the value of 14.

14

Table 14-1 Representation of a few decimal numbers

10^3 1000s	10^2 100s	10^1 10s	10^0 1s	Decimal Value
0	0	0	0	0
0	0	0	1	1
0	0	0	2	2
0	0	1	0	10
0	0	1	4	14
0	1	0	1	101
0	1	1	0	110
0	3	2	1	321
0	9	9	9	999
1	4	6	8	1468

Constructing values in the binary system works the same way as in the decimal system, except that you have only two symbols to use, so each successive column represents a value only two times greater than the column to its right. The column values for binary numbers are 1, 2, 4, 8, 16, 32, and so on. In other words, the column values are 2^0, 2^1, 2^2, 2^3, 2^4, 2^5, and so on. Table 14-2 shows a few binary numbers and their corresponding decimal values. The values 0 and 1 appear the same way in both systems, but the decimal 2 requires two columns in the binary system because no symbol for 2 is available. Instead, to represent 2 in the binary system you place a 1 in the twos column and zero in the ones column. As in the decimal system, leading zeros are not required to represent a number, but they are understood to mean that a number is smaller in value than one with more filled column positions.

When you pronounce a binary number such as 101, say "one zero one" or "one oh one." Do not say "one hundred and one."

TIP

You can construct any binary number's decimal value by adding the column values of those columns that contain a 1. For example, Table 14-2 shows that the binary number 10100 contains 1s in the 16s and 4s columns. Therefore, the decimal value of 10100 is 16 + 4, or 20.

Table 14-2   Representation of a few binary numbers

2^8	2^7	2^6	2^5	2^4	2^3	2^2	2^1	2^0	
256s	128s	64s	32s	16s	8s	4s	2s	1s	Decimal Value
0	0	0	0	0	0	0	0	0	0
0	0	0	0	0	0	0	0	1	1
0	0	0	0	0	0	0	1	0	2
0	0	0	0	0	0	0	1	1	3
0	0	0	0	0	0	1	0	0	4
0	0	0	0	0	0	1	0	1	5
0	0	0	0	0	0	1	1	0	6
0	0	0	0	0	0	1	1	1	7
0	0	0	0	0	1	0	0	0	8
0	0	0	0	1	0	1	0	0	20
0	0	1	0	1	1	0	0	1	89
0	1	0	0	0	0	0	0	1	129
0	1	0	0	0	0	1	1	1	135
0	1	1	1	1	1	1	1	1	255
1	0	1	0	0	0	0	0	1	321
1	1	0	0	0	0	0	0	0	384

When you examine Table 14-2, you see that it quickly takes many more binary digits than decimal digits to represent a value. For example, the value 2 requires only a single digit in the decimal system, but requires two positions in the binary system. The value 321 requires nine digits in the binary system—1s in the columns representing 256, 64, and 1, and 0s in all the other columns.

When you use the decimal system, there is no "highest possible column." That is, you can represent any number, no matter how large, by adding enough columns to support the value. The same is true of the binary system.

The odometer in your car uses the decimal system. In older cars with a mechanical odometer, after you had driven 9 miles, a gear forced the column second from the right to "turn over" to a 1, and the far right column became 0 again. Although newer cars use a magnetic sensor or optical pickup, they still use the decimal system, and each column "rolls over" when the column to its right passes 9. You can think of the binary system in the same way. After you pass the binary value 1, the column second from the right becomes 1 and the far right column becomes 0, resulting in binary 10, or decimal 2. After binary 11 (decimal 3), the far right column becomes 0, forcing the next column from the right to be 0, forcing the third column from the right to be 1. The result is binary 100, or decimal 4.

UNDERSTANDING WHY COMPUTERS USE THE BINARY SYSTEM

Imagine that there are no computers, and that you are the first to attempt to invent an electronic data storage device. You decide to build your storage device from common hardware store supplies, and you want to store values at least up to several thousand. If you need to store a number such as 321, you have several options about the type of hardware to install in your device:

- You can use a huge dial with thousands of settings representing every possible value. Such a device would be very expensive to build and calibrate, and cost perhaps $1,000.

- You can use four or five dials with 10 settings each, and a system similar to the decimal system. For example, to store 321 using four dials, you would set the far left dial to zero, set the second dial to 3, the third dial to 2, and the fourth dial to 1. Such 10-way switches, like a dimmer switch sold in a hardware store, might cost $40 each. If you used four dials to store each number, you could store values up to 9,999 for $160 per number.

14

- You can use 15 or 16 two-way toggle switches, like regular light switches on a wall. You could create a code where a specific sequence of ons and offs represents each possible value. Such switches might cost only 15 cents each. If you think of the digit 1 representing On switches, and the digit 0 representing Off switches, then you would be using the binary system. Table 14-2 shows that the value 321 would require at least nine on-off switches. Larger numbers would require more switches, but at 15 cents each, it would cost only $2.25 to store any value requiring up to 15 switches (the decimal equivalent of 32,767). The cost would be many times less than using complicated 10-way switches.

If you use ordinary hardware components, two-way switches are the cheapest. Of course, computers don't use ordinary hardware components; they use circuitry that is far less expensive per switch. However, in the integrated circuits that modern computers do use, two-way switches are still cheaper than any more complex system. For this reason, all computers store values as a series of 1s and 0s. Every piece of data is stored in this fashion—letters and special symbols as well as numbers.

Every computer system uses a code to represent values, although different systems use different codes. Many personal computers use a system called ASCII (American Standard Code for Information Interchange), in which eight binary digits are used to represent a character. For example, in ASCII, the character A is represented by 01000001. Many mainframe computer systems use a separate code named **EBCDIC (Extended Binary Coded Decimal Interchange Code)**, in which, for example, the character A is 11000001. Most C++ compilers also support Unicode, which is a 16-bit coding scheme. For example, the letter A is stored in computer memory as a set of 16 zeros and ones as 0000000001000001. (By design, this number is the same numeric value as the ASCII code for A.) The reason for using 16 bits is to support all the characters from large foreign alphabets such as Greek, Hebrew, and Chinese. The representation of A using each code is slightly different, but the precise binary code is unimportant. What is important is that each system recognizes an A when it sees one.

TIP   You first learned about the ASCII character set in Chapter 1. You first learned about Unicode in Chapter 13. For more information about Unicode, visit *www.unicode.org*.

Because every computer system uses binary digits to store data, computer professionals have developed a vocabulary with which they can talk about storage. Computer professionals use the term **bit** as shorthand when they refer to a single **bi**nary dig**it**. Eight binary digits are called a **byte**, which on many systems is the amount of storage required to store a single character such as an alphabetic letter or punctuation mark. Thus, every time you store a letter or other character in a computer system, you are actually storing eight separate digits that represent the character; in other words, you are storing one byte.

TIP   The far left bit in a byte is called the high-order bit; the far right bit is the low-order bit.

USING INDIVIDUAL BITS TO STORE DATA

You have several options for storing the values 0 and 1 within fields in a class you create. For example:

- You can store 0 or 1 in a **double** field.

- You can store 0 or 1 in an **int** field.

- You can store 0 or 1 in a single bit field.

On most computer systems, the 0 or 1 stored in an **int** requires less storage than the same value stored in a **double**. In all computer systems, the 0 or 1 stored in a bit takes far less room than the same value stored in either an integer or a **double**. When you need to create a field that contains a wide possibility of values, such as an ID number or an inventory quantity, it makes sense to use an integer. When you need to create a class field that might hold only the value 0 or 1 (for example, a flag that indicates true or false), you can still use an integer, but you can also use a single bit. The advantage to using a single bit is that you consume far less storage space. Depending on your computer, a single integer might occupy four bytes of storage. If you use bits to store true or false information, you can hold up to eight pieces of such information in one byte. That means bits give you the potential to store 32 times the information you would be able to store in an integer space.

TIP You could also use the **bool** data type to store a flag. The **bool** data type requires one byte, so it would save more room than using an **int**. However, it would still require eight times the space of a bit.

You declare a field to be a single bit by placing a colon and a 1 after the variable declaration. Thus, the declaration **int aFlag:1;** declares a variable named **aFlag** that occupies one bit of storage. It can hold only one of two values—0 or 1.

For example, Figure 14-3 shows two classes that can hold information about an automobile driver. The information is used to determine insurance premium rates. Each class holds fields for an ID number and several true or false fields, such as whether the driver is male or over 25 years old. The only difference between the two classes is that the **DriverUsingInts** class uses integers to store the true or false values, and the **DriverUsingBits** class uses single bits for the same purpose. (The bit designations in the **DriverUsingBits** class are highlighted.) For simplicity, neither of these classes contains any functions.

14

```
class DriverUsingInts
{
    private:
            int idNum;
            int isMale;
            int isOver25;
            int hasPreviousTickets;
            int tookDriversEd;
            int residesUrbanArea;
            int ownsMultipleVehicles;
            int drivesOver10MilesToWork;
};
class DriverUsingBits
{
    private:
            int idNum;
            unsigned int isMale:1;
            unsigned int isOver25:1;
            unsigned int hasPreviousTickets:1;
            unsigned int tookDriversEd:1;
            unsigned int residesUrbanArea:1;
            unsigned int ownsMultipleVehicles:1;
            unsigned int drivesOver10MilesToWork:1;
};
```

Figure 14-3   `DriverUsingInts` and `DriverUsingBits` classes

Figure 14-4 shows a **main( )** function that declares one object of type **DriverUsingInts** and one object of type **DriverUsingBits**. The function contains three **cout** statements. The first uses the **sizeof()** operator to display the size of an integer in the computer on which the program is run. Figure 14-5 shows the output on a computer in which integers are stored in four bytes. The other two **cout** statements, shaded in Figure 14-4, display the size of the declared **DriverUsingBits** and **DriverUsingInts**. Figure 14-5 shows that the first object's size is 32, but the second object's size is only 8.

TIP

Recall that the **sizeof( )** function is used to show the size in bytes of any object or type. You first learned about the **sizeof()** function in Chapter 1.

```
int main()
{
    DriverUsingInts anotherDriver;
    DriverUsingBits aDriver;
    cout<<"Size of an int on this system is "<<
        sizeof(int)<<endl;
    cout<<"Size of DriverUsingInts is "<<
        sizeof(anotherDriver)<<endl;
    cout<<"Size of DriverUsingBits is "<<
        sizeof(aDriver)<<endl;
}
```

Figure 14-4   Program that declares a `DriverUsingInts` and a `DriverUsingBits`

Figure 14-5   Output of program in Figure 14-4

When you examine the output in Figure 14-5, you see that the `DriverUsingInts` object requires 32 bytes of storage—four bytes for each of its eight integer fields. On the other hand, the `DriverUsingBits` object requires only eight bytes of storage—four bytes for the integer `idNum` and just one `int` (four bytes) for all the other fields added together. In fact, because there are eight bits in a byte, and four bytes in an `int`, and since only seven bits are used for the seven flag fields within the `DriverUsingBits` class, there actually is a little room to spare. In fact, 25 additional pieces of information could be stored for a `DriverUsingBits` object without using any additional memory.

TIP   If you use fewer than eight bits as fields in a class, the computer rounds up the storage requirements to the next whole number of bytes. That is, if you store any number of bits from one to eight, you must use an entire byte of storage; if you store nine to 16 bits, you must use two entire bytes of storage, and so on.

TIP   When you create a class with several bit fields, some systems place them in order from left to right within a byte; others place them from right to left. In other words, bit operations are machine dependent.

The advantage to storing a data field in a bit instead of a byte is the amount of storage space saved. When you write a program that declares a single object, it doesn't make much difference whether the object requires eight or 32 bytes of storage. The benefit comes

14

when you store thousands or millions of such objects, or when you transmit those objects across data communication lines. If you are an Internet user, you most likely have been frustrated with the wait time necessary when large objects are sent to you via e-mail, or when you try to download large objects from a Web site. The smaller an object is, the faster you can send it over a network or telephone lines to another user.

When you declare a field to be a bit field, the field type must be `int` or `unsigned int`. When a field is type `int`, it can hold both positive and negative numbers—the far left bit is reserved to hold the sign and the other seven bits represent the value. When a field is type **unsigned int**, then it must be positive, because no bit is reserved for a sign, and all eight bits are used to store the value. The advantage to using `unsigned int` when storing bit fields is that when no bit is needed for a sign, more data can be stored. You declare a field to be an unsigned `int` in one of two ways—you can use the type name `unsigned int`, or you simply can use `unsigned`, which the compiler interprets as `unsigned int`.

When you declare bit fields, you can assign values to them in the same way you assign values to ordinary non-bit fields. That is, you can use an integer constant or integer variable that holds a 1 or 0 and assign it to a bit field, and C++ takes care of the conversion. Similarly, the comparison operators—such as == , <, and >—work with bits in the same way they work with integers.

If you assign a value other than 0 or 1 to a bit field, only the far right bit is stored. All even numbers contain a 0 in the far right position, and all odd numbers contain a 1 in the far right position.

You cannot use the address operator (&) with a bit field. You can only access addresses of whole bytes or larger objects.

When you want to store a 0 or 1, you can use a single bit. If you want to store larger values, you need more bits. Table 14-2 shows that you need at least two bits of storage to represent the value 2 or 3. Similarly, you need three bits to represent 4, 5, 6, or 7. When you want to store a small value that requires more storage space than a bit, but not as much as a byte or an integer, you simply increase the number following the colon in the declaration of the bit field. For example, `int aField:2;` declares a field that is two bits in size. Within a two-bit field, you can store four values—00, 01, 10, and 11. If you examine Table 14-2, you can see that these four values are the equivalents of the decimal values 0, 1, 2, and 3.

CONVERTING A GROUP OF BIT FIELDS TO AN INTEGER VALUE

For convenience, you can picture a group of bit fields as a single byte or integer. For example, consider the partial `Employee` class definition shown in Figure 14-6. Besides an ID number, every `Employee` contains eight yes-or-no fields that indicate `Employee` attributes, such as whether the `Employee` is full-time, and whether the `Employee` requires a deduction for medical insurance.

```
class Employee
{
    private:
        int idNum;
        unsigned isFullTime:1;
        unsigned deductMedicalInsurance:1;
        unsigned deductDentalInsurance:1;
        unsigned deductLifeInsurance:1;
        unsigned deductUnionDues:1;
        unsigned deductSavingsBonds:1;
        unsigned deductRetirementPlan:1;
        unsigned deductCharitableContribution:1;
};
```

Figure 14-6   Partial `Employee` class definition

When you store 0s and 1s in the bit fields for an object, you can think of them as individual fields or as a single unit. For example, an `Employee` who is not full-time—and who elects the dental insurance, life insurance, and savings bond options, but no others—appears in computer memory as 00101100. (The far right 0 represents the first field listed within the class—`isFullTime`.) If you treat this group of flags as a binary number and assign the binary numbering system column values to each column, then the Employee's deduction group value is 32 + 8 + 4, or 44 in the decimal system. With 1s representing yes and 0s representing no, the `Employee`'s eight separate flags form the binary number 00101100. (The far right 0 represents the first field listed within the class—`isFullTime`.) If you treat this group of flags as a binary number and assign the binary numbering system column values to each column, then the `Employee`'s deduction group value is 32 + 8 + 4, or 44 in the decimal system.

Suppose you need to select `Employee`s who have elected the three options—life insurance, dental insurance, and savings bonds—for some purpose; perhaps you are going to offer a discounted deduction for `Employee`s who elect these three specific options and no others. You can use an `if` statement such as the following to select the appropriate `Employee`s and display a message:

```
if(deductMedicalInsurance == 0 &&
        deductDentalInsurance == 1 &&
        deductLifeInsurance == 1 && deductUnionDues == 0 &&
        deductSavingsBonds == 1 && deductRetirementPlan == 0 &&
        deductCharitableContribution == 0)
            cout<<" Special combination!"<<endl;
```

Alternatively, you can use the knowledge that an `Employee` who elects those three options holds a combined value of 44 in the bit fields, and use a statement similar to the following:

```
if(codes == 44)
        cout<<" Special combination!"<<endl;
```

Certainly the second option is easier to write, although it is more cryptic. If you use such a technique, then you should document the meaning of the 44 in a program comment, or create a named constant that holds the desired value. Figure 14-7 shows a complete `Employee` class, including a `convertBitsToInt()` function that calculates the combined decimal value of the bit fields that are part of the class.

The `Employee` class `setFields()` function prompts the user for an `Employee`'s ID number and for yes-or-no answers to questions regarding the values of each of the bit fields within the class. Because the `cin` operator uses the address of the variable for which you are reading a value, and because you cannot use the address of a bit, the `setFields()` function requires a temporary integer object for data entry. The temporary object accepts the input value, which is then assigned to the appropriate bit field.

```
class Employee
{
    private:
        int idNum;
        unsigned isFullTime:1;
        unsigned deductMedicalInsurance:1;
        unsigned deductDentalInsurance:1;
        unsigned deductLifeInsurance:1;
        unsigned deductUnionDues:1;
        unsigned deductSavingsBonds:1;
        unsigned deductRetirementPlan:1;
        unsigned deductCharitableContribution:1;
    public:
        void setFields();
        void showEmployee();
        unsigned convertBitsToInt();
};
```

Figure 14-7   The `Employee` class

```cpp
void Employee::setFields()
{
    int temp;
    cout<<endl<<"Enter ID number ";
    cin>>idNum;
    cout<<"Enter 1 or 0 for yes or no ";
    cout<<"to each of the following questions."<<endl;
    cout<<"Is Employee full time? ";
    cin>>temp;
    isFullTime = temp;
    cout<<"Medical insurance? ";
    cin>>temp;
    deductMedicalInsurance = temp;
    cout<<"Dental insurance? ";
    cin>>temp;
    deductDentalInsurance = temp;
    cout<<"Life insurance? ";
    cin>>temp;
    deductLifeInsurance = temp;
    cout<<"Union? ";
    cin>>temp;
    deductUnionDues = temp;
    cout<<"Savings bonds? ";
    cin>>temp;
    deductSavingsBonds = temp;
    cout<<"Retirement plan? ";
    cin>>temp;
    deductRetirementPlan = temp;
    cout<<"Charitable contribution? ";
    cin>>temp;
    deductCharitableContribution = temp;
}
void Employee::showEmployee()
{
    cout<<"ID #"<<idNum<<" ";
    cout<<deductCharitableContribution<<
        deductRetirementPlan<<deductSavingsBonds<<
        deductUnionDues<<deductLifeInsurance<<
        deductDentalInsurance<<deductMedicalInsurance<<
        isFullTime;
}
unsigned Employee::convertBitsToInt()
{
    unsigned temp;
    temp = deductCharitableContribution * 128
        + deductRetirementPlan * 64
        + deductSavingsBonds * 32
        + deductUnionDues * 16
        + deductLifeInsurance * 8
        + deductDentalInsurance * 4
        + deductMedicalInsurance * 2
        + isFullTime * 1;
    return temp;
}
```

14

Figure 14-7   The Employee class (continued)

TIP

In the `convertBitsToInt()` function in Figure 14-7, multiplying `isFullTime` by 1 does not change the value of `isFullTime`. The multiplication is explicitly stated for consistency, because all the other bit fields are multiplied by their place values.

TIP

In the `convertBitsToInt()` function in Figure 14-7, you might prefer using a named constant for each of the values that is a power of 2 (128, 64, and so on). This example does not use named constants so the example remains short and easier for you to follow.

TIP

To avoid the long string of multiplication operations in the `convertBitsToInt()` function, you could create the following version of the function:

```
unsigned Employee::getCodes()
{
    int *p = &idNum;
    ++p;
    return *p;
}
```

In this version, a pointer is set to the address of `idNum`, and then the pointer is incremented so it holds the address of the first bit of the integer whose bits contain the `Employee` codes. The value of the integer at this address, rather than just the value of one bit, is returned.

The `showEmployee()` function displays the field bit values for demonstration purposes. A fully developed `Employee` class would probably contain a more descriptive `showEmployee()` function that spells out the `Employee`'s status with regard to each of the deduction options. The `Employee` class `convertBitsToInt()` function shown in Figure 14-7 uses the binary system column values to construct an integer from the separate bit fields.

Figure 14-8 contains a `main()` function that uses the `Employee` class. An array of `Employee` objects is declared and, in a `for` loop, each `Employee` is assigned values from the keyboard. The second `for` loop displays each `Employee`'s values in turn, including the calculated code's value. This program looks for `Employee`s who have selected the dental insurance, life insurance, and savings bond options (but no others); checks each `Employee`'s calculated code against the value 44; and displays a message for the appropriate `Employee`s. Figure 14-9 shows a typical execution of the program. You can see from the output that each `Employee`'s bit field values correspond to a decimal number, and that any `Employee` whose bit field values equal 44 (only the first `Employee` in the sample execution) receives the "Special combination!" message.

```
int main()
{
    const int NUM_EMPS = 3;
    const unsigned int DENTAL_LIFE_AND_BONDS = 44;
    Employee emps[NUM_EMPS];
    int x;
    unsigned codes;
    for(x = 0; x < NUM_EMPS; ++x)
        emps[x].setFields();
    cout<<endl<<"Employee summary:"<<endl;
    for(x = 0; x < NUM_EMPS; ++x)
    {
        emps[x].showEmployee();
        codes = emps[x].convertBitsToInt();
        cout<<"    "<<codes<<endl;
        // 44 is the code for dental insurance, life
        // insurance, and savings bonds only
        if(codes == DENTAL_LIFE_AND_BONDS)
            cout<<"  Special combination!"<<endl;
    }
}
```

Figure 14-8   A main() function using the Employee class

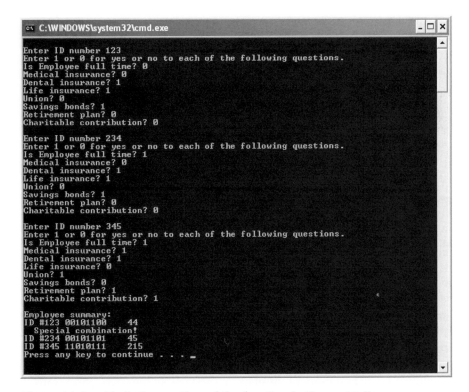

Figure 14-9   Typical execution of the function in Figure 14-8

14

USING THE BITWISE AND OPERATOR WITH A MASK

Comparing an object's bit fields to a decimal value is efficient when you want to find objects with a specific stored pattern. However, the job becomes more difficult when you want to select objects with multiple possible patterns. Suppose, for example, that you want to find all **Employee**s who carry any type of insurance—medical, dental, or life. The bit values for an **Employee** with these three deductions and no others are shown in Figure 14-10. Such an **Employee** has combined bit values that equal the decimal number 14. However, if you want to find all **Employee**s who take deductions for any type of insurance, you cannot just compare each **Employee**'s code value to 14. Many other **Employee** combinations also contain "on" bits for at least one of the three insurance types, but contain other on bits as well. For example, an **Employee** who is full-time and takes deductions for all three insurance types, but takes no other deductions, is represented by 00001111, or 15. Another **Employee** who is not full-time, but takes every possible deduction, including all three insurance deductions, is represented by 11111110, or 254. Additionally, some **Employee**s take the medical insurance option, but not the dental or life insurance. Others take the life insurance only, and so on. There are many numeric combinations for which at least one of the three insurance fields is 1, and it would take many if statements to compare an **Employee** with every possible valid combination that includes at least one of the three insurance fields.

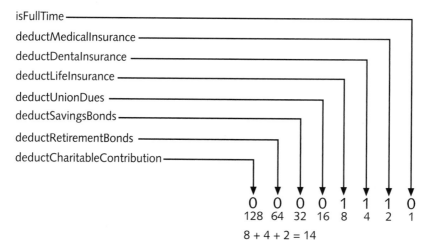

Figure 14-10   Representation of **Employee** with three kinds of insurance, but no other deductions

C++ provides you with a special set of operators called bitwise operators that you can use in situations like the one just described. **Bitwise operators** let you manipulate individual bits of integer or character values. One such operator is the **bitwise AND operator**, which is written as a single ampersand (&). You have already used the AND operator (without the word bitwise) by placing two ampersands between two Boolean expressions. For example, the following C++ statement displays a message when two conditions are true— **gradePoint** is at least 3.0, and **creditsEarned** are at least 30.

```
if(gradePoint >= 3.0 && creditsEarned >=30)
    cout<<"Eligible for honor society";
```

The bitwise AND operator does not compare variable values. Instead, it compares the individual bits of its two operands and produces a result based on the bit values. The result value contains a 1 in any columnar positions where both bitwise AND operands contain a 1; the result value contains a 0 in all other bit positions. For example, suppose value1 contains the bit pattern 10101010, and value2 contains the bit pattern 00001111. Figure 14-11 shows how the expression result = value1 & value2; is evaluated.

value1	1	0	1	0	1	0	1	0
value2	0	0	0	0	1	1	1	1
result	0	0	0	0	1	0	1	0

Figure 14-11   Using the logical bitwise AND operator with two values

TIP   In C++, the ampersand is polymorphic because it takes one meaning when used between two operands (the bitwise AND operator) and a different meaning when used to the left of a variable (the address operator). In other words, & is an overloaded operator.

Figure 14-11 shows that the far right column of value1 contains 0, and the far right column of value2 contains a 1. Because both operands, value1 and value2, do not contain a 1 in the far right column, the far right bit in the result is 0. (In other words, false AND true results in false.) Figure 14-11 also shows that value1 and value2 both contain 1s in the column that is second from the right. Therefore, the result field also contains a 1 in its corresponding column. In other words, if both operands contain a 1 in a column, so does the result, and if either or both the operands contain a 0 in a column, so does the result.

A common use for bitwise operators is to create a mask. A **mask** is a value whose only purpose is to filter values from other variables. Figure 14-12 shows three possible Employee objects and the result that ensues when you mask their bit values with an ALLINSURANCE mask set to 00001110. The first two Employee objects shown in Figure 14-12 carry at least one of the types of insurance. Although the results of the bitwise AND operation differ for the two Employees, both operations result in a nonzero value. The third Employee represented in Figure 14-12 carries no insurance. When the bit values of this Employee are compared to ALLINSURANCE with the bitwise AND, the result is zero because there are no bit fields for which both the Employee and the mask hold a 1 in the same position.

14

	retirement contributions	union savings		dental life	full-time medical		
Employee with dental insurance only	0	0	0	0	0	1	0	0
ALLINSURANCE	0	0	0	0	1	1	1	0
result	0	0	0	0	0	1	0	0

	retirement contributions	union savings		dental life	full-time medical		
Employee with every deduction	1	1	1	1	1	1	1	1
ALLINSURANCE	0	0	0	0	1	1	1	0
result	0	0	0	0	1	1	1	0

	retirement contributions	union savings		dental life	full-time medical		
full-time union Employee with no insurance	0	0	0	1	0	0	0	1
ALLINSURANCE	0	0	0	0	1	1	1	0
result	0	0	0	0	0	0	0	0

Figure 14-12 Using the logical bitwise AND operator with three Employees and an insurance mask

> **TIP**
> Consider a multiple choice test for which the test taker fills in bubbles to select answers. To compute a score, you can create a cover sheet with holes that correspond to the correct answers, hold the sheet over the completed exam, and count the number of filled-in bubbles you see. The cover sheet is a real-world example of a mask.

Figure 14-13 shows a program that declares several **Employee** objects and allows the user to enter values. In the first highlighted statement in the figure, the **ALLINSURANCE** mask is initialized to the value 14, which is the value that indicates true for all three insurance bits. In the second highlighted statement, the mask is used with a bitwise AND and with each **Employee** object to determine whether each **Employee** has any of the three forms of insurance. When an **Employee** has none of the three forms of insurance, the result of the mask is a zero, which is interpreted in the **if** statement as false. Thus, if an **Employee** carries none of the three forms of insurance, the "Has no insurance" message displays.

Figure 14-14 shows the end of a typical execution of the program. The first four **Employee**s have some form of insurance; for example, **Employee** 201 has all three insurance types. The last **Employee** does not carry any insurance; therefore, the mask result for the last **Employee** is zero, and the **if** statement determines that the **Employee** has no insurance.

```
int main()
{
    const int NUM_EMPS = 5;
    Employee emps[NUM_EMPS];
    int x;
    unsigned codes;
    const unsigned ALLINSURANCE = 14;
    for(x = 0; x < NUM_EMPS; ++x)
        emps[x].setFields();
    cout<<endl<<"Employee summary:"<<endl;
    for(x = 0; x < NUM_EMPS; ++x)
    {
        emps[x].showEmployee();
        codes = emps[x].convertBitsToInt();
        cout<<"     "<<codes<<endl;
        if(codes & ALLINSURANCE)
            cout<<"   Has some insurance"<<endl;
        else
            cout<<"   Has no insurance"<<endl;
    }
}
```

Figure 14-13   A main( ) function that uses an insurance mask to filter Employee bit fields

Using a mask is convenient. In the program in Figure 14-13, using the mask improves program efficiency; you can select records of **Employee**s who take all three types of insurance by making a single logical comparison. If you could not use the mask, then you would have to make separate comparisons using **if** statements with each of the three insurance fields.

When you use the bitwise AND operator, you can assign the result to a variable, as in the following statement:

```
result = value1 & value2;
```

You can also perform a bitwise comparison and assignment in one operation using &=. The following statement performs a bitwise AND comparison between **value1** and **value2**, and assigns the results to **value1**:

```
value1 &= value2;
```

14

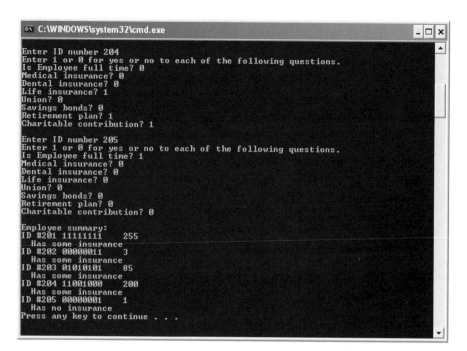

Figure 14-14 Typical execution of function in Figure 14-13

Using the Bitwise Inclusive OR Operator

The **bitwise inclusive OR operator** (|) compares the bits of its two operands, and produces a result in which each bit is a 1 if either of the operand's corresponding bits is a 1. Figure 14-15 shows an example that uses the bitwise OR operator. When either or both of the column's bits hold a 1, then the result bit also holds a 1. In other words, the result holds a 0 in a column only if both operands to the bitwise OR hold a 0 in the corresponding column.

value1	1	0	1	0	1	0	1	0
value2	0	0	0	0	1	1	1	1
result	1	0	1	0	1	1	1	1

Figure 14-15 Using the bitwise OR operator with two values

One reason to use the bitwise inclusive OR operator is to turn on specific bit fields within an object. For example, consider objects created from the **Employee** class in Figure 14-7. Suppose an organization decides to offer two new free benefits, a retirement plan and medical insurance, to all **Employee**s, whether they have previously elected those benefits or not. You can create a mask that holds 1s in those two positions and perform a bitwise OR with the mask and an `Employee`'s bit fields. Figure 14-16 shows some possible results. When you use the bitwise OR with any `Employee` and the `NEW_BENEFIT_MASK` that holds 1s in the `deductRetirementPlan` and `deductMedicalInsurance` fields, the result contains "on" fields for any options the `Employee` had originally. Additionally, the result contains on bits in the retirement and medical option fields whether the `Employee` originally held the benefits or not.

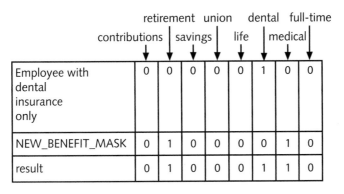

	retirement	contributions	savings	union	life	dental	medical	full-time
Employee with dental insurance only	0	0	0	0	0	1	0	0
NEW_BENEFIT_MASK	0	1	0	0	0	0	1	0
result	0	1	0	0	0	1	1	0

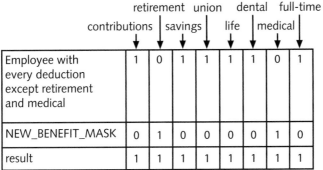

	retirement	contributions	savings	union	life	dental	medical	full-time
Employee with every deduction except retirement and medical	1	0	1	1	1	1	0	1
NEW_BENEFIT_MASK	0	1	0	0	0	0	1	0
result	1	1	1	1	1	1	1	1

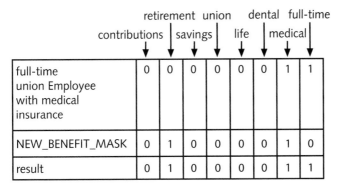

	retirement	contributions	savings	union	life	dental	medical	full-time
full-time union Employee with medical insurance	0	0	0	0	0	0	1	1
NEW_BENEFIT_MASK	0	1	0	0	0	0	1	0
result	0	1	0	0	0	0	1	1

Figure 14-16   Using the bitwise OR operator with three `Employee` objects and a mask

14

TIP

In Chapter 13, you used a bitwise OR with format flags to control the appearance of output.

Figure 14-17 shows a function you can add to the **Employee** class to assign an unsigned integer's bit values to an **Employee**'s bit fields. If an argument to **convertIntToBits( )** is at least 128, it means the far left bit in the argument is on, so a 1 is assigned to the **deductCharitableContribution** field, and the argument is reduced by 128. If the remaining value in the argument is at least 64, then it means the next bit is on, and 1 should be assigned to the **deductRetirementPlan** field. The procedure continues until each **Employee** bit field has been assigned its correct value.

```
void Employee::convertIntToBits(unsigned code)
{
    if(code >= 128)
    {
        deductCharitableContribution = 1;
        code -= 128;
    }
    else
        deductCharitableContribution = 0;
    if(code >= 64)
    {
        deductRetirementPlan = 1;
        code -= 64;
    }
    else
        deductRetirementPlan = 0;
    if(code >= 32)
    {
        deductSavingsBonds = 1;
        code -= 32;
    }
    else
        deductSavingsBonds = 0;
    if(code >= 16)
    {
        deductUnionDues = 1;
        code -= 16;
    }
    else
        deductUnionDues = 0;
    if(code >= 8)
    {
        deductLifeInsurance = 1;
        code -= 8;
    }
    else
        deductLifeInsurance = 0;
```

Figure 14-17   Function that assigns an integer to **Employee** bit fields

```
    if(code >= 4)
    {
        deductDentalInsurance = 1;
        code -= 4;
    }
    else
        deductDentalInsurance = 0;
    if(code >= 2)
    {
        deductMedicalInsurance = 1;
        code -= 2;
    }
    else
        deductMedicalInsurance = 0;
    if(code >= 1)
    {
        isFullTime = 1;
        code -= 1;
    }
    else
        isFullTime = 0;
}
```

Figure 14-17   Function that assigns an integer to `Employee` bit fields (continued)

TIP

To avoid the long string of comparison operations in the `convertIntToBits()` function, you could create the following version of the function:

```
void Employee::convertIntToBits(unsigned code)
{
    int *p;
    p = &idNum;
    ++p;
    *p = code;
}
```

In this version, a pointer is set to the address of `idNum`. Then the pointer is incremented so it holds the address of the first bit of the integer whose bits contain the `Employee` codes. The value of the integer at this address, which is the start of the list of bit fields, is assigned the code argument.

The `main()` function in Figure 14-18 establishes a `NEW_BENEFIT_MASK` with a value of 66. The value is set to 66 because an integer with the `deductRetirementPlan` and `deductMedicalInsurance` bits turned on has 1s in the columns valued at 64 and 2. The program creates an array of `Employee` objects and assigns values to each `Employee`'s fields. The second `for` loop within the program is used to display each `Employee`'s field values, convert the bits to an integer, perform a bitwise `OR` on the bits with the `NEW_BENEFIT_MASK`, set the `Employee`'s bits with the new value, and display the `Employee` data again. When you examine

14

the end of a typical execution, as shown in Figure 14-19, you see that no matter whether each `Employee` stored 1s in the `deductRetirementPlan` and `deductMedicalInsurance` bits prior to the bitwise OR (the second and second-to-last bits), each `Employee` contains 1s in these fields afterward.

```cpp
int main()
{
    const int NUM_EMPS = 5;
    Employee emps[NUM_EMPS];
    int x;
    unsigned codes;
    const unsigned NEW_BENEFIT_MASK = 66;
    for(x = 0; x < NUM_EMPS; ++x)
        emps[x].setFields();
    for(x = 0; x < NUM_EMPS; ++x)
    {
        cout<<"Before mask: ";
        emps[x].showEmployee();
        codes = emps[x].convertBitsToInt();
        codes = codes | NEW_BENEFIT_MASK;
        cout<<"    After mask: ";
        emps[x].convertIntToBits(codes);
        emps[x].showEmployee();
        cout<<endl;
    }
}
```

Figure 14-18   A `main( )` function that turns on `Employee` bit fields using an inclusive bitwise OR

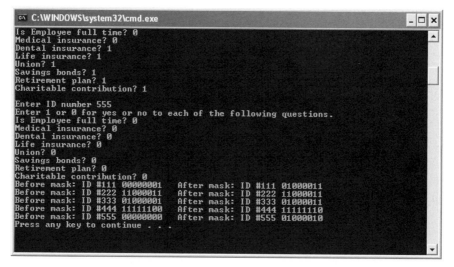

Figure 14-19   Output of typical execution of function in Figure 14-18

When you use the inclusive bitwise OR operator, you can assign the result to a variable, as in the following statement:

```
codes = codes | NEW_BENEFIT_MASK;
```

You can also perform a bitwise comparison and assignment in one operation using |=. The following statement performs an inclusive OR comparison between codes and NEW_BENEFIT_MASK, and assigns the result to codes:

```
codes |= NEW_BENEFIT_MASK;
```

TIP The bitwise inclusive OR operator (l) sets each bit in the result to 1 if the corresponding bit in either or both operands is 1. In contrast, the **bitwise exclusive OR operator** (^) sets each bit in the result to 1 only if exactly one of the corresponding bits in the operators is 1.

TIP The **bitwise complement operator** (~) sets each bit in the result to 1 if the corresponding bit in the operand is 0 and each bit in the result to 0 if the corresponding bit in the operand is 1. For example, if the bit values of someCode are 11110000, then the bit values of myCode = ~someCode are 00001111. Complements are important to computer professionals in part because the complement of a binary number plus 1 equals the negative of the same value.

SHIFTING BITS

You can use the **bitwise left shift operator** (<<) to shift bits to the left and the **bitwise right shift operator** (>>) to shift bits to the right. Each of these operators requires two operands—the one on the left holds the bits that are shifted, and the one on the right is the number of positions to shift.

For example, Figure 14-20 shows the bit representation of a byte, and the results after shifting one bit to the left—the equivalent of using the expression result = value1 << 1;. The bit pattern in value1 represents 46 (which you can prove by adding the values of the columns that contain 1s). When each bit is moved one position to the left, the far left position of value1 is lost and a zero is added to the vacated far right position in the result. The result value becomes 92—two times the original value of value1.

Decimal value of position	128	64	32	16	8	4	2	1
value1	0	0	1	0	1	1	1	0
Result after left shift	0	1	0	1	1	1	0	0

0

Figure 14-20   Shifting bits to the left

14

TIP

You left shift in the decimal system when you add a zero to the right of a value. The value 436 becomes 10 times larger, or 4360, when you left shift. The corresponding process in the binary system, adding a zero to the right side of a value, makes the value two times larger.

TIP

The bitwise shift operators are polymorphic; that is, they are overloaded. The << and >> operators are used for input and output as well as for bit shifting.

If you use the expression `result = value1 << 2;`, `result` becomes four times `value1`. For any number n, shifting n bits to the left is the same as multiplying by two to the n power. As with other binary operators, you can shift and assign in one operation using `<<=` or `>>=`.

The program in Figure 14-21 shows two ways of multiplying 5 by 2 to the third power. In the first part of the program, a variable named `num` is set to 5, and a loop is executed to multiply 2 by 2 by 2 to determine 2 to the third power before multiplying by 5 and displaying the answer. In the second part of the program (shaded), `num` is reset to 5 and the bitwise left shift operator performs the same task in one statement. The results, shown in Figure 14-22, are identical. Not only does shifting bits require less code, it also executes much more quickly.

Like the bitwise left shift operator, the bitwise right shift operator provides the same result as dividing by two to the power of the right operand. Again, the advantage is that the bitwise right shift operator works faster and requires less code.

```
#include<iostream>
using namespace std;
int main()
{
    int power = 3;
    int base = 2;
    int result;
    int x;
    int num = 5;
    result = base;
    for(x = 1; x < power; ++x)
        result *= base;
    result *= num;
    cout<<"Result after looping is "<<result<<endl;
    num = 5;
    result = num << power;
    cout<<"Result after shifting is "<<result<<endl;
}
```

Figure 14-21   Program demonstrating bitwise left shift operator

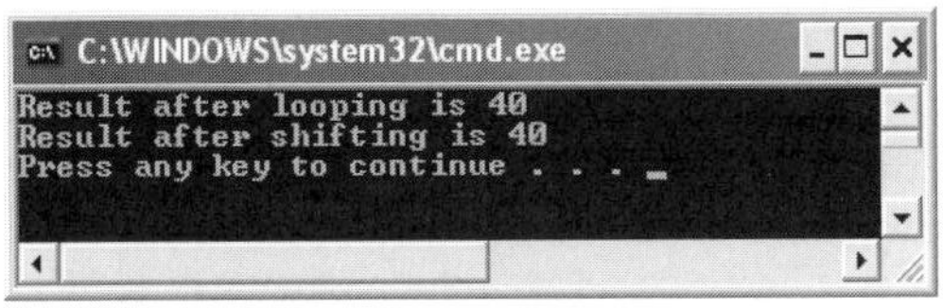

Figure 14-22 Output of program in Figure 14-21

UNDERSTANDING RECURSION

Recursion occurs when a function is defined in terms of itself. A function that calls itself is a **recursive function**. Many programming languages do not allow a function to call itself, but C++ programmers can use recursion to produce some interesting effects. Figure 14-23 shows a simple example of recursion. In this program, the `main()` function calls the `infinity()` function. The `infinity()` function displays "Help!" and calls itself again (see the highlighted statement). The second call to `infinity()` displays "Help!"; and generates a third call. The result is a large number of repetitions of the `infinity()` function. The output is shown in Figure 14-24.

```
#include<iostream>
using namespace std;
void infinity()
{
    cout<<"Help! ";
    infinity();
}
int main()
{
    infinity();
}
```

14

Figure 14-23 An example of recursion

Every time you call a function, the address to which the program should return at the completion of the function is stored in a memory location called the **stack**. When a function ends, the address is retrieved from the stack and the program returns to the location from which the function call was made. For example, suppose a `main()` function calls `functionA()` and that `functionA()` calls `functionB()`. When the `main()` function calls `functionA()`, a return address in `main()` is stored in the stack, then `functionA()` begins execution. When `functionA()` calls `functionB()`, a return address in `functionA()` is stored in the stack and `functionB()` begins execution. When `functionB()` ends, the `functionA()` return address is retrieved from the stack and program control returns to complete `functionA()`. When `functionA()` ends, the return address in the `main()` function is retrieved from the stack and program control returns to the `main()` function to complete it.

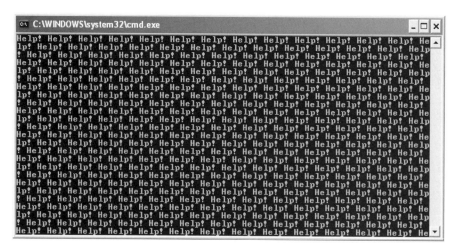

Figure 14-24 Output of program in Figure 14-23

When the `main()` function in Figure 14-23 calls the `infinity()` function, the stack receives the address to which the logic should return within `main()`. However, the `infinity()` function does not end until `infinity()` is called again, and a second return address is stored in the stack. You can picture the new return address as being stored "on top of" the first address. However, this address is never retrieved from the stack, because when this second version of the `infinity()` function executes, it, too, executes yet another repetition of `infinity()` and a third return address is stored in the stack. Because `infinity()` never reaches its end, and keeps calling another function (itself), eventually the stack overflows with too many stored return addresses. If you can imagine a computer with an infinite amount of memory allocated to the stack, then in theory, this program never ends. Instead, it keeps storing return addresses in the stack, but never retrieves any of them. In reality, many compilers will end the recursive calls after an excessive number of repetitions.

Of course, there is no practical use for an infinitely recursive program. Just as you must be careful not to create loops that can't end, when you write recursive functions, you must provide a way for the recursion to stop eventually.

Figure 14-25 shows an example of an application that uses recursion productively. The program calls a recursive function which computes the sum of every integer, from 1 up to and including the function's argument value. For example, the sum of every integer up to and including 3 is 1 + 2 + 3, or 6, and the sum of every integer up to and including 4 is 1 + 2 + 3 + 4, or 10.

When thinking about cumulative summing relationships, remember that the sum of all the integers up to and including any number is that number plus the sum of the integers for the next lowest number. In other words, the sum of the digits up to and including 4, is 4 plus the sum of the digits up to and including 3. The recursive `cumulativeSum()` function in Figure 14-25 uses this knowledge, so that for any argument, `num`, that is passed in with a value greater than 1, the function returns a value that is `num` plus the cumulativeSum( ) of num - 1. The main( ) function in Figure 14-25 calls the cumulativeSum( ) function ten times in a loop to show the cumulativeSum( ) of every integer from 1 through 10. Figure 14-26 shows the output of the program in Figure 14-25.

```cpp
#include<iostream>
using namespace std;
int cumulativeSum(int num)
{
    int returnVal;
    if(num == 1)
        returnVal = num;
    else
        returnVal = num + cumulativeSum(num - 1);
    return(returnVal);
}
int main()
{
    const int LIMIT = 10;
    int num;
    for(num = 1; num <= LIMIT; ++num)
    cout<<"When num is "<<num<<
        " then cumulativeSum(num) is "<<
        cumulativeSum(num)<<endl;
}
```

Figure 14-25   Program that uses a recursive cumulativeSum( ) function

Figure 14-26   Output of program in Figure 14-25

14

If you examine Figures 14-25 and 14-26 together, you can see that when 1 is passed to the cumulativeSum( ) function, the if statement within the function determines that the argument is equal to 1, the returnVal becomes 1, and 1 is returned for output.

On the next pass through the for loop, 2 is passed to the cumulativeSum( ) function. When the function receives 2 as an argument, the if statement within the function is false, and the returnVal is set to 2 plus the value of cumulativeSum(1). This second call to cumulativeSum( ) using 1 as an argument returns a 1, so when the function ends, it returns 2 + 1, or 3.

On the third pass through the `for` loop within the `main( )` function, 3 is passed to the `cumulativeSum( )` function. When the function receives 3 as an argument, the `if` statement within the function is false and the function returns 3 plus the value of `cumulativeSum(2)`. The value of this call is 2 plus `cumulativeSum(1)`. The value of `cumulativeSum(1)` is 1. So ultimately, `cumulativeSum(3)` is 3 + 2 + 1.

Following the logic of a recursive function is a difficult task, and programs that use recursion are error-prone and hard to debug. For these reasons, some business organizations forbid their programmers from using recursive logic within their programs. Additionally, many of the problems solved by recursive functions can be solved in a more straightforward way. Examine the program in Figure 14-27. Using a nested loop and no recursive function, this program produces identical output to that in Figure 14-26. The program in Figure 14-27 deals with the same problem in a more straightforward fashion.

```
#include<iostream>
using namespace std;
int main()
{
    int num;
    int total;
    const int LIMIT = 10;
    total = 0;
    for(num = 1; num <= LIMIT; ++num)
    {
        total += num;
        cout<<"When num is "<<num<<
            " then the cumulative sum of num is "
            <<total<<endl;
    }
}
```

Figure 14-27   Nonrecursive program that computes cumulative sums

 TIP
A humorous illustration of recursion is found in this sentence: "In order to understand recursion, you must first understand recursion." A humorous dictionary definition is "Recursion: See Recursion." These examples are funny because they contain an element of truth. In useful recursion algorithms however, there is always a point at which the infinite loop is exited. That is, there is always a point at which the base case, or exit case, is reached.

USING A RECURSIVE FUNCTION TO SORT A LIST

It is possible to quickly sort a list using a recursive sorting function. To use this sorting method, you employ a "divide and conquer" technique known as a **quick sort** or **pivot sort**. Using this technique, you select a point within a list that represents a middle position, and then divide the list into two sublists. (See Figure 14-28.) Then you swap the positions of pairs of values until all the values in the first sublist are less than the value in the middle position, and all the values in the second sublist are more than the value in the middle position. Subsequently, each sublist is divided in half and rearranged so all the low values are in one sublist and all the high values are in the other. You keep dividing lists into increasingly small sublists until there is only one element in a sublist. At that point, the values are sorted.

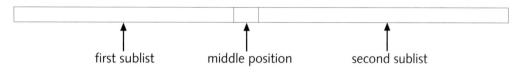

first sublist   middle position   second sublist

Figure 14-28 A list with two sublists and a middle position

You can solve the sorting problem by breaking down the work into several functions. The simplest function, named `swap( )`, appears in Figure 14-29. This function takes the address of two values, named `val1` and `val2`, as arguments. Then the function reverses the positions of the values. A temporary location holds `val1`, `val2` replaces `val1`, and the `temp` value (which is `val1`) replaces `val2`.

```
void swap(int &val1, int &val2)
{
    int temp;
    temp = val1;
    val1 = val2;
    val2 = temp;
}
```

Figure 14-29   The `swap( )` function

14

Figure 14-30 shows the `splitList( )` function. It accepts an array of integers and two integers representing the starting and ending subscripts in the list. The middle position, also known as the pivot point, is calculated by averaging the start and stop values. The middle position and its value are stored, and the middle value is moved to the beginning of the list. Then every value in the list (after the first one) is compared to the first value (which used to be the middle value). If any value is less than the original middle value, the value is exchanged with a value from the other side of the middle (that is, from the other sublist). At the end of the function, the middle value is returned to the middle of the list.

TIP

Some programmers prefer to use a random position as the pivot point for a sort instead of using the middle position.

```
int splitList(int nums[], int start, int stop)
{
    int midValue, midPoint, mid, x;
    mid = (start + stop) / 2;
    swap(nums[start],nums[mid]);
    midPoint = start;
    midValue = nums[start];
    for(x = start + 1; x <= stop; ++x)
        if (nums[x] < midValue)
        {
            ++midPoint;
            swap(nums[midPoint],nums[x]);
        }
    swap(nums[start], nums[midPoint]);
    return midPoint;
}
```

Figure 14-30   The splitList() function

The sort() function in Figure 14-31 is the recursive function. It accepts a list of numbers and a start and stop position. As long as the values of start and stop are not the same (as long as start is smaller than stop), the list is split in two and sort() is called twice recursively, using the first half of the list and the second half of the list.

```
void sort(int nums[], int start, int stop)
{
    int midPoint;
    if(start < stop)
    {
        midPoint = splitList(nums, start, stop);
        sort(nums, start, midPoint - 1);
        sort(nums, midPoint + 1, stop);
    }
}
```

Figure 14-31   The sort() function

Figure 14-32 shows a main() function that sorts an array of seven integers. It displays the values, calls sort(), and displays the values again. Figure 14-33 shows the output.

```
int main()
{
     const int NUM_VALS = 7;
     int nums[NUM_VALS] = {7,2,5,6,4,1,3};
     int x;
     cout<<"At start: ";
     for (x = 0; x < NUM_VALS; ++x)
         cout<<nums[x]<<" ";
     cout<<endl;
     sort(nums, 0, NUM_VALS-1);
     cout<<"At end:    ";
     for(x = 0; x < NUM_VALS; ++x)
         cout<<nums[x]<<" ";
     cout<<endl;
}
```

Figure 14-32   A main() function that uses sort()

Figure 14-33   Output of program in Figure 14-32

The output produced by the recursive sorting program is not remarkable; you can achieve the same results with many other types of sorts that do not involve recursion. Sorts that are written nonrecursively are also easier to understand and debug. However, this sorting function works very well and executes much more quickly than most other sorting methods. This sorting method is an example of a useful form of recursion that programmers sometimes employ.

14

You Do It

Working with an Enumeration

In the next steps, you create an application that uses an enumeration of department names for a business college.

1. Open a new file in your C++ editor. Type the statements you need to start a main() function that will use an enumeration:

```
#include<iostream>
using namespace std;
int main()
{
```

2. Add an enumeration to hold the department names in the business college:

```
enum Depts {ACCT, BUS, CIS, MRKTG, MGMT};
```

3. Next add a loop control variable, and two doubles that will hold a student's credits in a department and total credits earned:

```
int x;
double credits;
double total = 0;
```

4. Use the enumeration values in a for loop that prompts for credits earned in every department from ACCT through MGMT. Keep a running total of the credits. When the loop ends, display the total and add a closing curly brace for the program.

```
for(x = ACCT; x <= MGMT; ++x)
{
   cout<<"Enter credit hours earned in department "<<
      (x + 1)<<" ";
   cin>>credits;
   total += credits;
}
cout<<"Total credits earned is "<<total<<endl;
}
```

5. Save the file as **DeptEnumeration.cpp** and compile and execute the program. A typical execution appears in Figure 14-34.

Figure 14-34 Typical execution of DeptEnumeration.cpp

Working with Bits

In the next set of steps, you create a Driver class with two bit fields and declare some objects that hold values in the fields.

1. Open a new file in your C++ editor. Type the first statements you need to write the program.

```
#include<iostream>
#include<string>
using namespace std;
```

2. Create a `Driver` class that includes an `idNum` and `lastName`, and two bit fields that hold gender and age designations. Use the `unsigned` type for the bit fields. Include a constructor that requires values for all four fields, and a `showDriver()` function. Notice that the variables in the constructor argument list are three `int`s and a `string`. The values that will be used to assign values to the `genderCode` and `ageCode` fields are simply integers—they do not have to be any special type of field just because they will be assigned to bit fields.

```
class Driver
{
    private:
        int idNum;
        string lastName;
        unsigned genderCode : 1;
        unsigned ageCode : 1;
      public:
        Driver(int, string, int, int);
        void showDriver();
};
```

3. Within the `Driver` constructor, you make all the appropriate data assignments.

```
Driver::Driver(int id, string name, int gender, int age)
{
    idNum = id;
    lastName = name;
    genderCode = gender;
    ageCode = age;
}
```

4. The `showDriver()` function includes enumerations for the gender and age codes. These enumerations make clear the meanings of the more cryptic 0s and 1s. The function displays all the fields, substituting the strings "Male", "Female", "Not over 25", and "Over 25" for the code values.

```
void Driver::showDriver()
{
    enum Gender {MALE = 0, FEMALE};
    enum Age {YOUNG = 0, OLD};
    cout<<"ID #"<<idNum<<" Name: "<<lastName<<" Gender: ";
    if(genderCode == MALE)
        cout<<"Male    ";
    else
        cout<<"Female     ";
    if(ageCode == YOUNG)
        cout<<"Not over 25";
    else
        cout<<"Over 25";
    cout<<endl;
}
```

14

5. Write a `main( )` function that declares one `Driver` object of each type (a younger and older male and a younger and older female) by using the 0 and 1 codes. Then show the four objects to confirm that the assignments were made correctly.

```
int main()
{
    Driver firstDriver(222,"Wallace", 0, 0),
        secondDriver(333,"Parker", 0, 1),
        thirdDriver(444,"Larson", 1, 0),
        fourthDriver(555,"Hernandez", 1, 1);
    firstDriver.showDriver();
    secondDriver.showDriver();
    thirdDriver.showDriver();
    fourthDriver.showDriver();
}
```

6. Save the file as **Driver.cpp**. Compile and run the program. The output looks like Figure 14-35.

Figure 14-35 Output of Driver.cpp program

Using a Multi-Bit Field

In the next set of steps, assume that you want to include a field within the `Driver` class you just created, and that you allow only three or fewer vehicles per `Driver`. You could use an integer to hold the vehicle number, but you require only two bits, because 0, 1, 2, and 3 are represented in binary as 00, 01, 10, and 11. You can add a field that holds a number of vehicles without increasing the size of `Driver` objects by adding a two-bit field to the `Driver` class.

1. If necessary, open the **Driver.cpp** file. Immediately save it as **Driver2.cpp**.

2. At the end of the list of `Driver` class fields (after the `ageCode` field), add a new two-bit field that holds the number of vehicles being insured with this `Driver`.

```
unsigned numVehicles:2;
```

3. Within the `public` section of the declarations for the `Driver` class, add a required integer parameter to the `Driver` constructor argument list. This parameter holds the number of insured vehicles. The new prototype is:

```
Driver(int, string, int, int, int);
```

4. Change the `Driver` class constructor implementation to accommodate the new parameter and to assign it to the new `numVehicles` field.

```cpp
Driver::Driver(int id, string name, int gender, int age,
int cars)
{
    idNum = id;
    lastName = name;
    genderCode = gender;
    ageCode = age;
    numVehicles = cars;
}
```

5. Replace the last line of the `showDriver()` function. Currently it is `cout<<endl;`. The new line displays the number of vehicles as follows:

```cpp
cout<<"    Driver has "<<numVehicles<<" vehicle(s)."<<endl;
```

6. Within the `main()` function, add a number of vehicles to the constructor call for each `Driver`.

```cpp
Driver firstDriver(222,"Wallace", 0, 0, 0),
       secondDriver(333,"Parker", 0, 1, 1),
       thirdDriver(444,"Larson", 1, 0, 2),
       fourthDriver(555,"Hernandez", 1, 1, 3);
```

7. Save the file as **Driver2.cpp**. Compile and execute the program. The output appears in Figure 14-36. The correct number of vehicles appears with the other information regarding each `Driver`.

Figure 14-36 Output of Driver2.cpp program

WORKING WITH RECURSION

In the next set of steps, you create a recursive drawing function so you can experiment with the way recursion works.

1. Open a new file in your C++ editor. Type the statements you need to start this program.

```cpp
#include<iostream>
using namespace std;
```

2. Write a recursive **draw( )** function. The function accepts two arguments—a character that is drawn on the screen, and an integer that represents the number of times to draw the character. If the number of times to draw is greater than 0, the character is output and the **draw( )** function is called again, using a number that is one less than the original number. In other words, the **draw( )** function produces num characters.

```
void draw(char ch, int num)
{
    if(num > 0)
    {
        cout<<ch;
        draw(ch,num - 1);
    }
}
```

3. Next, write a recursive **display( )** function. Its three arguments include a symbol to be drawn, an offset number, and a length. If the length is greater than 0, the function calls **draw( )** twice. The first time it calls **draw( )**, it passes a space and the offset value to **draw( )**, so **draw( )** produces **off** number of spaces as output. The second time it calls **draw( )**, it passes the symbol and the length, so it produces **len** number of **sym** outputs. After a newline output, the **display( )** function calls itself using the same symbol, but an offset that is two more than the previous offset, and a length that is four less than the previous length. The **display( )** function keeps calling itself until the **len** variable is reduced to 0 or less.

```
void display(char sym, int off, int len)
{
    if(len > 0)
    {
        draw(' ', off);
        draw(sym, len);
        cout<<endl;
        display(sym, off + 2, len - 4);
    }
}
```

4. Next, write a **main( )** function that uses the **display( )** function. Initialize an offset variable to 0 and prompt the user for a length and symbol to use as initial arguments to **display( )**.

```
int main()
{
    char symbol;
    int offset = 0;
    int length;
    cout<<"Enter length ";
    cin>>length;
```

```
        cout<<"Enter symbol ";
        cin>>symbol;
        cout<<endl<<endl;
        display(symbol, offset, length);
    }
```

5. Save the program as **DrawingRecursion.cpp**. Compile and execute the program. Figure 14-37 shows the output when the user enters 30 and an asterisk in response to the prompts. The **main( )** function calls the **display( )** function using the asterisk, 0, and 30 as arguments. The **display( )** function calls **draw( )** twice. The first time it uses 0 spaces, and the second time it uses 30 asterisks. Then **display( )** calls **draw( )** two more times, using two spaces and 26 asterisks. The third set of calls to **draw( )** uses four spaces and 22 asterisks, respectively. The result is an inverted pyramid.

Figure 14-37   Typical execution of DrawingRecursion.cpp program

6. Run the program several times using different symbols and lengths until you understand how the two recursive functions operate.

14

Chapter Summary

❐ An enumeration is a programmer-defined set of integer constants represented by identifiers. The named constants are called enumerators. You create an enumeration using the keyword **enum** followed by a type name and, in curly braces, a list of identifiers that represent numeric values. Using enumerations rather than literal constants makes programs easier to read and maintain.

❐ The binary system is used to store computer data; the binary numbering system uses only two digits: 0 and 1. In the integrated circuits that modern computers use, two-way switches are cheaper to use than any more complex system. A bit is a binary digit; eight binary digits are called a byte.

❑ When you need to create a class field that might hold only the value 0 or 1, you can use a single bit. You declare a field to be a single bit by placing a colon and a 1 after the variable declaration; the field type must be `int` or `unsigned int`. To store larger values, you increase the number following the colon in the declaration of the bit field.

❑ When you store 0s and 1s in the bit fields for an object, you can think of them as individual fields or as a single unit.

❑ Bitwise operators let you manipulate individual bits of integer or character values. The bitwise `AND` operator, which is written as a single ampersand (&), compares the individual bits of its two operands and produces a result based on the bit values. The result value contains a 1 in any columnar positions where both bitwise `AND` operands contain a 1; the result value contains a 0 in all other bit positions. You can use the bitwise operators to create a mask, a value whose only purpose is to filter values from other variables. The bitwise inclusive `OR` operator (|) compares the bits of its two operands, and produces a result in which each bit is a 1 if either of the operand's corresponding bits is a 1.

❑ You can use the bitwise left shift operator (<<) to shift bits to the left and the bitwise right shift operator (>>) to shift bits to the right. Each of these operators requires two operands—the one on the left holds the bits that are shifted, and the one on the right is the number of positions to shift. For any number n, shifting n bits to the left is the same as multiplying by two to the n power. The bitwise right shift operator provides the same result as dividing by two to the power of the right operand.

❑ Recursion occurs when a function is defined in terms of itself; a function that calls itself is a recursive function. Every time you call a function, the address to which the program should return at the completion of the function is stored in a memory location called the stack. When a function ends, the address is retrieved from the stack and the program returns to the location from which the function call was made. When you write recursive functions, you must provide a way for the recursion to stop eventually. Following the logic of a recursive function is a difficult task, and programs that use recursion are error-prone and hard to debug.

❑ It is possible to quickly sort a list using a recursive sorting function. To use this sorting method, you employ a "divide and conquer" technique known as a quick sort or pivot sort.

KEY TERMS

An **enumeration** is a programmer-defined set of integer constants represented by identifiers.

Enumerators are the named constants in an enumeration.

The **binary system** is an arithmetic system that uses only 1s and 0s.

The **decimal system** is an arithmetic system that uses the digits 0 through 9.

EBCDIC (Extended Binary Coded Decimal Interchange Code) is a coding system used in many mainframe and midrange computers.

A **bit** is a **bi**nary di**git**.

A **byte** is eight binary digits; on many systems it is the amount of storage required to store a single character, such as an alphabetic letter or punctuation mark.

When a field is type `unsigned int`, then it must be positive, because no bit is reserved for a sign, and all eight bits are used to store the value.

Bitwise operators let you manipulate individual bits of integer or character values.

The **bitwise AND operator** (&) compares the individual bits of its two operands and produces a result in which each bit is a 1 where both operands contain a 1 and 0 in all other bit positions.

A **mask** is a value whose only purpose is to filter values from other variables.

The **bitwise inclusive OR operator** (|) compares the bits of its two operands, and produces a result in which each bit is a 1 if either of the operand's corresponding bits is a 1.

The **bitwise exclusive OR operator** (^) sets each bit in the result to 1 only if exactly one of the corresponding bits in the operators is 1.

The **bitwise complement operator** (~) sets each bit in the result to 1 if the corresponding bit in the operand is 0, and each bit in the result to 0 if the corresponding bit in the operand is 1.

The **bitwise left shift operator** (<<) shifts bits to the left. For any number n, shifting n bits to the left is the same as multiplying by two to the n power.

The **bitwise right shift operator** (>>) shifts bits to the right. For any number n, shifting n bits to the right is the same as dividing by two to the n power.

Recursion occurs when a function is defined in terms of itself.

A function that calls itself is a **recursive function**.

The **stack** is a memory location that holds addresses to which functions should return.

Quick sort and **pivot sort** are names for recursive sorting methods.

14

REVIEW QUESTIONS

1. A programmer-defined set of integer constants represented by identifiers is
   _____.

   a. a `const`

   b. a `struct`

   c. an enumeration

   d. illegal in C++

2. The binary system uses the digits _____.

   a. 0 and 1

   b. 0, 1, and 2

   c. 1 and 2

   d. 0 through 9

3. The decimal system and the binary system differ in _____.

    a. the maximum number of columns you can use to represent a number

    b. the meaning of 0 in the far right column

    c. the number of times larger each column's value is than the column on its right

    d. all of the above

4. The binary number 1100 is equivalent to the decimal number _____.

    a. 2

    b. 12

    c. 14

    d. 1100

5. The decimal number 20 is equivalent to the binary number _____.

    a. 11000

    b. 10100

    c. 1010

    d. 111000

6. The primary reason two-way switches are used for computer storage is that _____.

    a. they are the most natural for humans to understand

    b. they are less prone to electrical failure than switches with more settings

    c. they are the cheapest to build

    d. it is simply traditional

7. There are _____.

    a. eight bits in a byte

    b. eight bytes in a bit

    c. eight bytes in a character

    d. eight integers in a bit

8. You declare a bit field by placing _____ between the field name and an integer.

    a. a semicolon

    b. a colon

    c. two colons

    d. a space

9. The advantage to storing a piece of data in a bit instead of a byte is that

   _____.

   a. input and output operations are easier

   b. the code is less prone to error

   c. programs are easier to debug

   d. storage space is saved

10. The most common meanings of 0 and 1, respectively, are _____.

    a. true and false

    b. false and true

    c. on and off

    d. yes and no

11. If you declare a character as `char someChar = 'A';`, you can print the address of the far right bit with the statement _____.

    a. `cout<< &someChar;`

    b. `cout<<&someChar:0;`

    c. `cout<<&comeChar:7;`

    d. none of the above

12. The bitwise `AND` operator is _____.

    a. `&`

    b. `|`

    c. `<<`

    d. `>>`

13. If `byteA` contains 10000001 and `byteB` contains 10100000, then what is the value of `byteA & byteB`?

    a. 10100001

    b. 00100001

    c. 10000000

    d. 00000000

14. A value whose only purpose is to filter values from other variables is a

    _____.

    a. cast

    b. queue

    c. sieve

    d. mask

14

15. You would most likely use a bitwise inclusive OR to _____.

    a. make decisions

    b. filter out off bits

    c. turn on specific bits

    d. perform multiplication by powers of 2

16. If someNum = 6, then someNum >>= 1 equals _____.

    a. 0

    b. 3

    c. 6

    d. 12

17. A function that calls itself is _____.

    a. recursive

    b. refractory

    c. repulsive

    d. reactionary

18. What is the output of the following program?

```
int recursive(int x)
{
      int result;
      if(x == 0)
            result = x;
      else
            result = x * (recursive(x - 1));
      return   result;
}
int main()
{
      cout<<recursive(0);
}
```

    a. 0

    b. 1

    c. 2

    d. 4

19. Using the same `recursive()` function from Question 18, what is the output of the following program?

```
int main()
{
    cout<<recursive(2);
}
```

a. 0

b. 1

c. 2

d. 4

20. What is the output of the following program?

```
int recursive(int x)
{
    int result;
    if(x == 1)
        result = x;
    else
        result = x * (recursive(x - 1));
    return result;
}
int main()
{
    cout<<recursive(2);
}
```

a. 0

b. 1

c. 2

d. 4

14

EXERCISES

1. a. Create a function named `branchInfo()` that accepts an integer argument and displays the correct contact data for each of five branch offices of a loan company (manager's name, street address, and phone number).

   b. Write a `main()` function that contains an enumeration for the five branch office names. For example, you might choose to call the offices NORTH, SOUTH, EAST, WEST, and CENTRAL. Display the contact data for all five offices using the enumerations in a loop. Save the file as **UsingAllEnumerations.cpp**.

c. One branch office (you can choose any one you like) needs to send form letters to its customers to announce that it is adding evening hours every night until 9 pm. Write a program that displays form letters to 10 customers of the branch offices. Store the customer names in a string array and display the same short letter to each in sequence. The application contains the same enumerations as in part b, but you use the data only for the office for which the form letters are being produced. Save the file as **UsingOneEnumeration.cpp**.

2. a. Create an enumeration to represent the four standard suits of cards (CLUBS, DIAMONDS, HEARTS, and SPADES). Create another enumeration for the words that represent card point-value names (TWO, THREE, and the rest of the number cards through TEN; then JACK; QUEEN; KING; and ACE. In many card games, the ACE is considered to have a higher value than the KING.) Display the numeric suit and point-value names of all 52 cards. Save the file as **CardDeck.cpp**.

b. Create a **Card** class with data fields for suit and card point value. Include a constructor that accepts arguments for the data fields. Also include overloaded greater-than and less-than operators for comparing card values. Create an overloaded == operator; two cards are equal if they have the same suit and value. Randomly select two **Card** objects from a deck, making sure they are different. (Appendix E contains information on random number generation.) Display both **Card** objects and determine which is higher or whether they have the same value. Save the file as **DealTwoCards.cpp**.

c. Create a card game called Clubs. Two players each receive five randomly chosen cards. Each plays one card at a time. The higher card wins a point, but any club beats any value of another suit. For example, the five of hearts beats the three of spades, but the two of clubs beats both of them. On any turn, if both players' cards have the same value and neither is a club, then no points are awarded. Write an application in which you deal five cards to each of two players. Display each match and keep score. Save the file as **GameOfClubs.cpp**.

d. Modify the GameOfClubs application so it uses just one deck of cards. That is, no duplicate cards should appear during the game. Save the file as **GameOfClubsOneDeck.cpp**.

3. Create a **GraduationCandidate** class. Include fields for a **GraduationCandidate** ID number, and last and first names. Also include bit fields that indicate the following:

   ❑ Has the **GraduationCandidate** completed 120 credit hours?

   ❑ Has the **GraduationCandidate** completed 45 hours in his or her major?

   ❑ Has the **GraduationCandidate** paid all campus parking and traffic tickets?

   ❑ Has the **GraduationCandidate** paid all library fines?

   ❑ Has the **GraduationCandidate** paid all graduation fees?

The class includes appropriate functions to set and display all the fields. When you display a GraduationCandidate, include a decision as to whether the GraduationCandidate can graduate. Create a main( ) function that instantiates several GraduationCandidate objects, and demonstrate that your functions work correctly. Save the file as **GraduationCandidates.cpp**.

4. a. Create a CustomerProfile class. Each CustomerProfile contains a last name, phone number, and bit fields indicating whether the customer

    ❑ works full-time

    ❑ owns a home

    ❑ owns a dog

    ❑ owns a computer

    ❑ has a credit card

    ❑ gives to charity on a regular basis

    ❑ subscribes to magazines

    Also include appropriate functions to set and retrieve CustomerProfile values.

    b. Suppose an organization wants to solicit homeowners to home improvement loans. Write a program that allows you to create an array of at least 10 CustomerProfiles, then select homeowners and display them. Save the file as **CustomerHomeowners.cpp**.

    c. Using the same CustomerProfile class, write a program that allows you to select customers who own both a dog and a computer, so you can send them advertisements about a new pet-oriented Web site. Save the file as **CustomersWithComputersAndDogs.cpp**.

5. a. Create a Student class. Include appropriate fields and functions, including eight bit fields that store characteristics of your choice, such as whether the student is a smoker or an early riser.

    b. Write a program that creates 10 Student objects and a separate object that stores data about you. Then allow the program to select the most compatible roommates from the array of other Students. For example, if four of the roommate candidates each have five of the preferred characteristics, and no candidates have more, then select those four as possible roommates. Save the file as **BestRoommates.cpp**.

    c. Write a program that creates 10 Student objects and a separate object that stores data about you. Prompt the user for data for the 11 objects, then allow the program to select the most compatible roommate for you from the array of other Students. Display all the roommate candidates, and then the most compatible one. If two or more candidates share the distinction of having the most compatible characteristics, then choose one of them randomly. Save the file as **RandomRoommate.cpp**. (Appendix E contains information on random numbers.)

14

6. a. Create a `TempEmployee` class. Besides a name, phone number, and hourly pay rate, include at least six bit fields that store capabilities such as whether the temp employee is proficient in word processing or whether the employee can lift heavy weights over 50 pounds. Create any functions you need to support the class.

   b. Write a program that creates 10 `TempEmployee` objects and assign values to them. Create a separate `TempEmployee` object and allow the user to enter data values that specify the characteristics desired in a temporary employee for a specific job. Write the program so that it selects and displays data for only those employees who match all the necessary criteria. If no employees match all the criteria, display a message. Save the file as **TempEmployees.cpp**.

   c. Write a program that creates 10 `TempEmployee` objects and prompt the user to assign values to them. Create a separate `TempEmployee` object and allow the user to enter data values that specify the characteristics desired in a temporary employee for a specific job. Write the program so that it selects and displays data for the best employee for the job. (The best `Employee` for a job might have more skills than the requested ones, but must not be missing any requested skills.) If multiple employees match all the selected criteria, choose the ones with the lowest pay rate. If no employees match all the criteria, choose the ones who match the most criteria. Save the file as **TempEmployees2.cpp**.

7. Write a program that prompts the user for an `unsigned int` value. Compute and display the result when the bits are shifted one position to the left. Save the file as **ShiftToLeft.cpp**.

8. Write a recursive function named `power()` that takes two integers as arguments. The function finds the value of the first integer raised to the power of the second integer. Base your recursive function on the knowledge that for any two numbers x and n, $x^n = x * x^{n-1}$. Write a `main()` function that demonstrates that the `power()` function works correctly. Save the file as **Power.cpp**.

9. Write a recursive function that calculates the factorial of its integer argument. Base your recursive function on the knowledge that for any number n, the value of n factorial (usually written as $n!$) is $n * (n-1) * (n-2) * (n-3)...* 1$. Write a `main()` function that demonstrates that the function works correctly. (On many systems, you must use a value of 16 or lower to achieve correct results; the factorial of higher numbers is larger than the value that can be stored in an integer.) Save the file as **Factorial.cpp**.

10. Each of the following files in the Chapter14 folder contains syntax and/or logical errors. Determine the problem in each case, and fix the program. Save your solutions by adding "Fixed" to the filename, as in **DEBUG14-1Fixed.cpp**.

    a. DEBUG14-1.cpp

    b. DEBUG14-2.cpp

    c. DEBUG14-3.cpp

    d. DEBUG14-4.cpp

CASE PROJECT 1

CASE
PROJECTS

You have been developing a **Fraction** class for Teacher's Pet Software. Each **Fraction** contains a numerator, denominator, a whole-number portion, and access to several functions you have developed, including overloaded operators. Complete these tasks:

a. Create a **Problem** class for a teacher who wants to test her students on three **Fraction** problem types:

- ❑ Adding **Fraction**s that both have a numerator of 1

- ❑ Adding **Fraction**s that have the same denominator

- ❑ Adding **Fraction**s whose sum is less than 1

The **Problem** class contains four **Fraction** objects and three bit fields, each representing one of the above conditions. Create a function that assigns the correct bit field values to an unsigned integer, based on the user's selected **Problem** criteria. Pass this unsigned integer to the **Problem** constructor. The constructor then sets the appropriate bit fields and randomly assigns two **Fraction** values as operands in the **Problem** and computes their sum as the third **Fraction** value. The fourth **Fraction** value holds the user's attempted answer to the addition problem. The **Fraction**s used in the **Problem** must meet the user's criteria. For example, a user might choose to use **Fraction**s that both have a numerator of 1 and whose sum is less than 1, but that do not necessarily have the same denominator. In that case, a **Problem** such as 1/3 + 1/5 would be an acceptable **Problem**. You can make changes to the existing **Fraction** class as necessary. Write a **main( )** function that prompts the user for **Problem** criteria, then instantiates at least five **Problem** objects and displays them. Accept the user's answer for each **Problem**, and display a message indicating whether the user's answer is correct. Save the file as **Problem.cpp**.

b. Write a **main( )** function that declares an array of 10 **Fraction** objects. Write a recursive **sort( )** function that places the **Fraction** objects in ascending order. Save the file as **AscendingFractionSort.cpp**.

c. Write a **main( )** function that declares an array of 10 **Fraction** objects. Write a recursive **sort( )** function that places the **Fraction** objects in descending order. Save the file as **DescendingFractionSort.cpp**.

14

CASE PROJECT 2

You have been developing a `BankAccount` class for Parkville Bank that contains several fields and functions, including overloaded operators. You have also created child classes derived from the `BankAccount` class: `CheckingAccount`, `SavingsAccount`, and `CheckingWithInterest`. Complete these tasks:

a. Create a `BankLoan` class that derives from `BankAccount`. The `BankLoan` class inherits the account number and balance (loan amount) from its parent, and also includes fields that hold the loan term (in months) and the annual interest rate charged. The `BankLoan` class also contains bit fields that store data about the type of loan—whether it is a mortgage, automobile loan, home improvement loan, or student loan. For every loan, only one of these bits can be on. Additional bit fields indicate whether the `BankLoan` customer also has a checking account, savings account, or interest-bearing checking account with the bank. None, some, or all of these bits indicate that the customer's account types can be on. Write a `main()` function that prompts the user for five `BankLoan` objects. When data entry is complete, display the five `BankLoan` values. Save the file as **BankLoans.cpp**.

b. Write a `main()` function that declares an array of 10 `BankLoan` objects. Write a recursive `sort()` function that places the `BankLoan` objects in ascending order based on account number. Save the file as **AscendingLoanSort.cpp**.

c. Write a `main()` function that declares an array of 10 `BankLoan` objects. Write a recursive `sort()` function that places the `BankLoan` objects in descending order based on loan amount. Save the file as **DescendingLoanSort.cpp**.

A

GETTING STARTED WITH MICROSOFT VISUAL STUDIO 2005

In this appendix, you will:

♦ Prepare to write an application using Microsoft Visual Studio 2005

♦ Write, compile, and execute a program

PREPARING TO WRITE AN APPLICATION USING MICROSOFT VISUAL STUDIO 2005

The C++ applications you create using this book are console applications. **Console applications** are executed at the command line in the console window, and are typically designed without a graphical user interface. They are compiled into a stand-alone executable file. Writing console applications is a good way to learn new programming techniques without having to be concerned with the details of a graphical user interface. However, if you are using an integrated development environment (IDE) such as Microsoft Visual Studio 2005, you can refer to the instructions in this appendix for writing C++ applications using that tool.

There are several advantages to using an IDE:

- Some of the code you need is already created for you.

- The code is displayed in color, so you can more easily identify parts of your program. Reserved words appear in blue, comments in green, and identifiers in black.

- If error messages appear when you compile your program, you can double-click on an error message and the cursor will move to the line of code that contains the error.

- Other debugging tools are available.

To start writing a Visual Studio 2005 application:

1. Open Microsoft Visual Studio 2005. Usually, you can do this by clicking **Start**, pointing to **All Programs** then **Microsoft Visual Studio 2005**, and then clicking **Microsoft Visual Studio 2005**. Alternatively, after you click **Start**, Microsoft Visual Studio 2005 might appear in the Start menu. Another possibility is that your computer has a desktop icon for Microsoft Visual Studio 2005 that you can double-click to open.

2. Examine the Microsoft Development Environment that appears on your screen. It should look similar to Figure A-1. The environment contains many elements with which you probably are familiar. For example, a title bar appears at the top edge of the window, containing the title Microsoft Development Environment and Minimize, Restore, and Close buttons in the upper-right corner. The horizontal menu bar near the top of the window contains familiar options including File, Edit, View, and so on.

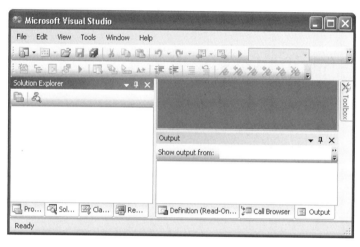

Figure A-1   The Microsoft Visual Studio window

3. Click **File** on the menu bar, point to **New**, and then click **Project**. (Alternatively, press **Ctrl + Shift + N** on the keyboard, or click the **New Project** button on the toolbar). The New Project window appears as shown in Figure A-2. In the Project Types pane, at the left, if the Visual C++ menu is not expanded, you can click the + to the left of Visual C++, and then click **Visual C++**. In the Templates pane at the right, click the **Win32 Console Application** icon. At the bottom of the window, in the Name text box, type a name for your application (for example, FirstProgram) and select a location where the project will be stored. (The Solution Name will automatically be entered for you to match the Project Name.) You can store your project on a hard drive, network drive, USB drive, or Zip disk, but do not store it on a floppy disk. Even the smallest Visual Studio C++ programs generate so many files that they immediately fill a floppy disk. Click **OK**.

A

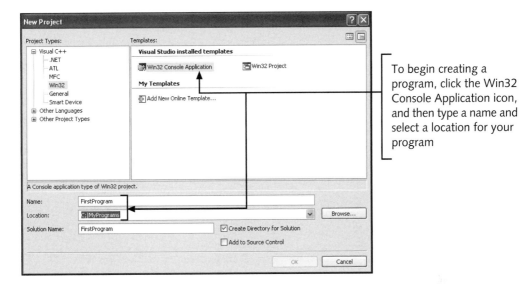

To begin creating a program, click the Win32 Console Application icon, and then type a name and select a location for your program

Figure A-2   The New Project window

TIP

Your screen might look different from Figure A-2. For example, you might see more available templates.

4. The Win32 Application window appears. Click **Finish** to accept the wizard's default settings.

5. The FirstProgram window (or the name you used for your project in Step 3) appears as shown in Figure A-3; the project name appears in the title bar. Below the title bar, the familiar File, Edit, View menu bar appears. On the left side, the Solution Explorer lists all the files associated with this project. The right side of the window contains two panes. The top pane is the **editor**—an area similar to a word processor in which you type your program code. A program appears there, already written. This prewritten program is intended as a template to help you get started when writing certain applications. You will delete most of this program and write your own. The bottom pane is the output window—the area in which warning and error messages will appear when you attempt to compile your program.

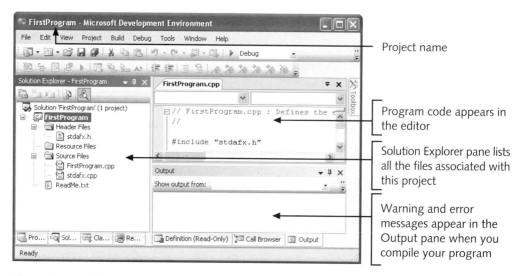

Figure A-3 The FirstProgram window

Project name

Program code appears in the editor

Solution Explorer pane lists all the files associated with this project

Warning and error messages appear in the Output pane when you compile your program

TIP
Your FirstProgram window might vary slightly. For example, the Solution Explorer might appear on the right side of the screen. You can drag it to any location you want. If you do not see the Solution Explorer, click View on the menu bar and then click Solution Explorer.

WRITING, COMPILING, AND EXECUTING A PROGRAM

To write, compile, and execute an application:

1. In the editor pane of the FirstProgram window, delete all the automatically generated code, except the preprocessor directive `#include "stdafx.h"`. Below that directive, enter the following code:

```
#include <iostream>
using namespace std;
int main()
{
    cout << "Hello World!";
}
```

TIP
You can place the `#include<iostream>` directive within the `stdafx.h` file instead of within your program. Do this now only if you are comfortable adding the statement to the existing file.

2. On the menu bar, choose **Build** and then **Compile**, or, alternatively, press Ctrl + F7 on the keyboard. The Output pane should indicate that your program compiled with 0 warnings and 0 errors. If not, you can proceed to Step 4.

3. Select **Debug** and then **Start Without Debugging**, or, alternatively, press Ctrl + F5 on the keyboard. If a dialog box appears with the message, "This project is out of date: Would you like to build it?", click **Yes**. If there are no compiler errors, an output window appears as in Figure A-4. The message "Hello World!" displays, followed immediately by "Press any key to continue…". Press any keyboard key and the output window disappears.

Figure A-4   Output of FirstProgram

4. If your program did not produce the output shown in Figure A-4, then you must examine the code for syntax errors. Make sure your program exactly matches the program in Step 1, including all capitalization and punctuation, and try selecting **Debug** and **Start Without Debugging** again. Even if your program did execute, purposely introduce an error by removing the semicolon at the end of the `cout` statement. Then choose **Build** and **Compile** again.

5. Examine the Output pane at the bottom of the window, as shown in Figure A-5. The error message indicates the location of the file containing the error and, in parentheses, the line number where the error was detected. An error number appears, followed by "syntax error" and a brief description of the error—in this case, "missing ';' before '}'". When you double-click the error message, the insertion point in the editor pane is repositioned to the approximate location of the error. In this example, the insertion point moves to the line containing the closing curly brace for the program. Even though the actual error is the missing semicolon in the previous line, the compiler does not "miss" the semicolon until the closing curly brace is encountered. Frequently, a C++ error will be discovered close to, but not in the exact location, where you need to make a correction.

Figure A-5   Build error message

TIP   Note that one mistake can generate many error messages. Correct the errors in order, as one correction may eliminate several error messages. Note also that the error messages will not always be helpful and the compiler will not always be able to correctly identify the cause of the error. The Help system will sometimes provide additional insight into the problem. Move the insertion point to the line with the error message and press F1 to get context-sensitive help.

6. Retype the missing semicolon at the end of the **cout** statement, and choose **Debug** and then **Start Without Debugging** again. This time the program executes successfully.

7. To exit Visual Studio, click **File** on the menu bar, and then choose **Exit**. Alternatively, you can click the **Close** button. If you have not saved the most recent changes you made in the editor, you will be prompted to save the files; usually you want to choose **Yes**.

B

GETTING STARTED WITH OTHER C++ COMPILERS

> **In this appendix, you will:**
> ♦ Write an application in Visual Studio 6.0
> ♦ Write an application using Unix and Linux systems
> ♦ Write an application using a standard C++ compiler

USING MICROSOFT VISUAL STUDIO 6.0

TIP

Depending on the version of your compiler and the installation options chosen, the appearance of your screen and the wording of some error messages might differ slightly from those in this appendix.

Writing a C++ program in Microsoft Visual Studio 6.0 is similar to using Microsoft Visual Studio 2005.

To write and run a C++ program in Visual Studio 6.0:

1. Start Microsoft Visual Studio C++ using an icon on your desktop, if possible. Otherwise, click **Start**, point to **All Programs**, point to **Microsoft Visual Studio 6.0**, and then click **Microsoft Visual C++ 6.0**.

2. Click **File** on the menu bar, and then click **New**.

3. In the New window, select the **Projects** tab, and then click **Win32 Console Application**. Type a project name, select a disk location, and click **OK**.

4. In the Win32 Console Application window, select **An empty project**, then click **Finish**. If a New Project Information window appears, click **OK**.

5. The Integrated Development Environment (IDE) appears. On the menu bar in the IDE, click **File** and **New**.

6. Click **C++ source file**. Enter a filename into the Name dialog box. Then click **OK**.

7. Enter the following code in the editor:

```
#include <iostream>
using namespace std;
int main()
{
   cout << "Hello World!";
}
```

8. On the menu bar, choose **Build** and then **Compile**, or, alternatively, press Ctrl + F7 on the keyboard. The bottom of the window should indicate that your program compiled with 0 warnings and 0 errors. If not, see Appendix A for help in resolving compiler errors.

9. Select **Build** and then **Execute**, or press Ctrl + F5 on the keyboard. If a dialog box appears with the message, "This project configuration is out of date. Would you like to rebuild it?", click **Yes**. If there are no compiler errors, an output window appears containing the message "Hello World!", followed immediately by "Press any key to continue...". Press any keyboard key and the output window disappears.

An Easy, Alternative Way to Start a Visual Studio 6.0 C++ Program

1. Type your C++ program into any editor—for example, Notepad. If you use WordPad or some other more sophisticated editor than Notepad, be sure to save the file as **Text Only** so that formatting codes are not included in the document.

2. Save the file with a .cpp extension. Most editors want to attach their own extension to a filename. For example, by default, Notepad documents end in .txt. In Notepad, you can change the extension to .cpp when you save the file by entering the filename in quotes, as in "MyProgram.cpp". Alternatively, you can type the filename and extension without quotes, click the Save as type list arrow, and choose **All Files**. You also could save the file with a .txt extension and rename it later.

3. Locate the saved .cpp file in My Computer or Windows Explorer. Double-click the file icon and Visual C++ will start automatically.

B

USING UNIX OR LINUX SYSTEMS

1. Write your C++ program using a text editor. Editors often available on Unix and Linux systems include vi, Emacs, and XEmacs. In the Common Desktop Environment on Sun/Solaris and HP workstations, the editor is dtedit. On Solaris/Open Windows, you can use the Open Windows text editor.

2. Enter the following program into your editor:

```cpp
#include <iostream>
using namespace std;
int main()
{
  cout << "Hello World!";
}
```

3. Save the file as **MyProgram.cpp**. To compile the program, at the command line, type the compiler name, the executable program you want to create, and the name of the source code file. In most systems, the C++ compiler is named c++ or g++. For this example, you might type **c++ -o MyProgram MyProgram.cpp**

TIP

The C++ compiler might be named CC, c++, or g++. For Borland's version 5.5 compiler, it is bcc32.

4. If the compilation produces error messages, correct the errors in the source file, save it, and compile again.

5. When the program compiles with no errors, you can execute the program by typing the program name at the command line.

TIP

With some Unix shells, you must run your program at the command line preceded with a dot and a slash, as in "./MyProgram", instead of just "MyProgram".

PREPARING TO WRITE AN APPLICATION USING A STANDARD C++ COMPILER

If you are using a compiler that is not ANSI/ISO compliant, make the following changes to each example used in this book:

1. Replace `#include<iostream>` with `#include<iostream.h>`.

2. Remove **using namespace std;**.

3. At the end of the `main()` function, you might receive an error message indicating that `main()` should return a value. If so, do one of the following:

   a. Add a final statement just before the closing brace so that `main()` returns a value. For example, add the following:

      ```
      return 1;
      ```

      This is the preferred solution.

   b. Change the `main()` function header from `int main()` to `void main()`. If `main()` is a `void` function instead of an `int` function, no return value is necessary.

C

OPERATOR PRECEDENCE AND ASSOCIATIVITY

In this appendix, you will:

♦ Learn about the precedence and associativity of C++ operators

When more than one operation appears in a C++ expression, the operations are carried out based on their precedence and associativity. Table C-1 shows the operator precedence from highest to lowest for each C++ operator. Each operator in a cell in the table has equal precedence with the others that share its cell. You can always override precedence using parentheses.

Table C-1 Operator precedence

Operator	Name or Meaning	Associativity
::	Scope resolution	None
.	Member selection (object)	Left to right
–>	Member selection (pointer)	Left to right
[ ]	Array subscript	Left to right
( )	Function call	Left to right
( )	Member initialization	Left to right
++	Postfix increment	Left to right
--	Postfix decrement	Left to right
typeid( )	Type name	Left to right
const_cast	Type cast (conversion)	Left to right
dynamic_cast	Type cast (conversion)	Left to right
reinterpret_cast	Type cast (conversion)	Left to right
static_cast	Type cast (conversion)	Left to right
sizeof	Size of object or type	Right to left
++	Prefix increment	Right to left
--	Prefix decrement	Right to left
~	One's complement	Right to left
!	Logical not	Right to left
–	Unary minus	Right to left
+	Unary plus	Right to left
&	Address-of	Right to left
*	Indirection	Right to left
new	Create object	Right to left
delete	Destroy object	Right to left
()	Cast	Right to left
.*	Pointer-to-member (objects)	Left to right
–>*	Pointer-to-member (pointers)	Left to right
*	Multiplication	Left to right
/	Division	Left to right
%	Modulus	Left to right
+	Addition	Left to right
–	Subtraction	Left to right
<<	Left shift	Left to right
>>	Right shift	Left to right

Table C-1   Operator precedence (continued)

Operator	Name or Meaning	Associativity
<	Less than	Left to right
>	Greater than	Left to right
<=	Less than or equal to	Left to right
>=	Greater than or equal to	Left to right
==	Equality	Left to right
!=	Inequality	Left to right
&	Bitwise AND	Left to right
^	Bitwise exclusive OR	Left to right
|	Bitwise inclusive OR	Left to right
&&	Logical AND	Left to right
||	Logical OR	Left to right
e1?e2:e3	Conditional	Right to left
=	Assignment	Right to left
*=	Multiplication assignment	Right to left
/=	Division assignment	Right to left
%=	Modulus assignment	Right to left
+=	Addition assignment	Right to left
–=	Subtraction assignment	Right to left
<<=	Left-shift assignment	Right to left
>>=	Right-shift assignment	Right to left
&=	Bitwise AND assignment	Right to left
|=	Bitwise inclusive OR assignment	Right to left
^=	Bitwise exclusive OR assignment	Right to left
throw *expr*	throw expression	Right to left
,	Comma	Left to right

D

FORMATTING OUTPUT

In this appendix, you will:

♦ Learn why output values might need to be formatted
♦ Use the `fixed` and `setprecision()` manipulators
♦ Use the `printf()` function

WHY OUTPUT VALUES MIGHT NEED TO BE FORMATTED

When you first learn to program you must cope with the logic of input, processing, output, decision making, looping, and array manipulation. You must also learn about classes, objects, inheritance, and polymorphism. Making a program produce correct output is an achievement, and in the scope of things, the format of the output is a small matter. For example, if the result of a mathematical calculation displays as 1.5, 1.50, or 1.50000, the meaning is the same. Many programmers are happy with a displayed result as long as it is arithmetically correct. However, if displaying values to a specific number of decimal places is important to you, you can use the techniques described in this appendix.

TIP

In Chapter 13, you learn the details of the manipulators you can use to format output. If you have already covered Chapter 13, you will find that much of this appendix repeats what Chapter 13 covers. This appendix is intended for users who want a quick reference to formatting output before understanding the complete details of the formatting functions.

By default, C++ displays numeric values in the "cheapest" way possible. That is, if a value can be displayed with fewer trailing digits without losing meaning, it is. For example, Figure D-1 shows an application that declares a **double** which is assigned the value 1.50. When the value is displayed, as Figure D-2 shows, it becomes only 1.5.

```
#include <iostream>
using namespace std;
int main()
{
    double money = 1.50;
    cout<<"Money is $"<<money<<endl;
}
```

Figure D-1 Program that displays a `double`

Figure D-2 Output of program in Figure D-1

C++ provides several ways to improve the appearance of the output.

USING THE `fixed` AND `setprecision()` MANIPULATORS

If you want to control the number of positions shown to the right of the decimal point, you can use the `fixed` and `setprecision()` manipulators.

Besides manipulators, you can use format flags and `ostream` member functions to format output. These techniques are described in Chapter 13.

TIP

The program in Figure D-3 uses the `fixed` and `setprecision()` manipulators (shaded). The `fixed` manipulator is not followed by parentheses, but the `setprecision` manipulator is, and the argument placed within the parentheses is the number of decimal places that display. You send these manipulators to the `cout` object with the insertion operator, in the same way you send variables or constants. When paired, these manipulators produce output to the specified number of decimal places. Figure D-4 shows the output of the application in Figure D-3.

Any C++ manipulator, such as `setprecision()`, that takes an argument requires the inclusion of the `iomanip` file in your program. The `include` statement is shaded in Figure D-3.

TIP

D

```
#include<iostream>
#include<iomanip>
using namespace std;
int main()
{
    double money = 1.50;
    cout<<fixed<<setprecision(2)<<
        "Money is $"<<money<<endl;
}
```

Figure D-3 Program using `fixed` and `setprecision` manipulators

```
C:\WINDOWS\system32\cmd.exe
Money is $1.50
Press any key to continue . . .
```

Figure D-4 Output of program in Figure D-3

When the `setprecision()` argument is smaller than the number of digits in the output value, the value is rounded to the requested number of decimals.

TIP

You can also use the `width()` manipulator to set a field display size. For example, the statement `cout<<width(10)<<24;` displays eight blanks followed by 24. When you use the `fixed` and `setprecision()` manipulators, all subsequent output is affected. When you use the `width()` manipulator, you must reuse it before each subsequent output you want displayed in a fixed-size field.

TIP

In Chapter 13, you learn more about these manipulators and others. You also learn to create customized manipulators.

TIP

USING THE printf() FUNCTION

In C++, you can use the printf() function to display output. (Unlike cout, you also can use printf() in the C programming language.) For example, Figure D-5 shows how to display a string followed by a newline character ('\n'). Figure D-6 shows the output.

```
#include <iostream>
using namespace std;
int main()
{
    printf("Hello, world!\n");
}
```

Figure D-5   Program using printf()

Figure D-6   Output of program in Figure D-5

TIP   Programmers working for different organizations develop programming conventions that are used when writing programs within their organizations. Your instructor or employer might prefer that you use cout and manipulators instead of the printf() function when formatting output.

When you want to display formatted numbers, you can add format specifications to the call to the printf() function. **Format specifications** describe the appearance of the values displayed and always begin with a percent sign (%). When you write a printf() statement, you can use a format string that includes a format specification, followed by data arguments. For example, Figure D-7 shows two printf() statements that each contain a format string that includes a format specification. Each string includes the words "An integer:" and a specification that ends with the newline character. In the first printf() statement in Figure D-7, the format specification is "%d". The symbol "d" means "decimal integer," that is, a base 10 number. (Alternatively, you can use "i".) In the second printf() statement in the figure, a field width is added—the specification is "%5d" and the output displays right-aligned in a field of five characters. Figure D-8 shows the output for the program.

```cpp
#include <iostream>
using namespace std;

int main()
{
    int anInt = 23;
    printf("An integer: %d\n", anInt);
    printf("An integer: %5d\n", anInt);
}
```

Figure D-7   Using integer formatting

Figure D-8   Output of program in Figure D-7

For floating-point numbers, you can use the %f format specification. Figure D-9 shows a program containing four `printf()` statements. The first uses just the %f format flag; you can see from the output in Figure D-10 that the two values are displayed to their default six decimal places. When `printf()` encounters the first format specification, it converts the first argument after the specification (`aDouble`) to the proper format and inserts it in the correct position in the string. When it encounters the second format specification, it uses the second argument (`anotherDouble`).

If there are more arguments in a `printf()` call than there are format specifications, the extra arguments are ignored. The results are undefined if there are not enough arguments for all the format specifications.

```
#include <iostream>
using namespace std;
int main()
{
   double aDouble = 45.6;
   double anotherDouble = 67.599;
   printf("%f is a double and %f is another double\n",
         aDouble, anotherDouble);
   printf("%.2f is a double and %.2f is another double\n",
         aDouble, anotherDouble);
   printf("%10.2f is a double and %10.2f is another double\n",
         aDouble, anotherDouble);
   printf("%-10.2f is a double and %-10.2f is another double\n",
         aDouble, anotherDouble);
}
```

Figure D-9   Program containing four `printf()` statements displaying `doubles`

Figure D-10   Output of program in Figure D-9

The second `printf()` statement in Figure D-9 uses a precision indicator, which is a decimal point followed by a size. When each value is displayed to two decimal places, 45.6 gains a rightmost zero, and 67.599 is rounded to 67.60. In the third `printf()` statement, a width is added to the precision. Displaying each value using the specification "%10.2f" causes each value to display right-aligned in a field of 10 with two decimal places. Notice that the decimal point "counts" as one of the places in the output field.

The final `printf()` statement in Figure D-9 uses a minus sign in front of the field size. The minus sign is a flag that causes the output to display to the left within the indicated field size, rather than to the right.

In summary, the general form for a format specification is:

```
% [flags] [width] [.precision] type
```

- The % is required.

- The optional flag can be a minus sign (–) to indicate left alignment. You can use a plus sign (+) to force a sign to display with any signed numeric field. Several other flags are also available. You can find them at:

  http://msdn.microsoft.com/library/default.asp?url=/library/en-us/vclib/html/ _crt_format_specification_fields_.2d_.printf_and_wprintf_functions.asp

- The optional width is an integer. If you precede the width with a 0, as in "%05d", then zeros fill the width to the left of the right-aligned value.

- The optional precision is a dot followed by a number of decimal places. The default precision is 6. If the precision value is 0, or if the dot appears with no number following it, then the decimal point is not displayed.

- The type is required. Its value can be **d** for integer, or **f** for floating point. You can also use **i** for integer, **c** for character, **s** for string, and several others.

TIP

You should ensure that format specification strings are not user-defined. For example, consider a program that prompts the user to enter his name and stores the input in a string variable called name. To print name, do not do this:

```
printf(name);
```

If the user has entered %s as part of the name, the program will crash. Instead, display the name as follows:

```
printf("%s", name);
```

E

GENERATING RANDOM NUMBERS

In this appendix, you will:

♦ Generate random numbers

♦ Generate numbers in a specified range

♦ Prove the fairness of the `rand()` function

Random numbers are useful in many programming situations. In particular, games and quizzes need random numbers to make the applications interesting. You do not want to be presented with a deck of cards dealt in the same sequence in every game or an alien who always travels the same path. Similarly, to have an effective study aid, you might not want to be asked questions in the same order every time you attempt a quiz. Computer simulations also need random numbers to generate random events such as what genetic combinations will occur in an animal's offspring or the number of patients utilizing a hospital emergency room during a given time period.

The C++ standard library provides a facility for generating random numbers using the **rand() function**. The numbers generated by this function aren't truly random; they are **pseudo random**; that is, they are generated in a sequence that gives the illusion of being random, but the sequence eventually repeats. For extremely scientific applications, you might want to find or purchase true random number generators, but for games and simple simulations, the rand() function is sufficient and useful.

TIP

All computer-generated random numbers are pseudo random. The prefix pseudo, which means "false," is used to distinguish this type of number from a "truly" random number generated by a random physical process such as radioactive decay.

GENERATING RANDOM NUMBERS

The `rand()` function generates a random number between 0 and the constant `RAND_MAX`. The value of `RAND_MAX` differs in different computer systems. The application in Figure E-1 displays its value on your computer. For example, Figure E-2 shows a typical execution of the application in Figure E-1.

```
#include <iostream>
using namespace std;
int main()
{
    cout<<"The value of RAND_MAX: "<<RAND_MAX<<endl;
}
```

Figure E-1 Determining the value of `RAND_MAX`

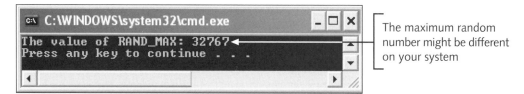

The maximum random number might be different on your system

Figure E-2 Output of program in Figure E-1

TIP

On some compilers, you might need to include the statement `#include<cstdlib>` to use the `rand()` function and the `RAND_MAX` constant.

TIP

The value 32767 that appears in the output in Figure E-2 is the largest value that can be contained in two bytes (16 bits). It is one less than the value of 2^{15}.

The `rand()` function returns an integer that you can display. Figure E-3 shows a program that displays 10 random numbers in a loop.

```
#include <iostream>
using namespace std;
int main()
{
   const int NUM = 10;
   int x;
   for(x = 0; x < NUM; ++x)
      cout<<rand()<<endl;
}
```

Figure E-3   Generating 10 random numbers

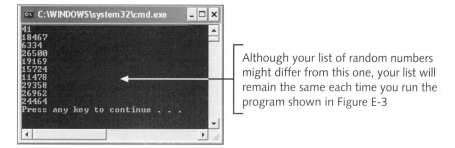

Although your list of random numbers might differ from this one, your list will remain the same each time you run the program shown in Figure E-3

Figure E-4   Output of program in Figure E-3

If you execute the application in Figure E-3 several times, the output always looks exactly like Figure E-4. That is, although the 10 output values appear to be random, they are the same set of values every time the program executes. If, for example, the values are used to select questions from a test bank, then students using the application will be presented with the same sequence of questions whenever they run the program. In that case, the random numbers are not very useful.

You can use the **srand()** **function** to **seed**, or initialize, the random number generator. The **srand()** function takes an integer argument that sets the starting point for the sequence of generated numbers. However, if you use an integer constant to seed the random number generator, then the generated numbers will still follow the same sequence every time you execute the application. A common way to more truly randomize generated numbers is to use the current time. The **time()** function returns the number of seconds that have elapsed since January 1, 1970. Because the time will always be different every time a program executes, the sequence of generated numbers will also be different. The call to **srand()** can be written as:

```
srand((unsigned)time(NULL));
```

TIP

To use the time() function, you include the header <ctime> at the top of the file. The value returned by time() is cast to unsigned integer before being sent to srand().

TIP

The srand() function takes an argument of type unsigned, so the value returned by time() is cast to the unsigned type. You use NULL as the argument to time() when you do not need to store the actual time.

TIP

Calling rand() before calling srand() produces the same sequence of generated numbers as calling srand() and passing 1 to it.

Figure E-5 shows the same application as in Figure E-3 with two shaded additions—the #include statement and the call to srand(). Figure E-6 shows two subsequent executions; each contains a unique list of random numbers.

```cpp
#include <iostream>
#include <ctime>
using namespace std;
int main()
{
    const int NUM = 10;
    int x;
    srand((unsigned)time(NULL));
    for(x = 0; x < NUM; ++x)
        cout<<rand()<<endl;
}
```

Figure E-5   Generating 10 random numbers

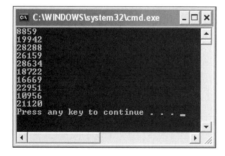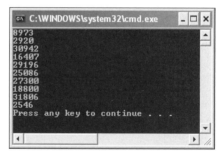

Figure E-6   Two executions of program in Figure E-5

GENERATING RANDOM NUMBERS IN A SPECIFIED RANGE

The values listed in the output in Figure E-6 are too large for many applications. For example, you might only need random numbers in the range 0 through 9 to use as a subscript to randomly choose an item stored in an array. There are several ways to generate numbers in a specified range. One of the simplest methods is to use the modulus operator and a value that is one more than the highest number you want. For example, when you divide a number by 10, the remainder is always a value from 0 through 9. Figure E-7 shows an application that generates 20 random numbers under 10. Figure E-8 shows a typical execution.

```cpp
#include <ctime>
#include <iostream>
using namespace std;
int main()
{
   const int DIVISOR = 10;
   const int NUM = 20;
   int x;
   int result;
   srand((unsigned)time(NULL));
   for(x = 0; x < NUM; ++x)
   {
      result = rand()% DIVISOR;
      cout<<result<<"  ";
   }
   cout<<endl;
}
```

Figure E-7   Generating random numbers 0 through 9

Figure E-8   Typical execution of program in Figure E-7

To generate numbers in a range that starts with a value other than 0, you can just add a value to the number generated using the modulus. For example, the following generates random values from 1 through 10:

```cpp
result = 1 + (rand()% DIVISOR);
```

Proving the Fairness of the rand( ) Function

The application in Figure E-9 generates 100,000 random numbers in the range 0 through 9. As each value is generated, 1 is added to the corresponding cell in an array (see the shaded statement.) After all 100,000 numbers have been generated, the array values are displayed. Each value should be generated about 10,000 times. Figure E-10 shows that the application does generate each of the in-range values close to that number of times.

```cpp
#include <ctime>
#include <iostream>
using namespace std;
int main()
{
    const int MAX = 10;
    const int NUM = 100000;
    int x;
    int result;
    int count[NUM] = {0};
    srand((unsigned)time(NULL));
    for(x = 0; x < NUM; ++x)
    {
        result = rand() % MAX;
        count[result]++;
    }
    cout<<"Summary"<<endl;
    for(x = 0; x < MAX; ++x)
        cout<<x<<" occurred "<<count[x]<<" times"<<endl;
}
```

Figure E-9   Program that counts occurrences of values generated by rand( )

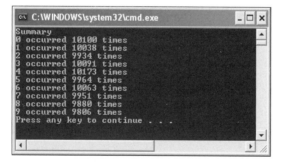

Figure E-10   Typical execution of program in Figure E-9

TIP

Robert R. Coveyou of Oak Ridge National Laboratory once titled an article, "The generation of random numbers is too important to be left to chance."

Glossary

#define name — An internal name for the group of statements that make up the definition of a class.

#endif — A C++ directive that means that you have reached the end of the block of code that you are defining; usually used with an `#ifndef directive`.

#ifndef — A C++ directive that allows you to test whether a class has already been defined in a project; it means "if not defined"; must be used with an `#endif directive`.

#include — A preprocessor directive that tells the compiler to include a file as part of the finished product.

\n — The escape sequence that indicates a new line of output in C++.

abstract data type (ADT) — A type you define (for example, a class), as opposed to types that are defined by C++ (for example, `int` or `double`).

abstraction — The process of extracting the relevant attributes of a process or object; it simplifies your concept of the process or object, allowing you to ignore nonessential details.

access modifier — A modifier that assigns accessibility to the declared variables that follow it. Access modifiers include `public`, `private`, and `protected`.

accumulate — To process individual records one at a time in a loop while adding numeric data to a total.

actual parameter — A parameter used in a function call; it holds the value that actually will be used by the function.

add and assign operator (+=) — An operator that adds the right-hand operand to the left-hand operand.

addition operator (+) — A binary arithmetic operator used to perform addition.

address operator (&) — A unary operator used to refer to the memory address of a variable.

alias — An alternate name.

allocate memory — To allot storage for and assign a name to a field.

ambiguity — A situation in which the compiler cannot tell which version of a function to use.

ANSI/ISO Standard — A set of C++ syntax rules developed by a joint committee of the American National Standards Institute (ANSI) and the International Standard Organization (ISO).

application program — A type of program that you apply to a task. Also called an **application**.

argument — The passed value in a function call.

arithmetic operator — A symbol that performs arithmetic.

arithmetic precedence — The set of rules of order of performance of arithmetic operations. Operators with higher precedence are performed first in an arithmetic statement with multiple operations.

array — A list of individual items that all have the same type.

assignment — The act of explicitly stating the value of a variable.

assignment operator — The equals sign (=).

associativity — The rule that dictates the order in which an operator works with its operands or actions within an expression are carried out.

atexit() function — A function that requires a function name as its argument; this function is then registered with `atexit()`, which means the named function is called automatically whenever the `exit()` function executes.

auxiliary function — A function that performs an action or service, such as sorting data or searching for data. Also called a **facilitator**.

base class — A class from which another is derived. Also called a **parent class**, **superclass**, or **ancestor**.

binary operator — An operator that takes two operands, one on each side of the operator.

binary system — An arithmetic system that uses only 1s and 0s.

bit — A binary digit; each bit represents a 1 or 0 in memory.

bitwise AND operator (&) — An operator that compares the individual bits of its two operands and produces a result in which each bit is a 1 where both operands contain a 1 and 0 in all other bit positions.

bitwise complement operator (~) — An operator that sets each bit in the result to 1 if the corresponding bit in the operand is 0 and each bit in the result to 0 if the corresponding bit in the operand is 1.

bitwise exclusive OR operator (^) — An operator that sets each bit in the result to 1 only if exactly one of the corresponding bits in the operators is 1.

bitwise inclusive OR operator (|) — An operator that compares the bits of its two operands, and produces a result in which each bit is a 1 if either of the operand's corresponding bits is a 1.

bitwise left shift operator (<<) — An operator that shifts bits to the left. For any number n, shifting n bits to the left is the same as multiplying by two to the n power.

bitwise operator — An operator that lets you manipulate individual bits of integer or character values.

bitwise right shift operator (>>) — An operator that shifts bits to the right. For any number n, shifting n bits to the left is the same as dividing by two to the n power.

black box — A device into which you cannot see to discover how it works, but it works nevertheless.

block — A group of statements between a set of opening and closing braces.

block comment — A comment that begins with a single slash and an asterisk (/*) and ends with an asterisk and a slash (*/); it might be contained on a single line or continued across many lines.

bool — The keyword used to declare Boolean variables that have only two possible values—true or false.

Boolean data type variable — A variable declared using the `bool` data type, which has only two possible values—true or false.

Boolean expression — An expression that evaluates as true or false.

byte — Eight binary digits; on many systems it is the amount of storage required to store a single character such as an alphabetic letter or punctuation mark.

call to the function — The statement that executes a function. Also called a **function call**, **call to the method**, or **method call**.

camel casing — The style of naming identifiers in which the name begins with a lowercase letter and subsequent words within the identifier are capitalized.

cast — To transform a value to another data type.

catch block — To handle a thrown object, you include one or more `catch` blocks in your program immediately following a `try` block. It contains statements that execute when an exception is thrown.

chain operations — To allow several operators to be used within the same statement.

char — The keyword used to declare a character variable.

character data type variable or **character variable** — A variable in which characters may be stored and declared with the keyword `char`. A variable that holds values such as 'A' or '&'.

check digit — A digit added to a number (either at the end or the beginning) that validates the authenticity of the number.

cin — An object that fetches values from the keyboard.

class — A category of objects. Also a user-defined, complex data type. By default, its data fields are private.

class client — A function that is a user of a class.

class template — A class in which at least one type is generic or parameterized.

cohesion — A measure of how well the operations in a function relate to one another. In highly cohesive functions, all operations are related.

comment — A statement that does not affect the compiling or running of a program; it is an explanatory remark that the programmer includes in a program to make notes, explain programming choices, or clarify what is taking place.

compile — To transform programming code into machine language.

compiler — A program that translates an entire program at one time.

composition — To use a class object within another class object.

compound assignment operator — An operator that performs two tasks, one of which is assignment.

conditional operator (?) — An operator that provides a concise way to express two alternatives. Also called the **if operator**

constructor — A function that is called automatically each time an object is created; it has the same name as its class.

container class — A template class that has been written to perform common class tasks; the purpose of container classes is to manage groups of other classes.

control structures — The basic logic components used in programs—sequence, selection, and loop.

copy constructor — A constructor that executes when you pass an object to a function, making a local copy.

count-controlled loop — A loop whose execution is controlled by counting the number of repetitions.

coupling — A measure of the strength of the connection between two functions; it expresses the extent to which information is exchanged by functions. Coupling is either **tight coupling** or **loose coupling**, depending on how much one function depends on information from another.

cout — The simplest object used for C++ output.

C-style string — A character-array string.

dangling reference — An error that occurs when a pointer is left with a null value.

data field — One piece of data, such as a first or last name, phone or Social Security number, or salary.

data file — A file that contains records that are logically related.

data hierarchy — A structure that represents the relationships between the sizes of data units that business professionals most often use.

data record — A number of data fields that are logically connected because they pertain to the same entity.

data structure — A user-defined, complex data type. Also called a **structure**.

data type — The characteristic of a variable that defines what kind of values may be stored in the variable, how much storage it occupies, and what kinds of operations can be performed on it.

database — A group of related files.

dead code — Statements that can never execute.

dead logical path — A path containing unreachable code.

deallocated memory — Memory that is no longer assigned to anything in an application.

decimal system — An arithmetic system that uses the digits 0 through 9.

declaration section — The part of a class that contains the class name, variables (attributes), and function prototypes.

declare a variable — To provide a name for the memory location where the computer will store the variable value and notifying the computer what type of data to expect. In contrast, when defining a variable, an initial value for the variable is also supplied.

decrement — To reduce by one.

default constructor — A constructor that does not require any arguments.

default exception handler — A statement that catches any type of object not previously caught; you create a default exception handler by creating a `catch` block with an ellipsis (…) as its argument.

default parameter — A parameter to a function for which an automatic value is supplied if you do not explicitly use one.

define a variable — To provide a name for the memory location where the computer will store the variable value, notifying the computer what type of data to expect, and providing a value. In contrast, when only declaring a variable, no initial value for the variable is supplied.

definite loop — A loop that must execute a specific number of times.

delete operator — An operator that frees previously allocated memory.

delimiter character — A character that terminates data entry or separates data fields.

dereference — To use an asterisk with a pointer when you want to use a value stored in the pointer.

derived class — A **child class**, **subclass**, or **descendant**.

descendant — A class extended from an existing class.

destructor — A function that is called automatically each time an object is destroyed; it has the same name as its class, preceded with a tilde.

divide and assign operator (/=) — An operator that divides the operand on the left by the operand on the right.

division operator (/) — A binary arithmetic operator used to perform division.

documentation — Explanations or instructions that help readers of program code understand the purpose of the code.

dot operator — A period (.), which is used to separate an object and a field name.

double — A keyword used to declare floating-point values.

do-while statement — A statement that controls a loop that tests the loop-continuing condition at the end, or bottom, of the loop.

dual-alternative if — A program structure that takes one action when its Boolean expression is evaluated as true, and uses an else clause to define the actions to take when the expression is evaluated as false. Also called an **if-else structure**.

dummy argument — An argument hat is not used within the function but exists only to provide a unique function prototype.

dynamically allocate memory — To allocate memory during the execution of a program (as opposed to when the program is compiled).

EBCDIC (Extended Binary Coded Decimal Interchange Code) — A coding system used in many mainframe and midrange computers.

echo — To repeat input as output.

editor — A simplified version of a word processor in which you type your program statements.

element — A single object in an array.

encapsulate — To hide or contain the variables and instructions within a module, making the module independent of all other modules, and therefore more reusable.

encapsulation — The principle of containing variables locally in their functions. Also called **data hiding**.

endl — The end line manipulator; inserting **endl** into the output stream causes a new line plus all waiting output to become visible.

end-of-file indicator — A key combination that indicates completion of data entry.

enumeration — A programmer-defined set of integer constants represented by identifiers.

enumerator — The named constant in an enumeration.

error message — A notification of a fatal errors from the compiler.

escape sequence — A sequence of characters in which the first character serves only to "escape" from the usual meaning of the second character.

exception — An error that occurs during execution of object-oriented programs, so-named because, presumably, it is not a usual occurrence. Also an object that contains information that is passed from the place where a problem occurs to another place that will handle the problem.

exception handling — The set of object-oriented techniques used to manage execution-time errors.

exception object — An object created when an exception occurs and contains information about the exception.

exception specification — A declaration of a function's possible **throw** types.

exdented style — The program coding style in which the braces in a function each occupy a line of their own and align to the left.

executable — A program that is runnable.

execute — To have a computer use a written and compiled program.

exit() function — A function that forces a program to end.

explicit cast — A deliberate cast; you can perform an explicit cast in one of two ways: by typing **static_cast<data type>** in front of an expression, or by using a type name within parentheses in front of an expression.

extensible — The quality of a class that makes it extendable; that is, you can create a new class that inherits from it.

extensible language — A language to which you can add your own data types.

extraction operator (>>) — An operator used with **cin** or another **istream** object to obtain input.

family of functions — A group of functions that generates from the same template.

fatal error — An error that prevents a program from executing.

field — The simple component that is an attribute of a class.

file mode — An attribute that indicates how a file is opened, for example, for input or output.

fixed manipulator — A manipulator that allows you to output a specified number of decimal places.

flag variable — A variable that you use to mark an occurrence.

float — A keyword used to declare floating-point values.

floating point — A type of variable that stores numbers with decimal places.

flushing the buffer — To force all waiting output to become visible.

for statement — A statement that can be used as alternative to the **while** statement; it typically contains sections that initialize, compare, and alter a loop control variable. Also called a **for loop**.

formal parameter — A variable listed in a function header.

format flag — The argument that determines the state of the **cout** object. Also called a **state flag**.

format specification — When used with the **printf()** function, the format specification describes the appearance of the values displayed and always begin with a percent sign (%).

forward reference — A statement that lets the compiler know that a class exists, and that the details will come later.

friend class — A class in which all functions can access the non-**public** members of another class.

friend function — A function that can access the non-**public** members of a class, even though the function itself is not a member of the class.

function — A small program unit that performs a task or group of tasks. In different programming languages, the counterpart to a function is known as a **subroutine**, **procedure**, **module**, or **method**.

function declaration — A statement that notifies the calling function that the definition, or details of, the named function will come later. Also called a **function prototype**.

function header — The initial three-part line of code in a C++ function that contains a return type, identifier, and optional parameter list. Also called a **header**.

function template — A function that uses variable data types.

function's return type — The type of object or variable that the function returns to the function that calls it. Also called the **function's type**.

functional cohesion — A measure of how well all function operations contribute to the performance of only one task.

garbage value — An uninitialized variable, which has an unknown value and is of no practical use.

generalization and specialization — A principle, which inheritance supports, that base classes are more general, and derived classes are more specialized cases of their base classes.

generic — Describes an argument that can stand for any number of C++ types. Also called a **parameterized** argument.

get() **function** — A function that takes a character argument and returns a reference to the object that invoked the **get()** function.

getline() function — A function that reads characters into an array, up to a size limit or until the newline character is encountered, whichever comes first.

global variable — A variable known to all functions in a program.

has-a relationship — A characteristic that describes the relationship of a class to its fields. Also called a **composition relationship**.

header — The initial three-part line of code in a C++ function that contains a return type, identifier, and optional parameter list. Also called a **function header**.

header file — A file that contains predefined values and routines.

hex manipulator — A manipulator that displays numbers in hexadecimal form.

hexadecimal — The base 16 numbering system.

high-level I/O — Formatted input/output; that is, bytes are grouped into meaningful units such as integers, **doubles**, and class object types.

identifier — A name provided to a variable or other C++ element.

if-else-if — A structure in which a new decision rests within the **else** clause of another decision.

ignore() function — A function that skips any additional characters left in the input stream after data is accepted..

implementation section — The part of a class that contains the functions.

implicit — Automatically determined. For example, the designation of a parameterized type is determined not by naming the type, but by the compiler's ability to determine it.

implicit cast — The automatic cast or transformation that occurs when you assign a value of one type to a type with higher precedence.

in scope — A variable between the time it is declared and when its block of code ends; usually this is when a variable appears between braces in a program. Also called **accessible**.

inaccessible — A class member that cannot be used from the current location.

increment — To increase by one.

inherit — To assume or traits of previously created objects, thereby reducing the time it takes to create new objects.

inheritance — The principle that knowledge of a general category can be applied to more specific objects. Specifically, inheritance in C++ means you can create classes that derive their attributes from existing classes.

initialization list — A list that provides constructor-required values for the member-objects; it is the part of the constructor header to the right of the colon.

initialize — To assign a first value to a variable. *See* **define a variable**.

inline function — A small function with no overhead, because program control never transfers to the function. Rather, a copy of the function statements is placed directly into the compiled calling program.

inner loop — A loop that falls entirely within the body of another loop.

input — The data provided by an outside source to the computer program so that the data can be manipulated.

input buffer — A holding area for waiting input.

insertion operator (<<) — An operator used to insert whatever is to the right into a **cout** or other **ostream** object.

inspector function — A function that returns information about an object's state, or display some or all of an object's attributes. Also called an **access function**.

instance — A specific item that belongs to a class; one occurrence of a class.

instantiate — To declare or create an object.

`int` — The keyword used to declare an integer variable.

integer — A number (either positive or negative) without a decimal point. Also, a type of variable that stores whole numbers.

integer data type variable — A variable that stores an integer value, and is declared with the keyword `int`.

integral data type — A type that holds an integer—a number (either positive or negative) without a decimal point. The data types `bool`, `char`, `int`, `long`, and `short` are integral; `double` and `float` are not.

interactive program — A program in which the user interacts with the program statements.

interface — An object that intercedes between you and the inner workings of an object. Also a means of entry into a method.

interpreter — A program that translates programming language instructions one line at a time.

invoke the method — To call a function.

is-a relationship — A relationship in which one item is an object that is an instance of a class. Also used to describe the relationship of a descendent object to its ancestor.

iteration — A repetition.

iterator — A variable that is used only to count the executions of a loop.

keyword — A word that is part of a programming language.

library — A collection of useful classes.

lifetime of a variable — The time during which it is defined, from declaration to destruction.

line comment — A comment that begins with two slashes (//) and continues to the end of the line on which it is placed.

link — To integrate outside references to a program.

linked list — A chain of objects, each of which consists of at least two parts—the usual components of the object itself and a pointer to another object.

local variable — A variable known only in a limited scope.

logical AND (&&) — An operator you use to create a compound Boolean expression in which two conditions must be true for the entire expression to evaluate as true.

logical error — An error that occurs when you use a statement that, although syntactically correct, doesn't do what you intended.

logical OR (||) — An operator you use to create a compound Boolean expression in which at least one of two conditions must be true for the entire expression to evaluate as true.

long double — The keyword used to declare floating-point values.

loop body — The part of a loop that contains the statements that execute within the loop.

loop control variable — A variable that controls the execution of a loop body.

loop structure — A program organization in which the program repeats actions while a condition remains unchanged.

low-level I/O — Unformatted input/output; that is, bytes are transferred into and out of memory without regard to the type of data they represent.

Lvalue — A variable located on the left side of assignment statements to which values legally can be assigned.

machine language — A computer's on-off circuitry language; the low-level language made up of 1s and 0s that the computer understands.

`main()` — The function that every C++ program contains; the first function that executes in an application.

maintenance programming — Programming that involves making modifications and improvements to existing systems.

manager function — A function that creates and destroys objects for you.

manipulator — A function used to manipulate, or change, the state of the `cout` object. Also called a **manipulator function**.

mask — A value whose only purpose is to filter values from other variables.

member-object — An object contained within another class.

memberwise copy — A copy of an object in which the value of each field or member of the object is copied to its counterpart in another object.

memory address — A value that identifies each location where a piece of data can be stored.

message — A passed object that contains information.

method — A group of statements that can be executed as a unit.

mixed expression — An expression in which the operands have different data types.

modulus and assign operator (%=) — An operator that finds the modulus when you divide the left-hand operand by the right-hand operand and assigns the result to the left-hand operand.

modulus operator (%) — A binary arithmetic operator used to perform modulus. The modulus operator gives the remainder of integer division; it can be used only with integers.

multiple inheritance — Inheritance that occurs when a child class derives from more than one base class.

multiplication operator (*) — A binary arithmetic operator used to perform multiplication.

multiply and assign operator (*=) — An operator that multiplies the left-hand operand by the right-hand operand

mutator function — A function that changes an object's state or attributes. Also called an **implementer**.

name mangling — The process by which the compiler creates unique names with all the information a compiler needs to distinguish identically named, overloaded functions.

named constant — A named memory location whose contents cannot change during execution of the program.

namespace — A mechanism for grouping features you want to include in a program

negative value operator (-) — A unary operator that indicates a negative value.

nested if — An `if` structure that rests entirely within another `if` structure, either within the `if` or the `else` clause.

nested loop — A loop contained in another loop.

new operator — A C++ operator you use the to dynamically allocate memory.

newline — An invisible character that forces the next output to appear on a new line.

non-default constructor — A constructor that requires at least one argument.

non-fatal error — A warning; a program containing only warnings and no errors can execute.

not operator (!) — An operator that reverses the true/false value of an expression.

null character — A character is represented by the combination '\0' (backslash and zero), or by using the constant `NULL` that is available if you use the statement `#include<iostream>` at the top of any file you compile.

numeric variable — A variable that holds values such as 13 or -6.

object — Any thing; an instance of a class.

object code — The output from compilation, which is statements that have been translated into something the computer can use.

object-oriented programming — A group of techniques that requires you to analyze the objects with which you are working, organize them into classes, and learn about inheritance and polymorphism.

oct manipulator — A manipulator that displays values in octal form.

octothorp — The pound sign (#).

one's complement operator (~) — The operator that makes every bit become its opposite. Also called the **bitwise complement operator**.

one-dimensional array — An array whose elements are accessed using a single subscript. *See* **two-dimensional array**.

open() function — A function that opens a data file.

operator overloading — The process by which you apply operators to your own abstract data types.

operator function — A function that overloads a built-in operator. For example, the **operator--()** function overloads the decrement operator, and the **operator+()** function overloads the + symbol.

out of bounds — Memory locations that are beyond the boundaries of an array.

out of scope — A variable outside the block in which the variable was declared. Also called **inaccessible**.

outer loop — A loop that completely contains another loop.

output — The information produced by a program.

overhead — The cost of doing business involved in calling a function.

overloading — To create multiple functions with the same name, but different argument lists.

override — To substitute one version of a function for another or to take precedence over.

parallel arrays — Corresponding arrays in which values in the same relative locations are logically related.

parameter — Data that a function obtains from another function.

parameterized manipulator — A manipulator that takes an argument.

parametric overloading — The use of functions that are distinguished by their number or types of arguments.

parent class — An original class that has been extended, or inherited from.

parentheses operator (operator()) — An operator you use to make multiple assignments within a class.

persistent storage device — A device such as a disk or a CD, retains data when power is lost. Also called a **permanent storage device**.

pivot sort — A type of recursive sorting method.

pointer variable — A variable that can hold memory addresses. Also called a **pointer**.

pointer-to-member operator — An operator that looks like an arrow and is used between an object's pointer and an object's field or function. It is constructed by using a dash followed by a right angle bracket (or greater-than sign).

polymorphism — The technique object-oriented programs use to carry out the same operation in a manner customized to the object.

positive value operator (+) — A unary operator that indicates a positive value.

postfix increment operator — The ++ after a variable that increases the value by one.

posttest loop — A loop in which the loop control variable is tested after the loop body executes.

precision — A measure of accuracy or number of significant digits of floating-point numbers.

precision() function — A function that controls the number of significant digits you see in the output of a floating-point number.

predicate function — A function that tests the truth of a condition.

prefix increment operator — The ++ before a variable that increase the value by one.

preprocessor — A program that runs before a C++ program is compiled.

preprocessor directive — A statement that tells a program, called the preprocessor, what to do before compiling the program.

pretest loop — A loop in which the loop control variable is tested before the loop body is executed.

priming read — An input statement that initializes a variable before a loop begins. Also called a **priming input statement**.

primitive — A data type that is a built-in, simple type such as int, char, or double. Also called **scalar**.

principle of least privilege — A programming principle that says you should give a process only the authority it needs to accomplish its job.

private — A field not available for use outside the class.

procedural program — A computer program that consists of a series of steps or procedures that take place one after the other.

production program — A real-life program in use by a business.

program — The set of instructions written to perform computerized tasks. Also called **software**.

program maintenance — The upkeep of professional programs over time.

programming — To write instructions that enable a computer to carry out a single task or a group of tasks.

programming language — A computer language such as Visual Basic, Pascal, COBOL, RPG, C#, C++, Java, or Fortran, used to write programs.

prompt — A statement that requests input from the user, often explaining what is expected.

protected access specifier — An access specifier that allows members to be used by class member functions and by derived classes, but not by other parts of a program.

pseudo random — Numbers that are generated in a sequence that gives the illusion of being random, but the sequence eventually repeats.

public — A field available to functions outside the class.

pure polymorphism — The situation in which one function body is used with a variety of arguments.

qualifier — A word that qualifies, or restricts, the ordinary capabilities of the named type.

queue — A data structure in which elements are removed in the same order they were entered, often referred to as FIFO (first in, first out).

quick sort — A type of recursive sorting method.

rand() function — The facility for generating random numbers provided in the C++ standard library.

real number — A number that includes decimal positions, such as 98.6, 1000.0002, and –3.85. Also called a **floating-point number**.

recursion — When a function is defined in terms of itself.

recursive function — A function that calls itself.

reference variable — A variable that acts as an alias for another variable. Also called a **reference**.

relational operator — An operator that evaluates the relationship between operands. **==** means equivalent to, **>** means greater than, **<** means less than, **>=** means greater than or equal to. **<=** means less than or equal to, and **!=** means not equal to.

reliability — The dependability and trustworthiness of a module or class.

resetiosflags() manipulator — A manipulator that turns off bit codes for the attributes named as arguments.

return value — A value sent from a subfunction to the function that called it.

run — To issue a command to execute, or carry out, program statements.

scope — The attribute of a variable defines where it can be accessed in a program.

scope resolution operator (::) — An operator that allows you to refer to a global variable when a local one has taken precedence.

seed — To initialize a random number generator.

selection structure — A program organization in which the program performs different tasks based on a condition.

semantic error — An error that occurs when you use a correct word in the wrong context.

sentinel value — A value that determines when a loop will end.

sequence structure — A program organization in which steps execute one after another, without interruption.

set_new_handler() function — A function that handles the problem of insufficient memory.

setf() function — A function that takes arguments that set the bits of `cout`; that is,

the arguments turn the bits in the format flag on.

setiosflags() manipulator — A manipulator that turns on bit codes for the attributes named as arguments.

setprecision() manipulator — A manipulator that specifies the number of significant digits displayed; combined with the fixed manipulator, you control the number of decimals that display.

setw() manipulator — A manipulator that allows you to set the width of a field for output.

showbase manipulator — A manipulator that displays octal numbers with a leading 0 and hexadecimal numbers with a leading 0x so you do not mistake them for base 10 (decimal) numbers.

signature — A function's prototype.

single inheritance — A child class deriving from a single parent.

single-alternative selection — A selection in which an action takes place only when the result of the decision is true.

source code — Program statements.

srand() function — A function that seeds, or initializes, the random number generator.

stack — A data structure in which elements are removed in the reverse order from which they were entered, referred to as LIFO (last in, first out). Also a memory location that holds addresses to which functions should return.

stacking — To make multiple calls to the same operator function.

statement — A segment of C++ code that performs a task; it is similar to an English sentence.

static — A class field for which only one memory location is allocated, no matter how many class objects you instantiate. All members of the class share a single storage location for a `static` data member of that same class.

static function — A function you can use without a declared object.

static variable — A variable that doesn't belong to a specific object; it belongs to the class, and you can use it even if you never instantiate an object. Also called a **class variable**, **class field**, or **class-wide field**.

stream — A sequence of bytes used in an input or output operation.

string — A C++ value expressed within double quotation mark s. Also called a **literal string**.

string constant — A value within double quotes.

stub — A simple routine that does nothing (or very little); you incorporate it into a program as a placeholder.

subfunction — A function used by a `main()` function.

subscript — A number that indicates the position of the particular array element being used.

subscript operator (`operator[]`)— An operator declared like any other function, but is called in a manner similar to accessing an array element.

subtract and assign operator (– =) — An operator that subtracts the right-hand operand from the left-hand operand.

subtraction operator (–) — A binary arithmetic operator used to perform subtraction.

switch statement — An alternative to a series of `if` statements. The keyword `switch` identifies the beginning of the statement. Then the expression in parentheses is evaluated. After the opening curly brace, a series of case statements separate the actions that should occur when the department equals each case.

syntax — The rules of a language.

syntax error — The incorrect application of a programming language's rules.

template class — A class that is generated by a class template. The terms are often used interchangeably.

template function — A function generated by a function template. The terms often are used interchangeably.

temporary data storage — Data that exists in computer memory; it is lost when power is lost.

test — To use sample data to determine whether program results are correct.

this pointer — The pointer that holds the memory address of the current object that is using a class function. It is automatically supplied every time you call a non-static member function of a class.

throw an exception — To send an error object to a calling function when an object-oriented program detects an error within a function. A `throw` resembles a return statement in a function, except that the execution of the program does not continue from where the function was called.

time() — A function that returns the number of seconds that have elapsed since January 1, 1970.

try block — One or more statements that the program attempts to execute, but which might result in thrown exceptions.

two-dimensional array — An array accessed using two subscripts; the first represents a row and the second represents a column. *See* **one-dimensional array**.

typedef — A C++ statement that provides a synonym for an identifier in a C++ program; it is a way to create a shorter, easier-to-remember nickname for an unwieldy identifier.

typename — A C++ keyword that can replace **class** in a template definition in some C++ compilers.

unary operator — An operator that requires only one operand.

Unicode — An extended, international coding system.

unifying type — The data type of the value in an arithmetic expression to which all the types in the expression are converted.

unsetf() function — A function that can be used to deselect a bit in the format flag.

unsigned int — A data type for a positive field value; no bit is reserved for a sign, and all eight bits are used to store the value.

unwinding the stack — To return from each called function to the one that called it.

user — A person who runs, and probably benefits from, the output provided by a program.

variable — A named memory location whose contents can change.

virtual — A C++ keyword that indicates a base class should be used only once, even though more than one of its children is also being used as a base to another class.

void — Nothing or empty.

warning — A notification of a non-fatal error by the compiler.

while loop — A repetition structure that executes as long as a tested expression is true.

whitespace — Any number of spaces, tabs, and Enter characters.

width() function — A function that defines the size of the output field in which the next output will be displayed.

Index